NAFTA
REVISITED

ACHIEVEMENTS AND CHALLENGES

INSTITUTE FOR INTERNATIONAL ECONOMICS

NAFTA REVISITED

ACHIEVEMENTS AND CHALLENGES

GARY CLYDE HUFBAUER
AND JEFFREY J. SCHOTT
Assisted by Paul L. E. Grieco and Yee Wong

Washington, DC
October 2005

Gary Clyde Hufbauer, Reginald Jones Senior Fellow since 1992, was the Marcus Wallenberg Professor of International Finance Diplomacy at Georgetown University (1985–92), deputy director of the International Law Institute at Georgetown University (1979–81), deputy assistant secretary for international trade and investment policy of the US Treasury (1977–79), and director of the International Tax Staff at the US Treasury (1974–76). He has written extensively on international trade, investment, and tax issues, with a particular focus on economic sanctions and NAFTA. He is coauthor or coeditor of *Awakening Monster: The Alien Tort Statute of 1789* (2003), *The Benefits of Price Convergence: Speculative Calculations* (2002), *NAFTA and the Environment: Seven Years Later* (2000), *Fundamental Tax Reform and Border Tax Adjustments* (1996), *Western Hemisphere Economic Integration* (1994), *Measuring the Costs of Protection in the United States* (1994), *NAFTA: An Assessment* (rev. ed. 1993), *North American Free Trade: Issues and Recommendations* (1992), *Economic Sanctions Reconsidered: History and Current Policy* (2d ed. 1990), and others.

Jeffrey J. Schott, senior fellow, joined the Institute in 1983. He was a senior associate at the Carnegie Endowment for International Peace (1982–83) and an international economist at the US Treasury (1974–82). He is the author, coauthor, or editor of *Free Trade Agreements: US Strategies and Priorities* (2004), *Prospects for Free Trade in the Americas* (2001), *Free Trade between Korea and the United States?* (2001), *The WTO after Seattle* (2000), *NAFTA and the Environment: Seven Years Later* (2000), *Launching New Global Trade Talks: An Action Agenda* (1998), *Restarting Fast Track* (1998), *The World Trading System: Challenges Ahead* (1996), *WTO 2000: Setting the Course for World Trade* (1996), *The Uruguay Round: An Assessment* (1994), *Western Hemisphere Economic Integration* (1994), *NAFTA: An Assessment* (rev. ed. 1993), *North American Free Trade: Issues and Recommendations* (1992), *Economic Sanctions Reconsidered* (2d ed. 1990), among others.

Paul L. E. Grieco, doctoral student at Northwestern University's Department of Economics, was a research assistant at the Institute for International Economics. He coauthored "The Payoff to America from Global Integration" in *The United States and the World Economy: Foreign Economic Policy for the Next Decade* (2005).

Yee Wong, doctoral student at the Massachusetts Institute of Technology, was a research assistant at the Institute for International Economics. She coauthored *China Bashing*, International Economics Policy Brief PB04-5 (Institute for International Economics, 2004).

**INSTITUTE FOR
INTERNATIONAL ECONOMICS**
1750 Massachusetts Avenue, NW
Washington, DC 20036-1903
(202) 328-9000   FAX: (202) 659-3225
www.iie.com

C. Fred Bergsten, *Director*
Valerie Norville, *Director of Publications
and Web Development*
Edward Tureen, *Director of Marketing*

Typesetting by BMWW
Printing by Kirby Lithographic Company, Inc.

Printed in the United States of America
07 06 05   5 4 3 2 1

Library of Congress Cataloging-in-Publication Data

Hufbauer, Gary Clyde
  NAFTA revisited: achievements and challenges / Gary Clyde Hufbauer and Jeffrey J. Schott.
     p. cm.
     Includes bibliographical references and index.
     ISBN 0-88132-334-9
     1. Free trade—North America.   2. North America—Economic integration.   3. Canada. Treaties, etc. 1992 Oct. 7.   4. Foreign trade and employment—North America.   I. Schott, Jeffrey J., 1949–   II. Title.

HF1746.H85 2005
382'.917—dc22   2005043365

The views expressed in this publication are those of the authors. This publication is part of the overall program of the Institute, as endorsed by its Board of Directors, but does not necessarily reflect the views of individual members of the Board or the Advisory Committee.

Contents

Preface

For more than two decades, the Institute has conducted a series of studies on economic integration in North America. The first, *The United States and Canada: The Quest for Free Trade* (1987) by Paul Wonnacott, analyzed the potential gains from a free trade agreement (FTA) between the United States and Canada and served as a useful guide for the ongoing trade negotiations. After the talks were concluded, Jeffrey Schott and Murray G. Smith produced the first comprehensive assessment of the pact in *The Canada–United States Free Trade Agreement: The Global Impact* (1988).

These studies set an important pattern for future Institute work on trade negotiations. For major initiatives, we first analyze the problems that require redress, the potential trade and welfare gains from doing so, and the international implications of the venture. This work establishes a blueprint for trade talks and a benchmark for assessing the ultimate outcome. We then conduct a comprehensive assessment of the benefits and costs of the agreement, after it is completed, and the unfinished business that negotiators left on the table.

Even while the Canada-US FTA was still a major event, the North American Free Trade Agreement (NAFTA) was thrust upon the scene with potentially broad economic and political consequences. When Mexico requested an FTA with the United States in 1990, then President George H. W. Bush could not refuse and Canada could not afford to stay out of the talks. Unlike the Canada-US pact, which joined two countries already closely linked by trade and investment and highly similar in levels of development, the talks with Mexico represented the first significant attempt to link a developing country with developed nations in a reciprocal FTA. NAFTA thus required a focus on development issues not previously stressed in trade negotiations, raised new concerns about labor and environmental policies, and addressed governance issues long ignored in bilateral and multilateral trade pacts. Not surprisingly, NAFTA quickly became a lightning rod for social concerns regarding trade and globalization.

For the past 15 years, Institute studies conducted by Gary Hufbauer and Jeffrey Schott have been an essential resource for understanding the NAFTA debate. In 1992, the Institute published *North American Free Trade: Issues and Recommendations*, which examined the state of economic integration among the three countries and exposed the problems that would need to be addressed in comprehensive negotiations. After the talks concluded, we released their *NAFTA: An Assessment* (1993), which analyzed the negotiated results, including the side accords on labor and the environment, and recognized and scored the major achievements while criticizing the pact's major shortcomings. The two books were widely cited in the ratification debates in all three countries and contributed importantly to an understanding of NAFTA among informed journalists and scholars.

The Institute has continued its work on NAFTA, and its potential evolution, ever since the agreement entered into force. In August 2001, Robert Pastor authored a far-reaching vision, *Toward a North American Community*, with radical recommendations for deeper political institutions between the three partners and more ambitious financial transfers from the United States and Canada to spur growth in Mexico. Until the terrorist strikes of September 11, 2001, Presidents Bush and Fox and Prime Minister Chretien seemed disposed to explore new avenues for NAFTA cooperation, and the Institute in fact hosted a major discussion of those issues with President Fox at the close of his widely heralded state visit with President Bush on September 7, 2001. After the strikes, of course, the policy agenda shifted sharply toward security concerns.

Today, NAFTA continues to be almost as controversial as it was during the ratification debate in the US Congress in the summer and fall of 1993. Both supporters and opponents of further trade liberalization cited the NAFTA experience in justifying their position, for example, in the congressional debate over the Central American Free Trade Agreement (CAFTA) in the summer of 2005. To provide a factual basis for this ongoing debate, Hufbauer and Schott's new study, *NAFTA Revisited: Achievements and Challenges*, evaluates NAFTA's performance since its entry into force, comparing actual experience with both the objectives of the agreement's supporters and the charges of its critics. They analyze future challenges and opportunities in the trade and investment relationships among the three partner countries and their broader implications for new trade initiatives throughout the hemisphere.

By economic standards, NAFTA has been a great success for all three countries, contributing to unprecedented growth in regional trade and investment. Intraregional merchandise trade in North America now exceeds $700 billion annually, and cross-border direct investment is extensive. Hufbauer and Schott examine what has been achieved and what has been left undone. They assess the overall economic gains and commercial results in key sectors such as autos, agriculture, and energy, as well as the operation of the dispute settlement and labor and environmental provisions. In so doing, they expose the critical development challenges that face Mexico if it is to take full advantage of the NAFTA partnership.

NAFTA Revisited: Achievements and Challenges makes an important contribution by recommending what needs to be done, over the medium term, to deal with the ongoing trade and investment problems confronting regional economic integration. Since September 11, the NAFTA partners have been confronted with an increasingly competitive and security-conscious global environment. Hufbauer and Schott offer proposals for resolving durable impediments to regional trade and investment, including those in the politically sensitive but strategically vital energy sector, and they offer practical solutions for thorny problems in migration, labor, and the environment. We offer their new book as a potential road map for the future of North America in the same way that their earlier studies provided a road map for much of what has been accomplished to date.

The Institute for International Economics is a private, nonprofit institution for the study and discussion of international economic policy. Its purpose is to analyze important issues in that area and to develop and communicate practical new approaches for dealing with them. The Institute is completely nonpartisan

The Institute is funded by a highly diversified group of philanthropic foundations, private corporations, and interested individuals. Major institutional grants are now being received from the William M. Keck, Jr. Foundation and the Starr Foundation. About 33 percent of the Institute's resources in our latest fiscal year were provided by contributors outside the United States, including about 16 percent from Japan. Funding for this study was received from the Ford Foundation, the John D. and Catherine T. MacArthur Foundation, Merck & Co., and the Charles Stewart Mott Foundation. The Embassy of Canada is supporting our dissemination of the volume.

The Institute's Board of Directors bears overall responsibilities for the Institute and gives general guidance and approval to its research program, including the identification of topics that are likely to become important over the medium run (one to three years) and that should be addressed by the Institute. The director, working closely with the staff and outside Advisory Committee, is responsible for the development of particular projects and makes the final decision to publish an individual study.

The Institute hopes that its studies and other activities will contribute to building a stronger foundation for international economic policy around the world. We invite readers of these publications to let us know how they think we can best accomplish this objective.

C. Fred Bergsten
Director
August 2005

Acknowledgments

The authors wish to thank C. Fred Bergsten, Richard N. Cooper, Kimberly Elliott, Malcolm Fairbrother, Robert C. Fisher, Antonio Ortiz Mena, Theodore Moran, Edwin Truman, Ralph Watkins, and Paul Wonnacott for useful suggestions and comments.

1

Overview

In June 1990, Mexican President Carlos Salinas de Gortari and US President George H. W. Bush announced a daring initiative: the creation of a free trade area between the United States and Mexico. When formal negotiations began one year later, Canada—spurred on by fears that its benefits from the 1989 Canada-US Free Trade Agreement (CUSFTA) might be diluted—joined the project. Negotiations on the North American Free Trade Agreement (NAFTA) proceeded to create one of the world's largest free trade blocs.[1] Upon entering into force in January 1994, NAFTA represented a $6 trillion economy with a population of 360 million. Ten years later, the NAFTA area grew to a $12.5 trillion economy with a population of 430 million.

Of course North American economic integration was well under way long before NAFTA—building on the 1965 Canada–United States Automotive Agreement (commonly known as the 1965 Auto Pact), initiation of the Mexican *maquiladora* program of 1965,[2] Mexican economic reforms from the mid-1980s, accession to the General Agreement on Tariffs and Trade (GATT) in 1986, and the CUSFTA in 1989. For many decades before 1990, the United States accounted for the predominant share of trade and

---

1. The European Union has more members, a larger population, and somewhat larger GDP than NAFTA. By contrast with NAFTA, the European Union is a customs union with a common external tariff and substantial supranational institutions.

2. The Mexican maquiladora program (initially termed the Border Industrialization Program) was developed to create assembly jobs in border communities when the United States terminated its *bracero* program in 1964 (see chapter 2 on labor).

foreign direct investment (FDI) in both Canada and Mexico.[3] Moreover, during the three years from announcement to completion of the negotiations, US trade with Mexico and Canada grew almost twice as fast as merchandise trade with other countries. North American economic integration would have continued to deepen—even *without* NAFTA—in response to new technology and competitive pressures in the world economy. But progress would likely have been slower.

Overall, the three economies of North America have grown significantly during the first decade of NAFTA. Average annual real GDP growth over 1994–2003 was 3.6 percent for Canada, 3.3 percent for the United States, and 2.7 percent for Mexico (despite the sharp recession in 1995). While all three countries grew faster than the OECD average during this period, Mexico's progress was insufficient to address its long-run development challenges and well below its estimated potential growth rate.[4]

Since NAFTA, intraregional merchandise trade has doubled; US FDI in Canada and Mexico increased even faster. How much NAFTA has contributed to growth and efficiency is a tough analytical question that challenges scholars. It is important to emphasize, however, that NAFTA obligations are only part of the story. The trade and investment pact is only one component of the rich complex of economic relations among the three countries. Macroeconomic events—the Mexican peso crisis of 1994–95, the US high-tech boom of the 1990s, and Canadian budget and monetary discipline—clearly shaped the depth and pace of economic integration. The effects of the agreement are difficult to disentangle from these and other events in the North American and global economies.

For the United States, NAFTA was an economic opportunity to capitalize on a growing export market to the south and a political opportunity to repair the sometimes troubled relationship with Mexico. At the same time, NAFTA was seen as a way to support the growth of political pluralism and deepening of democratic processes in Mexico and as part of the long-term response to chronic migration pressures.

In addition, US officials hoped the regional talks would spur progress on the slow-paced Uruguay Round of multilateral trade negotiations, while providing a fallback in the event that those talks faltered. NAFTA reforms promised to open new doors for US exporters—who faced Mexi-

---

3. In 1990, US trade (exports and imports) with Canada and Mexico totaled $170 billion and $57 billion, respectively; Canada-Mexico trade ran about $2.5 billion. US and Canadian companies invested heavily in each other's economy (combined FDI of about $95 billion), and US firms accounted for $10 billion in FDI in Mexico.

4. The OECD (2004d) estimates that Mexico's annual potential growth rate could be raised to 6 percent with structural and regulatory reforms. It argues that unless Mexico implements structural reforms to improve education and infrastructure and increase competition in the business sector, the Mexican economy will lag behind its 6 percent potential. See "Tequila Slammer—The Peso Crisis, Ten Years On," *The Economist*, January 1, 2005.

can industrial tariffs five times greater on average than US tariffs—to a growing market of almost 100 million people. US officials also recognized that *imports* from Mexico likely would include higher US content than competing imports from Asia, providing an additional benefit. Increased Mexican sales in the US market would in turn spur increased Mexican purchases from US firms.

For Mexico, NAFTA represented a way to lock in the reforms of the *apertura*, or "market opening," that President Miguel de la Madrid inaugurated in the mid-1980s to transform Mexico's formerly statist economy in the wake of the devastating debt crisis of the 1980s. Mexico needed more rapid growth to provide new opportunities for its young, expanding population. Given the legacy of the debt crisis of 1982, low domestic savings, and an increasingly overvalued peso, the most practical way to propel growth was to import goods and capital, creating more competition in the Mexican market.

An FTA with the United States was crucial to maintain secure access to Mexico's largest market and to blunt efforts to roll back Mexican reforms.[5] NAFTA obligations sharply raised the political cost of reversing economic reforms and made it easier to deflect protectionist demands of industrial and special interest groups. The trade pact thus was an integral part of the plan to create a more stable policy environment so that Mexico could attract greater FDI inflows—with its embedded technology and management skills—to build and finance growth.

For Canada, the latecomer to the NAFTA table, the objectives were less ambitious. Initially, Canadian officials suspected that a new agreement with Mexico would erode the hard-fought gains of the CUSFTA, which had come into force only in 1989. Canadian unions felt that Mexico's low wages would undercut Canada's competitive advantage in the US market, possibly diverting US FDI away from Canada. Trade between Canada and Mexico was small, the prospective deal seemed unlikely to redress CUSFTA shortcomings on trade remedies, and Canadians were less worried about migration flows than their US counterparts.[6] However, as it became clear in September 1990 that the United States and Mexico were going to move ahead with or without Canada, the Canadian government decided that it had more to gain by joining the negotiations than by stay-

---

5. President Carlos Salinas de Gortari used NAFTA ratification as political cover to reform the use of *ejido* lands (communal agricultural property). The Mexican Congress permitted the sale and consolidation of ejido lands when it ratified NAFTA, an important step toward the creation of economically viable agricultural units.

6. At first, Industry Minister John Crosbie vehemently denied any rumors of CUSFTA expansion: "It doesn't matter to us how many powerful US senators are for free trade with Mexico. . . . There is an absolute zero pounds per square inch of pressure on the Mexico question." Quoted in "Canada Is Free to Turn Down Mexico Deal, Crosbie Says," *The Toronto Star*, June 27, 1989, B2.

ing on the sideline.[7] Involvement allowed the government to minimize the risks to Canada of US-Mexico free trade and offered an opportunity to extract new commercial concessions from the United States.

At the time of its ratification, NAFTA was hailed by some and derided by others. Even after more than a decade of hindsight and data, the political debate over NAFTA remains confused and divisive. Much of what was promised from NAFTA could never be achieved solely through a free trade deal; much of what has occurred since NAFTA was ratified cannot be attributed to policy changes that the trade pact mandated.

Critics continue to berate the NAFTA partners for missed opportunities and misplaced priorities; some continue to recite misguided analysis put forward a decade ago during the NAFTA ratification debate. Before the pact was even concluded, NAFTA served as a lightning rod for attacks by labor and environmental groups against trade liberalization. NAFTA critics charged that the pact would encourage footloose plants to leave the United States and Canada, that low-wage Mexican jobs would displace US workers, and that the threat of relocation would suppress wage demands. While one would expect such effects to some degree, the critics grossly exaggerated their magnitude. Ross Perot's infamous "sucking sound" claims proved totally unfounded. Yet legendary tales still resonate in public debate.

However, NAFTA critics also cite an array of concerns that are harder to dismiss: continued high levels of illegal immigration, slow progress on environmental problems, growing income disparities (particularly within Mexico), weak growth in real wages, and trafficking of illegal drugs. Some of these problems are correlates of economic integration and higher incomes, though NAFTA is only a small part of the story. Nonetheless, these issues are often cited as evidence of a "failed NAFTA."

To their credit, the NAFTA critics have shone a spotlight on important problems, but most of them fail to offer constructive remedies. To redress decades of environmental abuse or labor and migration problems—not to mention the scourge of drugs and related crime—will require major initiatives well beyond the scope of a trade pact. NAFTA was never designed to address all the ills of society—though some political leaders during the ratification debate made inflated promises about trade's medicinal powers.

This book assesses NAFTA's first decade and speculates on prospects for deeper economic integration. Individual chapters provide detailed analysis of what has happened in three important sectors of the North American economy, which together account for nearly a third of intraregional trade (autos, agriculture, and energy); the varied implementation of key components of the trade accord (dispute settlement, labor, and en-

---

7. See "Canada Joins Trade Talks, Crosbie Foresees Deal with US, Mexico by End of 1991," *The Globe and Mail*, September 25, 1990, B1.

vironmental provisions); and US-Mexico migration. The concluding chapter offers recommendations for reforms by the NAFTA countries that could enhance the benefits of their partnership.

This chapter starts with a historical context for NAFTA, including why it arose, how it was received, and how contemporary events have affected North America since the pact came into force. From this perspective, we assess how well the NAFTA partners have achieved the goals set out in the agreement itself—as opposed to passing judgment on political leaders' promises voiced during the overheated ratification debate. We consider NAFTA's effect on trade, investment, and employment, as well as the operation of NAFTA's dispute settlement provisions, and its side accords on labor and the environment.

Against the modest benchmarks set out in the agreement, NAFTA has been a success: The North American economy is more integrated and more efficient today than it would have been without NAFTA. Our assessment is critical in some dimensions: We find that important NAFTA institutions lacked adequate mandates and funding; consequently, they fell short of aspirations. However, we believe NAFTA's failures are best addressed by building on its successes. Looking to the future, we highlight areas where North American partners can make progress on new challenges.

NAFTA in Historical Context

Trade agreements do not operate in a vacuum. How well the partners take advantage of the opportunities the pacts create depends importantly on overall macroeconomic policy and political stability in the region. In this regard, the three partners navigated rough shoals in the inaugural decade of NAFTA. Mexico's financial problems in NAFTA's early years provided an acid test for the regional alliance. The security demands of the post–September 11 era may pose greater challenges over the long haul. To understand how regional trade and investment have adapted to events, we first examine the economic and political forces that have shaped North American economic integration since NAFTA's entry into force in January 1994.

The Making and Selling of NAFTA

Like all trade agreements, NAFTA is the outgrowth of complex negotiations both within and between nations. The negotiation of the NAFTA text took 14 months of haggling, with side agreements added later; the result is a far cry from an ivory tower FTA. More than 100 pages of restrictive rules of origin, especially in the textile, apparel, and automotive industries, are both trade-distorting and protectionist.[8] Mexico retained its monopoly for the state oil company, Petróleos Mexicanos (Pemex), a symbol of national sovereignty and the cash cow of Mexican public finance.[9] Free trade in agriculture between the United States and Mexico was delayed up to 15 years for the most import-sensitive products; the United States and Canada continued to exclude important farm products from free trade obligations. Other departures from the free trade ideal could be listed (for examples, see Hufbauer and Schott 1993).

Supporters of free trade minimized their criticisms of NAFTA's protectionist features, seeing them as the price of getting an agreement at all. Moreover, in the United States, free trade opponents—an ideologically diverse array including H. Ross Perot, Patrick Buchanan, and the AFL-CIO—likewise focused on the big picture. They were dead set against the agreement and succeeded in making NAFTA a leading issue in the 1992 US presidential campaign.

President George H. W. Bush was NAFTA's strongest supporter in the election, but the most virulent attacks on NAFTA came not from his Democratic rival, Bill Clinton, but from primary challenger Patrick Buchanan (and his political ally, if ideological opposite, Ralph Nader) and then from third-party candidate Ross Perot. These men charged that NAFTA would cause a "giant sucking sound" of US capital and jobs fleeing to Mexico, while also endangering the sovereignty of the United States. Environmental groups charged that Mexico would become the pollution haven of North America, attracting firms that wanted to evade higher US and Canadian standards. Bush defended NAFTA as a tool for job creation and said it was the greenest trade agreement ever (Hufbauer and Schott 1993). The "greenest" claim was true, but since environmental concerns were not previously incorporated in trade agreements, the standard was not demanding.

NAFTA presented a challenge and an opportunity for the Democratic presidential candidate, "New Democrat" Bill Clinton. Generally supportive of NAFTA, Clinton criticized Bush on the details: "If I had negotiated that treaty, it would have been better."[10] Clinton argued that NAFTA needed to be improved by adding side agreements on workers' rights, environmental protection, and import surges. His nuanced position was

8. FTAs generally include rules of origin to prevent "trade deflection"—imports from non-FTA countries into the FTA member with the lowest most-favored nation (MFN) tariff for transshipment to other FTA members. However, the NAFTA rules of origin go far beyond the measures necessary to prevent trade deflection.

9. The Mexican Constitution bars all foreign companies from petroleum exploration and distribution. Mexican politicians see Pemex as a symbol of national patrimony and as the source of about 30 percent of government revenues. As a result, however, Pemex has been drained of funds needed for infrastructure and technology investments.

10. See "Mexico's President Hedges on Trade Pact Deals," *Washington Post*, October 10, 1992, C1.

successful in uniting the Democratic party under a banner of "fair trade" during the election.

Once elected, President Clinton persuaded Mexican President Carlos Salinas and Canadian Prime Minister Brian Mulroney to negotiate his proposed side agreements in order to secure NAFTA ratification in the US Congress. The resulting agreements, the North American Agreement on Environmental Cooperation (NAAEC) and the North American Agreement on Labor Cooperation (NAALC), were largely consultative mechanisms. Each created a supranational commission with limited means of enforcement to ensure that countries abide by their own laws.[11] The third side agreement on safeguards was nothing more than a clarification of the NAFTA text itself.

Although the side agreements won few converts from the anti-NAFTA side,[12] they did provide President Clinton with the political cover necessary to steer NAFTA through Congress (Destler 1995). To further smooth relations with his own party, Clinton attached a $90 million transitional adjustment assistance program to the NAFTA legislation (NAFTA-TAA).[13] NAFTA-TAA provided limited training and income support for workers displaced by trade or investment with Canada or Mexico, though the qualifying criteria glossed over the actual link between lost jobs and NAFTA (see chapter 2 on labor). To sweeten the NAFTA deal for the 14-member House Hispanic caucus, and particularly Representative Esteban Torres (D-CA), whose support turned on the issue, the United States and Mexico established a North American Development Bank (NADBank) to finance infrastructure projects (primarily wastewater treatment plants) on both sides of the border.[14] However, NADBank financing rates were so high, and qualification conditions so onerous, that in five years (by 1999) the bank had committed to only five loans. More recently, activity has increased, and as of March 2004, the bank had approved 76 projects with a total authorized financing of $642 million, $186 million of which had actually been disbursed.[15]

---

11. The NAALC and NAAEC are analyzed in greater detail in chapters 2 and 3 on labor and environment, respectively.

12. A few environmental groups, such as the National Wildlife Federation, were among the converts. Subsequently, the meager impact of the NAAEC disillusioned them.

13. See "Clinton Turns Up Volume on NAFTA Sales Pitch," *Congressional Quarterly Weekly Report*, October 23, 1993, 2863.

14. The United States and Mexico both authorized $225 million in paid-in capital and callable capital of $1.5 billion each to capitalize NADBank. As of March 2004, NADBank had received $349 million in paid-in capital and $2 billion in callable capital; see www.nadbank. org/english/general/general_frame.htm (accessed on April 22, 2005) and NADBank/BECC (2004).

15. The total authorized financing for the 52 approved projects in the United States is $340 million. The 24 approved projects in Mexico have total authorized financing of $302 million (NADBank/BECC 2004). For more information, see chapter 3 on environment.

Beyond these embellishments, Clinton's primary strategy for gaining NAFTA's passage could be summed up in three words: "jobs, jobs, jobs." Although most economists agree that employment levels are determined by macroeconomic policy in the short run, and labor skills coupled with workforce flexibility in the long run, both sides of the NAFTA debate put job gains or losses at the center of their talking points.[16] Clinton was not the first to push this argument: Robert Zoellick, counselor at the State Department in the George H. W. Bush administration, suggested that the "bottom line" of NAFTA was the creation of 44,000 to 150,000 jobs over four years (Zoellick 1991). While this number sounds large, it was tiny compared with US employment at the time, some 110 million. Mickey Kantor, President Clinton's first US Trade Representative (USTR), raised the estimate slightly to 200,000 in only two years.[17] Our own estimate was about 170,000 over several years—which we considered statistically insignificant (Hufbauer and Schott 1993, table 2.1). Not to be outdone, NAFTA opponents Ross Perot and Pat Choate projected job losses of up to 5.9 million.[18]

The jobs argument did little to convert anyone, though it may have hardened political positions. Clinton's Democratic administration was forced to rely on Republican support to ratify NAFTA. On November 17, 1993, the House of Representatives voted to pass NAFTA by a vote of 234 to 200; 132 Republicans and 102 Democrats supported the measure, while 143 Democrats and 56 Republicans plus the lone independent opposed it. Three days later, NAFTA passed the Senate by 61 to 38, with 34 Republicans and 27 Democrats voting in favor, and 10 Republicans and 28 Democrats against.

On January 1, 1994, NAFTA came into force. On the same day, Zapatista rebels in the southern Mexican state of Chiapas launched their uprising. Within a year, Mexico would be in financial crisis, and Clinton would ask Congress to bail out its new free trade partner.

The Peso Crisis of 1994–95

The peso crisis of late 1994–95, less than a year after NAFTA came into force, dramatically shaped the perceptions of the pact. To opponents, the

---

16. As then–Deputy Assistant Secretary of the Treasury for Economic Policy J. Bradford De-Long laments, political expediency usually trumps economics: "providing a short-run employment boost equivalent to an interest rate reduction of 0.1% gets turned into 'jobs-jobs-jobs' in the White House Briefing Room and then in the pages of the newspaper. . . . [National Economic Advisor Gene] Sperling always tried to keep the balance between number and quality of jobs: 'good jobs at good wages.' Clinton—on the few occasions I saw him in small groups—would always say, 'Yes, yes, I know, Gene. But that's too complicated. I need to simplify.' And he would always simplify to the 'more jobs' rather than the 'better jobs' position" (DeLong 2004).

17. See Mickey Kantor, "At Long Last, A Trade Pact to Be Proud Of," *Wall Street Journal*, August 17, 1993, A14.

18. See "NAFTA—The Showdown," *The Economist*, November 13, 1993.

temporal connection between NAFTA ratification and Mexico's economic collapse was too powerful to be mere coincidence. To supporters, the peso crisis was rooted in macroeconomic policy mistakes, far removed from the trade and investment bargain struck within NAFTA.

January 1994 marked both the start of the first year of NAFTA and the final year of the *sexenio* of the Salinas administration. Salinas anticipated a triumphal exit from Los Pinos and, with American support, an international perch as the director-general of the new World Trade Organization (WTO).

Salinas did several things—with varying degrees of disclosure—as he prepared for a glorious departure. Most publicly, in keeping with the tradition of the Partido Revolucionario Institucional (PRI) whereby each president selected his successor, Salinas anointed Luis Donaldo Colosio, his social development secretary, as the PRI candidate for president. Less obviously, but also consistent with PRI tradition, Salinas launched an off-the-books election-year spending splurge. To help finance Mexico's growing current account deficit—which reached almost 7 percent of GDP in 1994—Salinas authorized the Mexican Treasury to issue *tesobonos*, debt instruments with a new flavor. Tesobonos were short-term bills denominated in pesos but with a currency adjustment clause that effectively insured repayment in dollars. This feature attracted foreign investors, who were not inclined to buy high-yielding *cetes*, Mexican Treasury bills denominated solely in pesos.

In public pronouncements, Salinas asserted he would defend the dollar band—then about 3.3 pesos to the dollar.[19] Alongside these financial maneuvers, Salinas tolerated lax private banking practices, some of which bordered on the corrupt (La Porta, López-de-Silanes, and Zamarripa 2002). Mismatched banking assets and liabilities (currency and maturity) and "connected lending" were the order of the day.[20] Finally, and most secretively—but again in PRI tradition—some members of the Salinas family collected illicit payoffs, especially from the privatization of public corporations. While there is no hard evidence that President Salinas himself took kickbacks, his brother Raul Salinas collected bribes amounting to tens of millions of dollars. All these actions were to haunt Mexico, and President Salinas personally.

The first disquieting notes had relatively little to do with the end-of-term machinations of the Salinas presidency. First came the Zapatista rebellion, on January 1, 1994, in the southern state of Chiapas. Grievances in Chiapas had practically no link to NAFTA, but the symbolic date chosen for the rebellion deliberately coincided with the pact's entry into force.

---

19. Salinas's determination to defend the peso echoed that of President Lopez Portillo on the eve of the 1982 debt crisis. Lopez Portillo's vow to defend the peso "like a dog" is frequently misattributed to Salinas.

20. Mexican banking regulations supposedly limited currency and maturity mismatches, but the banks were able to find ways around the rules.

The Zapatistas saw in NAFTA a symbolic manifestation of the huge attention the Mexican government paid to the modern northern states and the neglect of the historically poor southern states. Concerns were heightened further when Colosio was assassinated in March 1994 while campaigning in Tijuana. To this day, theories and rumors abound in Mexico: Drug killing? Political killing? Nominated to take Colosio's place was Ernesto Zedillo, a well-regarded but relatively unknown technocrat and cabinet member who had never before held elective office.

Meanwhile, pumped up by federal spending and a consumer buying binge, the Mexican current account deficit continued to widen. Savvy Mexican investors, and a few foreign holders of Mexican tesobonos, grew nervous. They sold, sending dollars out of Mexico and depleting central bank reserves.[21]

The Banco de Mexico did not respond according to orthodox central bank doctrine. To maintain a fixed exchange rate, the bank should have allowed the domestic monetary base to shrink and peso interest rates to rise as dollars were withdrawn.[22] Instead, it purchased Mexican Treasury securities in sufficient volume to maintain the monetary base—and stave off soaring interest rates in an election year. This response ensured that as the year wore on and political troubles unfolded, the dollar reserve position of the Banco de Mexico would dwindle dramatically.

The crisis broke almost as soon as newly inaugurated President Ernesto Zedillo returned to Mexico City from the December 1994 Summit of the Americas held in Miami. The government first devalued the peso by 15 percent; then, unable to hold this line, it allowed the peso to float (Whitt 1996). The peso quickly collapsed from 3.4 to 7.2 per dollar, before recovering to 5.8 in April 1995 (OANDA Corp. 2004). Prices soared 24 percent in the first four months of 1995; December-over-December inflation for 1995 was 52 percent (INEGI 2004). With soaring inflation, domestic demand in real terms contracted sharply.

In January 1995, the Clinton administration crafted an international financial rescue package of historic proportion and committed the United States to almost $20 billion in immediate US assistance to Mexico, plus $30 billion from other sources—despite opposition in Congress and reservations by key donors in the International Monetary Fund (IMF).[23] In re-

---

21. Moreover, the Federal Reserve was raising short-term US interest rates in 1994. The target federal funds rate was raised six times from 3 percent in January to 5.5 percent in November, giving investors a further reason to shift dollars out of Mexico.

22. The extreme form of orthodox doctrine is a currency board system in which the monetary base responds one-for-one to any change in the central bank's foreign exchange reserves.

23. Much of the US support was channeled through the Exchange Stabilization Fund, thus avoiding the need for congressional approval. The total rescue package was roughly $50 billion, including $18 billion committed by the IMF, $5 billion from the Bank for International Settlements, $1 billion from four Latin American countries, and $1.5 billion from investment banks (Williamson 1995).

turn, Mexican policymakers introduced stringent controls on monetary and fiscal policy. Due to NAFTA obligations, however, Mexico largely abstained from the traditional dollops of trade protection and capital controls usually deployed by developing countries in response to balance-of-payments problems. Harsh medicine induced a deep but short-lived recession. By 1996, the Mexican economy had revived. The US loans were fully repaid, with interest, ahead of schedule in January 1997.

In sum, NAFTA facilitated the recovery of the Mexican economy in three ways:

- The US-inspired financial rescue package helped Mexico restructure its short-term dollar-denominated debt and ease its liquidity crisis. The US Treasury loans were all repaid ahead of schedule, yielding a net profit of almost $600 million (Rubin 2003, 34).

- Because of NAFTA obligations, Mexico followed a textbook recovery program based on fiscal constraint, tight money, and currency devaluation, rather than trade and capital controls.

- Open access to the US market, backed by NAFTA obligations, helped prevent an even more drastic recession in Mexico by spurring an export-led recovery in 1995–96.

If NAFTA had not been in place, the United States would surely have mounted financial assistance for Mexico, but the NAFTA partnership very likely enlarged the size of the rescue package and accelerated the speed of its delivery.[24]

Did NAFTA Contribute to the Peso Crisis?

Some critics argue that NAFTA negotiators could and should have done more to guard against prospective financial crises. Two arguments are used to blame the crisis on NAFTA: inadequate monitoring of financial institutions and "irrational exuberance" over Mexico's economic prospects.

Inadequate Surveillance. Arguably, NAFTA negotiators could have agreed to mutual surveillance of monetary, fiscal, and exchange rate policies and to mutual surveillance of banks and other financial institutions. Some analysts called for the negotiation of a side pact on macroeconomic policy to ensure more frequent consultations among the region's treasury and cen-

---

24. By contrast, in the Mexican debt crisis of 1982, US support was far smaller and more measured; see Cline (1995). The Mexican recovery also was much slower. As Rubin (2003, 34) noted, "After the 1982 crisis, Mexico took seven years to regain access to capital markets. In 1995, it took seven months." Moreover, US exports to Mexico declined almost 50 percent in 1983 from their precrisis peak and didn't regain that level until 1988. In 1995, US exports dropped 9 percent from the previous year but surpassed precrisis levels in 1996.

tral bank officials (Williamson 1995). These subjects would be novel in an FTA. Even the European Union did not get around to mutual surveillance of macroeconomic policies until the Maastricht Treaty of 1992, and even today the regulation of European banks and other financial institutions remains a matter for national authorities. Low-key tripartite swap and consultation arrangements had been in place before the peso crisis. Evidently these were insufficient to head off financial mismanagement in Mexico City.

Moreover, it must be acknowledged that Washington would not welcome Canadian or Mexican criticism of US macroeconomic policy, and reciprocal sentiments prevail in Ottawa and Mexico City. Recent US corporate and accounting scandals ranging from Enron to mutual funds demonstrate two things: Mexico has no monopoly on lax regulation within North America, and no financial regulator has an unblemished record of initiating preemptive reform before something blows up. This is not an argument for abandoning regulatory vigilance; rather it is an observation that commends strengthened surveillance (at the national and multilateral levels).

In retrospect, NAFTA can be criticized for going light on macroeconomic and financial surveillance. But there was no appetite in the Bush or Clinton administrations to take on this agenda, and it would have met stiff resistance in Ottawa and Mexico City. It is a counsel of perfection to argue that free trade and investment in North America should have awaited macroeconomic and financial rectitude. Those goals are certainly worthy, but they remain distant beacons for North America.

Overconfidence. Did overconfidence in the wake of NAFTA intensify the rush of "hot money" into Mexico, increasing its vulnerability to crisis? Ratification of NAFTA in 1993, together with Mexican accession to the Organization for Economic Cooperation and Development (OECD) in May 1994, did create a heady mood. Wall Street awarded higher ratings to Mexican securities. Investors became less critical of Mexico, instead assuming that the economic gains to Mexico from NAFTA would translate into quick financial returns. However, we think it is unfair to blame NAFTA for fiscal splurge in Mexico and other machinations of the PRI. NAFTA enabled the Mexican kabuki show to go on longer than it might otherwise have (as foreign investors willingly acquired high-yielding tesobonos), but it did not put the show on stage.

Current Account since the Crisis

The peso crisis forced a dramatic reduction of Mexico's then unsustainable current account deficit, which reached 7 percent of GDP in 1994. Since then, the Mexican current account balance has remained in the sustainable range and has attracted little attention (table 1.1). Larger trade

Table 1.1 Overview of the Mexican current account, 1994–2004 (billions of US dollars)

	1994	1995	1996	1997	1998	1999	2000	2001	2002	2003	2004
Current account balance											
Billions of US dollars	−29.7	−1.6	−2.5	−7.7	−16.1	−14.0	−18.2	−18.2	−14.1	−8.7	−7.4
Percent of GDP	7.0	0.5	0.8	1.9	3.8	2.9	3.1	2.9	2.2	1.4	1.1
Receipts											
Merchandise exports	60.9	79.5	96.0	110.4	117.5	136.4	166.5	158.4	160.8	164.9	188.0
Nonfactor services	10.3	9.7	10.6	11.1	11.5	11.7	13.7	12.7	12.7	12.6	13.9
Factor services	3.4	3.8	4.2	4.6	5.0	4.5	6.1	5.1	4.1	3.8	5.1
Total transfers	3.8	4.0	4.6	5.3	6.0	6.3	7.0	9.4	10.3	13.9	17.1
Of which household remittances	3.5	3.7	4.2	4.3	5.6	5.9	6.6	8.9	9.8	13.4	16.6
Total	78.4	97.0	115.3	131.3	140.1	158.9	193.3	185.6	187.9	195.2	224.2
Payments											
Merchandise imports	79.3	72.5	89.5	109.8	125.4	142.0	174.5	168.4	168.7	170.5	196.8
Nonfactor services	12.3	9.0	10.2	11.8	12.4	13.5	16.0	16.2	16.7	17.1	18.6
Factor services	16.4	17.1	18.1	17.3	18.3	17.4	20.9	19.1	16.5	16.2	16.1
Total transfers	—	—	—	—	—	—	—	—	—	—	0.1
Total	108.0	98.6	117.8	139.0	156.1	172.9	211.4	203.8	201.9	203.9	231.6

— = less than $50 million

Sources: Banco de Mexico (2005), OECD (2004a, 2005).

surpluses with the United States have been offset by growing trade deficits with the rest of the world.[25] Growing remittances (almost entirely from Mexican immigrants in the United States) have contributed significantly to Mexican foreign exchange earnings, outpacing FDI in 2003 and reaching $16.6 billion in 2004.

Current Challenges to Economic Integration

The peso crisis is now long past. While a fresh financial crisis cannot be ruled out, the prospects are more distant due to the tight fiscal and monetary policies pursued by Mexican officials.[26] But other problems continue to challenge the pursuit of economic integration in North America and the promise of greater prosperity in Mexico.

Mexico's Democratic Challenge

In 2000, the seven-decade political domination of the PRI ended with the election of Vicente Fox of the Partido Acción Nacional (PAN) to the Mexican presidency, the first peaceful transfer of power between political parties in modern Mexico.[27] The role of NAFTA, and the broader Mexican economic opening, in the realization of greater democracy are difficult to assess, although closer external scrutiny made the 2000 election much harder to rig.

Greater democracy has been a blessing for Mexico, but it has put demands on governance that did not exist under the one-party rule of the PRI. In the PRI era, the Mexican Congress dutifully approved the president's policies with little debate; the president secured support for his policies from state governments through revenue sharing and PRI party discipline. Without these carrots and sticks, Mexican leaders now need to forge coalitions among different parties and interest groups. In the long run, this process may lead to better and more stable policies; in the short run, however, it has often produced stalemate in Congress and the nation at large.

To be specific, President Fox has not enjoyed the same sway over the Mexican Congress and state governors as his predecessors. Nor has his administration been effectively managed. Fox's attempts to reform the Mexican tax system yielded modest results in 2004; his proposals to reform Mexican energy policies hit a stone wall (Ramírez de la O 2004).[28]

---

25. Like the United States, Mexico imports most of its consumer electronics from Asia.

26. In January 2005, Moody's Investor Service raised Mexico's currency rating to Baa1, two levels above the lowest investment grade rating (*New York Times,* January 7, 2005, 5).

27. Although the PRI governed Mexico continuously for seven decades, with the party always choosing the occupant of Los Pinos, power did change hands peacefully between discordant factions within the PRI.

These failures have already affected the competitiveness of Mexican industry in home and world markets.

NAFTAphobia Redux

The mantra of "No More NAFTAs" of Pat Buchanan and Ross Perot was revived in 2004, complemented by attacks from antiglobalization polemicists. During the Democratic presidential primaries in early 2004, the 10-year-old trade agreement again became a campaign theme. Strong anti-NAFTA rhetoric played particularly well in midwestern manufacturing states and southern textile-producing areas. North Carolina Senator John Edwards, the son of a textile mill worker and eventual vice presidential candidate, declared he would have voted against NAFTA if he had had the chance.[29] Edwards blamed NAFTA in particular and trade in general for the sharp decline in US manufacturing employment in recent years: "I saw what happened in my hometown when the mill closed. . . . [T]hese trade policies are killing your jobs."[30] The eventual Democratic nominee, Massachusetts Senator John Kerry, who voted in favor of NAFTA in 1993, argued that NAFTA should be renegotiated to cover more comprehensive labor and environmental obligations and enforcement procedures.[31]

While the inherently protectionist "trade policies are killing your jobs" argument is a campaign favorite, another group contends that free trade harms the developing world. Perennial presidential candidate Ralph

---

28. Mexico raised only 10 percent of its GDP in taxes in 2003, well below other countries at its stage in development (SHCP 2004, annex A). Consequently, the country remains highly dependent on Pemex revenues to finance government expenditures. Transfers from Pemex and oil-related rights and royalties accounted for 6.6 percent of GDP, with excise taxes bringing total oil-related revenue to 7.9 percent of GDP in 2003 (SHCP 2004, annex A). See Ramírez de la O (2004) for an accounting of Mexican finances that separates tax from nontax rather than oil from nonoil related revenue. In November 2004, the Mexican Congress approved a reform law; Mexican corporate income tax will gradually be reduced from a 33 percent statutory rate in 2004 to 28 percent by 2007. While the corporate tax reforms are a step in the right direction, the Mexican budget still depends inordinately on Pemex revenues—leaving Pemex little financial capacity for new investment. Moreover, the national tax revenues are completely inadequate to fund needed highways, ports, and other infrastructure.

29. In his run for the Senate in 1998, Edwards campaigned against NAFTA and fast-track trade negotiation authority, later renamed trade promotion authority (TPA).

30. See "In Ohio, Trade Talk Resonates," *Baltimore Sun*, February 25, 2004, 17A.

31. In response to a question on how to fix NAFTA, Kerry said, "I want to put [changes] into the body of the treaty. I know the Republicans don't like that approach. But I believe it's important for sustaining the consensus on trade. And I'm not talking about draconian, counterproductive standards. I'm talking about doing reasonable things. . . . I'm for the trade laws we passed being implemented. In NAFTA, we have labor [and environmental] protections in the side agreements. But they have not been enforced." (See "John Kerry's To-Do List; Create Jobs, Get Tough with China, and Redefine NAFTA All High on the Democratic Hopeful's Agenda," *BusinessWeek Online*, February 26, 2004.)

Nader, along with Naomi Klein, led the "anticorporate" movement, relying heavily on worker exploitation anecdotes in the low-wage textile and apparel industries.[32] The error we see is the implication that the developing countries would be helped by protection in the North, which interrupts trade and investment. For example, Klein observes that most of the workers in the Philippines factory she visited are the children of rural farmers (Klein 2002, 219–21) but ignores the fact that for rural farmers in the developing world, factory employment is a big step up. In a study on factory employment in Vietnam, Glewwe (2000) noted that at 42 cents per hour, "wages paid by joint ventures and [foreign-owned businesses] are but a small fraction of the wages paid for comparable work in the U.S. and other wealthy countries, [though] these workers are still better off than they would be in almost any other job available in Vietnam." Indeed, empirical research by Graham (2000, table 4.2) found that US affiliates in low-income countries tend to pay twice the local manufacturing wage—which implies a high multiple of rural earnings.

Many critics of NAFTA (and free trade more broadly) form an ideological alliance around environmental and labor standards. A favored idea is to create rules against imports that are produced in violation of enumerated labor and environmental standards. To a considerable extent, such rules would deny comparative advantages to developing countries. NAFTA rules of origin and antidumping actions illustrate how new standards could be misused (or abused) to create nontariff barriers that promote neither the environment nor workers' rights.[33]

Balancing Trade and Security

The terrorist attacks of September 11, 2001, brought security to the forefront of the North American agenda. Following the attacks, the United States sharply elevated security measures along its borders, causing lengthy delays. Firms that ship goods across the NAFTA borders must now consider the "security tax" of border delays and the risk of a total

---

32. Anticorporate and antiglobalist arguments often call up images of 19th century worker tenements and textile sweatshops in the United States to bring home the reality of present-day conditions in the developing world. See Klein (2002) and Public Citizen (2004), founded by Ralph Nader, for an exposition of the anticorporate argument.

33. NAFTA's excessively strict rules of origin suppress trade both by keeping foreign goods out and by forcing firms to keep lengthy paper trails to certify NAFTA origin. Similar problems could quickly arise with respect to imposing labor and environmental standards on trade. Who would certify that they were being upheld? If standards are applied and enforced at the national level, how much exploitation is too much? Should the standards apply to all industries or only those that export? And what type of enforcement measures would best promote compliance? In a constructive vein, Elliott and Freeman (2003) suggest that a "market for standards" can be fostered in trade agreements, whereby developed-world consumers can be encouraged by labeling and other means to award higher value to goods that were manufactured or grown under demonstrably acceptable working and environmental conditions.

border shutdown. The potential for security barriers of the future to replace trade policy barriers of the past is all too real.

In response to September 11, the United States negotiated two separate bilateral agreements—Smart Borders and the Border Partnership Action Plan with Canada and Mexico, respectively. These initiatives are designed to both improve security and minimize delays. However, the basic structure of border inspections—which was designed to collect tariffs and detect smuggling, not combat terrorism—remains in place. Better approaches must be implemented to plan for the eventuality of an attack (Dobson 2002, Goldfarb and Robson 2003). In the short run, there are reasons for envisioning how a security imperative might promote deeper US-Canada rather than US-Mexico bilateral cooperation.[34] Hufbauer and Vega-Cánovas (2003), among others, argue for an entirely new system of border management. The crux of their proposal is to allow joint inspections of low-risk trade to take place at a secure site at the point of origin and away from the border and then pass through the border with minimal delay. Tamper-proof containers and GPS tracking and other technologies could be used to ensure that precleared cargo remained secure from origin to destination. Preclearance would significantly reduce the strain on border inspectors. As a step in this direction, the Fast and Secure Trade Program was initiated to allow low-risk carriers a streamlined method of clearing customs. However, only 4.4 percent of trade crossing the US-Canada border uses the program. Ontario Premier Dalton McGuinty has urged cooperation to publicize the program and improve its effectiveness.[35] In the final chapter, we discuss our own proposals for improved border cooperation.

Assessing NAFTA

Different analysts use different standards to assess the NAFTA record. We try to judge the three countries on how well they have met the objectives that NAFTA negotiators set out in Article 102, which are summarized as follows:

- promote increased regional trade and investment;

---

34. Given the shared language and culture, the history of close cooperation on defense and intelligence issues, and effective Canadian government response toward terrorist threats, Bailey (2004) argues that national and public security cooperation with Canada will evolve more quickly than that with Mexico.

35. Delays are endemic on both the US-Mexico and US-Canada borders, due both to increased security measures and the dramatic increase in trade that came with NAFTA. McGuinty worries that "Border delays are making Ontario industry increasingly uncompetitive . . . [and] function as a quasi-tariff on Ontario goods and services heading south" (see "Wheels of Trade Seize Up at World's Busiest Border," *Financial Times*, August 3, 2004, 3; and BNA 2004).

- increase employment and improve working conditions and living standards in each country;

- provide a framework for the conduct of trilateral trade relations and for the management of disputes;

- strengthen and enforce environmental laws and basic workers' rights; and

- work together to promote "further trilateral, regional, and multilateral cooperation to expand and enhance the benefits of this Agreement."

Against these yardsticks, we find that NAFTA has been largely, but not totally, successful.

Trade and Investment

NAFTA has contributed to a sharp expansion of regional trade since the early 1990s. Table 1.2 summarizes US bilateral merchandise trade with its NAFTA partners. Since 1993, the year before NAFTA came into force, through 2004, US merchandise exports to and imports from Mexico have increased by 166 and 290 percent, respectively.[36] Total two-way US-Mexico merchandise trade has grown 227 percent; in contrast, US trade with non-NAFTA countries increased only 124 percent in the same period. Likewise, US-Canada trade continued the robust expansion inspired by the CUSFTA in 1989. Since 1989, US exports to and imports from Canada rose 140 and 190 percent, respectively; total US-Canada trade roughly kept pace with trade growth with the rest of the world. Trade with NAFTA partners in 2004 accounted for 31 percent of total US merchandise trade, up from 29 and 26 percent in 1993 and 1989, respectively.

Of course, an increase in trade *with* NAFTA partners is not in itself evidence of an increase in trade *because of* NAFTA. In appendix 1A, we survey the literature on the effects of NAFTA on trade volumes in North America. As in most integration arrangements, ex ante projections of trade growth seem to have underestimated the impact of NAFTA on the three economies. But we don't really know by how much. Estimates using computable general equilibrium and gravity models of the amount of two-way trade generated due to NAFTA vary greatly. Depending on the model selected, the trade gains from NAFTA range from modest (as low as 5 percent of two-way US-Mexico trade) to very large (greater than 50 percent of two-way trade). Disentangling the effect of NAFTA on trade

---

36. Much of the increased trade with Mexico reflects the expansion of assembly operations. Mexican plants registered under the maquiladora program and the Program for Temporary Imports used to make Exports (Programa de Importación Temporal para Producir Artículos de Exportación, or PITEX) accounted for 81 percent of total Mexican exports to the United States in 2003.

from the other events in the past decade is difficult, but the available evidence points to a strong positive impact.

Decadal trade statistics mask two distinct periods of trade integration: the US-led boom of the 1990s and the US-led recession and slow recovery since 2000. In the initial period, US exports to its NAFTA partners doubled in value and increased twice as fast as non-NAFTA shipments, while US imports from the region increased even more (though only slightly faster than imports from the rest of the world). The US trade deficit with the NAFTA region rose from $9 billion in 1993 to $77 billion in 2000. Canada accounted for the larger share of the increase in the NAFTA deficit, some $42 billion, whereas the deficit with Mexico increased by $26 billion. At the same time, the US trade deficit with the rest of the world rose $301 billion.

NAFTA trade actually declined in 2000–03 before rebounding in 2004. Overall, US trade with its NAFTA partners rose 8.7 percent during 2000–04; exports grew by only 3.6 percent, while US imports increased by 12.8 percent. However, US exports to Mexico actually declined slightly compared with a modest increase of 6.4 percent ($11 billion) in shipments to Canada.[37]

Has US trade with Mexico "hit a wall"? One explanation for the drop in US exports is the sharp drop in Mexican demand during 2000–03, when Mexican GDP growth averaged only 0.7 percent compared with Canada's modestly higher 2.3 percent. "When the US economy sneezes, the Mexican economy catches a cold," and US exports take a hit—but that story is too simple. Despite stronger growth in 2004, the introduction of highly competitive suppliers from East Asia has severely cut into the US share of the Mexican market in several important sectors (see appendix 1B).

Taken together, trade in autos and parts, agriculture, and energy account for roughly one-third of intraregional trade. Later chapters discuss these sectors in more detail, but each deserves a preview in this chapter. We then assess the impact of the broader increase in trade and investment.

Autos

Autos and auto parts account for 20 percent of total intra-NAFTA trade, the largest single sector. Liberalization began well before NAFTA, but the agreement extended the process. Since the 1965 Auto Pact and the CUSFTA essentially integrated auto trade between Canada and the United States, NAFTA's greatest contribution to the auto sector was to bring Mexico into the fold. NAFTA phased out purely national content requirements, but as a political price, it tightened the CUSFTA rules of origin and associated North American content requirements. NAFTA also phased out so-called trade-balancing requirements (a Mexican policy device) as well as tariff and nontariff barriers within the finished auto and parts trade.

---

37. USITC Interactive Tariff and Trade Dataweb, 2005, http://dataweb.usitc.gov (accessed on March 15, 2005).

Table 1.2   US merchandise trade with NAFTA partners, 1989–2004
(billions of US dollars)

Partner	1989	1990	1991	1992	1993	1994	1995	1996	1997
Canada									
Exports	78.3	83.0	85.1	90.2	100.2	114.3	126.0	132.6	150.1
Imports	88.2	91.4	91.1	98.5	110.9	128.9	145.1	156.5	168.1
Total	166.5	174.3	176.3	188.7	211.1	243.2	271.1	289.1	318.2
Balance	−9.9	−8.4	−6.0	−8.3	−10.7	−14.7	−19.1	−23.9	−17.9
Mexico									
Exports	25.0	28.4	33.3	40.6	41.6	50.8	46.3	56.8	71.4
Imports	27.2	30.2	31.2	35.2	39.9	49.5	61.7	73.0	85.9
Total	52.2	58.6	64.5	75.8	81.6	100.3	108.0	129.8	157.3
Balance	−2.2	−1.8	2.1	5.4	1.7	1.3	−15.4	−16.2	−14.5
World									
Exports	363.8	393.0	421.9	447.5	464.9	512.4	583.0	622.8	687.6
Imports	473.4	473.4	496.0	488.8	532.1	580.5	663.8	743.5	870.2
Total	837.2	866.4	917.9	936.3	997.0	1,092.9	1,246.9	1,366.3	1,557.8
Balance	−109.6	−80.4	−74.1	−41.3	−67.2	−68.1	−80.8	−120.7	−182.6
NAFTA									
Exports	103.2	111.3	118.4	130.8	141.8	165.1	172.3	189.3	221.5
Imports	115.4	121.5	122.3	133.7	150.9	178.4	206.8	229.5	253.9
Total	218.6	232.9	240.8	264.4	292.7	343.5	379.2	418.8	475.4
Balance	−12.2	−10.2	−3.9	−2.9	−9.1	−13.3	−34.5	−40.1	−32.4
Non-NAFTA									
Exports	260.5	281.6	303.4	316.7	323.0	347.3	410.7	433.5	466.1
Imports	358.0	351.9	373.7	355.2	381.2	402.0	457.0	514.0	616.3
Total	618.5	633.5	677.1	671.9	704.2	749.4	867.7	947.5	1,082.4
Balance	−97.5	−70.2	−70.3	−38.5	−58.2	−54.7	−46.3	−80.5	−150.2

Source: USITC Interactive Tariff and Trade Dataweb, http://dataweb.usitc.gov (accessed on March 15, 2005).

Phaseout periods of up to 10 years were granted to give the Mexican industry (including foreign-owned assembly plants) time to adjust.

The growth in auto trade owes both to Mexican domestic reforms and NAFTA liberalization. Mexico has attracted substantial investment from the United States, Japan, and Germany, increasing its auto production from 1.1 million units in 1993 to 1.8 million in 2002 (Ward's Communications 2003).[38] Mexican auto trade in 2003 was five times greater than in 1993; the auto sector accounted for 22 percent of Mexico's total exports in 2003.[39] Much of the trade increase can be attributed to specialization, as

---

38. A unit is a passenger car, truck (light or medium/heavy), or a bus. Light trucks have accounted for most of the production increase in Mexico.

39. This figure includes engines, wire harnesses, motor vehicle seats, and fuel pumps, which are not classified in Harmonized Schedule chapter 87.

1998	1999	2000	2001	2002	2003	2004	Percent change, 1989–2004	Percent change, 1993–2004	Percent change, 2000–04
154.2	163.9	176.4	163.7	160.8	169.5	187.7	139.8	87.4	6.4
174.8	198.3	229.2	217.0	210.6	224.2	255.9	190.1	130.7	11.7
329.0	362.2	405.6	380.7	371.4	393.6	443.6	166.5	110.1	9.4
−20.7	−34.4	−52.8	−53.2	−49.8	−54.7	−68.2			
79.0	87.0	111.7	101.5	97.5	97.5	110.8	343.7	166.1	−0.8
94.7	109.7	135.9	131.4	134.7	138.1	155.8	473.3	290.3	14.7
173.7	196.8	247.6	232.9	232.3	235.5	266.6	411.2	226.9	7.7
−15.7	−22.7	−24.2	−29.9	−37.2	−40.6	−45.1			
680.5	692.8	780.4	731.0	693.3	723.7	816.5	124.5	75.7	4.6
913.9	1,024.8	1,216.9	1,142.0	1,163.5	1,259.4	1,469.5	210.4	176.2	20.8
1,594.4	1,717.6	1,997.3	1,873.0	1,856.8	1,983.1	2,286.0	173.1	129.3	14.5
−233.4	−331.9	−436.5	−410.9	−470.3	−535.7	−652.9			
233.2	251.0	288.2	265.2	258.3	266.9	298.5	189.1	110.5	3.6
269.6	308.0	365.1	348.4	345.3	362.2	411.8	256.8	173.0	12.8
502.7	559.0	653.3	613.6	603.7	629.2	710.3	224.9	142.7	8.7
−36.4	−57.1	−77.0	−83.2	−87.0	−95.3	−113.3			
447.3	441.9	492.3	465.8	434.9	456.8	518.1	98.8	60.4	5.2
644.3	716.7	851.8	793.6	810.2	897.2	1,057.7	195.4	177.5	24.2
1,091.6	1,158.6	1,344.0	1,259.3	1,253.2	1,354.0	1,575.8	154.8	123.8	17.2
−197.0	−274.9	−359.5	−327.8	−383.3	−440.4	−539.6			

parts manufacturers and assembly plants have been reoriented to take advantage of economies of scale. As a result, supply lines for finished vehicles routinely cross national boundaries, as parts and assembly work is performed wherever it is most efficient.[40] In Canada and the United States, this process was far along when NAFTA came into force, but it has deepened in the NAFTA decade. While international supply lines are a boon to efficiency, reliance on just-in-time manufacturing processes makes the industry very sensitive to border disruptions.

40. Because trade statistics are kept as gross value rather than value added, international supply lines probably inflate trade figures in the auto sectors. For example, the value of a part that is produced in Mexico and then shipped to the United States for assembly will be counted as intra-NAFTA trade again if the assembled vehicle is shipped back to Mexico for sale. It is not unusual for auto parts to cross national borders several times during the production process (Hart 2004).

Agriculture

Agriculture remains the make-or-break issue for multilateral and regional trade agreements. This is equally true of NAFTA. US agricultural trade with NAFTA partners has more than doubled in value over 1993–2003 and has grown twice as fast as agricultural trade with the rest of the world.[41] While agriculture accounts for only about 5 percent ($35 billion) of total intraregional trade in NAFTA, this number understates its political sensitivity. Several NAFTA disputes have taken place in agriculture; we highlight the US-Canada disputes over softwood lumber and the Canadian Wheat Board, and US-Mexico disputes over sugar and high-fructose corn syrup, in chapter 5 on agriculture.

NAFTA does not have a unified text on agriculture. Instead there are three separate bilateral agreements: between the United States and Canada, the United States and Mexico, and Canada and Mexico. The US-Canada agreement maintains significant restrictions and tariff rate quotas held over from the CUSFTA, particularly on trade in sugar, dairy, and poultry. By contrast, the US agreement with Mexico is in theory far more liberalizing but with long phaseout periods for trade restrictions on sensitive products.[42] Despite these long phaseout periods, Mexico has not made the infrastructure investment necessary to restructure its agrarian economy. The extent to which small Mexican farmers, cultivating traditional crops, have suffered is a matter of dispute. Chapter 5 on agriculture suggests that critics have exaggerated the adverse effects of NAFTA.

In the case of corn, the Mexican government chose not to enforce the tariff-rate quota NAFTA authorized, so the actual phaseout period was much shorter than was negotiated. Mexico is not self-sufficient in corn production, and the Mexican government waived at least $2 billion in tariff revenues, using the argument that cheaper corn imports were necessary to meet growing domestic livestock demand and control inflation.

Energy

Energy trade has long been a key component of North American economic integration. Although prices are volatile, energy accounts for about 7 percent of intra-NAFTA trade, of which US imports from Canada and Mexico represent the lion's share. The value of total US energy imports from NAFTA partners was $56 billion in 2003.[43] The United States imports

---

41. See table 5.2 in chapter 5 on agriculture.

42. Moreover, the United States has sidestepped its commitments on sugar, and both countries are using phytosanitary standards for protectionist purposes.

43. Defined as imports of coal (SITC 32), crude oil (333), refined oil (334), propane and butane (342), natural gas (343), and electricity (351) as reported by USITC Interactive Tariff and Trade Dataweb 2005, http://dataweb.usitc.gov (accessed on March 15, 2005).

more petroleum from Canada (2.1 million barrels per day in 2003) than from Saudi Arabia (1.8 mmb/d); Mexico is a close third with 1.6 mmb/d (EIA 2004b, table S3). Canada is by far the leading source of US natural gas imports; Canadian pipelines accounted for 3.8 trillion of a total 4 trillion cubic feet of natural gas imported by the United States in 2002. Mexico has gone from roughly balanced natural gas trade with the United States (importing 61 billion cubic feet and exporting 54 billion cubic feet in 1999) to become a significant net importer (importing 263 billion cubic feet and exporting only 2 billion cubic feet in 2002) (EIA 2004c, table 9). This shift of fortune reflects inadequate investment and rising demand rather than a shortage of Mexican reserves.

While both the CUSFTA and NAFTA liberalized energy investment between the United States and Canada, Mexico opted out of NAFTA's provisions in order to maintain its constitutional ban on foreign investment in the energy sector. As a result, inadequate investment has handicapped the Mexican oil and gas industry, threatening to make Mexico a net energy importer by the end of the decade. North American demand for energy is expected to grow by 1.5 percent annually through 2025 (EIA 2004a, table A1). Unless there is a dramatic push for greater energy production within North America and sharply increased conservation efforts, much of this demand will have to be met with extra-NAFTA imports.

Effects of Increased Trade

The increase in trade within North America since NAFTA is impressive. However, income gains depend importantly on whether intra-NAFTA trade resulted in an equivalent increase in global trade or whether the intra-NAFTA gains merely reflect trade diversion—shifting trade from countries that are otherwise more competitive but whose exports continue to face tariff barriers in the NAFTA region.

In a few industries, most notably textiles and apparel where "yarn forward" rules of origin were imposed specifically to make US textile firms the preferred suppliers for Mexican apparel manufacturers, NAFTA has indeed fostered trade diversion.[44] Burfisher, Robinson, and Theirfelder (2001) point out the connection between trade diversion and rules of origin: Industries with the strictest rules of origin appear to be the same ones where NAFTA has had a diversionary effect. Fukao, Okubo, and Stern (2002) empirically verify the diversionary effects of NAFTA on textile and apparel trade by examining the relationship between the US tariff barrier faced by a supplying country and the growth in its share of the US import

---

44. Since "yarn forward" rules strictly limited Mexican purchases of Asian fabrics, they severely limited the growth of Mexican apparel exports to the US market. At the same time, they diverted Mexican yarn and fabric purchases from Asian to US suppliers.

market.[45] Importantly, the authors do not find diversionary tendencies when they examine other important trading industries, such as autos and electronics.

The World Bank (2003, chapter 6) notes that the increase in Mexico's share of aggregate NAFTA imports from 1994 to 2001 (from about 6 percent to over 9 percent) mirrors the growth of Mexico's share of non-NAFTA imports (from 0.2 to 0.4 percent)—suggesting that the increase in Mexico's aggregate import share is not due to diversionary factors. The wider range of products traded provides additional evidence of NAFTA trade creation. In 1993, 5,814 tariff lines covered all Mexican exports to the United States; by 2002, this figure had expanded to 8,328.[46] On balance, the empirical studies find that NAFTA tends to promote trade creation far more than trade diversion.

The success of NAFTA comes despite its restrictive rules of origin. Such rules determine which products are eligible for NAFTA trade preferences. Rules of origin were built into NAFTA (as in nearly all FTAs) for the announced purpose of preventing "trade deflection." Without such rules, third-country exporters could ship their wares to the NAFTA country with the lowest tariff rate and then reexport them duty-free throughout the free trade region. The idea is to preclude products largely made in non-NAFTA countries from receiving NAFTA benefits.

That said, the NAFTA rules of origin had an intended and protectionist side effect in selected sectors (notably textiles and apparel and autos): to restrict the use of intermediate goods from outside NAFTA. Unintentionally, the rules created administrative barriers to trade on goods within NAFTA—by forcing importers to maintain a lengthy paper trail on components used in highly fabricated goods. These side effects impose significant burdens on NAFTA producers. For example, Carrère and de Melo (2004) found that compliance costs entailed by rules of origin significantly offset, and in some cases outweigh, market access preferences granted under NAFTA—particularly in textiles and apparel.

Recognizing this problem, NAFTA trade ministers agreed in July 2004 to liberalize rules of origin affecting more than $20 billion in trade of foodstuffs and consumer and industrial products (NAFTA Free Trade Commission Joint Statement, July 16, 2004). We argue that such incremental reforms should be broadened. Distortions that rules of origin generate

---

45. Among 60 industries classified at the two-digit level, the authors detected evidence of trade diversion in 15 cases. Of these, four are within textiles and apparel. See Fukao, Okubo, and Stern (2002, tables 1 and 2).

46. See the World Bank's World Integrated Trade Solution database at http://wits.world bank. org (accessed on February 23, 2004). Mexico did not report tariff line data in 1993, so we cannot compare the number of products exported to Mexico pre- and post-NAFTA. The growth in tariff line trade between Canada and the United States is much smaller, due to stronger integration before NAFTA.

should be redressed by harmonizing and reducing the most-favored nation (MFN) tariffs of all three countries, thereby eliminating the incentive for trade deflection, the legitimate rationale, if not the real reason, for such rules (see the final chapter for our policy recommendations on this issue).

Services

Intraregional trade in services also increased significantly during NAFTA's first decade.[47] However, the growth was less pronounced than in merchandise trade, and NAFTA reforms made a difference in only a few sectors. For some services, notably tourism, barriers were already very low before the trade agreements were ratified. For others, such as trucking and maritime transport, the barriers were not only high but also almost impervious to liberalization. Moreover, the number of NAFTA temporary work visas for professional workers was tiny, not enough to have much effect on the recorded flows of cross-border services income. The CUSFTA and NAFTA (beyond the WTO commitments made under the auspices of the General Agreement on Trade in Services, GATS) greatly liberalized some services sectors, particularly financial services, but other sectors were barely affected.

Overall, US services trade with its NAFTA partners grew more slowly than both merchandise and services trade with the rest of the world (table 1.3). From 1993 to 2003, US two-way trade in services with its NAFTA partners rose from $44 billion to $74 billion, or by 70 percent. Services trade with Canada and Mexico grew 78 and 59 percent, respectively. The US services trade *surplus* in 2003 with the NAFTA region was $12.5 billion—about the same as in 1993. However, services trade growth in NAFTA was slower than growth with non-NAFTA countries (91 percent). In all, 14.2 percent of total US services trade was with NAFTA in 2002, down slightly from 15.7 percent in 1993.

Table 1.4 provides data on services trade by sector; these data do not include services provided both ways between affiliates and their parent corporations. In most sectors, both payments and receipts have grown significantly. However, in the telecommunications sector, payments to Canada and Mexico have both decreased, reflecting a sharp decline in so-called accounting rates (termination charges by the call-delivering carrier).

In the case of Mexico, telecom liberalization has been slow in coming. In response to a law giving the former state monopoly, Teléfonos de Mexico (Telmex), the right to negotiate terms and conditions for the ter-

---

47. Services trade data are much less comprehensive than merchandise trade data. With 48 million persons crossing the Canada-US border each year, and with telephones and computers allowing lawyers, architects, and other professionals to carry on international business from their own desks, it seems likely that official statistics significantly underestimate the exchanges taking place.

Table 1.3   US trade in cross-border services with NAFTA partners, 1989–2003 (billions of US dollars)

Partner	1989	1990	1991	1992	1993	1994	1995	1996	1997
Canada									
Exports	13.3	15.7	17.8	17.3	16.9	17.0	17.7	19.3	20.3
Imports	8.6	9.1	9.7	8.3	8.9	9.7	10.8	12.2	13.7
Total	22.0	24.8	27.5	25.6	25.8	26.7	28.5	31.5	34.0
Balance	4.7	6.6	8.1	9.0	8.0	7.3	6.9	7.1	6.6
Mexico									
Exports	4.8	8.6	9.7	10.5	10.4	11.3	8.7	9.4	10.8
Imports	6.7	6.7	7.1	7.3	7.4	7.8	7.9	8.9	9.8
Total	11.6	15.3	16.7	17.7	17.8	19.2	16.6	18.3	20.6
Balance	−1.9	1.9	2.6	3.2	3.0	3.5	0.8	0.5	0.9
World									
Exports	117.9	137.2	152.4	163.6	171.1	186.1	203.1	221.4	237.9
Imports	85.3	98.2	99.9	102.0	107.8	118.3	126.8	136.9	150.0
Total	203.2	235.4	252.4	265.6	278.9	304.4	329.8	358.3	387.8
Balance	32.6	39.0	52.5	61.6	63.3	67.7	76.3	84.5	87.9
NAFTA									
Exports	18.1	24.3	27.4	27.7	27.3	28.3	26.4	28.7	31.1
Imports	15.4	15.9	16.8	15.6	16.3	17.5	18.7	21.2	23.5
Total	33.5	40.1	44.2	43.3	43.7	45.8	45.2	49.9	54.6
Balance	2.8	8.4	10.6	12.1	11.0	10.7	7.7	7.6	7.6
Non-NAFTA									
Exports	99.8	113.0	125.0	135.9	143.8	157.8	176.6	192.6	206.8
Imports	69.9	82.3	83.2	86.4	91.5	100.8	108.0	115.7	126.4
Total	169.7	195.3	208.2	222.3	235.2	258.6	284.6	308.4	333.2
Balance	29.9	30.6	41.9	49.4	52.3	57.0	68.6	76.9	80.3

Source: BEA (2004a, table 2).

mination of *all* international calls, the United States brought a WTO case against Mexico in 2002.[48] The dispute settlement panel ruled substantially in favor of the United States in April 2004, and Mexico chose not to appeal. The Mexican government agreed to revise its law to comply with the panel recommendations by 2005. The new rules should benefit US carriers routing calls into Mexico as well as the affiliates of AT&T and MCI operating in Mexico.

One of the major sticking points of NAFTA implementation has been the liberalization of cross-border trucking. Eighty percent of bilateral trade between the United States and Mexico moves by truck (Moore 2004). NAFTA was intended to gradually allow Mexican trucks to operate in the entire United States and vice versa—first in border states by De-

---

48. See WTO case *Mexico—Measures Affecting Telecommunications Service*, WT/DS204, available at docsonline.wto.org. This was the first WTO case based solely on the General Agreement on Trade in Services (GATS).

	1998	1999	2000	2001	2002	2003	Percent change	
							1989–2003	1993–2003
	19.3	22.5	24.4	24.5	24.3	26.7	100.6	58.0
	15.1	16.1	17.6	17.6	18.4	19.1	121.6	114.5
	34.4	38.5	42.0	42.1	42.7	45.9	108.8	77.5
	4.2	6.4	6.8	6.9	5.9	7.6		
	11.6	12.8	14.3	15.2	15.9	16.6	244.2	59.7
	9.8	9.5	11.0	10.5	11.1	11.7	73.5	57.6
	21.4	22.3	25.3	25.7	27.0	28.3	144.8	58.8
	1.8	3.3	3.3	4.6	4.8	4.9		
	243.8	264.7	283.5	275.5	279.5	294.1	149.4	71.9
	163.6	180.5	204.7	201.6	205.2	228.2	167.6	111.7
	407.4	445.2	488.1	477.1	484.7	522.3	157.0	87.3
	80.2	84.2	78.8	73.9	74.3	65.9		
	30.9	35.3	38.7	39.7	40.2	43.3	138.8	58.6
	24.9	25.6	28.6	28.1	29.5	30.8	100.6	88.7
	55.8	60.8	67.3	67.8	69.7	74.1	121.2	69.9
	6.0	9.7	10.1	11.6	10.7	12.5		
	212.9	229.4	244.8	235.8	239.3	250.8	151.3	74.4
	138.6	155.0	176.1	173.5	176.8	197.4	182.3	115.8
	351.5	384.4	420.9	409.3	415.1	448.1	164.1	90.5
	74.3	74.5	68.7	62.3	63.5	53.4		

cember 1995, then finally throughout the two nations in January 2000.[49] Both political foot-dragging and judicial challenges delayed implementation of this provision. President Clinton first delayed implementation of the trucking agreement in 1995, citing concerns about the safety of Mexican trucks voiced by the International Brotherhood of Teamsters. After several years of inaction, Mexico charged the United States with violating its NAFTA obligations. No one was surprised when the NAFTA arbitration panel ruled, in February 2001, that the US ban on Mexican trucking was illegal. In November 2002, President Bush agreed to bring US practice into compliance, but regulations implementing his decision were im-

49. The United States agreed to allow Mexican operation of cross-border trucking services in border states three years after the *signing* of NAFTA, which occurred in December 1992, while full-country access was to be allowed six years after the agreement *entered into force*— January 1994 (NAFTA, vol. II, annex I, I-U-20). A copy of the NAFTA text is available at www.nafta-sec-alena.org/DefaultSite/index_e.aspx?DetailID=78 (accessed on July 18, 2005).

Table 1.4 US unaffiliated services trade with NAFTA partners, selected sectors, 1993–2003 (millions of US dollars)

Partner/sector	1993 Receipts	1993 Payments	1994 Receipts	1994 Payments	1995 Receipts	1995 Payments	1996 Receipts	1996 Payments	1997 Receipts	1997 Payments	1998 Receipts
Canada											
Travel	7,458	3,692	6,252	3,914	6,207	4,319	6,900	4,670	6,945	4,904	6,245
Passenger fares	1,191	260	1,186	302	1,284	306	1,339	391	1,361	470	1,478
Other transport	1,791	2,012	1,973	2,330	2,275	2,513	2,394	2,790	2,414	3,037	2,317
Education	343	8	383	8	403	9	425	10	439	12	445
Financial services	428	97	389	121	580	190	593	173	593	200	768
Insurance	262	366	258	412	313	407	318	374	359	412	361
Telecommunications	252	361	244	391	299	381	294	350	305	332	306
Business, professional, and technical services	1,023	351	1,376	374	1,230	629	1,637	681	1,879	1,197	1,802
Mexico											
Travel	5,119	5,159	4,866	5,334	2,857	5,316	3,004	5,972	3,438	6,480	3,818
Passenger fares	554	641	733	601	515	569	761	650	859	777	958
Other transport	495	397	567	476	420	481	549	525	567	800	549
Education	120	95	131	112	151	119	153	157	167	170	183
Financial services	230	66	231	75	160	79	249	125	282	82	261
Insurance	31	0	27	0	23	0	30	1	43	1	57
Telecommunications	180	884	195	966	251	1,067	350	1,162	445	1,104	464
Business, professional, and technical services	546	82	714	105	683	102	648	89	796	136	854

n.a. = not applicable

Source: BEA (2004a, tables 3.9–3.18, 5.9–5.18).

mediately challenged in court on grounds that an environmental assessment was required—under the National Environmental Policy and Clean Air Act—before Mexican trucks could roll on US highways. In June 2004, the US Supreme Court unanimously ruled that the administration's decision to comply with NAFTA does not require an environmental assessment.[50] However, the border remains closed to Mexican trucks pending the adoption of special regulations to ensure that they operate in a safe and clean manner. This delay has added to cross-border transportation costs, increased turnaround times at assembly plants, and worsened border pollution as older drayage trucks idle in lines to clear customs.

The liberalization of financial services has profoundly altered the Mexican banking sector. Mexico had negotiated a long phase-in period for financial-sector liberalization but chose to accelerate the pace in the wake of the peso crisis. Also, while Mexico was required to open the financial-services sector only to North American firms, it chose global liberalization. In response, the foreign share of Mexican banking assets has increased from 1 percent in 1994 to 90 percent in 2001 (ECLAC 2003, table III.2), lead-

---

50. See *Department of Transportation v. Public Citizen*, Docket No. 03-358, laws.findlaw.com/us/000/03-358.htm (accessed on June 30, 2005).

1998	1999		2000		2001		2002		2003		Percent change, 1993–2003	
Payments	Payments	Receipts	Payments	Receipts	Payments	Receipts	Payments	Receipts	Payments	Receipts	Receipts	Payments
5,692	6,740	6,233	7,188	6,284	6,595	6,345	6,268	6,489	6,844	6,376	−8.2	72.7
587	1,540	712	1,640	795	1,768	685	1,717	594	2,114	406	77.5	56.2
2,910	2,484	3,226	2,641	3,700	2,478	3,337	2,544	3,589	2,614	3,634	46.0	80.6
14	474	14	511	19	568	18	617	28	647	56	88.5	579.5
228	981	203	1,009	247	1,049	177	934	154	1,035	161	141.8	66.8
429	415	278	412	308	392	343	459	554	660	525	151.7	43.4
310	321	223	442	199	434	238	585	256	681	281	170.2	−22.2
1,477	2,448	2,145	2,820	2,522	2,897	2,073	2,954	2,267	3,000	2,786	193.3	693.7
6,396	4,114	5,805	5,162	6,646	5,320	6,711	5,688	7,061	5,861	7,404	14.5	43.5
809	961	957	1,028	923	949	828	1,329	794	1,158	862	109.0	34.5
958	690	1,070	683	1,318	720	1,031	790	993	882	1,040	78.2	162.0
179	192	172	211	182	223	203	267	201	294	221	144.2	131.6
31	347	54	383	46	376	60	309	87	388	99	68.4	49.8
2	70	3	82	5	91	9	125	16	164	13	429.3	n.a.
1,017	376	794	537	1,133	426	810	495	794	541	815	200.6	−7.8
123	952	129	723	155	932	181	938	215	1,116	260	104.4	217.1

ing a trend in foreign banking acquisitions throughout Latin America. Spanish banks BBVA and Santander made major acquisitions. BBVA controls BBVA Bancomer, currently Mexico's largest bank with $46 billion in assets, and BBV-Probursa, with $28 billion in assets, while Santander purchased Banca Serfin ($20 billion) and established the subsidiary Banco Santander Mexicano (UNCTAD 2004, table 88). Citigroup and Bank of America of the United States and Scotiabank of Canada also invested heavily in the Mexican market. Citigroup's $12.5 billion purchase of Banco Nacional de Mexico (Banamex) in 2001, at the time Mexico's largest bank, was unthinkable in a pre-NAFTA environment; Banamex now has $40 billion in assets (UNCTAD 2004, table 88).

One consequence of this financial transformation is a drastic reduction of "connected lending," motivated by political and family relationships rather than sound commercial principles. Another consequence is a flourishing market for home mortgages and the growth of middle-class home ownership, long lacking in Mexico.[51]

---

51. See "Revolution in Mexico: Affordable Housing," *Wall Street Journal*, December 15, 2004, B1; and "Mexico's Working Poor Become Homeowners," *New York Times*, December 17, 2004, 1.

Direct and Portfolio Investment

One of Mexico's key objectives in NAFTA has been to attract FDI—from the United States, Canada, and beyond. For that reason, Mexico implemented its NAFTA obligations regarding investment on an MFN basis. The trade pact itself has fostered FDI by ensuring that firms with assembly plants in Mexico could import US and Canadian components and export finished products duty-free to the north. More important, NAFTA's rights and obligations toward private investors have contributed—in conjunction with stable and conservative macroeconomic policies—to a more inviting environment for FDI in Mexico.

Since NAFTA entered into force, Mexico has enjoyed an FDI boom; based on data reported in the UNCTAD *World Investment Report* (table 1.5), the stock of FDI in Mexico grew from $33 billion in 1994 to $166 billion by year-end 2003, despite the tribulations of the 1994–95 peso crisis.[52] Based on US data, the stock of US FDI in Mexico increased from $17 billion in 1994 to $61.5 billion at year-end 2003 (table 1.6). About half of the US stock of FDI was accumulated after 1998 and reflects major investments in both financial services (led by Citibank's purchase of Banamex in 2001) and manufacturing. Mexico has attracted FDI not only from the United States but also from other countries (see table 1.5) and is now host to a larger stock of FDI than all other developing countries except China and Hong Kong.[53]

However, like other developing countries, Mexico faces strong competition from China for FDI in manufacturing industries (particularly textiles and apparel). The China threat heightened in 2003, when FDI inflows to Mexico fell to $11.4 billion (down from $15.1 billion in 2002). Mexico's decline as a destination for FDI was consistent with broader trends: FDI flows to the developing world fell 34 percent from a peak of $252 billion in 2000 to $158 billion in 2002, before partially recovering to $172 billion in 2003 (UNCTAD *World Investment Report 2004*). The decrease in FDI has been spread across almost all sectors of the economy (table 1.7), though low-skill, labor-intensive sectors—notably electronics assembly and the textile and apparel industries—have been particularly susceptible to competition from China. Nonetheless, preliminary data for 2004 indicate a resurgence of FDI in Mexico, particularly in the auto sector, with inflows valued at $16.6 billion.

Unlike Brazil and Argentina, Mexico does not have commodity endowments (except in the petroleum sector) that complement China's develop-

---

52. In fact, the "insurance policy" of NAFTA may have given confidence to foreign investors in Mexico's recovery from the peso crisis, encouraging investment at fire sale prices (Schott 1997).

53. Note, however, the inconsistencies between the UNCTAD *World Investment Report* data (table 1.7) and the US Bureau of Economic Analysis data (table 1.8).

Table 1.5 Realized FDI inflows and stocks in Mexico, by investing country or region

a. FDI inflows, 1994–2004 (billions of US dollars)

	1994	1995	1996	1997	1998	1999	2000	2001	2002	2003	2004	Share 1994–2004
Total FDI	15.1	9.7	10.1	14.2	12.4	13.3	16.9	27.7	15.3	11.7	16.6	
Estimates[a]	4.4	1.4	2.3	2.0	4.0	0	0	0	0	0	.8	
Notified FDI	10.7	8.3	7.8	12.2	8.4	13.3	16.9	27.7	15.3	11.7	16.1	100.0
By origin:												
Canada	0.7	0.2	0.5	0.2	0.2	0.6	0.7	1.0	0.2	0.2	0.3	3.3
United States	5.0	5.5	5.3	7.5	5.5	7.2	12.1	21.3	9.7	6.4	6.9	62.2
European Union	1.9	1.8	1.1	3.2	2.1	3.8	2.9	4.2	4.3	4.3	7.3	24.8
Japan	0.6	0.2	0.1	0.4	0.1	1.2	0.4	0.2	0.2	0.1	0.1	2.4
Switzerland	—	0.2	—	—	—	0.1	0.2	0.1	0.4	0.3	1.1	1.8

— = less than $50 million
FDI = foreign direct investment

a. Estimates of investment not notified to the Registro Nacional de Inversiones Extranjeras (RNIE), which are not attributed to any investing country. Estimates before 1999 include all reinvestment and exchanges between companies and their affiliates. These were included in notifications since 1999. Since 2002, the RNIE has made estimates of reinvestment that occurred but have not yet been reported.

Notes: Data presented are not comparable to official statistics before 1994. Pre-1994, statistics reflect realized investment in addition to unrealized notifications for the year reported. The data presented show realized investment credited to the year the investment took place. The peak in FDI in 2001 is due to the $12.5 billion acquisition of Banamex by Citigroup.

Source: Secretaría de Economía (2005a).

(table continues next page)

Table 1.5   Realized FDI inflows and stocks in Mexico, by investing country or region *(continued)*

b. Inward FDI stock, 1994–2003 (billions of US dollars)

	1994	1995	1996	1997	1998	1999	2000	2001[a]	2002[a]	2003[a]
Total	33.2	41.1	46.9	55.8	63.6	78.1	97.2	140.4	155.1	165.9
Canada	.7	.7	1.7	1.8	1.8	2.0	2.4	3.9	4.1	4.3
United States	23.5	26.1	27.9	33.4	35.0	42.9	55.0	88.3	97.6	103.6
European Union	6.0	7.5	8.1	10.3	17.6	20.9	26.8	33.3	37.5	41.4
Japan	1.6	.8	.8	1.3	1.5	2.8	3.3	3.6	3.8	3.9
Switzerland	1.2	2.0	2.2	3.0	2.5	2.9	2.8	3.0	3.4	3.7

a. Because UNCTAD does not report FDI position by country of origin, we estimate that increases in FDI stock are proportional to the national share of FDI inflow for 2001 to 2003 (table 1.5a).

Sources: OECD (2004a, 2005); UNCTAD *World Investment Report 2004.*

Table 1.6 **US outward direct investment position (stock) at year-end, NAFTA and world** (historical cost basis, billions of US dollars)

Sector	Canada 1994	Canada 2003	Mexico 1994	Mexico 2003	World 1994	World 2003
Mining[a]	10.4	24.3	.1	.4	67.6	98.7
Utilities	n.a.	1.0	n.a.	.7	n.a.	26.9
Manufacturing						
Food	4.0	4.3	2.7	1.7	24.9	22.7
Chemicals	5.8	13.1	2.3	4.0	47.9	90.3
Primary and fabricated metals	2.2	4.1	n.a.	n.a.	9.8	23.0
Machinery	2.1	3.1	n.a.	1.1	25.0	21.4
Computer and electronic products	n.a.	5.3	n.a.	1.8	n.a.	57.6
Electrical equipment, appliances, and components	1.1	1.5	.9	.9	19.6	9.7
Transportation equipment	9.4	17.9	1.8	n.a.	28.0	45.4
Total	34.0	74.9	10.1	20.1	201.0	378.0
Wholesale trade	6.9	12.7	1.3	2.0	59.0	140.6
Information	n.a.	2.2	n.a.	1.2	n.a.	47.5
Depository institutions	.9	2.7	n.a.	16.9	27.4	63.7
Finance (except depository institutions) and insurance	13.0	34.2	2.2	7.2	195.9	299.8
Professional, scientific, and technical services	3.3	2.0	.4	.4	27.0	40.6
Other industries	5.8	38.5	n.a.	12.6	35.0	693.1
All industries	74.2	192.4	17.0	61.5	612.9	1,788.9

n.a. = not available

a. Values for 1994 are petroleum only.

Notes: Starting in 1999, the Bureau of Economic Analysis (BEA) updated its categorization for FDI abroad. Some investment may have shifted categories as a result of reclassification.

Source: BEA (2004b).

ment needs. But it does have two key advantages: geographic proximity to the world's largest market and membership in NAFTA. These factors do not guarantee success in the global competition for FDI, but they provide positive incentives if complemented by other investment-friendly policies. Unfortunately, Mexico has not fully benefited due to a variety of homegrown problems related to the general business environment.[54] To be specific, worries about personal safety (mugging and kidnapping),

---

54. An element of the country's 2005 tax reform legislation further threatens to discourage FDI. The amendment restricts the definition of business activities under the Mexican tax code. Because business activities are not explicitly defined in the US-Mexico tax treaty (and several other Mexican tax treaties), several payments generally thought of as business profits would become subject to a 25 percent withholding tax (e.g., technical assistance, advertising, financial services, construction services, time sharing, and reinsurance). Several lawyers who have examined the amendment believe that the Mexican Supreme Court will find it unconstitutional; it came into force on January 1, 2005. See McLees (2004) and McLees et al. (2004).

Table 1.7 Realized FDI flows into Mexico, by sector, 1994–2004 (millions of US dollars)

Sector	1994	1995	1996	1997	1998	1999	2000	2001	2002	2003	2004	1994–2004 share
Manufacturing	6,207	4,858	4,815	7,295	5,157	8,994	9,502	6,032	6,500	5,045	8,246	49.3
Food, beverages, and tobacco	1,809	651	502	2,953	731	1,041	1,201	974	1,337	898	1,010	8.9
Machinery and metal products	1,889	2,893	2,212	2,757	2,344	5,396	4,445	3,362	2,926	2,597	3,869	23.6
Chemical products, including derivatives of petroleum, rubber, and plastics	646	573	1,197	820	1,166	950	1,444	412	1,133	687	1,857	7.4
Mineral nonmetallic products	54	90	37	6	20	236	143	102	–81	77	782	1.0
Basic metals	1,344	143	325	106	54	269	282	243	60	8	42	2.0
Other subsectors	466	509	542	653	842	1,102	1,986	940	1,126	778	687	6.5
Services	2,100	1,475	1,704	2,016	1,518	2,263	6,690	15,962	5,429	3,152	5,181	32.2
Real estate	222	65	64	59	59	179	329	143	152	49	100	1.0
Professional and technical services	266	140	211	144	313	703	1,143	954	411	566	68	3.3
Financial services and insurance	716	952	1,111	969	627	379	4,343	14,034	4,249	1,811	4,519	22.9
Restaurants and hotels	723	103	167	571	208	322	437	366	351	319	320	2.6
Other subsectors	174	216	150	273	312	680	438	465	267	407	174	2.4
Other	2,354	2,012	1,297	2,871	1,642	1,951	590	5,641	3,200	3,176	2,420	18.4
Total	15,067	9,667	10,055	14,216	12,360	13,207	16,781	27,635	15,129	11,373	16,602	100.0
Total notified	10,661	8,344	7,818	12,186	8,319	13,207	16,781	27,635	15,129	11,373	15,846	
Estimates[a]	4,405	1,322	2,238	2,030	4,041	0	0	0	0	0	756	

a. Estimates of investment not notified to the Registro Nacional de Inversiones Extranjeras (RNIE), which are not attributed to any host sector. Estimates before 1999 include all reinvestment and exchange between companies and their affiliates. These were included in notifications since 1999. Since 2002, the RNIE has made estimates of new investment and reinvestment that occurred but have not yet been reported.

Source: Secretaría de Economía (2005a).

widespread corruption, the absence of a stable legal framework, poor highways, and looming energy shortages all discourage new investment. However, these concerns vary widely among the 31 Mexican states. Nuevo Leon and Aguascalientes are known for a good business environment; Chihuahua and Jalisco have a different reputation.[55]

Since 2000, Mexican FDI flows appear to have shifted from manufacturing toward financial services, transport, and communications. FDI inflows at the sectoral level can fluctuate dramatically from one year to the next, due to expensive acquisitions of established Mexican firms. This was a pronounced feature in financial services, but so much of the industry is now in foreign hands that additional large FDI inflows in this sector seem unlikely.

The increase in cross-border investment between the United States and Canada has been less dramatic. Two-way FDI stocks between Canada and the United States increased from $104 billion in 1989 to $298 billion by year-end 2003, a gain of 187 percent. By contrast, US two-way FDI with non-NAFTA countries increased by 333 percent between 1989 and 2003. Even before the CUSFTA was ratified, Canada and the United States had a mature two-way investment relationship, so the incremental liberalization was a small spark compared with new opportunities elsewhere. Much of Canada's post-NAFTA investment in Mexico has been concentrated in mining and tourism, two industries where Canada has traditionally been competitive.

Longitudinal data on private portfolio investment are unreliable, but a few inferences can be drawn from stocks of portfolio capital as of 2001–02. At the end of 2001, private US holdings of foreign securities (equities and long-term and short-term debt) totaled some $2.3 trillion. Of this amount, $201 billion represented claims against Canadian issuers and $48 billion against Mexican issuers. In other words, claims against Canada were 9 percent of the global total, and those against Mexico were only 2 percent. Both figures were substantially less than the share of US merchandise exports destined for NAFTA partners (22 and 14 percent, respectively). Conversely, at the end of 2002, private portfolio investment in the United States totaled $4.4 trillion. Of this amount, $208 billion represented claims held by Canadian investors and $52 billion by Mexican investors. As shares of the relevant totals, claims held by both Canadian and Mexican investors (5 and 1 percent, respectively) are much smaller than Canadian and Mexican exports (18 and 12 percent, respectively).

Nevertheless, through direct investment, a great deal of financial integration has taken place within North America—for example, the Manulife–

---

55. In 2003, Mexico was ranked third—behind China and the United States—in the A. T. Kearney FDI Confidence Index, but it fell to 22 in the 2004 rankings. The index is derived from a worldwide survey of business executives. Lack of reforms—particularly in energy, infrastructure, and telecom—were cited as reasons for Mexico's decline (GBPC 2004).

John Hancock merger, the acquisition of Harris Bank by the Bank of Montreal, the acquisition of Banamex by Citigroup, and the equity share operations of TD Waterhouse. Even without massive cross-border portfolio flows, the mortgage security, equity, and insurance markets should become more tightly linked—especially with the help of a sound regulatory environment in all three countries.[56]

Summarizing the investment picture, it appears that the CUSFTA and NAFTA did little to enhance the already mature direct investment relationship between Canada and the United States. The growth of two-way US-Canada FDI lagged significantly behind two-way non-NAFTA FDI by the United States. By contrast, NAFTA significantly enhanced the direct investment relationship between Mexico and the United States. Two-way US-Canada and US-Mexico portfolio investment stocks are not particularly large, when contrasted with merchandise trade, but the most meaningful financial integration has probably taken place through cross-border mergers and new corporate subsidiaries.

While NAFTA appears to have boosted FDI in Mexico, the effect in Canada is hard to discern. In the United States, the effect has been minimal—no surprise considering the size of the US economy relative to its NAFTA partners. While complaints are still voiced about US plant closings and relocations to Mexico, in fact US FDI in Mexico has averaged less than one-half of 1 percent of nonresidential investment in the United States each year. Footloose plants are bad news for affected workers and their communities but represent a statistically insignificant share of US business investment. Furthermore, it is impossible to say whether these plants moved *because of* NAFTA or would have left in search of lower labor costs regardless. Nevertheless, in retrospect it is clear that US business groups worked hard to negotiate and ratify NAFTA partly because they anticipated the benefits resulting from cross-border investments.

Business Cycle Synchronization

A case can be made for free trade to have both synchronizing and desynchronizing effects on national business cycles. Synchronizing effects result from the stronger influence of partner-country demand on local business conditions. Desynchronizing effects result from production specialization within each country—increasing the country's exposure to industry-specific shocks. More time must pass before NAFTA's impact on the business cycles within North America can be definitively assessed. Preliminary studies appear to show, however, that synchronizing effects are

---

56. In Mexico, the effects of the peso crisis have dissipated enough to allow a $100 million issue of mortgage-backed securities by Hipotecaria Nacional, a leading mortgage lender. Since the number of Mexican households is projected to nearly double from 22.3 million in 2000 to 42.2 million in 2020, there is urgent need for a secondary mortgage market to capitalize homebuilding ("A Mexican Bond that's as Safe as Houses?" *Financial Times*, August 23, 2004, 25).

dominant. Kose, Meredith, and Towe (2004) find that regional factors became stronger determinants of the Mexican business cycle in 1994–2002 than in 1980–93. Cañas and Coronado (2004) confirm this result and point out that because over 80 percent of US-Mexican trade is intraindustry, the synchronizing effects should be expected to dominate. Cardarelli Kose (2004) adapt the model of Kose, Meredith, and Towe to evaluate the Canadian business angle and finds that while the regional factor has been important since the 1960s, its importance has grown since the early 1980s.

Increased synchronization, if it persists, will underscore the case for closer macroeconomic consultation within North America. Notably absent from the NAFTA experience has been any significant convergence in prices between Canada and the United States.[57] Engel and Rogers (1996) used price index changes (measured by standard deviations) across US and Canadian city pairs to determine a "border effect," controlling for the distance between cities. They could not find a significant convergence in cross-border prices as a result of the CUSFTA or NAFTA. Baldwin and Yan (2004), using prices of individual goods rather than indices, also found that the hypothesis that trade liberalization in North America would lead to price convergence was "not supported by the data." This result stands in contrast to the European experience (Rogers, Hufbauer, and Wada 2001; Engel and Rogers 2004) and invites the hypothesis that exchange rate volatility may be an obstacle to price convergence in North America.

To date, consultations between the three central banks and finance ministries are episodic and ad hoc; they have no institutional standing within NAFTA. NAFTA included no mechanisms for macroeconomic cooperation between member states, although Rubin (2003, chapter 1) reports that the US response to the 1994 peso crisis was stronger thanks to the creation of NAFTA. Since that time, stability has returned to the Mexican economy, and cooperation on macroeconomic policy has been limited to informal consultations between central banks and finance ministries. Given the economic preponderance of the United States in the region, sovereignty concerns are likely to obstruct closer forms of cooperation. The US Congress does not want to give Mexico or Canada a voice in the Federal Reserve System or a say on spending or tax priorities. Both Mexico and Canada would resist any formal US role in setting their fiscal and monetary policies. Indeed, the common currency debate underscores fierce Canadian resistance to "monetary domination" by Washington.

Remittances

Remittances have become an important source of foreign income for Mexico. Since 1994, when Mexico began keeping records on household remit-

---

57. Given the income and demographic differences between Mexico and its NAFTA partners, less price convergence would be expected between Mexico and the United States or Canada.

tances, they have grown from $3.5 billion to $16.6 billion in 2004, or by 374 percent (see table 1.1). The surge has coincided with an explosion in new services provided by banks and wire companies to facilitate remittances.[58] Approximately 9.9 million Mexican-born residents live in the United States.[59] A sizable fraction of them send a portion of their earnings home to relatives. In 2003, remittances from foreign sources ($13 billion) actually surpassed foreign inflows from FDI. NAFTA bears little relationship to the remittance story; rather, the growth reflects a larger migrant population and new technology that makes remittance transactions cheaper, faster, and safer. Remittances are expected to continue growing, raising the profile of immigration issues in the US-Mexico relationship (see chapter 8 on migration).[60]

Employment and Wages

What impact did NAFTA have on employment in each country? The short answer is positive, though less than promised by politicians and more than predicted by pundits. Economists know that employment gains essentially depend on macroeconomic policies, a flexible labor force, worker skills, and effective use of technology. Attempting to evaluate NAFTA based strictly on a jobs gained/lost measure leads analysts into a mercantilist trap of "exports good, imports bad" and distracts from the true source of gains from trade—more efficient production on both sides of the border.

NAFTA coincided with an extended period of strong economic growth in the United States—and positive knock-on effects for its neighbors. Employment levels increased in all three countries. US employment rose from 110 million in 1993 to 134 million in 2003 (BLS 2004a) and in Canada from 12.9 million to 15.7 million (Statistics Canada 2004). Jobs in the formal sector in Mexico increased from 32.8 million to 40.6 million (STPS 2004). But not every worker or community benefited, and national trade

---

58. HSBC, Citibank, Bank of America, and Western Union all have specific facilities geared toward remittances. Among the new facilities are accounts by which money deposited in the United States can be withdrawn by a relative abroad via ATM, regardless of whether the relative has a bank account. See Devesh Kapur and John McHale, "Migration's New Payoff," *Foreign Policy*, November 2003, 48–57.

59. Of these, roughly 1.6 million are naturalized US citizens, 3.5 million are nonnaturalized legal residents, and approximately 4.8 million are undocumented. See www.migration information.org (accessed on January 13, 2004).

60. In 2003, Mexican households received over 42 million remittance transactions, of which 88 percent were wire transfers and 10 percent were money orders. The average remittance was $321. To take advantage of the US-Mexico remittances market, Spain's Banco Bilbao Vizcaya Argentaria SA (BBVA) purchased Mexico's largest bank, Grupo Financiero Bancomer for $4.1 billion ("Mexican Migrants Send Home Dollars," *Financial Times*, January 31, 2004, 2, and "Spanish Bank Makes Bid in Move to Improve its Position in the US," *Wall Street Journal*, February 3, 2004, A8).

adjustment assistance programs remain inadequate to the task. This section surveys what happened in each country with regard to employment and wages; more detailed analysis is in chapter 2 on labor.

United States

Like any trade agreement with a small economy, NAFTA never had the potential for luring droves of US firms abroad or sucking millions of US jobs into Mexico or Canada. Yet the original NAFTA political debate in the United States was centered on prospective job gains and losses. While claims by the most strident NAFTA critics have been discredited, some— such as the Economic Policy Institute—continue to rehearse the jobs-lost story. Using multipliers based on the bilateral trade balance, Scott (2003) argues that NAFTA caused a net loss of 879,280 jobs, and he has disaggregated the figure by US states. Such analysis is fundamentally flawed.[61]

To most economists, the debate over NAFTA and jobs is surreal. Trade pacts can affect the composition and quality of jobs by shifting output from less productive into more productive sectors. This process contributes to the normal churning associated with job creation and job dislocation in the huge US economy (see table 1.8a). Using data from the Bureau of Labor Statistics (BLS) Mass Layoff Statistics Program, Kletzer and Litan (2001) found that churning "dislocates" more than 1 million jobs per year through mass layoffs in the United States.[62] Most of these workers "relocate" to other jobs, though in the process roughly 25 percent of them suffer pay cuts of 30 percent or more.[63] Trade pacts are far from the most prominent cause of job churn—and have only a third-order impact on the absolute level of employment.

Table 1.8 reports *overall* employment trends in the United States from the advent of NAFTA through 2003. Of course, NAFTA was a very small part of the overall picture. According to the Current Employment Survey, US employment expanded by about 15.6 million over this period, roughly in line with the expansion of the total US labor force. The lower part of the table is less familiar; it displays the gross job gains and losses over the period as calculated by the BLS using the Quarterly Census on Employment

---

61. The use of a multiplier to calculate employment effects from the bilateral trade balance rests on shaky theoretical ground. For example, does an increase in television exports from Mexico really cost US jobs, considering almost no TVs are manufactured in the United States, or do Mexican imports displace imports from Asia? Furthermore, Scott's method assumes that the entire increase in bilateral trade with Mexico is attributable to NAFTA—a flattering but unlikely assumption.

62. A mass layoff is defined as a job loss action associated with 50 or more claims against an establishment's unemployment insurance account over a five-week period.

63. Some 34 percent of dislocated workers report earning the same amount or more in their postdisplacement job. On average, workers take postdisplacement jobs that pay 17 percent less than their previous wage.

Table 1.8   US employment and NAFTA

a. US employment statistics (millions)

	1994	2003	Change
Current Employment Survey			
Seasonally adjusted employment	114.3	129.9	15.6
Seasonally adjusted labor force	131.1	146.8	15.8
Quarterly Census on Employment and Wages			
Gross job gains (1994–2003)	327.8		
Gross job losses (1994–2003)	312.9		
Difference	14.9		

Source: BLS (2004a, 2004b, 2004c).

b. NAFTA total US job predictions (thousands)

	Gain	Loss	Net	Years
Perot and Choate[a]		5,900	−5,900	n.a.
Kantor	200		200	2
Zoellick			44 to 150	4
Hufbauer and Schott	316	145	171	5

a. Perot and Choate calculated jobs "at risk" due to NAFTA; no time period was specified.

Sources: Perot and Choate (1993); *Wall Street Journal* (August 17, 1993, A14); Zoellick (1991); and Hufbauer and Schott (1993).

c. Estimated annual NAFTA effects on US employment (thousands per year)

	Gain	Loss	Net	As of
NAFTA-TAA and jobs supported by exports	100	58	42	December 2002
Scott	88	186	−98	December 2002
Hinojosa-Ojeda et al.[a]	74	23	51	December 1997

n.a. = not applicable

a. Hinojosa-Ojeda et al. (2000) use data from 1990–97 in their analysis, arguing that the Canada-US Free Trade Agreement and Mexican market opening, and associated trade impact, pre-date NAFTA.

Sources: Public Citizen's NAFTA-TAA database, 1994–2002; Scott (2003); and Hinojosa-Ojeda et al. (2000).

and Wages (a separate measure from the monthly Current Employment Survey). Over the NAFTA period, *every quarter* an average of 7.6 percent of total employment (10.5 million jobs at current employment levels) was displaced and 7.9 percent (11 million jobs) was created (BLS 2004c).[64] Oft-

---

64. The Quarterly Census counts a job gained only when an establishment opens or expands and a job lost only when an establishment closes or contracts. Therefore, persons changing jobs due to voluntary quits or retirement are not counted as long as the position remains intact. The size of the job churn is massive, but it is also surprisingly stable. Since 1994, the percentage of jobs lost has never been below 6 percent per quarter, and the percentage of jobs gained has never been below 7 percent.

reported statistics on net job gains or losses are the outcome of this massive churn process.

Tables 1.8b and 1.8c summarize some of the predictions and estimates of NAFTA's effect on US employment. All these estimates—even the most extreme—are minuscule compared with overall employment trends. Many focus only on jobs gained or alternatively jobs lost, without considering the other side of the churning equation. A one-sided look is questionable since the intended result of increased trade is to deploy labor more efficiently. Trying to tease out employment effects in the US economy of a trade agreement with two countries that, combined, are 18 percent of the US size (at purchasing power parity) may be a fool's errand. Nevertheless, our own estimate is included in table 1.8b.

Based on the NAFTA-TAA program, about 525,000 US jobs were dislocated in import-competing industries through 2002 when the program was consolidated with general TAA (about 58,000 jobs per year).[65] While this is the most solid figure available on the US impact, it contains elements of under- and overstatement. The figures are understated because not all workers who are displaced due to NAFTA apply for NAFTA-TAA benefits. They are overstated because NAFTA-TAA certification requires only showing that imports from Canada or Mexico adversely affected the job or that the firm moved to Canada or Mexico; no evidence was required that NAFTA liberalization *caused* either the imports or the relocation of the firm.

Comparable data are not collected on US jobs created in the United States in export industries. Given recent employment to value added ratio in manufacturing, we estimate that 8,500 manufacturing jobs are supported by every $1 billion of US exports.[66] Applying this coefficient to the average annual gain in US exports to NAFTA countries between 1993 and 2003, about $12.5 billion per year, over 100,000 *additional* US jobs were supported each year by the expansion of North American trade, though not necessarily as a direct result of NAFTA.[67] Even more important, Lewis and Richardson (2001, 24–27) found that export-oriented firms pay wages 13 to 16 percent higher than the national average.

---

65. See Public Citizen's NAFTA-Transitional Adjustment Assistance (NAFTA-TAA) Database, 1994–2002, www.citizen.org/trade/forms/taa_info.cfm (accessed on April 20, 2004).

66. In 2001, the manufacturing sector employed 15.9 million employees while manufacturing value added was $1,853 billion (*Statistical Abstract of the United States: 2003*, 123rd ed., US Census Bureau, table 987). Our calculation assumes that $1 billion of exports equates to $1 billion of manufacturing value added (taking into account shipments of components between manufacturing firms). This method, in contrast to the method adopted by the USTR (see following footnote), ignores labor employed in nonmanufacturing sectors that supply inputs to the manufacturing sector.

67. USTR (2004) estimates that US goods and services exports "supported" 11.6 million US jobs in 1999. The study uses a ratio of 12,000 jobs per billion dollars of exports, significantly above our own estimate, to calculate the number of jobs directly and indirectly supported by exports (indirect jobs are those outside manufacturing).

Widespread fears that integrating Mexico into the North American auto industry would cause job flight and wage collapse north of the Rio Grande have not materialized. While the US auto and auto parts employment level (SIC 371), like the manufacturing sector as a whole, is lower than it was in 1994 (reflecting declines in manufacturing employment since 1998), it is hard to attribute the change to Mexican production. Indeed, Mexican auto employment has also declined, reflecting substantial productivity gains and the manufacturing slowdown during the economic downturn in 2001–02. While the wage premium paid to US autoworkers over other manufacturing production workers has declined slightly, it is still high, $8.63 per hour.[68]

Canada

In contrast to the United States and Mexico, Canadian employment levels rose steadily during 2000–03, from 14.9 million to 15.7 million. In manufacturing, employment has remained nearly flat at 2.3 million. But while Canada has maintained or modestly increased its employment levels, the "productivity gap" between the United States and Canada has widened. Indeed, labor-market watchers in Canada have been seriously concerned with the widening productivity gap.

Labor productivity is the leading determinant of the national standard of living, so it comes as no surprise that Canada's lagging productivity growth, relative to the United States, is viewed with alarm. According to convergence theory, free trade agreements should spur productivity growth in both countries, but especially in the smaller and less productive country, Canada.[69] Trade should allow specialization and more efficient allocation of labor, facilitate technology transfers and information sharing (or spillovers), intensify competition and incentives to innovation, and facilitate economies of scale. However, since the CUSFTA came into force in 1989, Canada has experienced average annual productivity growth of 1.58 percent, compared with annual US productivity growth of 1.85 percent. The gap was particularly pronounced after 1995, with US productivity growth averaging 2.36 percent compared with only 1.64 percent for Canada (Sharpe 2003, figure 3).

Cardarelli and Kose (2004) believe that the larger impact of information technology (IT) on the US economy can explain much of the difference in productivity growth. NAFTA played a minuscule role in the IT component of the US productivity boom of the late 1990s. Canadian firms, with a few notable exceptions, neither produced nor adopted the new IT tech-

---

68. Calculated as the difference between the average per hour cost of employee compensation of production workers in SIC 371 and all manufacturing production workers. Data are from BLS (2003).

69. According to Trefler (2004), Canadian industries that faced the deepest tariff cuts under the CUSFTA raised their labor productivity by 15 percent, which translates into a compound annual growth rate of 1.9 percent.

Table 1.9   Real wages and productivity trends (1994 = 100)

a. In nonmaquiladora manufacturing[a]

Year	Real output per worker	Real productivity	Real monthly income per worker	Real wages
1987	69.7	70.6	71.3	72.1
1988	74.0	73.9	71.0	70.8
1989	78.7	78.2	77.3	76.8
1990	79.6	78.7	80.0	79.2
1991	82.8	81.6	84.9	83.7
1992	86.2	84.9	92.3	90.8
1993	90.7	90.5	96.5	96.1
1994	100.0	100.0	100.0	100.0
1995	114.1	115.5	87.5	88.5
1996	119.2	119.4	78.8	79.0
1997	117.8	117.2	78.3	77.9
1998	119.1	118.5	80.5	80.1
1999	115.8	114.6	81.8	80.9
2000	118.7	117.2	86.6	85.7
2001	119.8	118.6	92.4	91.7
2002	123.4	122.4	94.1	93.5
2003	125.4	124.7	95.3	94.8

b. In maquiladora manufacturing[b]

Year	Real value added per worker	Real productivity	Real monthly income per worker	Real wages
1990	96.2	99.6	96.2	99.7
1991	97.7	103.8	94.2	100.2
1992	95.7	99.7	95.9	99.9
1993	96.9	99.8	95.8	98.7
1994	100.0	100.0	100.0	100.0
1995	103.3	103.2	94.0	93.9
1996	98.7	96.9	88.8	87.1
1997	102.3	85.3	90.4	75.4
1998	110.4	92.5	94.0	78.8
1999	113.7	94.8	96.0	80.1
2000	113.2	94.5	100.3	83.7
2001	128.9	108.6	109.4	92.2
2002	141.1	118.9	115.5	97.4
2003	144.8	121.0	115.5	96.5

a. Pre-1994 statistics correspond to the 129 classification system, which was discontinued in 1995. Post-1994 statistics correspond to the 205 classification system, which was introduced in 1994. Data for real productivity are measured as peso-denominated gross output per hour worked. Nonmaquiladora value added data from the Encuesta Industrial Mensual were not available.

b. Data for real productivity are measured as peso-denominated value added per hour worked. Official Mexican productivity measures are typically reported on the basis of gross output; see INEGI (2002) and footnote 77.

Source: INEGI (2004).

those in the CEIP study.[77] Whereas CEIP reports that productivity in non-maquiladora manufacturing increased 59 percent between 1993 and 2003, we calculate a 25 percent increase between 1994 and 2003.[78]

The divergence between productivity and real wages during the peso crisis is not surprising. In 1995–96, real wages fell sharply due to rapid inflation; meanwhile employment and hours decreased more than output, causing a rise in productivity. To some extent, the fall in real wages represented a correction of the 1990–93 period, when real wage growth outstripped productivity.[79] For the whole period between 1994 and 2003, real wages fell 5.2 percent, while productivity rose 24.7 percent. However, since the peso crisis, wages have been catching up with productivity gains. Wages rose 21.7 percent between 1997 and 2003 while productivity gained only 6.4 percent. We disagree with the CEIP study that these data demonstrate the "decoupling of wages from productivity" (Audley et al. 2003, 25). However, sluggish productivity gains in recent years are a cause for concern.

To this point, our discussion has focused on nonmaquiladora manufacturing.[80] Maquiladoras—in-bond factories that produce exclusively for export—are a growing proportion of Mexican manufacturing. They represented 30 percent of total manufacturing employment in 1994, rising to 45 percent in 2003. The maquiladora workforce is generally less productive and less well paid than nonmaquiladora manufacturing discussed

---

77. Our calculations use the raw series Valor de Producción divided by Horas/Hombre Trabajadas (both series are from the Encuesta Industrial Mensual), deflated by the producer price index. INEGI, the official Mexican statistics service, commonly reports the series presented by CEIP (INEGI 2002, figure 22). INEGI calculates dollar-denominated productivity using the gross output method (i.e., output including the cost of intermediate inputs). Our statistics are calculated with a peso-denominated measure of output and therefore are more appropriate when comparing productivity with real wages. A second productivity series produced by INEGI (INEGI 2002, figure 14), sourced to the Sistema de Cuentas Nacionales (National Accounts) is peso-denominated (and also based on gross output) and roughly corresponds to our constructed series through 2000 (the latest available year). Banco de Mexico (2005) publishes a productivity series based on employment rather than hours worked. This series also corresponds roughly to the one we have constructed. See INEGI (2002) for more on the methodology of Mexican productivity statistics.

78. Due to classification changes in 1994, we do not report a growth rate between pre- and post-1994 data. All of the indices presented in table 1.9 are based such that 1994=100. The same change in classification systems caused the apparent decline in the number of maize farmers between 1993 and 2003, reported in the CEIP study. Using only the new census methodology, the World Bank (2004) shows an increase in the number of maize farmers between 1994 and 2004.

79. As mentioned earlier, Mexico introduced a new classification system in 1994. Therefore, caution should be used when drawing conclusions about changes between 1993 and 1994. We examine the movement of productivity and real wages from 1990 to 1993, a period that uses the old classification system.

80. However, it should be noted that companies registered under PITEX accounted for about one-quarter of the Mexican manufacturing labor force. These include all auto manufacturers and most parts suppliers. PITEX firms enjoy almost the same benefits as maquiladora firms.

above. Table 1.9b presents the trends in maquiladora manufacturing since 1990 (the earliest year data are available). Real wages decline over the period, again due to the peso crisis. However, since 1997, maquiladora real wage earnings have grown 28 percent, while productivity was up 42 percent.[81] In contrast to wage statistics expressed in hourly terms, real monthly income per worker rose by the lesser figure of 20 percent, reflecting fewer hours worked by each employee. Box 1.1 explains the boom and bust, and recent recovery, in the maquiladora sector.

The most likely explanation as to why real wage gains have lagged behind productivity growth is the large pool of unskilled Mexican labor. Rural agricultural laborers work under much harsher conditions and earn far less pay than urban workers, especially those in the manufacturing sector. Rural workers respond to higher urban wages by migrating from the farm to the city. Internal migration increases the supply of unskilled manufacturing labor and suppresses wage increases, though it often spells a dramatic improvement in the lives of erstwhile rural inhabitants. Since 1994, the share of agricultural employment in Mexico fell from 26 percent of total employment to 18 percent in 2001 (World Bank, *World Development Indicators* 2004). Over the same period, employment in maquiladoras, which employ mainly unskilled workers, doubled to over 1 million (INEGI 2004). Rural to urban migration is a necessary part of development; in 2003, the agricultural sector produced only 5 percent of Mexican GDP (World Bank, *World Development Indicators* 2004). Given that agriculture still employs almost a fifth of Mexican workers, the migration phenomenon, and its effect on manufacturing wages, will continue for the foreseeable future. As it proceeds, *average per capita income* will rise, even if manufacturing wages lag behind productivity growth.

Over the long term, average real wages for the entire population—rural as well as urban workers—are strongly linked to *national* labor productivity.[82] Productivity growth has been disappointing in Mexico. The prediction by NAFTA supporters that free trade would foster strong productivity growth has so far materialized only in export-oriented industries, such as autos (OECD 2004b). Mexico needs more, not less, productivity growth in services and agriculture, as well as manufacturing. Real wage growth will follow.

Per Capita Income Convergence

Whether or not Mexican GDP per capita income is "converging" to US levels due to NAFTA (or for other reasons) is the subject of hot debate and

---

81. Table 1.9b measures productivity on a value added basis, rather than a gross output basis.

82. Hanson (2003) argues that Mexican states with greater exposure to multinational firms, FDI, foreign trade, and migration enjoyed higher wage growth in the 1990s. Hanson finds a strong positive correlation between Mexican wage growth and the share of FDI in state GDP.

Box 1.1   The maquiladora boom and bust

Maquiladoras—Mexican firms with special legal status originally restricted to produce exclusively for export—are a closely watched feature of the Mexican economy.[1] A common modus operandi characterizes maquiladoras: import components, add value (mainly through labor), and export products (almost entirely to the United States). Mexican firms could follow the same business model without becoming a maquiladora, but membership had its privileges.[2] In the pre-NAFTA era, privileges took the form of duty rebates for imported inputs and a preferential corporate tax regime.

NAFTA has eroded the advantages of being a maquiladora. First, NAFTA extended free trade for components originating in North America to all firms, maquiladora or not. Second, in 2000, NAFTA ended duty rebates on imports of non-NAFTA components. Third, in the wake of NAFTA, Mexico cut back on the corporate tax benefits awarded to maquiladoras. Nevertheless, the maquiladora sector boomed during the 1990s and was often cited as evidence of NAFTA's success (table 1.10).

In 2001, the Mexican economy turned sour, and NAFTA opponents seized on maquiladora contraction as evidence that NAFTA did not work after all. Mexican protectionists cited shrinking maquiladora employment as evidence of debilitating competition from low-wage workers in China. The underlying causes of the maquiladora bust are primarily cyclical, and the decline in employment, while severe, must be considered in relation to the expansion of the late 1990s, which was equally steep (table 1.10).[3] As the US economy recovered, the maquiladora industry showed signs of recovery.[4] We believe the following forces contributed to the decline of maquiladoras, in order of importance:

- **US economic recession.** Some 98 percent of maquiladora output is exported to the United States, and much of this consists of intermediate goods. The largest

---

1. In 1993, Mexican legislation was modified to permit maquiladoras to sell 50 percent of their output to the domestic market. Under NAFTA, the export orientation requirement has been gradually phased down to 20 percent. However, in practice, maquiladoras still export most of their output.

2. In the 1960s, US, European, and Japanese firms invested in the Mexican automotive industry to supply the domestic market (which was then highly protected). When the maquiladora program was created in 1965, a parallel program, PITEX, was created to give these existing foreign investors equivalent tax benefits. At the beginning of 2005, there were 3,016 maquiladora firms and 3,665 PITEX firms in operation. For a description of the benefits available to maquiladora and PITEX firms, see "Exports from Mexico: Comparing Tax Benefits of Maquiladora vs. PITEX Regimes," *North American Free Trade and Investment Report* 15, no. 3, February 15, 2005, 1.

3. Most commentators count the decline from the peak maquiladora employment in October 2000 (1.35 million workers). From this base, employment is down 21 percent as of January 2004 (1.06 million). However, the January 2004 employment level is roughly equal to that of January 1999.

4. During January–August 2004, 800 new maquiladora companies were established in Mexico, which is 30 percent more than the same period in 2003—due to the improved health of the US economy and a modest real depreciation of the peso. See Morales (2004).

(box continues next page)

Box 1.1 *(continued)*

maquiladoras are foreign-owned and are organized so that they can be easily idled.[5] Gruben (2004) describes the role of maquiladoras as that of "shock absorbers" for the US manufacturing economy.[6]

- **NAFTA Section 303,** which ended the duty rebates on maquiladora imports of non-NAFTA components came into effect in 2001. Section 303 was especially severe on Asian-owned electronics maquiladoras, some of which reported an overnight production cost hike of 20 percent (GAO 2003). Some of these firms decided to shut down rather than absorb the tariff charges on imported components.[7]

- **Mexican tax law** was changed in 2000 to classify maquiladoras as "permanent establishments" and therefore subject to Mexican income tax. This both raised maquiladora tax liability and invoked a complex web of regulations for determining tax liability.[8] In 2002, maquiladoras were subjected to the Impuesto Sustantivo de Crédito al Salario, a payroll tax. The response was so negative that it was phased out in 2004. Maquiladora advocates claim the repeal will recover 50,000 jobs (UNCTAD 2004, box 1).

- **Competition from the developing world** severely affected textile and apparel maquiladoras and continues to do so. Competition comes not only from China (which benefited from the end of Multi-Fiber Arrangement quotas in January 2005) but also from the Caribbean and Central America. The Caribbean Basin Trade Partnership Act (CBTPA) grants Caribbean countries tariff-free status in the United States subject to rules of origin akin to preferences granted to Mexico under NAFTA.[9] When the Central American Free Trade Agreement (CAFTA) enters into force, those countries will also be granted "NAFTA parity."

- **The strong peso** had a marked impact as well. Just as the weak peso helped stimulate the maquiladora boom in the late 1990s, the overvalued peso in 2001–02 worked in the opposite direction (especially when coupled with an undervalued Chinese renminbi; see figure 1B.1).[10]

---

5. By number, about half of the maquiladoras are Mexican-owned, but these tend to be smaller firms that provide contract assembly services to foreign companies.

6. Maquiladoras made a comeback in 2004, due to the improved health of the US economy. The US upturn, and a modest real depreciation of the peso, are the significant factors that presage a rosier economic picture for maquiladoras.

7. To buffer these firms and avert more shutdowns, under its Programs for Sectoral Promotion, the government of Mexico issued a decree in November 2000 to allow duty suspensions for components that were not available in North America.

8. The tax structure is still evolving, and the Mexican Supreme Court has overruled some, not all, of the tax changes. Gerber (1999) explains the menu of tax options available to maquiladoras before the Supreme Court decision.

9. However, the CBPTA rules of origin are more onerous than NAFTA rules. This has limited the growth of apparel exports from the Caribbean to the US market.

10. The peso has actually depreciated somewhat in real terms against the dollar since April 2002, after appreciating steadily throughout the late 1990s.

Table 1.10 Maquiladora industry, 1990–2003

Year	Firms (units)	Employment (thousands)	Real value added[a] (billions of 2003 pesos)
1990	1,703	446.4	4.8
1991	1,914	467.4	5.1
1992	2,075	505.7	5.4
1993	2,114	542.1	5.8
1994	2,085	583.0	6.5
1995	2,130	648.3	7.4
1996	2,411	753.7	8.3
1997	2,717	903.5	10.3
1998	2,983	1,014.0	12.5
1999	3,297	1,143.2	14.5
2000	3,590	1,291.2	16.3
2001	3,630	1,198.9	17.1
2002	3,003	1,071.2	16.8
2003	2,860	1,062.1	17.1

a. Deflated with the Mexican national producer price index.
Source: INEGI (2004).

is part of the NAFTA controversy over the connection between openness, economic growth, and poverty reduction (box 1.2). To convey a broad impression, table 1.12 shows OECD data on the evolution of GDP and GDP per capita for NAFTA members, using market exchange rates.

The World Bank (2003) used a regression of the US-Mexico GDP per capita ratio to make the case that NAFTA, modeled as a dummy variable covering the period 1994–2002, increased the rate of convergence between the United States and Mexico relative to the period 1960–2002. Their estimates controlled for the episode of pre-NAFTA liberalization (1986–93) and the peso crisis (October 1994 to March 1995). The model suggests that the effect of NAFTA was to increase the rate of convergence between US and Mexican per capita income. Weisbrot, Rosnick, and Baker (2004) strongly question these results. Claiming to use more authoritative data, they estimate the same model and find that NAFTA may have actually raised the ratio between US and Mexican GDP per capita, causing divergence rather than convergence.[83] This debate is far from settled. As the World Bank authors freely admit, the "combination of big events and a

---

83. The World Bank (2003) used adjusted GDP per capita data from the World Bank's *World Development Indicators*. Weisbrot, Rosnick, and Baker (2004) reproduced the study using data from the Penn World Tables and OECD national accounts to find a contradictory result.

Box 1.2 Poverty and income inequality in Mexico

Some scholars argue that the distributional impact of NAFTA within Mexico provides a cautionary tale. Although middle- and upper-class Mexican professionals have prospered since NAFTA, as have the northern states such as Nuevo Leon and Sonora, it is less clear that life has improved for unskilled and rural Mexicans, or the southern states such as Chiapas and Oaxaca.

In statistical terms, the poverty rate in Mexico, defined by the World Bank as the share of population living below $2 a day, declined from 42.5 percent in 1995 to 26.3 percent in 2000. Trade inspired by NAFTA arguably contributed to this improvement. Total Mexican exports might have been about 25 percent lower without NAFTA, and FDI might have been 40 percent less without NAFTA (World Bank 2003). Even though poverty has lessened, it is still high in Mexico. By comparison, the poverty rate in Chile was only 9.6 percent in 2000 (table 1.11).

One reason for the continuing high level of Mexican poverty is inequality. Measured by the Gini coefficient, Mexico has about the same inequality as other large countries in Latin America.[1] The Mexican Gini coefficient declined slightly from 53.9 in 1994 to 51.4 in 2002.[2] By comparison, the Gini coefficient in the United States is around 45.

The key to poverty reduction is faster economic growth. In the long run, economic growth requires better human capital.[3] According to the OECD 2000 Program for International Student Assessment, Mexico ranks last in the OECD on the combined score for reading and literacy among 15-year-old students.[4] Reducing the education gap is essential if Mexico hopes to compete in the global economy.

Mexican growth is also constrained by inadequate physical infrastructure (highways, urban roads, water, and sewerage), corruption, and low savings. According to Transparency International, Mexico ranks 64 out of 146 countries with a score of 3.6 against a clean score of 10.[5] The OECD notes a recent business survey that suggests new firms had to pay extraofficial sums around $4,000 to start a business in Mexico (OECD 2004d). The gross national saving rate in Mexico is around 18 percent of GDP, well below Asian levels.

---

1. In rural Mexico, however, where about 65 percent of the extreme poor live, inequality has worsened. The richest 10 percent of rural households increased their share of total rural income from 27 percent in 1994 to nearly 32 percent in 1998. See ECLAC (2001) and World Bank (2004).

2. The Gini coefficient measures income inequality within a population, ranging from zero for complete equality to 100 for perfect inequality. See World Bank (2003).

3. Hanson (2003), for example, found that during 1990–2000, the better-educated Mexican workers enjoyed higher wage growth.

4. Based on completion rates of upper secondary level education over the last generation, Mexico fell from rank 29 to 30. Meanwhile, South Korea moved from rank 24 to 1. See OECD (2004b).

5. The Transparency International Corruption Perception Index ranks countries based on perceptions of the degree of corruption as seen by business people and country analysts and ranges between 10 (highly "clean") and 0 (highly corrupt). In 1995, Mexico received a score of 3.18.

Table 1.11   Income inequality and poverty in Mexico

Country	Percent of population below $2/day[a]		Human Poverty Index rank[b]	Gini coefficient[c]		
	1995	2000	2003	1990	1997	2002
Argentina	n.a.	14.3	n.a.	50.1	53.0	59.0
Brazil	n.a.	22.4	18	62.7	63.8	63.9
Chile	20.3	9.6	3	55.4	55.3	55.9
Mexico	42.5	26.3	12	53.6	53.9	51.4
Canada	n.a.	n.a.	12	40.0	43.0	42.0
United States	n.a.	n.a.	17	42.8	45.9	45.0

n.a. = not available

a. Setting the poverty line at $2/day reflects the World Bank methodology, which uses purchasing power parity at 1993 prices. For 2000, international poverty lines were equivalent to $65.48 per month (1993 purchasing power parity).

b. The Human Poverty Index is based on the United Nations HPI-1 and HPI-2 human poverty indices. The HPI-1 index for developing countries measures deprivation in longevity, education, and standard of living. The HPI-2 index (for selected high-income OECD countries) includes the three dimensions in HPI-1 plus social exclusion.

c. The Gini coefficient measures income inequality within a population. The coefficient ranges from zero for complete equality (all residents receive exactly the same income) to 100 for perfect inequality (a single resident receives the total national income; other residents receive no income).

Sources: World Bank *World Development Indicators*, 2004; United Nations *Human Development Report*, 2004; ECLAC (2004); World Bank (2003); Statistics Canada, *Analysis of Income in Canada*, 2002; US Census Bureau, *Money and Income in the United States*, 1998 and 2002.

short experience with NAFTA increases the difficulty of empirically identifying the impact of the agreement on income and productivity gaps."

In a more general and longer-term study, Arora and Vamvakidis (2004) make the case that increased trade with rich countries improves the growth rate of developing countries. They report several panel regressions across 101 countries over the period 1960–99. After controlling for demographics, investment, human capital, macroeconomic stability, trade openness, and other common drivers of growth, their study found that a 1 percent higher growth rate in the rich trading partners of a developing country (weighting the partners by exports) corresponds to a 0.8 percent increase in the growth rate of the developing country itself. Similarly, Bhalla (2002) argues that globalization disproportionately benefits the poorest households (the lowest 20 percent) in developing countries. Bhalla estimates that every 10 percent increase in total income in those countries is associated with a 5 percent decline in the poverty level. We report these global results while waiting for more complete evidence on NAFTA. As of now, however, it does not appear that Mexico's GDP has converged toward the US level.

Other panel studies have found empirical links between increased trade openness and growth. Dollar and Kraay (2004) present regressions explaining national growth rates using (among other variables) decadal changes in a country's openness to trade (measured as X+M/GDP) as an

Table 1.12 GDP and per capita GDP of the NAFTA countries, 1989–2004

	1989	1990	1991	1992	1993	1994	1995	1996	1997	1998	1999	2000	2001	2002	2003	2004
GDP at market exchange rates (billions of 2000 US dollars)																
Canada	534	535	524	528	541	567	582	592	617	642	678	714	727	752	767	790
Mexico	393	413	431	446	455	475	446	469	501	526	545	581	581	585	592	617
United States	6,988	7,110	7,075	7,292	7,486	7,792	8,002	8,280	8,661	9,035	9,409	9,765	9,790	10,024	10,330	10,783
GDP per capita, at market exchange rates (in 2000 dollars)																
Canada	19,599	19,339	18,701	18,641	18,869	19,560	19,897	20,006	20,649	21,313	22,326	23,280	23,441	23,982	24,254	n.a.
Mexico	4,907	5,088	5,088	5,177	5,184	5,319	4,946	5,088	5,330	5,490	5,606	5,886	5,804	5,765	5,765	n.a.
United States	27,998	28,200	27,773	28,321	28,707	29,514	29,907	30,637	31,681	32,636	33,713	34,575	34,479	34,775	35,488	n.a.
GDP annual growth (percent)																
Canada	2.6	0.2	-2.1	0.9	2.3	4.8	2.8	1.6	4.2	4.1	5.6	5.3	1.9	3.4	2.0	3.0
Mexico	4.2	5.1	4.2	3.6	2.0	4.4	-6.2	5.2	6.8	5.0	3.6	6.6	0.0	0.7	1.3	4.2
United States	3.5	1.7	-0.5	3.1	2.7	4.1	2.7	3.6	4.5	4.3	4.1	3.8	0.3	2.4	3.1	4.4
GDP per capita annual growth (percent)																
Canada	0.9	-1.3	-3.3	-0.3	1.2	3.7	1.7	0.6	3.2	3.2	4.8	4.3	0.7	2.3	1.1	1.3
Mexico	2.2	3.7	0.0	1.7	0.1	2.6	-7.0	2.9	4.8	3.0	2.1	5.0	-1.4	-0.7	0.0	2.3
United States	2.6	0.7	-1.5	2.0	1.4	2.8	1.3	2.5	3.3	3.0	3.3	2.6	-0.3	0.9	2.1	3.4

n.a. = not available

Sources: OECD (2004a, 2005); IMF *World Economic Outlook* database, 2005.

independent variable. On the basis of data from 101 countries, their findings indicate that a 100 percent increase in trade openness would result in a 25 to 48 percent increase in per capita income growth over a decade (Dollar and Kraay 2004, table 4).[84] Cline (2004, 228–38) surveys an earlier version of the Dollar-Kraay analysis and other studies and finds that all report significant and positive correlations between increased trade intensity and per capita income. Additional calculations indicate that free trade substantially reduces global poverty.[85] Within the Mexican context, these results suggest the wisdom of opening domestic markets to international trade, through NAFTA and other initiatives.

Dispute Settlement

Indirectly, NAFTA was designed to *increase* the number of trade disputes between the partner countries! The reason is straightforward: the larger the volume of trade, the greater the possibility of trade friction. Anticipating this equation, an important part of the negotiating strategy for Canada and Mexico was to restrain US antidumping (AD) and countervailing duty (CVD) actions and establish trilateral dispute settlement mechanisms to cover issues that might arise under the pact.

In the end, NAFTA incorporated *six* dispute settlement processes to manage and expedite the resolution of disputes among the three countries.[86] While AD and CVD cases are by far the most numerous, the most controversial dispute provisions cover investor-state disputes under Chapter 11. When investor rights were first conferred, the Chapter 11 provisions were relatively uncontroversial; in fact, they were hailed as a better forum than national courts for resolving investment disputes. In practice, however, the rules (e.g., the ban on indirect expropriation under Article 1110 and the minimum standards under Article 1105) have fostered litigation by business firms against a broader range of government activity than originally envisaged. We summarize in chapter 4 the caseloads under each class of NAFTA disputes and analyze in some detail the most contentious cases.

---

84. Birdsall and Hamoudi (2002), however, disagree with the methodology adopted by Dollar and Kraay. Specifically, they claim that using the trade/GDP ratio to measure trade openness is a poor proxy for government policy because it overstates the importance of trade policy in economic growth and excludes the "commodity dependence" variable. By including the effects of commodity-dependent exports, Birdsall and Hamoudi (2002) estimate a lower induced growth in per capita income.

85. After recalculating country poverty elasticities, Cline estimated that complete free trade could lift 440 million people out of poverty. His original estimate was 540 million. See technical correction to Cline (2004), www.iie.com/publications/chapters_preview/379/errataiie 3659.pdf (accessed on December 30, 2004).

86. The six processes are Chapter 11 (investment), Chapter 14 (financial services), Chapter 19 (antidumping and countervailing duties), Chapter 20 (functioning of the agreement), the NAALC (labor), and the NAAEC (environment).

In general, the dispute settlement process has worked relatively well in cases where the NAFTA obligations were clearly defined (including most Chapter 19 cases involving AD and CVD) but poorly in big cases where domestic politics have blocked treaty compliance (notably, US-Mexico trucking, Canada-US softwood lumber, and US-Mexico sugar and high-fructose corn syrup [HFCS]). In areas where the specific procedures were intentionally cumbersome, and relied heavily on consultation rather than litigation (the side pacts and general disputes under Chapter 20), most actions have been hortatory. Even the WTO dispute settlement mechanism, however, has difficulty resolving politically sensitive cases (e.g., beef hormones and genetically modified organisms). The procedures for disputes on financial services (Chapter 14) remain untested.

Labor and the Environment

The North American Agreements on Labor Cooperation and on Environmental Cooperation (NAALC and NAAEC, respectively) were negotiated and appended to the NAFTA in 1993 at the behest of President Clinton to encourage US ratification of the pact. These side agreements had three specific objectives: monitor implementation of *national* laws and regulations pertaining to labor and the environment, provide resources for joint initiatives to promote better labor and environmental practices, and establish a forum for consultations and dispute resolution in cases where domestic enforcement proves inadequate.

Despite a slow and cumbersome start, the pacts have begun to show results. Both side pacts primarily focused on oversight of national laws and practices, sponsoring comparative studies, training seminars, and regional initiatives to promote cooperative labor and environmental policies. These efforts seem small in relation to the magnitude of the problems, but they have directed fresh attention and resources to old issues.

Dispute settlement provisions in the two side pacts were a major US objective, but the record to date has been mixed. Both Mexico and Canada resisted the incorporation of penalties in the side pacts and only accepted a compromise process that was long on consultation and short on adjudication. Contrary to expectations, there has been no flood of environmental dispute cases under the NAAEC, indeed not a single state-to-state case has been adjudicated. Even when environmental cases run the adjudication gauntlet, only a factual record (with no recommendation) is released, and no follow-up takes place.

Beyond dispute settlement, the side pacts have promoted increased cooperation on transboundary problems. They have directed additional attention, and a small amount of new resources, to labor and environmental problems. While fears of "downward harmonization" have not been substantiated, progress to date pales in comparison with the scarcity of water and the burden of pollution. In fact, the absence of specific environmental indicators makes it difficult to set spending priorities, although the current level of public funding is surely inadequate. The trade pact cannot reverse decades of environmental abuse nor can it turn the spigot on billions of dollars of remedial funding. But the Commission for Environmental Cooperation (CEC) could do more to focus attention on areas where environmental conditions are substandard. With better information on environmental conditions, and a better assessment of needed environmental investments, the CEC could make a major contribution to informed policy making in all three countries.

Trilateral, Regional, and Multilateral Cooperation

The final touchstone, based on NAFTA Article 102, is quite broad. We consider NAFTA's contribution toward furthering regional and multilateral trade agreements and also whether cooperation within NAFTA has led to deeper cooperation in other areas of North American concern, most notably energy and migration policy.

For better or worse, many of these issues are linked politically. For the United States, faster economic growth in Mexico is critical to improving security on the southern border, while deeper post–September 11 cooperation with Canada is essential to ensure the efficient flow of goods and people across the long northern border. Mexico's economic prospects depend on radical reform of Mexican tax and energy policies to allow extensive investment in a sector that has been closed to foreign investment for seven decades. While this should be a standalone priority for Mexico, political realities may require more attention to the plight of Mexican migrants in the United States as an unstated quid pro quo. At the same time, much more could be done to address border environmental and health issues—led by urban water shortages and pollution—but only with substantial financial support from the US and Mexican federal governments.

Furthering Trade Negotiations

While NAFTA contains an accession provision, it has not been used so far. At the Summit of the Americas in Miami in December 1994, Chile was hailed as a future NAFTA partner. While the "four amigos" of Miami are joined together in a series of bilateral FTAs, they have made no effort to consolidate their ties into a common pact. Based on this experience and others, it seems likely that the Free Trade Area of the Americas (FTAA), if concluded, will coexist with NAFTA and other bilateral and regional pacts.

Although NAFTA itself has not expanded, its provisions have served as precedents for bilateral FTAs between the United States and other countries. Successive agreements—with Jordan, Chile, Singapore, Australia, Morocco, Central America–Dominican Republic, Bahrain, and others under negotiation—have drawn heavily on their predecessors, with NAFTA serving as the primary template. The basic NAFTA model has been refined in the years since the agreement. Most notably, environment and labor standards have been moved from side agreements into the treaty text. In response to sovereignty concerns, investor-state dispute settlement provisions have been weakened and ill-advised capital-market provisions have been added, but nothing akin to chapter 19 arbitration exists in post-NAFTA agreements.

Indirectly, NAFTA played a role in facilitating the liberalization of world trade at the multilateral level. The agreement helped provide the final push to the completion of the Uruguay Round, which was signed in April 1994. Mexico has become a world leader in bilateral FTAs, compiling agreements with 32 countries, including pacts with the 15-member European Union in 2002 and Japan in 2004.

US-Mexican Migration

The question of migration was too hot to handle in NAFTA negotiations. Proponents of NAFTA claimed that the agreement would support Mexican development and thereby stem the flow of unauthorized migrants to the United States in the long term; after 10 years, however, the economic incentive to come to the United States—legally or illegally—remains as strong as ever. In fact, the population of unauthorized Mexican immigrants—who constitute the majority of unauthorized immigrants in the United States—is growing faster than the total unauthorized immigrant population. Although statistics on undocumented immigrants are only rough estimates, table 1.13 displays US government figures on the number of unauthorized immigrants living in the United States. According to these estimates, the population doubled between 1990 and 2000, with an annualized increase of 400,000 per year.

Philip Martin, in chapter 8 on migration, offers a possible explanation for the surge in Mexican immigration: a "NAFTA migration hump." In Martin's scenario, NAFTA increased migration in the short term—due to dislocations in the Mexican economy, primarily in agriculture. Eventually, long-term declines will follow the "hump" as a result of faster development and an aging Mexican population.

For compelling reasons, both humanitarian and economic,[87] the Mexican government has attempted to open a dialogue on "regularizing" the status of its emigrant workers. In early September 2001, President Fox eloquently raised the question with President Bush and Congress during a visit to Washington and received a sympathetic hearing. But the September 11 terrorist attacks made border security an antiterror issue rather than an immigration issue. In 2004, President Bush sought to revive his earlier proposal for a guest worker program for Mexican migrants; possi-

---

87. Household remittances—many of them from illegal migrants in the United States—have become an important source of foreign exchange to the Mexican economy; see table 1.1.

Table 1.13   Estimated unauthorized resident population in the United States, 1990 and 2000 (thousands)

Country/state	1990	2000	Growth (percent)	Percent of total unauthorized population in 2000
By origin				
Mexico	2,040	4,808	135.7	68.7
El Salvador	298	189	−36.6	2.7
Guatemala	118	144	22.0	2.1
Colombia	51	141	176.5	2.0
Honduras[a]	42	138	228.6	2.0
China	70	115	64.3	1.6
By residence				
California	1,476	2,209	49.7	31.6
Texas	438	1,041	137.7	14.9
New York	357	489	37.0	7.0
Illinois	194	437	125.3	6.2
Florida	239	337	41.0	4.8
Arizona	88	283	221.6	4.0
Total	3,500	7,000	100.0	100.0

a. Includes 105,000 Hondurans granted temporary protected status in December 1998.

Source: USCIS (2003).

bly the Bush administration will press Congress for legislation in 2006 or 2007. So far, however, US-Mexican collaboration on migration policy—predicted to be a logical outgrowth of NAFTA cooperation—continues to languish on the policy drawing board.

Energy Security

The text of NAFTA leaves the continent a long way from an integrated North American energy market. This is particularly unfortunate when oil prices are above $60 per barrel, and turmoil appears to be a long-term descriptor of the Middle East. As between the United States and Canada, NAFTA built on the CUSFTA by liberalizing energy investment in addition to trade. However, Mexico opted out of energy investment liberalization and also took exceptions on trade liberalization to protect its state monopoly in petroleum and electricity. US officials agreed, noting that the FTA negotiation should not be used to revise the Mexican Constitution.

Predictably, therefore, NAFTA has had little effect in reforming the Mexican energy sector. Over the next decade, Mexico must invest heavily in energy production and distribution or endure slower growth on ac-

---

88. In 1999, the Zedillo government announced that over $59 billion in investment in power generation and infrastructure alone would be required to meet Mexican demand growth through 2009 ("Meeting Mexico's Electricity Needs," *North American Free Trade and Investment Report* 14, no. 2, January 31, 2004, 3). Nothing like this amount is built into Mexican investment plans. In fact, nearly all of Pemex's revenue surplus is drained off to support the federal budget.

count of widespread energy shortages.[88] So far, Mexico clings stubbornly to provisions in its 1917 Constitution that declare all subsoil minerals the property of the Mexican people (i.e., the state) and prohibit private investment in the energy sector. President Fox tried but failed to enact even modest proposals directed at electricity generation and distribution. Underproduction, rising costs, and energy shortages thus loom on the horizon for Mexico. For energy resource–rich Mexico, inadequate supplies of energy will continue to act as a drag on economic growth.

North America's energy needs over the next 25 years can only be described as massive. Whether they will be met at current prices is an open question. Continental consumption is expected to rise by an average 1.5 percent a year through 2025 (EIA 2004a). Energy consumption in the United States dwarfs that in Canada or Mexico; however, the growth rate in Mexican energy demand may well be the fastest over the next 20 years. If current trends continue, the continent will drastically increase its energy imports.

In the United States, energy policy episodically overlaps with "energy independence," usually defined as a reduced reliance on foreign oil, especially from the Middle East. Energy security should instead be considered in a regional context. Canada correctly feels it has a part to play in the US energy strategy; Mexico can contribute as well. Several proposals should be considered to better equip North America to meet the growing demand.[89]

Canada and the United States both have an interest in coming to agreement over appropriate routes for natural gas pipeline construction. The tar sands of Alberta and natural gas deposits in the Mackenzie Delta are promising sources of future Canadian production. At a minimum, Canadian oil and natural gas deposits should play a role as part of a North American "insurance policy" (in addition to the Strategic Petroleum Reserve) against acute shortages. Moreover, the United States and Canada should be working together to improve the reliability of energy transmission systems—especially electricity. This need was highlighted by the August 2003 blackout that spread across the northeast United States and eastern Canada, turning the lights out in both New York and Toronto.

Energy integration in hydrocarbons and conventional electricity has progressed between Canada and the United States since the CUSFTA entered into force in 1989. Looking to the future, Provincial Premier Dalton McGuinty envisions that Ontario will build multiple nuclear plants to satisfy its future energy needs. These plants could conceivably serve the

---

89. Moreover, if the United States chooses to enact a petroleum import duty, as a means both of promoting conservation and raising revenue, petroleum originating in Mexico and Canada should be excluded from the duty. However, the preference should be conditioned on Canadian and Mexican willingness to charge the same duty on their own petroleum imports.

northeastern United States as well, sidestepping America's not-in-my-backyard (NIMBY) complex over nuclear power.

Mexico's failure to invite energy investment from private firms is a missed opportunity for all three countries, although the costs fall most heavily on Mexico. Basically, Mexico has three choices: find tax revenue elsewhere and allow Pemex to reinvest its financial surplus in exploration and development; invite private energy producers into Mexico to drill for oil and gas; or slide into the ranks of energy-importing countries. While the decisions to find alternative revenue sources or open its energy fields to private (and foreign) investment rest with Mexico alone, other steps can be taken to advance energy cooperation on the continent. For example, the growing demand for natural gas presents an opportunity for Mexico and the United States to cooperate on liquefied natural gas (LNG) regasification terminals in Mexico. These terminals could supply both partners with imports from the Pacific region (e.g., Indonesia, Australia, and Peru), sidestepping another NIMBY complex in US coastal cities.

Rules of Origin Reform

In certain "sensitive" sectors (e.g., textiles, apparel, and some electronics) NAFTA rules of origin were intentionally distorting. Some progress has been made since NAFTA was ratified. In response to industry suggestions, NAFTA members have negotiated changes that allow somewhat more foreign content and reduce the administrative costs of qualifying for NAFTA treatment. The first changes were negotiated for alcoholic beverages, petroleum, pearl jewelry, headphones with microphones, chassis fitted with engines, photocopiers, and some food additives. These went into effect in January 2003 in Canada and the United States and in July 2004 in Mexico.

As noted earlier, in July 2004, NAFTA countries reached a "tentative" agreement for revised origin rules for a second group of products, which account for over $20 billion in trilateral trade: spices and seasonings, precious metals, speed drive controllers, printed circuit assemblies, household appliances (except televisions), loudspeakers, thermostats, and toys.[90] These reforms came into force in January 2005 in Canada and the United States but still await ratification by the Mexican Senate.[91]

In a separate announcement, negotiators agreed to end the 55 percent value added requirement and allow the use of imported uppers in footwear; these rules will go into effect in January 2006.[92] So far, changes in

---

90. See "Ministers Agree to Change NAFTA Rules of Origin on Nine Product Groups," *Inside US Trade*, July 23, 2004, 1.

91. See "The Continued Liberalization of NAFTA Rules of Origin," *North American Free Trade and Investment Report* 15, no. 2, January 31, 2005, 1.

92. Strict rules of origin have been blamed for the overall decline in US footwear imports from Mexico since 1997 and a 22 percent drop in US imports from Mexico in the first five months of 2004 ("NAFTA Chiefs Ease Footwear Rules," *Footwear News*, July 26, 2004, 14).

the rules of origin have been ad hoc, and more such changes are expected. However, ministers have "temporarily set aside" consideration of harmonizing MFN duty rates.[93]

NAFTA Institutions

NAFTA was designed with minimal institutional structures; none of the partners wanted to grant authority to a new regional bureaucracy. The restraint was too severe. NAFTA's skeletal institutional structure has impeded the achievement of certain core objectives.

In terms of political power, the institutional structure in NAFTA and the European Union are polar opposites. The NAFTA Commission—composed of the trade ministers of each country—is neither seen nor heard, aside from a semiannual meeting and joint statement. Beneath the commission more than 30 working groups toil on topics as diverse as goods, investment and services, rules of origin, agricultural subsidies, government procurement, sanitary and phytosanitary measures, and worn clothing. Working groups are intended to be apolitical bodies that explore and make recommendations. While the Working Group on Rules of Origin played an instrumental role in drawing up proposed reforms, and other groups have in some cases served as a forum to resolve disputes through negotiation, they remain weak and solely advisory. The NAFTA Secretariat is responsible for administering the dispute settlement processes (with the exception of those established under the side agreements); it also provides day-to-day assistance to the working groups and the commission. It has insufficient resources to do either job well.[94]

The Bottom Line

The first lesson is the most fundamental. NAFTA was designed to promote economic growth by spurring competition in domestic markets and promoting investment from both domestic and foreign sources. It has worked. North American firms are now more efficient and productive. They have restructured to take advantage of economies of scale in production and intraindustry specialization. US-Mexico trade has grown twice as fast as US trade outside of NAFTA, and foreign investment in Mexico has soared—from both North American and outside sources.

The US and Canadian economies have performed well during the NAFTA era, growing by average annual rates of 3.3 and 3.6 percent, re-

---

93. See "Ministers Agree to Change NAFTA Rules of Origin on Nine Product Groups," *Inside US Trade*, July 23, 2004, 1.

94. Pastor (2001) regards NAFTA's institutional structure as grossly inadequate and proposes the establishment of several new trinational bodies, including a North American Court on Trade and Investment and a North American Parliamentary Group.

spectively, over that period (OECD 2004a). Mexican growth has been a disappointment. Although Mexico grew at an annual rate of 2.7 percent between 1994 and 2003 (despite its sharp recession in 1995 following the peso crisis), this is well below Mexico's potential growth.[95] For better or worse, growth numbers cannot in the main be attributed to NAFTA—indeed NAFTA was a tiny factor in the US boom of the 1990s. While the agreement has played a positive role, particularly in Mexico, sectors that were shielded from NAFTA—particularly energy in Mexico—have also been shielded from its positive effects.

While NAFTA succeeded in its core goal—eradicating trade and investment barriers—trade pacts only create opportunities; they do not guarantee sales or new investment. In some cases, expectations (or fears) were overblown. NAFTA never had the potential for luring droves of US firms or sucking millions of US jobs into Mexico. Nor could NAFTA create "jobs, jobs, jobs" or significantly raise wages in the United States. Those gains essentially depend on good macroeconomic policies, a flexible labor force, better worker skills, and effective use of information technologies. With regard to the Mexican agricultural sector in particular, but on a wider basis as well, adjustment costs were underappreciated. Programs that were designed to alleviate adjustment burdens were inadequately funded.

In contrast to the European Union, the institutional mechanisms of NAFTA were designed to minimize interference with "business as usual" in the member states. A low level of commitment accurately reflected the political temperament of the time: There was no interest in a North American echo of European supranationalism. But NAFTA institutions were left with such minimal mandates and meager funding that they barely meet their original expectations. The prime example is NADBank, which approved only five loans in its first five years of existence. The pace has picked up sharply but still remains far below levels that would perceptibly improve border environmental conditions. Other institutions that focused on labor and the environment—the Commission for Labor Cooperation (CLC) and the Commission for Environmental Cooperation (CEC)—are similarly underfunded and have little power to influence national practices.

The dizzying mix of ad hoc NAFTA arbitration panels and standing committees (featuring six dispute settlement processes) if nothing else blurs the public image of NAFTA adjudication. In some cases, such as Chapter 20 hearings, the practice of nonbinding advisory opinions was intended to leave ultimate interpretation of NAFTA obligations in the hands of national authorities. In other cases, supposedly binding arbitration has not resolved long-running disputes because they were just too

---

95. The OECD estimates that Mexico's potential growth rate could be lifted to 6 percent through improvements in infrastructure and education ("Tequila Slammer—The Peso Crisis Ten Years On," *The Economist*, January 1, 2005).

big—particularly the marathon battles involving Mexican trucking and Canadian softwood lumber. This led Canadian Prime Minister Paul Martin to complain that "we've got to find a way that disputes can not only be settled, but be settled permanently."[96] On the other hand, NAFTA critics charge that Chapter 11 was a giveaway to foreign investors, citing $13 billion of claims filed, even though Chapter 11 awards to date amount to only $35 million.

A free trade area raises the premium on cooperation between partners. But the assumption that NAFTA would lead to closer cooperation on the environment, water resources, migration, and other issues has not been borne out—with the significant exception of the 1994–95 peso crisis. Meanwhile, border security concerns—not an issue during NAFTA negotiations—are now central to the national security of the United States. Security concerns have been dealt with on an ad hoc and bilateral basis rather than in a trilateral fashion.

With the benefit of hindsight, many of NAFTA's successes and failures appear predictable. The primary focus of the agreement was to reduce barriers to investment and trade, and it succeeded in that goal. NAFTA was able to bring the continent closer to free trade; this alone will not guarantee prosperity, but without free trade, prosperity would prove more elusive. The agreement improved the quality of life in North America but clearly not enough. Other ingredients are essential—good governance, good infrastructure, and good education, which are conspicuously short in many parts of North America, not only in Mexico.

The bottom line is that NAFTA is a great building block, but much remains to be built. In the rest of this book, we analyze particular sectors and issues and offer recommendations for constructive work.

References

Anderson, James E., and Eric van Wincoop. 2003. Gravity with Gravitas: A Solution to the Border Puzzle. *American Economic Review* 93, no. 1 (March): 170–92.

Arora, Vivek, and Athanasios Vamvakidis. 2004. *How Much Do Trading Partners Matter for Economic Growth?* IMF Working Paper 04/26. Washington: International Monetary Fund.

Audley, John, Demetrios G. Papademetriou, Sandra Polanski, and Scott Vaughan. 2003. *NAFTA's Promise and Reality: Lessons from Mexico for the Hemisphere.* Washington: Carnegie Endowment for International Peace.

Bailey, John. 2004. Security Imperatives of North American Integration. In *NAFTA's Impact on North America*, ed. Sidney Weintraub. Washington: Center for Strategic and International Studies.

Baily, Martin Neil. 2001. *Macroeconomic Implications of the New Economy.* Working Paper 01-9. Washington: Institute for International Economics. www.iie.com/publications/wp/2001/01-9.pdf (accessed on December 30, 2004).

Baldwin, John, and Beiling Yan. 2004. The Law of One Price: A Canada/US Exploration. *Review of Income and Wealth* 50, no. 1 (March): 1–10.

---

96. See "NAFTA Needs Fixing, PM Says," *The Globe and Mail*, July 8, 2004, A4.

Banco de Mexico. 2005. Indicadores Económicos y Financieros. www.banxico.org.mx/site BanxicoINGLES/eInfoFinanciera/FSinfoFinanciera.html (accessed on May 27, 2005).

BEA (Bureau of Economic Analysis). 2004a. *Cross-Border Trade and Services through Affiliates, 1986–2002.* www.bea.gov/bea/di/1001serv/intlserv.htm (accessed on January 5, 2005).

BEA (Bureau of Economic Analysis). 2004b. *US Direct Investment Abroad: Balance of Payments and Direct Investment Position Data.* www.bea.gov/bea/di/di1usdbal.htm (accessed on March 26, 2004).

Bhalla, Surjit. 2002. *Imagine There's No Country: Poverty, Inequality, and Growth in the Era of Globalization.* Washington: Institute for International Economics.

Birdsall, Nancy, and Amar Hamoudi. 2002. *Commodity Dependence, Trade and Growth: When 'Openness' Is Not Enough.* Working Paper Number 7. Washington: Center for Global Development.

BLS (Bureau of Labor Statistics). 2003. Hourly Compensation Costs for Production Workers in Manufacturing, 30 Countries or Areas, 40 Manufacturing industries, Selected Years 1975–2001. www.bls.gov/fls/flshcind.htm (accessed on January 27, 2004).

BLS (Bureau of Labor Statistics). 2004a. Current Employment Statistics. www.bls.gov/ces/ (accessed on January 5, 2005).

BLS (Bureau of Labor Statistics). 2004b. Current Population Survey. www.bls.gov/cps/ (accessed on March 12, 2004).

BLS (Bureau of Labor Statistics). 2004c. Business Employment Dynamics. www.bls.gov/bdm/ (accessed on March 12, 2004).

BNA (Bureau of National Affairs). 2004. Ontario Premier McGuinty Proposes Binational Zone Preclearance at Border. *BNA International Trade Reporter* 21, no. 26 (June 24): 1075.

Bradford, Scott C., Paul L. E. Grieco, and Gary Clyde Hufbauer. 2005. The Payoff to America from Global Integration. In *The United States and the World Economy,* C. Fred Bergsten and the Institute for International Economics. Washington: Institute for International Economics.

Brown, Drusilla K. 1992. The Impact of a North American Free Trade Area: General Equilibrium Models. In *Assessing the Impact of North American Free Trade,* eds. Nora Lustig, Barry P. Bosworth, and Robert Z. Lawrence. Washington: Brookings Institution.

Brown, Drusilla K., Alan V. Deardorff, and Robert M. Stern. 1992. A North American Free Trade Agreement: Analytical Issues and Computational Assessment. *The World Economy* 15: 11–29.

Burfisher, M. E., S. Robinson, and K. Theirfelder. 2001. The Impact of NAFTA on the United States. *Journal of Economic Perspectives* 15, no. 1: 125–44.

Cañas, Jesus, and Roberto Coronado. 2004. US-Mexico Trade: Are We Still Connected? *El Paso Business Frontier* 2004, no. 3. Federal Reserve Bank of Dallas, El Paso Branch.

Cardarelli, Roberto, and M. Ayhan Kose. 2004. *Economic Integration, Business Cycle, and Productivity in North America.* IMF Working Paper WP/04/138. Washington: International Monetary Fund.

Carrère, Céline, and Jaime de Melo. 2004. *Are Different Rules of Origin Equally Costly? Estimates from NAFTA.* Discussion Paper Series 4437. London: Center for Economic Policy Research (June).

CBO (Congressional Budget Office). 2003. *The Effects of NAFTA on U.S.-Mexican Trade and GDP.* Washington (May).

Cline, William R. 1995. *International Debt Reexamined.* Washington: Institute for International Economics.

Cline, William R. 2004. *Trade Policy and Global Poverty.* Washington: Institute for International Economics.

Deichmann, Uwe, Marianne Fay, Jun Koo, and Somik V. Lall. 2002. *Economic Structure, Productivity, and Infrastructure Quality in Southern Mexico.* World Bank Policy Research Working Paper 2900 (October). Washington: World Bank.

DeLong, J. Bradford. 2004. Looking Back at the NAFTA Ratification Debate. *Semi-Daily Web Journal.* www.j-bradford-delong.net/movable_type/2004_archives/000119.html (accessed on February 19, 2004).

DeRosa, Dean A., and John Gilbert. 2003. Technical Appendix: Quantitative Estimates of the Economic Impacts of US Bilateral Free Trade Agreements. Paper prepared for the Conference on Free Trade Agreements and US Trade Policy, Institute for International Economics, Washington, May 7–8, 2003.

DeRosa, Dean A., and John Gilbert. 2005. The Economic Impacts of Multilateral and Regional Trade Agreements in Quantitative Economic Models: An Ex Post Evaluation. ADR International Ltd. and Utah State University. Photocopy (June).

Destler, I. M. 1995. *American Trade Politics, 3d ed.* Washington: Institute for International Economics.

Dobson, Wendy. 2002. *Shaping the Future of the North American Economic Space: A Framework for Action.* Border Papers Commentary 162. Toronto: C. D. Howe Institute.

Dollar, David, and Aart Kraay. 2004. Trade, Growth, and Poverty. *The Economic Journal* 114, no. 493 (February): 22–49.

ECLAC (Economic Commission for Latin America and the Caribbean). 2001. *Social Panorama of Latin America 2000–01.* Santiago: United Nations (September).

ECLAC (Economic Commission for Latin America and the Caribbean). 2003. *Foreign Investment in Latin America and the Caribbean, 2002 Report.* Santiago: United Nations.

ECLAC (Economic Commission for Latin America and the Caribbean). 2004. *Social Panorama of Latin America 2004.* Briefing Paper. Santiago: United Nations.

EIA (Energy Information Administration). 2003a. *International Energy Outlook 2002.* Washington.

EIA (Energy Information Administration). 2003b. *Petroleum Supply Annual 2002.* Washington.

EIA (Energy Information Administration). 2004a. *International Energy Outlook 2004.* Washington.

EIA (Energy Information Administration). 2004b. *Petroleum Supply Annual 2003*, volume 1. Washington.

EIA (Energy Information Administration). 2004c. *Natural Gas Annual 2002.* Washington.

Elliott, Kimberly Ann, and Richard B. Freeman. 2003. *Can Labor Standards Improve Under Globalization?* Washington: Institute for International Economics.

Engel, Charles, and John Rogers. 1996. How Wide Is the Border? *American Economic Review* 86, no. 5 (December): 112–25.

Engel, Charles, and John Rogers. 2004. European Product Market Integration after the Euro. *Economic Policy* 19, no. 39 (July): 347–84.

Feenstra, Robert C., and Gordon H. Hanson. 1995. *Foreign Direct Investment and Relative Wages: Evidence from Mexico's Maquiladoras.* NBER Working Paper 5122. Cambridge, MA: National Bureau of Economic Research (May).

Fox, Alan K. 2004. Evaluating the Success of a CGE Model of the US-Canada and North American Free Trade Agreements. Paper presented at the Empirical Trade Analysis Conference on Strengthening Analytical Capabilities to Support Trade Negotiations, January 22–23. Washington: Woodrow Wilson International Center for Scholars.

Fukao, K., T. Okubo, and R. M. Stern. 2002. *An Econometric Analysis of Trade Diversion under NAFTA.* Research Seminar in International Economics Discussion Paper 491. Ann Arbor, MI: University of Michigan.

GAO (US General Accounting Office). 2003. *Mexico's Maquiladora Decline Affects U.S.-Mexico Border Communities and Trade; Recovery Depends in Part on Mexico's Actions.* GAO Report 03-891. July. www.gao.gov/new.items/d03891.pdf (accessed on September 25, 2003).

GBPC (Global Business Policy Council). 2004. FDI Confidence Index 7. Alexandria, VA: A. T. Kearney, Inc.

Gerber, James. 1999. *Whither the Maquiladora? A Look at Growth Prospects for the Industry after 2001.* San Diego Dialogue Working Paper #E-99-1. April. http://sandiegodialogue.org/pdfs/Maquila%20doc.pdf (accessed on October 16, 2003).

Glewwe, Paul. 2000. Are Foreign-Owned Businesses in Vietnam Really Sweatshops? *University of Minnesota Extension Service* 701 (Summer). www.extension.umn.edu/newsletters/ageconomist/components/ag237-701a.html (accessed on April 21, 2004).

Goldfarb, Danielle, and William B. P. Robson. 2003. *Risky Business: US Border Security and the Threat to Canadian Exports*. Border Papers Commentary 177. Toronto: C. D. Howe Institute.

Gould, David. 1998. Has NAFTA Changed North American Trade? *Economic Review* (First Quarter): 12–23. Dallas, TX: Federal Reserve Bank of Dallas.

Gradwohl, Carlos, and John Salerno. 2004. 2005 Mexican Tax Reform Approved. *North American Free Trade and Investment Report* 14, no. 21.

Graham, Edward M. 2000. *Fighting the Wrong Enemy: Antiglobal Activists and Multinational Corporations*. Washington: Institute for International Economics.

Gruben, William C. 2004. Have Mexico's Maquiladoras Bottomed Out? *Southwest Economy* (January/February). www.dallasfed.org/research/swe/2004/swe0401c.pdf (accessed on March 25, 2004).

Hanson, Gordon H. 2003. *What Has Happened to Wages in Mexico Since NAFTA?* NBER Working Paper 9563. Cambridge, MA: National Bureau of Economic Research.

Hart, Michael. 2004. A New Accommodation with the United States: The Trade and Economic Dimension. In *The Art of State, Volume II: Thinking North America*, eds. Thomas J. Courchene, Donald Savoie, and Daniel Schwanen. Montreal: Institute for Research and Public Policy.

Helliwell, John F. 1998. *How Much Do National Borders Matter?* Washington: Brookings Institution.

Hinojosa-Ojeda, Raúl, David Runsten, Fernando De Paolis, and Nabil Kamel. 2000. *The US Employment Impacts of North American Integration After NAFTA: A Partial Equilibrium Approach*. Research Report NAID-RR-010-00. Los Angeles, CA: North American Integration and Development Center, University of California at Los Angeles. http://naid.sppsr.ucla.edu/pubs&news/nafta2000.html (accessed on January 5, 2005).

Hufbauer, Gary Clyde, and Jeffrey J. Schott. 1993. *NAFTA: An Assessment* (rev. ed.). Washington: Institute for International Economics.

Hufbauer, Gary Clyde, and Gustavo Vega-Cánovas. 2003. Whither NAFTA? In *The Rebordering of North America: Integration and Exclusion in a New Security Context*, eds. Peter Andreas and Thomas J. Biersteker. New York: Routledge.

INEGI (Instituto Nacional de Estadística Geografia e Informática). 2002. El ABC de los Indicadores de la Productividad. Aguascalientes, Mexico.

INEGI (Instituto Nacional de Estadística Geografia e Informática). 2004. Banco de Información Económica. http://dgcnesyp.inegi.gob.mx/BDINE/BANCOS.HTM (accessed on April 21, 2004).

Klein, Naomi. 2002. *No Logo*. New York: Picador.

Kletzer, Lori G., and Robert Litan. 2001. *A Prescription to Relieve Worker Anxiety*. International Economics Policy Brief 01-2. Washington: Institute for International Economics.

Kose, M. Ayhan, Guy M. Meredith, and Christopher M. Towe. 2004. *How Has NAFTA Affected the Mexican Economy? Review and Evidence*. IMF Working Paper WP/04/59. Washington: International Monetary Fund.

Krueger, Anne O. 1999. *Trade Creation and Trade Diversion Under NAFTA*. NBER Working Paper 7429. Cambridge, MA: National Bureau of Economic Research.

La Porta, Rafael, Florencio López-de-Silanes, and Guillermo Zamarripa. 2002. *Related Lending*. NBER Working Paper 8848. Cambridge, MA: National Bureau of Economic Research.

Lewis, Howard, and J. David Richardson. 2001. *Why Global Commitment Really Matters!* Washington: Institute for International Economics.

McCallum, John. 1995. National Borders Matter: Canada-U.S. Regional Trade Patterns. *American Economic Review* 85, no. 3 (June): 615–23.

McLees, John A. 2004. US-Mexico Tax Treaty Override Risk in Pending Mexican Legislation. *North American Free Trade and Investment Report* 14, no. 20 (May 31).

McLees, John, Mary C. Bennett, Haime Gonzalez-Bendiksen, and Jaime Rojas-Merino. 2004. Mexico Redefines Business Profits to Limit Benefits Under Its Tax Treaties. *Tax Notes International* (December 6): 849–51.

Moore, Cassandra Chrones. 2004. US Supreme Court Finally Removes Decade-long Road-block to US-Mexican Trucking. *Free Trade Bulletin* 13. Washington: Cato Institute (July).

Morales, Ana. 2004. After Three-Year Slump, Maquiladora Industry Recovers; Lack of Reforms Could Hamper Growth. *North American Free Trade and Investment Report* 14, no. 21.

NADBank/BECC (North American Development Bank/Border Environment Cooperation Commission). 2004. Joint Status Report 2004 (March 31). www.nadbank.org/Reports/Joint_Report/english/status_eng.pdf (accessed on July 22, 2004).

OANDA Corp. 2004. FXHistory: Historical Currency Exchange Rates. www.oanda.com/convert/fxhistory (accessed on February 27, 2004).

OECD (Organization for Economic Cooperation and Development). 2004a. *Annual National Accounts Statistics Volume I—Comparative Tables, volume 2004, release 03*. Paris. Accessed via http://new.sourceoecd.org (September 1, 2004).

OECD (Organization for Economic Cooperation and Development). 2004b. *Education at a Glance 2004*. Paris (September).

OECD (Organization for Economic Cooperation and Development). 2004c. OECD Foreign Direct Investment Statistics, 2003. www.oecd.org/dataoecd/14/3/8264806.xls (accessed on May 14, 2004).

OECD (Organization for Economic Cooperation and Development). 2004d. *Economic Surveys: Mexico*. Paris.

OECD (Organization for Economic Cooperation and Development). 2004e. *OECD Reviews of Regulatory Reform: Mexico*. Paris.

OECD (Organization for Economic Cooperation and Development). 2005. *Annual National Accounts Statistics Volume I—Comparative Tables, volume 2005, release 01*. Paris. Accessed via http://new.sourceoecd.org (May 27, 2005).

Pastor, Robert A. 2001. *Toward a North American Community: Lessons from the Old World to the New*. Washington: Institute for International Economics.

Perot, Ross, with Pat Choate. 1993. *Save Your Job, Save Our Country: Why NAFTA Must Be Stopped—Now!* New York: Hyperion.

Public Citizen. 2004. Global Trade Watch. www.citizen.org/trade (accessed on April 15, 2004).

Ramírez de la O, Rogelio. 2004. Tax Reform in Mexico. *Hemisphere Focus* XII, no. 7. Washington: Center for Strategic and International Studies.

Rogers, John H., Gary Hufbauer, and Erika Wada. 2001. *Price Level Convergence and Inflation in Europe*. Working Paper 01-1. Washington: Institute for International Economics. www.iie.com/publications/wp/2001/01-1.pdf (accessed on December 30, 2004).

Rose, Andrew K. Forthcoming. Which International Institutions Promote International Trade? *Review of International Economics*. http://faculty.haas.berkeley.edu/arose/Rec Res.htm.

Rose, Andrew K. 2004. Do We Really Know that the WTO Increases Trade? *American Economic Review* 94, no. 1 (March): 98–114.

Rubin, Robert. 2003. *In an Uncertain World: Tough Choices from Wall Street to Washington*. New York: Random House.

Schott, Jeffrey. 1997. NAFTA: An Interim Report. In *Trade: Towards Open Regionalism*, eds. Shahid Javed Burki, Guillermo E. Perry, and Sara Calvo. Washington: World Bank.

Scott, Robert. 2003. *The High Price of Free Trade*. EPI Briefing Paper 147. Washington: Economic Policy Institute.

Secretaría de Economía. 2005a. Informe Estadístico sobre el Comportamiento de la Inversión Extranjera Directa en Mexico. www.economia.gob.mx/?P=1175 (accessed on May 27, 2005).

Secretaría de Economía. 2005b. Sistema de Informacíon Arancelaria vía Internet. www.economia-snci.gob.mx/sic_sistemas/siavi/entrada.php (accessed on May 27, 2005).

Sharpe, Andrew. 2003. *Are Americans More Productive Than Canadians?* Discussion Paper Series 1. Bellingham, WA: Center for International Business, Western Washington University.

SHCP (Secretaría de Hacienda y Crédito Público). 2004. Quarterly Report on Public Finances and Public Debt: Fourth Quarter of 2003. www.shcp.gob.mx/english/docs/qr03/qr403.pdf (accessed on June 30, 2005).

Statistics Canada. 2004. Employment by Industry and Sex. www.statcan.ca/english/Pgdb/labor10a.htm (accessed on May 27, 2004).

STPS (Secretaría del Trabajo y Previsión Social). 2004. Encuesta Nacional de Empleo (ENE). www.stps.gob.mx/01_oficina/05_cgpeet/302_0058.htm (accessed on May 27, 2004).

Tafoya, Audry, and Ralph Watkins. 2005. Production Sharing Update: Developments for 2003. *Industry Trade and Technology Review.* USITC Publication 3762: 9–30.

Trefler, Daniel. 2004. The Long and Short of the Canada-US Free Trade Agreement. *American Economic Review* 94, no. 4 (September): 870–95.

UNCTAD (United Nations Conference on Trade and Development). 2004. *World Investment Directory 2004—Volume IX: Latin American and Caribbean.* Geneva: United Nations.

INS (US Immigration and Naturalization Service). 2003. Estimates of the Unauthorized Immigrant Population Residing in the United States: 1990 to 2000. Washington. http://uscis.gov/graphics/shared/statistics/publications/Ill_Report_1211.pdf (accessed on July 20, 2005).

USDA (US Department of Agriculture, Economic Research Service). 2005. Agricultural Exchange Rate Data Set. http://www.ers.usda.gov/data/exchangerates/ (accessed on January 24, 2005).

USTR (Office of the United States Trade Representative). 2004. State-by-State Trade Information: United States Exports. Washington. Photocopy.

Wall, Howard J. 2003. NAFTA and the Geography of North American Trade. *Federal Reserve Bank of St. Louis Review* 85, no. 2 (March/April): 13–26.

Ward's Communications. 2003. Ward's Motor Vehicle Data 2003. Southfield, MI.

Weisbrot, Mark, David Rosnick, and Dean Baker. 2004. *NAFTA at Ten: The Recount.* Center for Economic and Policy Research Briefing Paper. Washington: Center for Economic and Policy Research.

Whitt, Joseph A., Jr. 1996. The Mexican Peso Crisis. *Federal Reserve Bank of Atlanta Economic Review* (January/February): 1–20.

Williamson, John. 1995. Statement before the Foreign Affairs Committee of the Canadian Senate, Ottawa, February 15. Photocopy.

World Bank. 2003. *Lessons from NAFTA for Latin America and the Caribbean Countries: A Summary of Research Findings.* Washington.

World Bank. 2004. *Poverty in Mexico.* Washington (June).

Zoellick, Robert B. 1991. *North American Free Trade Agreement: Extending Fast-Track Negotiating Authority.* Washington: United States State Department.

Appendix 1A
NAFTA and Trade Generation: Review of the Literature

Researchers have used two methods to attempt to answer the question, "How much trade did NAFTA create?" The first applies an ex ante construct: A computable general equilibrium (CGE) model compares the difference in trade with NAFTA against a hypothetical world without NAFTA. NAFTA itself is modeled as simply lower (or zero) tariff rates and ad valorem equivalents of nontariff barriers. This is a bare-bones conceptualization of the agreement. The second method applies an ex post regression: A gravity model explains the size of trade between nations in terms of several control variables.[97] NAFTA's presence or absence for a given year is one of the variables. Any trade expansion associated with the NAFTA dummy variable is attributed to NAFTA.

CGE models could be (and were) deployed before NAFTA came into force, and this was an advantage. The disadvantage is that CGE models rely on a complex network of assumptions, and the results may change substantially with a small change in the assumed framework.[98] Also, these models take into account only quantifiable barriers to trade, not investment liberalization, dispute settlement, or other parts of the agreement that have an indirect effect on trade flows.

- Brown (1992) surveyed CGE models of NAFTA and found that while all of the models considered predicted an increase in trade within North America on account of NAFTA, the increase varied from less than 5 to over 40 percent of total trade depending on the assumptions.

- Burfisher, Robinson, and Theirfelder (2001) found the consensus of CGE modelers seemed to be that "the [welfare] effects of NAFTA would be positive but small for the US, and positive and large for Mexico."

- Fox (2004) assessed the performance of the Michigan model for NAFTA (Brown, Deardorff, and Stern 1992) and added capital, labor, and balance of trade shocks to account for at least some of the exogenous events that occurred in the NAFTA era.[99] Using this model, Fox calculated that NAFTA generated a welfare gain of 0.1 percent of GDP

---

97. These models are called gravity models because two control variables are always country size and distance. Like Sir Isaac Newton's theories on gravitational pull, trade is directly related to country size (measured in GDP terms) and inversely related to distance.

98. Some particularly hotly debated assumptions are constant versus increasing returns to scale, static versus dynamic effects, and the appropriate values of Armington elasticities. Brown (1992) provides a useful overview of the choices that must be made when constructing a CGE model.

99. All of these events are regarded as exogenous in the model, but NAFTA might have triggered or augmented some of them. The Brown, Deardorff, and Stern model accounts for capital accumulation and economies of scale as a result of the reduction in trade barriers.

for the United States, 0.7 percent for Canada, and 1.6 percent for Mexico. He then compared the model's predictions with the observed changes in trade flows. Fox concludes, "Initial results suggest that while the model does a reasonable job of capturing the general pattern of trade, it fails to simulate the magnitude of trade, especially in cases where observed trade growth is substantial."

Gravity models have the advantage of relative simplicity. Since NAFTA is one of the explanatory variables within a regression model, the coefficient on the presence or absence of NAFTA (modeled as a one or zero dummy variable) purports to capture the full effect of NAFTA, through direct and indirect channels. Simplicity can also be a fault: A gravity model may attribute some influence to NAFTA that is due to contemporary, unobserved events. Moreover, gravity model analysis works by comparing the size of trade flows before and after NAFTA entered into force. Since NAFTA liberalization was phased in over several years, to say that NAFTA fully took effect in 1994 is an oversimplification. Bearing these limitations in mind, here is a summary of gravity model results:

- Gould (1998) examined quarterly data from 1980 to 1996 in a gravity model framework and found that NAFTA was responsible for a 16.3 percent increase in US exports to Mexico and a 16.2 percent increase in US imports from Mexico. The gains in US bilateral imports and exports with Canada were much smaller, 8.6 and 3.9 percent, respectively. Between Canada and Mexico, the effect of NAFTA was estimated to be negative (but with no significance). Indeed, of all six estimations, only the estimate of US exports to Mexico was statistically significant at a 90 percent confidence level.

- Krueger (1999) examined pooled time series of intra- and extra-NAFTA bilateral trade data in a gravity model framework. She found that NAFTA had a positive effect, estimating a 3 percent increase in trade when both countries were in NAFTA, but again the result was statistically insignificant.[100]

- Wall (2003) examined Canadian bilateral trade data from 1990 to 1998 between Canadian provinces and US states and Mexico, supplemented with international data. By treating states and provinces as individual units, Wall is able to alleviate the data scarcity problem.[101] Employing a vector of NAFTA dummies for each bilateral relationship

---

100. Krueger (1999) uses data from odd years between 1987 and 1997. Her study includes non-NAFTA countries and seeks to find the effect on trade if both partners belong to NAFTA.

101. Mexico is treated as a single entity. For the purposes of estimation, Canadian provinces are aggregated into three regions, while US states are aggregated into 10 regions. To assess the effect of trade diversion, eight non-NAFTA countries, aggregated into two regions (Europe and Asia), are also included.

between states and provinces, the estimation yields a majority of statistically significant results showing an increase in Canada's trade with the United States (14.3 percent in exports and 29.2 percent in imports, once reaggregated to the national level) and with Mexico (11.5 percent in exports and 48.2 percent in imports).[102]

- Helliwell (1998), following McCallum (1995), examined the same state-province data and found that the "border effect"—the difference between state-province and state-state trade, controlling for size and distance—between the United States and Canada fell from about 20 in 1988 to 12 after the ratification of the CUSFTA and NAFTA.[103] Anderson and van Wincoop (2003) argue that the McCallum method, which estimates the border effect only from the Canadian perspective, exaggerates the effect. Starting from a theoretical perspective, they estimate a model that suggests that the border effect is 10.7 from the Canadian perspective but only 2.5 from the US perspective (using data from 1993, the fourth year under the CUSFTA).[104]

- Rose (2004, forthcoming) examined world bilateral trade data from the IMF and used a panel regression to find that trade is 118 to 156 percent higher between countries in a regional trading agreement than those that are not.[105] This analysis assumes that all regional agreements (e.g., European Union, NAFTA, and Mercosur) amplify trade to the same extent.

DeRosa and Gilbert (2005) examine the predictive capability of both gravity and CGE models. According to the authors, "although both models are found to be quite accurate in some instances, the overall results do not make a strong case for the accuracy of either the empirical gravity model or the applied CGE model in predicting trade flows."

For the gravity model, DeRosa and Gilbert estimate gravity equations using two econometric techniques and data up to 1993 to "predict" that an

---

102. Since data are not available for trade between US states and Mexico, no state-by-state estimation was made for US-Mexican trade.

103. In other words, in 1988, Canadian provinces were 20 times more likely to trade with another province than a US state of the same size and distance; in 1993, they were only 12 times more likely to do so. Helliwell stresses a border effect of 1 should not be a policy goal, since cultural and other nondistorting differences between countries create a preference for intranational trade relations.

104. As with the McCallum and Helliwell numbers, these values relate the likelihood to trade across the border to the likelihood to trade between states or provinces. Anderson and van Wincoop also estimate that trade across the border would be 1.8 times higher if the United States and Canada were a single political unit.

105. In Rose (forthcoming, table 1) this number is reported in log terms, 0.78 (exp [(0.78)] −1 = 1.18). The higher coefficient, 0.94, is reported in Rose (2004, table 1). These estimates employ the country fixed-effects estimation technique; other econometric techniques have produced higher estimates of this coefficient.

FTA would increase bilateral trade between 185 and 250 percent (in real terms).[106] The predictions are based on FTAs in existence before 1993. In fact, real bilateral trade between the United States and Canada grew 70 percent between 1988, the year before the CUSFTA came into effect, and 1999, the final year in the dataset. (Andrew Rose compiled the dataset.)[107] Between 1993, the year before NAFTA, and 1999, US bilateral trade with Mexico grew 118 percent. Based on this analysis, NAFTA somewhat underperformed previous FTAs, possibly because North American trade was already relatively unhampered by barriers before the CUSFTA and NAFTA.

Turning to one variant of CGE models, DeRosa and Gilbert looked at forecasts generated from the plainest of "plain vanilla" Global Trade Analysis Project (GTAP) models. The model they examined utilized not only the contemporary GTAP databases (for 1995, 1997, and 2001)—a common practice in all CGE models—but also the GTAP model structure. The "plain vanilla" GTAP model structure assumes perfect competition (no monopolistic price markups), constant returns to scale (no scale economies or network economies), no factor productivity gains (stimulated either by foreign competition or by learning from foreign products and processes), and no induced investment (to take advantage of larger markets or new technology). In combination, these assumptions rule out most of the trade and welfare gains from policy liberalization that have been identified in recent empirical research (see Bradford, Grieco, and Hufbauer 2005).

The "plain vanilla" CGE model forecasts little change—in fact, small declines—in US-Canada and US-Mexico trade as a consequence of NAFTA liberalization. The forecast largely reflects the fact that in this model structure, adverse terms-of-trade effects for the exporting country exceed predicted trade volume gains. In addition, changes in the trade regime over the analyzed period may have been small, because many of the highest barriers are phased out slowly under NAFTA. Moreover, the calibration of the plain vanilla GTAP model to actual data is done in a way that attributes the bulk of trade expansion to factor endowment growth and higher total factor productivity—and trade liberalization is not allowed to change either of these drivers.

Accounting for changes in factor endowments and productivity ex post, the plain vanilla model comes moderately close to calculating the actual level of trade between country pairs in North America, but it does not explain why the basic trade drivers changed between two points in time. Our conclusion from this exercise is that for the CGE approach to be useful in predicting FTA outcomes, the model structure should be "flavored" by varying the assumptions enumerated earlier.

---

106. The two econometric techniques are clustered ordinary least squares (OLS) and generalized least squares with random effects.

107. Andrew Rose's dataset is publicly available in STATA format at http://faculty.haas.berkeley.edu/arose/RecRes.htm (accessed on June 14, 2005).

Appendix 1B
Trends in Mexican Imports since 2000

Table 1B.1 displays total Mexican imports by exporting country according to Mexican customs statistics. Mexico's total imports rose by 13 percent ($22 billion) between 2000 and 2004, but the share of imports from the United States fell from 73 to 56 percent (a $17 billion decline, but note the discrepancy between Mexican and US statistics).[108] Most of the seven-point drop in the US import share was due to increased Mexican imports from Asian countries, whose share rose 11 points from 12 to 23 percent. Mexican imports from China rose 397 percent to $14 billion in 2004; China's import share increased from 2 to 7 percent. The other gainers in import share were the European Union, up from 9 to 11 percent, and South American countries, up from 2 to 5 percent.

Weak demand for US products and increased competition from other nations (primarily Asian nations, led by China but including a resurgent Japan) contributed to the drop in the US share of Mexican imports. Increases in European market shares do not appear to be significant in industries where US exports are falling most sharply. While undervalued Asian currencies, led by the Chinese renminbi (figure 1B.1), may have played a role in the share decrease, "fundamentals," such as labor costs, are also at work.[109] In many industries, the share of imports from Asian countries has soared from near zero. In these cases, threshold effects (e.g., Asian "discovery" of the Mexican market and economies of scale in shipping) make it highly unlikely that US market share will fully recover even if Asian exchange rates are dramatically realigned. Indeed, in sectors where labor costs significantly affect the cost of production, Asian imports may continue to expand even after a revaluation of the Chinese renminbi.

Table 1B.2 displays import and share data on seven Harmonized Schedule (HS) two-digit industries, which together accounted for more than 60 percent of Mexican imports from the world and from the United States since 2000. These industries account for a dominant portion of the decline in imports from the United States.

Almost 90 percent of the total decline ($6 billion) in Mexican imports from the United States since 2000 occurred in electrical machinery and parts (HS 85), mainly due to slack demand. Total imports of HS 85 by Mexico fell $2 billion. However, this decline was accompanied by the influx of Asian competitors—China, Japan, and Taiwan. The import share claimed by China rose from 2 to 12 percent, while the import share for all

---

108. Unless otherwise indicated, all data are from Secretaría de Economía, Sistema de Inteligencia Comercial, www.economia-snci.gob.mx/sic_php/ (accessed on June 1, 2005).

109. While the renminbi is nominally pegged to the dollar, China experienced deflation or near-zero inflation between 1998 and 2002; whenever China's inflation rate is lower than the US inflation rate, the renminbi depreciates against the dollar in real terms (see figure 1B.1).

Table 1B.1 Mexican imports by country, selected years

Country/region	Billions of US dollars					Share of total imports (percent)					Change 2000–04		
	1994	2000	2002	2003	2004	1994	2000	2002	2003	2004	Percent	Import share gain/loss	Billions of US dollars
North America	**56.4**	**131.6**	**111.0**	**109.5**	**116.2**	**71.1**	**75.4**	**65.8**	**64.2**	**59.0**	**−11.7**	**−16.4**	**−15.4**
United States	54.8	127.5	106.6	105.4	110.8	69.1	73.1	63.2	61.8	56.3	−13.1	−16.8	−16.7
Canada	1.6	4.0	4.5	4.1	5.3	2.0	2.3	2.7	2.4	2.7	32.6	0.4	1.3
Central America	**0.2**	**0.5**	**0.7**	**0.9**	**1.3**	**0.2**	**0.3**	**0.4**	**0.5**	**0.7**	**186.7**	**0.4**	**0.8**
South America	**2.6**	**4.0**	**5.4**	**6.5**	**9.0**	**3.3**	**2.3**	**3.2**	**3.8**	**4.6**	**125.1**	**2.3**	**5.0**
Brazil	1.2	1.8	2.6	3.3	4.3	1.5	1.0	1.5	1.9	2.2	140.8	1.2	2.5
Chile	0.2	0.9	1.0	1.1	1.5	0.3	0.5	0.6	0.6	0.7	63.8	0.2	0.6
European Union	**9.1**	**15.0**	**16.6**	**18.0**	**21.8**	**11.4**	**8.6**	**9.9**	**10.6**	**11.1**	**45.0**	**2.5**	**6.8**
Germany	3.1	5.8	6.1	6.2	7.1	3.9	3.3	3.6	3.6	3.6	24.1	0.3	1.4
Italy	1.0	1.8	2.2	2.5	2.8	1.3	1.1	1.3	1.5	1.4	52.3	0.4	1.0
Spain	1.3	1.4	2.2	2.3	2.9	1.7	0.8	1.3	1.3	1.4	99.5	0.6	1.4
Asia	**9.5**	**20.3**	**31.4**	**31.9**	**44.4**	**11.9**	**11.6**	**18.6**	**18.7**	**22.6**	**119.0**	**10.9**	**24.1**
China	0.5	2.9	6.3	9.4	14.4	0.6	1.7	3.7	5.5	7.3	399.2	5.7	11.5
South Korea	1.2	3.9	3.9	4.1	5.3	1.5	2.2	2.3	2.4	2.7	36.9	0.5	1.4
Japan	4.8	6.5	9.3	7.6	10.6	6.0	3.7	5.5	4.5	5.4	63.7	1.7	4.1
Total	**79.3**	**174.5**	**168.7**	**170.6**	**196.8**	**100.0**	**100.0**	**100.0**	**100.0**	**100.0**	**12.8**	**0.0**	**22.4**

Source: Banco de México (2005).

Figure 1B.1 Peso and renminbi real exchange rate versus dollar

depreciation against dollar, January 2000 = 100

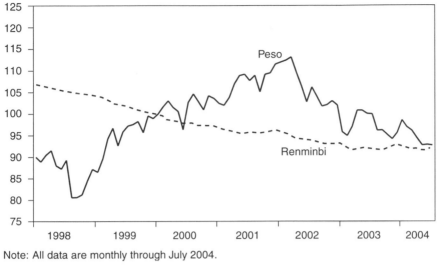

Note: All data are monthly through July 2004.

Source: USDA (2005).

three nations plus South Korea soared from 12 to 32 percent. The US share declined from 77 to 44 percent. Two forces are behind this shift: First, with rising income, middle-class Mexicans are purchasing more consumer electronics, almost all from Asia. Second, components made in China are displacing US parts in maquiladora assembly plants.[110]

China has also made its presence felt strongly in HS 84 (boilers, mechanical appliances, machinery and parts). Mexican imports in this category rose by $8.4 billion since 2000, while imports from the United States fell by $1.5 billion. Imports from China escalated from only $400 million in 2000 to $4.6 billion in 2004. Since 2000, the US market share dropped from 67 to 46 percent, while China gained 12 percentage points bringing its share to 14 percent. Computers and parts, and countertop appliances were responsible for much of the increase in imports from China to Mexico.

In the auto industry (HS 87), the $2 billion decline in imports from the United States occurred while total imports rose only slightly. Competition reduced the US import share from 72 to 58 percent. Brazil increased its shipments from $700 million to $1.7 billion in response to the auto agreement between the two countries. Japan doubled its shipments and increased its import market share to 7 percent, while Germany's share fell 1 percent on weaker sales. Argentina, while still a small player in the

---

110. Between 2000 and 2003, China's share of imported components rose from 1 to 7 percent. The US share dropped from 81 to 69 percent. See Tafoya and Watkins (2005).

Table 1B.2   Mexican imports by country, selected sectors, 1994–2004
(millions of US dollars and percent)

	1994	2000	2001	2002	2003	2004	Change 2000–04 Level	Change 2000–04 Percent
Total and US imports to Mexico								
All imports	79,346	174,458	168,396	168,679	170,958	197,303	22,845	13.1
US imports	54,791	127,534	113,767	106,557	105,686	114,978	−12,556	−9.8
Subtotal of listed categories:								
World subtotal	40,737	113,039	110,649	108,556	108,390	125,264	12,225	10.8
Percent of all imports	51.3	64.8	65.7	64.4	63.4	63.5	−1.3	−2.0
US subtotal	29,598	85,452	75,096	67,911	65,993	67,746	−17,706	−20.7
Percent of US imports	54.0	67.0	66.0	63.7	62.4	58.9	−8.1	−12.1
Imports of HS 27: Combustible minerals and oils								
Total	1,468.1	5,305.7	5,308.2	4,452.7	5,688.7	7,493.6	2,188	41.2
Share of total imports	1.9	3.0	3.2	2.6	3.3	3.8	0.8	24.9
United States	1,127.5	4,181.9	3,976.9	3,302.3	4,592.3	5,634.1	1,452	34.7
Share of HS 27 imports	76.8	78.8	74.9	74.2	80.7	75.2	−3.6	−4.6
Share of US imports	2.1	3.3	3.5	3.1	4.3	4.9	1.6	49.4
Saudi Arabia	0.5	237.6	176.9	172.1	160.4	252.3	14.7	6.2
Share of HS 27 imports	0.0	4.5	3.3	3.9	2.8	3.4	−1.1	−24.8
Venezuela	31.8	71.8	118.6	136.3	67.1	251.2	179.4	250.0
Share of HS 27 imports	2.2	1.4	2.2	3.1	1.2	3.4	2.0	147.8
Colombia	4.8	41.2	62.3	6.1	28.2	179.3	138.1	334.8
Share of HS 27 imports	0.3	0.8	1.2	0.1	0.5	2.4	1.6	207.9
Australia	0.0	54.3	73.9	86.3	220.9	162.5	108.2	199.4
Share of HS 27 imports	0.0	1.0	1.4	1.9	3.9	2.2	1.1	112.0
China	21.2	91.6	96.0	161.7	80.6	157.6	65.9	72.0
Share of HS 27 imports	1.4	1.7	1.8	3.6	1.4	2.1	0.4	21.8
Imports of HS 39: Plastics and plastic manufactures								
Total	4,403.4	10,443.4	9,926.1	10,535.7	11,575.5	12,665.1	2,222	21.3
Share of total imports	5.5	6.0	5.9	6.2	6.8	6.4	0.4	7.2
United States	3,876.3	9,302.8	8,508.0	8,917.3	9,557.9	10,186.1	0,883	9.5
Share of HS 39 imports	88.0	89.1	85.7	84.6	82.6	80.4	−8.7	−9.7
Share of US imports	7.1	7.3	7.5	8.4	9.0	8.9	1.6	21.5
China	31.8	101.0	172.1	223.5	269.1	386.4	285.4	282.7
Share of HS 39 imports	0.7	1.0	1.7	2.1	2.3	3.1	2.1	215.6
Japan	105.8	153.7	233.1	261.6	329.2	372.7	219.0	142.5
Share of HS 39 imports	2.4	1.5	2.3	2.5	2.8	2.9	1.5	100.0
South Korea	16.6	122.3	132.5	161.5	207.3	289.3	167.0	136.5
Share of HS 39 imports	0.4	1.2	1.3	1.5	1.8	2.3	1.1	95.0
Germany	79.2	176.3	174.5	188.5	328.7	288.9	112.7	63.9
Share of HS 39 imports	1.8	1.7	1.8	1.8	2.8	2.3	0.6	35.2
Imports of HS 48: Paper and paper products								
Total	2,079.8	3,599.4	3,332.9	3,318.9	3,337.4	3,667.5	0,068	1.9
Share of total imports	2.6	2.1	2.0	2.0	2.0	1.9	−0.2	−9.9
United States	1,759.0	3,195.1	2,820.6	2,726.7	2,662.9	2,962.4	−0,233	−7.3
Share of HS 48 imports	84.6	88.8	84.6	82.2	79.8	80.8	−8.0	−9.0
Share of US imports	3.2	2.5	2.5	2.6	2.5	2.6	0.1	2.8

(table continues next page)

Table 1B.2 *(continued)*

	1994	2000	2001	2002	2003	2004	Change 2000–04 Level	Change 2000–04 Percent
Canada	73.1	93.8	109.6	109.8	122.6	140.9	47.1	50.2
Share of HS 48 imports	3.5	2.6	3.3	3.3	3.7	3.8	1.2	47.4
Germany	38.7	29.4	31.7	56.8	65.9	75.0	45.5	154.8
Share of HS 48 imports	1.9	0.8	0.9	1.7	2.0	2.0	1.2	150.1
Finland	26.6	16.0	34.2	54.7	51.6	52.6	36.7	229.5
Share of HS 48 imports	1.3	0.4	1.0	1.6	1.5	1.4	1.0	223.4
Spain	19.2	22.9	29.6	37.5	40.2	51.7	28.7	125.1
Share of HS 48 imports	0.9	0.6	0.9	1.1	1.2	1.4	0.8	121.0
Imports of HS 73: **Manufactures** **of iron and steel**								
Total	2,414.5	5,027.0	4,380.9	4,131.1	4,056.6	4,797.3	−0,230	−4.6
Share of total imports	3.0	2.9	2.6	2.4	2.4	2.4	−0.5	−15.6
United States	1,967.0	4,183.7	3,426.1	3,108.2	3,059.7	3,371.6	−0,812	−19.4
Share of HS 73 imports	81.5	83.2	78.2	75.2	75.4	70.3	−12.9	−15.6
Share of US imports	3.6	3.3	3.0	2.9	2.9	2.9	−0.3	−10.6
Japan	103.1	179.4	207.3	258.4	193.9	222.3	42.9	23.9
Share of HS 73 imports	4.3	3.6	4.7	6.3	4.8	4.6	1.1	29.8
China	9.8	53.7	76.8	90.4	118.9	200.9	147.3	274.5
Share of HS 73 imports	0.4	1.1	1.8	2.2	2.9	4.2	3.1	292.5
Germany	57.1	146.6	138.0	136.7	138.3	173.3	26.7	18.2
Share of HS 73 imports	2.4	2.9	3.1	3.3	3.4	3.6	0.7	23.0
Taiwan	27.6	56.2	69.3	87.5	93.2	154.0	97.9	174.3
Share of HS 73 imports	1.1	1.1	1.6	2.1	2.3	3.2	2.1	187.4
Imports of HS 84: Nuclear **reactors, boilers,** **mechanical appliances,** **and machinery**								
Total	11,356.0	25,339.7	27,354.8	27,997.1	29,221.1	33,734.8	8,395	33.1
Share of total imports	14.3	14.5	16.2	16.6	17.1	17.1	2.6	17.7
United States	7,006.9	16,880.7	16,141.6	14,938.6	14,571.0	15,389.1	−1,492	−8.8
Share of HS 84 imports	61.7	66.6	59.0	53.4	49.9	45.6	−21.0	−31.5
Share of US imports	12.8	13.2	14.2	14.0	13.8	13.4	0.1	1.1
China	43.4	414.7	683.7	1,386.4	3,272.0	4,581.4	4,166.6	1,004.7
Share of HS 84 imports	0.4	1.6	2.5	5.0	11.2	13.6	11.9	729.8
Japan	736.5	1,427.1	1,574.4	1,666.0	1,393.4	2,089.6	662.5	46.4
Share of HS 84 imports	6.5	5.6	5.8	6.0	4.8	6.2	0.6	10.0
Germany	828.4	1,721.7	1,953.6	1,663.8	1,687.5	1,957.4	235.7	13.7
Share of HS 84 imports	7.3	6.8	7.1	5.9	5.8	5.8	−1.0	−14.6
South Korea	133.6	653.4	803.3	1,114.6	1,322.9	1,483.1	829.7	127.0
Share of HS 84 imports	1.2	2.6	2.9	4.0	4.5	4.4	1.8	70.5
Malaysia	51.6	102.8	718.1	637.9	1,492.9	1,143.5	1,040.7	1,011.9
Share of HS 84 imports	0.5	0.4	2.6	2.3	5.1	3.4	3.0	735.2
Imports of HS 85: **Electrical machinery** **and parts**								
Total	15,704.6	46,262.7	43,235.1	39,695.3	37,216.7	44,432.2	−1,831	−4.0
Share of total imports	19.8	26.5	25.7	23.5	21.8	22.5	−4.0	−15.1
United States	11,450.0	35,393.0	28,432.9	23,397.1	21,257.3	19,545.3	−15,848	−44.8
Share of HS 85 imports	72.9	76.5	65.8	58.9	57.1	44.0	−32.5	−42.5
Share of US imports	20.9	27.8	25.0	22.0	20.1	17.0	−10.8	−38.7

(table continues next page)

Table 1B.2 Mexican imports by country, selected sectors, 1994–2004
(millions of US dollars and percent) *(continued)*

	1994	2000	2001	2002	2003	2004	Change 2000–04 Level	Change 2000–04 Percent
China	88.8	904.9	1,385.4	2,254.6	3,150.4	5,379.3	4,474.4	494.5
Share of HS 85 imports	0.6	2.0	3.2	5.7	8.5	12.1	10.2	519.0
Japan	1,437.1	2,174.5	3,863.9	4,355.9	3,100.1	4,437.2	2,262.8	104.1
Share of HS 85 imports	9.2	4.7	8.9	11.0	8.3	10.0	5.3	112.5
South Korea	351.2	1,517.7	1,507.6	1,614.6	1,572.5	2,411.1	893.4	58.9
Share of HS 85 imports	2.2	3.3	3.5	4.1	4.2	5.4	2.1	65.4
Taiwan	257.7	818.3	1,553.1	2,082.7	1,219.0	1,976.0	1,157.7	141.5
Share of HS 85 imports	1.6	1.8	3.6	5.2	3.3	4.4	2.7	151.4
Imports of HS 87: Motor vehicles and parts								
Total	3,310.5	17,061.2	17,110.9	18,425.6	17,294.4	18,473.8	1,413	8.3
Share of total imports	4.2	9.8	10.2	10.9	10.1	9.4	−0.4	−4.3
United States	2,411.7	12,315.0	11,789.7	11,520.8	10,291.7	10,657.4	−1,658	−13.5
Share of HS 87 imports	72.8	72.2	68.9	62.5	59.5	57.7	−14.5	−20.1
Share of US imports	4.4	9.7	10.4	10.8	9.7	9.3	−0.4	−4.0
Brazil	190.0	706.5	894.1	1,073.8	1,482.4	1,660.4	953.8	135.0
Share of HS 87 imports	5.7	4.1	5.2	5.8	8.6	9.0	4.8	117.0
Germany	152.7	1,457.5	1,492.1	1,664.5	1,525.4	1,389.7	−67.8	−4.6
Share of HS 87 imports	4.6	8.5	8.7	9.0	8.8	7.5	−1.0	−11.9
Japan	129.2	861.7	668.5	857.8	947.0	1,300.3	438.6	50.9
Share of HS 87 imports	3.9	5.1	3.9	4.7	5.5	7.0	2.0	39.4
Canada	107.6	881.6	945.9	1,528.3	1,075.8	1,055.1	173.6	19.7
Share of HS 87 imports	3.3	5.2	5.5	8.3	6.2	5.7	0.5	10.5
Argentina	1.2	45.6	78.0	269.5	331.2	466.5	420.9	922.8
Share of HS 87 imports	0.0	0.3	0.5	1.5	1.9	2.5	2.3	844.6

Source: Secretaría de Economía (2005b).

industry, now accounts for 2.5 percent of Mexico's auto import market compared with very little in 2000.

In iron and steel (HS 73), total Mexican imports fell by $200 million while the decline in US imports was four times greater. Asian countries again eroded the US market share. The US market share fell from 83 to 70 percent, while the collective share of Japan, China, and Taiwan rose from 6 to 12 percent. Chinese shipments rose almost fourfold to $201 million; imports from Taiwan jumped from $56 million to $154 million. Germany, the only other large player in the industry, saw only a small increase in its shipments to Mexico from $147 million to $173 million.

2

Labor

Proponents of NAFTA in the United States, who claimed that opening up the Mexican market to US exports and investment would create thousands of jobs, magnified the importance of labor issues. During NAFTA negotiations, however, virulent opposition centered on threatened job losses and feared deterioration of wages and working conditions in the United States—stemming from intense low-wage competition south of the Rio Grande and lax enforcement of Mexican labor standards. Yet after NAFTA was ratified, Ross Perot's "giant sucking sound" was never heard. Instead, the United States created more than 2 million jobs per year between 1994 and 2000. The employment boom, however, had little to do with NAFTA and everything to do with the "new economy."

This is not to suggest that NAFTA was of no consequence. It simply puts the economic dimensions of NAFTA in proper perspective. US trade with Mexico is growing fast and is far from negligible, but two-way trade is marginal for the United States when compared with the economic size of the United States. US-Mexico two-way merchandise trade (exports plus imports) in 2004 reached $267 billion, or about 2.3 percent of US GDP in 2004.[1] Much of the two-way trade would have occurred without NAFTA. Even if additional US exports and imports created by NAFTA altered labor conditions in particular industries, the overall impact on a labor force of 147 million Americans was small.

One reason is that the initial impact of NAFTA trade was small. Another reason is that the ripple effects of trade impacts originating in Texas

---

1. Trade data are from the USITC Interactive Tariff and Trade Dataweb, 2005. GDP data ($11.7 trillion) are from the US Bureau of Economic Analysis (BEA 2005).

or the auto industry get quickly dampened as they move through the vast US labor market. In this respect, the market for US labor differs enormously from the market for 10-year treasury bonds. The labor market is highly segmented, unlike the bond market. In the bond market, additional demand or supply of $20 billion instantly ripples through, changing the price of all bonds. In the labor market, additional demand or supply of a few percentage points in one segment affects the wages in other segments slowly, if at all.

While forces external to NAFTA shaped the overall contours of the Canadian and US labor markets, it remains important for political economy reasons to evaluate the impact of North American trade on labor conditions. Labor concerns remain the rallying point of opposition not only against any deepening of NAFTA but also against new trade pacts promoting "NAFTA-like" conditions in the Western Hemisphere (the Free Trade Area of the Americas [FTAA] and the Central American Free Trade Agreement [CAFTA]) and agreements aimed at broad multilateral trade reforms under the auspices of the World Trade Organization.

Critics often ascribe to NAFTA the economic developments that have taken place since the pact entered into force, whether NAFTA caused them or not. Caveats must thus be recited before quantifying the impact of NAFTA on jobs and labor demand. First, trade is only one among many factors affecting labor. Business cycles, technological change, and macroeconomic policies are all more important (Baily 2002). Second, it is difficult to separate the effects of a particular trade agreement, NAFTA in this case, from the effect of increased global trade. With these caveats, what can be said about NAFTA's impact?

Facts about Fears

Labor issues were important in all three North American countries while NAFTA was being negotiated, but for different reasons. In the United States, employment and wages became a primary measuring rod for evaluating NAFTA. Ross Perot famously asserted that a "giant sucking sound" would be heard as US jobs migrated south of the border; the Clinton administration countered by claiming that hundreds of thousands of jobs would be created on balance if NAFTA were ratified. For better or for worse, how a proposed trade agreement will affect employment is probably the most often asked question in the United States.

In Canada, labor issues were important but less important than questions of sovereignty. NAFTA itself did not generate a great deal of labor concerns in Canada because Canada had very little exposure to Mexico. Rather, debates within Canada over labor have evolved as Canada has become more integrated with the United States. At first, some Canadians were concerned that their publicly funded social programs would be at risk if Canadian firms were exposed to US competitors that had lower corporate taxes. This fear has turned out to be largely unfounded, and Canadian attention has shifted to emigration, cross-border labor mobility of highly skilled workers, and whether the most productive Canadian workers are being lured to the United States.[2]

In Mexico, labor-related issues were less contentious than in the other two countries and at the same time more diffused. Some employees in the state sector feared layoffs, but most recognized that the potential trade and investment NAFTA generated would boost Mexican employment. Ironically, most of the attention to labor issues in Mexico came not from Mexicans but from opponents of NAFTA in the United States who claimed that NAFTA would exacerbate already bad labor practices in Mexico. This strain of opposition led to the creation of the labor side agreement to NAFTA.

United States

Job Losses

"Job counting" has become a popular, if misinformed, way to evaluate NAFTA. From the start, most serious economists emphasized that the net effect on employment would be very small relative to the size of the US economy. As table 2.1 indicates, unemployment in the United States fell after NAFTA was signed, but macroeconomic factors affect unemployment much more than trade agreements.

Before the agreement was ratified, several studies attempted to predict the impact of NAFTA on employment. Predictions ranged from a net gain of 170,000 US jobs by 1995—calculated by multiplying projected US net exports to Mexico by Department of Commerce estimates of jobs supported per billion dollars of exports—to as many as 490,000 US jobs lost between 1992 and 2000, resulting from an expected $20 billion reduction in the US capital stock provoked by a shift of investment from the United States to Mexico (Koechlin and Larudee 1992).

---

2. According to Richard Harris, labor-market integration for skilled workers under NAFTA could bring significant efficiency gains to Canada. Cross-border labor mobility between the United States and Canada, for example, would create knowledge spillovers between the two countries. "Brain circulation," or the idea that rapid international knowledge spillovers would recirculate and increase the rate of knowledge diffusion through a two-way flow between Canada and the United States, would replace the fear of "brain drain." Given that proportionately more Canadians choose knowledge occupations, firms and organizations in knowledge-intensive sectors will have more incentives to locate in Canada. See Harris (2004), Harris and Schmitt (2001), and Mercenier and Schmitt (2003). We thank Wendy Dobson for this observation and for providing written comments to an earlier draft.

Table 2.1 Annual average US employment, 1990–2004
(millions of workers)

Year	Total workforce	Employed	Of which: Part time	Unemployed	Unemployment rate (percent)
1990	125.8	118.8	25.4	7.0	5.6
1991	126.3	117.7	27.2	8.6	6.8
1992	128.1	118.5	27.7	9.6	7.5
1993	129.2	120.3	27.9	8.9	6.9
1994	131.1	123.1	26.6	8.0	6.1
1995	132.3	124.9	26.4	7.4	5.6
1996	133.9	126.7	26.1	7.2	5.4
1997	136.3	129.6	26.0	6.7	4.9
1998	137.7	131.5	25.5	6.2	4.5
1999	139.4	133.5	25.2	5.9	4.2
2000	142.6	136.9	24.9	5.7	4.0
2001	143.7	136.9	26.0	6.8	4.8
2002	144.9	136.5	27.0	8.4	5.8
2003	146.6	137.8	28.1	8.8	6.0
2004	147.4	139.3	28.2	8.1	5.5

Source: US Department of Labor (2005a).

A crude and misleading interpretation of these estimates would regard them as jobs gained or lost in the overall labor force. A more nuanced interpretation would regard them as jobs directly affected by additional imports or exports, even if (as most studies emphasized) the direct impact would be neutralized by offsetting forces in the US economy—creating or displacing jobs in other sectors.

Estimates of NAFTA's impact on US jobs continue to be far apart. On the negative side, one study claimed that "NAFTA eliminated 879,280 actual and potential jobs between 1994 and 2002," an assertion that amounts to around 110,000 US jobs lost on account of NAFTA each year (Scott 2001). This study uses three-digit Standard Industrial Classification (SIC) trade data and the Bureau of Labor Statistics (BLS) 192-sector employment table to estimate the impact of changes in merchandise trade flows on labor requirements in these 192 industries. The figure of 879,280 jobs lost was allocated to individual states on the basis of their share of industry-level employment in each three-digit industry.

On the positive side, another study found that new exports to Canada and Mexico during NAFTA's first five years created 709,988 jobs, or about 140,000 jobs annually. This number was calculated by multiplying increased merchandise exports to Mexico and Canada during NAFTA's first five years by the Department of Commerce average figure of jobs supported per billion dollars of exports (Bolle 2000).[3] Another group of researchers likewise concluded that trade with Mexico has a net positive effect on US employment (Hinojosa-Ojeda et al. 2000). Box 2.1 provides a comparison between the two sides and highlights criticisms of each.

Against these estimates, the NAFTA-Transitional Adjustment Assistance (NAFTA-TAA) program, created as part of NAFTA-implementing legislation, provided actual data about workers adversely affected by trade with and investment in Mexico and Canada. "Adversely affected" means workers "who lose their jobs or whose hours of work and wages are reduced as a result of trade with, or a shift in production to, Canada or Mexico" (US Department of Labor 2002c). "Secondary workers" (upstream and downstream workers who are indirectly affected by trade with or shifts in production to Canada and Mexico) are eligible as well. NAFTA does not have to be the cause of the job loss for a worker to qualify for NAFTA-TAA. Through 2002, when the NAFTA-TAA program was consolidated with general Trade Adjustment Assistance (TAA), the US Department of Labor had certified 525,000 workers (about 58,000 workers per year) as adversely affected.[4] Of the total number of workers certified under NAFTA-TAA, over 100,000 are from the apparel industries. Another 130,000 certifications are concentrated in fabricated metal products, machinery, and transport equipment.

NAFTA-TAA certification may have overestimated the pain of job losses because not all workers certified actually lost their jobs, and some who did lose their jobs were quickly reemployed. On the other hand, the NAFTA-TAA figures probably underestimated the number of job losses because the program was unknown to many workers, because workers indirectly displaced often were unaware that NAFTA was at the origin of their woes, and because the application process was cumbersome. Despite these limitations, NAFTA-TAA is probably the best record of the direct impact of additional NAFTA imports on US labor. No comparable certification process exists for the direct impact of additional NAFTA exports on US employees.

Despite the heated debate over the numbers, the reality is that the effect of NAFTA is small compared with the turnover of the US labor market. Even in a year like 2000, when unemployment was at a 30-year low, the

---

3. The number of jobs supported by new exports was calculated by multiplying the value of export growth each year expressed in billions of dollars by the corresponding estimate for the number of workers supported by each additional billion dollars of exports, correcting for productivity changes and inflation. In 1994, the number of workers supported by an additional billion dollars in exports was estimated at 14,361 jobs; in 1995, 13,774 jobs; in 1996, 13,258 jobs; and so on. The number declines each year because of productivity gains and inflation.

4. Data are from Public Citizen's NAFTA-TAA database, 1994–2002, www.citizen.org/trade/forms/taa_info.cfm (accessed on May 26, 2005).

Box 2.1   What job losses from NAFTA?

The *most extreme* estimate of job losses from NAFTA is 879,280 actual and potential jobs lost between 1994 and 2000, according to Robert E. Scott (2001) of the Economic Policy Institute. Scott's estimate is based on his calculations of how many more jobs there would be if the US trade deficit with Canada and Mexico were the same in 2002 as it was in 1993, adjusting for inflation.

Blaming NAFTA for 100 percent of the growth in the US trade deficit with Canada and Mexico ignores the macroeconomic determinants of these two bilateral trade deficits. The growth in the US trade deficit with Canada and Mexico is in line with, but slightly *lower* in percentage terms than, the growth in the total US trade deficit.

Even assuming Scott's estimates were plausible, over half of the alleged job loss comes from the growth in the US trade deficit with Canada, which competes with high-value US products. Scott concedes that the US economy created 20.7 million jobs between 1992 and 1999, or *27 times* the number of jobs allegedly lost due to NAFTA. The estimated 879,280 jobs lost over seven years due to NAFTA is less than 15.2 million US workers displaced during seven years.[1]

A group led by Raúl Hinojosa-Ojeda makes a much better estimate of jobs at risk due to imports from NAFTA countries. They estimate that imports from NAFTA countries put at risk *at most* 94,000 jobs per year. Under more realistic assumptions, only 50,625 jobs per year are at risk due to imports from NAFTA countries. US exports to NAFTA countries provide 73,845 jobs per year, for a *net effect* of 23,220 jobs created per year due to trade with NAFTA partners.

Furthermore, Hinojosa-Ojeda et al. (2000) make their calculations *disregarding* whether NAFTA caused the change in trade and in employment. Thus, the actual effect of NAFTA on both jobs created and jobs at risk is much lower.

Overall, even under the most extreme assumptions, the effect of NAFTA on US employment is small relative to the size of the US economy and macroeconomic forces.

---

1. Data are based on US Department of Labor biennial surveys of worker displacement, featured in supplements to the Current Population Survey (CPS). CPS Displaced Worker Surveys focus on workers who lost or left jobs they held for at least three years, also known as long-tenured workers. See Helwig (2004) and Hipple (1999).

US economy displaced 2.5 million workers (Kletzer 2001).[5] Even if the most pessimistic estimate is correct—an adverse NAFTA impact (considering only imports) of 110,000 jobs lost annually—the figure comes to less than 5 percent of total annual displacement in the labor force, which is tiny compared with annual gross job creation turnover. For example, in 2003 some 22.9 million American workers left their old jobs, while some 2.4 million workers found new jobs.

Stagnant Real Wages and Rising Inequality

NAFTA opponents contend that competition from cheap unskilled Mexican labor will depress real wages of unskilled American workers and

---

5. Displacement is defined as a layoff resulting from the closure or substantial restructuring of a plant.

widen the earnings gap between skilled and unskilled workers. NAFTA supporters discount this effect, arguing that the higher productivity of US workers, unskilled as well as skilled, largely or entirely offsets the nominal cost advantage of low Mexican wages.

Data on US real wages show that compared with high-skilled workers, unskilled workers did poorly during most of the past 30 years. As a result, average real wage growth in the United States was sluggish between the 1970s and the mid-1990s. This trend changed in the mid-1990s, when economic expansion started translating into significant real-wage growth for unskilled workers and a sustained rise in the average real wage. Indeed, between 1993 and 2004, 81 percent of the newly created US jobs were in industry and occupation categories paying above-median wages (Council of Economic Advisers 1999, 2004).

Technological change is the major force driving both relative and average real wages in the United States. US output per worker in the 1950s and 1960s grew at an average annual rate of 2.8 percent but slowed to only 1.2 percent between the 1970s and the early 1990s. This sluggish performance came to an end in the mid-1990s, and US labor productivity grew at around 2.4 percent a year from 1995 through 2000, increasing to 5.4 percent a year in 2002 (Council of Economic Advisers 2004). The spurt reflected information technology (IT) and other "new economy" forces (Baily 2001).

To the extent that higher output per worker determines real-wage gains (a very good long-term explanation), weaker increases in productivity, not an expansion of trade, would explain the slower growth of real wages between 1970 and the mid-1990s (Scheve and Slaughter 2001). Buttressing the productivity explanation, real-wage stagnation was most pronounced in the services sectors, which are mostly nontradables and which historically attracted little foreign direct investment (FDI).[6]

In addition to average trends, there were notable changes in relative wages. Earnings inequality in the United States is strongly associated with skill differences, and the growth of the US skill premium was a major feature of the wage story between 1970 and 2000. In the early 1980s, nonproduction (more-skilled) workers earned 50 percent more than production (less-skilled) workers; by the mid-1990s, the skill premium was over 70 percent (Scheve and Slaughter 2001, figure 4.1). Most economists agree that technological change explains about half of the rising US skill premium while trade and immigration forces account for around 10 and 5 percent, respectively.[7]

---

6. FDI in finance, telecommunications, retailing, and other services sectors picked up sharply in the 1990s.

7. Data are from the *Economic Report of the President 1997*, as quoted in Scheve and Slaughter (2001). See also Cline (1997), who finds slightly different sensitivities of the skill premium to trade and immigration.

US data on relative product prices support the hypothesis that trade was *not* a major factor driving relative wages. According to trade theory, if trade were the explanation for changing relative wages,[8] either between industries or between skill categories, relative product prices in the United States should have fallen in import-competing sectors, especially those that employ large numbers of low-skilled workers. Research a decade ago could uncover no such movement in US relative product prices (Lawrence and Slaughter 1993).

Other data confirm the small impact of NAFTA on US wages and inequality. Wage levels in the four states with the most NAFTA-TAA certifications (as a percentage of the state labor force)—namely North Carolina, Arkansas, Tennessee, and Alabama—do not differ significantly from wages in the four states with the fewest NAFTA-TAA certifications—Maryland, Nevada, Nebraska, and Oklahoma (see tables 2.2 and 2.3). Furthermore, the wage gap between the highest and lowest percentiles in the labor force is similar for the two groups of states.

Despite the small overall effect of NAFTA on wages, the effect on those directly affected by increased trade is not negligible. About a quarter of manufacturing workers displaced by trade suffer considerable wage losses—not unlike other manufacturing workers separated from their jobs for reasons having nothing to do with trade. Against popular myth, not all trade-displaced workers end up in low-paying retail jobs. According to a recent study of US manufacturing workers, only about 10 percent of reemployed displaced workers go into retail trade. Although the average wage loss of reemployed displaced workers is sizable (about 13 percent), there are great disparities within the group: 36 percent of displaced workers find new jobs with equal or higher levels of earnings; at the other extreme, 25 percent suffer wage losses of over 30 percent. Workers with lower skill levels suffer the largest percentage losses (Kletzer 2001).

Maquiladora Industry and US Labor. Several studies have examined the effect of imports on US employment and earnings, but no one has tried to rigorously assess the effect of maquiladora growth on US employment and earnings. Since maquiladoras are a sensitive issue in the US labor movement, we thought the connection ought to be explored. To do so, we constructed a dataset of maquiladora employment by four-digit SIC

---

8. Stolper and Samuelson spelled out the relationship between goods prices and factor prices in their landmark 1941 article, "Protection and Real Wages." According to the Stolper-Samuelson theorem, trade liberalization should raise wages of workers employed relatively intensively in sectors where relative prices are rising (export sectors) and reduce wages for workers employed relatively intensively in sectors with declining prices (import-competing sectors).

Table 2.2 NAFTA-TAA certifications by US state, 1994–2002
(thousands of workers)

State	NAFTA-TAA	Labor force	Percent of labor force affected by NAFTA
Texas	34.7	10,641	0.33
North Carolina	32.2	4,014	0.80
Pennsylvania	27.4	6,096	0.45
California	22.4	17,421	0.13
New York	19.9	8,950	0.22
Tennessee	18.4	2,866	0.64
Georgia	18.1	4,192	0.43
Michigan	12.5	5,236	0.24
Indiana	12.4	3,115	0.40
Alabama	11.4	2,168	0.53
Illinois	11.2	6,396	0.17
Wisconsin	10.8	3,049	0.35
Virginia	10.7	3,746	0.29
Missouri	10.2	2,957	0.35
Arkansas	10.2	1,277	0.80
Washington	10.1	3,020	0.33
New Jersey	9.0	4,254	0.21
Ohio	8.1	5,911	0.14
Florida	7.7	7,800	0.10
South Carolina	7.5	2,015	0.37
Kentucky	7.4	1,994	0.37
Oregon	7.3	1,817	0.40
Louisiana	7.0	2,048	0.34
Arizona	4.3	2,446	0.18
Massachusetts	3.9	3,368	0.11
Colorado	3.8	2,335	0.16
Minnesota	3.5	2,827	0.12
Idaho	3.4	688	0.49
Utah	3.2	1,134	0.28
Maine	2.9	690	0.42
Mississippi	1.8	1,308	0.14
Connecticut	1.7	1,716	0.10
Kansas	1.6	1,441	0.11
West Virginia	1.3	811	0.17
Montana	1.0	473	0.21
South Dakota	0.9	407	0.23
Alaska	0.9	328	0.28
Wyoming	0.7	270	0.25
Iowa	0.7	1,606	0.04
New Mexico	0.7	858	0.08
Oklahoma	0.6	1,662	0.03
Vermont	0.4	3433	0.12
North Dakota	0.4	337	0.12
New Hampshire	0.4	704	0.06
Maryland	0.4	2,884	0.01
Puerto Rico	0.4	1,317	0.03
Nebraska	0.3	949	0.03
Nevada	0.3	1,035	0.02
Total	366.0	142,917	0.26

Note: NAFTA-TAA certification requires a connection to any Mexico or Canada trade, not necessarily trade induced by NAFTA. NAFTA-TAA represents the total number of certifications during 1994–2002. Labor force figures are based on 2002 data.

Sources: Public Citizen's NAFTA-TAA database, 2005; and US Department of Labor (2002a).

Table 2.3　Wages and wage inequality in selected US states

State	Percent of labor force affected by NAFTA	Low wages, 10th percentile (dollars/hour)	High wages, 90th percentile (dollars/hour)	High/ low wages
States most affected by NAFTA				
North Carolina	0.80	6.54	25.04	3.8
Arkansas	0.80	5.91	21.93	3.7
Tennessee	0.64	6.30	24.49	3.9
Alabama	0.53	5.94	23.47	4.0
States least affected by NAFTA				
Oklahoma	0.03	6.14	22.70	3.7
Nebraska	0.03	6.48	23.58	3.6
Nevada	0.02	6.53	25.00	3.8
Maryland	0.01	7.16	34.27	4.8

Sources: Public Citizen's NAFTA-TAA database, 2005; US Department of Labor (2002a); and Rassell and Pho (2001).

industry in 1992 and 1997. Then we matched the maquiladora employment data with data on US employment and compensation.[9]

Table 2.4 shows the results of "fixed-effects" regressions. After allowing for inherent differences between industries (the fixed effects), this analysis determines whether changes in the independent variables (sales, imports, maquiladora employment, and a dummy variable for productivity gains) explain changes in the dependent variable (US employment). The US economic census was taken in 1992 and 1997, which are fairly representative of pre-NAFTA and post-NAFTA time periods. As expected, employment increases with sales. The dummy variable for the 1997 observations, interpreted as a productivity effect, is negative and significant (higher productivity reduces employment). Global imports reduce employment, but the magnitude of the effect is very small. However, employment in maquiladoras shows no statistically significant effect on US employment.

This finding should not come as a great surprise. Before NAFTA, US firms used maquiladoras to take advantage of cheap labor without paying tariffs at the border. NAFTA actually makes maquiladoras less economically important because almost all manufactured goods can now be traded duty-free. Furthermore, maquiladoras use inputs that are pro-

---

9. Data on maquiladora employment are from various issues of *Complete Twin Plant Guide* (a publication of Solunet). Because our data lacked complete coverage, we estimated maquiladora employment by determining the ratio of employment in each industry to the total number of maquiladora workers accounted for by Solunet and multiplied these ratios by the total number of maquiladora workers reported by INEGI (2002a). Data on imports are from the USITC Interactive Tariff and Trade Dataweb, 2002, and data on sales and employment are from the US Census Bureau (1997).

Table 2.4 Effect of maquiladora employment on US employment and worker compensation

Independent variable	Coefficient	t-stat
US employment (dependent variable)		
US sales	0.783	43.4
US imports	−0.027	−3.6
Maquiladora employees	0.000	0.1
Year 1997	−0.043	−7.8
Number of SIC industries: 772		
Number of observations: 1,544		
Within R-squared:[a] 0.73		
US worker compensation (dependent variable)		
US sales	0.052	5.3
US imports	−0.007	−1.6
Maquiladora employees	0.000	0.2
Year 1997	0.018	5.9
Number of SIC industries: 772		
Number of observations: 1,544		
Within R-squared:[a] 0.14		

a. Within R-squared is the percentage of explained time-series variation in the dependent variable, as opposed to the percentage of explained total variation. Most of the total variation is attributable to differences between industries and is controlled.

Note: All variables are in natural logarithm form except the 1997 dummy variable.

duced in the United States, which reduces the overall effect of maquiladoras on US employment. Critics of NAFTA seem to believe that if maquiladoras did not exist, the entire manufacturing process would take place in the United States and thus generate more US jobs. The economic reality is that if maquiladoras did not exist, the entire manufacturing process, in many cases, would take place outside the United States, and the finished product would be imported.

The fixed-effects model of US employment shows a reasonably good fit to the data. By contrast, a similar model for total compensation per worker in each industry does not perform well. The model for compensation is the same as the model for employment, except for a different dependent variable (real US compensation rather than US employment). The signs are the same as in the employment model, except for the 1997 dummy variable, which is positive (real compensation increases with productivity). While the independent variables in the model do not perform well as a group at explaining real compensation, the significance of the maquiladora variable is the question of greatest interest. The estimates indicate that the level of maquiladora employment does not appear to reduce real compensation in US industries.[10] These results suggest that the

---

10. To be sure, total US imports are partly a function of maquiladora activity, and therefore the effect of maquiladoras may be partly subsumed into the import variables. However, even if the import variables are omitted, the maquiladora coefficient is still insignificant.

feared effect of maquiladoras on US jobs and earnings has been greatly exaggerated.

In sum, while NAFTA plays a very limited role in the overall determination of real and relative wages in the United States, some unskilled workers who are laid off as a consequence of trade with Mexico and Canada suffer a significant loss of earnings. The solution for these individuals lies not in rolling back NAFTA nor in stopping other trade negotiations but in policies that directly address the problems—such as wage insurance and other adjustment programs.[11] In fact, Congress and the president embraced this core solution in the Trade Act of 2002. The Act roughly tripled the level of adjustment assistance (from $400 million to $1.2 billion annually), extended coverage to some secondary workers (those indirectly affected), and provided a health insurance subsidy for laid-off workers. As an alternative to trade adjustment assistance, older dislocated workers can claim wage insurance for up to 50 percent of the wage gap between old and new jobs (with a $5,000 cap per worker).

Deterioration of Labor Conditions

NAFTA skeptics argue that the agreement will eventually translate into a convergence of North American labor practices toward the lowest common denominator—a slow march to the bottom. Jurisdictions with better labor regulations will supposedly lose investment and eventually cut their regulatory standards to keep business from relocating.

The AFL-CIO claims that liberal trade and investment rules not only weaken the bargaining power of workers in wage negotiations but also undermine workplace health and safety regulations (AFL-CIO 1999) and that "NAFTA's main outcome has been to strengthen the clout and bargaining power of multinational corporations, to limit the scope of governments to regulate in the public interest, and to force workers into more direct competition with each other—reinforcing the downward pressure on their living standards, while assuring them fewer rights and protections" (AFL-CIO 2002).

The linchpin of this argument is a tide of investment toward Mexico and away from the United States. While investment flows to Mexico have been strong since NAFTA negotiations began, the flows are primarily not at the expense of investment in the United States. The United States remains among the top FDI destinations in the world and was a net receiver of FDI during 1996–2001.[12] Total FDI inflows as a percentage of GDP in

---

11. Hufbauer and Rosen (1986) advocated these ideas. For a modern restatement, see Kletzer and Litan (2001) and Kletzer (2001).

12. In other words, FDI inflows to the United States have exceeded FDI outflows in recent years. Since 2001, however, the United States has not been a net receiver of FDI.

the United States increased from under 1 percent in the early 1990s to 3 percent in 2000.[13]

Meanwhile, average annual US FDI flows to Mexico rose from $2 billion during the pre-NAFTA period (1990–93) to $5.7 billion during the post-NAFTA decade (1994–2003).[14] While the rise is significant, the level is very modest compared with $1.7 trillion of US gross private domestic investment in 2003. After NAFTA was enacted, from 1994 to 2002, 1,351 businesses relocated from the United States to Mexico and 334 relocated to Canada, according to Public Citizen's NAFTA-TAA database.[15] This represents less than 200 annually, or about 4 percent of total annual US business relocations. By comparison, between 1996 and 1999, about 4,000 firms on average moved between states each year.[16]

Mexico has been the main target of criticism regarding labor standards. However, the United States is not free from criticism. The US record is particularly faulted on freedom of association, child labor, and migrant worker protection.[17] The International Labor Organization (ILO) has often pointed out inconsistencies between US labor law and the ILO concept of freedom of association. First, the ILO argues, employer "free speech" allows firms to mount unfair campaigns against union organization (Gross 1995). A 1996 study commissioned by the Labor Secretariat of the Commission for Labor Cooperation (created under the North American Agreement on Labor Cooperation [NAALC]) found that plant-closing threats are often used as an antiunion strategy (Bronfenbrenner 1997). An update of that study using data from surveys of National Labor Relations Board (NLRB) certification elections in 1998 and 1999 found that 51 percent of firms used plant-closing threats during organizing campaigns (Bronfenbrenner 2000).[18]

---

13. FDI inflows to the United States topped $300 billion in 2000. They dropped to $159 billion in 2001 along with a slowdown in the worldwide FDI boom (BEA 2004b), reaching just $29.8 billion by 2003. As a result, total FDI inflows as a percentage of GDP in the United States declined from 1.6 percent in 2001 to 0.27 percent in 2003.

14. Based on US Bureau of Economic Analysis data for US direct investment abroad, capital outflows during 1990–2003, available at www.bea.doc.gov/bea/di/di1usdbal.htm#link1 (accessed on May 30, 2005).

15. See Public Citizen's NAFTA-TAA database, 1994–2002, www.citizen.org/trade/forms/taa_info.cfm (accessed on May 26, 2005).

16. See Brandow Company Releases US Business Migration Report, press release, September 3, 1999. www.prweb.com/releases/1999/9/prweb9093.php (accessed on June 24, 2002).

17. Human Rights Watch (2000) called for congressional legislation to address weak enforcement of labor standards and legal obstacles that hinder freedom of association, by comparison with international standards.

18. The survey data cover more than 5 percent of the 6,207 NLRB union certification elections in 1998 and 1999. This is the largest comprehensive database on private-sector union certification election campaigns to date.

Although some safeguards exist, the US "permanent replacement" doctrine poses a risk to employees who go on strike. Under this doctrine, new hires may permanently replace workers on strike. Moreover, statutory exclusions of the National Labor Relations Act (NLRA) mean that federal labor legislation does not cover millions of workers (agriculture workers, domestic employees, and independent contractors).

Regarding child labor, a Human Rights Watch report denounced both legislated standards and weak enforcement of child labor legislation on US farms. The Fair Labor Standards Act allows children to be employed in farms from a younger age than in other jobs (12 versus 14); there is no limit on the hours children may work in agriculture; and the Act does not require overtime pay for agricultural work.

Finally, the rights of migrant workers are often abused. Those holding a work permit seldom report an abuse, since their visa status depends on continued employment. Illegal immigrant workers are in constant fear of deportation. Making a fuss on the job can trigger a report to the US Citizenship and Immigration Services (USCIS).

Deunionization

The labor movement in the United States has had a dismal run over the last 25 years.[19] Union membership as a percentage of the US workforce has steadily fallen from 23 percent in 1977 to 13 percent in 2003. The total number of union members decreased by 4 million, despite the creation of over 50 million new jobs since the mid-1970s.

Popular explanations for the deunionization trend include increased domestic and international competition, structural changes in the labor force, deregulation of highly unionized sectors, declining recruiting efforts of unions, and decreasing interest of workers. Labor unions cite international trade as the key reason for their demise. Baldwin (2003) analyzed the role of international trade and other factors in US deunionization between 1977 and 1997. Following is a summary of his main findings:

- The decline in unionization is not exclusive to manufacturing, the sector of the economy most involved in international commerce. The proportion of unionized workers declined in primary industries, construction, and services as well. Exceptions to the downward trend in union membership are in services supplied by federal, state, and local governments. Even so, unionization rates fell among more-educated workers.

- Structural change in industry composition was not a major factor explaining deunionization. Only about a fifth of the decrease in the overall unionization rate can be attributed to shifts in the industry distribution of workers from highly unionized to less unionized industries.

---

19. This section draws from Baldwin (2003).

- A small drop in the earnings premium of union over nonunion workers accompanied deunionization. The ratio of average weekly earnings of union members to nonunion workers fell from 1.4 to 1.3 overall and from 1.19 to 1.16 in manufacturing.

- From 1977 to 1987, union workers (mostly with 12 years or less of schooling) suffered more job displacement pressure from imports and gained less from the employment-creation effects of exports than could be expected given their relative importance in the respective labor forces. The net employment impact during the period was a loss of 690,000 union jobs, about 24 percent of the total union jobs lost during the period.

- From 1987 to 1997, however, union workers faced less job displacement pressure from imports and enjoyed more job creation from exports than could be expected on the basis of their numbers in the respective labor forces. The net employment impact of trade on union workers was a gain of 387,000 jobs.

Canada

Canada experienced two key changes in the labor market during the 1990s: (1) industrial restructuring that followed the economic crisis of the late 1980s and early 1990s and (2) rationalization of Canadian social programs, which, among other things, reformed the unemployment program. Industrial restructuring, combined with the IT revolution and economic boom in the United States, spurred Canadian employment. Employment increased from 12.8 million to 16 million between 1993 and 2004, and the unemployment rate fell from 11 to 7 percent. Against this larger economic backdrop, the Canada-US Free Trade Agreement (CUSFTA) and NAFTA created a certain amount of political noise.

Erosion of Social Safety Nets

Canadian fears about competing with the United States echo US fears about competing with Mexico. One fear some Canadians hold is that increased integration with the United States will undermine the Canadian social safety net and put downward pressure on labor standards through scaled-back government programs. A particular worry is that provincial governments will not be able to maintain their universal healthcare programs (Helliwell 2000).

Canadian labor markets are highly unionized, and government standards play a bigger role than in the United States. Unemployment benefits, social welfare programs, and minimum wages are more generous. Canadian health care is also universally available and provided to a national standard. Since access to health care, along with healthcare stan-

Table 2.5 Healthcare spending in North America, 1990 and 2002 (percent of GDP)

Country	1990	2002
Canada	9.0	9.6
Mexico	4.4	6.1
United States	11.9	14.6

Source: OECD (2004c).

dards, are particular worries, the comparative statistics are worth noting. The Canadian federal and provincial governments have provided universal health insurance since 1960. In the United States, government-assured health insurance covers only 33 percent of the population, while private insurance brings the US total coverage up to 85 percent of the population. On the basis of these differences, some Canadians fear that economic pressures will threaten their universal healthcare system.

These fears are overblown, as Canadians increasingly recognize. If the Canadian healthcare system were more costly than the US system, there would be reason to worry. However, the public system in Canada consumes 9.6 percent of GDP while the mixed public/private system in the United States consumes 14.6 percent of GDP (see table 2.5). In Canada, publicly funded health care enables employers to avoid costly private systems. To the extent healthcare costs figure in business location decisions, Canada is a cheaper place to do business. Furthermore, as table 2.6 indicates, total public spending on labor-market programs is much higher (relative to GDP) in Canada than in the United States or Mexico.

Canada's large public deficit in the early 1990s (8 percent of GDP) prompted a political reaction that led to substantial cuts in spending on health and education. By 2004, Canada featured one of the best public budget positions among developed countries (a general government surplus of 1.8 percent of GDP) (IMF, *World Economic Outlook* 2002). Yet, the Canadian healthcare system still provides universal coverage, and despite budget cuts, real public spending per capita on health care in Canada rose 1.8 percent annually between 1990 and 2000 (OECD 2004c).

Changes in the social safety net will come about if Canadians lose faith in their system and turn to the US model. The opposite could also happen. In the larger scheme of things, deeper economic integration is a comparatively weak force. If economic integration determined the size of social safety nets, Nevada and California would have similar systems. So would Alberta and British Columbia. They do not.

Increased economic integration with the United States does not force any country to adopt US-style social policies.[20] Countries choose their

---

20. There is concern, however, that Wal-Mart, the giant US retailer, might stifle the establishment of unions in Canada. Since 1994, Wal-Mart has acquired more than 100 outlets from

Table 2.6 Active and passive labor-market public spending, 2001 (percent of GDP)

Country	Active spending	Passive spending
Mexico	0.06	n.a.
United States	0.14	0.57
Canada	0.42	0.80

n.a. = not available

Note: Active spending includes public employment, adult job training, youth job training, subsidized private employment, and measures for the disabled. Passive spending includes unemployment compensation and compensation for early retirement.

Source: OECD (2004b).

own social programs and adjust their resources to the program and vice versa. Canadians can have as much welfare state as they are willing to pay for. The benefits of trade and financial globalization include faster GDP growth, which can make available more resources for safety net spending, if that's what a country chooses.

Brain Drain

The social safety net is Canada's yesteryear worry. The worry now is the loss of high-skilled workers to the United States. Migration from Canada to the United States is not a new phenomenon. At the beginning of the 20th century, Canadian-born individuals living in the United States represented 20 percent of the Canadian population. At the beginning of the 21st century, the percentage was down to about 2 percent (Helliwell 2000, 2001). The Canadian concern today, however, is not numbers but quality—some of the best may be moving south.

Statistics Canada reports that 22,000 to 35,000 Canadians—or 0.1 percent of the population—moved to the United States annually during the 1990s. While this rate is lower than historical levels, it increased after the mid-1990s and involved mostly high-tech and highly skilled workers. While 21 percent of Canadians have a university degree, 94 percent of Canadians working in the United States were university graduates.[21] As these num-

---

a Canadian retailer and currently owns 262 stores across Canada. Among these, the Wal-Mart store in Quebec was unionized in August 2004. In February 2005, the store was shut down because, according to Wal-Mart, declining store revenue and escalating union demands forced the first Wal-Mart closing in Canada. See Clifford Kraus, "For Labor, A Wal-Mart Closing in Canada is a Call to Arms," *New York Times*, March 10, 2005.

21. The all-Canada statistic is based on the share of Canadian adult population (aged 25 to 64 years old) that completed a university degree in 2001. See OECD (2004d). The proportion of Canadians working in the United States with university degrees is based on beneficiaries of H-1B work visas in 2001. See US Department of Homeland Security, Office of Immigration, *Statistical Yearbook 2004.*

bers increase, so do fears that Canada will face a shortage of skilled labor and eventually lose out in the "new economy." Before the dotcom bubble burst, the debate centered on high-tech Canadians headed for Silicon Valley.

On the other side of the ledger, Canada is a net receiver of immigrants. Four times as many university graduates entered Canada from abroad as left for the United States. According to the Canadian census, from 1998 to 2003, around 71,000 degree holders entered Canada annually. During the same period, the annual average of Canadian university graduates leaving for the United States was about 12,000.[22]

High Canadian taxes, better US job opportunities, and higher salary levels are among the causes most cited for Canadian emigration. A survey in 2000 shows that migrants rank these factors as follows: first, job opportunities; second, better salaries; and third, lower taxes (Helliwell 2000). Income tax differences are estimated to account for about 10 percent of Canadian migration to the United States—a small proportion, but the only factor public policy can directly influence (Wagner 2000).

There are also some signs of a shortage of skilled labor in Canada. While hiring difficulties that Canadian employers experienced in the late 1990s were the result of a tight labor market at the end of a prolonged boom, Canada will face an increasing shortage of skilled labor, including in construction, energy, and healthcare sectors.[23] The Conference Board of Canada estimates that Canada faces a shortfall of nearly one million workers by 2020.[24] As a result, immigration fulfills most of the shortages in high-skilled professions and trades.[25]

---

22. Data on immigrants to Canada who hold university degrees are based on Citizenship and Immigration Canada (CIC) estimates of immigrants holding a bachelor's degree or higher. Canadian university graduates working in the United States are based on the number of Canadian beneficiaries under the US nonimmigrant temporary work program known as the H-1B program. See US Department of Homeland Security, Office of Immigration, *Statistical Yearbook* 2001 and 2004; and CIC (2000, 2003).

23. For an empirical analysis, see Gingras and Roy (2000). As more Canadian nurses reach retirement age, the Canadian government expects to have a shortage of more than 100,000 nurses by 2011. See Conference Board of Canada (2004). Labor shortage also forced Petro Canada to suspend an oil sands project in May 2003 and gradually led major Canadian energy companies to secure government approval to import nearly 700 skilled foreign workers for oil sands projects. See James Stevenson, "Foreign Labor Stirs Up Political Passions," *Canadian Press*, March 29, 2005; and Deborah Yedlin, "Labor Shortage Threatens Oil Patch," *Globe and Mail*, May 2, 2003. We thank Wendy Dobson for this observation and for providing written comments to an earlier draft.

24. According to Watson Wyatt human resources consultants, demographic changes, including rising life expectancy and lower fertility rates, will inflict a severe labor shortage on Canada by 2030. The number of workers for every retiree in Canada is projected to decline from 3.7 in 2000 to 2 by 2030. See Elizabeth Church, "Serious Labor Shortage Looms," *Globe and Mail*, January 27, 2004, B2; and Government of Canada (2001).

25. Immigrants represent a growing share of highly skilled professions in Canada and are often overrepresented in engineering and natural science occupations. Immigrants generally have a higher level of education than native Canadians. See Conference Board of Canada (2004).

Table 2.7 Flow of nonimmigrant professional workers to the United States, 1989–2003

	Under CUSFTA		Under NAFTA	
Year	Total number of workers (TC visa)	Of which: Spouses and children (TB visa)	Total number of workers (TN visa)	Of which: Spouses and children (TD visa)
1989	2,677	140		
1990	5,293	594		
1991	8,127	777		
1992	12,535	1,274		
1993	16,684	2,408		
1994	5,031	498	19,806	5,535
1995			23,904	7,202
1996			26,987	7,694
1997			n.a.	n.a.
1998			59,061	17,816
1999			68,354	19,087
2000			91,279	22,181
2001			95,479	21,447
2002			73,699	15,331
2003			59,446	12,436

n.a. = not available

Source: US Department of Homeland Security, Office of Immigration, *Statistical Yearbook 2004*.

NAFTA's contribution to Canada's brain drain was unintended and unanticipated. NAFTA temporary visas (TN visas) were designed to facilitate the mobility of professional workers in North America as an adjunct to cross-border business. The number of immigrants holding TN visas increased rapidly, peaking at over 95,000 in 2001 before falling sharply in the post–September 11 era (table 2.7). Most are Canadians; just over 2,500 came from Mexico. However, the rapid growth of TN visas primarily reflected the greater ease of obtaining a TN visa relative to other types of visas, rather than increased trade and investment resulting from the CUSFTA and NAFTA. In our recommendations, we propose an expansion of the TN program, but this recommendation has more consequence for Mexico than Canada.

NAFTA seems to be a secondary factor in the recent increase in Canadian migration to the United States. Incentives to migrate are tied to labor-market conditions, especially relative salaries. A shortage of high-tech and healthcare workers in the United States drove the high mobility in the 1990s. Other, more permanent, institutional characteristics (higher salaries, lower taxes) probably played a lesser role.

Mexico

The most significant event for Mexican labor markets in the 1990s was the 1994–95 peso crisis. The Mexican economy contracted by over 6 percent in 1995, slashing Mexican employment and wages. Employment creation picked up by mid-1996; overall employment numbers increased from 31.3 million in 1993 to 39.7 million in 2003. Real wages for the majority of workers have largely recovered. Against this difficult background, NAFTA has mainly had a positive impact on the Mexican labor ledger.

One of the NAFTA promises to Mexican workers was more and better jobs. Table 2.8 indicates that between 1993 and 2003, the number of employed workers increased by more than 8 million, and the percentage of the working-age population that is employed increased from 84 to almost 98 percent. Some of those workers have their jobs because of increased trade and investment induced by NAFTA. While there were large net job losses in 1995 due to the recession in Mexico, and a small downturn in 2001, for the period as a whole Mexico averaged annual employment growth of 3.3 percent.[26]

Over 1994–2004, the average annual growth of the Mexican economy was 2.9 percent. Nearly one-third of this growth came from export activities.[27] Mexican firms with FDI, which are mostly exporting firms, generally pay higher wages. Average salaries in foreign-funded companies are 48 percent higher than the national average, and employment in foreign-funded companies accounts for about 25 percent of jobs created in Mexico (Lustig 2001). Contrary to the expectation that foreign investment would be concentrated in the lowest-skilled activities, the principal impact of FDI in manufacturing was to raise the demand for semi-skilled workers and the wage premium paid to them.[28] Moreover, after liberalizing trade through NAFTA, the percentage of electronic components produced domestically in the Mexican computer industry increased. In 2005, private developers were building a new $1 billion industrial park, "Silicon Border," to compete directly with Chinese manufacturers and lure semiconductor manufacturers with the help of a 10-year tax break.[29]

---

26. Mexican annual employment growth is based on the average annual growth of formal-sector employment during 1994–2004. See IMSS (2005) and table 8.4 in chapter 8 on migration.

27. Based on World Bank *World Development Indicators* 2005 data for Mexican exports of goods and services as a share of GDP during 1994–2003.

28. According to Gordon Hanson, US manufacturing firms in Mexico raised the average skill intensity of production in both the United States and Mexico, thereby raising the demands and earnings of relatively higher-skilled workers in both countries. See Hanson (2003) and Feenstra and Hanson (2001).

29. Modeled after other Asian industrial parks, the key advantages of the Silicon Border include a parallel supply chain that is closer to West Coast manufacturing than are Asian suppliers. See "Despite Obstacles, Silicon Border Stands Good Chance of Success," *Miami Herald*, March 19, 2005. In 2000, the "Little Silicon Valley" cluster near Guadalajara reached 125 com-

Table 2.8 Labor force in North America, 1993 and 2003 (in millions)

	Canada		Mexico		United States		Total	
	1993	2003	1993	2003	1993	2003	1993	2003
Population	28.7	31.6	94.2	102.3	258.1	291.0	381.0	425.0
Labor force (working age 15–65)	14.6	17.0	37.2	40.7	131.0	146.5	182.8	204.3
Percent of total population	51	54	40	40	51	50	48	48
Official unemployment rate (percent)	11.4	7.6	3.2	2.6	6.9	6.0		
Employed	12.9	15.7	31.3	39.7	120.3	137.7	164.5	193.2
Percent of working-age population	88.2	92.4	84.2	97.5	91.8	94.0	90.0	94.6
Agriculture	.6	.4	8.0	6.5	3.3	2.3	11.9	9.2
Percent in sector	4	3	26	16	3	2	7	5
Industry	2.8	3.5	7.0	9.9	28.9	16.9	38.7	30.4
Percent in sector	22	22	22	25	24	12	24	16
Services	9.5	11.8	16.0	23.2	88.1	103.5	113.6	138.5
Percent in sector	74	75	51	58	73	75	69	72

Source: OECD (2004a).

Financial crises have significant and persistent effects on real wages.[30] The financial crisis of 1982 burst the economic bubble that Mexico enjoyed after the oil shocks of the 1970s. As an oil exporter, Mexico enjoyed lush revenues until the early 1980s and was able to borrow freely in the New York capital markets. The drastic fall in oil prices in the early 1980s triggered a financial meltdown; in the aftermath, real wages in the Mexican manufacturing sector plummeted to a much lower equilibrium. The center column of table 2.9 shows that the same thing happened after the 1994–95 peso crisis. Mexican manufacturing wages fell over 20 percent in real terms from 1994 to 1997. In 2003, average real wages in the manufacturing sector were still 5 percent below 1994 levels, although wages had gained 22 percent from their postcrisis trough in 1997.[31] In contrast, real

---

panies, including Mexican-owned companies, employing 90,000 workers. See Diane Lindquist, "Guadalajara is Mexico's 'Silicon Valley'," *San Diego Union Tribune,* October 23, 2000.

30. The primary example is the Mexican "tequila crisis" of 1994–95, when the breakdown of the peso fixed exchange rate against the dollar caused the currency to drop by about 50 percent in six months. In turn, real wages declined, and thousands of Mexicans defaulted on credit card and other loans in the wake of sharply higher interest rates. We thank Wendy Dobson for this observation.

31. Our calculations use the raw series "Remuneraciones" divided by "Persona Ocupada" (both series are from STPS 2005c), deflated by the consumer price index. The Banco de Mexico (2004) publishes a productivity series based on employment rather than hours worked. This series also corresponds roughly to the one we have constructed.

Table 2.9   Real wages in manufacturing in Mexico

	Nonmaquiladora[a]		Maquiladora	
Year	Real monthly income per worker (1994 = 100)	Real wages (1994 = 100)	Real monthly income per worker (1994 = 100)	Real wages (1994 = 100)
1987	71.3	72.1	—	—
1988	71.0	70.8	—	—
1989	77.3	76.8	—	—
1990	80.0	79.2	96.2	99.7
1991	84.9	83.7	94.2	100.2
1992	92.3	90.8	95.9	99.9
1993	96.5	96.1	95.8	98.7
1994	100.0	100.0	100.0	100.0
1995	87.5	88.5	94.0	93.9
1996	78.8	79.0	88.8	87.1
1997	78.3	77.9	90.4	75.4
1998	80.5	80.1	94.0	78.8
1999	81.8	80.9	96.0	80.1
2000	86.6	85.7	100.3	83.7
2001	92.4	91.7	109.4	92.2
2002	94.1	93.5	115.5	97.4
2003	95.3	94.8	115.5	96.5

— = not applicable

a. Pre-1994 statistics correspond to the 129 classification system, which was discontinued in 1995. Post-1994 statistics correspond to the 205 classification system.

Source: INEGI (2005a, 2005b).

monthly income per worker in maquiladoras actually increased by 15 percent over the decade and by 30 percent after the peso crisis (see table 2.9). Other salient features of the Mexican labor market are summarized below:

- Mexican statistics show about a 4 percent unemployment rate in 2004, which sounds pretty good, but the definition of Mexican unemployment includes only those who have worked *less than one hour* in the past week.

- The percentage of employed working 35 or more hours a week (indicating full-time employment) increased from 71 to 77 percent between 1993 and 2002, then declined to 71 percent in 2004. Meanwhile, the percentage of workers with no pay dropped from 14 percent in 1993 to 8 percent in 2004.

- The percentage of workers earning less than one minimum salary (many workers in Mexico work more than one job) is down to 24 percent (from 35 percent), and the percentage of workers with social security and related coverage rose to 33 percent (from 29 percent) for 1993–2004.

Compared with the United States and Canada, there were few fears about the effect of NAFTA on labor conditions in Mexico. Labor conditions in Mexico are so poor that most analysts believed that NAFTA could only help by creating jobs and attracting foreign investment. However, three Mexican fears are worth mentioning. First, some observers were concerned that NAFTA (and globalization in general) would worsen income inequality in Mexico. Second, workers in small Mexican firms feared that their employers would not be able to compete against large multinational firms. Finally, workers in the state sector feared that they would lose their jobs as state-owned enterprises were privatized.

Income Inequality and Labor Conditions

Income inequality is severe in Mexico, which had a Gini index of 51.4 in 2002. By comparison, the most recent US Gini index was 45 and the Canadian Gini index was 42 (World Bank 2002).[32] Furthermore, the economic security of Mexican workers has episodically dropped during the last decade, primarily as a result of the peso crisis in 1994–95 and more recently due to the US economic slowdown between 2000 and 2002.

Child labor remains one of the most serious problems in Mexico. The United Nations Children's Fund (UNICEF) estimates that 16 percent of the child population (or 3.6 million children) works in Mexico, often in conditions that lack basic health and safety measures.[33] Few NAFTA opponents claimed that NAFTA would make a bad child labor scene worse. Since ratification, however, events indicate that the scene remains bad. NAFTA cannot be the cure for abysmal child labor practices. In Mexico, as in most other countries, child labor has little connection with multinational firms, or firms involved in international trade. Child labor is largely a phenomenon of rural life and low-end service-sector activities.

---

32. The Gini index measures income inequality within a country, with higher values indicating more inequality. The maximum value of the Gini index is 100, corresponding to a state where one person has all the income. African countries generally have the highest income inequality (Gini indices in the 60s). The minimum value is 0, corresponding to an equal income for everyone. European countries generally have the least inequality (Gini indices in the 20s).

33. Based on the UNICEF definition of child labor (children between the ages of 5 and 14) and Mexican Secretaría del Trabajo y Previsión Social (STPS) estimates for the population of children (between the ages of 5 and 14). See STPS (2005a) and UNICEF (2004, 2005).

Table 2.10 Department of Labor and unemployment insurance spending in North America, 1994–2003
(billions of dollars)

	Canada		Mexico		United States	
Year	Amount	Percent of GDP	Amount	Percent of GDP	Amount	Percent of GDP
Department of Labor spending						
1994	24.6	4.4	0.1	0.02	37.8	0.5
1995	25.3	4.4	0.1	0.02	32.8	0.4
1996	25.7	4.3	0.1	0.02	33.2	0.4
1997	18.6	3.0	0.1	0.02	31.1	0.4
1998	17.7	3.0	0.0	0.01	30.6	0.3
1999	18.3	2.9	0.0	0.01	33.0	0.4
2000	18.6	2.7	0.1	0.01	31.9	0.3
2001	19.4	2.7	n.a.	n.a.	39.8	0.4
2002	19.7	2.7	n.a.	n.a.	64.7	0.6
2003	20.5	2.4	n.a.	n.a.	70.7	0.6
Unemployment insurance spending						
1994	14.2		—		21.6	
1995	12.0		—		21.3	
1996	11.0		—		21.8	
1997	10.3		—		19.8	
1998	8.4		—		19.6	
1999	8.9		—		20.6	
2000	8.6		—		20.6	
2001	8.3		—		31.7	
2002	9.7		—		41.7	
2003	10.8		—		41.3	

n.a. = not available
— = Mexico does not have an explicit unemployment insurance program. Partial alternatives to unemployment compensation are social security and other pension programs (IMSS and ISSTE). In 2003, these programs distributed $22 billion, mostly for old-age support.

Sources: Treasury Board of Canada Secretariat (2004), Fox (2001), US Government Printing Office (2004), US Department of Labor (2004a), Mexican Federal Government (2004), and personal communication with Carlota Serna, 2001. Canadian and Mexican values converted to US dollars using annual exchange rates reported by the International Monetary Fund.

While the Mexican government has tried to address enforcement problems for child labor and other abuses, the budget of the Secretaría de Trabajo y Previsión Social (STPS), the Mexican Labor Department, is insufficient to enforce existing labor standards (see table 2.10). More important, Mexico does not have an explicit government program of unemployment insurance.[34] On the bright side, spending on social security and the num-

34. While social security and pension programs (IMSS and ISSTE) provide partial alternatives to unemployment compensation in Mexico, it is unknown how much these programs are used to alleviate unemployment.

ber of workers covered have increased significantly since 1994. In addition, Mexico implemented a new program for employment, training, and defense of labor rights—the Programa de Empleo Capacitación y Defensa de los Derechos Laborales 1995–2000.

Furthermore, the STPS signed agreements with all of the state labor authorities in 1998 to implement new regulations on workplace inspections and provide federal training of state inspectors. STPS officials report that compliance is reasonably good at most large companies. Problems are concentrated in small companies, and federal inspectors are stretched too thin for effective enforcement when companies do not comply voluntarily.

The Maquiladora Sector

Maquiladoras are another hot-button issue. The Mexican maquiladora program started in 1965 and allowed multinational corporations to ship US inputs to Mexico for further processing before being reimported into the United States. Under the maquiladora program, the value of US inputs is not subject to US tariffs when the finished goods are reimported to the United States.

NAFTA did not enhance the maquiladora program and in fact made it less relevant. Before NAFTA, the US content of some products was not subject to tariffs under the maquiladora program. After NAFTA, the US content of those products is still not subject to tariffs, but the tariffs against Mexican value added are phased out as well. Not surprisingly, one researcher found that NAFTA has had no effect on maquiladora employment. Gruben (2001) finds that US industrial production and relative wage levels adequately explain maquiladora employment and that the existence of NAFTA does not add explanatory power to the model.

Continuing prior trends, however, maquiladoras have become a more important component of Mexican trade since NAFTA. As figure 2.1 indicates, in 1993 maquiladoras accounted for about 25 percent of total Mexican imports and a little more than 40 percent of total Mexican exports. Following the 1994–95 financial crisis and subsequent depreciation of the peso, nonmaquiladora imports into Mexico contracted faster than maquiladora imports, and exports diversified into new product lines. The share of total imports into Mexico purchased by maquiladoras has stayed near 35 percent since 1995 while the maquiladora share in total Mexican exports has grown to almost 50 percent.

If NAFTA has not had much of a causal effect on maquiladora trade, how has tighter integration with the United States affected maquiladoras? In 1994, the Mexican border states accounted for 82 percent of the maquiladora plants and 85 percent of the maquiladora value added. By 2004, there had been a small relative shift inland, with border states accounting for 79 percent of the plants and 79 percent of the value added (figure 2.2).

Figure 2.1   Maquiladoras and Mexican trade, 1991–2002

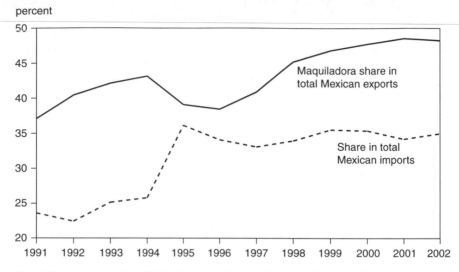

percent

Note: Shares are calculated by first aggregating monthly data. 2002 ratio is based on data from January through June.

Source: INEGI (2002a).

This inland shift has many explanations. Traditionally, maquiladoras have been concentrated in northern Mexico because the roads in Mexico were poor, particularly in central and southern Mexico. Recently, the roads have been improved somewhat, but modest infrastructure improvement is not the main explanation. There are reports that wages along the border are getting too high and that plant managers become frustrated when a large number of employees work only for a short period in the maquiladora and then depart to illegally enter the United States.

Little evidence suggests that the maquiladora program has helped or hurt wages in Mexico. Maquiladora workers are paid less than manufacturing workers as a whole, but the average skill requirements for maquiladora workers are lower. Table 2.9 does show, however, that real wages in the maquiladora sector were close to their pre-1995 levels by 2003. Within the maquiladora sector, the ratio of wages in the border states to wages in other states has shrunk since 1996, after rising sharply at the onset of NAFTA. The trend in the relative wage ratio, which is illustrated in figure 2.3, may reflect the decision of some maquiladora firms to move farther inland.

Despite the sharp increase in real wages, the post-2000 period was not particularly good for the maquiladora sector. Maquiladora employment peaked at 1.35 million in October 2000 and declined to 1.14 million by October 2004, a decline of almost 16 percent (INEGI 2005a). Based on general

Figure 2.2 Value added in maquiladoras, 1980–2004

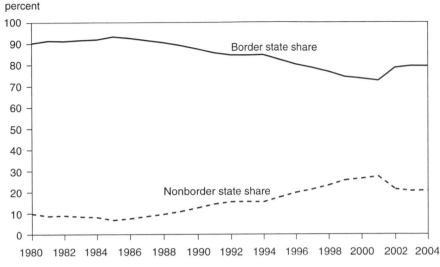

percent

Note: Shares are calculated by first aggregating monthly data. 2004 shares are calculated based on data from January through October.

Source. INEGI (2005c).

trends, 2005 looks to be a better year for maquiladoras, but continued growth depends heavily on the US economy's strength.

Small Firms and the State Sector

NAFTA has supported Mexican employment on balance by attracting foreign investment and promoting trade. However, many small and medium-sized Mexican firms have gone out of business both because of the 1994–95 financial crisis and because they could not compete with multinational firms. Between 1993 and 2000, the number of manufacturing firms operating in Mexico fell by 9.4 percent, while employment rose by 11.5 percent (Calderon-Madrid and Voicu 2004, table 3).[35] Overall, according to official statistics, unemployment is low in Mexico, only 2.6 percent at the end of 2004 (STPS 2005b). While official figures are understated, the downside of NAFTA on the Mexican labor force has been temporary dislocation rather than persistent unemployment.

NAFTA may have accelerated the process of "sifting and sorting" within Mexican manufacturing, forcing less productive firms out of busi-

---

35. Calderon-Madrid and Voicu (2004) analyze the Mexican manufacturing sector using data from the Encuesta Industrial Anual (EIA); therefore their analysis excludes maquiladora and other "in-bond" firms.

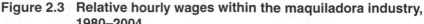

Figure 2.3   Relative hourly wages within the maquiladora industry, 1980–2004

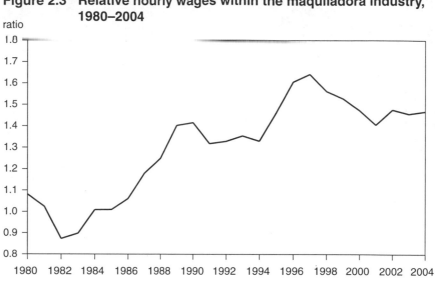

Note: Ratio is calculated by first averaging monthly data. 2004 ratio is based on data from January through October.

Source: INEGI (2005c).

ness, thereby freeing resources for more productive firms. On the basis of firm-level data covering all sectors of Mexican manufacturing, Calderon-Madrid and Voicu (2005) conclude that total factor productivity (TFP) was a dominant indicator of company survival. Depending on the sector, a firm that was 20 percent less productive than its own industry average was between 15 and 27 percent more likely to exit the marketplace.[36] Furthermore, the authors found that productivity growth was strongest in firms that engage in external commerce. Greater use of intermediate imports and a higher proportion of exports to sales were both associated with higher productivity growth.

Mexican workers in the state sector were at best lukewarm about NAFTA. In the past 15 years, Mexico has undergone a wave of privatization, and NAFTA accelerated a larger trend. Workforce reduction usually accompanies privatizations, obviously unpopular among separated employees. While Mexico has made enormous progress in shifting from a state-dominated to a market-dominated economy, the state sector is still substantial. NAFTA has had little effect on Petróleos Mexicanos (Pemex), the state-owned petroleum company, and Comisión Federal de Electricidad (CFE), the state-owned electricity company. Mexico essentially opted out of liberalizing the energy sector when NAFTA was negotiated. Mexico

---

36. This estimate controls for import penetration, size, age, and liquidity. Interestingly, import penetration was a significant factor only within the textiles industry.

has delayed an inevitable dose of political pain yet still faces the persistent reality that the country will eventually need to reform Pemex and CFE. When reforms happen, they will surely include a downsizing of bloated labor forces in the energy sector.

Independent Unions in Mexico

Mexican labor organization practices are changing as a delayed feature of the liberalization movement that started in the 1980s. Following were the landmarks in this process:

- *The debt crisis of 1982.* International financial institutions insisted on a degree of liberalization in exchange for loans and aid.

- *GATT accession in 1986.* This definitively ended the period of import substitution industrialization.

- *Economic reform between 1988 and 1994.* President Carlos Salinas de Gortari increased openness to international trade and investment.

- *The peso crisis of 1994–95.* Sharp devaluation of the peso sparked militant mass movements in rural areas and a political shift that increased votes for the Partido Acción Nacional (PAN) and the Partido de la Revolución Democrática (PRD).

- *Two landmark events in 1997.* In July, the Partido Revolucionario Institucional (PRI), Mexico's ruling party since 1929, lost control of the Mexican Congress. In August, the death of Fidel Velazquez, the long-serving and powerful leader of the Confederación de Trabajadores Mexicanos (CTM), punctuated the difference between old and new relations between labor and government.

- *The election of Vicente Fox in 2000.* The democratization process ended 71 years of PRI rule and opened the way for further changes in the corporatist relationship between labor and government.

Greater political openness has translated into a more open approach to labor organization in Mexico. This new approach is reflected in the following events:

- Creation of an independent organization of workers in 1997. The Unión Nacional de Trabajadores (UNT) is a breakaway coalition of 200 Mexican unions comprising between 1 million and 2 million workers (La Botz 1998).

- Decrease in the ranks of the official unions, the Congreso del Trabajo (CT) and the CTM. In the early 1990s, the CT claimed to represent over 10 million workers. Today, government statistics estimate its membership at about 1 million. Similarly, the number of CTM members declined from over 5 million to around half a million.[37] While early numbers were almost certainly inflated, the official unions are surely losing members.

- The Mexican Supreme Court ruling in April 2001 that obligatory union membership was unconstitutional.[38]

No one expected NAFTA to be a boon for unions, but the new environment in Mexico is opening the door for greater cooperation between labor unions in the NAFTA countries. Leadership changes within the US labor movement have also increased interest in forging cross-border alliances. Until the 1990s, US labor unions had little interest in organizing across borders (with the notable exception of Canadian auto workers). During the NAFTA debate, US labor opposition focused on winners (Mexican workers) and losers (US workers), stressing job competition rather than workplace cooperation. US labor leaders often portrayed Mexican workers as desperate, abused, and compliant—a portrait that insulted Mexico. Since the debate, practical cooperation has begun to replace rhetorical combat.

Contacts between Mexican and US unions are still low but have gone beyond the "meet and greet" level. Cross-border exchanges have increased, especially in the automotive, textile, and telecom industries. As the Mexican independent labor movement grows, US and Canadian unions are increasingly willing to establish relationships with Mexican labor groups. Mexico's Frente Auténtico del Trabajo, for example, has open relationships with more than a dozen labor unions and federations from the north. A decade ago, Francisco Hernandez, leader of the Mexican telephone workers union, proposed the creation of a trinational labor coalition (Sosa 1995), and US unions are increasing their permanent representation in Mexico.

The United Auto Workers (UAW) and the AFL-CIO have supported maquiladora workers in litigation against US corporations for violating Mexican labor law. In one of these legal battles, a US court granted standing to Mexican workers, a decision that led to a settlement favorable for the workers. While the case did not establish a legal precedent—it was settled before reaching the appellate court—it showed Mexican workers that they can pursue legal remedies in the United States and revealed the potential benefit of cross-border organizing (Browne 1995).

---

37. Data are from the United Electrical, Radio, and Machine Workers of America (2000). According to the CTM Secretariat, membership in 2001 was 493,000.

38. Historically, Mexican unions, especially the CTM, had a close affiliation with the PRI as well as overwhelming control over company workforces. One consequence of the Mexican Supreme Court ruling is that more than one union can now represent a company's employees. See Jose de Cordoba, "Labor Decision Strikes at Mexico's PRI," *Wall Street Journal*, April 19, 2001; and Andrea Mandel-Campbell, "Campaigners Seek to Loosen Grip of Company Unions," *Financial Times*, May 1, 2001.

Table 2.11   Population distribution in Mexico, 1980–2000
(millions, percent of total in parentheses)

	1980	1990	1995	2000	Percent born in-state (as of 1995)
Mexico federal district	8.8 (13)	8.2 (10)	8.5 (9)	8.6 (9)	76
Border states	10.7 (16)	13.2 (16)	15.2 (17)	16.6 (17)	74
Other states	47.3 (71)	59.8 (74)	67.4 (74)	72.2 (74)	81
Total	66.8	81.2	91.1	97.5	80

Sources: INEGI (2005b) and www.citypopulation.de/Mexico.html (accessed in January 2005).

Other examples show that assistance works both ways. The United Electrical Workers called on Mexican organizers to help mobilize the vote of Mexican immigrants in a labor campaign in Milwaukee (Moberg 1997). Furthermore, coalitions of nongovernmental organizations (NGOs) and labor organizations from all three NAFTA countries have brought forward most citizen claims under the North American labor side agreement.

Internal Migration

Although international migration (the subject of the next section) is probably the most salient issue in US-Mexico relations, internal migration within Mexico is related and also important. As table 2.11 shows, only about three-quarters of Mexican federal district and border state residents were born in that state; by comparison, in other states, about 81 percent of the residents were born within the state. Movement from one border state to another could account for some of this difference, but most of it probably reflects migration northward within Mexico. However, the share of the total Mexican population that lives in the border states has remained almost constant since 1980, suggesting that the inward internal migration is largely offset by emigration to the United States.

The economic base in Mexico was shifting northward well before NAFTA went into effect. Table 2.12 indicates that the share of GDP from border states had increased to nearly 24 percent in 2002, up from 19 percent in 1980. This relatively sharp increase in production, combined with a more moderate increase in population growth, reflects growth in per capita income in the border states (table 2.13). Between the financial crisis in 1995 and 2000, real per capita income rose 17 percent in the border states compared with 13 percent in other states.[39] This difference will continue to at-

---

39. In fact, wage growth has been much higher in regions with higher levels of FDI and higher exposure to foreign trade. See Hanson (2003).

Table 2.12   Contribution of border states and Mexico federal district to Mexican GDP, 1970–2002 (percent)

Year	Border states	Mexico federal district
1970	21.1	27.6
1975	20.3	26.1
1980	19.0	25.2
1985	19.4	21.0
1993	21.5	23.8
1995	23.2	22.8
2000	24.2	22.5
2002	23.6	23.2

Source: INEGI (2005a).

Table 2.13   Per capita income in Mexico (in 2000 pesos)

	1995	2000	Growth (percent)
Border states	25,577	29,845	17
Mexico federal district	45,123	53,723	19
Other states	13,443	15,148	13
Total	18,424	21,062	14

Source: INEGI (2005a).

tract Mexicans from poorer regions, but the promise of even higher incomes in the United States will tempt many to continue their journey north.

As the economic base has gravitated toward northern Mexico, it has also gravitated toward the cities, especially cities in the border region. As table 2.14 illustrates, in 1950, 57 percent of the Mexican population lived in rural areas. By 2000, that share had fallen to 25 percent, while 26 percent now live in cities of 500,000 or more. In the border states, the percentage of people living in urban and semiurban settings is over 86 percent compared with 73 percent in other states (table 2.15). Between 1990 and 2000, the total population of Mexico grew about 20 percent, but seven cities in the border region have grown much faster over the same period (table 2.16). Cities like Juárez and Tijuana have grown more than 50 percent in the last decade, causing congestion and pollution but also soaring property values (see chapter 3 on environment).

In conclusion, substantial evidence documents the phenomenon of internal migration within Mexico. The dominant features are migration from southern Mexico and movement from rural to urban areas (especially in the border region). These movements correspond with the greater role that

Table 2.14   Population concentration in Mexico, 1950–2000
(percent of total population)

	1950	1970	1990	1995	2000
Rural (less than 2,499 people in town)	57	41	29	27	25
Semiurban (2,500 to 14,999 people in town)	17	22	14	14	14
Urban (more than 15,000 people in city)	26	37	58	60	61
Of which:					
Less than 100,000 people in city	11	14	13	14	14
Less than 500,000 people in city	7	12	23	21	21
More than 500,000 people in city	9	11	21	26	26

Source: INEGI (2002a).

border states have claimed in the Mexican economy and the better opportunity that the border states offer to escape poverty. For many migrants, however, northern Mexico is just a stop on the way to the United States.

International Migration

Two issues strongly color popular US perceptions of NAFTA: One is migration, the other is the 1994–95 peso crisis. Unlike the impending peso crisis, the problems surrounding Mexican migration to the United States were very familiar to NAFTA negotiators in the early 1990s. At the time, they were seen as "too hot to handle" in a trade agreement. Beyond some verbal fencing and a very limited TN visa program, the NAFTA text steered clear of immigration questions.[40]

Ducking immigration issues did not, of course, put an end to the debate. Indeed, perhaps the most vexing question between Mexico and the United States is the issue of undocumented workers. Legal immigration from Mexico numbered between 130,000 and 200,000 persons annually in the past few years (compared with a total figure from all countries of 737,000 annually on average between 1997 and 2000). Over 95 percent of legal Mexican immigrants enter under family reunification visas. Within the undocumented category are two groups: those who already reside in the United States, a group whose number reached nearly 8 million in 2004, and those who come to the United States to work, a number running about 275,000 per year.[41] While important distinctions can be made be-

---

40. President Carlos Salinas, in pushing NAFTA, once remarked that the United States had a choice: either import Mexican tomatoes or accept Mexican tomato pickers. In reality, the United States does both.

41. See US Department of Homeland Security, Office of Immigration, *Statistical Yearbook 2003*. In 2000, the unauthorized resident population born in Mexico accounted for 69 percent of the total.

Table 2.15 Urbanization in Mexico, 2000 (percent)

	Percent urban
Border states	86.2
Other states	72.9
Total	74.6

Source: INEGI (2002a).

tween the two groups, the whole issue of unauthorized immigration is highly charged. On the Mexican side, the government considers the legalization of immigrant workers a matter of human rights and social justice—and a necessary step in the economic integration of North America. In terms of economic benefits, legalization would help ensure that the Mexican economy receives a growing flow of worker remittances. (In 2004, Mexican remittances totaled $17 billion, some 2.6 percent of Mexican GDP.)[42] Moreover, the legalization of millions of Mexicans working in the United States would improve their economic prospects and enable many to return to Mexico as successful entrepreneurs.

Feelings are equally strong on the US side. Some Americans flat-out oppose any increase in immigration. More immediately, the attack on September 11 and the deterioration of the US economy dampened the serious consideration that had been given to Mexican immigration in the fall of 2001. The fact that many of the terrorists overstayed their visas cast a huge shadow over any legalization initiative. The recession and rising unemployment gave fresh impetus to groups that oppose the opening of the border to migrant workers. According to polls, after September 11, the American people grew more apprehensive about what they perceive as weak border control and voiced stronger support for enforcing immigration laws.

Against this background, NAFTA contained a small initiative: the TN visa program. TN visas are issued to professionals for "temporary" work assignments. To get a TN visa, the applicant must qualify within designated job categories, meet the education or professional criteria, and have a sponsoring letter from his US employer. The number of TN visas for Mexico was initially capped at 5,500 annually, but the number of TN visas for Canadians is potentially unlimited.

As table 2.17 demonstrates, in fiscal 2003, the USCIS recorded just 1,269 TN visa entrants from Mexico, well under the already low annual ceil-

---

42. Banco de Mexico Governor Guillermo Ortiz estimated that Mexican remittances would reach $20 billion in 2005. In 2003, remittances surpassed foreign investment to become Mexico's second largest source of revenue after oil. The International Monetary Fund (IMF) recognizes the growing importance of remittances for developing countries and argues that remittance-financed consumption in Mexico exerts a significant multiplier effect on the economy. "Mexico's Central Bank Predicts Remittances Will Reach $20 Billion for 2005," *Associated Press*, May 23, 2005; IMF (2005); and "Monetary Lifeline," *The Economist*, July 29, 2004.

Table 2.16   Population growth in Mexican cities near the US border

City	State	Population 1990	Population 1995	Population 2000	Growth, 1990–2000 (percent)
Ciudad Juárez	Chihuahua	798,499	1,011,786	1,218,817	52.6
Tijuana	Baja California	747,381	991,592	1,210,820	62.0
Mexicali	Baja California	601,938	696,034	764,602	27.0
Chihuahua	Chihuahua	530,783	627,662	671,790	26.6
Reynosa	Tamaulipas	282,667	337,053	420,463	48.7
Matamoros	Tamaulipas	303,293	363,487	418,141	37.9
Nuevo Laredo	Tamaulipas	219,468	275,060	310,915	41.7
Nogales	Sonora	107,936	133,491	159,787	48.0

Sources: INEGI (2002a).

ing for TN visas.[43] The likely reason for low utilization is that alternative H-1B (temporary worker) visas require approximately the same documentation and offer better terms. Like TN visas, H-1B visas are issued on the basis of employer letters, but H-1B visas are not limited to a detailed job list. Moreover, the initial term for an H-1B visa is three years (renewable for another three years), whereas TN visas have an initial term of one year (but can be renewed every year if the person maintains a residence abroad). In 2004, the cap of 5,500 on Mexican TN visas was abolished, and the application process simplified. These changes may eventually increase the number of TN visa entrants.

TN visas are given to skilled workers, and most research shows that immigration exerts no perceptible impact on the earnings of skilled citizens. However, immigration does have negative consequences for the wages of low-skilled workers in the United States because immigration substantially increases the supply of low-skilled labor. One study finds that for citizens without a college degree, immigration reduces wages by $1,915 (12 percent) per year (Camarota 1998). Fear of reduced wages is one of the driving forces against liberalization of immigration in North America. Nevertheless, in an attempt to enlist them as union members, the AFL-CIO has endorsed amnesty for illegal immigrants currently in the United States. It is difficult to isolate the effects of immigration on wages without detailed data on workers, wages, and immigration. However, we can generate some ideas about these effects by looking to aggregated wage data along the southern US border. We picked seven US cities along the border (Brownsville, El Paso, Laredo, Las Cruces, Tuscan, Yuma, and San Diego) that presumably have experienced a good deal of legal and illegal immigration from Mexico. We then compared the average wage and wage

---

43. The term "visa entrants" refers to persons entering the United States. Many TN visa holders may enter more than once within a year.

Table 2.17 Legal migration into the United States, fiscal 2003

	Total	Family-sponsored preferences	Employment-based preferences	Relatives of US citizens	Other
Immigrants					
World	705,827	158,894	82,137	332,657	132,100
Canada	16,555	1,730	6,328	7,785	712
Mexico	114,984	29,526	3,151	78,200	4,107

	Total	Specialty workers (H-1B visa)	Other temporary workers (H2 visa)	Intracompany transferees (L1 visa)	NAFTA workers (TN visa)	Other
Nonimmigrants						
World	1,269,840	360,498	116,927	298,054	59,446	434,915
Canada	116,563	20,947	5,213	15,618	58,177	16,608
Mexico	130,327	16,290	75,802	15,794	1,269	21,172

Source: US Department of Homeland Security, Office of Immigration, *Statistical Yearbook* 2004.

growth in these cities with the overall average for cities in the respective states. Table 2.18 indicates that the average wage is lower than the state city average in all seven cases, in both 1993 and 2003.

Does this mean NAFTA is in fact hurting US wages? No—NAFTA did not liberalize immigration law or inhibit its enforcement. Table 2.19 shows that wages in these seven cities have remained below the state city averages ever since 1970, long before NAFTA. Between 1970 and 1995, six of the seven cities fell further behind; however, between 1995 and 2003, only four of the cities continued their relative descent. These tables suggest that cities with an abundance of low-skilled labor attract firms that need low-skilled labor and pay wages that correspond to skills required. The pull on illegal migration is part of this labor-market mix. The consequent industry structure in these US cities limited their participation in the boom of the 1990s and more broadly in US economic development over the past 30 years. The long-term solutions are faster growth and better worker skills in Mexico, thereby curbing the supply of low-skilled labor on both sides of the border.

NAFTA's Labor Provisions

A Sketch of North American Labor Law

The heated NAFTA debate and the ensuing negotiation of a labor side agreement created a misleading sense that North American labor standards might be on the political agenda. But the NAALC, the side agreement on labor, was no more than a quarter-step toward common North American

Table 2.18 Average annual wage per job in border cities pre- and post-NAFTA (current dollars)

Area	1993	2003	Growth (percent)
Texas MSA average	27,264	37,517	38
Brownsville-Harlingen-San Benito	17,414	23,181	33
El Paso	20,144	27,228	35
Laredo	17,762	24,951	40
Three-city average	18,440	25,120	36
Three-city average as percent of Texas MSA average	68	67	
New Mexico MSA average	22,349	31,556	41
Las Cruces	19,029	25,597	35
Las Cruces as percent of New Mexico MSA average	85	81	
Arizona MSA average	23,634	35,268	49
Tucson	21,878	32,510	49
Yuma	18,396	25,451	38
Two-city average	20,137	28,981	44
Two-city average as percent of Arizona MSA average	85	82	
California MSA average	28,985	42,056	45
San Diego	26,013	39,299	51
San Diego as percent of California MSA average	90	93	
Seven–border city average	20,091	28,317	41
Four-state MSA average	25,558	36,599	43
Seven–border city average as percent of four-state MSA average	79	77	

MSA = metropolitan statistical area

Source: Bea (2004c).

labor rights. Given the economic disparity between Mexico and its northern partners, and given sovereignty concerns in all three countries, common standards are not a realistic possibility. Each of the NAFTA countries has its own long history of labor regulations, legislative processes and procedures, and unique approaches to enforcement. There was no chance that NAFTA would suddenly supersede decades of domestic political compromise on labor legislation in each country.

Canada

The Canadian Constitution does not address labor rights or minimum labor standards.[44] As a general rule, in Canada, federal labor law does not

---

44. The Canadian Charter of Rights and Freedoms guarantees freedom of association, freedom of expression, and the right to assembly. However, in *Re Public Service Employee Relations Act* (1987), the Canadian Supreme Court ruled that "freedom of association" does not include collective bargaining or the right to strike.

Table 2.19 Average wage per job as a percent of state MSA average

Area	1970	1975	1980	1985	1990	1995	2000	2003	Change 1970–95	Change 1995–2003
Brownsville-Harlingen-San Benito, TX	69	73	70	66	67	67	60	62	–2	–5
El Paso, TX	88	85	79	79	78	77	71	73	–10	–5
Laredo, TX	73	73	71	67	66	69	66	67	–4	–3
Las Cruces, NM	95	91	86	85	83	81	79	81	–14	0
Tucson, AZ	96	97	97	94	92	92	87	92	–4	1
Yuma, AZ	83	90	91	84	79	76	68	72	–7	–4
San Diego, CA	90	92	90	90	90	90	90	93	0	3

MSA = metropolitan statistical area

Source: BEA (2004c).

supersede provincial labor law. The federal government has primary labor jurisdiction over a few sectors, namely federal government employees and workers in activities of "national, international, and interprovincial importance." These sectors account for about 10 percent of the workforce. Provincial labor legislation covers the remaining 90 percent of workers. As a result, Canada has 11 labor legislation systems, one for the federal sector and territories and one for each of the 10 provinces.

Administrative labor boards (composed of worker, employer, and provincial government representatives) oversee enforcement of labor legislation in most provinces. Quebec has a labor commissary and a labor tribunal for this purpose. Employer-employee joint committees develop and supervise work safety and health standards. Inspections can be carried out without prior notice or warrants. Abatement orders are frequently issued for violations, but fines are uncommon.[45] Canadians favor cooperation and voluntary compliance when it comes to enforcement.

Legislation in Canada is much more union-friendly than in the United States, and unionization levels are higher in Canada. Union density in Canada reached 30 percent of the labor force in 2004 (72 percent in the public sector, 18 percent in the private sector overall, and over 30 percent in the manufacturing sector) (Statistics Canada 2004). By contrast, in the United States, under 13 percent of workers were union members in 2003 (42 percent of government workers, 9 percent in the private sector overall, and 15 percent in manufacturing) (US Department of Labor 2002b). In other words, the role of unions is about twice as great in Canada as in the United States.

---

45. See the NAALC Web site, www.naalc.org/english/pdf/canada.pdf (accessed on June 24, 2002).

Mexico

Mexican labor law is based on Article 123 of the 1917 Constitution, which gives the federal Congress exclusive authority to enact labor laws. All Mexican workers are subject to the minimum employment standards set forth in the Constitution and the 1970 Ley Federal del Trabajo (LFT). The LFT is enforced in the 33 national jurisdictions (31 states, the federal district, and the federation of federal government). Enforcement of the LFT is divided between federal, state, and local authorities. The STPS is responsible for ensuring enforcement at the federal level. Mexico has three review mechanisms for compliance with safety and health standards: government inspection, private-sector verification, and joint committees. Penalties are not frequently imposed.

Mexican labor law is highly progressive, but its enforcement is very weak. On paper, Mexico's protection of workers' rights is greater than in Canada or the United States, but reality is another story. The gap between theory and practice underscores the point that new standards at the NAFTA level might have little effect in Mexico. Besides, the deeper NAFTA gets into labor issues, the more important sensitive enforcement issues will become.

In Mexico, more than 30 percent of the labor force is unionized, including half of the workers under federal jurisdiction. The Mexican government and the labor unions have traditionally had a close political relationship, and the government is often involved in settling disputes. Indeed, the Mexican Constitution requires that labor arbitration boards include a government representative, and traditional ties between government and unions historically allowed the government to control the vote of the union representative (Ruhnke 1995).

As the poorest country in North America, Mexico has more limited social programs than the United States or Canada. Mexico has no unemployment insurance program and has a large informal labor sector, where wages and working conditions are usually poor and where labor protection does not exist. While there are plans to grant universal health care under the Mexican Popular Health Insurance Program by 2010, it remains an aspiration.[46]

The United States

The US Constitution does not specifically address labor rights or standards, but constitutional interpretation has had a major impact on US

---

46. Currently, under the Mexican Popular Health Insurance Program, families pay fees on a sliding scale based on income and location; the poorest people do not pay. Under Article 4 of the Mexican Constitution, "every person has a right to receive medical treatment when deemed necessary." See Adrienne Bard, "National Healthcare Plan Would Insure the Poor," *Miami Herald*, January 8, 2005.

labor law. The First Amendment to the Constitution, protecting freedom of assembly, has been extended by Supreme Court decisions to cover related labor rights (pickets, leafleting, boycotts, and political participation). The Constitution gives Congress the power to regulate trade between states, and this power has been extended by additional Supreme Court decisions to cover labor legislation. As a consequence, a mixture of federal and state laws, judicial decisions, and administrative regulations governs US labor law. Under the Supremacy Clause of the US Constitution, federal laws or regulations preempt state laws when they conflict. Workplace safety and health are regulated by the Occupational Safety and Health Administration (OSHA) and enforced mainly through federal inspections. These require either employer consent or a warrant. Fines are frequently imposed for violations.

The NLRA mainly regulates employer-employee relations. The NLRA established the NLRB to hear disputes between employers and employees. The NLRB's general counsel can independently investigate and prosecute cases. If not subject to the NLRA, then other federal or state statutes cover employers and employees.[47]

How does NAFTA fit in? Given this mosaic, it is unrealistic to expect detailed harmonization of labor standards at the North American level. But much can be done to agree on core labor standards and enforce their compliance. We offer some proposals in the final section.

The NAFTA Text

The original NAFTA included several environmental provisions but hardly any clauses regarding labor rights. After reviewing the legislative record, the Bush administration concluded that Mexican labor standards are comparable to those in the United States. On paper, this is true: Article 123 of the Mexican Constitution, the cornerstone of Mexican labor legislation, gives Mexican workers the right to organize unions and to strike, and it guarantees a wide range of basic labor standards—from minimum wage to worker housing (Human Rights Watch 2001, 14). The Bush administration further argued that NAFTA would stimulate economic growth and thereby facilitate funding for adequate enforcement of existing labor laws.

This stance permitted the Bush administration to sidestep enforcement questions, and with enforcement put to one side, the NAFTA text made few references to labor issues. The preamble of the main agreement includes two general objectives regarding labor:

---

47. The Railway Labor Act governs labor relations in the railway and airline industries. Employees and agencies in the federal public sector are subject to the Federal Service Labor-Management Relations Act (FSLMRA), which is administered by the Federal Labor Relations Authority.

- "create new employment opportunities and improve working conditions and living standards" and

- "protect, enhance, and enforce basic workers' rights."

As a free trade agreement, NAFTA generally precludes governments from using trade protection to shield specific sectors from North American imports or to promote domestic employment and output (Campbell et al. 1999). Explicit provisions, however, ease the pressure on workers in vulnerable sectors. Fifteen-year transition periods on the road to free trade were stipulated for the most sensitive sectors; safeguard mechanisms (an "escape clause") can be invoked for injured industries; and strict rules of origin are supposed to "ensure that free-trade benefits of a NAFTA accrue to North American products and their workers."[48]

The "escape clause" in NAFTA, written at US insistence, allows tariffs to snap back to the most-favored nation (MFN) level when a domestic industry is severely injured. Additionally, the three countries can continue to impose antidumping and countervailing duties against imports from each other.[49] To prevent abuses of trade remedies, Chapter 19 of NAFTA includes a special dispute settlement procedure to contest final decisions of national authorities.[50]

The Labor Side Agreement

Introduction

Fear that free trade would worsen labor conditions did not originate with the negotiation of NAFTA. Indeed, "pauper labor" arguments were a staple of tariff debates throughout the 19th century. The novelty in NAFTA was the fierce resistance mounted by the US labor movement to an agreement with Mexico (compared with other postwar trade agreements), and the subsequent attempt to address labor issues within the framework of a trade agreement.

In 1991, organized labor fired its opening shot with a campaign against congressional authorization of fast track for NAFTA negotiations. Against this assault, President George H. W. Bush promised attention to environment and labor issues to win congressional votes for extension of fast-track procedures until June 1993. NAFTA negotiations were substantially

---

48. Testimony of Lynn Martin, US Secretary of Labor, before the Senate Finance Committee, Washington, September 10, 1992.

49. Antidumping and countervailing duties are not permitted on intraregional trade in some FTAs and customs unions, including the European Union and the Australia–New Zealand and Canada-Chile FTAs.

50. See chapter 4 on dispute settlement.

completed in August 1992, and the agreement was signed in December 1992 (Destler and Balint 1999, 9).

However, President-elect Bill Clinton vowed to delay ratification of the pact until new rights and obligations on labor and the environment supplemented it, as he had promised during the election campaign. Speaking in North Carolina in October 1992, Clinton argued that the basic trade agreement signed by President Bush did nothing to ensure that Mexico would enforce its own labor standards and that new "side agreements" were needed to forcefully correct these shortcomings. Only then would NAFTA reinforce a "high-wage, high-skill" path for America and merit ratification. Negotiations were reengaged in early 1993, and the side agreements were signed in August 1993 (Hufbauer and Schott 1993).

The labor side agreement has three specific objectives: First, the pact monitors implementation of *national* labor laws and regulations in each country, performing a watchdog role to alert countries about abuses of labor practices within each country. Second, the pact provides resources for joint initiatives to promote better working conditions and labor practices. Third, the pact establishes a forum for consultations and dispute resolution in cases where domestic enforcement is inadequate.

Despite a slow and cumbersome start, the pact has achieved modest results. Policy efforts have focused on oversight of national laws and practices, comparative studies, training seminars, and regional initiatives to promote cooperative labor policies. These efforts seem small in relation to the magnitude of labor problems, but they have directed additional attention and resources to identified issues.

Dispute settlement provisions were a major objective of the US initiative for the labor side agreement. In this area, the record has been mixed. Most cases are still under review—indeed a slow, deliberative process is by design. Mexico and Canada resisted the incorporation of dispute provisions and only accepted a compromise that was long on consultation and short on adjudication.

Disputes concerning unfair labor practices (primarily denial of the right of association) have benefited from the glare of publicity. Thirty-one cases have been submitted to the national administrative offices (NAOs) as of May 2005 (19 in the United States, 8 in Mexico, and 4 in Canada).[51] Nearly two-thirds of these cases were filed since 1998, and most of these new cases are still under review. Trade sanctions have not been a factor in any of the cases.[52]

---

51. Complete details of labor complaints filed under NAALC are available at www.dol. gov/ilab/programs/nao/status.htm (accessed on May 16, 2005).

52. In the Han Young case (1998), Mexican workers at the Han Young Hyundai maquiladora plant alleged that the Mexican government failed to protect the workers' right to freedom of association. Workers wanted a union to address occupational and safety violations, and the company was eventually fined as the result of STPS labor inspections under Mexican law and not pursuant to the NAFTA labor side agreement. See US Department of Labor (1998).

Differences Between the Labor and Environment Side Agreements

The labor side accord initially proposed by the United States mirrored the environmental side agreement. It contemplated the creation of an independent secretariat with the power to investigate citizens' complaints and with remedies for persistent nonenforcement of existing laws.[53] However, pressure from the US business community and unwavering opposition from Canada and Mexico resulted in significant differences between the environmental and labor texts as finally negotiated—the North American Agreement on Environmental Cooperation (NAAEC) and the NAALC.

First and foremost, labor-related issues are more politically charged than environmental matters. Consequently, the NAFTA members were more reluctant to cede authority over labor questions to supranational institutions. This was particularly true for Mexico, where union power played a key role in the traditional political game.[54] However, the United States was no exception; at home, US business was more concerned about lurking dangers in the labor side agreement than in the environment side agreement.

Secondly, the domestic political climate in the three countries influenced the ultimate outcome. In the United States, President Clinton was able to enlist the support of environmental NGOs for his side agreement. The labor constituency, on the other hand, adamantly opposed NAFTA. Nothing in a side agreement—short of a European-style social charter setting common standards, enforceable through domestic courts and international sanctions—would satisfy organized labor in the United States (Mayer 1998).

The Mexican government strongly opposed enforcement tools that could be used to restrict trade or compromise Mexican sovereignty. However, as the side agreement negotiations stretched, public support within Mexico for NAFTA eroded. Fearing a domestic backlash and complications for the 1994 presidential election, Mexican negotiators were willing to search for a face-saving compromise, one that did not erode traditional government control over the labor unions.

Canada also opposed the US side agreement proposal. While Canada's position was closer to that of the United States, Canada's new liberal government, fresh from a constitutional crisis, was not willing to "sell out" to the United States and allow for new trade sanctions in the side agreements (Mayer 1998).

The biggest contention was the establishment of a supranational institution. While Canada, Mexico, and the United States agreed on the need

---

53. For details on the environmental side agreement, see Hufbauer et al. (2000) and chapter 3 on environment.

54. The PRI, in power in Mexico for over 70 years, relied heavily on its special relationship with official trade unions and the business world to maintain its rule.

for an international body to oversee the agreement, they differed sharply on the power, independence, and enforcement mechanisms available to the new institution.

The Mexican government disliked the notion that an international institution might review Mexican labor questions given the special relationship between unions and the PRI. Canadians adamantly opposed the use of trade sanctions as an enforcement mechanism. US business and even some labor groups were uneasy with the idea of a powerful international institution.

To paper over these differences, the United States proposed that NAOs handle citizen complaints. The NAOs would be located within each member's department of labor. With national governments deciding whether claims merited international consultation, the idea of an independent supranational body was quietly buried. Thus the scope of the NAALC was limited to ensuring that each country followed its own laws. Enforcement questions were resolved on a bilateral basis. Between the United States and Mexico, fines and suspension of trade benefits are the potential enforcement mechanisms. Trade sanctions do not apply to Canada, and Canadian courts will impose fines (if at all).[55]

All this was accompanied by the usual solemn promises from each government to improve labor standards, increase cooperation, and enhance domestic enforcement of existing labor legislation.

The NAO in each country has the power to review labor law matters in the other NAFTA members. However, NAOs are national institutions, and any decision to "meddle" in the labor affairs of another NAFTA member would be approached with great caution. In sum, despite the labor side agreement, labor matters are still essentially a national issue.

Labor advocates did not favor NAFTA with or without a side agreement. They feared job losses, worsening of labor conditions, and lower wages. From the outset, organized labor in the United States denounced the NAALC as inadequate and correctly recognized that the lofty stated goals would not be achieved. However, based on the more limited standards set out in the NAALC text, there has been some success in terms of consultation on labor issues. The biggest payoff from the labor side agreement was that it enabled NAFTA to pass the US Congress. However, this gain was tarnished because critics were able to disrupt trade liberalization efforts for the rest of the 1990s by claiming that NAFTA had made inadequate progress on labor issues.

The North American Agreement on Labor Cooperation

The NAALC aims to promote labor rights by obliging parties to enforce their domestic labor laws. Additionally, the agreement obliges govern-

---

55. For a detailed analysis of the negotiation process of the labor side agreement, see Mayer (1998).

ments to ensure public access to administrative and judicial enforcement procedures.

Part one of the NAALC contains an ambitious list of objectives: improving working conditions, promoting labor principles, exchanging information, cooperating in labor-related activities, furthering effective enforcement of labor laws, and fostering transparency in labor law administration. Part two gives each party the right to establish its own domestic labor standards qualified by a commitment to high labor standards. Each party shall promote adequate enforcement and guarantee due consideration to alleged violations of labor law.

Part three of the NAALC establishes the Commission for Labor Cooperation (CLC) and the NAOs, defines their structure, powers, and procedures. Part four establishes the mechanisms for cooperation and evaluation. Finally, part five provides a mechanism for resolution of disputes over "persistent" nonenforcement of select labor standards.

The side agreement identifies 11 labor principles and divides them into three tiers. Access to remedies for inadequate enforcement varies according to the tier:

- The first tier is limited to NAO review and ministerial oversight. A committee of experts cannot evaluate the enforcement of labor principles in this tier, and no penalties are provided for noncompliance. This tier applies to matters concerning freedom of association, collective bargaining, and the right to strike.

- In the second tier are principles subject to NAO review, ministerial consultations, and evaluation by a committee of experts—but still no arbitration of disputes and no imposition of penalties. This tier covers principles concerning forced labor, gender pay equity, employment discrimination, compensation in case of injury or illness, and protection of migrant labor.

- Principles in the third tier get the full treatment: NAO review, ministerial consultations, evaluation and arbitration, and ultimately monetary penalties. This tier is limited to child labor, minimum wages, and occupational safety.

Institutions under the NAALC

Commission for Labor Cooperation. The labor side agreement created the CLC to oversee the implementation of the NAALC and promote cooperation. This commission is made up of a ministerial council, consisting of each country's top labor official; a trinational secretariat that provides technical support to the council and reports on labor law and enforcement issues; and an NAO in each of the three NAFTA countries. The NAO, which operates at the federal level, gathers and supplies information on labor matters, and provides a review mechanism for labor law issues in the territory of the other parties. Additionally, the three countries can call on national advisory committees representing labor and business organizations and governmental committees representing federal, state, and provincial governments.

The Secretariat. The CLC Secretariat was initially established in 1995 in Dallas and later moved to Washington, DC. Its functions are to assist the council on the implementation of the agreement, promote cooperative activities, and prepare reports on North American labor issues. However, the budget of the CLC Secretariat is extremely limited, about $2 million annually. The secretariat can do little more than pay office rent and staff salaries. Within its tight budget, the secretariat has produced comparative studies on North American labor markets and labor laws and several reports on specific labor issues: plant closings, labor practices in the apparel industry, and employment of women. Additionally, the secretariat has supported working groups focusing on income security, worker compensation, and productivity trends.

National Administrative Offices. The NAOs provide a point of contact between labor ministries in the three countries and with the CLC Secretariat. The primary function of the NAOs is to provide information for reports and evaluations of labor matters and receive complaints regarding another country's failure to enforce its domestic labor laws. The NAOs can initiate their own investigations and accept citizen submissions. To date, the NAOs of the three countries have been shy in using their authority (Human Rights Watch 2001). The NAALC gives the labor departments of each of the NAFTA signatories freedom to define the role of its NAO. Consequently, the NAOs differ in important aspects.

The Canadian NAO, for example, has tried to extend the reach of the NAALC with a proposal that national labor tribunals take into account the aspiration to high labor standards agreed in the NAALC. Mexico's NAO, on the other hand, has limited its role to presenting the facts included in public submissions, without further investigation or findings. The US NAO tries not to interpret the NAALC but instead provides detailed analyses of citizen complaints (Human Rights Watch 2001). The US Department of Labor has limited its NAO to cases citing inadequate national enforcement of labor laws, thereby avoiding any investigation of labor conditions in specific companies operating in Canada and Mexico. This limitation reduces conflicts, but it also precludes the NAO from getting to the root of many labor problems (Lopez 1997).

Citizen Submissions and Dispute Settlement. The NAALC provides a government-to-government dispute settlement mechanism for cases where cooperative efforts fail. Before reaching the arbitration stage, disputes must pass through cooperative consultation and evaluation procedures. A party may request ministerial consultations with another party regarding any matter within the scope of the agreement. But higher levels of review apply only to enforcement of the 11 labor principles covered by the NAALC (following the three-tier system explained above)—when the matter is trade-related and covered by mutually recognized labor laws.

One NAO can initiate consultations with the NAO of another country regarding labor law, labor law administration, and labor-market conditions. Additionally, citizens and NGOs can file submissions, with their respective NAOs, regarding labor law enforcement in other countries. After reviewing the submission, if the domestic NAO determines the submission merits action, it may request consultations with the foreign NAO. Once the NAOs have consulted, ministerial consultation may be recommended.[56]

If the matter remains unresolved after ministerial consultations, any party can request the establishment of an Evaluation Committee of Experts (ECE) to analyze the matter and issue a report. For matters unresolved by an ECE, disputing parties can request consultations and eventually the formation of an arbitration panel. Ultimately, arbitration can lead to monetary fines (see box 2.2). However, to date, the remedy of arbitration and monetary fines remains untested. Through May 2005, the NAOs created by the NAALC had received 31 citizen submissions (see appendix table 2A.1). Nineteen were filed with the US NAO (17 involved allegations against Mexico and two against Canada), eight with the Mexican NAO (all eight regarding US labor practices), and four with the Canadian NAO (two raised allegations against Mexico and two raised allegations against the United States).

Most submissions have focused on the enforcement of obligations relative to the 11 labor principles agreed upon in the NAALC. However, a few submissions have raised questions about other articles of the NAALC, namely Article 4 "appropriate access to labor tribunals" and Article 5 "fair, equitable and transparent labor proceedings."

Twenty-four of the citizen submissions referred to freedom of association issues (15 filed in the United States, six filed in Mexico, and three filed in Canada). Most of these cases alleged violations of other labor rights as well, mostly health and occupational safety and minimum employment standards. The remaining citizen submissions addressed issues dealing with child labor, gender discrimination, protection of immigrant workers, and the right to strike.

Of the 31 distinct cases filed with the NAOs (two cases were filed with two NAOs at the same time), seven were denied review, three were withdrawn, and one was settled before completion of the review process. The re-

---

56. Any party may request ministerial consultations with another party regarding any matter within the scope of the agreement without first receiving an NAO recommendation to do so.

Box 2.2   NAALC part V dispute resolution timeline and procedures

The North American Agreement on Labor Cooperation (NAALC) provides a government-to-government dispute settlement mechanism for cases where cooperative efforts fail. Following the final report of the Evaluation Committee of Experts, a NAFTA member government can initiate consultations with another NAFTA member if the government lodging the dispute believes the other country has persistently failed to effectively enforce its labor laws regarding child labor, minimum wage standards, or workplace safety. If the disputing parties fail to reach agreement within 60 days of the request for consultations, either party may request a special session of the council (comprising labor ministers from each NAFTA country). The council must convene within 20 days of the request and try to mediate the dispute. The council may call upon technical advisers and make recommendations. If the council cannot resolve the dispute within 60 days, an arbitral panel may be convened at the request of either party, with a two-thirds vote of the council.

The arbitral panel examines whether the party complained against has shown a persistent pattern of failure to effectively enforce occupational safety, child labor, or minimum wage labor standards. The disputants are allowed to make initial and rebuttal written submissions and are entitled to at least one hearing before the panel. The panel may seek advice from experts, with the consent of the disputing parties. Within 180 days after the first panelist is selected, the panel must submit an initial report containing its findings. If the country is found to exhibit a persistent pattern of failure to enforce its labor standards, the report will make recommendations, normally in the form of an action plan. The disputants have 30 days to submit written comments on the report, and the panel must issue a final report to the disputants within 60 days of the release of the initial report. The disputing parties must give the report to the council within 15 days after it is presented to them. The final report will be published five days after it is submitted to the council.

(box continues next page)

maining 20 resulted in 14 case reports, 13 of which recommended ministerial consultations. The outcome of the consultations was six ministerial agreements between Mexico and the United States, one ministerial agreement between Canada and Mexico, plus several studies and outreach sessions.

To date no submission has progressed beyond the consultation stage. Submissions regarding access to fair tribunals, freedom of association, and the right to strike only warrant review and consultation. However, even submissions covering rights that warrant access to arbitration mechanisms have ended with ministerial consultations. The ultimate solution coming out of consultations appears to be workshops or conferences.

Four-Year Review of the NAALC. Article 10 of the NAALC requires the Council of Ministers, the governing body of the CLC, to review the "operation and effectiveness" of the NAALC "within four years after the date of entry into force of this Agreement." In September 1997, in accordance with this requirement, the council appointed a Review Committee of Experts, issued an invitation to the public to submit written comments, and

Box 2.2 *(continued)*

The disputing parties will then agree on an action plan, which "normally shall conform with the determinations and recommendations of the panel" (Article 38). If an agreement cannot be reached on an action plan, a complaining party may request that the arbitral panel be reconvened, though no earlier than 60 days or later than 120 days after the date of the panel's final report. The panel will either approve an action plan proposed by the party complained against, create its own action plan, or impose a monetary fine. If an action plan is not agreed upon, and a panel solution has not been requested within the required time frame, the last action plan submitted by the offending party will be used.

If the complainant believes that the offending country is not fully implementing the agreed action plan, it may request that the labor panel be reconvened, though no earlier than 180 days after the action plan was decided upon. The panel shall determine within 60 days of being reconvened whether the action plan is being fully implemented. If the panel determines that the action plan is not being fully implemented, a monetary fine may be imposed of up to 0.007 percent of total trade in goods between the disputing parties during the most recent year for which data are available. If the complaining party believes that the offending party is still not complying with the determinations after 180 days, it may request that the panel be reconvened. The panel must determine whether the party is complying within 60 days of being convened. In the case of the United States and Mexico, if the panel determines that there is still no compliance, the country filing the complaint may impose tariffs equal to the monetary fine. Trade sanctions, however, cannot be imposed against Canada. Instead, Canada has agreed to make the panel determination legally binding under the Canadian courts—an "order of the court."

Source: McFadyen (1998).

consulted with advisory bodies.[57] A summary report with the results was published at the end of 1998, accompanied by conclusions and recommendations of the council along the following lines:[58]

- The NAALC is relatively new and untried. A second review, promised in 2002, should provide a clearer picture of its effectiveness. (As of 2005, the second review was still a work in progress.)

- The NAALC institutions have followed their mandate, but they have not been fully utilized. NAOs should launch their own evaluations and not rely solely on public submissions to trigger investigations.

---

57. The advisory bodies that contributed to the review process were the national advisory committees of Mexico and the United States and the national governmental committees of Canada and Mexico.

58. See the NAALC Web site, www.naalc.org/english/publications/review.htm (accessed on June 24, 2002).

- Given the size and diversity of the North American labor market, and the limited resources available to the secretariat, the secretariat should formulate a long-term plan and resource requirements.

- Greater uniformity in consultations and evaluation procedures among the three NAOs would improve public communications. NAOs should develop a multiyear work plan for their cooperative initiatives.

These recommendations remain to be implemented. While the CLC has developed a long-term plan, the three governments have yet to approve it.

Effects of the NAALC on North American Labor

The NAALC does not enforce labor standards. Instead, the agreement relies on each country to enforce its own labor laws. The function of the NAALC is to provide a forum for cooperation and a limited mechanism to evaluate labor issues. Under the NAALC, instances of noncompliance can be investigated following a citizen's complaint or a party's request.

Since the CLC Secretariat does not have the power to develop factual records (unlike the Commission for Environmental Cooperation), submissions have to be filed with the NAO of each country. To bring a case against his own country, a citizen must file with another country. Ultimately, the NAO civil servants investigate the performance of bureaucrats abroad, not the actions of the employers or unions involved in the complaint.[59] With all these limitations, perhaps it is not surprising that since NAFTA took effect, only 31 citizen complaints have been filed in a North American labor market of 200 million workers.

The NAALC has been criticized for its limited scope. To be blunt, the NAALC does not envisage a supranational tribunal to judge alleged violations, nor does it provide remedies for workers whose rights are violated. What the NAALC does provide is a meeting place for governments and labor organizations from the three NAFTA members, a consultation and cooperation mechanism, and a constrained dispute settlement arrangement. What has been achieved with such tools?

Cooperation has provided technical assistance to government officials and promoted interaction between labor representatives in the three countries. However, the NAALC has had practically no impact on North American labor-market conditions. The sheer size and complexity of the North American labor market are daunting, sovereignty concerns are overriding, and very little can be done to overcome enforcement shortcomings on an annual budget under $2 million.

---

59. See "Nafta's Do-Gooder Side Deals Disappoint: Efforts to Protect Labor, Environment Lack Teeth," Wall Street Journal, October 15, 1997.

Labor Adjustment Programs in North America

There is ample evidence that trade in general and NAFTA in particular play a limited role in shaping US labor markets. NAFTA's impact on labor markets is proportionally greater in Canada and Mexico, but the labor backlash is by far greatest in the United States.

Labor-market churning is part of economic progress. Workers quit their jobs all the time in search of better prospects. Even during periods of rapid economic growth, workers lose their jobs involuntarily. Job losses impose substantial costs on workers in terms of forgone income during the unemployment period and even after, if finding new employment means a lower salary. These costs exist whether the cause of the job loss is technological change, economic downturn, or increased trade. To ease worker concerns, governments can promote programs that reduce the economic hardship by providing temporary income support, wage insurance, health coverage assistance, and incentives for rapid reemployment.

The three North American countries address the needs of unemployed workers in their own way. Canada regards NAFTA adjustment as part of the continuing process of restructuring caused by technological change and globalization. Canadian employment insurance provides 14 to 45 weeks of benefits per year. Unemployed workers receive 55 percent of average earnings to a maximum of $277 a week (workers in low-income families may receive up to 80 percent of their average earnings). Mexico does not have specific programs for trade-related displacement nor does it provide employment insurance. However, displaced workers have the right to receive severance pay in the amount of three months of salary plus 20 days per year worked.

Employers in the United States are not required to provide healthcare benefits for employees. However, if health coverage is provided, dismissed employees can pay the group rate premiums and receive group health coverage for 18 months. In the United States, each state determines unemployment payments and duration of benefits. Maximum benefits range between $180 and $359 per week.

The United States is the only NAFTA party with specific programs for trade-displaced and NAFTA-displaced workers. Since 1962, US workers affected by increased imports have been eligible for supplemental unemployment insurance under TAA. Benefits are provided for a maximum of 52 additional weeks if the worker is enrolled in a training program. A similar program, the NAFTA-TAA, was established under the North American Free Trade Agreement Implementation Act of 1993. The Department of Labor's NAFTA-TAA program provided assistance to workers displaced by imports from Canada and Mexico or a shift of production to Canada and Mexico (e.g., production for consumption in those countries or for export to third countries). Eligibility for NAFTA-TAA did not depend on a demonstrated link to NAFTA trade concessions. All that was required was a connection to trade or investment in Mexico or Canada. Workers under this program are entitled to federal training programs up to two years, income support while training (equivalent to their unemployment insurance), job search allowances, and relocation assistance.

In fiscal 2001, Congress appropriated $407 million for TAA and NAFTA-TAA programs. On average, since fiscal 2001, 163,000 workers have been certified annually for assistance under these two trade adjustment programs.[60] By comparison, in 2001, federal funding for nontrade job loss assistance amounted to $1.6 billion and provided support to an estimated 927,000 workers.[61] State unemployment insurance benefit outlays were estimated at $42 billion for fiscal 2003 (US Department of Labor 2004b).

In August 2002, President Bush signed into law the Trade Act of 2002, which inter alia contained new trade promotion authority and an expansion of the TAA program, tripling the amount of money available for TAA programs. This act folded NAFTA-TAA into the broader TAA program. Highlights of the new TAA include

- coverage of some "secondary workers" who are dislocated when their companies lose sales to firms that are adversely affected by imports;

- a 65 percent refundable tax credit to pay for health insurance of participants in the TAA program;

- coverage of slightly more workers who are displaced when their firms shift production to a country that has a preferential trade agreement with the United States or (at the discretion of the department of labor) other countries as well; and

- wage insurance for workers over the age of 50. This five-year program will pay part of the difference in wages when older workers are displaced by trade and take a new job that pays less than the previous job. Wage insurance is available only after the worker starts the new job—the idea is to encourage laid-off workers to find a new position rather than subsist on unemployment benefits and questionable training programs.

The new TAA is clearly a step in the right direction. However, much more needs to be done in order to allay workers' fear of trade. We make recommendations on adjustment assistance in the concluding section of this chapter.

---

60. To prevent job churning, workers are eligible for these benefits once every four years.

61. See Trade Adjustment Assistance: Improvements Necessary, but Programs Cannot Solve Communities' Long-Term Problems, testimony by Loren Yager before the Senate Finance Committee, July 20, 2001, www.senate.gov/~finance/072001lytest.pdf (accessed on June 24, 2002).

Conclusion and Recommendations

Reform of the NAALC

We advocate a *smaller*, but more focused, mandate for the NAALC. The starting point for reform is candid recognition that the NAALC was designed as a political mechanism to ensure US ratification of NAFTA.[62]

Since the NAALC has failed to persuade labor opponents—either before or after the NAFTA vote—to support regional trade integration, one could question whether it should be continued. But international institutions, once created, are hard to eradicate, no matter how ineffective. Moreover, in the spirit of eventually creating a "North American Community"— broader in scope than trade and investment issues—a North American mechanism should exist for addressing labor issues.[63]

In this spirit, we recommend the way to start is with a very severe pruning of the NAALC's mandate. Our goal is to trim the NAALC back to its most effective branches and then to strengthen those branches.

Recommendations for the NAALC

- Provide the CLC with adequate funding. To date, the three countries have contributed equal amounts to the meager CLC budget (about $700,000 each). The vast difference in the size of the three North American economies would justify scaling the contributions to the size of North American merchandise trade flows. Under such a formula, the United States would increase its share of the CLC budget.

- Canada, Mexico, and the United States should agree to revamp the labor review process into a monitoring system based on agreed labor standards in four areas: discrimination, child labor, coerced labor, and workplace health and safety standards. An independent board that both reports to the CLC and publishes its findings should do the monitoring. By focusing on the four core areas, the CLC will avoid diluting its impact with forays into subjects where there is no prospect of agreement on appropriate standards (e.g., freedom of association).

---

62. There is extensive debate in the economic literature on the suitability of incorporating and enforcing labor standards through international trade agreements. See, for example, Maskus (1997). NAFTA and more recent FTAs contain labor-related provisions that go far beyond what is covered in multilateral trade negotiations. Indeed, WTO members excluded labor standards from the Doha Round negotiations. Paragraph 8 of the Doha declaration mentions labor but only to "reaffirm our declaration made at the Singapore Ministerial Conference regarding internationally recognized core labour standards. We take note of work under way in the International Labour Organization (ILO) on the social dimension of globalization."

63. For the concept of a community, see Pastor (2001).

- Workers are entitled to know in advance if a plant might be relocated because of labor cost, tax cost, or other cost differences. In the context of labor negotiations, however, such threats can be and are idly made. Our recommendation is that the relocation "threats" should be subject to a "false advertising" test. When the relocation issue is raised in labor negotiations, companies should be required to furnish detailed comparative cost figures in a format approved by the NLRB and labor boards in Canada and Mexico.

- The US Worker Adjustment and Retraining Notification Act of 1988 generally entitles workers—with significant exceptions—to 60 days' advance notice of plant closings or mass layoffs, and the workers are entitled to back pay if the firm fails to provide sufficient notice. Our recommendation would strengthen this provision by requiring documentation of comparative cost differences, if a firm raises the prospect of international relocation in labor negotiations.[64]

Temporary Visas

Under Chapter 16 of NAFTA, temporary entry is available for business persons provided that they do not pose a threat to public health and safety or national security and provided that they meet the eligibility requirements. The eligibility requirements state that the person must be a citizen of a North American country, have a letter indicating that he or she is crossing the border to temporarily work in a business activity that is international in scope, fall within one of the 63 enumerated high-skilled professions, and meet the minimum educational or licensing requirements or both for that profession. Liberalizing the requirements so that blue-collar workers also are eligible would increase the integration of the North American labor market and provide an alternative to cyclical illegal immigration.

Recommendations for the TN Visa Program

- Any legal resident of a country in North America should be eligible for temporary entry rather than just citizens.

- Temporary entrants should specify in their applications the date they will return to their home country. If a temporary entrant needs to stay longer than originally anticipated, he or she can file another application.

---

64. All firms should be required to adhere to this documentation regulation without exception. Unlike the Worker Adjustment and Retraining Notification Act, exceptions are not needed because firms that are seriously considering international relocation will have already spent considerable resources investigating cost differentials before the labor negotiations.

- Any worker that meets the basic eligibility criteria should be permitted to apply for a temporary entry visa, regardless of occupation or level of education. In other words, the list of 63 enumerated professions and associated requirements should be discarded. However, to discourage abuse, employers should be required to guarantee a job for the duration of the visa and pay a salary at least 5 percent above the prevailing wage. A fine should be levied against any host firm that files a fraudulent letter on behalf of the applicant.

- The spouses and dependents of persons who are granted temporary entry should be permitted temporary entry for the same duration and should be permitted to work, without having to meet additional eligibility requirements.

International Migration

US-Canada and US-Mexico migration issues are entirely different. For Canadians, a more liberal TN visa program, without job restrictions, could make a major difference in some occupations. The United States and Canada should permit the free flow of labor, just as Australia and New Zealand do. While TN visa terms are also important to Mexico, they are not at the heart of the US-Mexico migration problem.[65] Other visa questions are more critical.

Recommendations on Migration from Mexico

The place to start is with the ongoing flow of migrant workers arriving in the United States. The United States should take up President Fox's challenge—put forward shortly before the September 11 attacks—to substantially enlarge the annual quota of Mexicans legally authorized to enter the United States on temporary (but renewable) work permits.

The way to tackle the flow problem is to expand the number of legal visas to, say, 300,000 persons from Mexico annually. These additional visas should be issued on a work skill basis (including unskilled workers), not on a family reunification basis (the dominant test for current visas). For this purpose, we would mesh the TN and H1-B visa programs. However (and this is where security is underlined), to obtain a temporary work permit, the Mexican applicant should undergo a background check designed to avert security threats. Once inside the United States, temporary permit holders would need periodically to inform the USCIS, using the Internet, of their address and place of employment. Permit holders could renew their permits as long as they were employed a certain number of months (say eight months) in each rolling 12-month period, had

---

65. The numerical limit on TN visas for Mexicans was abolished on January 1, 2004. However, other conditions severely limit the use of TN visas.

no felony convictions, and reported regularly to the USCIS. They could apply for US citizenship after a certain number of years (say a cumulative five years as temporary permit holders). In the meantime, they should accumulate public Social Security and Medicare rights, as well as any private health or pension benefits.

Coupled with this substantial, but closely regulated, increase in temporary work permits, the United States and Mexico should embark on a joint border patrol program to reduce the flow of illegal crossings. The program should include features such as enhanced use of electronic surveillance, ineligibility for a temporary work permit for three years after an illegal crossing or an illegal overstay, and short-term misdemeanor detention (say 30 days) in Mexico following an illegal crossing. No border patrol program will eliminate illegal crossings, but a joint program, coupled with a substantial temporary work permit initiative, could reduce the flow.

That leaves the very difficult question of perhaps 8 million undocumented immigrants, many of them Mexicans, who live and work in the United States. We do not have a magic solution. The foundation for our recommendations is the proposition that undocumented Mexicans have made permanent homes in the United States and are not going to pick up their lives and return to Mexico. Under a set of appropriate circumstances, therefore, they should be granted residence permits with eligibility for citizenship. The appropriate circumstances we envisage have two components—a threshold related to illegal crossings and standards for individual applicants.

- The resident permit program would be launched when the presidents of the United States and Mexico could jointly certify that the annual rate of illegal crossings of the southern border does not exceed 50,000 persons. This would entail a reduction of more than four-fifths in illegal crossings by Mexican nationals observed in recent years and a significant reduction in illegal crossings by Central and South Americans who enter the United States through Mexico. The residential permit program would be suspended in years when the presidents could not make this certification.

- Individual eligibility would require evidence that the person resided in the United States before the *announcement* of the program. Otherwise, eligibility standards would parallel those for temporary work permits.

- An applicant for a residence permit who could provide satisfactory evidence of residence in the United States before the announcement of the program would not be subject to deportation (whether or not he met other eligibility requirements) so long as the entrant periodically reports a place of residence to the USCIS and commits no felony after the issuance of the residence permit.

- Holders of residence permits would be immediately eligible for public Social Security and Medicare benefits, as well as private health and
  pension benefits. They could apply for citizenship after five years.

Labor Standards

Labor standards have become a prominent part of the political debate surrounding free trade agreements, but trade by itself will improve labor
standards only in the long run. In the meantime, the governments in
North America need to take proactive measures to ensure that appropriate labor standards are set and enforced.

Our recommendations key off the ILO's Declaration of Principles Concerning Multinational Enterprise and Social Policy and the OECD Guidelines for Multinational Enterprise. We recognize that while Canada, Mexico, and the United States officially endorsed the declaration and guidelines,
endorsement came only after heated battles and over the opposition of
many in the business community.[66] In practice, as surveys reported by the
Manufacturers Alliance show, US manufacturing firms generally exceed
local labor, environmental, and ethical standards (Preeg 2001a and 2001b).
The business community objects as much to prospective regulatory burdens as to costs incurred in meeting labor and environmental norms.

Recommendations for Improving Labor Standards

- Businesses with operations in two or three NAFTA countries should
  adopt common labor codes of conduct. These codes should reflect the
  OECD guidelines and the ILO declaration. Companies would self-
  certify their compliance. Randomly selected companies (say 10 percent per year) should submit to an independent audit to ensure that
  they observe the code.

- The self-certification program should be gradually extended to
  smaller companies that do business in two or more NAFTA countries.
  Oversight from both private-sector interest groups and the CLC
  would back up these self-regulatory efforts.

---

66. The four principles reflected in the ILO declaration are freedom of association and collective bargaining, no forced labor, no child labor, and nondiscrimination. While the United
States endorses the ILO declaration, since 1984 the United States has unilaterally defined
workers' rights in a fashion that differs from core labor standards enumerated in the ILO's
1998 Declaration on Fundamental Principles and Rights at Work. Specifically, the United
States defines "internationally recognized" workers' rights to include freedom of association
and collective bargaining, freedom from forced labor, freedom from child labor, and "acceptable conditions of work." So far, the United States has ratified only two core conven-
tions—105 on forced labor and 182 on child labor. See Elliott and Freeman (2003) and Elliott
(2004).

Worker Adjustment

Canada already has sufficient mechanisms to address displaced workers. Health insurance is universal in Canada, and Canadian unemployment programs are relatively generous. Mexico simply cannot afford a broad-based unemployment program. Consequently, our recommendations for worker adjustment focus on the United States, which has both the need and the resources for more comprehensive worker adjustment programs. However, we do have recommendations for specific sectors within Mexico.

Recommendations for Worker Adjustment

The existing safety net system for displaced US workers has done little to relieve anxiety among US workers about losing their jobs and does nothing to diminish their opposition to international trade. Despite the fact that a significant expansion of the TAA program was packaged with Trade Promotion Authority in 2002, few Democrats in the House of Representatives supported the final bill.

As Rosen (2002) notes, support for free trade agreements in opinion polls goes up if the question is framed to include the possibility of government support for workers who lose their jobs. While the new TAA program was widely described as a short-term way of "buying" congressional votes for TPA, its supporters see the new TAA as a way of reducing the distress of dislocated workers and building public support for more trade liberalization in the long run.

While the 2002 version of TAA (which folds in the NAFTA-TAA program) is an improvement, considerable scope exists for further expansion. For example, the arbitrary provision should be eliminated that restricts coverage to workers adversely affected by a shift in the firm's production to a country that has a free trade agreement with the United States (and not a shift to any other country). The TAA program should include workers, both upstream and downstream, regardless of where the imports come from, where production shifts to, or how old they are. Alleged budget constraints were cited as a justification for limiting the health insurance subsidy to 65 percent. There is room to increase the generosity of the subsidy and increase funding for other aspects of the TAA program as well. The limit on wage insurance to workers over 50 and the $5,000 per worker cap are just stingy. Improving the 2002 TAA program would help to further reduce the fear of imports in the United States.[67]

In Mexico, a very special problem arises in Pemex and the CFE. Labor opposition within these two state-owned companies severely hampers privatization reform in the energy sector. Because the energy sector is so crucial to North America (see chapter 7 on energy), we recommend a spe-

---

67. See Kletzer and Rosen (2005) for a more detailed discussion of TAA reform.

cial adjustment program for workers in this sector. In conjunction with reform in the sector, workers 55 years and older should be offered full pensions for early retirement.

References

AFL-CIO. 1999. *Resolutions: Book One.* www.aflcio.org/ (accessed on July 24, 2005).

AFL-CIO. 2002. *NAFTA's Seven-Year Itch.* www.aflcio.org/mediacenter/resources/upload/naftabenefitsnotdelivered.pdf (accessed on July 20, 2005).

Baily, Martin Neil. 2001. *Macroeconomic Implications of the New Economy.* Working Paper 01-9. Washington: Institute for International Economics.

Baily, Martin Neil. 2002. Persistent Dollar Swings and the US Economy. Paper presented at a conference at the Institute for International Economics, Washington, September 18.

Baldwin, Robert E. 2003. *The Decline of Labor Unions and the Role of Trade.* Washington: Institute for International Economics.

Banco de Mexico. 2004. Indicadores Económicos y Financieros. Producción. www.banxico.org.mx/eInfoFinanciera/FSinfoFinanciera.html (accessed on June 15, 2004).

BEA (US Bureau of Economic Analysis). 2004a. Frequently Requested National Income and Product Accounts (NIPA) Tables. Washington: US Department of Commerce. www.bea.gov/bea/dn/nipaweb/SelectTable.asp?Popular=Y (accessed on May 23, 2005).

BEA (US Bureau of Economic Analysis). 2004b. Foreign Direct Investment in the United States: Capital Inflows. Washington: US Department of Commerce. www.bea.gov/bea/di/fdi21web.htm (accessed on January 10, 2005).

BEA (US Bureau of Economic Analysis). 2004c. Regional Accounts Data. Washington: US Department of Commerce. www.bea.gov/bea/regional/reis/ (accessed on January 10, 2005).

BEA (US Bureau of Economic Analysis). 2005. Frequently Requested National Income and Product Accounts (NIPA) Tables. Washington: US Department of Commerce. www.bea.gov/bea/dn/nipaweb/SelectTable.asp?Popular=Y (accessed on May 23, 2005).

Bolle, Mary Jane. 2000. NAFTA: Estimated US Job "Gains" and "Losses" by State Over 5 Years. Congressional Research Service Report for Congress 98-782 E (February 2). Washington: Congressional Research Service.

Bronfenbrenner, Kate. 1997. Organizing in the NAFTA Environment: How Companies Use "Free Trade" to Stop Unions. *New Labor Forum* 1, no. 1 (Fall): 50–60.

Bronfenbrenner, Kate. 2000. Uneasy Terrain: The Impact of Capital Mobility on Workers, Wages, and Union Organizing. Report of the US Trade Deficit Review Commission (September). www.citizenstrade.org/pdf/nafta_uneasy_terrain.pdf (accessed on July 20, 2005).

Browne, Harry, ed. 1995. Workers Succeed in Cross-Border Bid for Justice. *BorderLines* 3, no. 10 (November). www.us-mex.org/borderlines/1995/bl18/bl18emosa.html (accessed on June 24, 2002).

Calderon-Madrid, Angel, and Alexandru Voicu. 2004. *Total Factor Productivity Growth and Job Turnover in Mexican Manufacturing Plants in the 1990s.* Discussion Paper 993. Bonn, Germany: The Institute for the Study of Labor (January).

Camarota, Steven A. 1998. The Wages of Immigration: The Effect on the Low-Skilled Labor Market. Washington: Center for Immigration Studies. www.cis.org/articles/1998/wagestudywages.pdf (accessed on July 20, 2005).

Campbell, Bruce, Andrew Jackson, Mehrene Larudee, and Teresa Gutierrez Haces. 1999. Labour-Market Effects under CUSFTA/NAFTA. www.ilo.org/public/english/employment/strat/publ/etp29.htm (accessed on June 24, 2002).

CIC (Citizenship and Immigration Canada). 2000. *Facts and Figures 2000: Immigration Overview*. Research and Statistics. Ottawa, Ontario. www.cic.gc.ca/english/research/menu-fact. html (accessed on May 30, 2005).

CIC (Citizenship and Immigration Canada). 2003. *Facts and Figures 2003: Immigration Overview*. Research and Statistics. Ottawa, Ontario. www.cic.gc.ca/english/research/ menu-fact.html (accessed on May 30, 2005).

Cline, William R. 1997. *Trade and Income Distribution*. Washington: Institute for International Economics.

Conference Board of Canada. 2004. *Performance and Potential 2004–2005 Report: How Can Canada Prosper in Tomorrow's World?* Ottawa.

Council of Economic Advisers. 1999. *20 Million Jobs: January 1993–November 1999*. Washington (December 3).

Council of Economic Advisers. 2004. *Economic Report of the President 2004*. Washington.

Destler, I. M., and Peter Balint. 1999. *The New Politics of American Trade: Trade, Labor, and the Environment*. POLICY ANALYSES IN INTERNATIONAL ECONOMICS 58. Washington: Institute for International Economics.

Elliott, Kimberly Ann, and Richard B. Freeman. 2003. *Can Labor Standards Improve Under Globalization?* Washington: Institute for International Economics.

Elliott, Kimberly Ann. 2004. *Labor Standards, Development, and CAFTA*. International Economics Policy Brief PB04-02. Washington: Institute for International Economics.

Feenstra, Robert C., and Gordon H. Hanson. 2001. *Global Production Sharing and Rising Inequality: A Survey of Trade and Wages*. NBER Working Paper 8372 (July). Cambridge, MA: National Bureau of Economic Research.

Fox, Vicente. 2001. First Government Report. http://informe.presidencia.gob.mx/ Informes/2001Fox1/docs/1erInforme-english.doc (accessed on September 4, 2002).

Gingras, Yves, and Richard Roy. 2000. Is There a Skill Gap in Canada? *Canadian Public Policy* XXVI, no. 1 (supplement). www.econ.queensu.ca/pub/cpp/July2000/Gingras&Roy.pdf (accessed on June 24, 2002).

Government of Canada. 2001. *Canada's Innovation Strategy*. Ottawa.

Gross, James A. 1995. *Broken Promise: The Subversion of US Labor Relations Policy, 1947–1994*. Philadelphia, PA: Temple University Press.

Gruben, William C. 2001. Was NAFTA Behind Mexico's High Maquiladora Growth? *Economic and Financial Review* (third quarter). Dallas, TX: Federal Reserve Bank of Dallas.

Hanson, Gordon H. 2003. *What Has Happened to Wages in Mexico Since NAFTA?* NBER Working Paper 9563 (March). Cambridge, MA: National Bureau of Economic Research.

Harris, Richard G. 2004. *Labor Mobility and the Global Competition for Skills: Dilemmas and Options*. HISSRI Working Paper 2004 D-20. Ottawa: Industry Canada (February).

Harris, Richard G., and Nicolas Schmitt. 2001. The Consequences of Increased Labor Mobility Within an Integrating North America. Burnaby, British Columbia: Simon Fraser University (November).

Helliwell, John F. 2000. Globalization: Myths, Facts, and Consequences. C. D. Howe Institute Benefactors Lecture, Ontario, October 23. www.cdhowe.org/PDF/helliwell.pdf (accessed on June 24, 2002).

Helliwell, John F. 2001. Canada: Life Beyond the Looking Glass. *Journal of Economic Perspectives* 15, no. 1 (Winter).

Helwig, Ryan. 2004. Worker Displacement in 1999–2000. *BLS Monthly Labor Review* (June). www.bls.gov/opub/mlr/2004/06/art4exc.htm (accessed on May 31, 2005).

Hinojosa-Ojeda, Raúl, David Runsten, Fernando DePaolis, and Nabil Kamel. 2000. *The US Employment Impacts of North American Integration after NAFTA: A Partial Equilibrium Approach*. Research Report NAID-RR-010-00. Los Angeles, CA: North American Integration and Development Center, University of California at Los Angeles. http://naid. sppsr.ucla.edu/pubs&news/nafta2000.html (accessed on June 25, 2002).

Hipple, Steven. 1999. Worker Displacement in the Mid-1990s. *BLS Monthly Labor Review* (July). www.bls.gov/opub/mlr/1999/07/contents.htm (accessed on May 31, 2005).

Hufbauer, Gary C., and Jeffrey J. Schott. 1993. *NAFTA: An Assessment*, rev. ed. Washington: Institute for International Economics.

Hufbauer, Gary Clyde, Daniel C. Esty, Diana Orejas, Luis Rubio, and Jeffrey J. Schott. 2000. *NAFTA and the Environment: Seven Years Later.* POLICY ANALYSES IN INTERNATIONAL ECONOMICS 61. Washington: Institute for International Economics.

Hufbauer, Gary Clyde, and Howard Rosen. 1986. *Trade Policy for Troubled Industries.* Washington: Institute for International Economics.

Human Rights Watch. 2000. Unfair Advantage: Workers' Freedom of Association in the United States under International Human Rights Standards (August). www.hrw.org/reports/2000/uslabor/ (accessed on June 24, 2002).

Human Rights Watch. 2001. *Trading Away Rights: The Unfulfilled Promise of NAFTA's Labor Side Agreement* (April). Washington. www.hrw.org/reports/2001/nafta/ (accessed on June 24, 2002).

IMF (International Monetary Fund). 2005. Workers' Remittances and Economic Development. *World Economic Outlook* (April). Washington. www.imf.org/external/pubs/ft/weo/2005/01/index.htm (accessed on May 26, 2005).

IMSS (Instituto Mexicano del Seguro Social). 2005. Asegurados en el IMSS por Sector de Actividad Económica, Anual 1983–2004. Centro de Estudios de las Finanzas Públicas. www.cefp.org.mx/intr/e-stadisticas/copianewe stadisticas.html (accessed in May 2005).

INEGI (Instituto Nacional de Estadística, Geografía e Informática). 2005a. Banco de Información Económica. dgcnesyp.inegi.gob.mx/bdine/bancos.htm (accessed on January 10, 2005).

INEGI (Instituto Nacional de Estadística, Geografía e Informática). 2005b. Estadísticas sociodemográficas.

INEGI (Instituto Nacional de Estadística, Geografía e Informática). 2005c. Indicadores económicos de coyuntura. www.inegi.gob.mx/inegi/ (accessed on July 20, 2005).

INEGI (Instituto Nacional de Estadística, Geografía e Informática). 2002a. XII Censo General de Población y Vivienda, 2000. www.inegi.gob.mx/default.asp?e–276 (accessed on July 20, 2005).

Kletzer, Lori G. 2001. *Job Loss from Imports: Measuring the Costs.* Washington: Institute for International Economics.

Kletzer, Lori G., and Robert E. Litan. 2001. *A Prescription to Relieve Worker Anxiety.* International Economics Policy Brief 01-2. Washington: Institute for International Economics and Brookings Institution. February.

Kletzer, Lori G., and Howard Rosen. 2005. Easing the Adjustment Burden on US Workers. In *The United States and the World Economy: Foreign Economic Policy for the Next Decade*, ed. C. Fred Bergsten. Washington: Institute for International Economics.

Koechlin, Timothy, and Mehrene Larudee. 1992. The High Cost of NAFTA. *Challenge* (September/October).

La Botz, Dan. 1998. Reform, Resistance and Rebellion Among Mexican Workers. *Borderlines* 6, no. 7 (September). www.us-mex.org/borderlines/1998/bl48/bl48work.html (accessed on June 24, 2002).

Lawrence, Robert Z., and Mathew J. Slaughter. 1993. International Trade and American Wages in the 1980s: Giant Sucking Sound or Small Hiccup? *Brookings Papers on Economic Activity, Microeconomics* 2: 161–211.

Lopez, David. 1997. Dispute Resolution Under NAFTA: Lessons from the Early Experience. *Texas International Law Journal* 32, no. 2.

Lustig, Nora. 2001. Life Is Not Easy: Mexico's Quest for Stability and Growth. *The Journal of Economic Perspectives* 15, no. 1 (Winter). Nashville, TN: American Economic Association.

Maskus, Keith E. 1997. *Should Core Labor Standards Be Imposed Through International Trade Policy?* World Bank Working Paper 1817. Washington: World Bank. www.worldbank.org/research/trade/pdf/wp1817.pdf (accessed on June 24, 2002).

Mayer, Frederick W. 1998. *Interpreting NAFTA: The Science and Art of Political Analysis*. New York: Columbia University Press.

McFadyen, Jacqueline. 1998. *NAFTA Supplemental Agreements: Four-Year Review*. Institute for International Economics Working Paper 98-4. Washington: Institute for International Economics. www.iie.com/catalog/WP/1998/98-4.htm (accessed on June 24, 2002).

Mercenier, John, and Nicolas Schmitt. 2003. *International Brain Circulation and Intra-Industry Trade*. Paper prepared for Conference on Trade and Labor Perspectives on Worker Turnover, University of Nottingham, June.

Mexican Federal Government. 2004. *Informe de Gobierno*. cuarto.informe.presidencia.gob. mx/index.php (accessed on May 10, 2005).

Moberg, David. 1997. The Resurgence of American Unions: Small Steps, Long Journey. *Working USA* (May/June).

OECD (Organization for Economic Cooperation and Development). 2002. *OECD Economic Survey Mexico 2002*. Paris.

OECD (Organization for Economic Cooperation and Development). 2004a. *Labor Force Statistics*. Paris.

OECD (Organization for Economic Cooperation and Development). 2004b. *Employment Outlook*. Paris.

OECD (Organization for Economic Cooperation and Development). 2004c. OECD Health Data 2004. Paris. www.oecd.org/document/16/0,2340,en_2649_34631_2085200_1_1_ 1_ 1,00.html (accessed on January 11, 2005).

OECD (Organization for Economic Cooperation and Development). 2004d. *Education at a Glance*. Paris.

Pastor, Robert A. 2001 *Toward a North American Community: Lessons from the Old World for the New*. Washington: Institute for International Economics.

Preeg, Ernest H. 2001a. *US Manufacturing Industry's Impact on Ethical, Labor, and Environmental Standards in Developing Countries: A Survey of Current Practices*. Washington: Manufacturers Alliance/MAPI and National Association of Manufacturers.

Preeg, Ernest H. 2001b. *Doing Rather Than Feeling Good About Labor and Environmental Standards in Developing Countries*. Washington: Manufacturers Alliance/MAPI (September).

Rassell, Edith, and Yvon Pho. 2001. *Scattered Showers for Labor Day 2001*. Washington: Economic Policy Institute.

Rosen, Howard. 2002. Reforming Trade Adjustment Assistance: Keeping a 40-Year Promise. Paper presented at the Institute for International Economics Conference on Trade Policy, Washington, February 26.

Ruhnke, Jill Sanner. 1995. The Impact of NAFTA on Labor Arbitration in Mexico. *Law and Policy in International Business* 26, no. 3 (Spring).

Scheve, Kenneth F., and Matthew J. Slaughter. 2001. *Globalization and the Perceptions of American Workers*. Washington: Institute for International Economics.

Scott, Robert E. 2001. NAFTA's Hidden Costs: Trade Agreement Results in Job Losses, Growing Inequality, and Wage Suppression for the United States. Washington: Economic Policy Institute. www.epinet.org/content.cfm/briefingpapers_nafta01_US (accessed on July 20, 2005).

STPS (Secretaría de Trabajo y Previsión Social). 2005a. Encuesta Nacional de Empleo, Población Total por Sexo y Grupos de Edad. www.stps.gob.mx/01_oficina/05_cgpeet/ 302_0074.htm (accessed on May 25, 2005).

STPS (Secretaría de Trabajo y Previsión Social). 2005b. Encuesta Nacional de Empleo, Población Economicamente Activa por Sexo y Grupos de Edad, Según Condición de Ocupación. www.stps.gob.mx/01_oficina/05_cgpeet/302_0151.htm (accessed on May 25, 2005).

STPS (Secretaría de Trabajo y Previsión Social). 2005c. Encuesta Nacional de Empleo, Annual de Tasa de Desempleo Abierto Alternativa. www.stps.gob.mx/01_oficina/05_cgpeet/ 302_0056.htm (accessed in May 2005).

Sosa, Ivan. 1995. La Falta de Coordinación Sindical Causa Debilidad del Acuerdo Laboral del TLC. *El Financiero* (February 1).

Statistics Canada. 2004. Unionization—An Update. *Perspectives on Labour and Income* 5, no. 12 (December). www.childcareadvocacy.ca/resources/pdf/union_update2004e.pdf (accessed on January 11, 2005).

Stolper, Wolfgang, and Paul A. Samuelson. 1941. Protection and Real Wages. *Review of Economic Studies* 9.

Treasury Board of Canada Secretariat. 2004. Departmental Performance Reporting. Human Resources Development Canada. www.tbs-sct.gc.ca/rma/dpr/dpre.asp (accessed on July 7, 2005).

UNCTAD (United Nations Conference on Trade and Development). 2002. Worker Remittances by Country. http://stats.unctad.org (accessed on September 3, 2002).

UNICEF (United Nations Children's Fund). 2004. *State of the World's Children.* New York.

UNICEF (United Nations Children's Fund). 2005. Information by Country. New York. www.unicef.org/infobycountry/index.html (accessed on May 25, 2005).

United Electrical, Radio, and Machine Workers of America. 2000. How the Mighty are Fallen: Congress of Labor and Confederation of Mexican Workers: The PRI's "Official" Federations in Decline. *Mexican Labor News and Analysis* V, no. 3 (March). www.ueinternational.org/Vol5no3.html (accessed on June 24, 2002).

US Census Bureau. 1997. Economic Census. Washington. www.census.gov/epcd/www/econ97.html (accessed on June 24, 2002).

US Department of Labor. 1998. Public Report of Review of NAO Submission 9702. National Administrative Office (April 28). www.dol.gov/ilab/media/reports/nao/pubrep9702.htm (accessed in January 2005).

US Department of Labor. 2001. *Review of the North American Agreement on Labor Cooperation.* Washington: National Administrative Office (June).

US Department of Labor. 2002a. Local Area Unemployment Statistics. Washington: Bureau of Labor Statistics. www.bls.gov/lau/home.htm (accessed on September 4, 2002).

US Department of Labor. 2002b. Union Members Summary (January 17). Washington: Bureau of Labor Statistics. www.bls.gov/news.release/union2.nr0.htm (accessed on June 24, 2002).

US Department of Labor. 2002c. *Employment and Training Administration Fact Sheet.* Washington. www.doleta.gov/programs/factsht/nafta.htm (accessed on June 24, 2002).

US Department of Labor. 2004a. Current Population Survey 2004. Washington: Bureau of Labor Statistics. www.bls.gov/cps/cpsatabs.htm (accessed on January 11, 2005).

US Department of Labor. 2004b. *Unemployment Insurance Outlook.* http://workforcesecurity.doleta.gov/unemploy (accessed on July 20, 2005).

US Department of Labor. 2005a. Current Population Survey 2005. Washington: Bureau of Labor Statistics. data.bls.gov/cgi-bin/surveymost?ln (accessed on May 27, 2005).

US Department of Labor. 2005b. North American Agreement on Labor Cooperation (NAALC): Status of Submissions. Washington. www.dol.gov/ilab/programs/nao/status.htm#i (accessed on May 16, 2005).

US Government Printing Office. 2004. Budget of the United States Government: Historical Tables. www.gpoaccess.gov/usbudget/ (accessed on July 20, 2005).

Wagner, Don. 2000. Do Tax Differences Cause the Brain Drain? *Policy Options* (December). www.irpp.org/po/archive/dec00/wagner.pdf (accessed on June 24, 2002).

World Bank. 2002. Distribution of Income or Consumption. Washington. www.worldbank.org/poverty/data/2_8wdi2002.pdf (accessed on September 3, 2002).

Appendix 2A

Table 2A.1 National Administrative Office (NAO) submissions on enforcement matters, 1996–2005

Submission	Filed	Claimant	Defendant	Claim	Status
Canada					
98-1	April 6, 1998	Canadian Office of the United Steelworkers of America et al.	Itapsa	Substantially same as US NAO submission no. 9703, including denial of freedom of association and lax enforcement of labor legislation covering occupational health and safety standards	Canadian NAO accepted submission for review in June 1998. Public meetings held in September and November 1998. The first part of the report addressing the freedom of association issues was released in December 1998. The second part of the report, released in March 1999, addressed the health and safety claims. Canada requested ministerial consultations with Mexico in March 1999. Consultations are pending.
98-2	September 28, 1998	Yale Law School Workers' Rights Project et al.	US government	Replicates Mexican NAO submission no. 9804	Canadian NAO, in light of a US Department of Labor and the Immigration and Naturalization Service memorandum of understanding, considered a review inappropriate and closed the file in April 1999.
99-1	April 14, 1999	LPA, Inc. and EFCO Corp.	US government	Failure to review labor law matters arising in another party's territory. Failure to effectively enforce domestic labor laws. (Section 8(a)(2) of the National Labor Relations Act)	Canadian NAO declined to accept the submission for review. The claimants filed an appeal in June 1999.
03-1	October 3, 2003	United Students Against Sweatshops (USAS) and Centro de Apoyo al Trabajador	Puebla	Replicates US NAO submission no. 2003-01	Canadian NAO accepted submission for review in March 2004. Public meeting held in May 2004. Canada requested ministerial consultations with Mexico in May 2005. Consulta-

Mexico

9501	February 9, 1995	Mexican Telephone Workers' Union	Sprint Corporation in the United States	Workers deprived of their freedom of association and the right to organize due to closure of Sprint subsidiary in San Francisco shortly before a union representation election	Ministerial consultations held. Resulted in: (1) A public forum held in San Francisco and (2) Initiation of Secretariat special study on "Plant Closings and Labor Rights." The Communications Workers of America filed an unfair labor practice case with the National Labor Review Board (NLRB). On December 27, 1996, the NLRB ordered Sprint to reinstate the dismissed workers and awarded backpay. Sprint filed an appeal with the US federal courts. In November 1997, the US federal courts reversed the NLRB ruling and ruled that Sprint closed its plant because the plant was losing money, not because the company feared the workers would vote to join a union.
9801	April 13, 1998	Oil, Chemical, and Atomic Workers' International Union (Local 1-675), Industrial and Commercial Workers' Union ("October 6"), the Labor Community Defense Union, and the Support Committee for Maquiladora Workers	Solec, Inc., California (manufacturer of solar panels)	Workers denied freedom of association, occupational safety, and health issues	Mexican NAO accepted submission for review in July 1998. In August 1999, a public report was issued requesting ministerial consultations. In May 2000, a ministerial agreement was signed by Mexico and the United States to address submissions 9801-02-02. As part of the agreement, the US Department of Labor will host government-to-government meetings to discuss the issues in review.

(table continues next page)

Table 2A.1 National Administrative Office (NAO) submissions on enforcement matters, 1996–2005 (continued)

Submission	Filed	Claimant	Defendant	Claim	Status
2005-01	April 13, 2005	Northwest Workers' Justice Project, Brennan Center for Justice (New York University School of Law), and Andrade Law Office	US government	Issues concerning rights of migrant workers under the H-2B visa program in Idaho, including freedom of association, right to organize and bargain collectively, right to minimum employment standards, safety and health, employment discrimination, protection of migrant workers, and compensation in cases of occupational injuries/illness	Not determined yet.
United States					
940001 and 940002	February 14, 1994	International Brotherhood of Teamsters and United Electrical, Radio, and Machine Workers of America, respectively	Honeywell Corporation and General Electric Corporation in Mexico	Workers deprived of their freedom of association and the right to organize into unions of their choice	Process terminated in October 1994 at NAO review stage due to insufficient evidence. US NAO recommended the development of trilateral programs addressing freedom of association and the right to organize and for public information and education regarding the North American Agreement on Labor Co-

Number	Date	Submitter(s)	Against	Issues	Outcome
940003	August 16, 1994	International Labor Rights Education and Research Fund, the National Association of Democratic Lawyers of Mexico, the Coalition for Justice in the Maquiladoras, and the American Friends Service Committee	Sony Corporation in Mexico	Workers deprived of their freedom of association, the right to organize, and minimum employment standards relating to hours of work and holiday work	Ministerial consultations held. Resulted in a two-year program of activities including seminars, workshops, meetings, and studies to address union registration and its implications. The US NAO issued a report in December 1996 based on a follow-up review of the issues and a related Mexican Supreme Court decision. (Allegations concerning minimum employment standards were not accepted for review.)
940004	September 12, 1994	United Electrical, Radio, and Machine Workers	General Electric Corporation in Mexico	Workers deprived of their freedom of association and the right to organize	Withdrawn in January 1995 before completion of review process.
9601	June 13, 1996	International Labor Rights Fund, Human Rights Watch/Americas, and the National Association of Democratic Lawyers of Mexico	Mexican government	Federal workers denied freedom of association and the right to organize (among other reasons cited: Mexican government failure to comply with international labor organization conventions to which it is a signatory). Questioned whether labor tribunals reviewing these issues are impartial	Ministerial consultations held on the status of international treaties, constitutional provisions, and protecting freedom of association. Resulted in NAFTA members agreeing to exchange information to permit a full examination of the issues raised. A seminar, open to the public, was held in Baltimore in December 1997. The allegation of impartiality of labor tribunals for the federal sector was found to be ungrounded. In December 1997, claimants requested reopening of the submission, asserting that some issues raised in the original submission were not adequately addressed. Finding that these issues had been sufficiently reviewed, the NAO declined the request.

(table continues next page)

Table 2A.1   National Administrative Office (NAO) submissions on enforcement matters, 1996–2005   *(continued)*

Submission	Filed	Claimant	Defendant	Claim	Status
9602	October 11, 1996	Communications Workers of America, Union of Telephone Workers of Mexico, and Federation of Goods and Services Companies of Mexico	Maxi-Switch in Mexico	Workers denied freedom of association and the right to organize	In April 1997, submitters withdrew the submission after the federal government instructed the local authorities to certify the independent union. The local authorities have not complied, and the dispute has been taken to the Mexican courts.
9701	May 16, 1997	Human Rights Watch, the International Labor Rights Fund, and the National Association of Democratic Lawyers of Mexico	Mexican government	Failure to enforce Mexican labor law prohibitions on discrimination against pregnant women. Also alleges that Mexico denies victims of sex discrimination access to impartial tribunals	In January 1998, the US NAO requested ministerial consultations on the effectiveness of Mexican laws and law enforcement in protecting against pregnancy-based gender discrimination. A ministerial consultations implementation agreement was signed in October 1998, and a conference on protecting the labor rights of working women was held March 1999. Outreach sessions in August 1999 and May 2000 followed the conference.

| 9702 | October 30, 1997 | Support Committee for Maquiladora Workers; the International Labor Rights Fund; the National Association of Democratic Lawyers of Mexico; and the Union of Metal, Steel, Iron, and Allied Workers' Union of Mexico. (Amendment filed by Maquiladora Health and Safety Support Network, Worksafe! Southern CA, the United Steelworkers of America, the United Auto Workers, and the Canadian Auto Workers) | Han Young factory in Mexico and Mexican government | Workers denied freedom of association and the right to organize. Also raises issues of failure by Mexico to enforce its laws on safety and health, wages, dismissal from employment, and profit sharing | The Mexican government recognized the results of a second election (secret ballot election held on December 12, 1997), which was won by the independent union. However, Han Young has subsequently refused to negotiate with the new union, and the responsible labor tribunal has permitted another election at the plant to challenge the representation by the independent union. The Mexican government levied a $9,000 fine against Han Young for health and safety violations. Following ministerial consultations between Mexico and the United States, a public seminar was held in June 2000 to promote freedom of association. |
| 9703 | December 15, 1997 | Echlin Workers Alliance, the Teamsters, the United Auto Workers, the Canadian Auto Workers, UNITE, the United Electrical, Radio and Machine Workers of America, the Paperworkers, the Steelworkers et al. | Itapsa export processing plant in Mexico | Workers denied freedom of association and the right to organize | The US NAO held a public hearing in March 1998, and issued its public report in July 1998 recommending ministerial consultations. In May 2000, the United States and Mexico signed a ministerial agreement for submissions 9702 and 9703. Under this agreement, the Mexican government held a public seminar in June 2000 to promote freedom of association and the right to collective bargaining. |

(table continues next page)

Table 2A.1 National Administrative Office (NAO) submissions on enforcement matters, 1996–2005 *(continued)*

Submission	Filed	Claimant	Defendant	Claim	Status
9801	August 17, 1998	Association of Flight Attendants and AFL-CIO	Aerovías de Mexico (Aeromexico), Mexican government	Workers denied freedom of association and the right to organize	NAO declined acceptance of the submission in October 1998 in accordance with procedural guidelines. NAO agreed to launch research evaluating how the three NAALC parties could reconcile national interests with the right to strike.
9802	September 28, 1998	Florida Tomato Exchange	Mexican government	Failure to enforce labor protection for children	NAO held submission in abeyance waiting for further information from claimants. No additional information was provided, and the case was closed in October 1999.
9803	October 19, 1998	International Brotherhood of Teamsters, Teamstérs Canada, the Quebec Federation of Labor, Teamsters Local 973 (Montreal), and the International Labor Rights Fund	McDonald's, Canadian government	Workers denied freedom of association and the right to organize	NAO accepted submission for review in December 1998. The c aimants requested the end of NAO review and in April 1999, claimants and the government of Quebec reached an agreement to have the issue evaluated by a provincial council.
9804	December 2, 1998	Organization of Rural Route Mail Couriers, Canadian Union of Postal Workers, National Association of Letter Carriers et al.	Canadian government	Workers deprived of the right to organize	In accordance with procedural guidelines, in February 1999, the NAO declined to accept the submission for review.

Case	Date	Submitter	Respondent	Issue	Action
9901	November 10, 1999	Association of Flight Attendants and Association of Flight Attendants of Mexico	Executive Air Transport, Inc., Mexican government	Workers deprived of the right to organize, bargain collectively, and minimum labor standards	In January 2000, the NAO accepted the submission for review. A hearing was held in March 2000 and a report issued in July 2000, recommending ministerial consultations. Ministerial consultations held in June 2002. Resulted in plans for a public seminar in Mexico to discuss different unions in each country and their relevant collective bargaining rights.
2000-01	July 3, 2000	Coalition for Justice in the Maquiladoras	Auto Trim and Custom Trim, Mexican government	Occupational safety and health issues	NAO accepted submission for review in September 2000. A public hearing was held in December 2000. In April 2001, a report was issued recommending ministerial consultations. Ministerial consultations held in June 2002. Resulted in the establishment of a bilateral working group on occupational safety and health issues. To date, the bilateral working group has focused on occupational safety and health management systems and voluntary protection programs, handling of hazardous substances, inspector and technical assistance staff training, and the development of the trinational web page.
2001-01	June 29, 2001	AFL-CIO and PACE	Duro Bag Manufacturing Corporation, Mexican government	Workers deprived of the right to organize and bargain collectively	NAO declined acceptance of the submission in February 2002 in accordance with procedural guidelines.

(table continues next page)

Fast-track authority was extended for two years, and the negotiations proceeded.

The "greening" of NAFTA produced notable results when the talks concluded in August 1992 but were not enough to satisfy presidential candidate Bill Clinton. During the election campaign in October 1992, Clinton criticized the pact for not dealing adequately with labor and environmental issues. He pledged not to implement NAFTA until a supplemental agreement had been concluded requiring each country to enforce its own environmental standards and establishing an "environmental protection commission with substantial powers and resources to prevent and clean up water pollution."[1]

Clinton's campaign commitments created high expectations among US environmental groups, expectations that were not fully met in the postelection negotiations. The August 1993 side agreement, labeled the North American Agreement on Environmental Cooperation (NAAEC), augmented NAFTA's environmental provisions and dispute settlement procedures, making the world's greenest trade accord still greener. The NAFTA side accord did not, however, deliver on some of Clinton's ambitious environmental promises. In particular, the Clinton administration did not choose to spend large sums of federal money on improving conditions in US and Mexican border communities. Meanwhile, Canada and Mexico preferred a less confrontational approach to dealing with environmental abuses and did not agree to US demands regarding enforcement provisions. Most environmental groups initially supported the "enhanced" NAFTA but became increasingly dissatisfied with government efforts to deal with environmental problems.[2] Eventually they soured on NAFTA and practically all other trade initiatives.

Does the NAFTA record on the environment since 1994 justify the criticism by environmental groups? Ten years is too short a period to redress decades of environmental abuse, but it is not too soon to assess NAFTA's achievements and shortcomings in meeting its environmental objectives. To that end, this chapter reviews (1) the environmental provisions of NAFTA and the NAAEC; (2) the trends in North American environmental policy; and (3) the situation at the US-Mexico border.

Overall, the NAFTA experience demonstrates that trade pacts can simultaneously generate economic gains from increased trade, avoid the dismantling of existing environmental protection regimes, and improve

---

1. Speech by Bill Clinton at North Carolina State University, October 4, 1992.

2. The largest environmental groups, known to their opponents as the "shameful seven," supported the NAFTA environmental side agreement: World Wildlife Fund, National Wildlife Federation, Natural Resources Defense Council, Defenders of Wildlife, Environmental Defense Fund, Conservation International, and Audubon Society. We thank John Audley for clarifying this sentence, which draws heavily on written comments he provided to an earlier draft.

environmental standards. But the NAFTA record does not demonstrate that a trade pact can reverse decades of abuse, nor can it turn the spigot on billions of dollars of remedial funding.

NAFTA's Environmental Provisions

NAFTA explicitly addresses environmental issues in its preamble and in five of its 22 chapters. Other chapters deal with environmental issues indirectly.

Preamble and Chapter 1

NAFTA's preamble ensures that the goals of the agreement are attained "in a manner consistent with environmental protection and conservation." Additionally, the preamble includes among NAFTA goals the "promotion of sustainable development" and the "strengthening of the development and enforcement of environmental laws and regulations."

Chapter 1 sets forth the agreement's basic rules of interpretation. In particular, Articles 103 and 104 confirm NAFTA's precedence over other international agreements—with the notable exception of the trade provisions in specified multilateral environmental agreements (MEAs). In other words, while Canada, Mexico, and the United States agreed that NAFTA takes precedence over GATT provisions, they recognized the legitimacy of incorporating trade measures (beyond those in NAFTA) as enforcement tools in MEAs.[3]

Chapters 7B and 9

Chapter 7B, on sanitary and phytosanitary (SPS) measures, allows the signatories to adopt or apply SPS measures more stringent than those established by international bodies. In other words, an unusually "tough" SPS standard is not automatically a prohibited trade barrier. To avoid abuses, Chapter 7B requires that SPS measures (1) not arbitrarily discriminate among like goods; (2) be based on "scientific principles"; (3) be repealed or abandoned when no scientific basis exists for them; (4) be based on a risk assessment, as appropriate to the circumstances; (5) be applied only to the extent necessary to attain the desired level of protection; and (6) not represent a bad-faith disguised restriction on trade.

---

3. Nonetheless, each country agreed—when complying with MEA obligations—to implement measures that were "least inconsistent" with NAFTA, if afforded options that were "equally effective and reasonably available."

Chapter 9 deals with technical barriers to trade and standards-related measures. It authorizes parties to choose "the levels of protection considered appropriate" and to adopt measures deemed necessary to attain the desired level of environmental protection, provided they are nondiscriminatory and do not create unnecessary obstacles to trade. While chapters 7B and 9 set limits on regulatory powers, NAFTA's SPS disciplines are less restrictive than those of GATT. For example, GATT requires in Article XX(b) that any standards-related environmental laws be "necessary" for the protection of human, animal, or plant life or health. GATT dispute settlement panels have interpreted "necessary" as meaning "least trade restrictive." NAFTA did not adopt the "least trade restrictive" test and differs from GATT in several other aspects.

NAFTA Article 710 explicitly states that the NAFTA provisions of Chapter 7B regarding SPS measures apply rather than those of GATT Article XX(b).

During the NAFTA ratification debate, US officials issued two clarifications regarding Chapter 7B. First, "necessary" is not to be interpreted as "least trade restrictive." Second, the appropriate "scientific basis" for an SPS measure is a matter for the regulating authority to decide, not the dispute settlement panel.[4]

NAFTA Chapter 9 does not contain an express "least trade restrictive" requirement, which means that governments have greater regulatory flexibility under NAFTA rules than under GATT rules.

In an arbitration case brought by a party under NAFTA's Chapter 7B or 9, the party challenging the law or regulation carries the burden of proof. By contrast, under GATT, a defending party must prove that its laws are consistent with the provisions of Article XX(b) or XX(g) regarding the conservation of exhaustible natural resources. In addition, in any challenge arising under NAFTA Chapter 7B or 9, the defending party may choose to have the case heard under either a NAFTA panel or a GATT panel—a choice that enables the defending party to apply the NAFTA rules.

North American Agreement on Environmental Cooperation

The environmental side agreement, or the NAAEC, was designed to encourage cooperative initiatives and to mediate environmental disputes. In addition, in 1993 the United States and Mexico signed the Border Environmental Cooperation Agreement (BECA), which furthered their joint efforts to deal with border problems by expanding on the 1983 La Paz Agreement. The border region was defined as the area lying 100 kilometers to the north and south of the US-Mexico boundary. The BECA established two new institutions: the Border Environment Cooperation Com-

---

4. These clarifications were put forward in the US Statement of Administrative Action issued as part of the legislative package to implement NAFTA in US law.

mission (BECC) and the North American Development Bank (NADBank) to evaluate, certify, and help fund environmental projects.

The NAAEC was more the product of the US legislative battle over NAFTA than the brainchild of collective environmental conscience among the governments of Canada, Mexico, and the United States. Regardless of the motivation, however, the NAAEC provided North America with a trilateral framework for environmental governance (Kirton 2000). Specifically, the NAAEC established a "framework . . . to facilitate effective cooperation on the conservation, protection, and enhancement of the environment" and set up an institution—the North American Commission for Environmental Cooperation (CEC)—to facilitate joint activities.

Part one of the NAAEC contains an ambitious set of objectives that include the protection and improvement of the environment, the promotion of sustainable development, and enhanced compliance with and enforcement of environmental laws and regulations. Part two obligates parties to periodically issue reports on the state of their environment; to develop environmental emergency preparedness measures; to promote environmental education; to develop environmental technology and scientific research; to assess environmental impacts; to use economic instruments for environmental goals; and to "ensure that [their] laws and regulations provide for high levels of environmental protection."

Part three of the NAAEC establishes the CEC and defines its structure—a Council of Ministers, a Secretariat, and a Joint Public Advisory Committee (JPAC)—its powers, and its procedures. Part four calls for cooperation in the interpretation and application of the NAAEC, the prior notification of proposed or actual environmental measures, and the prompt provision of information upon the CEC's request.

Part five deals with the resolution of disputes. In case of a "persistent pattern of failure" to enforce an environmental law, a party may request an arbitral panel. The request alone does not trigger arbitration; instead, a two-thirds vote of the Council is needed to form a panel. This panel can require implementation of an action plan to remedy nonenforcement of the offending nation's environmental law. Failure to comply with the plan can lead to suspension of NAFTA benefits—except when Canada is the defending party. So far there have been no complaints of "persistent failure to enforce," and hence this mechanism remains untested.

Commission for Environmental Cooperation

The operational goals of the NAAEC can be encapsulated in three parts—to improve environmental conditions through cooperative initiatives, to ensure appropriate implementation of environmental legislation, and to mediate environmental disputes. The CEC is the institutional structure created to achieve all three goals. The CEC consists of a governing body, the Council of Ministers; a Secretariat, which provides the Council with technical support; and a channel for nongovernmental organization (NGO) influence, namely JPAC.

The Council is composed of "cabinet-level or equivalent representatives" and meets at least once a year. Its functions include the promotion of environmental cooperation; approval of the CEC's annual budget; oversight of the agreement's implementation and the Secretariat's activities; assistance in the prevention and resolution of environment-related trade disputes; development of recommendations on environmental issues ranging from data analysis to enforcement; and cooperation with NAFTA's Free Trade Commission (FTC) to achieve NAFTA's environmental goals. For example, Article 10(6) of the NAAEC specifically directs the CEC to assist the FTC on environment-related matters and to act as a point of contact for NGOs and interested citizens. The implementation of Article 10(6), however, has been limited.[5]

Although the NAAEC supposedly facilitates cooperation between the CEC and the FTC, little contact has occurred between them. Since NAFTA entered into force, several NAFTA trade disputes have been "environment related," yet the CEC has not been involved in any of them. As discussed at length in chapter 4 on dispute settlement, NAFTA Chapter 11 cases involving investment disputes with direct environmental implications are particularly contentious (see box 3.1). Yet, trade and environment officials are only beginning to identify the appropriate ways to implement Article 11B provisions regarding investor-state disputes (Mann and von Moltke 1999).

The Secretariat is a permanent trilateral organization based in Montreal. It carries out the daily work of implementing the agreement, issues reports on environmental matters, and has some investigatory powers. Article 13 of the NAAEC allows the Secretariat to initiate investigations and prepare reports on "any matter within the scope of the annual program." In addition, Articles 14 and 15 authorize the Secretariat to develop a factual record in response to complaints of environmental nonenforcement submitted by individual citizens or NGOs.[6] A two-thirds vote of the Council is necessary to proceed either with Article 13 reports or Article 14–15 factual records.

---

5. Economic ministries in NAFTA parties are reluctant to see Article 10(6) invoked. As an example, when there was discussion about whether the CEC should have an active role in ongoing US-Canada softwood lumber disputes, several governmental agencies (e.g., US Department of Commerce, US Trade Representative, and the Canada Department of Foreign Affairs and International Trade) resisted. We thank John Audley for providing this example.

6. As of March 2005, NGOs filed 34 of the 50 cases. Based on authors' analysis of CEC submissions; also see Kirton (2000).

Box 3.1 Chapter 11 provisions and environmental regulation

Under Article 1110, the host country cannot expropriate the property of a foreign investor unless the expropriation is explicitly done for a public policy purpose, on a nondiscriminatory basis, in accordance with due process of law, and with fair compensation. These restrictions apply to direct measures and any indirect measures "tantamount to nationalization or expropriation." This language, and its application in individual cases, has prompted some commentators to complain that Chapter 11 arbitration panels can interpret the "tantamount to expropriation" phrase broadly to encompass "regulatory takings." Host governments are then required to compensate foreign investors for damages equivalent to the amount of profits lost on account of regulation designed to further domestic social policies (e.g., environment and human health and safety).

Article 1110 is the third most frequently cited breach of NAFTA obligation. Based on Article 1110 claims, both the Canadian and Mexican governments have paid compensation for regulatory measures with environmental overtones. In the *S.D. Myers* decision, the NAFTA Chapter 11 tribunal decided that the real intent of Canada's ban on the export of PCB waste was to protect the Canadian waste disposal industry from its US competitors. In November 2000, the Canadian government paid about $3.9 million to the US firm, S.D. Myers. In the *Metalclad* case, the Chapter 11 tribunal decided that the Ecological Decree used to protect rare cactus was arbitrarily invoked and amounted to "an act tantamount to expropriation." As a result, in August 2000, the tribunal ordered the Mexican government to pay $16.7 million in damages.

While both NAFTA tribunal decisions had environmental groups up in arms, the compensation represented less than 20 percent of initial claims and did not cover the investment costs of a new facility or lost revenues. Evidently the tribunals cast a skeptical eye not only on regulatory shell games but also on overblown claims. Moreover, learning from the NAFTA experience, recent US FTAs with Chile, Singapore, and Central America have adopted more restrictive language in their foreign investor–protection provisions compared with the original NAFTA text.

The JPAC is an innovative 15-member board that facilitates public input on CEC activities. The JPAC advises the Council on any matter within the scope of the NAAEC and provides relevant information to the Secretariat. Between 1995 and 2004, the JPAC met more than 40 times and provided advice to the Council on a wide range of issues. Most recently, the JPAC recommended that Mexico participate in the North American Pollutant Release and Transfer Register to help enforce regulatory measures. Other suggestions included requiring a national inventory of all polychlorinated biphenyl (PCB) sites in Mexico.

Article 43 of the NAAEC specifies that "each Party shall contribute an equal share of the annual budget of the Commission, subject to the availability of appropriated funds." Any NAFTA member thus has the ability to curtail the operation of the CEC by reducing or withholding financial support. Since 1995, however, each of the three countries has maintained its $3 million annual contribution to the CEC budget. Funding at this level seems inadequate for CEC's mandate and represents an insignificant fraction of the resources dedicated to the environment in North America.[7]

Citizen Submissions under Articles 14 and 15

Submission Process

Articles 14 and 15 of the NAAEC provide a process for any NGO or person to initiate a submission, or complaint, against a government for "failing to effectively enforce its environmental laws" (NAAEC Article 14(1)).[8] With the CEC Council's approval, the submission process can lead to further investigation and published findings in a factual record under NAAEC Article 15.

The procedures are outlined under the CEC Guidelines for Submissions on Enforcement Matters (1995). After receiving a submission that meets Article 14(1) submission requirements, there is no time limit for the Secretariat review.[9] If submission requirements have not been satisfied, however, the Secretariat will request the complainant to resubmit within 30 days. If the resubmitted complaint still does not meet formal requirements, the Secretariat will terminate action.[10] Provided that the submission meets the formal filing requirements, the Secretariat will initiate a

---

7. While small, the CEC budget compares favorably with the UN Environment Program, when both are scaled to the population served. Moreover, the CEC budget has leveraged other public monies directly and indirectly. For example, CEC grants are instrumental for providing financial and technical support to Mexican NGOs. During 1996–2003, CEC grants helped 109 public interest groups strengthen local enforcement during a period when direct financial support from the Mexican government was lacking. See Kirton (2000) and Silvan (2004). We thank Scott Vaughan for helpful comments on an earlier draft.

8. Specifically, to be considered by the CEC Secretariat, a submission must meet six formal requirements, including claims that "a Party is failing to effectively enforce its environmental law and should focus on any acts or omissions of the Party asserted to demonstrate such failure." Other requirements include that the complaint must "identify the applicable statute or regulation, or provision," "contain a succinct account of facts," "appear to be aimed at promoting enforcement rather than at harassing industry," "communicated in writing," and "address factors for consideration identified in Article 14(2)." See JPAC (2001) and CEC (1999).

9. The original guidelines, adopted in October 1995, were later revised in June 1999. A key amendment under the 1999 guidelines requires the CEC Secretariat to explain its reasons for making final determinations under Article 14(1). (In the original 1995 guidelines, the Secretariat only needed to provide reasons for dismissing a submission.) As a result of the change in the 1999 guidelines, citizen submissions have the benefit of past experience. Nevertheless, several submissions have been dismissed for deficiencies under Article 14(1). See JPAC (2001) and Markell and Knox (2003).

10. The Secretariat may also terminate complaints if they are already subject to a pending judicial or administrative proceeding, or if a factual record is not recommended. See JPAC (2001).

second review to determine whether to respond. The Secretariat's response is based on Article 14(2) and depends on four "factors for consideration": (1) Does the complaint allege harm to the complainant? (2) Will the complaint advance the goals of the NAAEC? (3) Have private remedies been pursued? (4) Is the complaint drawn largely from mass media reports? (CEC Guidelines 1995, Section 5).

Once it receives the complaint, the government has up to 60 days to submit a response. During this period, the government can provide additional information to the Secretariat, including whether environmental policies were further defined (subsequent to the facts alleged in the complaint) and whether the government has implemented policies that address the complaint (CEC Guidelines 1995, Section 9). Following the government's reply, the Secretariat decides whether the complaint merits the development of a factual record.

If the Secretariat recommends a factual record, the Secretariat requires a two-thirds mandate from the Council.[11] Once the Secretariat submits the draft factual record to the Council, "any party may provide comments to the accuracy of the draft within 45 days thereafter."[12] Again, a two-thirds vote from the Council is necessary to make the factual record publicly available.[13]

Outcome of Submissions

Since the establishment of the CEC in 1995, 50 submissions have been filed with the Secretariat, of which 10 warranted developing a factual record, 28 were terminated, 2 were withdrawn, and 10 are still pending (appendix table 3A.1). Among the citizen submissions on enforcement matters, 17 concerned Canadian enforcement, 24 concerned Mexican enforcement, and 9 concerned US enforcement.

Of the 28 terminated cases, the Secretariat determined that 14 submissions did not satisfy the formal filing requirements under Article 14(1). In eight cases, the Council voted against the development of a factual

---

11. The submission process will terminate if the Council does not approve the preparation of the final version of the factual record.

12. Specifically, factual records should include (1) a summary of the submission that initiated the process; (2) a summary of the response, if any, provided by the concerned Party; (3) a summary of any other relevant factual information; and (4) the facts presented by the Secretariat. Based on NAAEC Article 15(5). See NAAEC text, www.sice.oas.org/trade/nafta/env-9142.asp (accessed April 2005). See also CEC (1999).

13. After the Council approves making the factual record public, the factual record will be publicly available within 60 days of its submission to the Council. Independent of any Council decision to make the factual record public, a two-thirds vote by the Council also makes the factual record available to the JPAC. See JPAC (2001) and Hufbauer et al. (2000).

record.[14] Of the 10 pending cases, the Secretariat is reviewing two for their adequacy under Articles 14(1) and 14(2): *Coal-Fired Power Plants* and *Crushed Gravel*.[15] In two cases, the Secretariat has not yet decided whether to recommend the preparation of a factual record under Article 15(1).[16] The Council approved the development of factual records for five submissions, and the preparation of one factual record by the Secretariat is pending.[17]

While Council rulings and NAAEC factual records are nonbinding, the submission process has yielded positive results. After the final determination in the *Cozumel* case (SEM-96-001) against Mexico, former President Ernesto Zedillo declared the Cozumel Coral Reef a protected natural area in Quintana Roo, creating a precedent for reforming the law of environmental impact (Hufbauer et al. 2000 and Silvan 2004). In the *BC Logging* case (SEM-00-004) against Canada, the Canadian Department of Fisheries and Oceans addressed deficiencies in departmental procedures (CEC 2004b).

On the other hand, concerns are voiced that the Council lacks sufficient authority to implement recommendations flowing from the citizen submission process and that there is an inherent conflict of interest in a Council's determination when one of its member countries violated its own environmental laws. In addition, critics question whether the Council may be predisposed against cases involving the United States, since only one new submission (SEM-04-005) has been brought against the US government in the past five years, and large environmental NGOs are not using the process (Gardner 2004 and CEC 2004b).

Environmental Policy Trends in North America

Different levels of economic development in the three NAFTA countries mean diverse levels of environmental funding and different environmental priorities. In fiscal 2002, the United States spent $28 per capita on the

---

14. Reasons for not recommending the development of a factual record usually reflect shortcomings regarding requirements under Articles 14(1) and 14(2). Recommendations against a factual record were made in eight cases: *Quebec Hog Farms* (SEM-97-003), *Lake Chapala* (SEM-97-007), *Great Lakes* (SEM-98-003), *Cytrar I* (SEM-98-005), *Cytrar II* (SEM-01-001), *Mexico City Airport* (SEM-02-002), *Ontario Power Generation* (SEM-03-001), and *Cytrar III* (SEM-03-006).

15. *Coal-Fired Power Plants* (SEM-04-005) was filed on September 20, 2004, and *Crushed Gravel in Puerto Penasco* (SEM-005-001) was filed on January 12, 2005.

16. The Secretariat is considering whether to recommend a factual record for the *Lake Chapala II* (SEM-03-003) and *Quebec Automobiles* (SEM-04-007) submissions.

17. The Council approved factual records in the following cases: *Montreal Technoparc* (SEM-03-005), *Ontario Logging* (SEM-02-001), *Ontario Logging II* (SEM-04-006), *Pulp and Paper* (SEM-02-003), and *Tarahumara* (SEM-00-006). The Council has yet to approve the development of a factual record in the *Alca-Iztapalapa II* case (SEM-03-004).

environment, Canada spent $17, and Mexico $23.[18] Where the money is spent also differs markedly: In less-developed areas, environmental priorities are safe drinking water and basic infrastructures that provide minimum living standards. In more prosperous regions, where these basic services are provided, environmental initiatives focus on reclaiming damaged sites and saving flora and fauna.

Two concerns were raised during the NAFTA ratification process—the "downward harmonization" of US and Canadian environmental or public health standards and the creation of a "pollution haven" in Mexico. The evidence shows that neither of these fears has materialized.

United States and Canada

Since NAFTA was enacted, new health and environment-related laws—such as the Safe Drinking Water Act Amendments of 1996, the Food Quality Protection Act of 1996, and the Brownfields Revitalization Act of 2002—have been added to the US regulatory framework. The US Environmental Protection Agency (EPA) set several enforcement records in 1999: It collected $3.6 billion through enforcement actions and penalties for environmental cleanup, pollution control, and improved monitoring (up 80 percent from 1998) and received $166.7 million in civil penalties (up 60 percent from 1998), and it brought 3,945 civil, judicial, and administrative actions.[19]

However, environmentalists remain concerned about US environmental policy going forward for two reasons.[20] First, the proposed fiscal 2006 budget would cut the overall EPA funding by 5.6 percent to $7.6 billion.[21]

---

18. The figures were calculated by dividing environmental agencies' fiscal 2002 budgets in US dollars by estimated population. Data were obtained from www.inegi.gob.mx/, www.ec.gc.ca, and www.epa.gov.

19. See EPA, "1999 Enforcement Actions Under Title VI," www.epa.gov/ozone/enforce/enforce99.html (accessed February 2005). Since 1999, the EPA has not publicly released enforcement records. See www.epa.gov and "Dingell Criticizes EPA on Enforcement Slump," *Congress Daily*, January 31, 2003.

20. While no significant environmental legislation has been repealed in the United States, some environmentalists fear that policy initiatives tabled by the George W. Bush administration would weaken environmental safeguards. Recent proposals include opening the Arctic National Wildlife Reserve for oil and gas drilling and energy bill provisions that would exempt companies from the Clean Water Act. See Craig Welch, "For Good or Ill, Bush Clears Path for Energy Development," *Seattle Times*, September 26, 2004; Sierra Club, "George W. Bush and Clean Water," www.sierraclub.org/wwatch/cleanwater/index.asp, February 2005; and "Analysis: President Bush Promoting His Clear Skies Environmental Initiative," *NPR All Things Considered*, September 15, 2003.

21. Specifically, the proposed 2006 Clean Water State Revolving Fund would decrease from $1.35 billion in 2004 to $730 million in 2005. See Miguel Bustillo and Kenneth R. Weiss, "Bush Plan Could Drain Effort to Clean Up Waters," *Los Angeles Times*, February 9, 2005; and Felicity Barringer, "Clean Water Fund Facing Major Cuts," *New York Times*, February 8, 2005.

Second, there are questions about the enforcement of air and water quality standards. For example, in January 2004, the EPA proposed to modify, inter alia, rules issued under the Clean Air Act (1990) that regulate mercury and other toxic emissions from industrial sources. Under the Clear Skies initiative, power plants would be required to cut smog, soot, and mercury pollution by 70 percent by 2020—compared with the original Clean Air Act rules that require power plants to reduce their pollution by 90 percent by 2010. As of March 2005, however, the requisite legislation had not passed Congress.[22]

In its Action Plan for Innovation drafted in October 1999, the Office of Enforcement and Compliance Assurance outlined specific commitments that bolster the EPA's regulatory enforcement program. The Audit Policy facilitates compliance by providing incentives for companies to detect and disclose environmental violations. When companies volunteer such information to the EPA, it will waive or substantially reduce civil penalties by 75 to 100 percent (CEC 2001). Between 1997 and 2004, under the Audit Policy, the EPA settled about 600 cases for over 1,000 facilities, with reduced or no penalties levied on 969 of them (EPA 2004).

From an environmental perspective, NAFTA certainly encouraged Mexican production for export markets, but it did not shift export specialization toward more polluting sectors (Schatan 2000). An analysis of the composition of foreign direct investment (FDI) on a sectoral basis indicates that US FDI flows to Mexico in the post-NAFTA period declined in high pollution–incidence sectors such as chemicals and printed products.[23] Moreover, low pollution–incidence sectors, such as automotive products and services, received a growing share of FDI after NAFTA was ratified (Gallagher 2004a). Harmonization efforts also encourage a regionwide convergence toward higher levels of environmental standards that inhibit a regulatory "race to the bottom." In the electricity sector, moreover, NAFTA-associated processes are showing signs of positive outcomes. For example, the San Diego–based Sempra Energy recently built a power plant in Mexicali that meets neighboring California's pollution standards.[24]

---

22. In March 2005, the Clear Skies legislation failed on a 9-9 vote in the Senate Environment and Public Works Committee. Several EPA employees and environmental groups point toward the influence of utility lobbyists in shaping the Bush administration's mercury reduction proposal. New regulations issued under the Clean Water Act (1972) illustrate another attempt to modify existing environmental standards. In November 2004, the EPA issued proposals that would allow sewer operators to dump partially treated sewage into waterways. See Cousins, Perks, and Warren (2005) and National Wildlife Federation (2003), www.nrdc. org and www.nwf.org, respectively (accessed March 2005).

23. Kevin P. Gallagher (2004a) rejects the notion that Mexico became a pollution haven under NAFTA. In fact, employment in pollution-prone industries in the United States remained the same during the NAFTA era but actually declined in Mexico. See Kirton (1999).

24. Tim Weiner, "US Will Get Power, and Pollution, from Mexico," *New York Times*, September 17, 2002.

Canada's post-NAFTA environmental record has been less impressive in terms of regulatory activity. Quebec and Ontario adopted more permissive toxic waste disposal regulations to help local businesses compete, thereby giving an incentive for American industries to ship toxic waste to Canadian dump sites.[25] In 1998, almost one-third of all US hazardous wastes were shipped to a single facility in Sarnia, Ontario.[26] The number of environmental investigators employed by Environment Canada fell from 28 to 17 between 1995 and 1998 as a result of a 40 percent reduction in the agency's budget (BNA 2000). However, Canada's Budget 2005 commits spending of C$5 billion over five years in environmental initiatives.[27]

Budget cuts do not seem to have worsened environmental conditions across Canada. According to Environment Canada, Canadian environmental quality is improving: Air pollution levels are falling, and between 1995 and 2002, toxic chemical releases were reduced by 25 percent.[28] Moreover, according to the CEC, the Canadian government's efforts to reduce pollution have positively influenced companies such as Blount Canada Ltd., which transformed itself in 1998 from being the third largest emitter of trichloroethylene (TCE), a suspected carcinogen, to completely removing TCE from its plant.[29]

Mexico

A major environmental concern, especially in the United States, at the time of the NAFTA negotiations and in the run-up to congressional ratification, was the permissive character of Mexican environmental laws and particularly their weak enforcement. But Mexico's efforts to improve its

---

25. Enforcement of environmental standards in Quebec and Ontario was hindered by significant cuts in both provincial government budgets. We thank Scott Vaughan for clarifying this example, which draws heavily on written comments he provided to an earlier draft.

26. "Borderline Hazards: Controlling the Toxic Waste Trade," *Trio Newsletter of the NACEC* (spring 2002).

27. Two major examples of environmental investments outlined under Canada's Budget 2005 include about C$5 billion in green infrastructure projects and C$1 billion in the clean fund to fight climate change and smog. See BNA (2000), Environment Canada (2004), and "Government of Canada Highlights Budget 2005 Green Technology Investments," *Canada Newswire*, February 28, 2005.

28. While Environmental Defence Canada and the Canadian Environmental Law Association (CELA) report that overall chemical emissions jumped by 49 percent from 1995 to 2002, Environment Canada claims that sulfur dioxide emissions declined by 25 percent and carbon monoxide emissions declined by 19 percent over the same period. Jones, Griggs, and Fredricksen (2002). See also Kenneth Green, "Are We Losing the Fight Over Pollution?," op-ed, *The Fraser Institute*, December 22, 2004; and CELA and Environmental Defence Canada (2004).

29. Martin Mittelstaedt, "Ontario is Fifth Most-Polluted Area," *Globe and Mail*, July 21, 2001, A7.

environmental legislation started well before NAFTA was conceived. In 1988, the General Law of Ecological Equilibrium and Protection of the Environment (Ley General del Equilibrio Ecológico y la Protección al Ambiente, or LGEEPA) was approved, strengthening environmental regulation. Public environmental expenditures grew steadily, reaching almost $2 billion in 1991 (DiMento and Doughman 1998). After NAFTA entered into force, the Mexican government reorganized its administration of environmental issues in a new agency—the Environment and Natural Resources Secretariat (Secretaría de Medio Ambiente y Recursos Naturales, or SEMARNAT). In 1996, the LGEEPA was adapted to the growing environmental challenges by specifically establishing federal, state, and local jurisdiction over environmental matters. Major revisions included limiting disposal of hazardous waste to landfills only when recycling or secondary materials recovery is not technically or economically feasible and prohibiting the disposal of liquid hazardous waste in landfills (Jacott, Reed, and Winfield 2001).

In December 1998, Article 4 of the Mexican Constitution was amended to expand the scope of the LGEEPA by stipulating that "every person has the right to an environment suitable for his development and welfare." Greater decentralization was achieved in 1998 with the creation of a special line item of the budget for states and municipalities and again in 1999, when more autonomy was given to municipalities under Article 115 of the Constitution. Today, the official Mexican environmental norms are renewed and updated annually.

Environmental standards, however, do not ensure results unless they are accompanied by strong enforcement measures. The Mexican Federal Environmental Protection Agency (Procuraduría Federal de Protección al Ambiente, or PROFEPA) is charged with enforcement matters. In 1995, the Mexican government established an environmental auditing program to promote *voluntary* compliance; the program covers all public-sector industries as well as big private industrial groups. Through voluntary compliance, regulatory agencies can waive penalties and reduce inspections, provided that a regulated industry initiates environmental audits or pollution prevention to meet or exceed regulations. The PROFEPA completed almost 1,000 audits between 1995 and 1999. Almost 1,000 industries signed compliance action plans to correct environmental failures detected during that period. From 1995 to 1999, the 400 action plans entailed more than $800 million in environmental improvement expenditures in Mexico and cost an estimated $3.4 billion in environmental management (USTR 1997 and INEGI 2004a and 2004b).

Through its inspection program, the PROFEPA verifies compliance with environmental legislation. Over 1994–99, about 70,000 plants were inspected. Some 23 percent of the facilities complied with the legislation; 74 percent had minor irregularities; and 3 percent of the inspected plants had major environmental flaws. There seems to be little difference in the incidence of violations ascribed to *maquiladoras* compared with all national industrial companies (Jacott, Reed, and Winfield 2001).

In spite of improvements in Mexican environmental protection, numerous challenges remain. While big companies and public enterprises in Mexico have largely embraced the voluntary compliance program, 90 percent of Mexican firms are small and medium-sized companies. Many are financially strapped. Only 50 percent of medium-sized enterprises have wastewater treatment facilities, and most small firms lack environment-friendly equipment. The Mexican government provides some incentives to stimulate investment on environmental equipment, but the incentives have not had the hoped-for results, partly because of deficient marketing and partly because of the financial stress facing small companies.

Some commentators suggest that Mexico does not follow the "environmental Kuznets curve" (EKC) hypothesis since the modest rise in Mexican income per capita over the past decade has not led to a sharp reduction in environmental pollution. According to the EKC hypothesis, economic growth goes hand in hand with environmental degradation at low income levels; however, as income levels rise and reach a "turning point," public demand for environmental protection becomes sufficiently strong that environmental quality begins to improve. Put another way, environmental quality becomes a luxury good at higher levels of income. At the threshold where further income increases yield environmental improvement, the income elasticity of environmental demand can be said to be greater than one (Yandle, Bhattarai, and Vijayaraghavan 2004).

Grossman and Krueger (1991) were the first to model the relationship between environmental quality and economic growth. They estimated that the turning point for sulfur dioxide emissions ranges from $4,000 to $5,000 GDP per capita measured in 1985 US dollars. This is equivalent to about $6,700 to $8,450 GDP per capita in 2003 US dollars. Turning-point estimates in subsequent EKC studies range from $6,700 GDP per capita (in 2003 US dollars) to $28,100 GDP per capita (in 2003 US dollars), depending on the pollutant, the time period, and the countries covered (Yandle, Bhattarai, and Vijayaraghavan 2004). The heterogeneity of results demonstrates that no single "turning point" relationship fits all pollutants for all countries and time periods.[30] At best, EKC studies only roughly describe the relationship between environmental change and income growth.[31]

Given the wide range of EKC turning points and Mexico's current level of income (about $6,500 GDP per capita), it is not obvious that Mexico

30. In fact, according to Zarzoso and Bengochea-Morancho (2003), the relationship between sulfur dioxide emissions and income is not consistent with the EKC hypothesis. They use a panel dataset of 19 Latin American and Caribbean countries, including Mexico, during 1975–98.

31. Recent EKC studies dispute the "pollution haven" hypothesis and suggest that more intense trade activities actually lead to lower domestic emissions. According to Cole (2003), expanding trade correlates with lower sulfur dioxide emissions. See also Yandle, Bhattarai, and Vijayaraghavan (2004).

should be on the downward path.[32] Nevertheless, based on the original Grossman-Krueger estimate that the upper bound of the turning point is $5,000 GDP per capita (measured in 1985 dollars), some commentators fault Mexico for not behaving according to the EKC hypothesis.[33] According to Gallagher (2004a, 2004b), while "Mexico has passed the theoretical turning point of $5,000 GDP per capita," environmental degradation in Mexico "overwhelmed any benefits from trade-led economic growth." Gallagher based his assertion on a recent Instituto Nacional de Estadística, Geografía e Informática (INEGI 2004b) study that the financial cost of environmental degradation was about $36 billion per year during the late 1990s, while the benefits of economic growth were about $14 billion per year during the same period.[34]

However, Gallagher compares apples with oranges. According to INEGI's calculations, environmental costs are slowly declining as a percent of GDP. Costs were estimated at 10.8 percent in 1997 (the first year of INEGI's calculations) and fell to 10 percent in 2002. There is no indication, in INEGI's calculations or elsewhere, that *higher* Mexican GDP led to a *rising* share of environmental costs. The $36 billion cost figure cited by Gallagher is essentially the *inherited* pre-NAFTA level of environmental degradation experienced in Mexico. Based on INEGI statistics—which measure average rather than marginal relationships—the strongest claim that an environmentalist such as Gallagher might make is that when Mexican GDP increases by $14 billion annually, about 10 percent of the measured growth, or $1.4 billion annually, is offset by higher environmental costs. This is a far cry from the complaint that Mexican economic growth is a mirage, because it has been swamped by environmental costs.

Returning to basics, the EKC hypothesis is no more than a statistical assertion about the strength of market forces for and against pollution at different levels of income. The object of environmental regulation is to reinforce whatever market forces may exist to curtail pollution. Whether or not an EKC "turning point" describes contemporary Mexico, greater public efforts can certainly reduce the extent of environmental degradation that characterizes Mexican urban areas.

The US-Mexico Border

For over 30 years, the border area has undergone dramatic growth in population and industrialization. Unfortunately, the region's infrastructure

---

32. GDP per capita is in US dollars at current prices. Data are based on IMF *World Economic Outlook Database* 2005.

33. We thank Frank Loy and Paul Joffe for drawing our attention to this debate.

34. Measuring the costs of environmental deterioration is a difficult task. For details of the methodology used, see INEGI (2004b).

has not kept pace, leading to inadequate facilities for water supply, sewage treatment, and hazardous and solid waste disposal.

The problems on the Mexican side of the border result primarily from inadequate municipal finance and inadequate investment in environmental infrastructure. But an array of artificial financial constraints hobble Mexican municipalities. They depend on revenue-sharing from the federal and state governments to finance infrastructure projects. The revenue available to most communities is uncertain, because it depends on allocations made annually by legislative decree. Municipalities cannot raise capital outside the domestic market, since the Mexican Constitution prohibits states and municipalities from borrowing in foreign currencies or from foreign creditors.

As an alternative, communities can turn to Mexico's National Bank of Public Works and Services for environmental infrastructure project loans. However, most communities cannot reliably repay the principal and interest because their regular tax receipts are meager. Property taxes tend to be very low and poorly collected, while the value added tax paid on purchases of goods and services is collected and administered by the central government in Mexico City. Only 3 percent of the taxes that the Mexican federal government collects directly returns to the municipalities. In sum, dependence on the federal government, limited fiscal authority, and the absence of a civil service tradition (administrative staff turns over with every change of government) all contribute to impede progress on municipal environmental projects.

By comparison, US border municipalities have better environmental infrastructure. Property and sales tax payments on the US side of the border contribute substantially to the tax base of local communities, and these tax revenues are used to fund basic infrastructure. Local governments in the United States can also raise funds for infrastructure by issuing bonds. Civil service traditions generally provide for continuity of municipal administrators, ensuring repayment and keeping financing costs low.

The municipal finances of Tijuana and San Diego illustrate the disparity in resources available to local governments on opposite sides of the border. Tijuana's 2002 municipal revenue was $196 million (including $73 million from the federal government) to service a population of 1.2 million. In 2000, San Diego County's municipal revenue was $3 billion (including $74 million from the federal government and $1.7 billion from the state government) to service a population of 2.8 million. In other words, on a per capita basis, San Diego's municipal resources were 6.6 times as large as Tijuana's.

Another twin-cities comparison illustrates the same point: El Paso (population of 0.7 million) and Juárez (population of 1.2 million). El Paso's revenue was $331 million in 2000 (including $80 million from the federal government). On the Mexican side of the border, the revenue of the municipality of Juárez was $159 million in 2002 ($43 million from the federal

Table 3.1   Growth of cities near the US-Mexico border

City	State	Population 1990	1995	2000	Growth, 1990–2000 (percent)
Mexico					
Ciudad Juárez	Chihuahua	798,499	1,011,786	1,218,817	52.6
Tijuana	Baja California	747,381	991,592	1,210,820	62.0
Nuevo Laredo	Tamaulipas	219,468	275,060	310,915	41.7
United States					
El Paso	Texas	595,350	654,250	682,111	14.6
San Diego	California	2,512,365	2,623,697	2,824,809	12.4
Laredo	Texas	134,430	167,466	194,868	45.0

Sources: INEGI (2004a, 2004b), BEA (2004).

government). On a per capita basis, El Paso had 3.6 times the resources of Juárez.[35]

The growth of twin-plant activity on the border has contributed to environmental strains. Maquiladora incentives (favorable tariff and tax treatment) were first established in 1965 to attract foreign investment and provide employment for Mexican workers in the aftermath of the US *bracero* program. The maquiladora program succeeded especially in the border region. But the industrial boom was not accompanied by adequate infrastructure investments to handle industrial wastes and residues or by sewage treatment plants to accommodate the rapidly expanding border population. In 1997, Mexico's National Water Commission estimated that only 34 percent of collected wastewater was treated. Deplorable environmental conditions are the consequence.

Table 3.1 shows the growth of three pairs of twin cities between 1990 and 2000. All six cities grew faster than their respective national averages during this decade. Both sides of the border at Laredo have been growing at about the same rate—in excess of 40 percent over ten years. However, Tijuana and Juárez have grown much faster (62 and 53 percent, respectively) than their US counterparts, San Diego and El Paso (12 and 15 percent, respectively). The growth in population puts stress on ecosystems, but the fact that the population growth is concentrated on the southern side of the border, where fewer resources are devoted to environmental protection, makes the situation worse.

Despite regulatory and enforcement efforts, the maquiladora industry still poses a major environmental challenge. The number of maquiladora plants has increased by about 30 percent since the launch of NAFTA, from

---

35. El Paso County and San Diego County revenue from 1999 to 2000, US Census Bureau Government Finances 1999–2000 Report, www.census.gov/govs/estimate/00allpub.pdf. Municipal revenue information for Tijuana and Juárez from INEGI's Sistema Municipal de Bases de Datos (SIMBAD) program, www.inegi.gob.mx.

2,157 in January 1994 to about 2,817 in May 2005, providing jobs to almost 1.2 million workers (May 2005) and accounting for 46 percent of Mexico's total exports.[36]

The maquiladora boom is stressing communities along the border, which find themselves struggling for tax money to pay for roads, schools, electricity, and sewage systems. Tax revenues from the maquiladoras flow to the Mexican federal treasury. Even if all maquiladora taxes were returned to the states and municipalities, local governments would still face a revenue shortfall. A long-term solution requires that Mexican states and municipalities have real authority to collect and spend property taxes and infrastructure fees.

Hazardous waste generated by many maquiladora plants is a persistent and troublesome problem. The Mexican National Ecology Institute estimated that, in 1997, over 20 percent of the hazardous waste generated in Mexico came from maquiladora industries. Under the La Paz Agreement (Article XI, Annex III), "hazardous waste generated in the processes of economic production . . . for which raw materials were utilized and temporarily admitted, shall continue to be readmitted by the country of origin of the raw materials in accordance with applicable national policies, laws, and regulations." In other words, the United States must admit hazardous waste that maquiladoras generate from US raw materials; however, Mexico can instead choose to dispose of the waste locally. The La Paz Agreement requires the parties to notify one another about transboundary shipments of hazardous substances. Under Article III of the agreement, the country importing hazardous waste can regulate the method of shipment and disposal. As a policy matter, Mexican waste management laws require that wastes produced from US materials be returned to the United States for treatment or disposal. In other words, Mexico has generally required that hazardous waste from maquiladoras be shipped back to the United States. With the rapid growth of maquiladoras, there has been a concomitant increase in shipments to US disposal facilities. But the La Paz system has many shortcomings, as we describe below.

At NAFTA's launch, the Instituto Nacional de Ecología (INE) estimated only 1 million out of 8 million tons of hazardous waste generated in 1994 were adequately controlled. The EPA implemented a new hazardous waste tracking program known as HAZTRAKS in 1993 to track the amount of hazardous waste imported into the United States from Mexico and to regulate associated environmental violations. Mexico adopted a similar system, known as Sistema de Rastreo de Residuos Peligrosos. The HAZTRAKS database covers approximately 800 companies, or about 40 percent of all maquiladoras located in border states that shipped either

---

36. Based on the INEGI Banco de Información Económica (BIE) database, dgcnesyp.inegi. gob.mx/cgi-win/bdieintsi.exe/NIVJ10000100020001#ARBOL (accessed on August 10, 2005).

hazardous or nonhazardous waste from Mexico to the United States during 1997.[37] Nevertheless, reporting of returned hazardous waste slipped from 65 percent of maquiladoras in 1996 to 38 percent in 1998–99 (Varady, Lankao, and Hankins 2001). There are numerous "leakages" from the disposal and reporting systems: illegal dumping in the desert outskirts of Juárez, transportation spills, and abandoned factories—all followed or preceded by nonreporting.

The absence of environmental infrastructure provides economic incentives to dump illegally.[38] For example, in 1995 the Texas Natural Resource Conservation Commission surveyed 32 counties along the US-Mexico border and found a total of 1,247 illegal dump sites and estimated there were another 20,000 (Reed, Jacott, and Villamar 2000). According to a National Law Center for Inter-American Free Trade study, Mexico has only two fully operational treatment, storage, and disposal facilities (Reed 1998). Many maquiladoras are unwilling to pay the costs of legal dumping in a market of few suppliers. The more costly it is to comply with US environmental laws, the more incentives there are to illegally dump hazardous waste within Mexico. To make matters worse, a great deal of waste, hazardous and otherwise, is exported from the United States to Mexico.[39]

The result is numerous contaminated sites. Inadequate funding hinders cleanup of these sites. Superfund legislation does not cross the Rio Grande, and US public funds are not available to help dispose of toxic materials within Mexico. The problem exists throughout Mexico, not just along the border.[40] However, since 1994, private investment in hazardous waste collection, storage, and management facilities has sharply increased (NADBank 2002). Mexican authorities are also responding to the lack of available landfills by establishing a series of Integrated Centers for Handling, Recycling, and Disposal of Hazardous Waste (CIMARIs). To resolve waste management problems, CIMARIs work jointly with INE-approved companies that provide technology for waste treatment and recycling. By 1998, eight Mexican companies and their US partners had helped establish CIMARIs (Reed, Jacott, and Villamar 2000; Jacott, Reed, and Winfield 2001).

---

37. In 1997, INE received about 10,000 hazardous waste reports, covering about 10 percent of all companies, though accounting for about 30 percent of the estimated waste. See www.ine.gob.mx.

38. The World Bank (1994) noted that an estimated 80 percent of hazardous waste is not repatriated but remains stored on-site or is illegally disposed of in Mexico.

39. INE reports that the amount of waste flowing from the United States to Mexico is 20 to 30 times greater than the amount shipped from Mexico to the United States. See Reed (1998).

40. However, the Dirección de Residuos Sólidos Municipales reported the number of legal disposal sites was 76 in 2000. Hazardous waste disposal statistics reported in the next paragraph from INEGI, www.inegi.gob.mx.

Integrated Environmental Plan for the Border Region

For over a century, US and Mexican authorities have recognized the importance of cross-border environmental cooperation. In 1889, a bilateral treaty created the International Boundary Commission. In 1944, the Water Treaty converted the commission to the International Boundary and Water Commission. In 1983, the US and Mexican governments adopted a broader agenda with the signing of the Agreement for the Protection and Improvement of the Environment in the Border Area (the La Paz Agreement). During the course of NAFTA negotiations, the EPA and its Mexican counterpart (then known as SEDUE) developed an integrated environmental plan for the border region calling for the establishment of six working groups on water, air, solid waste, pollution prevention, contingency planning and emergency response, and cooperative enforcement and compliance. In 1996, the plan was updated and expanded, becoming the Border XXI Program.

Under the Border XXI Program, the United States and Mexico established work groups to implement specific objectives for border cleanup through infrastructure development and decentralized environmental management. Considerable effort has been expended on negotiating agreements with border states and tribes. The "Coordination Principles" agreement in May 1999, which was signed by all 10 border-state environmental agencies, together with EPA and SEMARNAT at the federal level, formalized binational interagency coordination. Environmental compliance was further institutionalized by the "Seven Principles" public-private agreement between the US-Mexico Chamber of Commerce on the one hand and BECC, EPA, and SEMARNAT on the other.

NAFTA tried to advance recovery efforts at the US-Mexican border by creating the NADBank and the BECC. These institutions are mandated to develop, certify, and finance environmental infrastructure projects along the US-Mexico border area. These specialized agencies are now examined in greater detail.

Border Environmental Cooperation Commission

The BECC provides technical assistance to border communities and certifies projects for consideration for NADBank finance. It focuses on water supply, wastewater treatment, and solid waste disposal. Under its technical assistance program, the BECC helps communities prepare their project proposals for certification. By December 2004, the BECC had authorized $30.3 million in technical assistance funds for 228 infrastructure projects in 131 communities (35 percent of the funds went to Mexican communities and 65 percent to US communities). Most of the funding was devoted to water and wastewater projects and a lesser amount to solid waste projects. In 2004, the BECC had certified 105 infrastructure projects that ultimately will entail total estimated expenditure of $2.2 billion. Of these projects, 36 are located in Mexico and 69 in the United States; they will benefit over 8 million border residents (NADBank-BECC 2004).

North American Development Bank

NADBank provides managerial assistance, direct loans, and loan guarantees that facilitate additional project finance from other lenders for BECC-certified environmental infrastructure projects. In addition, NADBank administers some EPA grant resources. Mexico and the United States contribute equally to NADBank resources. Both countries have fully authorized their $1.5 billion capital commitments. Of NADBank's $3 billion in capital, 15 percent ($450 million) consists of actual cash; the remaining $2.55 billion takes the form of callable capital—cash that the governments must provide to NADBank to meet debt obligations or guarantees, if required.[41]

To build capacity among border communities, the EPA, NADBank, and the World Bank have funded technical assistance to help state and local officials enforce environmental monitoring. Through NADBank's Border Environment Infrastructure Fund (BEIF), the EPA contributed an initial $170 million for water and wastewater infrastructure projects. By December 2004, $516.2 million in BEIF grant funds had been used for 54 construction and transition assistance projects in the poorest communities (NADBank-BECC 2004). NADBank also finances environmental projects through its own Loan and Guaranty Program and Solid Waste Environmental Program (SWEP) funds.

While NADBank's role as an investment banker is necessary to facilitate financing, its rates are unaffordable for smaller US communities with limited tax bases. Insufficient revenues to support financing also hinder Mexican border communities. Between 1994 and 2004, NADBank had committed to 29 projects in Mexico totaling up to $136 million.[42] In the early years, Mexican communities faced peso interest rates between 26 and 27 percent for 15-year NADBank loans.[43] Large US communities

---

41. As of March 2004, NADBank had received $348.8 million in paid-in capital and $1.976 billion in callable capital, representing 77.5 percent of its total subscribed capital. See www. nadbank.org/english/general/general_frame.htm (accessed on April 22, 2005), NADBank-BECC (2004), and US Treasury (2005).

42. Based on total financing disbursed for NADBank projects in Mexico as of December 2004. NADBank disbursed about $131 million for US projects. While 29 out of 36 projects in Mexico had total financing disbursed, the status of the remaining seven projects is unclear. NADBank does not explain these projects or their financing status. See NADBank-BECC (2004).

43. *Financial Times* Special Report, February 2001. By comparison, in 1999, the bank had two loans to US communities with variable rates ranging between 5.15 and 7.38 percent. The bank demanded higher rates from Mexican communities to cover its exposure to currency conversion risk and various default factors. US General Accounting Office Report to Congressional Requesters, "U.S.-Mexico Border: Despite Some Progress, Environmental Infrastructure Challenges Remain" (March 2000). See David Hendricks, "NADBank Is Doing More Good, Now That It's Allowed To," *San Antonio Express-News*, October 1, 2003.

often did not apply for NADBank loans as they found more attractive alternatives through various sources, including state revolving funds and municipal bonds. There is, however, growing momentum in NADBank-financed activities.[44] In August 2003, for example, NADBank provided a $28 million loan to pave roads in Baja border cities and is expected to lend up to $487 million for similar projects.

In the meantime, many Mexican border communities have sought infrastructure financing from other sources. State officials in Baja California, for example, negotiated a $240 million loan agreement with Japan's Financial Overseas Economic Development Fund, at rates lower than NADBank's, to help finance wastewater treatment and sewer improvement projects in Tijuana and Mexicali. NADBank still plays a role, though smaller than originally envisaged. For example, the bank created an $80 million water conservation fund to finance irrigation district projects along the Rio Grande.[45] The bank also approved $11.8 million in loans and grants for three small projects: a wastewater facility in Ciudad Acuña, a sanitary landfill in San Luis Rio Colorado, Mexico, and wastewater system improvements in Fabens, near El Paso.

To address criticisms that NADBank offers higher-cost financing in comparison with municipal bonds or state revolving funds, BECC-certified environmental projects are directly financed by the Loan and Guaranty Program, which is made more attractive through the Low Interest Rate Lending Facility (LIRLF) adopted in 2002. By December 2004, NADBank had authorized 24 Loan & Guaranty Program loans with a face value of $103.9 million. The World Bank's Programa Ambiental de la Frontera Norte de Mexico (PAFN) covering six Mexican border states has also provided funding to advance the Border XXI Program's goals.

Summing up, as of December 2004, NADBank has approved $697 million in loans and grants for 85 infrastructure projects. Most of the money (about $516 million) is in the form of grants; NADBank directly loaned only about $24 million.[46] In total, these 85 projects are expected to cost

---

44. In March 2005, Senator Hutchison (R-TX) introduced legislation to allow NADBank to guarantee tax-exempt bonds. Sponsors of the legislation argue that it would help NADBank leverage capital, help smaller communities to sell debt, and reduce borrowing costs. See Emily Newman, "Federal Guarantees: Bill Would Let NADBank Back Tax-Exempts," *The Bond Buyer*, March 28, 2005; and David Hendricks, "Border Would Benefit Under NADBank Legislation," *San Antonio Express*, March 23, 2005.

45. David McLemore, "New $80 Million Conservation Fund May Ease Border Dispute Over Water," *Dallas Morning News*, August 21, 2002.

46. According to John B. Taylor, US undersecretary of the Treasury, NADBank has directly loaned just $23.5 million in low-interest loans to finance projects since 1996 and disbursed only $11 million of that money, despite having a lending capacity of $2.7 billion. The majority of the approved $697 million, about 74 percent or $516 million, is in the form of grant funds from the NADBank Border Environment Infrastructure Fund. See Taylor (2002). See also Miramontes (2002) and NADBank-BECC (2004).

$2.3 billion (NADBank-BECC 2004). Investment in Mexico is scheduled to be around 57 percent of the projected $2.3 billion expenditure, despite the fact that environmental conditions are much worse on the Mexican side of the border.

Recognizing this imbalance, NADBank established a financial institution in Mexico, the Corporación Financiera de América del Norte (COFIDAN), to supplement its normal financing channels and facilitate lending to Mexican public institutions. As mentioned earlier, the Mexican Constitution contains a provision that prohibits Mexican states and municipalities from borrowing from foreign entities or in foreign currencies. With the creation of COFIDAN, NADBank can lend directly to municipalities. COFIDAN has made 12 loans to Mexican public entities (totaling $56.3 million) (NADBank-BECC 2002). To repeat an earlier point, however, the basic problem is the capacity to repay, which is severely constrained by the limited taxing authority of Mexican municipalities.

If the indicated relationship between funds granted, loaned, or guaranteed by NADBank and the resulting expenditure on infrastructure is maintained ($1 lent = $3.30 investment), NADBank and its program affiliates would have to grant, lend, or guarantee about $2.42 billion to achieve the $8 billion investment in infrastructure suggested in 1993 as minimally necessary for the recovery of the border region (Hufbauer and Schott 1993). NADBank activity, including funds administered for the EPA, has fallen well short of this level. Meanwhile, municipalities on the Mexican side have not had the resources for local cleanup programs. In 1995, the total population along the border was 10.6 million. In 2000, the estimated population in the border region was about 12 million. Border population is expected to increase to about 20 million by 2020. Allowing just for larger population, the minimal level of environmental cleanup expenditure today is substantially greater than it was a decade ago.

Three problems are contributing to the slow pace of environmental recovery at the border. First, no comprehensive assessments have been made of required environmental outlays. In other words, political leaders do not have reliable targets to shoot at. Second, the Mexican tax system fails to capture even a modest fraction of the spiraling property values to improve public infrastructure. And third, without fiscal autonomy, many Mexican border communities are too poor to finance environmental projects.

In addition to its financing mission, NADBank carries out other environmental activities. NADBank's Institutional Development Cooperation Program (IDP) provides assistance for studies that enhance the management of public utilities and training for utility managers and staff. The goal is to ensure the long-term viability of infrastructure projects. The IDP became fully operational in the spring of 1997 and is currently involved in 102 projects assisting 68 communities. The IDP projects are funded with NADBank earnings, and the annual budget more than doubled from $2 million in August 1997 to $5 million in 2004 (NADBank-BECC 2004).

NADBank managers are pushing for an expanded mandate to increase the bank's lending capacity. The proposals would make funds available for a greater range of environmental projects. At present, NADBank projects have to be related to water, wastewater treatment, and solid waste; the proposals would add new sectors to the list. These proposals also seek to cover a wider geographic area, expanding NADBank coverage from 100 to 300 kilometers north and south of the US-Mexico border. Finally, they would enlarge financial subsidies by providing more grants and doubling NADBank's low interest rate lending capacity for the poorest communities.

The Mexican and US governments have not yet agreed on the mandate change. Mexican President Vicente Fox has suggested that the capital base of NADBank be expanded from its present $3 billion to at least $10 billion, but in addition to border programs he wants to help fund more Mexican projects beyond the border region. Rather than allocating additional funding to NADBank, the George W. Bush administration was initially attracted to US Treasury Department proposals to merge the BECC and NADBank under a single institution in late 2001. However, facing opposition against the merger, in March 2002, Presidents Fox and Bush finally agreed to implement most initiatives outlined in a bipartisan bill sponsored by US Congressman Charlie Gonzalez (D-TX). Some of the bill's proposals to reform the BECC and NADBank include (1) launching a third-party audit of both NADBank and the BECC to identify structural efficiencies; (2) increasing the US contribution to BEIF consistent with NADBank's five-year outlook; (3) creating a single board of directors for NADBank and the BECC; and (4) increasing the capital devoted to NADBank's LIRF (which offers lower interest rates for border environmental projects).[47]

Conclusions and Recommendations

In determining whether NAFTA has improved or damaged the North American environment, it is critical to define the relevant baseline for comparison. Most environmentalists believe that conditions have deteriorated, partly because tougher environmental clauses were not built into the agreement. Most negotiators disagree: The side agreements the Clinton administration crafted in 1993 stretched the patience not only of Mexico and Canada but also of Republicans in the US Congress. In our view, the relevant counterfactual was not tougher provisions, but no NAFTA. Without NAFTA, the Mexican government would have had less incentive to pass environmental legislation or to improve its enforcement efforts,

---

47. Specifically, Presidents Bush and Fox agreed to create a $50 million grant program funded by NADBank's paid-in capital. See US Department of Treasury press release, NADBank fiscal 2002; Congressman Gonzalez press release, March 2002; and "Senate Passes Sweeping NADBank Reform,"*States News Service*, March 12, 2004.

and the achievements, modest though they are, of the CEC, NADBank, and BECC would not exist.

Despite the positive environmental incentives of NAFTA and the achievements of the environmental institutions created by the side agreements, NAFTA's environmental record affords ample room for improvement. Toward this end, we offer several recommendations.[48]

With Regard to the NAFTA Environmental Provisions

NAFTA countries should highlight the success of Chapters 7B and 9. These chapters demonstrate that free trade need not undermine appropriate regulatory authority and sovereignty. The fact that no claims have been litigated under these provisions shows that NAFTA countries recognize each other's right to establish appropriate levels of protection.

With Regard to NAAEC

The NAAEC was the first comprehensive environmental cooperation agreement associated with a trade agreement. However, it has two major shortcomings. First, the "nonenforcement" mechanism contained in Articles 22–36 of the NAAEC is disappointing. It deceives those who identified this mechanism with the "teeth" of the side agreement, and it continues to irritate Canadians and Mexicans, who begrudgingly consented to these procedures.[49] Indeed, the Canadians did not fully consent. This mechanism should be revised; its design should be changed to make it more functional. The potential withdrawal of NAFTA benefits should be replaced with civil fines, which would avoid differential penalties between Mexico and Canada and forestall the interruption of trade in sectors unrelated to the environmental practices in question.

Second, NAFTA governments have not given adequate support to the institution created to carry out the side agreement's goals—the CEC. In addition, CEC performance would benefit from a more focused agenda. Since its creation in 1994, the CEC has tried to be all things to all people—on a modest annual budget of $9 million. It has played too many roles to be truly effective in any of them: environmental information center, developer and controller of environmental indicators, promoter of environmen-

---

48. Chapter 4 on dispute settlement addresses the thorny issue of Chapter 11 investor-state disputes.

49. During NAFTA side-letter negotiations, the Mexican Ministry of Economy viewed environmental obligations as a potential threat to market liberalization. The ministry feared that environmental standards would be used for US protectionist purposes, rather than a genuine attempt to improve the environment. According to this view, Mexico's signature on the NAAEC was a "big mistake." See Deere and Esty (2002).

tal awareness and clean technology, producer of environmental reports, founder of environmental community projects, and arbiter of disputes. While the CEC launched an alphabet soup of initiatives (Trade and Environment, Strategic Plan, NABCI, SCCC, and NAGPI), the CEC has also been a model for openness and transparency. In an effort to build intergovernmental cooperation, the CEC could strengthen its focus on substandard environmental conditions that are closely linked to trade expansion and government inaction.[50]

If NAFTA members are serious about addressing common environmental problems, they will devote much greater ministerial attention to the CEC and significantly boost its minuscule budget. That said, foreseeable budget constraints should compel the CEC to focus its activities. With existing and foreseeable resources, the CEC can do two things well: (1) It can make use of the investigatory powers of Articles 13–15 to draw attention to environmental problems that are closely connected to North American trade; and (2) it can become a reputable source of North American environmental data to facilitate better policymaking.

Investigatory Powers

The CEC should produce reports under Articles 13–15 that shed light on specific environmental problems and lagging environmental enforcement where there is a North American trade connection. Unlike the past, the CEC should be authorized to propose solutions and issue recommendations that would encourage cooperative initiatives and prod enforcement of existing environmental laws in NAFTA countries. Article 13 reports, together with the factual records resulting from Article 14 citizen submissions, have had some positive results. In June 2002, the CEC released its multiyear Article 13 report on electricity restructuring, which addressed complex issues and reflected extensive public input. As a result, the CEC electricity report garnered significant attention from policymakers in Europe and elsewhere for both the content and process.[51] However, since 1995, only four Article 13 reports have been developed, and only 10 out of 50 citizen submissions have led to the development of factual records (see appendix table 3A.1). Against this background, NAFTA citizens have come to the disappointing but realistic conclusion that a trip to the CEC will not generate enough policy payoff to justify the time and energy required.

A revised and revived citizen submission process of the NAAEC should include provisions to ensure a more expeditious process. Furthermore, it

---

50. Some scholars note that OECD working groups for environmental enforcement regularly reference the CEC *Taking Stock 2001* report, which analyzed North American data to identify opportunities for pollution reduction. See CEC (2004a).

51. We thank Scott Vaughan for providing this example, which draws heavily on written comments he provided to an earlier draft. See CEC (2002).

should *require* the CEC to determine whether nonenforcement has occurred and to offer appropriate recommendations.

Environmental Data

The CEC should become the premier source of "hard" environmental data comparing levels and trends in Canada, Mexico, and the United States. As the recent CEC ten-year review suggests, the CEC could create a web-based North American Clearinghouse on Trade and Environment Linkages (CEC 2004b). To do so, it needs to refocus its publication style from long descriptive reports to comparative statistics modeled on the OECD's *Economic Outlook* and the IMF's *World Economic Outlook.* In its first five years, the CEC wrestled with heterogeneous environmental indicators and poor data collected in the three countries. Building on its prior work, the CEC should now be able to provide comparable indicators for the three countries, saving NAFTA citizens the trouble of searching for "hard" information hidden in discursive reports.

To the extent that data gaps remain, the CEC should invest in the development of useful and reliable indicators and data.[52] With the publication of clear and concise reports, the CEC would establish a reputation for providing useful information to interested citizens. In addition, readily available and highly regarded reports would allow the CEC to use the "public shame factor" to pressure governments to improve their environmental performance.

One of the major obstacles to efficient management of the North American environment has been the absence of comprehensive triennial assessments of environmental conditions in Canada, Mexico, and the United States, especially along the border. The absence of consistent environmental indicators makes it difficult to evaluate the environmental impact of NAFTA and to set priorities for public spending. We recommend the publication of a triennial North American environmental "report card" (in the style of the Fraser Institute's *Environmental Indicators—Critical Issues Bulletin*) and the organization of a public annual conference on the state of the environment in North America. The three NAFTA governments should provide funding for high-quality independent environmental analysis to be presented in these annual conferences. Similarly, the CEC, the BECC, and NADBank should take this opportunity to report on their activities, call attention to particular environmental problems, and present evaluation reports commissioned from independent consultants.

---

52. An example of a successful index that measures environmental sustainability is the Environmental Sustainability Index (ESI), created by the Yale Center for Environmental Law and Policy. ESI was released at the World Economic Forum in January 2005. Information about ESI is available at www.yale.edu/esi/ (accessed in March 2005).

With Regard to the US-Mexican Border

NADBank and the BECC have launched several projects to address the difficult environmental problems on the US-Mexico border. In addition, they provide an umbrella for interagency meetings between US and Mexican environmental agencies. As a result, collaboration has improved between local, national, and international agencies. Nevertheless, border conditions are bad and in some respects may be getting worse. NADBank and the BECC should assess what needs to be done in border communities to reach environmental levels comparable to those in nearby US cities and interior Mexican cities that are known for good environmental practices. As an example, NADBank and the BECC could encourage environmental enforcement by establishing and funding mechanisms for transferring environmental technology to Mexico.[53]

NADBank and the BECC should also promote financing mechanisms to ensure that worthwhile projects are implemented over the next decade. For NADBank to respond effectively to the needs of the border area, it should first assess the extent of the problem, examining each environmental problem in turn. Costs should be measured against two standards of environmental quality: representative nonborder communities in the United States and in Mexico. These independent assessments of the existing environmental problems, work programs necessary for recovery, and estimates of the associated costs required to provide cleanup and infrastructure in these border communities would achieve several goals. They would give the public a better appreciation of the price tag, help establish the priorities, and focus attention on finding new revenue sources.

In that regard, NADBank should offer appropriate financing (backed by environmental assessment districts and user fees) for hazardous waste sites in Mexico—near the plants that actually generate the waste. While the La Paz Agreement authorizes back-haul shipments of waste to the United States, there has never been much economic logic to this disposal system. The shipments are expensive and usually involve the transfer of dangerous cargo from one truck to another at the border. All too often, shippers simply dump their loads en route to US hazardous waste sites. Locating hazardous waste sites within Mexico—accompanied by much tighter surveillance systems—will reduce the incidence of opportunistic dumping in the Mexican desert.

As noted earlier, NADBank provides about one-fourth of the funding for infrastructure projects. The rest of the funding comes from international institutions and federal, state, and local governments. Hence border infrastructure projects must compete with other important goals for scarce

---

53. We thank Paul Joffe for providing the example in this paragraph, which draws heavily on written comments he provided to an earlier draft. See Joffe and Caldwell (2003).

public funds. However, there should be no shortage of funding. The border area is booming, and property values are soaring. Within this thriving economy, there are adequate resources to pay for the environment. To tackle the funding problem, NADBank and the BECC should create environmental assessment districts along the border region. These local institutions should be funded with environmental fees assessed on industries and housing in the area. The "polluter pays" principle should govern the setting of fees. Under the "polluter pays" principle, the direct link between the environmental impact of an industry or other local activity (such as operating old, polluting cars) would provide a disincentive to pollute and in turn would reduce future environmental problems. For activities that cannot be directly charged through a fee system, the assessment districts should rely on property taxes. Local taxes would both provide additional funding and make communities and industries more environmentally aware.[54]

Summing Up

In conclusion, the achievements of NADBank and the BECC fall well short of the aspirations of the environmental community. To improve the North American environment, especially at the US-Mexico border, these institutions, along with the CEC, should be strengthened in the next phase of NAFTA. The NAAEC was created in the context of a trade agreement to address environmental issues related to NAFTA. To gain public support for the trade agreement, US officials sold the environmental side agreement as the panacea for the environmental problems of North America. Political rhetoric grossly inflated expectations about the potential achievements, and the actual accomplishments were almost destined to disappoint.

The environmental problems of North America were not, at their core, the result of NAFTA, nor was the NAAEC devised to address all of them. It is difficult to quantify what amount of environmental deterioration is a direct consequence of increased trade. Furthermore, even if NAFTA is the main force, it is certainly not the sole driver of North American trade expansion.

Putting these linkages aside, significant improvements can be made to get better results from NAFTA's environmental institutions. The way for-

---

54. Recent World Bank studies point in this direction. Research found that traditional regulation relying on fines, plant shutdowns, prison sentences, and the like is not always successful because it requires strong enforcement mechanisms—monitoring, analysis, legal proceedings, and so on. All these mechanisms are subject to corrupt administration. The World Bank suggests that pollution charges (taxes) are more efficient than traditional penalties in providing the right incentives to reduce polluting activities. See World Bank (1999).

ward is to establish a systematic program that assesses gaps in the environmental performance of individual NAFTA member countries.[55] If an environmental "vision" can then be broadly agreed on, the stage will be set to clarify NAFTA's environmental institutions so that they can either meet public expectations or be relieved of the task.

The divergence between public expectations and NAFTA's environmental capacities can be reconciled in two ways: (1) modify the side agreement to address the flaws in its environmental institutions and enhance their ability to meet the environmental expectations of the North American public; or (2) frankly acknowledge the environmental limitations of NAFTA and its environmental side agreement and address environmental issues through non-NAFTA institutions and mechanisms.

NAFTA's environmental record clearly is imperfect. It makes more sense to tackle the shortcomings than to lament the existence of an FTA, as many environmentalists do, or to overlook the problems, as a very few diehard free trade advocates might. With the necessary tuning, NAFTA can become a trade agreement that both environmentalists and free traders appreciate.

References

Audley, John. 1997. *Green Politics and Global Trade: NAFTA and the Future of Environmental Politics*. Washington: Georgetown University Press.

BEA (Bureau of Economic Analysis). 2004. Regional Economic Accounts. Washington: US Department of Commerce. www.bea.gov.

BNA (Bureau of National Affairs). 2000. Canada: Fiscal 2000 Budget Commits C$700 Million for Development of Environmental Technology. *BNA International Environment Daily* (March 1).

CELA (Canadian Environmental Law Association) and Environmental Defence Canada. 2004. Shattering the Myth of Pollution Progress in Canada: A National Report (December). www.cela.ca/publications/cardfile.shtml?x=2063 (accessed in February 2005).

CEC (Commission for Environmental Cooperation). 1995. Guidelines for Submissions on Enforcement Matters Under Articles 14 and 15 of the NAAEC (June). Montreal. www.cec.org/citizen/guide_submit/index.cfm?varlan=english (accessed on April 20, 2005).

CEC (Commission for Environmental Cooperation). 2001. *Special Report on Enforcement Activities* (June). Montreal.

CEC (Commission for Environmental Cooperation). 2002. *Environmental Challenges and Opportunities of the Evolving North American Electricity Market*. Article 13 Report (June). Montreal. www.cec.org/files/PDF//CEC_Art13electricity_Eng.pdf (accessed on March 7, 2005).

CEC (Commission for Environmental Cooperation). 2004a. *Taking Stock 2001: North American Pollutant Releases and Transfers* (June). Montreal. www.cec.org/files/PDF/POLLUTANTS/TS2001-Report_en.pdf (accessed on March 7, 2005).

---

55. We thank Paul Joffe for providing the suggestion in this paragraph, which draws heavily on written comments he provided to an earlier draft. See Joffe and Caldwell (2003).

CEC (Commission for Environmental Cooperation). 2004b. *Ten Years of North American Environmental Cooperation*. Montreal. www.cec.org/pubs_docs/documents/index.cfm?varlan=english&ID=1522 (accessed on February 15, 2005).

CEC (Commission for Environmental Cooperation). 2005. *Status of Filed Submissions on Enforcement Matters under Articles 14 and 15 of the NAALC*. www.cec.org/citizen/status/index. cfm?varlan=english (accessed on July 15, 2005).

Cole, M. A. 2003. Development, Trade and the Environment: How Robust Is the Environmental Kuznets Curve? *Environment and Development Economics* 8, no. 4: 557–80.

Cousins, Emily, Robert Perks, and Wesley Warren. 2005. *Rewriting the Rules: The Bush Administration's First-term Environmental Record*. Washington: Natural Resources Defense Council (January).

Deere, Carolyn L., and Daniel C. Esty, ed. 2002. *Greening the Americas: NAFTA's Lessons for Hemispheric Trade*. Cambridge, MA: MIT Press.

DiMento, Joseph F., and Pamela M. Doughman. 1998. Soft Teeth in the Back of the Mouth: The NAFTA Environmental Side Agreement Implemented. *Georgetown International Environmental Law Review* 10, no. 3: 651–752.

Environment Canada. 2004. *Performance Report 2002–2003*. Ottawa. www.ec.gc.ca/dpr/index_e.htm (accessed in April 2005).

EPA (US Environmental Protection Agency). 2004. *FY 2004 End of Year Enforcement and Compliance Assurance Results*. Office of Enforcement and Compliance Assurance. Washington. www.epa.gov/compliance/resources/reports/endofyear/eoy2004/fy04results.pdf (accessed on April 22, 2005).

Gallagher, Kevin P. 2004a. *Free Trade and the Environment*. Stanford: Stanford University Press.

Gallagher, Kevin P. 2004b. Mexico-United States: The Environmental Costs of Trade-Led Growth. In *Globalization and the Environment: Lessons from the Americas*. Washington: The Heinrich Boell Foundation (June).

Gardner, Jane. 2004. Emerging Conflict of Interest: Analysis of Articles 14 and 15 of the NAAEC. Discussion Paper (April). Presentation at the Eleventh Regular Session of the CEC and JPAC, Puebla, Mexico, June. www.cec.org/pubs_docs/documents/index.cfm?varlan=english.ID=1645 (accessed on July 15, 2005).

Grossman, Gene M., and Alan B. Krueger. 1991. *Environmental Impact of a North American Free Trade Agreement*. NBER Working Paper 3914. Cambridge, MA: National Bureau of Economic Research.

Hufbauer, Gary C., and Jeffrey J. Schott. 1993. *NAFTA: An Assessment*. Washington: Institute for International Economics.

Hufbauer, Gary C., Daniel C. Esty, Diana Orejas, Luis Rubio, and Jeffrey J. Schott. 2000. *NAFTA and the Environment: Seven Years Later*. Washington: Institute for International Economics.

INEGI (Instituto Nacional de Estadística, Geografía, e Informática). 2004a. Gastos de Protección Ambiental. www.inegi.gob.mx/est/contenidos/espanol/rutinas/ept.asp?t=cuna6&c=1708 (accessed on July 15, 2005).

INEGI (Instituto Nacional de Estadística, Geografía, e Informática). 2004b. Sistema de Cuentas Económicas y Ecológicas de Mexico 1997–2002. www.inegi.gob.mx/prod_serv/contenidos/espanol/catalogo/default.asp?accion=12&tema=109000000&numero=1.9 (accessed on April 6, 2005).

Jacott, Marissa, Cyrus Reed, and Mark Winfield. 2001. The Generation and Management of Hazardous Wastes and Transboundary Hazardous Waste Shipments between Mexico, Canada and the United States 1990–2000. Austin, TX: Texas Center for Policy Studies (May).

Joffe, Paul, and Jake Caldwell. 2003. Mutually Supportive Trade and Environment Regimes. High-Level Roundtable on Trade and Environment, Cozumel, Mexico, September.

JPAC (Joint Public Advisory Committee). 2001. *Lessons Learned: Citizen Submissions Under Articles 14 and 15 of the NAAEC.* Montreal: Commission for Environmental Cooperation (June). www.cec.org/files/PDF/JPAC/rep11-e-final_EN.PDF (accessed on May 18, 2005).

Jones, Laura, Laura Griggs, and Liv Fredricksen. 2002. Environmental Indicators, 4th edition. *Critical Issues Bulletin* (April). Vancouver: Fraser Institute.

Kirton, John. 1999. *Environmental Research and Policy Endeavours in the NAFTA Context: Description and Evaluation.* Toronto: Centre for International Studies, University of Toronto (January).

Kirton, John. 2000. *Canada-US Trade and the Environment: Regimes, Regulatory Refugees, Races, Restraints and Results.* Toronto: Center for International Studies (EnviReform), University of Toronto (November).

Magraw, Daniel, and Steven Charnovitz. 1994. NAFTA's Repercussions: Is Green Trade Possible? *Environment* 36, no. 2 (March).

Mann, Howard, and Konrad von Moltke. 1999. *NAFTA's Chapter 11 and the Environment: Addressing the Impacts of the Investor-State Process on the Environment.* Winnipeg: International Institute for Sustainable Development.

Markell, David L., and John Knox, eds. 2003. *Greening NAFTA: The North American Commission for Environmental Cooperation.* Palo Alto, CA: Stanford University Press.

Miramontes, Victor. 2002. Potential Reform of the NADBank's Charter. Testimony before the US House Committee on Financial Services, May 19. Washington: US House of Representatives.

National Wildlife Federation. 2003. *Six Bush Administration Conservation and Wildlife Policies.* Washington. www.nwf.org/nwfwebadmin/binaryVault/SixBushAdministration ConservationPolicies.pdf (accessed on March 7, 2005).

NADBank (North American Development Bank). 2002. *2002 Annual Report.* San Antonio, TX.

NADBank-BECC (North American Development Bank and Border Environmental Cooperation Commission). 2002. *BECC-NADBank 2002 Joint Status Report.* San Antonio, TX.

NADBank-BECC (North American Development Bank and Border Environmental Cooperation Commission). 2004. *BECC-NADBank 2004 Joint Status Report.* San Antonio, TX. www. nadbank.org/Reports/Joint_Report/english/status_eng.pdf (accessed in February 2005).

Reed, Cyrus. 1998. Hazardous Waste Management on the Border: Problems with Practices and Oversight Continue. *Borderlines* 46, no. 5 (July).

Reed, Cyrus, Marisa Jacott, and Alejandro Villamar. 2000. *Hazardous Waste Management in the United States-Mexico Border States: More Questions than Answers.* Austin, TX: Red Mexicana de Acción Frente al Libre Comercio (RMALC) and Texas Center for Policy Studies (March).

Schatan, Claudia. 2000. Mexico's Manufacturing Exports and the Environment Under NAFTA. Prepared for the Commission for Environmental Cooperation, October.

Silvan, Laura. 2004. *CEC Makes a Difference in Mexico by Fostering Public Participation.* Montreal: Commission for Environmental Cooperation. www.cec.org/pubs_docs/ documents/index.cfm?varlan=english&ID=1512 (accessed on May 16, 2005).

Taylor, John B. 2002. Instability in Latin America: US Policy and the Role of the International Community. Testimony before the US Senate Committee on Banking, Housing and Urban Affairs, October 16. Washington: US Senate.

USTR (US Trade Representative). 1997. *Study on the Operation and Effects of the North American Free Trade Agreement.* Washington: Office of the US Trade Representative (July).

US Treasury. 2005. International Programs: FY2006 Budget Request. Washington: Office of International Affairs. www.treas.gov/offices/international-affairs/intl/fy2006/ (accessed on April 22, 2005).

Varady, Robert, Patricia R. Lankao, and Katherine Hankins. 2001. Managing Hazardous Materials Along the US-Mexico Border. *Environment* 43, no. 10: 22–36 (December).

World Bank. 1994. Mexico Northern Border Environment Project. World Bank Executive Project Summary. Washington.

World Bank. 1999. *Greening Industry: New Roles for Communities, Markets, and Governments.* Policy Research Report. New York: Oxford University Press.

Yandle, Bruce, Madhusudan Bhattarai, and Maya Vijayaraghavan. 2004. *Environmental Kuznets Curves: A Review of Findings, Methods, and Policy Implications.* Research Study 02-01. Bozeman, MT: Property and Environment Research Center (April).

Zarzoso, Inmaculada Martinez, and Aurelia Bengochea-Morancho. 2003. Testing for an Environmental Kuznets Curve in Latin American Countries. *Revista de Análisis Económico* 18, no. 1 (June).

Appendix 3A

Table 3A.1 CEC Article 14 submissions on enforcement matters, 1994–2005

ID number filing date	Claimant and defendant	Claim	Status
SEM-95-001 6/30/1995	Biodiversity Legal Foundation et al. vs. United States	Failure to effectively enforce some provisions of the Endangered Species Act of 1973 as a consequence of the Rescissions Act of 1995.	Process terminated. The Secretariat determined that "enactment of legislation which specifically alters the operation of pre-existing environmental law in essence becomes a part of the greater body of laws and statutes on the books." The Secretariat determined not to request a response from the concerned government party and, under guideline 8.1, the process was terminated on December 11, 1995.
SEM-95-002 8/30/1995	Sierra Club et al. vs. United States	Failure to effectively enforce all applicable federal environmental laws by eliminating private remedies for salvage timber sales as a consequence of the "Logging Rider" clause of the Rescissions Act of 1995.	Process terminated for the same reason stated in submission SEM-95-001. The Secretariat also concluded that the submission lacked a factual basis supporting the assertion of failure to effectively enforce environmental laws. The 30-day term expired without the Secretariat receiving a submission that conformed to Article 14(1). Under guideline 6.2, the process was terminated on January 7, 1996.
SEM-96-001 1/18/1996	Comité para la Protección de los Recursos Naturales et al. vs. Mexico	Failure to effectively enforce environmental laws during the evaluation process of a project involving construction and operation of a port terminal and related works in Cozumel.	Factual record released to the public on October 24, 1997. The CEC Council did not make any recommendations.
SEM-96-002 3/20/1996	Aage Tottrup, P. Eng. vs. Canada	Failure to effectively enforce environmental laws resulting in the pollution of specified wetland areas affecting the habitat of fish and migratory birds.	Process terminated because the same case has been brought before the Canadian court of law. The 30-day term expired without the Secretariat receiving new or supplemental information from submitter(s). Under guideline 8.1, the process was terminated on June 1, 1996.

(table continues next page)

Table 3A.1 CEC Article 14 submissions on enforcement matters, 1994–2005 *(continued)*

ID number filing date	Claimant and defendant	Claim	Status
SEM-96-003 9/9/1996; SEM-97-006 10/4/1997	The Friends of the Old Man River vs. Canada	Failure to effectively enforce the habitat protection sections of the Fisheries Act and the Canadian Environmental Assessment Act.	Process terminated because the same case has been brought before the Canadian court of law. The submission was refiled (as SEM-97-006) on October 4, 1997, following conclusion of Canadian legal proceedings. Final factual record publicly released on August 11, 2003.
SEM-96-004 11/14/1996	The Southwest Center for Biological Diversity and Dr. Robin Silver vs. United states	Failure to effectively enforce the National Policy Act with respect to the US Army's operation at Fort Huachuca. Specifically, expansion of the base will drain local water supply and destroy the ecosystem dependent on it.	Submission withdrawn. Matter is currently being examined by the Secretariat under Article 13.
SEM-97-001 4/2/1997	British Columbia (BC) Aboriginal Fisheries Commission et al. vs. Canada	Failure to enforce the Canadian Fisheries Act and to use its powers pursuant to the National Energy Board Act to ensure the protection of fish and fish habitat in BC rivers from ongoing and repeated environmental damage caused by hydroelectric dams.	The Secretariat transmitted a factual record on this case to the CEC Council on May 31, 2000. The factual record was released to the public on June 12, 2000. The CEC Council did not make any recommendations.
SEM-97-002 3/15/1997	Comité Pro Limpieza del Río Magdalena vs. Mexico	Failure to enforce Mexican environmental laws governing disposal of wastewater. Alleging that wastewater from Imuris, Magdalena de Kino, and Santa Ana is being discharged into the Magdalena River without prior treatment.	The Secretariat made publicly available documents related to the preparation of a factual record on March 22, 2002.
SEM-97-003 4/9/1997	Centre québécois du droit de l'environnement et al. vs. Canada	Failure to enforce several environmental protection standards regarding agriculture pollution originating from animal production facilities in Quebec.	The Secretariat has reviewed the response from Canada. On October 29, 1999 the Secretariat informed the CEC Council that this submission warrants developing a factual record. The CEC Council voted down the development of a factual record.

Submission	Submitter	Description	Status
SEM-97-004 5/26/1997	Canadian Environmental Defence Fund vs. Canada	Failure to enforce law requiring environmental assessment of federal initiatives, policies, and programs. In particular, failure to conduct an environmental assessment of the Atlantic Groundfish Strategy, as required by Canadian law, jeopardizing the future of Canada's east coast fisheries.	The Secretariat determined that submission criteria were not met. The 30-day term expired without the Secretariat receiving a submission that conformed to Article 14(1). Under guideline 6.2, the process was terminated on September 24, 1997.
SEM-97-005 7/21/1997	Animal Alliance of Canada et al. vs. Canada	Failure to pass endangered species legislation or regulations as required by the Biodiversity Convention to which Canada is a signatory.	The Secretariat determined that submission criteria were not met. The Secretariat determined that "until international obligations are implemented by way of statute . . . those obligations do not constitute the domestic law of Canada." The 30-day term expired without the Secretariat receiving a submission that conformed to Article 14(1). Under guideline 6.2, the process was terminated on June 25, 1998.
SEM-97-007 10/10/1997	Instituto de Derecho Ambiental vs. Mexico	Failure to effectively enforce the applicable environmental laws with respect to a citizen's complaint filed on September 23, 1996 in regard to the Hydrological Basin of the Lerma Santiago River-Lake Chapala. The citizen's complaint was submitted "with the view to declaring a state of environmental emergency in the Lake Chapala ecosystem, following administrative proceedings." Specifically, the submission alleges that Mexico failed to carry out the requisite administrative procedures provided by the LGEEPA.	Process terminated. The Secretariat determined not to recommend the preparation of a factual record.
SEM-98-001 1/9/1998	Instituto de Derecho Ambiental vs. Mexico	Failure of the federal attorney general and federal judiciary to effectively enforce the LGEEPA in relation to the April 22, 1992, explosions in the Reforma area of the city of Guadalajara, state of Jalisco.	Process terminated. The Secretariat determined that the revised submission, received on October 15, 1999, did not meet the Article 14(1) criteria.

(table continues next page)

Table 3A.1 CEC Article 14 submissions on enforcement matters, 1994–2005 *(continued)*

ID number filing date	Claimant and defendant	Claim	Status
SEM-98-002 10/14/1997	Hector Gregorio Ortiz Martinez vs. Mexico	Failure to effectively enforce the applicable environmental legislation in relation to a citizen's complaint regarding lumbering operations at the "El Taray" site in the state of Jalisco. Specifically, the submission alleges that the technical audit and inspection visit which were performed were inadequate response to the citizen submission and that the relevant authority failed to issue the appropriate ruling regarding damages and losses as provided by section 194 of the LGEEPA (in force at the time of the submission).	The Secretariat terminated the process on March 18, 1999. The subject matter of the dispute is expressly excluded from Article 14 review by the definition of environmental law in Article 45(2)(b) of the Agreement. The Secretariat determined that the revised submission did not meet the Article 14(1) criteria and terminated the process under guideline 6.3.
SEM-98-003 5/27/1998	Department of the Planet Earth et al. vs. United States	Failure of the US Environmental Protection Agency (EPA) to enforce domestic laws (the Clean Air Act, 1990) and treaty obligations with Canada with regard to regulation of solid waste and medical incinerator air pollution designed to protect the Great Lakes.	Process terminated. The Secretariat determined that inspection and monitoring allegations do not warrant a factual record. The Secretariat determined not to recommend the preparation of a factual record. Under guideline 9.6, the process was terminated.
SEM-98-004 6/29/1998	Sierra Club of British Columbia et al. vs. Canada	Failure to enforce provisions of the Fisheries Act with regard to protecting fish and fish habitat from the destructive environmental impacts of the mining industry.	The Secretariat transmitted a factual record on this case to the CEC Council on June 27, 2003. The factual record was released to the public on August 12, 2003.
SEM-98-005 7/23/1998	Academia Sonorense de Derechos Humanos vs. Mexico	Failure to effectively enforce all environmental legislation in regard to the operation of a hazardous landfill less than six kilometers away from Hermosillo, Sonora.	Under guideline 9.6, the process was terminated. The Secretariat determined not to recommend the preparation of a factual record.

SEM-98-006 10/20/1998	Grupo Ecológico Manglar, AC vs. Mexico	Failure to enforce and properly administer domestic and international environmental laws, including the LGEEPA, in relation to the establishment and operation of the Granjas Aquanova SA shrimp farm in Nayarit, Mexico.	The Secretariat submitted the factual record on this case to the CEC Council for review on March 7, 2003. The factual record was released to the public on June 23, 2003.
SEM-98-007 10/23/1998	Environmental Health Coalition vs. Mexico	Failure to effectively enforce environmental laws according to Mexican law and the La Paz Agreement in connection with the abandoned lead smelter in Tijuana, Baja California, Mexico.	The Secretariat transmitted a factual record on this case to the CEC Council on November 29, 2001. The factual record was released to the public on February 11, 2002.
SEM-99-001 10/18/1999; SEM-00-002 3/20/2000	Methanex Corporation vs. United States; Neste Canada Inc. vs. United States	Failure to effectively enforce environmental laws and regulations related to water resource protection and the regulation of underground storage tanks in California.	The Secretariat acknowledged receipt of the submission on October 20, 1999. The Secretariat requested a response from the US government on March 30, 2000. On April 20, 2000, this submission was consolidated with SEM-00-002. On June 30, 2000, the Secretariat terminated the case because the matter is the subject of a pending judicial or administrative proceeding.
SEM-99-002 11/19/1999	Alliance for the Wild Rockies et al. vs. United States	Failure to effectively enforce Section 703 of the Migratory Bird Treaty Act, which prohibits the killing of migratory birds without a permit.	The Secretariat transmitted a factual record on this case to the CEC Council on February 21, 2003. The factual record was released to the public on April 24, 2003.
SEM-00-001 2/9/2000; SEM-00-005 5/3/2000	Rosa María Escalante de Fernández vs. Mexico; Academia Sonorense de Derechos Humanos vs. Mexico	Failure to effectively enforce the LGEEPA in relation to the operation of the company Molymex, SA in Cumpas, Sonora, Mexico.	First submission dismissed due to lack of information. Documents related to the preparation of a factual record for the second submission on the same matter was submitted to the CEC Council on May 28, 2002. The factual record was released to the public on October 8, 2004.

(table continues next page)

Table 3A.1 CEC Article 14 submissions on enforcement matters, 1994–2005 *(continued)*

ID number filing date	Claimant and defendant	Claim	Status
SEM-00-003 3/2/2000	Hudson River Audubon Society of Westchester Inc. et al. vs. United States	Violation by the National Park Service of the US Department of Interior of the Migratory Bird Treaty Act and the Endangered Species Act by proposing the construction of a paved bicycle path through the Jamaica Bay Wildlife Refuge in Queens, New York.	Process terminated. The Secretariat determined that the revised submission did not meet the Article 14(1) criteria. Specifically, the Secretariat dismissed the submission because it alleges a prospective rather than an ongoing failure to effectively enforce environmental law.
SEM-00-004 3/23/2000	Suzuki Foundation et al. vs. Canada	Failure to enforce sections of the Fisheries Act against logging in British Columbia is disrupting fish habitat.	The Secretariat submitted the factual record on this case to the CEC Council for review on April 15, 2003. The factual record was released to the public on August 11, 2003.
SEM-00-006 6/9/2000	Comisión de la Solidaridad y Defensa de los Derechos Humanos vs. Mexico	Failure to effectively enforce its environmental law by denying Indigenous communities in the Sierra Tarahumara in the State of Chihuahua access to environmental justice.	On April 22, 2003, the Council voted to approve the development of a factual record. The Secretariat submitted the draft factual record to the CEC Council for review on April 6, 2005, for a 45-day comment period on the accuracy of the draft.
SEM-01-001 2/14/2001	Academia Sonorense de Derechos Humanos, AC Lic. Domingo Gutiérrez Mendívil vs. Mexico	Failure to enforce its environmental law by allowing the establishment of the Cytrar hazardous waste landfill in Sonora, Mexico.	The Secretariat received a response from the Mexican government on July 19, 2001. The CEC Council voted not to warrant a factual record for this case on December 10, 2002.
SEM-01-002 4/12/2001	Names Withheld vs. Canada	Failure to enforce environmental obligations under NAAEC. Specifically, the submission alleges the failure to issue a prohibitory order stopping exports into the United States of products containing the banned hazardous substance isobutyl nitrite.	Process terminated. The Secretariat determined that the revised submission did not meet the Article 14(1) criteria. Specifically, the submission criteria were not met because there was no evidence of defendant party's failure to effectively enforce its environmental laws.

Number / Date	Submitter	Summary	Status
SEM-01-003 6/14/2001	Mercerizados y Teñidos de Guadalajara, SA vs. Mexico	Failure to effectively enforce Articles 5, 6, and 7 of the NAAEC and Article 194 of the LGEEPA in relation to groundwater contamination caused by the firm Dermet.	Process terminated. The Secretariat determined that the revised submission did not meet the Article 14(1) criteria.
SEM-02-001 2/6/2002	Sierra Club et al. vs. Canada	Failure to effectively enforce section 6(a) of the Migratory Bird Regulations adopted under the Migratory Birds Convention Act, 1994 against the logging industry in Ontario. Specifically, the submission alleges that despite the estimated widespread destruction of bird nests, an access-to-information request revealed no investigations or charges in Ontario for violations of section 6(a).	Documents related to the preparation of a factual record for the second submission on the same matter were submitted to the CEC Council on March 24, 2004. The Secretariat requested the preparation of a factual record on June 30, 2004. The Secretariat published a work plan available to the public and stakeholders on April 4, 2005.
SEM-02-002 2/7/2002	Jorge Rafael Martínez Azuela et al. vs. Mexico	Failure to effectively enforce environmental laws resulting in noise emissions at Mexico City International Airport exceeding limits established in environmental law, causing irreversible damage to the thousands of persons living near the airport.	Process terminated because the Secretariat determined the case did not warrant the preparation of a factual record (guideline 9.6).
SEM-02-003 5/8/2002	Friends of the Earth et al. vs. Canada	Failure to effectively enforce the Pulp and Paper Effluent Regulations. In particular, the submission alleges Canada failed to meet its stated policy to seek to ensure compliance in the shortest possible time with no recurrence of violations, as well as its stated commitment to fair, predictable, and consistent enforcement.	The Secretariat requested the preparation of a factual record on March 1, 2004.
SEM-02-004 8/23/2002	Arcadio, Leoncio, Fernanda, and Milagro Pesqueira Senday vs. Mexico	Failure to effectively enforce Article 15 of the LGEEPA Hazardous Waste Regulations and the Mining Law and its Regulations. The submission alleges that the company Minera Secotec, SA de CV exploited the low-grade placer gold deposit of the "El Boludo" project without complying with several conditions of the environmental impact authorization.	Process terminated. Submission withdrawn on July 7, 2004.

(table continues next page)

Table 3A.1 CEC Article 14 submissions on enforcement matters, 1994–2005 *(continued)*

ID number filing date	Claimant and defendant	Claim	Status
SEM-02-005 11/25/2002	Angel Lara García vs. Mexico	Failure to enforce environmental laws with respect to a citizen's complaint about the manufacturing facility of ALCA, SA de CV, which releases highly toxic contaminants. The health and economic effects allegedly attributable to the emissions produced by the company are cited in the 183 documents submitted by the claimant.	Process terminated. The Secretariat determined that the revised submission did not meet the Article 14(1) criteria.
SEM-03-001 5/1/2003	Attorneys general of the states of New York, Connecticut, and Rhode Island et al. vs. Canada	Failure to effectively enforce sections 166 and 176 of the Canadian Environmental Protection Act and failure to effectively enforce section 36(3) of the Fisheries Act against the Ontario Power Generation's coal-powered facilities. Specifically, the submission alleges that emissions of mercury, sulfur dioxide, and nitrogen oxides pollute the air and water downwind, into eastern Canada and the northeastern United States.	Process terminated because the Secretariat determined the case did not warrant the preparation of a factual record (guideline 9.6).
SEM-03-002 5/14/2003	Movimiento Ecologista Mexicano AC et al. vs. Mexico	Failure to effectively enforce the applicable environmental legislation under LGEEPA in relation to a citizen's complaint regarding the Home Port Xcaret project. The citizen's complaint alleges that the EIA project "will irreparably affect and destroy the natural resources and coral ecosystems, gravely endangering countless marine species."	Process terminated. The Secretariat determined that the revised submission did not meet the Article 14(1) criteria.

Number / Date	Submission	Description	Status
SEM-03-003 5/23/2003	Instituto de Derecho Ambiental vs. Mexico	Failure to effectively enforce its environmental law with respect to the Hydrological Basin of the Lerma Santiago River-Lake Chapala. The submission alleges that Mexico failed to carry out the requisite administrative procedures provided by the LGEEPA. As a result, there is serious environmental deterioration and uneven water distribution in the basin, as well as the risk that Lake Chapala and its migratory birds will eventually disappear.	The Secretariat is reviewing the submission under Article 14(1). On March 31, 2004, the Secretariat received a response from the responding government Party and is considering whether to recommend a factual record.
SEM-03-004 6/17/2003	Ángel Lara García vs. Mexico	Failure to effectively enforce its environmental law with respect to the operation of a footwear materials factory by ALCA, SA de CV, in the Santa Isabel Industrial neighborhood of Iztapalapa Delegation in Mexico, DF. The submission alleges that Mexico failed to carry out the requisite administrative procedures provided by the LGEEPA in regards to the management of the factory's hazardous waste. As a result, there is serious environmental deterioration and the health of his family has been affected by the pollution generated by the factory.	The Secretariat requested the preparation of a factual record on August 23, 2004.
SEM-03-005 8/14/2003	Waterkeeper Alliance et al. vs. Canada	Failure to enforce section 36(3) of the federal Fisheries Act against the City of Montreal in regard to the discharge to the St. Lawrence River of toxic pollutants from the city's Technoparc site. As a result, polychlorinated biphenyls, polycylic aromatic hydrocarbons, and other pollutants are being discharged from Technoparc, the site of a historic industrial and municipal waste landfill.	The Secretariat requested the preparation of a factual record on April 19, 2004. The council approved the development of a factual record on August 20, 2004. The Secretariat posted a request for information relevant to the factual record on its Web site on February 8, 2005.
SEM-03-006 8/15/2003	Academia Sonorense de Derechos Humanos vs. Mexico	Failure to enforce its environmental law by allowing the establishment of the Cytrar hazardous waste landfill in Sonora, Mexico.	Process terminated because the Secretariat determined the case did not warrant the preparation of a factual record (guideline 9.6).

(table continues next page)

195

Table 3A.1　CEC Article 14 submissions on enforcement matters, 1994–2005 *(continued)*

ID number filing date	Claimant and defendant	Claim	Status
SEM-04-001 1/27/2004	Genaro Meléndez Lugo y José Javier et al. vs. Mexico	Failure to enforce environmental laws by not properly processing their complaint against the companies Ecolimpio de México, SA de CV, and Transportes J. Guadalupe Jiménez, SA, and by not penalizing those companies. The submitters claim that both companies operate in violation of the law, causing serious damage to the environment and their property.	Process terminated. The Secretariat determined that the revised submission did not meet the Article 14(1) criteria.
SEM-04-002 7/14/2004	Academia Sonorense de Derechos Humanos, AC, and Domingo Gutiérrez Mendívil vs. Mexico	Failure to enforce provisions of Mexican environmental law regarding the prevention, monitoring, oversight and control of air pollution in Hermosillo, Sonora. The submission alleges the failure to enforce and ensure compliance with the Mexican Official Standards (Normas Oficiales Mexicanas) on air pollution; the alleged lack of actions to prevent air pollution in properties and areas under state and municipal jurisdiction; the alleged failure to establish and update a National Air Quality Information System; and the alleged lack of defined state and municipal urban development plans indicating the zones where polluting industries may operate.	Process terminated. The Secretariat determined that the revised submission did not meet the Article 14(1) criteria.
SEM-04-003 9/7/2004	Centro de Derechos Humanos Tepeyac del Istmo de Tehuantepec, AC et al. vs. Mexico	Failure to enforce environmental laws by not processing or responding to a citizen complaint filed with PROFEPA on February 16, 2004. The submission alleges that the spillage of 68,000 liters of gasoline resulted in the death of fish in the Laguna Superior of the Gulf of Tehuantepec in Oaxaca, Mexico, harmed the environment, and endangered the health of the indigenous Zapotec community.	Process terminated. The Secretariat determined that the 30-day term expired without receiving a submission that met with the Article 14(1) criteria.

SEM-04-004 9/10/2004	The Friends of the Oldman River vs. Canada	The submission alleges that the federal government's 1998 "Decision Framework for the Determination and Authorization of Harmful Alteration, Disruption or Destruction of Fish Habitat" is not authorized by or compatible with the Fisheries Act or the Canadian Environmental Assessment Agency.	Process terminated. The Secretariat determined that the 30-day term expired without receiving a submission that met with the Article 14(1) criteria.
SEM-04-005 9/20/2004	Friends of the Earth et al. vs. United States	Failure to enforce the federal Clean Water Act against coal-fired power plants for mercury emissions. The submission alleges that the number of fish consumption advisories for mercury has risen from 899 to 2,347 since 1993, and that, according to the US EPA, 35 percent of the total lake acres and 24 percent of the river miles in the United States are now under fish consumption advisories. As a result, there is degradation of thousands of rivers, lakes, and other water bodies across the United States.	The Secretariat notified the submitters on December 16, 2004, that the submission did not meet all of the Article 14(1) criteria. On January 18, 2005, the submitters provided more information. On February 24, 2005, the Secretariat determined that the submission met the criteria of Article 14(1) and requested a response from the concerned government party in accordance with Article 14(2). The United States responded on April 25, 2005.
SEM-04-006 10/12/2004	Canadian Nature Federation et al. vs. Canada	Failure to enforce the Migratory Birds Convention Act, 1994, in regard to logging in four forest management units in Ontario. Section 6(a) of the Migratory Birds Regulation makes it an offence to disturb, destroy, or take a nest or egg of a migratory bird without a permit. The submission alleges that Environment Canada is primarily responsible for enforcing the Migratory Birds Convention Act, 1994 but that virtually no action has been taken to enforce section 6(a) of the Migratory Birds Regulation against logging companies, logging contractors, and independent contractors.	The Secretariat requested the preparation of a factual record on December 17, 2004. On April 4, 2005, the Secretariat published a work plan on its Web site or otherwise made it available to the public and stakeholders.

(table continues next page)

Table 3A.1   CEC Article 14 submissions on enforcement matters, 1994–2005   *(continued)*

ID number filing date	Claimant and defendant	Claim	Status
SEM-04-007 11/3/2004	Quebec Association Against Air Pollution vs. Canada	Failure to enforce Quebec's "Regulation respecting the Quality of the Atmosphere" and the Quebec Environment Quality Act with regards to emissions of hydrocarbons, carbon monoxide, and nitrogen oxides from post-1985 light vehicle models. The submission alleges that the only way to ensure effective enforcement of this legislation is through the establishment of a mandatory automobile inspection and maintenance program that would apply to the whole fleet of automobiles in Quebec on a frequent basis. As a result, this alleged failure has considerable negative impacts on the environment and public health.	The Secretariat received a response from the Canadian government on February ˉ, 2005, and began considering whether to recommend a factual record.
SEM-05-001 1/12/2005	Inmobiliaria J y B Empresas, SA de CV vs. Mexico	Failure to enforce environmental laws by not processing or responding to a citizen complaint filed with PROFEPA. The submission alleges that extraction activities have had a negative environmental impact and that Diamond Golf Internacional did not obtain the permits and authorizations required to carry out the mining activities.	The Secretariat received the submission on January 14, 2005. On February 16, 2005, the Secretariat determined that the submission met the criteria of Article 14(1) and requested a response from the concerned government party in accordance with Article 14(2).

LGEEPA = General Law of Ecological Equilibrium and Protection of the Environment
PROFEPA = Mexico's Federal Environmental Protection Agency
CEC = Commission for Environmental Cooperation
NAAEC= North American Agreement on Environmental Cooperation

Source: CEC (2005).

4

Dispute Settlement Systems

Building on the 1989 Canada-US Free Trade Agreement (CUSFTA), NAFTA contains formal dispute settlement provisions in six areas: Chapter 11 is designed to resolve investor-state disputes over property rights; Chapter 14 creates special provisions for handling disputes in the financial sector via the Chapter 20 dispute settlement process; Chapter 19 establishes a review mechanism to determine whether final antidumping (AD) and countervailing duty (CVD) decisions made in domestic tribunals are consistent with national laws; and Chapter 20 provides government-to-government consultation, at the ministerial level, to resolve high-level disputes. In addition, the NAFTA partners created interstate dispute settlement mechanisms regarding domestic environmental and labor laws under the North American Agreement on Environmental Cooperation (NAAEC) and the North American Agreement on Labor Cooperation (NAALC), respectively. This chapter examines the first four dispute settlement systems; the NAAEC and NAALC systems are evaluated in the environment and labor chapters of this book.

Before analyzing the framework for each NAFTA chapter, a brief review of the reasons for creating the NAFTA dispute settlement systems may be helpful. As a nation that trades heavily with the United States, Canada was primarily concerned about ensuring open access to the US market when it negotiated the CUSFTA.[1] Put succinctly, Canada wanted to en-

1. In 1986, two years before signing CUSFTA, exports to the United States represented about 75 percent of total Canadian exports, a proportion that increased to about 86 percent by 2003 (IMF Direction of Trade Statistics, November 2002, and Industry Canada Trade Data Online, October 2004). See Hart (2002).

sure that Canadian exports to California, for example, would face barriers no greater than New York exports to California. In the 1980s, Canada became increasingly concerned about the threat of US CVD and AD duties —provoked by adverse rulings on lumber, fish, and pork (Winham 1993). While the United States wanted to preserve its trade remedies to redress both Canadian public subsidies and private dumping, Canada wanted an agreement that would curtail overzealous application of trade measures against Canadian exports.

The preferred Canadian approach was harmonization of substantive trade remedy laws, but the United States was adamantly opposed to changes in its own unfair trade laws (Mena 2001). As a compromise, the United States and Canada agreed to create an innovative dispute settlement mechanism to review final national AD and CVD determinations and to defer talks on subsidies, AD, and CVD rules to the ongoing Uruguay Round of GATT negotiations. A few years later, when NAFTA loomed on the horizon, Canada wanted to make sure that its gains in CUSFTA were preserved in a trilateral agreement. Canada feared that a US-Mexico bilateral agreement might set the stage for backsliding on the dispute settlement provisions, which were not uniformly popular in the United States. Moreover, Canada wanted to make another run at harmonizing trade remedy laws.

Mexico's adherence to NAFTA's dispute settlement mechanisms was critical to assure its partners that Mexico was committed to faithfully implementing NAFTA reforms. Memories of the 1982 nationalization of banks, and its subsequent judicial controversy, fueled concerns about the value of Mexico's commitments. US investors and exporters also questioned the reliability of Mexico's judicial system.[2] In NAFTA, Mexico agreed to the basic principles of the Chapter 19 process, which are largely based on common-law tenets, as well as the other dispute settlement mechanisms.[3] Mexico viewed the NAFTA dispute settlement process as a tool for providing institutional legitimacy, which would help promote foreign direct investment (FDI).

The United States sought improvements on CUSFTA investment provisions by providing for international arbitration of investment disputes, by broadening the coverage of dispute procedures, and by prohibiting additional performance requirements not addressed in CUSFTA. US officials were satisfied with the Chapter 11 dispute settlement mechanism, which enabled private investors to seek a binding arbitration of their disputes

2. In November 1982, President Lopez Portillo nationalized a commercial bank, which local courts determined was a violation of the Constitution. Mexico's Supreme Court later controversially overturned this ruling. See Ramírez de la O (1993).

3. See Vega-Cánovas and Winham (2002). By contrast with common-law tenets, Mexico's legal system is built on a European-style civil code.

with NAFTA governments, and were not evidently worried that Chapter 11 might be used against the United States (IGPAC 1992).

Different expectations about the role of NAFTA panel determinations, particularly Chapter 19 binational panels, prevailed throughout the initial implementation of the agreement. Canada lobbied for resolving potential trade disputes through working groups.[4] Like Mexico, Canada envisioned a similar outcome from the NAFTA dispute settlement process—namely that greater rigor and restraint would be practiced in the application of domestic trade remedy law. The United States, on the other hand, already opposed to Canada's idea of harmonizing trade remedies, believed that tribunal decisions, particularly Chapter 19 panels, would follow domestic US standards of judicial review. These standards require deference to the factual conclusions of the initial examining body.

With this background in mind, we now turn to an overview of each NAFTA dispute settlement chapter.

Chapter 11

A big NAFTA innovation was the establishment of an international mechanism for investment disputes. Mexico had long been a champion of the Calvo doctrine, which called for strict regulation of foreign investment and required that disputes be adjudicated only in local courts. Under that doctrine, foreign investors had no recourse to diplomatic protection or the courts of their home states.[5] Pursuing its vision of strict regulation, in 1973 Mexico enacted the foreign investment law, which effectively limited foreign equity to a maximum ownership stake of 49 percent.[6] The National Foreign Investment Commission (NFIC) screened investments. Other regulations required that foreign-owned plants balance their imports with exports and locate outside the main urban areas, especially Mexico City (Ramírez de la O 1993). In 1993 (after NAFTA), a new foreign investment

---

4. NAFTA parties established a Working Group on Trade and Competition and a Working Group on Trade Law in 1993. The official function of the Working Group on Trade and Competition was to provide recommendations on issues affecting competition laws and policies and trade under NAFTA. The objectives of the Working Group on Trade Law included monitoring the success of Chapter 19 panels and antidumping laws and considering changes in those laws. Despite Canada's support for these pre-NAFTA working groups, some US industry associations resisted any discussion of potential trade cases during working group meetings.

5. The Calvo doctrine was invoked by Mexico and other Latin American nations to emphasize national sovereignty over foreign investment.

6. However, Mexico also allowed "neutral investment," namely foreign investment in nonvoting shares. These shares are not included in the computation of the proportion of a firm owned by foreign investors. See Cuevas, Messmacher, and Werner (2002).

law allowed foreign investors to fully own Mexican corporations; however, several sectors were excepted from the reforms. As of 2004, investment restrictions remained inter alia on Pemex and other state monopolies and radio and TV other than cable.

NAFTA investment provisions inaugurated a major change in Mexican policy toward foreign investors. By liberalizing its investment rules and accepting the international dispute resolution framework of Chapter 11, Mexico signaled investors that it was committed to a new regime. In the wake of the 1995 financial crisis, Mexico went further: It decided that the wisest course was to put out a welcome mat for foreign investors. The government rapidly opened to FDI sectors that had previously been reserved in NAFTA's annexes.[7]

While many investor provisions in Chapter 11 were carried over from CUSFTA, NAFTA was unique in adopting the "negative list" approach to reservations. In trade and investment agreements, the negative list approach means that a country must specifically identify industries or measures *not* covered by the relevant obligations. The agreement applies to everything else.[8]

National reservations that exclude sensitive industries or measures from investment protection provisions serve to highlight the residual areas of discrimination. The negative list acts like a NAFTA warning sign: "keep out." At the same time, it invites the attention of future negotiators. There are three types of reservations under Chapter 11: sectoral, reciprocal ("tit for tat"), and investment review reservations listed in Annexes 1, 2, and 3.[9]

Mexico reserved the largest number (89) of sectors. The United States and Canada carried over reservations from CUSFTA—50 and 48, respectively.[10] Sectoral reservations concentrate heavily on national treatment (Article 1102) and most-favored nation (MFN) rights for foreign investors (Article 1103). These exclusions represent 71 percent of all Mexican reservations, 76 percent of all US reservations, and 60 percent of all Canadian reservations. The most sensitive sector for all three NAFTA trading part-

---

7. According to Vega-Cánovas and Winham (2002), industries opened to FDI included railroads, telecommunications, satellite transmission, banking, and some petrochemicals.

8. By contrast, a "positive list" approach does not obligate a country to open its market unless it specifically lists sectors in its national schedule.

9. NAFTA Annex 1 provides the vehicle for investment review. In reserved sectors and subsectors, each party can invoke Annex 1 to add more restrictive measures. See Rugman and Gestrin (1993).

10. All members have absolute reservations on health and social services, while individual countries maintained absolute exceptions in specific sectors—for example, Canada excludes its cultural industries (newspapers, television programming, etc.) and large-scale water exports.

ners is the transportation sector, where each member scheduled extensive reservations.[11]

"Tit for tat" reservations, scheduled in Annexes 1 and 2, enable NAFTA countries to retaliate against another member's reservations as circumstances warrant. Among the three NAFTA partners, the United States retains the longest list of "tit for tat" reservations. US reservations cover mining, petroleum reserves, pipeline ownership, specialty air services, cable television, newspaper publishing, and ownership of US cultural industries. Canada has reservations against the US maritime sector and ownership of its waterfront land; and Mexico has reservations against US legal services (McMillan 2002).

More significantly, each country maintained investment thresholds or screening mechanisms. Canada's threshold for direct acquisition in financial services, transportation, uranium, and cultural industries was set at $5 million; and its threshold for indirect acquisitions was set at $50 million. The United States does not have investment thresholds, though under the 1988 Exon-Florio legislation the US president may refuse any investment that would endanger national security (McMillan 2002).

Mexico's investment thresholds were staggered throughout its NAFTA transition period: Controlling investment stakes in financial services were restricted to $25 million for a three-year period beginning in 1997 and then were to be increased to $75 million by 2000 and further raised to $150 million by 2003.[12] However, these investment thresholds were lifted when Mexico enacted its bank bailout legislation in March 1998, which further eliminated restrictions on foreign investment in Mexican commercial banks. This reform enabled Citibank to purchase Banco Confia as a retail subsidiary in 1998 for $195 million (and to acquire all of Banamex for $12.5 billion in 2001, now named Grupo Financiero Banamex). As of 2004, more than 80 percent of the Mexican banking industry is foreign-owned.[13]

Chapter 11 is unique (among NAFTA provisions) in allowing private investors to enforce government obligations under NAFTA Articles 1116

---

11. Under Annex 1, Mexico lists sectoral reservations in the energy, air and rail transport, agriculture, postal services, media ownership, and social services sectors; Canada lists reservations in cultural industries, air transport, social services, and agriculture; the United States lists reservations in maritime and air transport, radio communications, social services, and agriculture. See McMillan (2002).

12. See NAFTA Annex 1, Reservations and Exceptions to Investment at www.sice.oas.org/trade/nafta/naftatce.asp (accessed in November 2002). See Jonathan Friedland, "Mexican Congress Clears Bank Rescue," *Wall Street Journal*, December 14, 1998, and "Citibank Mexico, Banamex to Merge Bank Operations Monday," *Dow Jones International News*, November 7, 2001.

13. In the first quarter of 2004, five principal banks—Banamex, Bancomer, Santander Serfin, HSBC, and Scotiabank—were foreign-owned. Monica Campbell, "Mexico: Chase Is on for the Whole Enchilada," *The Banker*, June 1, 2004.

and 1117.[14] For NAFTA dispute settlement process purposes, the definition of investment is broadened to include minority interests, portfolio investment, and real property.[15] In the event that a state breaches one of NAFTA Chapter 11's substantive obligations, the investor may initiate an ad hoc arbitration tribunal, pursuant to Article 1120. The tribunals operate under the arbitration rules of either the International Center for Settlement of Investment Disputes (ICSID) or the United Nations Commission on International Trade Law (UNCITRAL).[16] Chapter 11 tribunals award monetary relief to the winning party.

By contrast, the WTO does not grant substantive rights to private parties or give them access to the dispute settlement mechanism. The WTO is designed as an interstate agreement. Nonparties to a dispute, such as private firms and nongovernmental organizations (NGOs), are limited at most to submitting amicus curiae briefs in panel hearings.[17]

For reasons not anticipated when Chapter 11 was drafted, protection of investor rights has since become the most contentious feature of the NAFTA dispute settlement system. NAFTA's substantive rules on investor rights were carried over from CUSFTA. These include investment liberalization rights for foreign investors (Article 1101), as well as guaran-

---

14. Mandatory investor-state arbitration, enforceable in US courts through the New York Convention, is present in several bilateral investment treaties (BITs) signed by the United States and many other countries. We thank Gary Horlick for this observation and for providing written comments to an earlier draft.

15. NAFTA Article 1139. In the *S.D. Myers* case, for example, investment in US-based waste disposal operations was compared with investment in similar Canadian waste disposal operations. See Cosbey (2002).

16. NAFTA arbitration rules allow investors to bring claims under the following conditions: the investor has suffered loss or damage due to the breach in NAFTA obligations (Articles 1116 and 1117); the disputing parties have attempted but failed to settle the claim through consultation or negotiation (Articles 1118 and 1120); arbitration was initiated within six months of the events giving rise to the claim (Article 1120); and the investor waives the right to initiate similar proceedings for compensation before domestic courts and other tribunals (Article 1121).

17. WTO Article V, as interpreted by the Appellate Body. Third parties may submit amicus curiae briefs, but neither panels nor the Appellate Body have a legal obligation to accept non-WTO member submissions. Since its ruling in the WTO *EU-Peru sardines* case (October 2002), the policy of the Appellate Body is to consider amicus curiae briefs on a case-by-case basis and accept them if the briefs are pertinent and useful to that particular case. If an amicus brief interferes with the "fair, prompt, and effective resolution of trade disputes," the Appellate Body can reject the consideration of any amicus curiae brief. Prior to the *EU-Peru sardines* case, the Appellate Body had not considered an amicus curiae brief pertinent to any WTO case. Most developing countries opposed the acceptance of amicus curiae briefs by WTO panels, arguing that amicus submissions might give nongovernmental organizations (NGOs) and private parties a greater role in dispute proceedings than some WTO members with limited resources. Correspondence with Amy Porges of Sidley, Austin, Brown & Wood LLP, Washington, DC and Debra P. Steger of Thomas & Partners, Ottawa, Canada, and comments from Patrick Macrory.

tees to protect existing investments established under conditions more favorable than those scheduled in the national reservations of individual NAFTA members (Article 1108).[18] However, the investor provisions that have sparked the most disputes filed under Chapter 11 are national treatment rights (Article 1102), MFN rights (Article 1103), minimum international standards of treatment (Article 1105), performance requirements (Article 1106), and especially provisions for compensation in the event of expropriation (Article 1110).

Articles 1102 and 1103 stipulate that a host country must treat foreign investors and their investments "no less favorably" than domestic investors or investors from any other country "in like circumstances."[19] Article 1103 is an extended version of the national treatment provisions contained in CUSFTA. This provision ensures that foreign investors based in North America will enjoy the best possible treatment among all foreign investors, even when one of the parties scheduled a NAFTA reservation against national treatment (Vega-Cánovas and Winham 2002). Article 1105 requires that NAFTA members meet minimum standards of "international law, including fair and equitable treatment and full protection and security." This provision is the functional equivalent of MFN treatment. Article 1106 prohibits governments from imposing certain types of performance requirements on investors.[20]

Several principles embodied in NAFTA Chapter 11 are also found in the WTO Agreement on Trade-Related Investment Measures (TRIMs) (as well as the Organization for Economic Cooperation and Development's [OECD]

---

18. Under Article 1108(4), no party may "require an investor of another Party, by reason of its nationality, to sell or otherwise dispose of an investment existing at the time the measure becomes effective." Other rights and obligations covered under Chapter 11 are compensation for acts of war or civil strife (Article 1105(2)), prohibitions on senior management nationality requirements (Article 1107), and an environmental protection provision—members are not allowed to reduce environmental standards as a way of attracting investment (Article 1114). It is worth noting that many Chapter 11 cases have a trade dimension.

19. There is some concern that since "fair and equitable treatment" is not further defined under NAFTA Chapter 11, the phrase could lead to mischief. The fear is that Chapter 11 arbitrators will not follow customary international law but instead will articulate their own standards on a case-by-case basis. As an extreme example, a foreign investor in the United States might lose its case before the US Supreme Court and then appeal to the NAFTA dispute settlement mechanism. In turn, NAFTA arbitrators could hypothetically overturn the US Supreme Court decision. Based on helpful comments from Theodore Moran. See Foy and Deane (2001).

20. As an example, governments cannot demand that firms use domestic inputs. The complete list of prohibitions on performance requirements includes government thresholds on exports of a given portion of production; using a given level of domestic content; making foreign exchange available based on the firm's levels of imports or exports; showing preference for domestic goods or services; requiring a firm to transfer its technology; or requiring a firm to locate production, provide employment, or offer specific services within its domestic territory.

ill-fated Multilateral Agreement on Investment, or MAI). The WTO accord prohibits (apart from scheduled exceptions) discrimination between foreign and domestic investors (national treatment) and between foreign investors from different countries (MFN treatment). It also limits the imposition of some of the performance requirements on foreign investors covered by NAFTA.[21] And it requires host states to compensate foreign investors for direct and indirect expropriations (Kurtz 2002).

Neither the CUSFTA nor the WTO TRIMs agreement grants private foreign investors the right to directly invoke and participate in dispute settlement cases (nor was such direct access contemplated in the MAI). But private investors are expressly given direct access to the NAFTA dispute settlement system under Chapter 11, and this has become one of its contentious features.[22] As a result, NAFTA member governments publicly narrowed the scope of foreign investment protections under Chapter 11, and the US government adopted more restrictive language in recent free trade agreements (FTAs) with Chile, Singapore, and Central America.[23]

The most criticized provision, Article 1110, is controversial because it attempts to balance investor rights against government measures to protect public welfare. Article 1110 of NAFTA states that a host country cannot expropriate from a foreign investor directly or indirectly, unless the expropriation is explicitly done for a public policy purpose, on a nondiscriminatory basis, in accordance with due process of law, and with fair compensation. These restrictions apply to direct or indirect measures "tantamount to nationalization or expropriation." This language, and its application in individual cases, causes some observers to fear that Chapter 11 arbitration panels will interpret the "tantamount to expropriation" phrase broadly to encompass "regulatory takings." Host governments would then be required

---

21. By contrast, the MAI would have required similar treatment of foreign investors in every province of Canada and every state of Mexico and the United States. NAFTA only requires that investors receive the best treatment provided in that province (or state). For complete details, see Appleton (2002).

22. Some practitioners, like Mark Cymrot of Baker & Hostetler LLP, argue that NAFTA governments are only beginning to see the potential implications of Chapter 11 as investment disputes face independent tribunals rather than governments. See Cymrot (2004). Specifically, NAFTA Chapter 11 actions can be brought not only by investors who are NAFTA nationals but also by any company incorporated in any one of the NAFTA countries. As an example, Sony United States, as an investor, could bring a Chapter 11 case against the United States. See Horlick and Marti (1997) and Dumberry (2001).

23. US Senator Max Baucus (D-MT), former chair of the Senate Finance Committee, called for an appellate mechanism in investor-state arbitration under future FTAs, a proposal that has since been adopted in the Central American Free Trade Agreement (CAFTA). The perceived overreaching influence of Chapter 11 led Congress to limit investor-state arbitration clauses in the US Trade Act of 2002. At Australian insistence, the recent Australia-US FTA excludes an investor-state dispute settlement clause. See Baker & Hostetler LLP (2004); also see Adam Liptak, "NAFTA Tribunals Stir US Worries," *New York Times*, April 18, 2004, A1.

to compensate foreign investors for damages equivalent to the amount of profits lost on account of regulation designed to further domestic social policies (e.g., environment, human health, and safety).[24]

In August 2000, an ICSID tribunal weighed in on the expropriation debate and made a relatively broad interpretation of expropriation under NAFTA. In the *Metalclad* case, the ICSID tribunal emphasized that expropriation is not limited to "outright seizure" but also includes "covert or incidental interference with the use of property which has the effect of depriving the owner, in whole or in significant part, of the use or reasonably-to-be-expected economic benefit of property even if not necessarily to the obvious benefit of the host State." The ICSID tribunal also decided that the motivation for the Ecological Decree, used by the local Mexican government to protect a rare cactus, was "not essential to the Tribunal's finding of a violation of NAFTA Article 1110."[25]

In contrast to the aggressive interpretation in the *Metalclad* case, other NAFTA Chapter 11 tribunal decisions have defined expropriation in more limited terms.[26] Moreover, new language in the US-Chile and US-Singapore FTAs limits the scope of investor protection and makes it very difficult for firms to claim that environmental or health measures are indirectly "tantamount to expropriation."

Chapter 14

Building upon financial-sector provisions established in CUSFTA Chapter 17, NAFTA Chapter 14 develops a general framework for the treatment of

---

24. A similar concern arises from the effort of conservative US scholars to argue that any regulation that adversely impacts a company's reasonable profit expectations could be considered an expropriation. The logical result is that, under the US Constitution, the regulating government body would need to indemnify the company for lost profits. Obviously this broad definition of expropriation would constrain regulatory regimes. We thank Theodore Moran for helpful written comments to an earlier draft. See Rose-Ackerman and Rossi (1999), van der Walt (1999), and Veloria (2002). See also "Interagency Group Struggles with Government Role in Investor Suits," *Inside US Trade*, March 22, 2002.

25. The ICSID tribunal found (in paragraph 111) that "the Tribunal need not decide or consider the motivation or intent of the adoption of the Ecological Decree." See *ICSID Award, Metalclad v. United Mexican States*, Case Number ARB (AF)/97/1, August 30, 2000. We thank Theodore Moran for providing the example in this paragraph, which draws heavily on written comments he provided to an earlier draft.

26. For different interpretations of expropriation under NAFTA, see the NAFTA tribunal determination in the *S. D. Myers* case and in *Pope & Talbot*. According to Daniel Price (2001), one of the lead US negotiators of NAFTA Chapter 11, negotiators tried to distinguish "between legitimate regulation on the one hand, bona fide and nondiscriminatory, and a taking on the other hand. We quickly gave up that enterprise. If the US Supreme Court could not do it in over 150 years, it was unlikely that we were going to do it in a matter of weeks."

banking, insurance, and brokerage. Chapter 14 uses a negative list for specific reservations, and these enable each country to maintain distinct prudential and protective regulation of financial sectors.[27] Canada scheduled a single reservation, whereas the United States listed 18, and Mexico initially had 26.

Canada's only reservation restricted the purchase of reinsurance by Canadian insurers from nonresident reinsurers. The United States adopted certain restrictions to complement its decentralized financial system. The exclusions focus on national treatment.[28] US reservations include citizenship and residence requirements for bank directors, home country reciprocity in order for a foreign institution to gain the status of a primary dealer in government debt, and the exclusion of foreign banks from owning domestic banks under some regional holding company laws.[29]

Mexico initially insisted on a very restrictive investment regime in financial services, focused primarily on limitations to Articles 1404 (Establishment) and 1407 (National Treatment). Mexico restricted foreign investment in existing financial institutions and ruled out foreign government ownership in an extensive list of financial institutions. Reflecting concerns that foreign financial affiliates would overrun Mexico's domestic financial industry, the Mexican government negotiated a comprehensive set of transitional limits.[30] As noted above, many of these restrictions were subsequently lifted as part of the Mexican government's response to the 1995 financial crisis.

NAFTA Chapter 14 allows foreign banks the right to establish themselves in member countries through branch offices. This provision was echoed in the WTO's Financial Services Agreement (1997). One of the key differences is the broader concept of "competitive opportunities" under Chapter 14. Under the WTO Financial Services Agreement, members agree to provide nondiscriminatory national treatment for scheduled financial services. NAFTA Chapter 14 went beyond this by requiring members to

---

27. See Annex 7 of the NAFTA Agreement, www.sice.oas.org/trade/nafta/naftatce.asp.

28. The United States does not, however, limit the right of establishment. See Rugman and Gestrin (1993).

29. Under NAFTA Chapter 14, the United States preserved restrictions in the Bank Holding Company Act (1956) and the International Banking Act (1978) that prevent foreign banks from enjoying the same treatment as domestic bank holding companies based in the same state in terms of their ability to expand into other states. This directly applies to NAFTA Article 1405 (National Treatment). See Chant (2002). As a practical matter, foreign banks can avoid these restrictions using alternative legal structures.

30. Transitional exceptions put caps on the authorized capital of each institution relative to the total capital of all institutions in the same financial sector. See Chant (2002).

provide "equal competitive opportunities" so that foreign providers will not be disadvantaged relative to domestic suppliers (Article 1405(6)).[31]

Chapter 14 also promotes competitiveness by allowing insurance companies to sell certain products, including reinsurance and cargo insurance, on a cross-border basis (NAFTA Article 1404).[32] Similarly, US and Canadian bonding companies can establish Mexican subsidiaries without any market share limitations. Through progressive liberalization, foreign investment in Mexican insurance companies was raised incrementally from 30 percent in 1994 to full ownership by 2000 (Kash 1997). Within the guidelines for financial liberalization in Chapter 14, Mexican restrictions on foreign ownership of banks and securities firms were initially subject to a gradual phaseout on a schedule extending through 2007.[33] This gradual liberalization timetable was scrapped in 1998, following Mexico's bank bailout legislation.

Principles for the provision of financial services cover regulatory safeguards (Article 1410),[34] the freedom of cross-border trade (Article 1404), the right of establishment (Article 1403), and national treatment (Article 1405). In addition, Chapter 14 includes special dispute settlement procedures (Articles 1412 to 1415).[35]

---

31. Exceptions are made with respect to national treatment that allow NAFTA members to pursue "reasonable measures for prudential reasons" (Article 1410) including protection of investors, depositors, and financial-market participants to whom a fiduciary duty is owed by a cross-border financial services provider; or maintenance of safety, integrity, or financial responsibility of financial institutions; or ensuring the integrity and stability of a party's financial system. For complete details, see Canada Department of Foreign Affairs and International Trade, www.dfait-maeci.gc.ca/nafta-alena/chap14-e.asp (accessed in November 2002).

32. Under NAFTA Chapter 14, Mexico also agreed to eliminate restrictions on its residents to purchase the following services from cross-border insurance providers: tourist insurance, cargo insurance for goods on international transit, and insurance for a vehicle in the transportation of cargo.

33. The initial restrictive provision stipulated that the proportion of total bank capital held by foreign banks was allowed to rise gradually to a maximum of 15 percent before the aggregate constraint disappears. Despite commitments to financial services liberalization, each NAFTA member reserved the right to tighten limits on market access and national treatment. See White (1994).

34. To preserve each country's sovereign monetary authority, regulatory safeguards ensure that each NAFTA party can maintain its autonomous right to monetary and exchange rate policies. As long as nondiscriminatory measures are applied to stabilization policies, each member country can pursue its own approach to regulation. For details see www.sice.oas.org/trade/nafta/chap-141.asp#A1402 (accessed in November 2002).

35. The special dispute settlement procedures are in Article 1412: Financial Services Committee; Article 1413: Consultations; Article 1414: Dispute Settlement; Article 1415: Investment Disputes in Financial Services. See www.sice.oas.org/trade/nafta/chap-141.asp #A1402 (accessed in November 2002).

An innovation in NAFTA Chapter 14 (by comparison with CUSFTA) is the mechanism for resolving disputes in the financial sector. In cases of investor-state disputes based on rights enumerated in Chapter 11, Article 1415 allows the defendant country to justify its public measures to the Financial Services Committee, which makes a binding determination. Committee members are drawn from government authorities responsible for financial services.[36]

Ultimately, financial-sector disputes can be subject to dispute settlement procedures under Chapter 20, where disputes will be referred to a tribunal that has limited authority to uphold or remand the decisions of national authorities. If the tribunal upholds a complaint, the home country of the complaining party may suspend benefits in the financial services sector (Chant 2002). This dispute settlement mechanism is untested: As of April 2005, no financial-sector disputes have been filed under either Chapter 14 or 20.

Chapter 19

Chapter 19 of NAFTA basically extended the provisions of Chapter 19 of the CUSFTA to Mexico. In CUSFTA negotiations, Canada sought to reform trade remedies that it labeled "contingent protection"—namely CVD and AD actions. This initiative was unacceptable to the United States. The compromise—reached in the eleventh hour of negotiations—was a new mechanism to review final determinations in CVD and AD cases, designed to substitute for and expedite the judicial review of administrative actions.

However, such an approach requires some degree of harmonization of AD and CVD administrative procedures. This did not pose a problem in CUSFTA given the similarities in US and Canadian practices. To facilitate Mexico's integration under the Chapter 19 dispute settlement process, negotiators adopted a two-pronged approach. One prong extended CUSFTA provisions within the NAFTA agreement itself; the other prong involved changes in Mexico's domestic trade remedy laws. The binational panel process has operated relatively well despite initial reservations over differences between Mexico's civil law system and the common-law US and Canadian legal systems.

The Chapter 19 panel process depends on the application of the domestic law of the party whose agency's determination is being challenged. In the context of NAFTA, Mexico adopted domestic trade remedy laws similar to those of the United States and Canada.[37] For example, as required

---

36. In addition to its dispute settlement function, the committee meets annually to review the financial services agreement. See Potter (1999).

37. Mexico knew that these changes would be required as well by the GATT in the Uruguay Round of multilateral trade negotiations.

under Article 1904(15), Mexico changed its domestic law that previously allowed CVD and AD duties to be levied within five days after receiving a petition. To facilitate Mexico's enforcement of trade laws, in 1993 the Government of Mexico enacted the Foreign Trade Act (Ley de Comercio Exterior, or LCE).[38] Mexico later amended the LCE to include provisions for judicial review and clarified the criteria for assessing AD and CVD.

To ensure that each NAFTA member fairly applies its own national trade remedy laws, Chapter 19 allows parties to challenge final administrative determinations before binational panels in lieu of appealing through national courts. Moreover, Chapter 19 retained the Extraordinary Challenge Committee (ECC) procedure established in the CUSFTA. This is a safeguard procedure to protect the integrity of the panel process. If a country alleges that a panel is biased or exceeded its authority, it can challenge the panel's decision before a three-person ECC.[39] This procedure was invoked three times under CUSFTA and three times under NAFTA (always by the United States).[40]

---

38. The LCE facilitates cooperation between antidumping authorities and the competition policy agency, the Federal Competition Commission (Comisión Federal de Competencia, or CFC).

39. Under Article 1904(13), the ECC process may be invoked if a party finds the NAFTA Chapter 19 tribunal decision was influenced by acts that threatened "the integrity of the binational panel review process." These actions include a panelist who is "guilty of gross misconduct, bias or a serious conflict of interest, or otherwise materially violated the rules of conduct." Other reasons for an ECC action include a panel "seriously [departing] from a fundamental rule of procedure; or if a panel "manifestly [exceeds] its powers, authority or jurisdiction set out in this Article" by "failing to apply the appropriate standard of review." The complete rules governing Chapter 19 are available at www.sice.oas.org/trade/nafta/naftatce.asp (accessed in November 2002).

40. The ECC process has been invoked only three times out of 101 NAFTA Chapter 19 cases. The United States initiated each ECC process and lost all three ECC decisions. The first ECC process was invoked by the United States in March 2000, after the Chapter 19 tribunal remanded the US Commerce Department's determination to impose final dumping margins on Gray Portland Cement and Clinker from Mexico (USA-97-1904-02). In October 2003, the ECC unanimously denied the US petition and affirmed the decision of the Chapter 19 panel. The second ECC process was invoked by the United States in September 2003, after the Chapter 19 tribunal remanded the US Commerce Department's decision to impose final dumping margins on pure magnesium from Canada (USA-CDA-2000-1904-06). This case was also resolved against the United States. The third ECC process was initiated by the United States in November 2004, after the Chapter 19 tribunal remanded the US Commerce Department's determination to impose 27 percent combined CVD and AD duties on Canadian softwood lumber with a specific instruction to enter a negative determination on injury and withdraw the countervailing duty order. The ECC rejected the US appeal in August 2005. See "US to Pursue Extraordinary Challenge of NAFTA Lumber Ruling," *Inside US Trade*, October 15, 2004; "Canadians See US Foot-Dragging on Formation of Lumber Panel," *Inside US Trade*, January 7, 2005; and "Canada Urges End of Lumber War After NAFTA ECC Rules Against United States," *Inside US Trade*, August 12, 2005. For details of the cases, see NAFTA Secretariat at www.nafta-sec-alena.org (accessed in August 2004).

Like CUSFTA before it, NAFTA does not have a body of substantive and procedural rules for handling AD and CVD cases.[41] Under NAFTA, each member applies its own national trade remedy laws, with no requirement to conform to a common template. NAFTA Chapter 19 is limited to establishing binational panels of five experts to review whether CVD and AD cases have been decided in a reasonable manner consistent with national law.

From the standpoint of US exporters to Mexico, Chapter 19 ensured that Mexico observed due process guarantees. From the standpoint of Canada and Mexico, Chapter 19 was meant to ensure that US administrative decisions are closely scrutinized.[42] In most cases, panel decisions have lowered US CVD and AD duties against Canadian and Mexican exports.[43] It is also worth noting that Canada and Mexico are subject to a lower intensity of US AD and CVD investigations than other countries, proportionate to trade volume. According to Patrick Macrory, since NAFTA was enacted, seven times as many AD and CVD orders have been filed against EU exports as Canadian exports, even though the total value of US imports from the European Union was not much higher than imports from Canada (Macrory 2002).[44]

As of June 2005, 103 panel reviews have been initiated under NAFTA Chapter 19.[45] But it is important to note that intra-NAFTA cases are increasingly appealed to the WTO rather than Chapter 19 panels. As of August 2004, the NAFTA partners have litigated 27 intra-NAFTA disputes

41. By contrast, WTO codes go to great lengths to define impermissible subsidies and dumping and to lay out the procedural rights and obligations of WTO members in trade remedy cases.

42. However, some international trade law experts argue that in Chapter 19 proceedings, the US government wrongly insists on "excessive deference" to the US Department of Commerce (DOC) and USITC rulings and that this deference perverts the appropriate standard of review. See Feldman (2004).

43. Besides softwood lumber, some 8 Canadian product lines are subject to AD or CVD orders. Based on USITC AD and CVD orders in place as of June 7, 2005, available at www.usitc.gov/trade_remedy/731_ad_701_cvd/investigations/antidump_countervailing/index.htm (accessed in July 2005). See appendix 4A.5 of this chapter for a compilation and summary of Chapter 19 cases. Also, Macrory (2002) counts product categories differently than in table 4.9.

44. The disparity in filings partly reflects a "mutual nonaggression" pact between the US and Canadian steel industries: Neither files AD or CVD complaints against the other. Since 2001, US imports from the European Union have surpassed those from Canada. In 2004, US imports from the European Union totaled $283 billion and US exports to the European Union reached $173 billion; by comparison, US imports from Canada were $256 billion, and US exports to Canada were $190 billion. Data are from US Census Bureau, Foreign Trade Statistics 2005.

45. Figures are based on research and press releases from the US DOC, US Trade Representative, and Canada Department of Foreign Affairs and International Trade.

under the WTO Dispute Settlement Mechanism.[46] An important reason is that the WTO has enunciated common standards and procedures for AD, CVD, and safeguard remedies, whereas NAFTA requires that national agencies faithfully apply their own standards and procedures.

However, WTO rulings do not invariably favor the country objecting to trade remedies. In June 2002, the WTO upheld the US law that establishes a time frame for implementing WTO rulings in AD and CVD cases.[47] In August 2004, the WTO Appellate Body sidestepped the issue of whether US AD calculations were inconsistent with the WTO Antidumping Agreement (see appendix table 4A.1 for a chronology of WTO decisions on lumber).[48] By contrast, in May 2004, the NAFTA Chapter 19 tribunal ruled that the US International Trade Commission (USITC) determination of injury in the same AD case against Canadian softwood lumber was inconsistent with US law. Then, in August 2004, the NAFTA Chapter 19 panel unanimously overturned the USITC finding of threat of injury in the softwood lumber case. Instead of reversing the case—the customary procedure under Chapter 19—the panel ordered the USITC to reverse itself in 10 days (see appendix table 4A.2 for a chronology of NAFTA decisions on lumber).[49] In this instance, the NAFTA arbitration panel rulings against the United States were stronger than anything issued by the WTO.

To provide a context for different determinations in the WTO and NAFTA, we compare the two dispute settlement mechanisms following our discussion of NAFTA Chapter 20.

Chapter 20

NAFTA Chapter 20 establishes the overall institutional framework for implementing NAFTA. While NAFTA Chapters 11, 14, and 19 are narrowly defined, Chapter 20 emphasizes the resolution of disputes through a variety of means: interstate consultations (including within the Free Trade

---

46. See the WTO Web site for a complete description of the 27 WTO cases, www.wto.org/english/tratop_e/dispu_e/distabase_wto_members3_e.htm (accessed in August 2004).

47. See Ricardo Reyes, "WTO Panel Rejects Canadian Challenge to US law," US Trade Representative press release, June 12, 2002, www.ustr.gov/Document_Library/Press_Releases/2002/June/section_index.html (accessed in August 2004).

48. See "WTO Appellate Body Rules Against Zeroing in Softwood Lumber Decision," *Inside US Trade*, August 13, 2004.

49. The Chapter 19 panel already remanded the case three times, but the USITC refused to comply. In the end, the NAFTA panel felt compelled to overturn the USITC decision. We thank Patrick Macrory for this observation and for providing written comments to an earlier draft. See "NAFTA Lumber Panel Orders ITC to Find No Injury Threat in 10 Days," *Inside US Trade*, September 3, 2004.

Commission), referral to a panel of independent experts, or resolution of the dispute through national courts by the complainant.

Substantive law issues addressed in Chapter 20 include the interpretation of the NAFTA itself; domestic measures of a party that may be inconsistent with the agreement; and national measures that might cause "nullification or impairment" of benefits arising under the Agreement (Article 2012). In July 2001, the NAFTA Free Trade Commission engaged in an important piece of legal interpretation: It narrowed the potential scope of Article 1105 by using new language to describe the minimum standard of treatment for foreign investors.[50]

Chapter 20 is similar in spirit to WTO consultation procedures, articulated in GATT Articles 22 and 23. Under NAFTA Chapter 20, the Free Trade Commission (a trilateral body of cabinet-level officers) conducts political consultations on matters arising from the implementation or interpretation of NAFTA obligations or resulting from changes in domestic or multilateral trade rules that affect NAFTA's operation. By virtue of these powers, the Free Trade Commission is responsible for overall political supervision of the NAFTA agreement.

Unlike CUSFTA Chapter 18, which required in Article 1806 recourse to "binding arbitration" to settle disputes over safeguard measures (as well as other matters, if mutually agreed), NAFTA removes the binding flavor of Chapter 20 panel arbitration. Instead, NAFTA members opted for closer consultations in the event an emergency measure, or safeguard action, is imposed.[51] While the NAFTA text provides the winning party an automatic right to retaliate in the absence of compliance,[52] the Free Trade Commission itself does not play an active role in submitting binding recommendations to member governments either on a public or confidential basis. Ad hoc consultation and standing committees at the ministerial level of the Free Trade Commission also sponsor technical studies and provide forums for general issues.

As of June 2005, Chapter 20 panel consultations reportedly have occurred only 10 times, compared with 103 panel reviews initiated under Chapter 19. Unlike other NAFTA dispute settlement procedures, Chapter 20 lacks any comprehensive, official record of formal consultation re-

---

50. For more information, see Canada International Trade Minister Pettigrew press release, webapps.dfait-maeci.gc.ca/minpub/Publication.asp?FileSpec=/Min_Pub_Docs/104441. htm (accessed August 2004).

51. According to Gilbert Winham (1993), the removal of binding arbitration in NAFTA Article 804 is consistent with the NAFTA philosophy of resolving disputes at the ground level before they become difficult.

52. Under Article 2019, if both parties cannot reach a "mutually satisfactory resolution" within "30 days of receiving the final [NAFTA Commission] report," the "complaining Party may suspend benefits of equivalent effect until . . . they have reached agreement on the resolution of the dispute." For complete details, see NAFTA Secretariat, www.nafta-sec-alena.org/DefaultSite/index_e.aspx?DetailID=176#A2018 (accessed March 2005).

quests compiled by the NAFTA Secretariat or individual governments. Some Chapter 20 cases have involved highly politicized disputes over trucking, sugar, and tomatoes. In these instances, consultations have had mixed results in promoting compliance with NAFTA obligations but have prevented episodes of "tit-for-tat" retaliation that could have undercut NAFTA reforms.

NAFTA and WTO Dispute Settlement Mechanisms Compared

Canada, Mexico, and the United States are members of the WTO as well as NAFTA. One consequence is overlapping jurisdiction between the NAFTA and the WTO dispute settlement mechanisms.[53] While the two systems have similarities, they also have key differences.

Decentralized System

Perhaps the biggest difference is that the WTO's Dispute Settlement Understanding (DSU) creates a single, integrated dispute resolution system for almost all Uruguay Round texts. This avoids potential procedural controversies when a dispute overlaps the boundaries between trade in goods, services, and intellectual property. By contrast, NAFTA contains several adjudication systems and standards of review. Chapter 11 panels are instructed to evaluate claims against the minimum norms set forth in the NAFTA text.[54] Chapter 19 panels are instructed to apply the domestic law of the importing NAFTA party to review administrative determinations in trade remedy cases. NAFTA's Chapter 20 establishes a political interstate dispute resolution mechanism, drawing on both NAFTA and international law.

---

53. At least two cases filed under Chapter 20 raised potential conflicts between NAFTA and WTO obligations: the *Canadian Agricultural Tariffs* case (CDA-95-2008-01) and the *Broom Corn Brooms* case (USA-97-2008-01). The *Agricultural Tariffs* case is particularly interesting. Before NAFTA, Canada used quotas to limit agricultural imports, and these were not disturbed by NAFTA. However, the WTO Uruguay Round accord required Canada to convert its agricultural quotas into new and higher tariffs. When this was done, the United States filed a complaint that Canada had breached its NAFTA obligation not to raise tariffs. In December 1996, the NAFTA Chapter 20 tribunal unanimously determined that Canadian agricultural tariffs conformed to NAFTA provisions. In the *Broom Corn Brooms* case Mexico alleged the United States failed to apply the appropriate injury test under the GATT Article XIX safeguards provision. The NAFTA Commission accepted this argument, and the United States withdrew its safeguard measures. See Abbott (1999) and Vega-Cánovas and Winham (2002).

54. NAFTA Chapter 11 on investment disputes is open to three arbitration procedures: ICSID, ICSID's "Additional Facility," and UNCITRAL.

Beyond the decentralized nature of the NAFTA system, other features distinguish dispute settlement under NAFTA from that under the WTO.[55]

Judges and Panelists

The WTO DSU is unique among commercial agreements in creating a permanent appellate body that reviews panel decisions. Panels of first instance normally consist of three persons. The WTO Secretariat maintains a roster of approximately 200 potential panelists; the DSU has detailed procedures for panel selection to avoid delays in constituting panels (which often occurs in the NAFTA context).[56] The WTO process also ensures third-party adjudication: It does not allow panelists to be citizens of either party to the dispute.

Through August 2004, WTO panels had issued 146 reports, which in turn generated 63 Appellate Body decisions.[57] In cases of WTO appellate review, a three-person panel is drawn from the standing seven-person Appellate Body.[58] The procedures for selection are confidential so that no government can predict which Appellate Body members will sit on its appeal. The seven Appellate Body judges are appointed to four-year terms, renewable once; the WTO Dispute Settlement Body (DSB) selects them through a consensus process.

By contrast, NAFTA maintains smaller rosters of panelists, ranging from 30 to 75 members depending on the chapter.[59] Under Chapter 11, the

---

55. NAFTA parties have the option of simultaneously pursuing disputes under NAFTA Chapter 19 and the WTO. However, if a dispute has already been initiated under either NAFTA Chapter 20 or the WTO, the NAFTA party can choose only one forum and cannot pursue cases in both multilateral dispute settlement processes (see Article 2007). There are also conditions when the NAFTA defendant country may request to pursue disputes only under NAFTA (see Article 2005). Specifically, the option to limit disputes to the NAFTA dispute settlement forum is allowed only for cases pertaining to environmental and conservation agreements, sanitary and phytosanitary measures, or standards-related measures.

56. Delays in constituting NAFTA panels have been damaging. By contrast, a relatively minor mechanical step under the WTO makes a huge difference. Under the WTO, any party to the dispute can ask the director-general to appoint panelists within 20 days. We thank Gary Horlick for this observation and for providing written comments to an earlier draft.

57. All WTO panel and Appellate Body reports are described at www.wto.org/english/tratop_e/dispu_e/stats_e.htm (accessed in October 2004).

58. However, all seven Appellate Body panelists consult on each case to ensure consistency of rulings. See Bacchus (2003) and Jackson (2000).

59. Immediately before the enactment of NAFTA, negotiators anticipated an increase in trade remedy disputes and expanded the roster of candidates to serve as panel members. See "US NAFTA Secretariat Expands Roster of Eligible Panelists," *Inside US Trade*, November 25, 1994. NAFTA Chapter 11 maintains a roster of 45 panelists appointed from the ICSID Panel of Arbitrators, Chapter 19 maintains a roster of 75 individuals, and Chapter 20 a roster of up to 30 members appointed by consensus for three-year terms, with possibility for renewal.

disputing parties appoint an ad hoc three-member tribunal selected from legal experts on the ICSID roster. Each NAFTA party to the dispute appoints a panelist, and the presiding arbitrator is appointed either by consensus between the disputants or by the ICSID secretary-general.[60] Despite initial fears that NAFTA tribunal decisions would be determined along national lines, studies suggest this has not been the trend (Howse 1998, Macrory 2002).

Under Chapter 14, financial disputes would ultimately be resolved by a panel comprising at least two arbitrators selected by each government from an agreed roster of 15 financial services experts, plus a chair selected by the two arbitrators. The Chapter 14 panel procedure has not yet been invoked.

Under Chapter 19, each litigant chooses two of the five panelists, and the panelists themselves choose the fifth. Panelists are drawn from a roster of 75 individuals, mainly international trade lawyers.[61] If there is an extraordinary challenge, three judges or former judges are selected as panelists.

Echoing criticisms of CUSFTA, there are, however, concerns about the standard of review[62] and the panel selection process under Chapter 19. US Senators Larry Craig (R-ID), Saxby Chambliss (R-GA), Lindsey Graham (R-SC), and Jeff Sessions (R-AL) have questioned the integrity of the NAFTA dispute settlement process. Specifically, they contend that the Canadian government's refusal, in the softwood lumber case, to remove a panelist with an alleged conflict of interest violates the dispute resolution rules. Similar arguments are voiced from representatives of Canadian interests. Elliot J. Feldman of Baker & Hostetler LLP argues that US panelists are chosen based on politics rather than impartiality and that the US government uses conflict-of-interest allegations to delay the panel selection process.[63] We suggest procedural reforms to address these concerns in the last section of this chapter.

---

60. If NAFTA disputing parties fail to agree upon the presiding arbitrator, the secretary-general will select the arbitrator from among a roster of 45 individuals agreed upon by NAFTA governments.

61. Chapter 19 urges NAFTA members (at US insistence) to include individuals who are "sitting or retired judges" on their roster. To date, however, there seems to have been only one Canadian judge on a binational Chapter 19 panel, while no American judge or former judge has served on a panel (NAFTA Annex 1901.2).

62. As an example, in both panel decisions over softwood lumber—the original CUSFTA and the subsequent ECC process—there were clear differences about whether panelists based their previous decisions on US legal principles. US members argued that Canadian panelists systemically misapplied the US standard of appellate review used to evaluate administrative law decisions. See Macrory (2002), Howse (1998), and Baker & Hostetler LLP (2004).

63. Feldman argues that the US government preemptively removed US panelists in the middle of the *Magnesium from Canada* case that seemed to be hostile to the US position. The US senators refer to the *Softwood Lumber* case as an example of how conflict of interest by one of the Canadian panelists breaches the NAFTA dispute resolution system. See Larry Craig, Saxby Chambliss, Lindsey Graham, and Jeff Sessions, letter to John Ashcroft, May 12, 2004. See Baker & Hostetler LLP (2004) and Feldman (2004).

Under Chapter 20, five panelists hear cases that reach the arbitration stage. A chairperson is first selected from a neutral country and then two panelists are selected from citizens of each disputing party.[64] Parties agree to choose a chair within 15 days of the date a panel request is delivered. If disputing parties cannot agree on a chair, they must draw lots and choose a nonnational panelist.

As of August 2004, three arbitration panels have been convened; 8 of the 15 panelists have been law professors.[65] By comparison with the WTO dispute settlement mechanism, NAFTA Chapter 20 remains primarily a forum for political consultation. Unlike the WTO DSU, however, arbitral panels under NAFTA Chapter 20 can provide only nonbinding recommendations; moreover, there is no appellate review of Chapter 20 panels.[66] Chapter 20 panels are limited to reviewing findings of fact to determine whether a member country's policy is consistent with its obligations under NAFTA.

Timelines

Article 12 of the WTO DSU requires panel reports to be issued within six to nine months after the case is brought, but it also allows the losing party to have a "reasonable period of time" (Article 21) to implement rulings. Under Article 21, the losing party can propose a period of time to comply with the panel determination, and the normal 15-month timeline "may be shorter or longer, depending upon the peculiar circumstances" (DSU Article 21.3).

By contrast, NAFTA has both tighter and looser timelines for arbitration. Chapter 11 has strict time limits on what disputing parties must do to initiate and/or respond to proceedings, but it does not set time limits on actual arbitration (Wilkie 2002). As a consequence, some cases have taken four years or more.[67]

---

64. A "reverse selection" panel process is designed to ensure impartiality. First, the chair of the panel is selected from a neutral third country, then each disputing party selects two additional panelists who are citizens of the other party (Article 2011).

65. See Gantz (1999). The citation of three panels refers to officially initiated dispute settlement panels under Chapter 20. See appendix 4A.3 for the list of known Chapter 20 cases and government consultations.

66. According to Gantz (1999), the NAFTA Free Trade Commission and Secretariat appear similar to the WTO Dispute Settlement Body (DSB) on paper, but in reality, the DSB and Secretariat are more impartial since members of the NAFTA Free Trade Commission also are officials of governments involved in NAFTA Chapter 20 disputes.

67. *Marvin Feldman vs. United States* (February 1998); *Loewen Group Inc. vs. Canada* (July 1998); *Sun Belt Water Inc. vs. United States* (November 1998); *Methanex Corporation vs. United States* (June 1999); *UPS of America Inc. vs. Canada* (May 2000); *ADF Group Inc. vs. Canada* (July 2000); *USA Waste vs. Mexico* (September 2000); and *Adams et al. vs. Mexico* (November 2000). For a description of the cases, see www.naftaclaims.com (accessed in March 2005). The cited dates indicate when cases were filed.

Chapter 19 panels have 315 days to submit their final determinations. After authorities in the importing country review the ruling, the exporting country has 30 days to submit its request for relief to the NAFTA importing country. If followed, this schedule would be shorter than resorting to judicial review through national courts. Through October 2002, the NAFTA dispute settlement tribunals on average decided cases within 18 months. While no case has been resolved within the 315-day schedule, the Chapter 19 binational system generally resolves disputes more quickly than either Canada's Court of International Trade or the US Federal Circuit.

Yet there is some concern that, without a permanent roster of panelists, the NAFTA dispute settlement process might be subject to delay. According to Eric J. Pan (1999), during 1994–99, the Chapter 19 dispute settlement mechanism took an average 502 days, and the Canadian Court of International Trade and US Federal Circuit took a combined average 1,210 days to resolve disputes. David A. Gantz (1999) also notes that inattention to Chapter 19 proceedings by NAFTA governments has led to endemic delay.[68] For example, in 1999, 6 of 11 active Chapter 19 cases were suspended during the proceedings, sometimes for more than six months.[69]

Elliot Feldman (2004) contends that, in the past few years, deliberate delay by the US government has made Chapter 19 proceedings slower on average than the Canadian Court of International Trade. Feldman notes that missed deadlines are often the norm and there are no effective penalties to curb delay. As a result, some Canadian producers are turning to the Canadian Federal Court of Appeal and the US Court of International Trade to adjudicate disputes, because they see Chapter 19 as too costly and lengthy.[70]

The Chapter 20 dispute settlement mechanism emphasizes consultations, good offices, conciliation, and mediation over arbitration. Most Chapter 20 disputes have been resolved during the prepanel stage. Compared with other dispute settlement chapters, the flexible nature of Chapter 20 is a liability because delays in the panel selection process only drag out politically sensitive issues—such as the Mexico-US trucking dispute and disagreements over Mexican sugar exports.[71]

---

68. For a complete list of cases and their timelines, please refer to appendix tables 4A.3, 4A.4, and 4A.5.

69. Most of the suspensions occurred because panelists resigned over alleged conflict of interest. We thank Patrick Macrory for this observation and for providing written comments to an earlier draft.

70. In May 2004, for example, the Heinz Company of Canada won a dispute in the Federal Court of Appeal against the Gerber Products Company (US). See Potter (2004) and Stobo (2004).

71. Panels are the last recourse under Chapter 20, and long delays in the panel selection process are normal. See Mena (2001).

Transparency

A key criticism of dispute resolution under both the NAFTA and the WTO is that settlement proceedings are closed to the public. Panel sessions and initial reports are kept confidential. Interested third parties are allowed only limited participation, fostering the confidential nature of the dispute settlement process.

Some NAFTA critics complain that secret notices of intent and confidential proceedings enable private interests to lobby governments with little public scrutiny (Mann 2001). As an example, during 1994–2004, the record indicates that notice of intent and arbitration proceedings were kept confidential in about 25 percent of cases filed under Chapter 11.[72] These may include some of the most controversial cases.

In an effort to make the Chapter 11 dispute settlement process more transparent, the NAFTA Free Trade Commission agreed in 2001 to limit the circumstances when documents could remain confidential and to encourage the publication of all other documents.[73] In July 2002, the US Congress directed US trade negotiators to pursue similar guidelines in all new US trade agreements.[74] In August 2004, NAFTA trade ministers supported open hearings under Chapters 11 and 20 dispute settlement mechanisms but not under Chapter 19 (WorldTrade Executive, Inc. 2004).

Finality and Enforceability of Decisions

Neither the WTO nor the NAFTA dispute settlement systems have independent authority over national legislatures or domestic courts. In the last analysis, it is up to national administrative, legislative, and judicial bodies to implement WTO and NAFTA decisions. For example, the WTO Appellate Body has the final say on the rights and obligations of members under various WTO agreements. It can authorize the winning member to

---

72. Descriptions of disputes submitted under Chapter 11, including proceedings that were confidential, are compiled by Todd Weiler at www.naftaclaims.com (accessed in March 2005).

73. The NAFTA Free Trade Commission stated that documents withheld from the public could include confidential business information and information that is protected from disclosure under a party's domestic law. See NAFTA Free Trade Commission, "Notes of Interpretation of Certain Chapter 11 Provisions," July 2001. All NAFTA Free Trade Commission interpretive notes are described at www.dfait-maeci.gc.ca/tna-nac/NAFTA-Interpr-e.asp (accessed in March 2005).

74. Section 2102 (b)(3)(H) of the Bipartisan Trade Promotion Authority Act of 2002 directs US negotiators to ensure "the fullest measure of transparency in the dispute settlement mechanism." Subsequently, the NAFTA tribunal in the *Methanex* case determined that future substantive hearings will be open to the public. For details, see the International Institute for Sustainable Development at www.iisd.org (accessed in March 2005).

take countermeasures against the losing member. But it cannot instruct national judges sitting in the courts of the losing member to enforce WTO decisions.

Notable differences exist between the WTO and NAFTA institutional mechanisms for encouraging member countries to accept dispute settlement decisions. WTO adoption of Appellate Body decisions is virtually automatic, since a "reverse consensus" of member countries is required to overturn a decision of the Appellate Body.[75] If disputing parties cannot agree upon mutually acceptable compensation within 20 days, the complaining party can retaliate by requesting that the DSB authorize the suspension of WTO obligations in an amount equivalent to the value of its impaired WTO trade rights (DSU Article 22). WTO dispute settlement procedures seldom lead to compensation settlements, so retaliation is the final recourse when countries that violate their WTO obligations do not comply with panel rulings (Anderson 2002).[76] While WTO decisions are ultimately backed up by compensation or retaliation, according to the DSU text, "neither compensation nor suspension of concessions or other obligations is preferred to full implementation of a recommendation to bring a measure into conformity with the covered agreements" (DSU Article 22). By comparison with the streamlined WTO system for encouraging compliance, the NAFTA works along several tracks.

Chapter 11

Under Chapter 11, arbitral awards are final. NAFTA Article 1136 requires each government to establish rules for enforcement of final awards.[77] The award can be enforced through either government-to-government arbitration under Article 2008, the ICSID Convention, or ultimately by domestic courts. As of August 2004, 6 out of 31 cases filed under NAFTA Chapter 11 have led to tribunal awards.[78] NAFTA governments have generally implemented these awards without resort to further proceedings. The only Chapter 11 arbitral award subject to a judicial review, the *Metalclad* case, was affirmed in favor of the investor. In *Metalclad*, the British

75. A "reverse consensus" under the WTO Agreement means that no WTO member, including the winning party, would accept the Appellate Body decision. So far this has not happened.

76. The WTO authorized retaliatory measures in eight cases during 1996–2004. See www.wto.org/english/tratop_e/dispu_e/distabase_e.htm (accessed in August 2004).

77. Article 1136(4) states that each disputing party should "provide for the enforcement of an award in its territory."

78. So far, US investors are most successful at winning tribunal awards. The NAFTA tribunal ordered the Canadian and Mexican governments to pay about $17 million each to US investors. The US government had to pay only for the cost of arbitration proceedings in the *USA Waste* case.

Columbia court denied an attempt by the government of Mexico to set aside the award.[79]

Chapter 14

NAFTA Chapter 14 provides a mechanism for settling financial disputes, via a Chapter 20 arbitration, but tribunal decisions are not binding on administrative agencies or national courts. The winning complainant's final recourse is retaliatory action (Articles 1414 and 1415).

Chapter 19

Chapter 19 is unique in providing the only mechanism for resolving AD and CVD trade disputes with binational panels (Baker & Hostetler LLP 2004). Chapter 19 panel decisions either uphold or remand (in whole or part) a final administrative agency determination in AD or CVD investigations. In the event of a remand, the original administering agency is supposed to reconsider its decision in light of the panel's determination.[80] As a consequence, compliance ultimately rests with national administrative agencies.[81] The dependence on national administrative agencies gives Chapter 19 flexibility but also raises questions about the finality of panel decisions. As an example, in the *Live Swine* case, carried over from CUSFTA, the US Department of Commerce (DOC) in May 1995 essentially ignored the Chapter 19 panel ruling that Quebec's Farm Income Stabilization Insurance (FISI) program did not create a countervailable subsidy.[82] The DOC reopened the *Live Swine* case several times, imposing

---

79. In the Chapter 11 arbitration proceeding of *Metalclad vs. United Mexican States*, the tribunal gave an award to Metalclad, but the amount of damages to be paid was reduced from the $90 million claim to an award of $16.7 million. For details, see the NAFTA Secretariat at www.nafta-sec-alena.org/DefaultSite/index_e.aspx (accessed in March 2005).

80. However, given that each Chapter 19 panel review is sui generis, each panel decision is unique and cannot be used as a precedent for future Chapter 19 cases. See Baker & Hostetler LLP (2004).

81. While international trade experts may argue that the Chapter 19 process gives substantial deference to the US DOC and USITC, some US Senate members and industry lobbyists disagree. In May 1995, 40 US industry associations protested the "judicial activism" of NAFTA Chapter 19 panels. Industry lobbyists argued the NAFTA panels had moved beyond their original mandate of deciding cases based on the applicable national law. US Senate leaders raised similar concerns in August 1995. See "Canada Presses for Substantive Results of NAFTA AD/CVD Group," *Inside US Trade*, June 16, 1995; "Dole, Finance Committee Members Warn Against NAFTA Panel System," *Inside US Trade*, August 1995; and "Coalition Letter on NAFTA Dispute Settlement," *Inside US Trade*, May 1995.

82. The US DOC found that two agricultural programs benefiting swine producers were specific subsidies because the actual number of recipients of benefits was small compared with potential beneficiaries. However, the Chapter 19 panel determined the DOC did not provide substantial evidence that swine producers received disproportionately large bene-

new CVDs, most recently in May 2004, despite rulings by the Chapter 19 panel.[83] The prolonged softwood lumber case may lead to a US court decision determining whether or not the US DOC must observe specific instructions in a Chapter 19 panel report.

Chapter 20

The trilateral nature of NAFTA implies that at least two of the three NAFTA member countries will be parties to each Chapter 20 dispute. Peer pressure to resolve a Chapter 20 dispute therefore comes from a small but intensely interested set of countries. By contrast, in the WTO system, peer pressure can come from a great many countries, even though only a few may be intensely interested in the dispute.

Often overlooked, Chapter 20 is potentially useful for enforcing NAFTA obligations. Under Article 2004, NAFTA parties can hold each other accountable to their implementation of the agreement.[84] Specifically, any NAFTA member country can initiate consultations under Article 2006.[85] If bilateral or trilateral consultations fail, the NAFTA party has recourse to mediation under Article 2007.[86] The final recourse is arbitration under Article 2008.[87]

---

fits under FISI. See Macrory (2002) and Feldman (2004). Also see *Live Swine from Canada*, USA-94-1904-01 and *Live Swine from Canada*, USA-91-1904-04, www.nafta-sec-alena. org/ DefaultSite/index_e.aspx (accessed in March 2005).

83. See Baker & Hostetler LLP (2004), Potter (2004), and Office of the Federal Register (2004).

84. Article 2004 allows for the resolution of Chapter 20 disputes between NAFTA parties "regarding the interpretation or application of this Agreement or wherever a Party considers that an actual or proposed measure of another Party is or would be inconsistent with the obligations of this Agreement or cause nullification or impairment in the sense of Annex 2004." Annex 2004 clarifies that a NAFTA member country can initiate a dispute if "any benefit . . . is being nullified or impaired" under the agreement in any of the following areas: trade in goods (except automotive and energy sectors), technical barriers to trade, cross-border services trade, and intellectual property. See NAFTA Chapter 20: Institutional Arrangements and Dispute Settlement Procedures, www.sice.oas.org/trade/nafta/chap-202.asp (accessed in March 2005).

85. Under Article 2006.1, "any Party may request in writing consultations with any other Party regarding any actual or proposed measure or any other matter that it considers might affect the operation of this Agreement." See NAFTA Chapter 20: Institutional Arrangements and Dispute Settlement Procedures, www.sice.oas.org/trade/nafta/chap-202.asp (accessed in March 2005).

86. A mediation includes a meeting before the NAFTA Free Trade Commission, which comprises cabinet-level representatives.

87. Under Article 2008.1, "any consulting Party may request in writing the establishment of an arbitral panel." See NAFTA Chapter 20: Institutional Arrangements and Dispute Settlement Procedures, www.sice.oas.org/trade/nafta/chap-202.asp (accessed in March 2005).

Table 4.1 Investor-state disputes under Chapter 11, 1994–2004

Claimant	Respondent		
	Canada	Mexico	United States
Canada	0	1	13
Mexico	1	0	0
United States	9	15	0
Total	10	16	13

Sources: US State Department, Office of the Legal Adviser, 2004, www.state.gov/s/l/c3439.htm; Canada Department of Foreign Affairs and International Trade, 2004; and Todd Weiler, www.naftalaw.org, 2004.

Noncompliance with a Chapter 20 ruling under NAFTA can theoretically lead to penalties. Under Article 2019 of NAFTA (like Article 22.2 of the WTO DSU), in the event of noncompliance, the winning complaining party can retaliate by suspending tariff concessions or other obligations covered by the trade agreement. As in the WTO, the ultimate penalty in NAFTA is retaliation. And like the WTO, difficult cases take a long time to resolve. Thus, both the sugar and trucking disputes between the United States and Mexico have been characterized by layered retaliatory threats and countermeasures between the parties.

Outcome of Dispute Settlement Cases

Chapter 11 Cases

Through January 2005, 39 investor-state disputes were initiated under Chapter 11.[88] The cases are summarized in appendix table 4A.4. Sixteen cases have been initiated against Mexico, 10 against Canada, and 13 against the United States (table 4.1).[89] US investors account for two-thirds of the cases initiated; only two cases have been initiated between Mexico and Canada. The number of cases filed has steadily increased over time.[90] US-Mexico cases are substantially more frequent, per billion dollars of US FDI in Mexico, than US-Canada cases (see table 4.2, which compares the number of disputes with the corresponding bilateral FDI).

---

88. For a complete description of cases, see Canada Department of Foreign Affairs and International Trade, www.dfait-maeci.gc.ca/tna-nac/nafta-e.asp (accessed in March 2005).

89. Cases initiated are based on notices of intention to arbitrate (whether or not a claim was filed).

90. Mark Clodfelter (2004) at the US State Department NAFTA Arbitration Division notes that a high proportion of Chapter 11 cases are rooted in trade disputes. He points out that the rise in Chapter 11 cases seems to be outrunning the availability of qualified arbitrators.

Table 4.2   FDI stock related to Chapter 11 disputes, 1994–2004

US FDI in	Bilateral FDI stock[a] (billions of dollars)	Chapter 11 cases	Cases per $1 billion FDI
Canada	173	9	0.05
Mexico	36	15	0.41

a. Average 1994–2003, based on FDI stock.

Sources: Bureau of Economic Analysis, US Commerce Department, 2004; and Mexico Ministry of the Economy, 2004.

As of August 2004, US investors had been wholly or partly successful in five decided Chapter 11 cases (see table 4.3, which compares the number of disputes won by the investor and state by country).[91] However, in none of the cases has the investor been awarded an amount close to its initial (probably overblown) claim. The cases in question are *Ethyl Corporation vs. Canada, Metalclad Corporation vs. Mexico, Azinian vs. Mexico, Marvin Feldman vs. Mexico, S. D. Myers vs. Canada, Pope & Talbot vs. Canada, Mondev International vs. United States, ADF Group Inc. vs. United States,* and *USA Waste vs. Mexico* (submitted twice) (see table 4.4, which compares settled Chapter 11 cases and arbitral awards).[92] Five cases have been withdrawn, and another 16 cases are pending determination. Tribunal awards to successful claimants have so far totaled around $35 million (see appendix table 4A.4 and table 4.4).[93] Arbitral awards are small relative to initial claims—on average, they amount to only 19 percent of the original claim. In the most extreme case so far (*Pope & Talbot*), the final NAFTA arbitral award represented only 0.5 percent of the original claim.[94] Nevertheless, the process shows that private investors can hold NAFTA governments accountable to their Chapter 11 obligations.

As of January 2005, 11 environment-related disputes had been brought under Chapter 11, seven of which were filed by US investors and four by a Canadian company. Among these cases, four each were filed against

---

91. Success is defined as a monetary award in favor of the respondent or claimant. Specifically, US investors won five cases with a monetary award and one case partly on legal grounds.

92. So far, 11 out of 13 settled cases received arbitral awards that are a fraction of the initial overblown claims. The remaining three cases were withdrawn before the commencement of arbitration. See table 4.4 for details.

93. Total awards amount to about $35 million damages plus interest and plus the cost of tribunal proceedings.

94. Pope & Talbot's initial claim was $130 million, but the NAFTA tribunal awarded final costs and damages totaling $461,566 plus interest. The small NAFTA arbitral award reflects the fact that Pope & Talbot lost all of its main claims. For details, see Canada Department of Foreign Affairs and International Trade, www.dfait-maeci.gc.ca/tna-nac/NAFTA-e.asp (accessed in March 2005).

Table 4.3   Outcome of investor-state disputes under Chapter 11, 1994–2004

Disposition	Canada	Mexico	United States
Total won by the investor/claimant	0	0	5
Total won by the state/respondent	0	0	1
Joint termination of case	4	2	4

Note: Winning is defined as a monetary award in favor of the claimant or respondent.

Sources: US State Department, Office of the Legal Adviser, 2004, www.state.gov/s/l/c3439.htm; Canada Department of Foreign Affairs and International Trade, 2004; and Todd Weiler, www.naftalaw.org, 2004.

Mexico and the United States, and three against Canada. Currently more than a quarter of all Chapter 11 cases involve environment-related issues.

Nearly half of all investor-state cases claimed violations under NAFTA Articles 1102 and 1105 (table 4.5). National treatment provisions in Articles 1102 and 1103 require governments to treat foreign investors based in any NAFTA member country no less favorably than domestic investors. Article 1105 requires members to observe the minimum standards of "international law." In an effort to address the criticism that arbitration panels had overextended Article 1105, in August 2001 the NAFTA Free Trade Commission issued an Interpretive Note stating that "[a] determination that there has been a breach of another provision of the NAFTA, or of a separate international agreement, does not establish that there has been a breach of Article 1105(1)."[95] In other words, the commission narrowed the interpretation of minimum standards of treatment to limit possibilities for firms to litigate based on any international law obligation.[96] The third most frequently cited breach of NAFTA obligation is Article 1110, which provides the basis for "regulatory takings" claims. We examine a few cases to highlight how these and other provisions have featured in Chapter 11 disputes.

S. D. Myers Inc. vs. the Government of Canada

In the S. D. Myers case, decided in October 2002 in favor of the US investor, the NAFTA tribunal dismissed the company's claims relating to expropriation and performance requirements but upheld its assertion that Canada violated its national treatment obligation. Until Canada's Poly-

---

95. For more information about the NAFTA Free Trade Commission's interpretation of Article 1105, see Canadian International Trade Minister Pettigrew's press release, webapps.dfait-maeci.gc.ca/minpub/Publication.asp?FileSpec=/Min_Pub_Docs/104441.htm (accessed in March 2005).

96. The NAFTA Free Trade Commission's interpretation of Article 1105 clarified that minimum standards of treatment correspond with customary international law.

Table 4.4   Comparison of settled Chapter 11 claims and arbitral awards

Case	Amount claimed (millions of dollars)	Amount awarded[a] (millions of dollars)
Ethyl Corporation	250.0	13.0
Metalclad Corporation	90.0	16.7
Azinian	17.0	—
Marvin Feldman	50.0	1.0
USA Waste[b]	60.0	—
S. D. Myers	20.0	3.9
Pope & Talbot[c]	507.6	0.5
Mondev	16.0	—
ADF Group Inc.	90.0	—
Methanex Corporation	970.0	4.0
Total	**2,070.6**	**39.0**

— = No award on costs made; each side pays its own expenses plus half the costs and expenses of the tribunal proceedings.

a. Tribunal awards plus interest. Three cases (Sun Belt, Ketcham, and Trammel Crow) that were withdrawn before the commencement of arbitration are not included.
b. USA Waste is counted twice as it was submitted twice.
c. Based on claims that the Canadian government violated five Chapter 11 obligations: Articles 1102, 1103, 1105, 1106, and 1110.

Sources: US State Department, Office of the Legal Adviser, 2004, www.state.gov/s/l/c3439. htm; Canada Department of Foreign Affairs and International Trade, 2004; Todd Weiler, www.naftalaw.org, 2004.

chlorinated Biphenyls (PCB) Waste Export Regulations were adopted in 1990, Canadian law favored domestic treatment and disposal of PCBs.[97] Meanwhile, the United States prohibited PCB imports until 1995, when the US Environmental Protection Agency (EPA) allowed S. D. Myers and nine other companies to import PCB waste from Canada for processing and disposal. S. D. Myers, an Ohio-based waste treatment company, was located closer to Canadian PCB wastes than its Canadian competitor. Consequently, S. D. Myers was poised to gain from EPA's new policy.

In response, the government of Canada quickly issued an interim order banning the export of PCBs. Canada justified this emergency environmental legislation as a means of implementing a multilateral agreement governing trade in toxic waste—namely the Basel Convention on the Control of Transboundary Movements of Hazardous Wastes. In turn, S. D. Myers challenged the Canadian government under Chapter 11 of the NAFTA, citing the following arguments:

■ *National treatment (Article 1102):* Canada's PCB Waste Export Interim Order prevented any PCB wastes from being exported to the United States.

---

97. Canada's 1990 PCB Waste Export Regulations banned export of PCBs to all countries except the United States. And Canada could not export PCBs to the United States unless the US EPA gave prior approval.

Table 4.5 Types of measures disputed under Chapter 11, 1994–2003

Article	Contest measures	Total	Percent
1102	National treatment	16	25
1103	Most-favored nation treatment	7	11
1104 and 1105	Standard of treatment	19	31
1106	Performance requirements	5	8
1110	Expropriation	11	18
1116 and 1117	Obligation under Chapter 15 (monopolies and state enterprises)	4	3
Total		62	100

Note: Multiple grounds are cited in each case.

Sources: US Department of State, Office of the Legal Adviser, 2004, www.state.gov/s/l/c3439.htm; Canada Department of Foreign Affairs and International Trade, 2004; and Todd Weiler, www.naftalaw.org, 2004.

- *Minimum standard of treatment (Article 1105):* S. D. Myers was denied proper treatment because the Canadian government did not consult before implementing the PCB export ban, which Myers asserted was required under Canada's domestic regulatory framework.

- *Performance requirements (Article 1106):* The PCB export ban amounted to a performance requirement—namely that contaminated waste could only be disposed in Canada.

- *Expropriation (Article 1110):* The PCB export ban eroded the value of the S. D. Myers investment in Canadian facilities, constituting a measure tantamount to expropriation.

The NAFTA tribunal decided that the real intent of Canada's ban on the export of PCB waste was to protect the Canadian waste disposal industry from its US competitors. Environmental groups criticized the *S. D. Myers* decision, arguing that the tribunal elevated investor rights over an international environmental agreement. They were particularly offended by the tribunal's suggestion that Canada should adopt a "least trade restrictive" policy (Public Citizen 2001). The tribunal suggested that to promote its domestic waste disposal industry, Canada could have subsidized domestic waste disposal firms and that such subsidies would not have been inconsistent with Canada's national treatment obligation or the Basel Convention.[98] Contrary to this suggestion, some environmental advocates argue that governments should have a free hand to use what-

---

98. The tribunal affirmed Canada's environmental obligations under the NAAEC. *S. D. Myers Inc. vs. Canada Partial Award* (November 13, 2000), at para. 247, 255. Complete details are at www.dfait-maeci.gc.ca/tna-nac/SDM-e.asp (accessed in March 2005).

ever trade restrictions they find appropriate to implement environmental policies.

The tribunal did not accept the "free hand" reasoning. Instead, in the *S. D. Myers* case, the tribunal found that the government of Canada, with protectionist intent, breached its national treatment obligation under NAFTA Article 1102. But the tribunal rejected claims that the PCB export ban additionally breached Article 1106 by requiring S. D. Myers to consume goods and services in Canada. The tribunal further decided that the ban was not "tantamount to nationalization or expropriation."[99]

Methanex Corporation vs. the United States

In 1999, the Vancouver-based Methanex Corporation, the world's largest producer and marketer of methanol, which is a principal ingredient of the gasoline additive MTBE, requested a NAFTA tribunal review. The final outcome of the Methanex claim could become a leading precedent for future Chapter 11 cases.

In July 1999, Methanex initiated a Chapter 11 claim for nearly $1 billion against the state of California, which banned MTBE on December 31, 2002 (the ban took effect on January 1, 2004).[100] The California ban on MTBE did not discriminate between imports and domestic production. Instead, a key issue in the opening round of litigation was whether the ban was based on "sound science" or practical politics. Methanex claimed that California did not act in the "least trade restrictive" manner to deal with treatment of groundwater pollution. Instead, according to Methanex allegations, the MTBE ban was used to protect Archer Daniels Midland Company (ADM), a major campaign donor for California Governor Gray Davis. ADM is a major US manufacturer of ethanol, the main alternative to MTBE as a gasoline additive.[101] Since federal law requires all gasoline to contain either MTBE or ethanol,[102] the California ban would shift the

---

99. In *S. D. Myers Inc. vs. Canada,* the tribunal also rejected the claim of an indirect expropriation. Direct expropriation refers to a "taking" by government authority, or seizing of private property, while indirect expropriation refers to measures that could erode all or nearly all the value of an investment property. See *S. D. Myers Inc. vs. Canada Partial Award,* para. 285.

100. Wendy Stueck, "Methanex to Take $86 Million Charge to Be the Last One for Fortier Plant, It Says," *Globe and Mail,* November 26, 2002, B6.

101. *The Financial Post* claims ADM produces more than 70 percent of the ethanol used in the United States. Media reports estimate ADM contributed $220,000 in donations to Governor Davis' 1998 campaign. Tony Seskus, "Methanex Loses the NAFTA Complaint: More Evidence Needed," *Financial Post,* August 8, 2002, FP11. Robert Collier, "Canadian Trade Challenge Falls Flat—But More Fights May Be Coming," *San Francisco Chronicle,* November 17, 2002, A14.

102. The stated rationale for this policy is to promote alternative energy sources to the use of petroleum.

state's additive market from the Canadian firm Methanex to domestic ethanol producers such as ADM.[103]

The state of California EPA justified the ban on grounds that MTBE is highly soluble in water and posed a significant risk of water contamination.[104] Methanex argued that the groundwater problems in California are due to leaky gasoline storage tanks and not the use of MTBE itself. In July 2000, the NAFTA Commission for Environmental Cooperation (CEC) dismissed submissions by Methanex to review California's environmental enforcement policies.[105] Meanwhile, Methanex challenged California under Chapter 11 of the NAFTA with the following arguments:[106]

- *National treatment (Article 1102):* The California Executive Order D-5-99, which banned MTBE, reflected a protectionist intent that improperly favored the US ethanol industry against foreign investors.

- *Minimum standard of treatment (Article 1105):* The California ban did not use the "least trade restrictive" method of solving the water contamination problem; campaign contributions allegedly violate principles inherent in Article 1105, namely that domestic decision making should be free from pecuniary interests; and a breach of Article 1102 (national treatment) is sufficient grounds to find a breach in Article 1105.[107]

---

103. The US Department of Agriculture's August 2002 report restates its position that ethanol is an energy-efficient additive. The report can be viewed at www.usda.gov/news/releases/ (accessed in March 2005). According to the Sierra Club, ethanol helps reduce carbon monoxide but increases smog. The Sierra Club marks ADM among the top ethanol producers, which together contributed $1.1 million to members of Congress via PAC and soft money contributions. Sierra Club's perspective ("The Bill that Industry Bought") is available at www.sierraclub.org/politics/lobbying/lobbying_details.asp (accessed in March 2005).

104. The decision is largely based on a 1998 University of California-Davis study that found "significant risks and costs associated with water contamination due to the use of MTBE," but there is disagreement about the toxicity of MTBE. California's Proposition 65 regulations require the state to list human carcinogens, but MTBE was not listed as a human carcinogen. The World Health Organization's International Agency for Research on Cancer also does not classify MTBE as a human carcinogen. The EPA classifies MTBE as a potential human carcinogen. See Public Citizen (2001) and Hufbauer et al. (2000).

105. In October 1999, Methanex filed a submission to the CEC requesting that it prepare a factual record on "California's failure to enforce its regulations concerning underground storage tanks." In July 2000, the CEC decided not to review the submission because the Methanex case was still pending arbitration under Chapter 11. For details about the CEC's determination, see www.cec.org/news/details/index.cfm?varlan=english&ID=2251 (accessed in March 2005).

106. Includes arguments added following the *Methanex Corporation Draft Amended Claim*, filed in February 2001. A complete description of the case is available at www.naftaclaims.com (accessed in March 2005).

107. Methanex argued that the principles of fair and equitable treatment embodied in Article 1105 include a minimum of four principles: (1) a decision maker purportedly acting in-

- *Expropriation (Article 1110):* The MTBE ban transferred market share in California's oxygenate market from Methanex to the domestic ethanol industry, which is tantamount to expropriation.

After considering the case for three years, the NAFTA tribunal sidestepped all these issues in an interim ruling handed down in August 2002. The interim ruling held that the NAFTA violations cited by Methanex, if true, applied to MTBE, not methanol. Since Methanex produces methanol and not MTBE, the tribunal ruled that Methanex was not directly affected by the California MTBE ban. In order to sustain its case, Methanex would need to show that methanol (not MTBE) was the object of discrimination. The tribunal's interim ruling was notable in its attempt to narrow the class of investors who might bring a Chapter 11 claim.

After Methanex submitted an amended claim in November 2002, the NAFTA tribunal invited third parties to submit amicus curiae briefs.[108] In June 2004, the tribunal also made final hearings open to the public.[109] The panel's final decision, issued in August 2005, rejected Methanex's amended claim.[110]

Metalclad Corporation vs. the Government of the United Mexican States

In the *Metalclad* case, a US investor purchased land in the early 1980s to establish a waste disposal facility in San Luis Potosi. Although Metalclad was granted a federal permit to construct a waste treatment facility, in December 1995 local municipal authorities denied permission, citing environmental problems. The governor of San Luis Potosi subsequently issued an Ecological Decree that declared the site of the landfill an ecological preserve for the protection of rare cactus. According to Greenpeace Mexico, environmental standards were violated at the site. An independent environmental impact analysis by the University of San Luis Potosi found that the facility was located on an alluvial stream and might con-

---

dependently and in the public interest must not be biased by pecuniary considerations; (2) state officials must act reasonably and in good faith; (3) nondiscrimination; and (4) a regulatory measure taken by a state must not be a disguised form of protection but instead must be the least trade restrictive of the reasonably available alternatives. See *Methanex Amended Claim, supra note* 101, para. 49.

108. For a complete description of claims filed in the Methanex case, see www.naftalaw.org (accessed in August 2004).

109. See ICSID press release, "Methanex v. United States: NAFTA/UNCITRAL Arbitration Rules Proceeding," January 30, 2004, www.worldbank.org/icsid/methanex.htm (accessed in March 2005).

110. For details on the final award, see www.state.gov/s/l/c5818.htm (accessed on August 15, 2005).

taminate the local water supply.[111] Metalclad was subsequently denied permission to continue construction of the landfill site at an ad hoc meeting of a distant town council.[112] In response, Metalclad filed a Chapter 11 claim in January 1997 based on the following arguments:

- **Minimum standard of treatment (Article 1105):** The lack of transparency in municipal law and the improper denial of a permit violated general obligations to grant fair and equitable treatment.

- **Expropriation (Article 1110):** The municipal authority's decision to refuse the operation of Metalclad's waste disposal facility was not for a public purpose and constituted both a direct and an indirect expropriation.

In one of the first NAFTA decisions based on general concepts of transparency and due process, the tribunal held that principles articulated in NAFTA Article 102(1) imposed an elevated transparency obligation under Article 1105.[113] The tribunal noted the absence of an established procedure for handling municipal construction permits and Metalclad's reliance on misleading advice from federal officials as examples of Mexico's failure to uphold its commitment to transparency under the NAFTA agreement.[114]

---

111. See Wheat (1995). Also see Public Citizen's report about environmental hazards posted on the organization's Web site, www.citizen.org/publications/release.cfm?ID=7076 (accessed in March 2005).

112. Metalclad was not notified of (and did not participate in) the town council meeting that considered the permit application; the NAFTA tribunal found that this procedure constituted a failure to ensure transparency. See Weiler (2001). See also *Award of the Tribunal: Metalclad Corp. vs. The United Mexican States*, August 2000, www.state.gov/s/l/c3752.htm (accessed in March 2005).

113. The tribunal did not fully explain what constituted "fair and equitable treatment," but its decision suggested that San Luis Potosi's behavior failed to observe the customary international law standards that must be respected under NAFTA Article 1105. The tribunal argued that the principle of transparency refers to the state's "duty to ensure that the correct position is promptly determined and clearly stated so that investors can proceed with all appropriate expedition in the confident belief that they are acting in accordance with all relevant laws." *Metalclad Award, supra note* 111, para. 76.

114. When the government of Mexico challenged the NAFTA tribunal decision, the Supreme Court of British Columbia upheld the tribunal award (on grounds discussed below) but decided against the panel's Article 1105 decision. The Canadian court held that the Chapter 11 tribunal exceeded its authority in determining that a breach of transparency constituted a violation of "fair and equitable" treatment. The recent NAFTA Free Trade Commission's interpretive note extends the Canadian court's argument by curtailing the creation of Article 1105 obligations out of other NAFTA commitments. VanDuzer (2002) contends there still exists uncertainty about Article 1105 standards despite the Commission's attempt to limit the scope of interpretation. Gastle (2002) argues that the Commission's interpretation of Article 1105 only provides for the "customary international law minimum standard of treatment of aliens."

More controversially, the tribunal decided Mexico had taken measures "tantamount to expropriation," contravening Article 1110.[115] The tribunal emphasized each NAFTA member's obligation to the "substantial increase in investment opportunities in the territories of the Parties" (NAFTA Article 102(c)). In examining the Ecological Decree issued by San Luis Potosi, the tribunal held that enforcing the decree would "constitute an act tantamount to expropriation."[116] This aspect of the NAFTA tribunal decision got some environmental groups up in arms. They claim the Metalclad decision unnecessarily broadens the definition of takings and could hinder traditional governmental regulatory functions.[117] However, the NAFTA tribunal awarded Metalclad only $16.7 million in damages, which represented 18.5 percent of the initial claim ($90 million) and did not include investment for a new facility or lost revenues. This suggests that the tribunal casts a skeptical eye not only on the regulatory shell game (municipal vs. federal authorities) but also on Metalclad's overblown claims (Hufbauer et al. 2000).

Pope & Talbot Inc. vs. Canada

Based on the 1996 US-Canada Agreement on Trade in Softwood Lumber (SLA), the government of Canada established quota limits on duty-free exports of softwood lumber from four Canadian provinces to the United States. In March 1999, Pope & Talbot, an Oregon-based timber company with subsidiaries in British Columbia, Canada, claimed Canada's SLA Export Control Regime violated investment provisions under NAFTA Chapter 11.

To facilitate the SLA, the Export Control Regime requires exporters of softwood lumber products originating from the provinces of Quebec, Ontario, Alberta, and British Columbia—together accounting for approximately 95 percent of Canada's softwood lumber exports to the United States—to obtain export permits and pay fees to export their products to

---

115. See *Metalclad Award, supra note* 111, para. 70 and 111. The tribunal defined expropriation in Article 1110 to include "not only open, deliberate and acknowledged takings of property, such as outright seizure . . . but also covert or incidental interference with the use of property which has the effect of depriving the owner, in whole or in significant part, of the use or reasonably-to-be expected economic benefit of property even if not necessarily of obvious benefit to the host State" (*Metalclad Award, supra note* 111, para. 103).

116. See *Metalclad Award, supra note* 111, para. 111.

117. Concurring in part with these concerns, Graham (2002) argues that compensating investors for diminution in value of investment under Chapter 11 is more likely to lead to nonoptimal results than application of the "polluter pays" principle. Other observers see corporations using Chapter 11 to respond to environmental protectionism. Under Chapter 11, foreign investors are allowed to challenge discriminatory environmental regulation without the political support previously necessary on the part of national governments. See Rugman, Kirton, and Soloway (1999), 154–55; and *Metalclad Award, supra note* 111, para. 92.

the United States.[118] Pope & Talbot argued that some lumber producers in British Columbia were treated more favorably and that the quota system, as implemented, discriminated against Pope & Talbot.[119] Specifically, Pope & Talbot raised the following arguments:[120]

- *National treatment (Article 1102):* Canada's implementation of the SLA discriminated against investors of lumber in provinces covered by the Export Control Regime by comparison with investors in other provinces.[121]

- *Minimum standard of treatment (Article 1105):* Canada's verification of softwood lumber quota audit violated international law standards.

- *Performance requirements (Article 1106):* Canada's Export Control Regime restriction on sales, coupled with performance requirements linked to exports, discriminate against Pope & Talbot.

---

118. Canada's Export Permit Regulations Act (1996) established requirements for exporting softwood lumber to the United States. These requirements were at issue in the *Pope & Talbot* case. At the heart of the underlying softwood lumber dispute are key differences in US and Canadian lumber industry trade policies. The Canadian government owns nearly all of Canada's forests (90 percent), Canadian logging and softwood lumber industries are highly integrated (75 percent), and Canadian stumpage fees are lower than the fees charged by private US forest owners. By contrast, most US timber (58 percent) is harvested from private land at market prices. See *Award on Merits Between Pope & Talbot Inc. vs. Government of Canada,* April 10, 2001, para. 86; and *Interim Award Between Pope & Talbot Inc. vs. Canada,* June 2000, para. 34 and 35. For complete details, see www.dfait-maeci.gc.ca/tna-nac/phases-en.asp#1 (accessed in November 2002). See also "Canada to Launch US Ad Campaign on Softwood Lumber Dispute," *Associated Press,* November 8, 2002; and Howse (1998).

119. When the SLA quota was established, the government of Canada granted the province of British Columbia 59 percent of Canada's total quota of lumber that Canadian companies can export to the United States duty-free; Quebec was given 23 percent. Pope & Talbot claimed that British Columbia's share was later dropped to 56 percent while Quebec's portion increased to 25.3 percent, a shift amounting to 500 million board feet less per year from British Columbia. Heather Scoffield, "US Firm Says Ottawa Bungled Lumber Pact," *Globe and Mail,* March 26, 1999, B7.

120. Pope & Talbot originally alleged a violation of MFN treatment as well as other claims, but the MFN issue was dropped by the time the *Interim Award* was issued on June 26, 2000. See *Memorial of the Investor,* January 28, 2000. For a complete account of all claims against Canada, see www.dfait-maeci.gc.ca/tna-nac/phases-en.asp#2 (accessed in November 2002). Pope & Talbot's claims against Canada under Article 1105 include the following issues: interpretation of Article 1105, discrimination of transitional adjustment provisions, unfair allocation of quota related to wholesale exports, inequitable reallocation of quota for British Columbia companies, unfair effect of Super Fee measures, secretive conduct of the Canadian government during the verification review process, and Canada's breach of administrative fairness. See *Award on Merits,* April 2001, www.dfait-maeci.gc.ca/tna-nac/phases-en.asp#2 (accessed in March 2005).

121. Canada claimed that its quota allocation provision was adjusted for new entrants under the SLA on an as-needed basis, and not according to provincial historical shares. See Government of Canada Statement of Defense, October 8, 1999, and Counter-Memorial of Canada, October 10, 2000, para. 359 to 438, www.dfait-maeci.gc.ca, www.naftaclaims.com (accessed in March 2005).

- *Expropriation (Article 1110):* Canada's Export Control Regime would interfere with business operations, constituting measures tantamount to expropriation under NAFTA Article 1110 and indirect expropriation under international law.

The NAFTA tribunal determined that Canada's implementation of the SLA Export Control Regime did not discriminate against foreign-owned companies. Moreover, the tribunal dismissed Pope & Talbot's claims regarding direct expropriation.[122] However, the tribunal decided that Canada's verification audit of Pope & Talbot was unreasonable and violated Article 1105.[123] Specifically, the tribunal suggested that Canada's export control regulations as administered (apparently to punish Pope & Talbot) sustained a claim of indirect expropriation. The tribunal concluded that Canada should pay compensation for damages arising from the verification audit and the cost of proceedings, totaling $461,566 plus interest.[124]

While Canada essentially won the case, some NGOs criticized the tribunal's decision to broaden the concept of fair and equitable treatment under NAFTA Article 1105 (Public Citizen 2001). However, the recent interpretive note issued by the NAFTA Free Trade Commission precludes the wholesale creation of Article 1105 obligations from the violation of other NAFTA provisions.[125]

---

122. See *Interim Award, supra note* 121, para. 64 to 80. The tribunal emphasized that the Export Control Regime did not place limitations on domestic sales of softwood lumber.

123. See *Interim Award, supra note* 121, para. 83 to 104. The tribunal invoked three arguments for its decision that Canada did not breach NAFTA Article 1102 obligations. First, the absence of US final determinations against exporters in noncovered provinces of the SLA partly reflects the fact that the SLA regime was designed to address CVD threats against covered provinces (British Columbia, Alberta, Ontario, and Quebec). Second, British Columbia, where Pope & Talbot has subsidiaries, faced a declining share of total Canadian exports to the United States, but not necessarily because of Canada's SLA export regime. The tribunal points toward new entrants requiring new quota allocations and preexisting market conditions before the SLA that show higher investment in new and existing mills in Quebec than in British Columbia. Third, the Super Fee that was introduced to settle the dispute over lower British Columbia stumpage fees did not discriminate against foreign-owned softwood lumber companies operating in British Columbia. However, the tribunal determined that Canada's behavior during the verification review violated Article 1105 obligations. According to the tribunal, Pope & Talbot was subjected to unfair treatment by the government of Canada, including "threats, [denial of] reasonable requests for pertinent information, [requirement] to incur unnecessary expense and disruption in meeting Softwood Lumber Department's requests for information, [forced expenditure of] legal fees and probably [suffered from] a loss of reputation in government circles." See *Award on Merits,* para. 181.

124. See *Interim Award, supra note* 121, para. 96 to 105, and *Memorial of the Investor re: Pope & Talbot, Inc.,* www.naftalaw.org (accessed in March 2005).

125. The NAFTA Free Trade Commission's interpretive note is described in Canadian International Trade Minister Pettigrew's press release, webapps.dfait-maeci.gc.ca/minpub/Publication.asp?FileSpec=/Min_Pub_Docs/104441.htm (accessed in March 2005).

Table 4.6 NAFTA disputes under Chapter 19: Complainants and respondents, 1994–2005

As petitionor/complainant	As respondent/defendant			
	Canada	Mexico	United States	Total
Canada	—	3	38	41
Mexico	2	—	31	33
United States	17	12	—	29
Total cases	19	15	69	103

a. Subsidiaries of private firms have initiated cases against the host government. Please refer to NAFTA Chapter 19 Dispute Settlement Tables for details about specific cases.

Source: NAFTA Secretariat, 2005, www.nafta-sec-alena.org.

Chapter 19 Cases

Since Chapter 19 reviews of final AD and CVD decisions began in 1994, NAFTA panels have convened in 103 cases. Most disputes are related to AD rather than CVD determinations. As the largest NAFTA user of trade remedy laws, the United States has been the main target of Chapter 19 disputes, facing more cases than Canada and Mexico combined (table 4.6). The United States has been the complainant in 29 cases and the respondent in 69 cases; Canada and Mexico defended decisions in 19 and 15 cases, respectively.

Under CUSFTA, nearly two-thirds of binational panel decisions against US agencies called for a remand.[126] This pattern holds under NAFTA Chapter 19. As of August 2004, the NAFTA Chapter 19 tribunal disagreed with US administrative decisions and partly remanded 11 cases against the United States and totally remanded 3 cases. Canada had 3 cases partly remanded and 1 case totally remanded. Mexico had 3 cases partly remanded and 3 cases totally remanded (table 4.7).[127] In addition, 41 cases have been terminated, and 68 cases are awaiting final tribunal decisions.

Most Chapter 19 cases resulted in the reduction of penalty duties. The ECC procedure has been invoked only thrice—in the *Gray Portland Cement and Clinker, Pure Magnesium,* and *Softwood Lumber* cases.[128] Despite Mex-

---

126. A remand is similar to a reversal. However, instead of entering its own judgment, the arbitration panel sends the case back to the administrative agency to reconsider its determination in light of the panel's ruling on the applicable law. As an example, an arbitration panel can remand a case if it concludes that the administrative agency provided insufficient evidence to back up its original decision.

127. While the United States and Mexico had nearly half of all their administrative decisions remanded, Canada had most of its agency determinations affirmed. See Vega-Cánovas and Winham (2002).

128. Some NAFTA scholars allege that the Chapter 19 ECC process is wrongly invoked to discipline panelists. Specifically, Potter (2004) argues that the ECC procedure has been

Table 4.7 Outcome of tribunal panel decisions under Chapter 19, 1994–2004

	Petitioning country		
Disposition	Canada	Mexico	United States
Affirmed in favor of respondent[a]	10	3	12
Remanded in favor of petitioner[a]	10	10	7
Remanded against respondent[a]	4	6	14
Ambiguous decision (terminated cases)	6	8	27
Pending cases	17	18	33
Total cases won as respondent[a]	10	2	12
Total cases won as petitioner[a]	9	8	7
Total cases involved as respondent or petitioner	18	14	63

a. Includes cases that are not unanimously decided but defined by being affirmed in part for the respondent or remanded in part for the respondent or petitioner.

Source: NAFTA Secretariat, 2004, www.nafta-sec-alena.org/english/index.htm.

ico's increasingly active use of AD and CVD measures, the United States and Canada have challenged Mexican decisions only 14 times, mostly involving iron and steel products.

While Chapter 19 disputes are not as hotly debated as Chapter 11 disputes, they represent significantly larger economic stakes. As table 4.8 indicates, the intensity of US-Mexico Chapter 19 cases, relative to bilateral trade flows, is somewhat greater than the intensity of US-Canada Chapter 19 cases. The vast majority of Chapter 19 disputes, about 80 percent, focus on nonagricultural products. This is not surprising, as US two-way trade with NAFTA partners in nonagricultural products that attract AD and CVD cases increased from $26 billion in 1994 to $49 billion in 2003.[129] Overcapacity and slow demand growth characterize iron, steel, cement, glass, and ceramic products. While they account for about 10 percent of US trade with NAFTA partners, these products represent about half of all Chapter 19 disputes.

Base metal products (i.e., iron and steel) are the leader, accounting for 38 out of 82 total NAFTA nonagricultural Chapter 19 cases (table 4.9). Cement, glass, and ceramic products accounted for 17 out of the 82 nonagricultural cases under Chapter 19 (table 4.9). Agricultural products ac-

---

abused and this has aroused cynicism in the Canadian business community toward the Chapter 19 process. As a result, Potter sees a growing trend to use the Canadian Federal Court of Appeal instead of Chapter 19. The US government has since initiated an ECC process, in November 2004, to reverse the NAFTA panel's adverse ruling against the USITC. See "US to Pursue Extraordinary Challenge of NAFTA Lumber Ruling," *Inside US Trade*, October 15, 2004.

129. Based on two-way trade of US exports and imports of base metals (i.e., iron, steel, and nickel), cement, glass, ceramic, and plastic products with Canada and Mexico.

Table 4.8   Bilateral two-way trade among NAFTA countries

Countries	Two-way trade[a] (billions of dollars)	Chapter 19 cases	Cases per $1 billion
US-Canada	336	55	.16
US-Mexico	181	43	.24

a. Average sum of total exports and imports 1994–2003.

Sources: Secretaría de Economía, Dirección General de Inversiones Extranjeras; Bureau of Economic Analysis, US Department of Commerce; and Canada Department of Foreign Affairs and International Trade, 2003.

count for 19 cases. As agricultural trade barriers are lowered in NAFTA, AD and CVD actions could become much more numerous. Softwood lumber exports from Canada—a product with characteristics shared by mainstream agricultural goods—have already been the object of several trade remedy disputes.

US-Canada Chapter 19 Trade Disputes

The Chapter 19 dispute settlement process has been relatively successful at resolving US-Canada trade disputes. So far, out of 54 US-Canada Chapter 19 disputes, 43 cases have been settled.[130] During 2002–03, Canada challenged ten US AD and CVD determinations on softwood lumber, tomatoes, and steel wire rod. The tomato cases were subsequently terminated, but the softwood lumber case has stretched the limits of the Chapter 19 arbitration process. As such, it deserves a more detailed examination.

For all the success of the Chapter 19 process, its most glaring failure—and NAFTA's continuing largest trade dispute—involves softwood lumber. Since 1982, the United States and Canada have been at odds over US CVD and AD actions against Canadian softwood lumber exports. Indeed, the dispute almost caused the CUSFTA talks to be stillborn in 1986, when the concern about softwood lumber sharply divided the Senate Finance Committee's vote that allowed talks to go forward.

The economic stakes are huge. In 2001, Canadian softwood lumber accounted for one-third of the US market and by 2003 represented $6.4 billion per year of exports for Canada.[131] Softwood lumber is the basis for single-

---

130. Settled cases are here defined as cases with a final panel decision and cases that have been jointly terminated by both the United States and Canada. As of July 2005, 22 US-Canada cases reached a final Chapter 19 panel decision; another 21 cases were jointly terminated. See appendix 4A.5 for details.

131. Canada is more distant from other markets, and the United States remains the most important export market for Canadian softwood lumber. Canadian exports of wood products to the United States as a share of total bilateral trade increased from 3.9 percent in 1990 to 4.7 percent in 2001. US exports of wood products as a share of total bilateral trade grew from 3.3 percent in 1990 to 3.7 percent in 2001. See Canada House of Commons (2002) and Statistics Canada (2004).

Table 4.9 Types of products at issue in Chapter 19 disputes by defendant countries, 1994–2005

Harmonized System section[a]	Type of product	Cases brought against			
		Canada	Mexico	United States	Total
Agricultural products					
I	Animal products (including fish)	2	2	8	12
II	Vegetables	n.a.	n.a.	3	3
III	Animal or vegetable fats and oils	n.a.	n.a.	n.a.	n.a.
IV	Prepared foodstuffs, nes	2	1	1	4
Subtotal		4	3	12	19
Nonagricultural products					
V	Minerals	1	n.a.	6	7
VI	Chemicals	n.a.	4	2	6
VII	Plastics	n.a.	1	n.a.	1
VIII	Leather	n.a.	n.a.	1	1
IX	Wood	1	n.a.	4	5
X	Pulp and paper	n.a.	n.a.	n.a.	n.a.
XI	Textiles and clothing	n.a.	n.a.	n.a.	n.a.
XII	Footwear	n.a.	n.a.	n.a.	n.a.
XIII	Glass, cement, and ceramics	1	n.a.	14	15
XV	Base metals (iron and steel)	7	6	28	41
XVI	Machines and electronic equipment	5	n.a.	1	6
XX	Other manufactures	1	n.a.	n.a.	1
Subtotal		16	11	56	83
Total	All products	20	14	68	102

nes = not elsewhere specified
n.a. = not available

a. Harmonized Commodity Description and Coding System. The basic commodity chapters are numbered 1 to 97. The chapters are grouped into sections numbered from I to XXI. The table refers to these sections.

Source: NAFTA Secretariat, 2005, www.nafta-sec-alena.org/english/index.htm.

industry economies in several Canadian towns, notably in British Columbia, where lumber is the most important manufacturing industry. To date, US import tariffs on softwood lumber have led to an estimated 15,000 layoffs in Canada, yet twice as many American mills as Canadian ones have shut down or reduced output.[132] Ironically, the adverse economic consequences of the softwood lumber dispute have made the Canadian lumber industry more efficient.[133] Bilateral disagreements can be traced both to

---

132. See "Canada, US Softwood Talks Break Down," Canada Broadcasting Corporation, February 26, 2003. For complete details, see www.cbc.ca (accessed in March 2005). See also *The Economist*, "The Softwood-Lumber Dispute," February 1, 2003.

133. According to *The Economist*, op. cit., average costs at Canadian mills have been reduced by an estimated $65 per thousand board feet of lumber, which includes added duties. As a result, Canadian mills can maintain their market share in the United States despite the pressure on realized prices. US industry sources apparently concur that AD duties on Canadian lumber exports led Canadian firms to ramp up production to reduce production costs. See also "US, Canada Resume Lumber Talks Amid Divisions Over Export Tax," *Inside US Trade*, February 21, 2003.

trade remedy measures pursued before and after NAFTA and to forest resource management practices.

As the CUSFTA negotiations demonstrated, the United States and Canada could not agree on trade remedy reforms. Subsequent bilateral efforts to resolve the dispute resulted in temporary fixes but no long-term framework for production and trade.[134] To reach a compromise, it appears that Canada will have to forgo its efforts to reform US trade remedy laws. Similarly, the United States will need to move away from solutions that are narrowly focused on market-based timber pricing methods.

A background understanding about different forest management practices is necessary before discussing details of the dispute. In the United States, private contracts or auctions determine timber prices, when timber is purchased from either the US Forest Service or privately owned lands. By contrast, in Canada, most timber is located on public (crown) lands, and the provinces control the crown forests. As a general matter, Canada severely limits the export of logs, preferring instead to export cut lumber. The provinces also assign Canadian companies long-term cutting rights in exchange for assured job numbers and sustainable forestry. Propelled by US mill producers and the Coalition for Fair Lumber Imports, the US government argues that Canada's low timber prices, both on account of log export restraints and low stumpage fees, confer provincial subsidies on domestic softwood lumber producers.[135] However, while the US Forest Service is burdened by costs for harvesting timber on public lands, Canada's provincial governments shift forest management costs to producers.[136]

The softwood lumber dispute was carried over from CUSFTA into NAFTA. After Canada unilaterally terminated the 1991 memorandum of

---

134. A memorandum of understanding (MOU) was agreed between the United States and Canada in 1991 and again in 1996. Shortly after each MOU expired or was unilaterally terminated, Canada initiated an SWL dispute against the United States. The United States has not brought an SWL dispute against Canada in either the WTO or NAFTA.

135. Arguing different reasons for the same result, the Indigenous Network of Economies and Trade (INET) submitted a brief contending that stumpage prices set by the Canadian government do not reflect the cost of aboriginal proprietary interests on lands where softwood lumber is harvested. Amicus curiae submissions to the WTO by INET in April 2002.

136. US forest management policies have limited domestic supply, partly because the US Forest Service does not allow as large a timber harvest on federal lands as economic factors might warrant, thus causing relatively higher stumpage prices. Even so, according to GAO reports (GAO 1998), the US government apparently loses money on its stumpage auctions. Roger Sedjo (1997) at Resources for the Future adds that Canada's dominance in the US SWL market is based upon its comparatively larger volume of native forests situated on accessible flat terrain. Sedjo argues that the United States can increase SWL production by intensively managing forests. The Economist ("The Softwood-Lumber Dispute," February 1, 2003) notes that European producers have recently increased SWL exports, helping depress prices by 10 percent from May 2002 to January 2003. See Michael Percy, "A Hard Look at the Softwood Lumber Dispute," University of Alberta ExpressNews, March 10, 2003, www.expressnews. ualberta.ca/expressnews/articles/ideas.cfm?p_ID=933&s=a (accessed in March 2005).

understanding (MOU) that specified a schedule of export taxes on Canadian softwood lumber exports, the United States imposed CVDs on imports from Canada. Canada then initiated a CUSFTA binational panel review. After the CUSFTA panel decided in favor of Canada, the United States filed an extraordinary challenge in 1994. The ECC panel upheld the panel decision but was split along national lines, a divisive trend that would define future softwood lumber disputes addressed under NAFTA.

A temporary remedy emerged from another MOU in 1996. The 1996 MOU allowed Canada to export 14.7 billion board-feet of lumber without paying export fees for the five-year duration of the pact. After the five-year agreement expired in 2001, the US DOC imposed a CVD of about 19 percent and an average AD duty of 10 percent.[137] Canada responded by filing six disputes against the United States in the WTO; Canada also initiated three cases under NAFTA Chapter 19, two of which are pending final panel decisions.[138] (See appendix tables 4A.1 and 4A.2, which catalog the recent history of NAFTA and WTO disputes over lumber.) In response, the United States filed an extraordinary challenge in November 2004 to reverse the NAFTA panel's ruling against the USITC.[139]

Meanwhile, the status of the Byrd Amendment hangs over the entire softwood lumber dispute.[140] The WTO Appellate Body has ruled that the

---

137. See Peter Watson, "Dispute Settlement Under FTA-NAFTA," *Policy Options*, June 1999.

138. In softwood lumber cases USA-CDA-2002-1904-02 and USA-CDA 2002-1904-03, NAFTA panels have remanded the case back to US agencies several times. See appendix 4A.5.

139. As the softwood lumber dispute intensifies, the United States and Canada seem to move further away from a negotiated bilateral compromise focusing on a sliding export tax. In January 2003, US proposals focused on a declining four-tiered tax schedule while Canada preferred a continuously sliding export tax that would fall as prices rise. One reason why Canada opposes the four-tiered export tax is that it would arbitrarily penalize Canadian lumber exports when prices are just below a tier. Another wrinkle: While the US DOC does not guarantee import duties would be revoked even if a Canadian province implemented all the policy changes, the US proposal includes province-specific policy frameworks that could lead to the revocation of import duties on lumber imported from some provinces but not others. See "Commerce Issues Second Draft Lumber Paper As Talks End Without Deal," *Inside US Trade*, February 7, 2003. See "Commerce Lumber Memo," *Inside US Trade*, January 31, 2003.

140. Currently all CVD and AD duties on Canadian softwood lumber are being held for possible distribution to domestic US lumber firms under the Continued Dumping Offset Act (the Byrd Amendment), against Canada's strenuous objections. In 2005, the "pot" of softwood lumber penalty duties will exceed $4 billion (increasing at $4 million per day). By March 2005, Canada (and the European Commission) announced intentions to retaliate against the US failure to repeal the Byrd Amendment. The Canadian government planned to impose a 15 percent tariff on US exports totaling about $3.5 million. Former US Under Secretary of Commerce Grant Aldonas emphasized that the prospect of the United States refunding duty deposits to Canada would be one of the last issues to be resolved. See "Commerce Issues Second Draft Lumber Paper As Talks End Without Deal," *Inside US Trade*, February 7, 2003; "Lumber Talks Break Off," *Inside US Trade*, February 28, 2003; and "Canada Byrd Retaliation Notice Could Lead to New Fight with United States," *Inside US Trade*, April 1, 2005.

Byrd Amendment violates the WTO, but so far there is no indication that Congress will repeal the law. Meanwhile, the US DOC continues to collect CVD and AD duty deposits on Canadian lumber exports. The softwood lumber dispute heated up when, in May 2002, the United States levied a 27 percent CVD/AD tariff on Canadian softwood lumber.[141] Faced with US penalty tariffs and stalled bilateral negotiations, Canada requested a WTO panel on April 3, 2003. In August 2004, the WTO Appellate Body upheld some US AD tariffs on Canadian softwood lumber but ruled against the US DOC zeroing methodology, a practice that tends to drive up the overall final AD margin.[142] In commentary, Canadian International Trade Minister James Peterson urged the US government to comply with recent (and more favorable) NAFTA panel rulings. On August 21, 2004, the NAFTA panel ordered the USITC to rescind the injury finding underlying the 27 percent CVD and AD duties on Canadian softwood lumber, emphasizing that the USITC "consistently ignored the authority" of the NAFTA Chapter 19 panel in the past.[143] Likewise, the WTO panel concurred that the US injury finding was flawed (WTO 2004). The fact that Canada has always appealed softwood lumber cases (after being initiated by the US DOC) underscores the high economic stakes of the lumber industry for Canada's economy.

Softwood lumber litigation is entering its third decade. In our view, the dispute will ultimately be resolved by negotiation, not further rounds of litigation. The pragmatic solution should include auction-based provincial timber sales, open to all bidders, for a significant portion of stumpage rights. Some Canadian provinces are receptive to adopting competitive timber auctions.[144] As Canada implements market-based lumber pricing

---

141. Canadian lumber firms allege that the highest sustainable rate for an export tax on SWL is 18 percent; they argue that the recent 27 percent penalty tariff would make it impossible for them to earn a profit. See "Lumber Talks Break Off," *Inside US Trade*, February 28, 2003.

142. However, government and private-sector sources believe the US government would interpret the WTO decision narrowly so that it would not affect US DOC administrative reviews or the use of zeroing calculations for dumping margins on other products such as steel. See "WTO Appellate Body Rules Against Zeroing in Softwood Lumber Decision," *Inside US Trade*, August 13, 2004.

143. See Steven Chase and Peter Kennedy, "Another Softwood Victory for Canada," *Globe and Mail*, September 1, 2004, B3.

144. The British Columbia Forestry Revitalization Plan proposal adopts the idea of selling timber on an auction-based system for 20 percent of Canada's government-owned timber. Auction results will then determine stumpage rates for the remaining 80 percent of crown timber. This new forest policy would resolve a key US complaint that stumpage fees act as a de facto subsidy by the Canadian government for its softwood lumber producers. See BNA (2003a).

measures, the United States should recalculate its CVDs on lumber derived from noncompetitive stumpage and totally exempt lumber derived from auction-based stumpage. Meanwhile, the "pot" of money potentially subject to distribution under the Byrd Amendment should be divided between US and Canadian producers, in a matter designed to balance the other components of the settlement.

US-Mexico Chapter 19 Trade Disputes

Since 1994, Mexico has initiated 31 cases against the United States under NAFTA Chapter 19. One was affirmed in favor of the United States, 9 panels remanded decisions in whole or part to US agencies, 8 cases were terminated, and 13 are awaiting final panel decisions (see appendix table 4A.5). The vast majority of Mexico's Chapter 19 complaints involve long-standing concerns over cement (14 cases).[145]

By contrast, the United States challenged Mexican administrative determinations only in 12 cases, and only eight have been initiated since 1995. More than half the US cases initiated against Mexico deal with steel and chemical products.[146] Most US-initiated disputes were decided in favor of the United States and remanded back to the Secretariat of Commerce and Industrial Development (Secretaría de Comercio y Fomento Industrial, or SECOFI), Mexico's Ministry of Trade and Industrial Development.[147] The most contentious case involves high-fructose corn syrup (HFCS), which is discussed in some detail below.

In February 1998, US exporters initiated a Chapter 19 case against Mexico's decision to impose AD duties on US exports of HFCS.[148] Shortly after, the United States also requested a WTO panel to challenge Mexican AD duties on HFCS imports from the United States (WTO 1998). In June 2002, the Chapter 19 panel's final decision suggested that Mexico's AD duties on US exports of HFCS were inconsistent with NAFTA's scheduled HFCS duty re-

---

145. During 1994–2004, US cement imports from Mexico totaled nearly $2 billion. Based on statistics from the USITC Dataweb 2003, US imports for consumption, available at www.dataweb.usitc.gov (accessed in March 2005).

146. Under Chapter 19, the United States initiated disputes against Mexico over steel (six cases), chemicals (two cases), sugar (one case), beef (two cases), and cement (one case). See appendix table 4A.5.

147. Specifically, six cases were remanded to SECOFI, two were affirmed, three were jointly terminated, and one case is pending.

148. Five major US exporters of HFCS joined the US Corn Refiners Association to file the NAFTA HFCS Chapter 19 case against Mexico (MEX-USA-98-1904-01): Cerestar USA, Inc.; Cargill, Inc.; A. E. Staley Manufacturing Co.; Archer Daniels Midland Co. (ADM); and CPC International, Inc. Two Mexican firms with ties to US producers joined the dispute: Almidones Mexicanos S.A. and Cargill Mexico S.A. See NAFTA Secretariat for complete details, www.nafta-sec-alena.org/DefaultSite/index_e.aspx (accessed in March 2005).

ductions.[149] By 2003, both WTO and NAFTA panel decisions concurred that Mexico failed to justify its AD determination on US HFCS exports.[150]

Meanwhile, in January 2002, the Mexican Congress imposed a 20 percent tax on soft drinks that use HFCS. The tax is just as effective in protecting Mexico's struggling sugar industry because almost all HFCS in Mexico is imported. Compounding the dispute, both the Mexican Supreme Court and Congress overruled the Fox administration's efforts to suspend the HFCS tax administratively.[151] In January 2003, US Corn Products International Inc., one of the largest US exporters of HFCS, initiated a Chapter 11 claim for $250 million against the Mexican 20 percent tax on soft drinks using HFCS rather than cane sugar.[152]

A collateral disagreement concerns the Mexican government's claim that the original NAFTA sugar side letter is invalid. The side letter, drafted under pressure by domestic US sugar groups, amended NAFTA's original terms by including Mexico's domestic consumption of HFCS in the calculation of Mexico's eligibility for free access to the US sugar market.[153]

Without political support to repeal the existing tax on HFCS imports, the Fox administration focused on bilateral industry negotiations.[154] Bilateral negotiations tried but failed to reach a compromise that would allow some US HFCS into Mexico and partly open the US market to Mex-

---

149. After SECOFI imposed AD tariffs, US exports of HFCS to Mexico declined from 186,000 tons to 2,000 tons. See "Briefing Room: Sugar and Sweetener Trade," US Department of Agriculture Economic Research Service, April 2002, table 14a. See also "Final Decision: Review of the Antidumping Investigation on Imports of High Fructose Corn Syrup, Originating from the United States of America" (MEX-USA-98-1904-01). The entire panel report is available at www.nafta-sec-alena.org/DefaultSite/index_e.aspx (accessed in March 2005).

150. According to the interim WTO panel decision (1999), SECOFI failed to take into account several basic factors in its injury determination: profits, output, and employment. See "WTO Panel Delivers Split Interim Decision on Mexico AD Action," *Inside US Trade*, October 15, 1999.

151. The Mexican Supreme Court held that the Fox administration acted illegally by suspending the tax. See "US Floats Temporary Sweetener Deal to Mexico, As HFCS Tax Revives," *Inside US Trade*, July 19, 2002.

152. In January 2002, the 20 percent tax prompted Mexican soft drink bottlers to switch from HFCS to sugar. (In turn, this makes Mexico's domestic market somewhat more attractive for sugar producers, compared with exporting to the United States above the NAFTA tier-two tariff.) According to the US National Corn Growers Association and Corn Refiners Association, US exports of HFCS have virtually been barred from the Mexican market. See BNA (2003b, 2003c) and "Zoellick to Raise Mexico Sugar in Hopes of Resolution this Year," *Inside US Trade*, February 28, 2003.

153. By including both domestic sugar and HFCS consumption, Mexico practically lost the possibility of unlimited duty-free access to the US market, should Mexico become a net surplus producer for two consecutive years. See Haley and Suarez (1999).

154. One proposal would guarantee Mexican access to the US sugar market up to 268,000 tons over three years starting in 2004. An equivalent amount of US HFCS would also enter Mexico. See "US Mexican Industries Make New Stab at Resolving Sweetener Dispute," *Inside US Trade*, April 23, 2004.

ico's surplus sugar. To date, US and Mexican trade officials have not been able to agree on the amount of Mexican access to the US sugar market, the portion of access that would be raw and refined, shipping patterns, how long the agreement would apply, and trade remedy rules governing sugar. Facing an impasse over sweetener negotiations, the United States initiated a WTO case against the Mexican HFCS tax in March 2004.[155] As NAFTA tier-two tariffs phase out through 2008, US-Mexico HFCS sweetener disputes will probably intensify.[156]

The web of sugar and HFCS disputes is all about dividing up a delicious pie of economic rent. None of the private parties to the dispute wants a truly competitive market for sugar: that would simply slash the price. What each party wants is to keep sugar prices high but to enlarge its own share of the market at another party's expense. To be sure, there are persuasive health reasons for keeping sugar prices high—and even raising them. But the compelling health argument does *not* mean that high prices should confer a windfall on sugar producers, the world norm today, and the norm under NAFTA. It makes no more sense to enrich "Big Sugar" than it would to foster a Tobacco Monopoly or Whisky Trust. If legislators are persuaded by health arguments to raise sugar prices, then sugar taxes should be the mechanism, not border protection. The revenue should be used both to augment public health budgets and to phase out acreage devoted to sugar production. In our chapter on agriculture, these themes are explored further.

Chapter 20 Cases

The NAFTA partners seldom resort to Chapter 20 panels: Only 11 cases were brought during 1994–2004, and only three of them have progressed to the stage of panel deliberations. All Chapter 20 disputes have involved the United States either as defendant (seven cases) or complainant (four cases). There have been no cases between Mexico and Canada. US-Mexico trade in agriculture (e.g., sugar, tomatoes, and broom corn) and trucking services have been the most frequent sources of dispute. Canada and Mexico also challenged the US Helms-Burton Act (echoing European complaints brought to the WTO).

Broom Corn Brooms Case

In 1997, Mexico initiated a Chapter 20 panel to resolve Mexican concerns about US emergency safeguard actions against broom corn brooms.[157]

---

155. In July 2004, a WTO panel was established to review the HFCS case.

156. Beginning in January 2003, US tier-two tariffs on Mexican sugar drop by 1.5 cents a pound each year until 2008, when US sugar tariffs are supposed to disappear.

157. According to Vega-Cánovas and Winham (2002), the Chapter 20 *Broom Corn Brooms* case is important in establishing precedents for reviewing USITC decisions by an international panel.

The Chapter 20 panel decided that the United States violated its NAFTA obligations by imposing tariffs on Mexican broom exports. In compliance with the NAFTA panel decision, the United States removed its safeguard measures and complied with the panel recommendations.

Cross-Border Trucking Case

A long-standing and commercially more important dispute between Mexico and the United States concerns cross-border trucking.[158] Potential spillovers into bilateral agricultural trade compound this complex case. More than 45 percent of cross-border trade in agriculture and agrifood products is perishable, and about 80 percent of the value of US-Mexico trade moves by truck.[159] US safety concerns, partly driven by domestic trucking interests, have delayed Mexican bus and truck access and indirectly prevented progress on cross-border traffic congestion. As a consequence, transportation delays, reaching as high as 23 hours, can act as a de facto tax on agrifood trade.[160]

After NAFTA was signed, efforts were made to facilitate anticipated liberalization of cross-border trucking under Chapter 12 (Cross-Border Trade in Services). Specifically, cross-border trucking was supposed to be permitted within commercial zones of certain US border states: California, Arizona, New Mexico, and Texas.[161] Under NAFTA, all other cross-border shipments were to be transferred through an inefficient drayage system, much as existed before the agreement: Under the drayage system, once Mexican trucks reach the US border, they must unload their container and hire short-haul drayage tractors to pull the trailers across the border. Long-haul trucks on the other side of the border then pick up the con-

---

158. A separate dispute, with parallel features, involves cross-border bus traffic. We do not cover the bus dispute in this section.

159. Based on USDA estimates. The United States exports animal and horticultural products to heavily populated Mexican areas such as Mexico City and Guadalajara. Mexico exports fresh fruits and vegetables from the northwest states of Sinaloa and Sonora through Nogales, Arizona to the western US states. US bulk exports in oilseeds and grain and Mexican perishable exports are made through Veracruz and other Mexican gulf ports to US east coast ports. See Coyle (2000). For economic concerns about cross-border trucking raised in a letter from Mexico's secretary of the economy to all US senators, see "Mexican Letter on Cross-Border Trucking," *Inside US Trade*, August 3, 2001.

160. According to studies done by Texas A&M International University, removing border bottlenecks could reduce travel time between Chicago and Monterrey, Mexico, by 40 percent. Transportation bottlenecks obviously threaten fresh and perishable agricultural products. "Mexican Letter on Cross-Border Trucking," *Inside US Trade*, August 3, 2001.

161. In effect, the United States lifted the 1982 Bus Regulatory Reform Act (BRRA) to facilitate Mexican truckers with access to US border states. The BRRA imposed a two-year moratorium on issuing new US highway authorizations to trucks based in a foreign country or those owned by foreign persons.

tainer trailers and take them to their destination in the United States. The reverse happens for shipments into Mexico.

After NAFTA was signed, the United States blocked Mexican truck access across the US border, citing truck safety concerns. Most observers believe that the real reason was fervent opposition from the Teamsters Union and some US trucking firms and that truck safety issues served as a convenient cover for deeper economic objections. Following consultations, Mexico initiated a Chapter 20 case against the United States in 1998, claiming that the United States failed to fulfill its NAFTA obligations. Canada sided with Mexico in its brief to the Chapter 20 panel, describing the cross-border trucking services dispute as "archaic." The Chapter 20 panel ruled against the United States, and in February 2001 the US government agreed to comply. The US Department of Transportation (DOT) passed regulations three months later to facilitate the NAFTA panel decision.[162] The DOT Trucking Regulations outline the necessary safety measures for Mexican trucks and buses to operate in the United States.

Meanwhile, the US Congress considered legislation offered by Senators Richard Shelby (R-AL) and Patty Murray (D-WA) that would raise new licensing obstacles to cross-border trucking. Faced with the prospect of President Bush's veto, in late November 2001 the US Congress adopted a compromise on truck safety standards that abandoned earlier proposals for electronic verification of the driver's license of every Mexican truck driver.[163]

In November 2002, President Bush ended the moratorium by allowing Mexican buses to operate beyond the commercial zone along the US-Mexico border.[164] President Bush also lifted a moratorium on Mexican investment in trucking and busing firms based in the United States.

---

162. Based on 2001 DOT Trucking Regulations, once Mexican trucks receive provisional authorization confirming that all safety conditions have been met, they can operate throughout the United States. See Sheppard (2002).

163. See "Congress Strikes a Deal on NAFTA Trucks Supported by White House," *Inside US Trade*, November 30, 2001. See also "US Congress and Bush Administration Reach Compromise," *SourceMex*, December 5, 2001.

164. Since 1982 (Bus Regulatory Reform Act), Mexican buses and trucks have been prevented from traveling into the continental United States due to a variety of environmental and safety regulations imposed by the DOT. On November 27, 2002, President Bush declared the US border open to Mexican buses. President Bush's proposal was significant in allowing Mexican companies to transport passengers in cross-border scheduled bus service rather than change carriers at the border. Around the same time, there were proposals to improve NAFTA's highway infrastructure by extending I-69 from Canada, through Michigan and Mississippi, ultimately reaching Mexico. The budget for NAFTA highway construction, however, is nonexistent. See Howard J. Shatz, "Opinion: Mexican Trucking on the Road to Trade Liberalization," *San Diego Union-Tribune*, December 18, 2002; Jerry Pacheco, "Cross-Border Trucking a Complex Issue," *Albuquerque Journal*, December 16, 2002; BNA (2003d); and "Paving NAFTA's Highway," *Christian Science Monitor*, December 9, 2002.

Domestic interest groups that support a delay, if not a complete ban, on Mexican trucks took the DOT to court over its licensing measures. Sensing a loss on truck safety issues, these groups invoked environmental concerns in their court suit. In January 2003, the Ninth Circuit agreed with the plaintiffs, holding that DOT must complete an environmental impact statement (EIS) before authorizing Mexican truck access to the United States beyond established border zones.[165] Meanwhile US opponents of Mexican trucking continued to raise safety issues in their press releases.

Legitimate criticisms of Mexican truck safety standards center on Mexican drayage trucks, which have higher failure rates because the economic incentives favor the use of older, less safe trucks for short distances. But truck safety arguments have less force for normal long-distance hauls. A 2001 study by the US DOT found that Mexican trucks operating in certain US border states are not significantly less safe than US trucks: The Mexican failure rate is only 5 percent higher than the US rate. Moreover, pessimistic forecasts that cross-border trucking will attract a flood of Mexican trucks onto US highways are probably ill-founded. The DOT estimates that lack of financing for Mexican truck operators will prevent a surge in the truck fleet serving the US market (Sheppard 2002).

All this has taxed the patience of the Mexican government. On March 12, 2003, Mexico proposed bilateral government consultations. In the absence of US compliance with the Chapter 20 panel, Mexico threatened to seek compensation for lost profits due to the cross-border trucking dispute.[166] Meanwhile, Mexico has blocked the entry of US trucks.[167] The US Supreme Court unanimously overturned the Ninth Circuit decision in June 2004. While the Fox administration views the Supreme Court's decision as solving a domestic conflict rather than US-Mexico differences over 2002 DOT regulations, the decision did underscore the importance of NAFTA commitments (EIU 2004, Moore 2004). As of May 2005, the Bush administration was upgrading its inspection program to resolve the remaining doubts on truck safety. The final outcome will test whether the United States can balance the demands of its NAFTA commitment, the protests of organized labor, and its obligation to ensure highway safety.

---

165. The court determined that the DOT failed Clean Air Act and National Environmental Policy Act requirements when a DOT study concluded that Mexican truck access to the United States would not have a significant impact on the environment. See "Court Blocks Bush Implementation of NAFTA Truck Panel," *Inside US Trade*, January 24, 2003; and "Congress Strikes a Deal on NAFTA Trucks Supported by White House," *Inside US Trade*, November 30, 2001.

166. According to the Mexican Economy Ministry, 1,500 Mexican truck companies submitted applications for permission to enter the United States; 200 US truckers are waiting for authorization to operate beyond the commercial zone; and 1,300 Mexican truckers are waiting for approval to operate within the commercial zone. See BNA (2003d).

167. In March 2003, the Mexican economic secretary temporarily cancelled the transportation chapter of NAFTA and decided to close off Mexico's northern border from US transport vehicles. See "Border Will Remain Closed to US Truckers," *Corporate Mexico*, March 7, 2003.

Conclusion and Recommendations

While the alarms over NAFTA Chapter 11 seem overblown, the short-comings of NAFTA Chapters 19 and 20 highlight the need for institutional improvements. Even though NAFTA governments have no desire to create supranational institutions (modeled along EU lines), stronger institutions would facilitate the resolution of disputes and strengthen the North American accord.

Institutional Consolidation

We think the place to start is with an agreed roster of panelists who would serve on all NAFTA cases for a period of six years. The roster might, for example, have 30 names (10 nominated by each country) from which five arbitrators would be selected in each case, whether it arises under Chapters 11, 14, 19, or 20 or involves labor or environmental questions. Just as federal judges hear a wide range of civil and criminal cases, panelists with a broad range of experience in international economic law can be selected. To attract qualified panelists, the NAFTA Secretariat should match the ICSID rate of about $2,400 per day. The big advantage of a single roster is that once panelists are named to a roster, they can be disqualified only on highly specific grounds (e.g., conflict of interest). Time delays in choosing panelists will be reduced, and panelists are more likely to know one another, cultivating a certain degree of "judicial collegiality."[168]

Second, NAFTA partners need to establish a joint funding pool to cover costs for proceedings, travel, and panelist fees. Canada maintains a permanent staff of 8 to 15 persons and an annual budget of more than $2 million. Mexico has 7 to 16 staff and an annual budget between $1 and $2 million. By contrast, the United States has 3 staff members and an average budget of about $1 million. Part of the problem is that the US Section on NAFTA is buried in the International Trade Administration (ITA) of the US DOC and lacks a separate line item in the budget. The chronic lack of funding in the US section causes Canada and Mexico to reimburse about 50 percent of the panel costs. To resolve this disparity in funding levels, and to raise the profile of the US commitment to NAFTA, James R. Holbein, former US secretary at the NAFTA Secretariat, has recommended that the US section be assigned its own line item in the budget, funded with at least $3 million annually, have at least 6 staff members, and report directly to the secretary of commerce (not through the ITA) (Holbein 2004).

---

168. As Gustavo Vega-Cánovas points out, panelists on the roster would need to subscribe to a high code of conduct, and a selection procedure (possibly a negative strike system) would need to be agreed to. Numerous other administrative features would also need to be worked out. We thank Vega-Cánovas for this observation.

As a profile-raising measure, NAFTA partners should consolidate their national NAFTA desks into a single staff, equally funded by all three parties. The staff members should have civil service protection and should all work in a single NAFTA headquarters building. We leave the choice of a headquarters site to political bargaining between the members.

Structural Changes: Chapters 11, 19, and 20

In addition to consolidating NAFTA staff in a single headquarters building and establishing a roster of semipermanent panelists, we offer structural recommendations for Chapters 11, 19, and 20.[169] Since these issues spark contentious debates, particularly in the US Congress, they will need to be bundled with NAFTA reforms in other areas to ensure congressional approval.

Chapter 11

Chapter 11 should harmonize investor-state dispute settlement provisions with US-Chile and US-Singapore FTAs, which clarify direct and indirect expropriation. The interpretation of Chapter 11 expropriation provisions is important, and the language in the Chile and Singapore FTAs indicates that environmental or health regulations would rarely constitute compensable indirect expropriation.[170] Moreover, both FTAs include changes that limit the scope of "expropriation." While NAFTA uses broad language to define indirect expropriation as measures that are "tantamount to nationalization or expropriation," the Chile and Singapore FTAs limit indirect expropriation to measures that "have an effect equivalent to direct expropriation."[171] Both FTAs also emphasize that the economic impact of government policies, by itself, does not establish the basis for indirect expropriation.

---

169. The Chapter 11 process has generally been successful, and Chapter 14 has never been invoked. In the chapters on environment and labor, we discuss how to strengthen dispute resolution in those agreements.

170. The Chile and Singapore FTAs narrow the protection against expropriation without compensation to "tangible or intangible property right or property interest" rather than to an "investment," as defined under NAFTA Chapter 11. Unlike NAFTA, the Chile and Singapore FTAs also include claims based on the breach of "an investment authorization," which some argue could open domestic regulatory programs to new areas of potential investor challenges. See Trade and Environment Policy Advisory Committee (TEPAC) Report, "US-Singapore FTA," February 27, 2003.

171. Direct and indirect expropriations are clarified under Article 15 investment provisions and the expropriation side letter in the US-Singapore FTA. Similarly, indirect and direct expropriation provisions are clarified under Article 10 investment provisions in the US-Chile FTA. See USTR (2003a, 2003b).

Chapter 11 should also include an appellate body mechanism for investor-state disputes resembling the recent Central American Free Trade Agreement (CAFTA) proposal.[172] Appellate mechanisms can be important for establishing clear jurisprudence in arbitration panels that are consistent with US investor protections (Butler et al. 2004, Peterson 2003). The Singapore and Chile FTAs, as an example, include language that could be used to establish an FTA appellate review mechanism or provide recourse to a future multilateral investment appellate body, options notably absent in NAFTA. In the context of CAFTA, an appellate body has been concretely proposed.

Chapter 19

While Chapter 19 served its purpose under CUSFTA—namely, expediting judicial review and providing a voice for Canada in US AD and CVD decisions—the Chapter 19 process under NAFTA has not fared as well. Decisions on Canadian complaints required an average of about 315 days under CUSFTA, compared with an average near 700 days under NAFTA.[173] Moreover, multiple remands and extraordinary challenges have marred the process. In light of this record, two alternative approaches should be considered.

One alternative is simply to maintain Chapter 19 provisions as they are currently written but set Chapter 19 panels within the context of the dispute settlement system reforms that we outlined above. Perhaps in this new setting, delays and frictions would be reduced in future Chapter 19 cases. But the institutional reforms we have suggested would not address the fundamental weakness in Chapter 19—the absence of a common NAFTA benchmark for judging national AD and CVD actions and the absence of agreed standards of NAFTA panel review.[174] Unless these fundamental difficulties are resolved, the Chapter 19 process will continue to encounter difficulty, especially in controversial big-ticket cases.

Alternatively, the NAFTA countries simply could abolish Chapter 19 and consign all disputes over AD and CVD determinations to the WTO.

---

172. The establishment of a CAFTA appellate mechanism is pending a decision over when to initiate the appeals process. At issue is whether only a serious error of law, or whether any error of law, is sufficient to initiate an appeal. See "Decision Close on CAFTA Investor-State Appellate Body Proposal," *Inside US Trade*, September 17, 2004.

173. The Chapter 19 decision process has proven slower on average than the US Court of International Trade. In the *Magnesium* case, for example, which was initiated in 2000, the NAFTA Chapter 19 panel did not reach a final decision until June 2004. See Potter (2004) and Feldman (2004).

174. The question of standard of review comes down to how much deference the NAFTA panel should give to the national administering agency. Should the panel remand only those agency findings that are clearly erroneous? Or should it also remand agency findings that are not adequately supported by the evidence? The latter test is a common standard in US courts.

The WTO dispute settlement mechanisms were still on the drawing board when NAFTA was ratified. They have now been working for nearly a decade, and numerous AD and CVD cases have been decided. If NAFTA members are willing to consider adopting WTO codes in Chapter 19 cases, they might as well go all the way and simply turn to the established WTO system to resolve AD and CVD disputes. In our view, this option makes the most sense.[175] We note, however, that WTO decisions that reverse an AD or CVD determination do not result in the refund of penalty duties collected prior to the WTO decision, unlike Chapter 19 decisions. If this feature is critical, NAFTA members could agree among themselves to a refund protocol, in the event of an adverse WTO ruling.

Chapter 20

Chapter 20 should be strengthened by adding provisions for binding arbitration and monetary awards. In theory, NAFTA parties can already enforce Chapter 20 panel reports by suspending equivalent benefits against the defendant party.[176] However, without binding arbitration, it is hard to get an impartial measure of equivalent benefits. Moreover, monetary awards inflict less collateral damage than trade sanctions and should thus become the preferred remedy.

Frequently overlooked, Chapter 20 includes significant provisions for addressing administrative failures under NAFTA. To add teeth to Chapter 20 decisions, NAFTA parties should first clarify that Chapter 20 Commission "reports" are in fact "decisions." Second, Chapter 20 should include a stipulation under Article 2018 that final Chapter 20 panel decisions "shall be binding."[177]

---

175. We recognize, however, that the Chapter 19 appeal process has been effective in resolving many cases, and the choice of Chapter 19 or the WTO (or both) has proved relatively favorable to Canada and Mexico. If the Chapter 19 process were not available, and if instead only the WTO ruled against the United States in the softwood lumber dispute, the United States might prolong the WTO compliance process much longer than it would prolong the Chapter 19 compliance process. We thank Patrick Macrory for this observation.

176. Under Article 2019, if the defendant party ignores Chapter 20 panel reports, the complaining party can retaliate by suspending benefits equal to the benefits denied by the defendant party's violations. See Feldman (2004). While Article 2019 parallels remedies available under the WTO dispute settlement system, NAFTA Chapter 20 is different from the WTO in at least one respect. Since Chapter 20 decisions are not binding, the Chapter 20 panel would neither evaluate whether sufficient evidence warranted retaliation by disputing parties nor whether parties adequately followed Chapter 20 panel recommendations.

177. The language of Chapter 20 binding decisions should follow the Chapter 19 ECC procedure. Specifically, Annex 1904.13 stipulates that Chapter 19 ECC decisions "shall be binding on the Parties with respect to the particular matter between the Parties that was before the panel."

References

Abbott, Frederick M. 1999. *The North American Integration Regime and Its Implications for the World Trading System*. New York: Jean Monnet Center for International and Regional Economic Law and Justice, New York University School of Law.

Anderson, Kym. 2002. *Peculiarities of Retaliation in WTO Dispute Settlement*. Center for International Economic Studies Discussion Paper 0207 (March). Adelaide, Australia: Center for International Economic Studies.

Appleton, Barry. 2002. *Comparing NAFTA and the MAI*. Washington: Appleton & Associates. www.appletonlaw.com.

Bacchus, James. 2003. Groping Toward Grotius: The WTO and the International Rule of Law. *Harvard International Law Journal* 44, no. 2 (Summer).

Baker & Hostetler LLP. 2004. Protecting Investors: Can Governments Stop the Music? Background paper prepared for the Canadian-American Business Council and CSIS (June).

BNA (Bureau of National Affairs, Inc.). 2003a. New British Columbia Forest Policy Intended to Resolve Softwood Lumber Fight. *BNA International Trade Reporter* 20, no. 14 (April 3).

BNA (Bureau of National Affairs, Inc.). 2003b. US Corn Syrup Exporter to Seek NAFTA Compensation for Mexican Tax. *BNA International Trade Reporter* 20, no. 5 (January 30).

BNA (Bureau of National Affairs, Inc.). 2003c. House Lawmakers Urge Mexican Envoy to Help Resolve Trade in Sweeteners. *BNA International Trade Reporter* 20, no. 12 (March 20).

BNA (Bureau of National Affairs, Inc.). 2003d. Mexico Seeks Urgent Meeting to Discuss Implementation of Cross-Border Trucking. *BNA International Trade Reporter* 20, no. 12 (March 20).

Butler, William, Rhoda H. Karpatkin, Daniel Magraw, and Durwood Zaelke. 2004. Separate Comments of TEPAC Members on the US-Central American Free Trade Agreement. Washington: Center for International Environmental Law (March 18).

Canada House of Commons. 2002. *Partners in North America: Advancing Canada's Relations with the United States and Mexico*. Report of the Standing Committee on Foreign Affairs and International Trade (December). Ottawa.

Chant, John F. 2002. *The Financial Sector in NAFTA. Two Plus One Equals Restructuring*. Vancouver: The Fraser Institute (November).

Clodfelter, Mark. 2004. Protecting Investors: Can Governments Stop the Music? Presentation at the Canadian-American Business Council and CSIS, Washington, June 16.

Cosbey, Aaron. 2002. *NAFTA's Chapter 11 and the Environment: A Briefing Paper for the CEC's Joint Public Advisory Committee*. Ottawa: International Institute for Sustainable Development (June).

Coyle, William T. 2000. Transportation Bottlenecks Shape US-Mexico Food and Agricultural Trade. *USDA Agricultural Outlook* (September). Washington: US Department of Agriculture.

Cuevas, Alfredo, Miguel Messmacher, and Alejandro Werner. 2002. *Changes in the Patterns of External Financing in Mexico Since the Approval of NAFTA*. México D.F.: Banco de Mexico (July).

Cymrot, Mark. 2004. Investment and Trade Disputes in North America: Government Apprehension and Institutional Failures. Presentation at the Canadian-American Business Council and CSIS, Washington, June 16.

Dumberry, Patrick. 2001. The NAFTA Investment Dispute Settlement Mechanism: A Review of the Latest Case Law. *Journal of World Investment* 2 (March): 151–95.

EIU (Economist Intelligence Unit). 2004. Mexico: Cross-Border Trucking Still Faces Hurdles (June 14).

Feldman, Elliot J. 2004. *Duties and Dumping: What's Going Wrong with Chapter 19?* Background Paper (June). Washington: Baker & Hostetler LLP.

Foy, P. G., and J. C. Deane. 2001. Foreign Investment Under Investment Treaties: Recent Developments Under Chapter 11 of the North American Free Trade Agreement. *ICSID Review Foreign Investment Law Journal* 16, no. 1.

Gantz, David. 1999. Dispute Settlement Under the NAFTA and the WTO: Choice of Forum Opportunities and Risks for the NAFTA Parties. *American University International Law Review* 14, no. 4.

GAO (US General Accounting Office). 1998. Forest Service Distribution of Timber Sales Receipts. Report to the Committee on Resources. Washington: House of Representatives (November).

Gastle, Charles M. 2002. NAFTA's Chapter 11 "Frontier Justice" Needs Reform. *The Lawyers Weekly* (December 6).

Graham, Edward M. 2002. Economic Issues Raised by Treatment of Takings under NAFTA Chapter 11. Washington: Institute for International Economics.

Haley, Stephen, and Nydia Suarez. 1999. US-Mexico Sweetener Trade Mired in Dispute. *USDA Agricultural Outlook* (September). Washington: US Department of Agriculture. www.ers.usda.gov/publications/agoutlook/sep1999/ao264g.pdf (accessed in March 2005).

Hart, Michael. 2002. *A Trading Nation: Canadian Trade Policy from Colonialism to Globalization.* Vancouver: University of British Columbia Press.

Holbein, James R. 2004. Chapter 19: Is the System Failing? Presentation at the Canadian-American Business Council and CSIS, Washington, June 16.

Horlick, Gary, and Alicia L. Marti. 1997. NAFTA Chapter 11: A Private Right of Action to Enforce Market Access Through Investments. *Journal of International Arbitration* 14, no. 1 (March). Norwell, MA: Kluwer Law International.

Howse, Robert. 1998. *Settling Trade Remedy Disputes: When the WTO Forum Is Better than the NAFTA.* C. D. Howe Institute Commentary. Toronto: C. D. Howe Institute.

Hufbauer, Gary C., Daniel C. Esty, Diana Orejas, Luis Rubio, and Jeffrey J. Schott. 2000. *NAFTA and the Environment: Seven Years Later.* Washington: Institute for International Economics.

IGPAC (United States Intergovernmental Policy Advisory Committee). 1992. Report on the North American Free Trade Agreement (September 15).

Jackson, John H. 2000. The Role and Effectiveness of the WTO Dispute Settlement Mechanism. *Brookings Trade Forum* (April). Washington: Brookings Institution.

Kash, David W. 1997. *NAFTA and Its Impact on the Surety and Insurance Business.* Phoenix, AZ: National Law Center for Inter-American Free Trade.

Kurtz, Jurgen. 2002. *A General Investment Agreement in the WTO? Lessons from Chapter 11 of NAFTA and the OECD Multilateral Agreement on Investment.* New York: Jean Monnet Center for International and Regional Economic Law and Justice, New York University School of Law (June).

Macrory, Patrick. 2002. *NAFTA Chapter 19: A Successful Experiment in International Trade Dispute Resolution.* C. D. Howe Institute Commentary (September). Toronto: C. D. Howe Institute.

Mann, Howard. 2001. *Private Rights, Public Problems: A Guide to NAFTA's Chapter on Investor Rights.* Winnipeg: International Institute for Sustainable Development.

Mann, Howard, and Konrad von Moltke. 1999. *NAFTA's Chapter 11 and the Environment: Addressing the Impacts of the Investor-State Process on the Environment.* Working Paper. Winnipeg: International Institute for Sustainable Development.

McMillan, Stephen. 2002. *NAFTA Chapter 11: Issues and Opportunities.* Australian APEC Study Center. Melbourne: Monash University (July).

Mena, Antonio Ortiz L. N. 2001. *Dispute Settlement Under NAFTA: The Challenges Ahead.* Mexico: Centro de Investigación y Docencia Económicas (CIDE) (May).

Moore, Cassandra C. 2004. US Supreme Court Finally Removes Decade-long Roadblock to US-Mexican Trucking. *CATO Free Trade Bulletin* no. 13 (July 8).

Office of the Federal Register. 2004. International Trade Commission, Live Swine from Canada, Investigation Number 701-TA-438. *Federal Register* 69, no. 94 (May 14).

Pan, Eric J. 1999. Assessing the NAFTA Chapter 19 Binational Panel System: An Experiment in International Adjudication. *Harvard International Law Journal* (Spring).

Peterson, Luke E. 2003. US-Chile FTA Text Released. Winnipeg: International Institute for Sustainable Development (May).

Potter, Simon V. 1999. Dispute Settlement After 10 Years of Free Trade. Presentation at a conference on Free Trade at 10, Washington, June.

Potter, Simon V. 2004. Chapter 19 of the NAFTA: An Emerging Canadian View. Presentation at the Canadian-American Business Council and CSIS, Washington, June 16.

Price, Daniel M. 2001. NAFTA Chapter 11, Investor-State Dispute Settlement: Frankenstein or Safety Valve. *Canada-United States Law Journal* 26, no. 1. Cleveland, OH: Case Western Reserve University School of Law.

Public Citizen. 2001. *NAFTA Chapter 11 Investor-to-State Cases: Bankrupting Democracy*. Washington (September).

Ramírez, de la O Rogelio. 1993. *The North American Free Trade Agreement from a Mexican Perspective*. Vancouver: The Fraser Institute.

Rose-Ackerman, Susan, and Jim Rossi. 1999. *Takings Law and Infrastructure Investment: Certainty, Flexibility and Compensation*. Yale Program for Studies in Economics and Public Policy Working Paper 220. New Haven, CT: Yale Law School (August).

Rugman, Alan M., and Michael Gestrin. 1993. *The Investment Provisions of NAFTA*. Vancouver: The Fraser Institute.

Rugman, Alan, John Kirton, and Julie Soloway. 1999. *Environmental Regulations and Corporate Strategy*. Oxford: Oxford University Press.

Sedjo, Roger A. 1997. *The Forest Sector: Important Innovations*. Discussion Paper 97-42 (August). Washington: Resources for the Future.

Sheppard, Hale E. 2002. The NAFTA Trucking Dispute: Pretexts for Noncompliance and Policy Justifications for US Facilitation of Cross-Border Services. *Minnesota Journal of Global Trade* 11, no. 2 (Summer).

Soloway, Julie A. 1999. Environmental Trade Barriers in NAFTA: The MMT Fuel Additives Controversy. *Minnesota Journal of Global Trade:* 8.

Statistics Canada. 2004. International Merchandise Trade: Annual Review. Ottawa: Ministry of Industry (June). www.statcan.ca/english/freepub/65-208-XIE/2003000/index.htm (accessed in March 2005).

Stobo, Gerry H. 2004. Through the Looking Glass: Chapter 19 Binational Panel Reviews. Presentation at the Canadian-American Business Council and CSIS, Washington, June 16.

USTR (United States Trade Representative). 2003a. Text of the US-Singapore FTA (May). Washington. www.ustr.gov/Trade_Agreements/Bilateral/Section_Index.html (accessed in March 2005).

USTR (United States Trade Representative). 2003b. Text of the US-Chile FTA (June). Washington. www.ustr.gov/Trade_Agreements/Bilateral/Section_Index.html (accessed in March 2005).

Van der Walt, A. J. 1999. The Constitutional Property Clause: Striking a Balance Between Guarantee and Limitation. In *Property and the Constitution*, ed. Janet Maclean. Oxford: Hart Publishing.

VanDuzer, J. Anthony. 2002. *NAFTA Chapter 11 to Date: The Progress of a Work in Progress*. Ottawa: Carleton University (January 18).

Vega-Cánovas, Gustavo, and Gilbert R. Winham. 2002. The Role of NAFTA Dispute Settlement in the Management of Canadian, Mexican and US Trade and Investment Relations. *Ohio Northern University Law Review* 28.

Veloria, Velma. 2002. Statement during the International Investment Agreement Seminar Series. National Policy Association and the Congressional Economic Leadership Institute. Washington (May).

Weiler, Todd. 2001. Substantive Law Developments in NAFTA Arbitration. *Mealey's International Arbitration Report* 17.

Wheat, Andrew. 1995. Toxic Shock in a Mexican Village. *Multinational Monitor Volume* 16, no. 10 (October).

White, William R. 1994. *The Implications of the FTA and NAFTA for Canada and Mexico*. Technical Report Number 70. Ottawa: Bank of Canada (August).

Wilkie, Christopher. 2002. *The Origins of NAFTA Investment Provisions: Economic and Policy Considerations*. Ottawa: Center for Trade Policy and Law, Carleton University (January).

Winham, Gilbert R. 1993. *Dispute Settlement in the NAFTA and the FTA*. Vancouver: The Fraser Institute.

WorldTrade Executive, Inc. 2004. NAFTA Commission Approves Measures to Simplify Rules of Origin and Dispute Settlement Measures. *North American Free Trade and Investment Report* (August 15).

WTO (World Trade Organization). 1998. Mexico Antidumping Investigation of HFCS from the United States—Consultation of the Panel Established at the Request of the United States (October). Geneva.

WTO (World Trade Organization). 2004. *Final Dumping Determination on Softwood Lumber from Canada*. Appellate Body Report, WT/DS264/AB/R (August 11). Geneva.

Appendix 4A

Table 4A.1 Chronology of WTO softwood lumber disputes, January 2002 to 2004

Date	Status
December 2001	WTO panel established to evaluate US antidumping (AD) determination against Canadian softwood lumber (SWL) exports to the United States (WTO DS 236).
May 2002	US Department of Commerce (DOC) final AD and countervailing duty (CVD) determinations: average CVD rate of 18.79 percent, average AD rate of 8.43 percent, and average combined rate of 27.22 percent.
September 2002	WTO final report determines that US CVD findings based on Canadian provincial stumpage programs violated some WTO obligations (WTO DS 236).
October 2002	WTO panel established to evaluate US CVD determination against Canadian SWL exports to the United States (WTO DS 257).
January 2003	WTO panel established to evaluate US AD determination against Canadian SWL exports to the United States (WTO DS 264).
May 2003	WTO panel established to evaluate US AD determination against Canadian SWL exports to the United States (WTO DS 277).
August 2003	WTO panel rejects some of the Canadian government claims and determines that US CVD actions are inconsistent with the WTO Agreement on Subsidies and Countervailing Measures (SCM) (WTO DS 257).
December 2003	WTO panel determines that the US International Trade Commission (USITC) AD determination violates WTO AD rules (WTO DS 264).
January 2004	WTO panel reverses WTO CVD panel's August 2003 finding. WTO panel determines that the DOC could use benchmarks other than market prices in "very limited circumstances," but WTO panel declines to specify whether comparison of US prices with Canadian stumpage prices is consistent with WTO rules (WTO DS 257).
March 2004	WTO panel rejects USITC AD injury findings (WTO DS 277).
April 2004	Final WTO panel report determines some elements of the US AD injury determination are inconsistent with US WTO obligations (WTO DS 264).
April 2004	The United States and Canada agree to adhere to the WTO CVD decision by December 17, 2004 (WTO DS 257).
June 2004	DOC preliminary determination in first administrative review: recalculates AD and CVD rates—imposes countrywide CVD rate of 9.2 percent and AD rate of 4 percent (about half of May 2002 rates).
July 2004	DOC issues revised, recalculated CVD determinations: New DOC recalculation could reduce the CVD cash deposit rate from 18.79 to 7.82 percent, but the CVD cash deposit rate is subject to further revisions until the WTO panel process is completed.
August 2004	WTO Appellate Body report upholds WTO panel findings that the US zeroing methodology violates WTO AD rules (WTO DS 264).
November 2004	WTO final determination on the CVD cash deposit rate is due.

Sources: WTO Dispute Settlement Body, www.wto.org/english/tratop_e/dispu_e/dispu_e.htm; Government of British Columbia, Ministry of Forests, www.for.gov.bc.ca/HET/Softwood/; and Office of the US Trade Representative, Monitoring and Enforcement, www.ustr.gov/Trade_Agreements/Monitoring_Enforcement/Dispute_Settlement/Section_Index.html.

Table 4A.2 Chronology of NAFTA softwood lumber disputes, January 2002 to 2004

Date	Status
April 2002	NAFTA panel established to evaluate US antidumping (AD) determination against Canadian softwood lumber (SWL) exports to the United States.
April 2002	NAFTA panel established to evaluate countervailing duty (CVD) determination against Canadian SWL exports to the United States.
May 2002	US Department of Commerce (DOC) final AD and CVD determinations: average CVD rate of 18.79 percent, average AD rate of 8.43 percent, and average combined rate of 27.22 percent.
May 2002	NAFTA panel established for US threat of injury determination (AD) against Canadian SWL exports to the United States.
July 2003	NAFTA panel remands US AD injury determination to DOC.
August 2003	NAFTA panel remands US CVD determination to DOC.
September 2003	NAFTA panel remands US AD injury determinations to US International Trade Commission (USITC).
January 2004	DOC revises CVD finding in response to NAFTA panel remand.
March 2004	NAFTA panel again remands US AD injury determination to DOC.
May 2004	NAFTA panel rejects USITC injury determination and again remands US AD injury determination to USITC.
June 2004	DOC preliminary determination in first administrative review: recalculates AD and CVD rates—imposes countrywide CVD rate of 9.2 percent and AD rate of 4 percent (about half of May 2002 rates).
June 2004	NAFTA panel instructs DOC to recalculate its CVD determinations.
July 2004	DOC issues revised, recalculated CVD determinations: New DOC recalculation could reduce the CVD cash deposit rate from 18.79 to 7.82 percent, but the CVD cash deposit rate is subject to further revisions until the NAFTA panel process is completed.
August 2004	NAFTA panel releases third report, which again determines that USITC findings do not support threat of injury and remands AD determination to USITC, ordering USITC to find no threat of injury within 10 days. If the United States initiates an Extraordinary Challenge Committee (ECC) procedure and the NAFTA panel decision is still upheld, then CVD and AD cases concerning USITC findings will be terminated and Canada will have won the SWL phase IV litigation.
October 2004	NAFTA panel will issue its finding on the July 2004 DOC CVD determination.
December 2004	DOC final administrative review is due: If DOC finds CVD and AD rates lower than 27.22 percent, then exporters should receive refunds. Otherwise, exporters will have to pay the difference. Either the United States or Canada can appeal the final administrative review to a NAFTA panel.

Sources: NAFTA Secretariat, Decisions and Reports, www.nafta-sec-alena.org/DefaultSite/home/index_e.aspx; Government of British Columbia, Ministry of Forests, www.for.gov.bc.ca/HET/Softwood/; and Office of the US Trade Representative, Monitoring and Enforcement, www.ustr.gov/Trade_Agreements/Monitoring_Enforcement/Dispute_Settlement/Section_Index.html.

Table 4A.3　Chapter 20 disputes under NAFTA, January 1994 to March 2003

Initial filing/ termination	Petitioner country	Defendant country	Subject of dispute	Status/outcome
February 1995/ settled December 1996 (CDA-95-2008-01)	United States	Canada	Canada's application of customs duties higher than those specified in NAFTA to certain US-origin agricultural products	Panel unanimously determined that the Canadian tariffs conformed with NAFTA provisions.
Consultations 1995/ active	United States	Mexico	Discrimination against US trucking firms	Consultations at NAFTA Commission meeting in 1995; discussions continue between governments.
Consultations January 1996/active	Mexico	United States	Tariff rate quota on tomatoes	Consultations were held on January 18, 1996. Bilateral negotiations on tomatoes ongoing.
Consultations April 1996/active	Canada and Mexico	United States	Cuban Liberty and Democratic Solidarity Act of 1996 (Helms-Burton Act)	Consultations were held on April 20, 1996 and May 28, 1996; discussed by NAFTA Commission on June 28, 1996.
October 1996/active	United States	Mexico	Alleged discriminatory regulations limiting truck size for local delivery	Consultations ongoing.
Consultations October 1996/active	Canada	United States	US Sugar-Containing Products Re-Export Program	Consultations requested on October 23, 1996 and held on November 20, 1996.
January 1997/settled January 1998 (USA-97-2008-01)	Mexico	United States	US safeguard action taken on broom corn brooms from Mexico, imports that allegedly caused injury to the US domestic industry	Panel determined that the United States violated its obligations and recommended that the United States bring its measure into compliance with NAFTA.
July 1998/settled February 2001 (USA-MEX-98-2008-01)	Mexico	United States	US restrictions on cross-border trucking services and on Mexican investment in the US trucking industry	Panel unanimously decided that the United States breached its NAFTA obligations.
April 1999/settled November 1999	United States	Canada	Certain measures and practices by Canada affecting sports fishing and tourism services	Province of Ontario revoked the provincial measures that were under investigation.
August 2000/active	Mexico	United States	US tariff rate quota on sugar	Bilateral negotiations on sugar ongoing.
March 2003/active	Mexico	United States	Discrimination against Mexican trucking firms	Mexico renewed government consultations on March 12, 2003.

Notes: The first column shows the date of request for panel review under Chapter 20 or date of initial consultations when no panel review has been requested. CDA: panels reviewing Canadian agency determinations; MEX: panels reviewing Mexican agency determinations; and USA: panels reviewing US agency determinations.

Sources: NAFTA Secretariat, Decisions and Reports 2002, www.nafta-sec-alena.org/english/index.htm; OAS Foreign Trade Information System, SICE Dispute Settlement Binational Panel Decisions and Arbitral Panel Reports 2002, www.sice.oas.org/dispute/natdispe.asp; Office of the US Trade Representative 2002, www.ustr.gov/Trade_Agreements/Monitoring_Enforcement/Dispute_Settlement/Section_Index.html.

Table 4A.4   Chapter 11 disputes under NAFTA, August 1995 to August 2004

Initial filing/ termination[a]	Petitioner and nationality	Defendant country	Subject of dispute	Status/outcome
August 1995/ no claim filed	Halchette Distribution Services, United States	Mexico	Claim unknown	Notice of intent to arbitrate filed; no further action taken
March 1996/ no claim filed	Signa S.A. de C.V., Mexico	Canada	Canadian regulations injured Mexican company's investment in Canada	Notice of intent set claim for $36.8 million; no further action taken
September 1996/ July 1998	Ethyl Corporation, United States	Canada	Canadian ban on MMT imports. Claimed $250 million for damages and expropriation	Case settled for $13 million; ban on MMT imports eliminated by the government of Canada prior to tribunal decision
October 1996/ August 2000	Metalclad Corporation, United States	Mexico	Government actions preventing the opening of a hazardous waste landfill. Claimed $90 million	Tribunal ordered Mexico to pay Metalclad $16.7 million in damages
December 1996/ November 1999	Desechos Sólidos de Naucalpan C.V. (Azinian), United States	Mexico	Claim for $17 million for seizure of property and breach of contract	Resolved in favor of the Mexican government; no award of costs made
February 1998/ December 2002	Marvin Feldman, United States	Mexico	Claim for $50 million for lost profits due to refusal to rebate excise taxes on cigarette exports	Tribunal ordered Mexico to pay Feldman $982,901 plus interest
June 1998/ June 2000	USA Waste, United States	Mexico	Claim for $60 million	Resolved in favor of the Mexican government but no award on costs incurred by Mexico; the United States ordered to pay for costs of arbitration proceedings

Date filed/status	Claimant	Respondent	Claim	Outcome
July 1998/ November 2000	S. D. Myers, United States	Canada	Claim for $20 million for losses due to export ban on PCB waste	Tribunal affirmed in part and remanded in part; resolved in favor of S. D. Myers for $3.87 million plus interest
July 1998/active	Loewen Group Inc., Canada	United States	Claim for $725 million for discrimination and expropriation due to a $550 million damage sentence in civil case	Tribunal determined that NAFTA did not give jurisdiction over an investor that was founded in Canada and reincorporated in the United States (June 2003); tribunal also noted that undue intervention in domestic matters by international arbitrators could "damage . . . the viability of NAFTA itself"
November 1998/ Withdrawn 1999	Sun Belt Water Inc., United States	Canada	Claim for $220 million for biased treatment by government of British Columbia in joint venture	Appears that claim is withdrawn
December 1998/ November 2002	Pope & Talbot Inc., United States	Canada	Claim for $130 million[b] for discriminatory implementation of Softwood Lumber Agreement	Tribunal dismissed 2 of the 4 claims made by Pope & Talbot Inc.; tribunal ordered Canada to pay Pope & Talbot $461,566 plus interest for damages and cost of tribunal proceedings
June 1999/ August 2005	Methanex Corp., Canada	United States	Claim for $970 million in damages due to California state ban on the use of MTBE (gasoline additive)	Tribunal ordered Methanex to pay for the cost of US legal fees and arbitration proceedings totaling nearly $4 million

(table continues next page)

Table 4A.4 Chapter 11 disputes under NAFTA (continued)

Initial filing/ termination[a]	Petitioner and nationality	Defendant country	Subject of dispute	Status/outcome
September 1999/ October 2002	Mondev International, Canada	United States	Claim for $16 million plus interest and legal costs for a failed 1978 mall development deal in Boston; Mondev sued and won a jury trial in 1994 but the verdict was reversed by the Massachusetts Supreme Judicial Court (SJC); Mondev contested SJC's decision	Panel unanimously rejected each of Mondev's claims (October 2002); no award on costs was made
May 2000/active	UPS of America Inc., United States	Canada	Claim for $100 million; UPS accuses Canada Post of subsidizing its courier services with revenue from its regular letter delivery service	Tribunal dismissed UPS Article 1105 claim and rejected Canada's jurisdictional challenge under Article 1102; consultations ongoing
July 2000/ January 2003	ADF Group Inc., Canada	United States	Claim for $90 million; ADF protests US Department of Transportation enforcement of US Federal Surface Transportation Assistance Act (1982) that requires federally funded state highway projects to use only US-produced steel	Tribunal dismissed ADF claims against the United States; tribunal ordered the US government and ADF to split the costs of the proceeding
September 2000/ June 2002	USA Waste, United States	Mexico	Resubmitted claim that the tribunal's initial decision would prevent USA Waste from bringing any additional claims relating to a possible breach of NAFTA obligation	Tribunal dismissed Mexico's argument that the tribunal lacked jurisdiction on this case; no award on costs was made

November 2000/active	Adams et al., United States	Mexico	Claim for $75 million for expropriation of land developed by Adams et al.	Notice of arbitration filed February 2001; no further action taken
December 2000/withdrawn 2000	Ketcham Investments, Inc. and Tysa Investments, Inc., United States	Canada	Claim for C$30 million as compensation for damages caused by Canada's regulation on softwood lumber	Claim withdrawn
December 2001/withdrawn April 2002	Trammel Crow Company, United States	Canada	Claim for $32 million; Trammel Crow alleges Canada's control over the Canada Post Corporation breaches its NAFTA obligations	Claim withdrawn
December 2001/active	Francis K. Haas, United States	Mexico	Claim unknown	Notice of intent to arbitrate filed December 2001; no further action taken
Unknown month 2001/active	Fireman's Fund Insurance Company, United States	Mexico	Claim for $100 million; Fireman's Fund accuses Mexican government of facilitating the purchase of debentures denominated in Mexican pesos and owned by Mexican investors but not facilitating the purchase of debentures denominated in US dollars and owned by Fireman's Fund	Award on jurisdiction filed July 2003; tribunal ruled that it could allow the Fireman's Fund expropriation claim to proceed but that it lacked jurisdiction to examine the investor's claims of violation of Chapter 11's rules on national treatment and minimum standards of treatment, as well as Chapter 14's rules on national treatment
Unknown month 2002/active	International Thunderbird Gaming Corporation, Canada	Mexico	Claim for $100 million for losses associated with the Mexican government's regulation, enforcement, and closure of gaming facilities	Notice of arbitration filed in 2002; consultations ongoing

(table continues next page)

Table 4A.4 Chapter 11 disputes under NAFTA *(continued)*

Initial filing/ termination[a]	Petitioner and nationality	Defendant country	Subject of dispute	Status/outcome
January 2002/active	Calmark Commercial Development Inc., United States	Mexico	Claim for $400,000 for actions taken by Mexico's judiciary that amounted to measures tantamount to expropriation	Notice of intent to submit claim to arbitration filed January 2002; no further action taken
February 2002/active	Robert J. Frank, United States	Mexico	Claim for $1.5 million as compensation for damages caused by Mexican government's expropriation of land occupied and developed by Robert J. Frank	Notice of arbitration filed in August 2002; no further action taken
March 2002/active	James Russell Baird, Canada	United States	Claim for $660 million as compensation for damages caused by US government regulation of methods for disposing nuclear and toxic waste beneath the seabed ("sub-seabed disposal"); Baird alleges that US Congress and Department of Energy retroactively and arbitrarily changed rules that placed a de facto ban on sub-seabed disposal, without submitting notices and publication requirements as necessary under NAFTA Article 718.3[c]	Notice of intent to submit claim to arbitration filed in March 2002; no further action taken

Date filed/status	Claimant	Respondent	Description	Status
April 2002/active	GAMI Investments, Inc., United States	Mexico	Claim for $55 million; GAMI says the Mexican government expropriated sugar mills owned by five subsidiaries of Grupo Azucarero México, S.A. de C.V., a company in which GAMI claims to hold a 14.18 percent ownership interest; GAMI also alleges the Mexican government regulated the sugar industry in a discriminatory and arbitrary manner	Resolved in favor of the Mexican government; no award of costs made
May 2002/active	Doman Industries Ltd., Canada	United States	Claim for $513 million; Doman accuses the US government of preventing it from selling softwood lumber products in the United States	Notice of intent to submit claim to arbitration filed in May 2002; no further action taken
May 2002/active	Tembec Corporation, Canada	United States	Claim for $200 million; Tembec accuses the United States of violating NAFTA Chapter 11 provisions when the USITC imposed antidumping and countervailing duties of 29 percent on Tembec's softwood lumber exports to the United States	Notice of arbitration and statement of claim filed in December 2004; in March 2005, the US government requested the establishment of a consolidation tribunal to address three Chapter 11 cases—Canzor, Terminal Forest Products, and Tembec Corporation
July 2002/active	Canfor Corp., Canada	United States	Claim for $250 million; Canfor alleges losses as a result of US antidumping, countervailing duty determinations on softwood lumber in March 2002	Notice of arbitration filed July 2002; consultations ongoing

(table continues next page)

Table 4A.4 Chapter 11 disputes under NAFTA (continued)

Initial filing/ termination[a]	Petitioner and nationality	Defendant country	Subject of dispute	Status/outcome
August 2002/active	Kenex Ltd., Canada	United States	Claim for $20 million; Kenex claims injuries resulting from the Drug Enforcement Administration's interpretation of the Controlled Substances Act as prohibiting the sale of products that cause THC to enter the human body	Notice of arbitration filed in August 2002; the US Court of Appeals for the Ninth Circuit granted Kenex petition and affirmed enforcement of NAFTA Chapter 11 obligations
January 2002/active	Corn Products International, United States	Mexico	Claim for $250 million; Corn Products International alleges the Mexican government's tax on high fructose corn syrup represented a breach of Mexico's NAFTA obligations	Notice of arbitration filed in October 2003; consultations ongoing
September 2002/active	Crompton Corp., United States	Canada	Claim $100 million for lost profit due to Canadian government's export ban of the pesticide Lindane	Amended notice of arbitration filed in September 2002; no further action taken
July 2003/active	Glamis Gold Ltd., Canada	United States	Claim $50 million for California regulations requiring backfilling and grading for mining operations in the vicinity of Native American sacred sites	Notice of arbitration filed in July 2003; consultations ongoing

September 2003/active	Grand River Enterprises et al., Canada	United States	Claim $340 million for violation of NAFTA Chapter 11 rules concerning national treatment, and expropriation, among others; Grand River alleges the 1998 settlement agreement between various state attorney generals and the major tobacco companies adversely impacted the future of competition and trade in the US cigarette industry	Notice of arbitration filed in March 2004; consultations ongoing
September 2003/active	**Terminal Forest Products Ltd., Canada**	**United States**	**Claim $90 million for alleged injuries resulting from certain US antidumping, countervailing duty, and material injury determinations on softwood lumber**	**Notice of arbitration filed in March 2004; consultations ongoing**
October 2003/active	Archer Daniels Midland Co. and A. E. Staley Manufacturing Co., United States	Mexico	Claim in excess of $100 million. ADM and Staley allege the Mexican government's tax on high-fructose corn syrup has forced it to stop production in Mexico and halt exports to Mexico	Notice of intent to submit claim to arbitration filed in October 2003; consultations ongoing
February 2004/active	Albert J. Connolly, United States	Canada	Claim unknown	Notice of intent to submit claim to arbitration filed in February 2004

(table continues next page)

Table 4A.4 Chapter 11 disputes under NAFTA *(continued)*

Initial filing/ termination[a]	Petitioner and nationality	Defendant country	Subject of dispute	Status/outcome
August 2004/active	Canadian Cattlemen for Fair Trade (CCFT), Canada	United States	Claim for $113 million. CCFT claims the US government's prolonged closing of the US-Canada border violated NAFTA Chapter 11 provisions	Notice of intent filed in August 2004; consultations ongoing
August 2004/active	North Alamo Water Supply Co., United States	Mexico	Claim up to $555 million for missed water payments; North Alamo Water Supply claims the Mexican government diverted water destined for the United States, violating the 1944 bilateral water treaty	Notice of intent filed in August 2004; consultations ongoing

Note: Environment-related cases are in bold.

a. Date of initial notice of intention to arbitrate (whether or not a claim was filed) and date of award or settlement (unless still active).
b. Damages claimed range from $30 million to $500 million depending on the source.
c. Damages claimed range from $660 million each for alleged violations (Articles 1102, 1103, or 1105) to $5.8 billion (Articles 1106 and 1110).

Sources: Mann and von Moltke (1999); Soloway (1999); Canada Department of Foreign Affairs and International Trade, www.dfait-maeci.gc.ca/tna-nac/dispute-e.asp; US Department of State, www.state.gov/s/l/c3433.htm; and Todd Weiler's Web site, www.naftaclaims.com (also known as www.naftalaw.org).

Table 4A.5 Chapter 19 disputes under NAFTA, January 1994 to present

Date of initial filing	Complainant	Respondent	Products subject to administrative determinations	Status/outcome
[CDA-94-1904-01] Unknown month/ terminated 1994	US producers	Canada	Finding of injury on certain fresh whole delicious, red delicious, and golden delicious apples in nonstandard containers for processing	Review terminated by joint consent of participants
[CDA 94-1904-02] January 1994/ settled July 1995	US producers	Canada	Finding of injury on synthetic baler twine with a knot strength of 200 pounds or less	Unanimously affirmed in part and remanded in part the agency's determination
[CDA-94-1904-03] August 1994/settled June 1995	US producers	Canada	Antidumping (AD) determination against certain corrosion-resistant steel sheet products	Unanimously affirmed in part and remanded in part the agency's decision; panel affirmed, with two partial dissenting opinions
[CDA-94-1904-04] September 1994/ settled July 1995	US producers	Canada	Determination to exclude certain corrosion-resistant steel sheet products	Unanimously affirmed the agency's determination
[MEX-94-1904-01] September 1994/ settled April 1998	US producers	Mexico	Final AD duty on flat-coated steel products	Unanimously remanded the determination to the agency twice, in each instance affirming part of the determination
[MEX-94-1904-02] September 1994/ settled October 1995	US producers	Mexico	Final AD and injury determination on cut-to-length steel plate industry	Panel majority, with two dissenting opinions, remanded the final determination to the investigating authority
[MEX-94-1904-03] December 1994/ settled September 1996	US producers	Mexico	Final AD duty determination on crystal and solid polystyrene	Panel majority, with one dissenting opinion and one concurring opinion, affirmed the agency (SECOFI) provided sufficient findings of fact and conclusions of law to support its final determination

(table continues next page)

269

Table 4A.5 Chapter 19 disputes under NAFTA, January 1994 to present *(continued)*

Date of initial filing	Complainant	Respondent	Products subject to administrative determinations	Status/outcome
[USA-94-1904-01] March 1994/settled September 1995	Canadian producers	United States	Countervailing duty (CVD) determination on live swine	Unanimously affirmed in part and remanded in part the agency's determination
[USA-94-1904-02] Unknown month/ settled October 1995	Mexican producers	United States	CVD determination on leather wearing apparel	Unanimously remanded the final determination at the request of Mexico's investigating authority
[CDA-95-1904-01] August 1995/settled November 1995	US producers	Canada	Finding of injury on certain malt beverages	Unanimously affirmed the agency's determination
[CDA-95-1904-02] Unknown month/ terminated 1995	US producers	Canada	Final AD determination on fresh whole delicious, red delicious, and golden delicious apples	Review automatically terminated by complainant
[CDA-95-1904-03] Unknown month/ terminated 1995	US producers	Canada	AD determination on machine tufted carpeting	Review automatically terminated by complainant
[CDA-95-1904-04] December 1995/ settled January 1997	US producers	Canada	Final AD determination on refined sugar	Unanimously affirmed in part and remanded in part the agency's determination
[MEX-95-1904-01] Unknown month/ terminated 1995	US producers	Mexico	AD duty determination on seamless line pipe	Review automatically terminated by the complainant
[USA-95-1904-01] January 1995/ settled July 1996	Mexican producers	United States	AD determination on porcelain-on-steel cookware	Unanimously affirmed in part and remanded in part the agency's determination

Case	Complainant	Country	Determination	Decision
[USA-95-1904-02] May 1995/settled September 1996	Mexican producers	United States	AD determination on gray Portland cement and cement clinker	Unanimously affirmed the US Department of Commerce's final determination
[USA-95-1904-03] June 1995/settled May 1996	Canadian producers	United States	Finding of AD on color picture tubes	Unanimously affirmed, with one concurring opinion, the decision of the US Department of Commerce
[USA-95-1904-04] July 1995/settled December 1996	Mexican producers	United States	Final AD determination on oil country tubular goods	Unanimously affirmed in part and remanded in part the agency's determination
[USA-95-1904-05] November 1995/settled March 1997	Mexican producers	United States	Final AD determination on fresh cut flowers	Unanimously remanded the agency's determination
[CDA-96-1904-01] Unknown month/terminated 1996	US producers	Canada	Final AD determination on bacteriological culture media	Review automatically terminated by complainant
[MEX-96-1904-01] Unknown month/terminated 1996	Canadian producers	Mexico	Final AD determination on cold-rolled steel sheet	Review automatically terminated by complainant
[MEX-96-1904-02] January 1996/settled December 1998	Canadian producers	Mexico	Final AD and countervailing determinations on rolled steel plate	Unanimously affirmed in part and remanded in part the agency's determination twice
[MEX-96-1904-03] February 1996/settled September 1997	Canadian producers	Mexico	Final AD determination on hot-rolled steel sheet	Unanimously affirmed in part and remanded in part
[USA-96-1904-01] Unknown month/terminated 1996	US producers	Mexico	Final AD determination on porcelain-on-steel cooking ware	Review automatically terminated by complainant

(table continues next page)

271

Table 4A.5 Chapter 19 disputes under NAFTA, January 1994 to present *(continued)*

Date of initial filing	Complainant	Respondent	Products subject to administrative determinations	Status/outcome
[CDA-97-1904-01] August 1997/settled August 1998	US producers	Canada	Finding of injury on certain concrete panels, reinforced with fiberglass mesh	Unanimously affirmed the agency's determination
[CDA-97-1904-02] December 1997/ settled December 1999	Mexican producers	Canada	Finding of injury on certain hot-rolled carbon steel plate	Unanimously remanded the agency's determination on standard of review; panel majority, with two dissenting opinions, affirmed the agency's determination on remand
[MEX-97-1904-01] Unknown month/ terminated 1997	Mexican producers	United States	Final countervailing determination on hydrogen peroxide	Review automatically terminated by joint consent of participants
[USA-97-1904-01] May 1997/settled February 2000	Mexican producers	United States	AD determination on gray Portland cement and clinker	Panel unanimously affirmed the agency's determination on remand; Extraordinary Challenge Committee (ECC) filed by the US government in March 2000
[USA-97-1904-02] May 1997/settled December 1998	Mexican producers	United States	AD determination on gray Portland cement and clinker	Panel affirmed, with one partial dissent, the agency's determination
[USA-97-1904-03] May 1997/settled September 1999	Canadian producers	United States	Final AD determination on corrosion-resistant carbon steel flat products	Panel unanimously remanded the determination to the agency twice
[USA-97-1904-04] Unknown month/	Canadian producers	United States	Final countervailing determination on pure and alloy magnesium	Panel review terminated by the requestors

Case	Requestor	Country	Determination	Outcome
[USA-97-1904-05] Unknown month/ terminated 1997	Mexican producers	United States	Final AD determination	Panel review terminated by the requestors
[USA-97-1904-06] Unknown month/ terminated 1997	Mexican producers	United States	Final AD determination on circular welded nonalloy steel pipe and tube	Panel review terminated by joint consent of participants
[USA-97-1904-07] August 1997/settled July 1999	Mexican producers	United States	Final AD determination on porcelain-on-steel cookware	Panel unanimously affirmed in part and remanded in part the agency's determination
[USA-97-1904-08] Unknown month/ terminated 1997	Canadian producers	United States	Final countervailing determination on steel wire rod	Panel review terminated by joint consent of participants
[CDA-USA-98-1904-01] June 1998/settled November 1999	Canadian producers	United States	Finding of injury on certain prepared baby food products	Panel unanimously affirmed the agency's determination
[CDA-USA-98-1904-02] September 1998/settled July 2000	US producers	Canada	Finding of injury on certain cold-reduced flat-rolled sheet products of carbon steel (including high-strength low-alloy steel)	Panel unanimously affirmed the agency's determination
[CDA-USA-98-1904-03] December 1998/settled April 2000	Canadian producers	United States	Finding of injury on certain solder joint pressure pipe fittings and solder joint drainage, waste and vent pipe fittings, made of cast copper alloy, wrought copper alloy or wrought copper	Panel unanimously affirmed the agency's determination
[USA-CDA-98-1904-01] April 1998/settled August 2001	Canadian producers	United States	Final AD determination on certain corrosion-resistant carbon steel flat products	Majority panel, with one partial dissenting opinion, remanded the agency's determination

(table continues next page)

Table 4A.5 Chapter 19 disputes under NAFTA, January 1994 to present *(continued)*

Date of initial filing	Complainant	Respondent	Products subject to administrative determinations	Status/outcome
[USA-MEX-98-1904-02] Unknown month 1998/active	Mexican producers	United States	Final AD determination on gray Portland cement and cement clinker	Panel unanimously affirmed in part the agency's determination; determination on remand due to be determined
[USA-CDA-98-1904-03] August 1998/settled November 1999	Canadian producers	United States	Final AD determination on brass sheet and strip	Panel unanimously affirmed in part and remanded in part the agency's determination
[USA-MEX-98-1904-04] Unknown month/ terminated 1999	Mexican producers	United States	Final AD determination on porcelain-on-steel cookware	Panel review terminated by joint consent of participants
[USA-MEX-98-1904-05] Unknown month 1998/settled June 2004	US producers	Mexico	Final AD determination on circular welded non-alloy steel pipe	Panel unanimously affirmed the third determination of remand to the agency
[MEX-USA-98-1904-01] February 1998/ settled June 2002	US producers	Mexico	Final AD determination on high-fructose corn syrup	Panel unanimously remanded the determination to the agency twice
[CDA-MEX-99-1904-01] Unknown month 1999/terminated 1999	Mexican producers	Canada	Finding of injury on certain hot-rolled carbon steel plate	Panel review terminated by joint consent of participants

[USA-CDA-99-1904-01] Unknown month/ terminated 1999	Canadian producers	United States	Final AD determination on certain corrosion-resistant carbon steel flat products	Panel review terminated by joint consent of participants
[USA-CDA-99-1904-02] Unknown month/ terminated 1999	Canadian producers	United States	AD determination on certain cut-to-length carbon steel plate	Panel review terminated by joint consent of participants
[USA-MEX-99-1904-03] April 1999/settled January 2004	Mexican producers	United States	Final AD determination on gray Portland cement and cement clinker	Panel affirmed, with two partial dissents, determination on remand
[USA-CDA-99-1904-04] Unknown month/ terminated 1999	Canadian producers	United States	Final AD determination on stainless steel round wire	Panel review terminated by joint consent of participants
[USA-MEX-99-1904-05] Unknown month/ terminated 1999	Mexican producers	United States	Final AD determination on porcelain-on-steel cookware	Panel review terminated by joint consent of participants
[USA-CDA-99-1904-06] Unknown month/ terminated 1999	Canadian producers	United States	Final CVD determination on live cattle	Panel review terminated by joint consent of participants
[USA-CDA-99-1904-07] Unknown month/ terminated 1999	Canadian producers	United States	Finding of injury on live cattle	Panel review terminated by joint consent of participants

(table continues next page)

Table 4A.5 Chapter 19 disputes under NAFTA, January 1994 to present *(continued)*

Date of initial filing	Complainant	Respondent	Products subject to administrative determinations	Status/outcome
[CDA-USA-2000-1904-01] Unknown month/ terminated 2000	US producers	Canada	Final AD determination on certain iodinated contrast media used for radiographic imaging	Panel review terminated by joint consent of participants
[CDA-USA-2000-1904-02] Unknown month 2000/settled January 2003	US producers	Canada	Finding of injury on certain iodinated contrast media used for radiographic imaging	Panel unanimously affirmed agency's determination
[CDA-USA-2000-1904-03] August 2000/settled April 2002	US producers	Canada	Final AD determination on certain top-mount electric refrigerators, electric household dishwashers, and gas or electric laundry dryers	Panel unanimously affirmed the agency's determination
[CDA-USA-2000-1904-04] August 2000/settled January 2002	US producers	Canada	Finding of injury on certain refrigerators, dishwashers, and dryers	Panel unanimously affirmed, with one concurring opinion, the agency's determination
[MEX-USA-2000-1904-01] May 2000/settled January 2004	US producers	Mexico	AD determination on imports of urea	Panel unanimously remanded agency's determination
[MEX-USA-2000-1904-02] Unknown month 2000/action	US producers	Mexico	Final AD determination on bovine carcasses and half carcasses, fresh or chilled	Panel unanimously affirmed in part and remanded in part the agency's determination; decision on remand due to be determined

Case number / dates	Party	Country	Determination	Status
[USA-CDA-2000-1904-01] Unknown month/ terminated 2000	Canadian producers	United States	Final AD determination on certain cut-to-length carbon steel plate	Panel review terminated by joint consent of participants
[USA-CDA-2000-1904-02] Unknown month/ terminated 2000	Canadian producers	United States	Final AC determination on certain corrosion-resistant carbon steel flat products	Panel review terminated by joint consent of participants
[USA-MEX-2000-1904-03] Unknown month 2000/active	Mexican producers	United States	Final AD determination on gray Portland cement and cement clinker	Decision to be determined
[USA-MEX-2000-1904-04] Unknown month/ terminated 2000	Mexican producers	United States	Final AD determination on porcelain-on-steel cookware	Panel review terminated by joint consent of participants
[USA-MEX-2000-1904-05] Unknown month 2000/active	Mexican producers	United States	Final AD determination on gray Portland cement and cement clinker	Decision to be determined
[USA-CDA-2000-1904-06] September 2000/ settled in August 2003	Canadian producers	United States	AD determination on pure magnesium	Panel unanimously affirmed the third determination on remand; Extraordinary Challenge Committee (ECC) filed by the US government in September 2003
[USA-CDA-2000-1904-07] August 2000/settled October 2002	Canadian producers	United States	Final CVD determination on pure magnesium and alloy magnesium	Panel unanimously remanded the determination to the agency twice

(table continues next page)

Table 4A.5 Chapter 19 disputes under NAFTA, January 1994 to present *(continued)*

Date of initial filing	Complainant	Respondent	Products subject to administrative determinations	Status/outcome
[USA-CDA-2000-1904-08] Unknown month/ terminated 2000	Canadian producers	United States	Final AD determination on certain corrosion-resistant carbon steel flat products	Panel review terminated by joint consent of participants
[USA-CDA-2000-1904-09] August 2000/active	Canadian producers	United States	Final AD and CVD determinations on magnesium	Majority panel, with one dissenting opinion, remanded the agency's determination; decision on remand to be determined
[USA-MEX-2000-1904-10] Unknown month 2000/active	Mexican producers	United States	Final AD determination on gray Portland cement and cement clinker	Decision due on September 22, 2005
[USA-CDA-2000-1904-11] Unknown month 2000/settled in April 2005	Canadian producers	United States	Final countervailing and AD determinations on carbon steel products	Majority panel, with one dissenting opinion, affirmed determination on remand
[ECC-2000-1904-01USA] April 2000/ settled in October 2003	United States	Mexico	AD determination on gray Portland cement and clinker	ECC panel rejected US arguments and affirmed the panel's decision to remand the agency's determination
[USA-CDA-2001-1904-01] Unknown month/ terminated 2001	Canadian producers	United States	Final AD determination on certain cut-to-length carbon steel plate	Panel review terminated by joint consent of participants
[USA-MEX-2001-1904-02] Unknown month/ terminated 2001	Mexican producers	United States	Final AD determination on porcelain-on-steel cookware	Panel review terminated by joint consent of participants

[USA-MEX-2001-1904-03] Unknown month 2001/active	Mexican producers	United States	Final AD determination on oil country tubular goods	Panel unanimously remanded the determination to the agency
[USA-MEX-2001-1904-04] Unknown month/active	Mexican producers	United States	Final AD determination on gray Portland cement and cement clinker	Decision to be determined
[USA-MEX-2001-1904-05] Unknown month 2001/active	Mexican producers	United States	Final AD determination on oil country tubular goods	Decision due on October 18, 2005
[USA-MEX-2001-1904-06] Unknown month 2001/active	Mexican producers	United States	Final AD determination on oil country tubular goods	Decision to be determined
[MEX-USA-2002-1904-01] Unknown month/terminated 2002	US producers	Mexico	Final countervailing determination on bovine carcasses and half carcasses, fresh or chilled	Panel review terminated by joint consent of participants
[USA-MEX-2002-1904-01] Unknown month 2002/active	Mexican producers	United States	Initiating investigation on Section 751(b) on gray Portland cement and cement clinker	Decision to be determined
[USA-CDA-2002-1904-02] Unknown month 2002/active	Canadian producers	United States	AD determination on certain softwood lumber products	Panel unanimously affirmed in part the agency's determination on remand; determination on third remand to be determined
[USA-CDA-2002-1904-03] Unknown month 2002/active	Canadian producers	United States	Final CVD determination on certain softwood lumber products	Panel unanimously affirmed in part and remanded in part the agency's third determination on remand

(table continues next page)

279

Table 4A.5 Chapter 19 disputes under NAFTA, January 1994 to present *(continued)*

Date of initial filing	Complainant	Respondent	Products subject to administrative determinations	Status/outcome
[USA-CDA-2002-1904-04] Unknown month/terminated 2002	Canadian producers	United States	Final AD determination on green-house tomatoes	Panel review automatically terminated by sole requestor
[USA-MEX-2002-1904-05] Unknown month 2002/active	Mexican producers	United States	Final AD determination on gray Port-land cement and cement clinker	Decision to be determined
[USA-CDA-2002-1904-06] Unknown month/terminated 2002	Canadian producers	United States	Final AD determination on green-house tomatoes	Panel review automatically terminated by sole requestor
[USA-CDA-2002-1904-07] Unknown month 2002/active	Canadian producers	United States	Finding of injury on certain softwood lumber products	Panel unanimously affirmed the third determination on remard; ECC filed by the US government in November 2004
[USA-CDA-2002-1904-08] September 2002/terminated 2003	Canadian producers	United States	Final CVD determination on carbon and certain alloy steel wire rod	Panel review terminated by joint consent of participants
[USA-CDA-2002-1904-09] Unknown month 2002/settled April 2005	Canadian producers	United States	Final AD determination on carbon and certain alloy steel wire rod	Panel unanimously affirmed the agency's determination
[MEX-USA-2003-1904-01] Unknown month 2003/active	Mexican producers	United States	Final CVD determination on sodium hydroxide (caustic soda)	Decision to be determined
[MEX-USA-2003-1904-02] Unknown	Mexican producers	United States	Final CVD determination on fresh red delicious and golden delicious	Decision to be determined

Case	Complainant	Country	Subject	Status
[USA-MEX-2003-1904-01] Unknown month 2003/active	Mexican producers	United States	AD determination on gray Portland cement and cement clinker	Decision to be determined
[USA-CDA-2003-1904-02] Unknown month 2003/active	Canadian producers	United States	Final CVD determination on alloy magnesium	Decision due on September 9, 2005
[USA-MEX-2003-1904-03] Unknown month 2003/active	Mexican producers	United States	AD determination on gray Portland cement and cement clinker	Decision to be determined
[USA-CDA-2003-1904-04] Unknown month 2003/terminated 2003	Canadian producers	United States	Final AD determination on certain durum wheat and hard red spring wheat	Panel review automatically terminated by sole requestor
[USA-CDA-2003-1904-05] Unknown month 2003/active	Canadian producers	United States	Final CVD determination on certain durum wheat and hard red spring wheat	Panel unanimously affirmed in part and remanded in part the agency's determination on remand; determination on another remand due August 8, 2005
[USA-CDA-2003-1904-06] Unknown month 2003/active	Canadian producers	United States	Finding of injury on certain durum wheat and hard red spring wheat	Majority panel, with one partial dissent, remanded the agency's determination; determination on remand due on October 5, 2005
[ECC-2003-1904-01USA] September 2003/active	United States	Canada	AD determination on pure magnesium	ECC panel unanimously affirmed the panel's decision to remand the agency's determination.
[ECC-2004-1904-01USA] November 2004/active	United States	Canada	Finding of injury on certain softwood lumber products	Decision to be determined

(table continues next page)

Table 4A.5   Chapter 19 disputes under NAFTA, January 1994 to present   *(continued)*

Date of initial filing	Complainant	Respondent	Products subject to administrative determinations	Status/outcome
[USA-CDA-2004-1904-01] Unknown month 2004/active	Canadian producers	United States	Final CVD determination on alloy magnesium	Decision to be determined
[USA-CDA-2004-1904-02] Unknown month 2004/terminated	Canadian producers	United States	Final AD determination on carbon and certain alloy steel wire rod	Panel review terminated by joint consent of participants
[USA-MEX-2004-1904-03] Unknown month 2004/active	Mexican producers	United States	AD determination on gray Portland cement and cement clinker	Decision to be determined
[USA-CDA-2005-1904-01] Unknown month 2005/active	Canadian producers	United States	Final CVD determination on certain softwood lumber products	Decision to be determined
[USA-CDA-2005-1904-03] Unknown month 2005/active	Canadian producers	United States	USITC implementation of the new determination under Section 129(a)(4) of the Uruguay Round agreement	Decision to be determined
[MEX-USA-2005-1904-01] Unknown month 2005/active	US producers	Mexico	AD determination on certain steel tubing	Decision due on May 8, 2006
[USA-CDA-2005-1904-04] Unknown month 2005/active	Canadian producers	United States	US Department of Commerce AD determination under Section 129 of the Uruguay Round of Agreements Act	Decision due on April 11, 2006

Note: CDA stands for panels reviewing Canadian International Trade Tribunal determinations; MEX for panels reviewing Mexican Ministry of Trade and Industrial Development (SECOFI) determinations; and USA for panels reviewing US Department of Commerce determinations.

Sources: NAFTA Secretariat, Decisions and Reports 2002, www.nafta-sec-alena.org/english/index.htm; OAS Foreign Trade Information System, SICE Dispute Settlement Binational Panel Decisions and Arbitral Panel Reports 2002, www.sice.oas.org/dispute/nafdispeasp.

5

Agriculture

The NAFTA agreement on agricultural trade consists of three bilateral agreements—between the United States and Mexico, the United States and Canada, and Canada and Mexico. The US-Canada agreement largely carried into NAFTA the tariff and nontariff barrier rules that had been adopted in the Canada-US Free Trade Agreement (CUSFTA). Under the CUSFTA, most agricultural tariffs between the United States and Canada were to be phased out by January 1998, and NAFTA adopted this schedule. However, Canada was allowed to maintain permanent tariff rate quotas (TRQs) on imports of dairy products, poultry, and eggs from the United States,[1] and the United States was allowed to maintain TRQs on imports of sugar, dairy products, and peanuts from Canada (appendix table 5A.1).[2] Although a tariff snapback provision remains in effect until 2008, Canada has rarely used

---

1. Under NAFTA, the overquota tariffs for products subject to a TRQ regime are the lower of either the existing tariff rate when NAFTA took effect or the current most-favored nation (MFN) rate. In-quota imports are charged the more favorable NAFTA tariff. Under NAFTA's TRQ arrangement, the members must gradually expand each quota while gradually eliminating the associated overquota tariff during the transition period. See USDA (2002a).

2. The TRQ system does not cover agricultural products subject to special safeguards (Article 703). Special safeguards apply only to Canada-Mexico and US-Mexico trade but not to Canada-US trade. When a special safeguard is applied, tariffs on goods listed in Annex 703.3 may be raised to higher levels if imports reach the quota levels specified in the tariff schedules. A NAFTA country, however, cannot simultaneously apply a safeguard against a good listed in Article 703 and invoke Chapter 8 emergency action on that good. Mexico, for example, uses special safeguards on imports of live swine, pork, potato products, fresh apples, and coffee extract. The United States applies special safeguards on selected horticultural crops. Sensitive agricultural commodities subject to Canadian special safeguards include fresh cut flowers, tomatoes, onions, cucumbers, broccoli, cauliflower, and frozen strawberries. See USDA (2002a).

it. Virtually the same restrictions limited agricultural trade between Mexico and Canada. As might be expected, some agricultural trade associations favored NAFTA while others opposed it. Box 5.1 summarizes the lineup of important trade associations.

In contrast to the US-Canada agreement, Mexico and the United States took far-reaching steps toward complete liberalization of agricultural trade. The ultimate goal of their bilateral agreement was to eliminate all import quotas and tariffs—with no exceptions. Liberalization was not, however, implemented on a rapid schedule, and the phaseout terms for sensitive products were often backloaded. Mexican tariffs on corn and dry beans were subject to a 15-year phaseout period, and the United States insisted on similar transition periods for tariffs on winter vegetables, orange juice, peanuts, and sugar (USDA 2002a). Appendix table 5A.1 gives duty rates on US-Mexico agricultural trade as of 2003, and box 5.2 summarizes the phaseout arrangements. Given these restraints, in 2000, just nine commodities—some of them minor agricultural products—represented 55 percent of the value of US-Mexico agricultural trade: beer,[3] coffee, tomatoes, cattle, peppers, cucumbers, grapes, cauliflower, and broccoli.

Mexican agriculture is passing through a familiar phase in the history of industrialization. As countries become richer, agriculture inevitably plays a smaller role in the economy and employs a smaller share of the

---

3. Beer, of course, represents a highly processed agricultural product, and the issues surrounding trade in beer (and other alcoholic beverages) are very different from those surrounding primary agricultural products. Since alcoholic beverage trade now faces few barriers in North America, beer issues are not discussed in this chapter.

Box 5.2 Timeline of NAFTA tariff phaseouts

January 1994	Elimination of Mexican tariffs on US sorghum, certain citrus fruit, fresh strawberries, and seasonal tariffs on oranges
	Elimination of US tariffs on Mexican corn, sorghum, barley, soymeal, apples, pears, peaches, fresh strawberries, beef, pork, and poultry, and of seasonal tariffs on oranges
January 1998	Elimination of leftover CUSFTA tariffs
	Completion of US-Mexico four-year transition period
	Elimination of Mexican tariffs on US pears, plums, and apricots
	Elimination of US tariffs on Mexican nondurum wheat, soy oil, and cotton, and of seasonal tariffs on oranges
January 2002	Elimination of Canadian agricultural tariffs on Mexican fish, meat, sugar, flour, dairy, and beer[1]
January 2003	Completion of US-Mexico nine-year transition period
	Elimination of Mexican tariffs on US wheat, barley, rice, dairy, soybean meal and soy oil, poultry, peaches, apples, frozen strawberries, hogs, pork, cotton, and tobacco, and of seasonal tariffs on oranges
	Elimination of US tariffs on Mexican durum wheat, rice, limes, winter vegetables, dairy products, and frozen strawberries
October 2007	Elimination of US-Mexico sugar tariffs
January 2008	Completion of US-Mexico 14-year transition period
	Elimination of US tariffs on Mexican frozen concentrated orange juice, winter vegetables, and peanuts
	Elimination of Mexican tariffs on corn and dry beans

1. Specifically refers to the following agricultural commodities by 2-digit Harmonized Tariff Schedule (HTS) code: fish and crustaceans (HTS 3); edible preparations of meat, fish, crustaceans, molluscs, or other aquatic invertebrates (HTS 16); sugars and sugar confectionery (HTS 17); and preparations of cereals, flour, starch or milk, and bakers' wares (HTS 19).

Note: Under NAFTA, traditional Mexican licensing requirements were converted to tariffs or tariff rate quotas (TRQs). As an example, in January 2003, Mexican quotas that were converted to tariffs covered wheat, tobacco, cheese, milk, and grapes (seasonal basis).

Source: US Department of Agriculture, Economic Research Service.

workforce. In figure 5.1, a cross-country regression covering about 76 countries illustrates how a 1 percent increase in income per capita is associated with a reduction in agriculture value added as a share of GDP by about 0.6 percentage points. Time-series analysis tells the same story. Just as the agricultural sector in advanced economies accounted for a declining share of GDP in the first half of the 20th century as income per capita increased, the agricultural share of GDP in South Korea declined from

Figure 5.1 Agriculture and income in selected countries, 2000

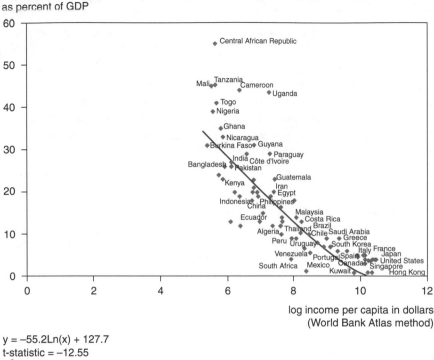

value added agriculture
as percent of GDP

log income per capita in dollars
(World Bank Atlas method)

$y = -55.2\ln(x) + 127.7$
t-statistic = -12.55
$R^2 = 0.71$

Note: The sample consists of 76 countries, both early and late growers.

Source: World Bank, *World Development Indicators* (2003).

about 25 percent in 1970 to 5 percent in 2000. Mexico will be following the same path for at least the next two decades. Agricultural production has been increasingly centered on large-scale farms, factory-type livestock lots, and capital-intensive food processing, putting pressure on small-scale farms, particularly on subsistence household farmers in Mexico.

Overview of Agricultural Trade in NAFTA

Trade and Agriculture

Media reports on NAFTA and agriculture tend to highlight the negative:[4] small farmers driven from the land, huge income disparities within the

---

4. See, for example, "Controversial Study Says NAFTA Has Little Direct Impact on Problems of Mexican Agriculture Sector," *SourceMex Economic News*, April 14, 2004; "US Consumer Group Report: NAFTA Has Hurt Farm Sector," *Reuters*, June 26, 2001; and "Agriculture Can Take No More: Demands Reconsideration of NAFTA," *Corporate Mexico*, March 3, 2003.

agricultural sector, trade barriers not reduced on schedule, and sanitary and phytosanitary (SPS) disputes. In response, much of this chapter dwells on agricultural problems rather than achievements. Stepping back from the litany of real and imagined agricultural woes, however, it is important to emphasize that agricultural trade has clearly prospered in the NAFTA era.

US agricultural exports to NAFTA partners increased by 93 percent during 1993–2003, while total US exports to the world expanded by only 39 percent (appendix table 5A.2). In 1993, the share of US agricultural exports to Canada and Mexico represented only 12 and 8 percent, respectively, of US agricultural exports to world markets. By 2003, US agricultural exports to Canada and Mexico increased to 16 and 13 percent, respectively, of US agricultural exports to the world (table 5A.2).

Between 1993 and 2003, US agricultural exports to NAFTA partners increased by very large percentages in key agricultural products: oilseeds (130 percent), grains and feeds (128 percent), vegetables and preparations (90 percent), and animals and animal products (69 percent). North America has become an increasingly important market for US agricultural exporters. Canada is now the largest importer of US agricultural goods, displacing Japan in 2002. Mexico surpassed the European Union as an export market for US agriculture in 2000 (Vollrath 2004). Similarly, between 1993 and 2003, Canadian and Mexican agricultural exports to the United States also increased significantly: beverages excluding fruit juices (319 percent), sugar and related products (244 percent), vegetables and preparations (197 percent), fruit and preparations (196 percent), fresh cut flowers (1,885 percent), and grains and feeds (131 percent) (table 5A.2).

Canadian and Mexican agricultural trade with the rest of the world expanded less rapidly than that with the United States (table 5A.2). For example, the average annual growth rate of US agricultural exports to Canada under NAFTA is 5.1 percent, while that for the rest of the world is only 1 percent (Myles and Cahoon 2004). During 1993–2003, Canadian and Mexican agricultural exports to world markets (excluding the United States) increased 52 percent compared with agricultural exports to the United States, which increased by 125 percent.[5] The United States thus remains a key market for Canadian and Mexican agricultural goods.[6] US agricultural imports from Canada and Mexico increased from $7.4 billion

---

5. Canadian and Mexican agricultural exports to the world (excluding the United States) are calculated based on total Canadian and Mexican agricultural world exports minus their exports to the United States. See UNCTAD's statistical database, 2003; and USDA Foreign Agricultural Service (FATUS) database, 2003.

6. Canadian agrifood exports to the United States increased from $6.8 billion in 1993 to $13.3 billion in 2003; total Canadian agrifood exports to the world increased from $12.2 billion to $20.5 billion in the same period. Similarly, Mexican agrifood exports to the United States increased from $2.4 billion in 1993 to $7.9 billion in 2003 while total agrifood exports to the world increased from $3.6 billion in 1993 to $9.3 billion in 2003. See Statistics Canada, Canada Trade Online, 2004; UN Food and Agriculture Organization FAOSTAT database, 2004; and USDA (2004c).

in 1993 to \$16.6 billion in 2003; Canadian and Mexican agricultural imports from the United States increased from about \$9 billion in 1993 to \$17.2 billion in 2003.[7]

US agricultural exports to Mexico increased from \$3.6 billion in 1993 to \$7.9 billion in 2003. US agricultural imports from Mexico likewise increased from \$2.7 billion in 1993 to \$6.3 billion in 2003. US agricultural trade with Mexico thus doubled between 1993 and 2003 (table 5A.2). US agricultural exports to Mexico sharply increased during 1993–2003 in fruit juices (175 percent), vegetables and preparations (267 percent), and grains and feeds (149 percent). Meanwhile, Mexican exports sharply expanded in sugar and related products (595 percent), beverages excluding fruit juices (584 percent), and grains and feeds (328 percent). Mexican horticultural exports to the United States, a large-volume category, increased by nearly 100 percent from \$1.8 billion in 1993 to \$3.5 billion in 2003.[8]

The expansion of US-Mexico agricultural trade in basic products accompanied the growth of foreign direct investment (FDI) in high-value processed foods. US FDI stock in the Mexican food processing industry more than doubled from \$2.3 billion in 1993 to \$5.7 billion in 2000. US FDI is concentrated in high-value products such as pasta, confectionery, and canned and frozen meats.

Canada's agricultural exports to Mexico represented only a small share of Canada's total food and agrifood product exports. Nonetheless, since 1993, Canadian agricultural exports to Mexico have increased by 149 percent, from \$300 million in 1993 to \$746 million in 2003 (table 5.1).[9] Six key agricultural products represent 88 percent of total Canadian agrifood exports to Mexico: meat, dairy, lentils, canary and canola seeds, wheat, and beer.

Sharp trade and investment gains in the NAFTA era do not mean that the agricultural sector, particularly in Mexico, has not had adjustment problems. In the aggregate, however, static and dynamic gains from expanded trade under NAFTA auspices probably exceed the adjustment costs within Mexico by a factor of five or higher. Estimates for the United States indicate that GDP gains from globalization amount to about 10 percent of GDP and exceed adjustment costs by a ratio of 20 to one (Bradford, Grieco, and Hufbauer 2005). William Cline (2004) concludes that an increase in the ratio of merchandise trade to GDP by 10 percentage points ultimately raises the GDP of a representative developing country by about

---

7. See USDA Foreign Agricultural Service (FATUS) database, 2003; and Canada House of Commons (2002).

8. As NAFTA has eliminated tariffs, SPS restrictions have become the trade barrier of choice in the horticultural sector. NAFTA avoided harmonizing SPS standards. Instead, each NAFTA country reserves the right to determine its own standards necessary to protect consumers from unsafe products or to protect domestic livestock and crops from invasive pests and diseases.

9. Canada's agrifood product imports from Mexico increased by 60 percent, from \$255 million in 1999 to \$409 million in 2003 (AAFC 2002b).

Table 5.1   Canadian agricultural trade with Mexico, 1993–2003 (millions of US dollars)

Year	Canadian exports to Mexico	Canadian imports from Mexico	Canadian trade balance
1993	300.0	136.0	164.0
1994	386.6	160.0	226.6
1995	316.9	197.2	119.7
1996	432.3	230.5	201.8
1997	396.3	255.2	141.1
1998	543.2	266.6	276.6
1999	534.3	254.2	280.1
2000	664.0	268.3	395.7
2001	785.8	282.4	503.4
2002	702.8	301.6	401.2
2003	745.8	409.0	336.8

Sources: SECOFI, Mexico's Ministry of Economy, 2003–04, Sistema de Información Empresarial Mexicano, www.secofi-siem.gob.mx/portalsiem (accessed in June 2003); Statistics Canada, Agriculture Economics Statistics, 2004; and Canadian Embassy in Mexico City.

5 percentage points. During the post-NAFTA era, Mexico's trade ratio has increased about 18 percentage points (IMF *International Financial Statistics Yearbook 2004*), indicating potential GDP gains of about 9 percentage points. Since agriculture contributed only 4 percent of Mexican GDP in 2003 (World Bank *World Development Report 2005*), it seems fairly certain that national gains to Mexico from trade liberalization will ultimately swamp income losses in the agricultural sector.

Nevertheless, the adjustment costs are both real and painful, particularly to affected farms and communities. At market prices, value added by Mexican agriculture dropped from around $32 billion in 1993 to around $25 billion in 2003 (World Bank's *World Development Report 1995* and *2005*). Over the same period, the number of Mexicans employed in rural agriculture declined from 8.1 million to 6.8 million.[10]

---

10. As an illustration of the adjustment burden, Mexican hog farms have attracted considerable notice. See, for example, Ginger Thompson, "NAFTA to Open Floodgates, Engulfing Rural Mexico," *New York Times*, December 19, 2002. According to an advocacy calculation by the Mexico Hog Farmers Association, a third of the 18,000 swine producers in Mexico will be forced out of business by the elimination of tariffs in January 2003. While no estimates have been published since the tariffs were removed, US pork and live swine exports to Mexico have soared. In response, Mexico has applied antidumping (AD) duties on US live swine exports and initiated AD investigations into US exports of various ham and pork products. See Anne Fitzgerald, "Mexico Goes Whole Hog for US Pork," *The Des Moines Register,* September 19, 2004; and "Mexico Lifts Duties on Live Swine, Keeps AD Investigation on US Pork," *Inside US Trade*, May 23, 2003.

Domestic Agricultural Policies

United States

In 1996, the United States enacted the landmark Federal Agriculture Improvement and Reform Act, also known as the Freedom to Farm Act. The Act attempted to gradually eliminate many traditional agricultural subsidies and decouple support payments from farm prices. Direct income payments were supposed to be phased out over seven years (1996–2002), and price supports and supply management programs were to be gradually eliminated.[11] The schedule for reduced income payments and price supports was based on optimistic predictions of future prices and expanded world markets. Not only were the price and market assumptions underlying the projections of the Freedom to Farm Act too rosy but also successive droughts and floods prompted Congress to pass a series of supplemental relief bills in the late 1990s that sharply increased US farm subsidies. Recent studies estimate that the Freedom to Farm Act programs and supplemental relief cost US consumers and taxpayers at least $19 billion annually in the late 1990s (Gardner 2000).

After several years of "emergency aid," the United States returned to a more permanent version of its erstwhile subsidy system. In May 2002, Congress enacted the Farm Security and Rural Investment Act (Farm Act of 2002), which will govern federal farm programs through 2007. The Farm Act provides income support for wheat, feed grains, upland cotton, rice, and oilseeds through three programs: direct payments, countercyclical payments, and marketing loans (table 5.2).[12] The US government also supports domestic producers through generous "loan" rates at which stocks can be forfeited to the Commodity Credit Corporation.[13] While

---

11. Under the Freedom to Farm Act, income support was given to eligible producers of wheat, feed grains, upland cotton, and rice during 1996–2002. The Act eliminated the Acreage Reduction Program, gradually reduced dairy price supports, and modified US peanut and sugar programs. However, the proposed Freedom to Farm Act budget, starting at $6 billion per year and then supposedly declining, frequently was supplemented due to falling agricultural commodity prices and aid after natural disasters. See Burfisher, Robinson, and Thierfelder (1998); and presentation by Dale Hathaway at the North American Committee Conference on Agriculture, Washington, March 21, 2003.

12. The 2002 Farm Act capped individual farmer subsidies at $360,000, but this limit is widely abused as farmers create legal entities with interests in the same land, each entitled to a payment. See "Harvesting Poverty: Welfare Reform for Farmers," *New York Times*, November 10, 2003.

13. The Commodity Credit Corporation is a government-owned institution, established to promote US agriculture. See David Orden's testimony before the US Committee on Agriculture, Nutrition, and Forestry, "Is It Time for Domestic Sugar Policy Reform?," July 26, 2000. See also LMC International (2003).

Table 5.2   Direct US and Canadian agricultural government payments, 2003 (millions of dollars)

Program	Preliminary forecast
United States	
Total direct payments[a]	17,380
Marketing loan gains[b]	712
Production flexibility contracts[c]	−300
Direct payments	7,702
Countercyclical payments	1,895
Loan deficiency payments	615
Compensation payment to peanut quota holders	250
National dairy market loss payments	900
Conservation[d]	2,286
Emergency assistance[e]	3,300
Miscellaneous[f]	20
Total	34,760
Canada	
Gross Revenue Insurance Plan	n.a.
Net Income Stabilization Account	518
Income disaster assistance	315
Western Grain Stabilization	n.a.
Provincial stabilization	510
Tripartite payments	n.a.
Crop insurance	1,222
Dairy subsidy	n.a.
Other	843
Total rebates reducing expenses	70
Total	3,477

n.a. = not available

a. This category includes only those funds paid directly to farmers within the calendar year.
b. In publications before May 2001, marketing loan gains were included in cash receipts rather than in government payments.
c. The enactment of the Farm Act 2002 terminated the authority for production flexibility payments.
d. This category includes all conservation programs. In publications before July 2003, this category included only payments to the Conservation Reserve Program, Agricultural Conservation Program, Emergency Conservation Program, and Great Plains Program.
e. This category includes all programs providing disaster and emergency assistance payments to growers. In publications before July 2003, this category included only emergency assistance payments attributed to supplemental legislation.
f. Miscellaneous programs and provisions vary from year to year. In publications before July 2003, this category included some program payments that are now considered either as conservation or ad hoc and emergency.

Sources: USDA (2004a); Statistics Canada, Agriculture Economics Statistics, 2004.

recent studies conclude that the 2002 Farm Act will have only a small incremental impact on world prices beyond the effects of the 1996 Freedom to Farm Act, high US wheat and corn subsidies draw considerable ire from NAFTA and other US trading partners.[14]

Under the 2002 Farm Act, the United States continued its export subsidies through the Export Enhancement Program (EEP). Until June 1995, 80 percent of EEP aid was allocated to wheat products. Between 1995 and 2002, the United States gradually phased out the EEP, replacing it with various export subsidy programs that helped US wheat producers stay competitive in third-country markets.[15] US dairy producers benefited from export subsidies under the Dairy Export Incentive Program, though the payments were only a modest $32 million in fiscal 2003.[16] Besides EEP and the dairy program, the United States operates huge "food aid" programs. In particular, the GSM-102 program provides $4.6 billion to support agricultural exports (including wheat) to third-country markets. The GSM-102 program is part of the Export Credit Guarantee Program (GSM-102 and GSM-103) that promotes wheat and other agricultural exports. The annual budget for this program totaled $5.7 billion in 2002.[17] Some portion of these funds confers benefits akin to export subsidies and will likely be phased out under the terms of a prospective World Trade Organization (WTO) accord on agriculture under negotiation in the Doha Round.

As a concession to its trading partners in the course of Uruguay Round negotiations, the United States withdrew its Section 22 waiver, which was adopted in 1955 and which allowed the United States to impose quotas

---

14. Studies estimate the 2002 Farm Act will have relatively small output effects, causing world prices to decline between 1.5 and 6 percent depending on the commodity. See Hathaway (2003). In particular, the extension of US export subsidies and country-of-origin label requirements were unpopular in Mexico and Canada, respectively. See Anson et al. (2003).

15. The US government maintains official allocations for wheat and grains under EEP but has not disbursed any of those funds since 1995. Currently, EEP funds only a few agricultural commodities: frozen poultry, table eggs, and vegetable oil. Interview with Debbie Seidband, policy analyst, USDA Foreign Agricultural Service, Grain and Feed Division, March 5, 2003.

16. Under the 2002 Farm Act, the US government established a new dairy payment program, the Dairy Market Loss Payments. The program supports the income of small dairy producers by providing countercyclical payments as an incentive to increase production at the margin. Despite high tariff rates on overquota imports into Canada, US exports of dairy and dairy-containing products to Canada have more than tripled from $75.9 million in 1994 to $254.6 million in 2002. See Orden (2003) and Myles and Cahoon (2004).

17. Other export subsidy programs include the Supplier Credit Guarantee Program and the Facility Guarantee Program. Details about the breakdown of funding for wheat exports under the GSM-102 federal program are not available. However, in 2002, GSM-102 registrations totaled $3 billion for exports to 11 countries and six regions. See USDA (2002d).

on imports that might undercut domestic support programs.[18] Without recourse to Section 22, the United States has found it more difficult to limit wheat imports from Canada—the main source of bilateral agriculture friction.

Canada

In 1991, Canada enacted the Farm Income Protection Act, which provided subsidies for grains and oilseeds through a voluntary insurance program organized and partly financed by the federal and provincial governments (table 5.2).[19] While subsidized exports from the United States and Mexico to world agricultural markets have increased recently, Canadian subsidized exports to world markets declined from 37 percent in 1995 to zero percent in 1998 (OECD 2000, 2003; Qualman and Wiebe 2002). In other words, so far as Canada is concerned, overt agricultural export subsidies are largely a thing of the past.[20]

According to the Organization for Economic Cooperation and Development (OECD), Canada's aggregate measure of support (AMS) has declined because of several policy reforms, including the elimination of internal transportation subsidies for western grains provided under the Western Grain Stabilization Act and phaseout of the Gross Revenue In-

---

18. Section 22 authority is based on the Agricultural Adjustment Act (1933), which allows the US government to impose fees or quotas on agricultural imports that threaten any USDA commodity stabilization program. After the Uruguay Round Agreement on Agriculture (1995), the United States agreed that Section 22 restrictions could be imposed only on imports from non-WTO countries. As a result, the United States can levy quantitative trade restrictions only on a WTO member as part of a Section 201 safeguard measure.

19. The Farm Income Protection Act provides crop loss protection through a production guarantee and reinsurance agreement. The production guarantee is based on a producer's probable yield: If current production falls below the farmer's production history, he will be eligible for an indemnity. The reinsurance agreement allows the federal government to provide additional funding to provinces when indemnities exceed accumulated premium reserves due to severe crop losses. See Alston, Gray, and Sumner (2000) and AAFC (2003b).

20. Only a fraction of US government export credits ($5.5 billion under the Export Credit Guarantee Program) can be classified as export subsidies. Nevertheless, by comparison with recent Canadian government funding for agricultural exports (totaling $33 million), the US government provides very substantial assistance. See BNA (2003a). However, the WTO Appellate Body *Dairy* ruling, in December 2002, determined that the Canadian Commercial Export Milk Program was in fact an export subsidy that violated WTO obligations. Both Canada and the European Union worry that the Appellate Body *Dairy* decision creates a new and higher standard, based on a comparison between export prices and the average cost of production, which makes it difficult for countries to prove that agricultural exports are not subsidized. Similarly, the recent WTO ruling in *Subsidies on Upland Cotton* characterized US export credit guarantee programs that benefit agricultural commodities as export subsidies in part. The exact measurement of export subsidies is being negotiated within the current WTO Doha Round talks. For a detailed analysis of US export credit guarantee programs, see Hanrahan (2004) and WTO (2004a).

Table 5.3 Average annual farm support by country/region
(producer support estimates)

Country/period	PSE in billions of dollars	Percent PSE	Producer NPC
Canada			
1986–88	5.7	34	1.40
2001–03	4.7	19	1.13
Mexico			
1986–88	–0.3	–1	0.91
2001–03	7.3	21	1.20
United States			
1986–88	41.8	25	1.19
2001–03	44.2	20	1.12
European Union			
1986–88	93.7	42	1.87
2001–03	101.7	35	1.34
OECD			
1986–88	238.9	38	1.58
2001–03	238.3	31	1.31

PSE = producer support estimate
NPC = nominal protection coefficient
OECD = Organization for Economic Cooperation and Development

Note: The table shows average PSE over the given period. PSE measures the annual monetary value of gross transfers from consumers and taxpayers to agricultural producers. The percentage PSE is the ratio of the PSE to the value of total gross farm receipts, measured by the value of total production (at farm gate prices), plus budgetary support. NPC measures the nominal rate of protection for consumers using the ratio between the average price paid by consumers (at farm gate) and the border price of imports, before tariffs or other restrictions.

Source: OECD, *OECD Agricultural Policies 2004: At a Glance.*

surance Program (OECD 2000, 61). The Canadian federal government also slashed federal spending on agriculture from $6.1 billion in 1991–92 to about $3.3 billion in 2001–02.[21] As a consequence, during the period between 1986–88 and 2001–03, Canada's producer support estimate declined by about 18 percent (table 5.3).

Nevertheless, domestic measures still ensure high internal prices for selected commodities. The Canadian government supports poultry, dairy, and eggs through supply management programs based on a combination of production and import quotas designed to maintain farm prices (especially in Quebec) at high levels. Moreover, Canada charters state trading enterprises that handle import and export sales. The most controversial is the Canadian Wheat Board (CWB), discussed further below.

21. See Agriculture and Agri-Food Canada (AAFC), *Farm Income, Financial Conditions, and Government Assistance Data Book,* 2004; and Qualman and Wiebe (2002).

Mexico

Following its accession to the General Agreement on Tariffs and Trade (GATT) in 1986, Mexico lowered its tariff protection and converted most import quotas to tariffs.[22] While Mexico maintained import quotas on some staple food products, notably corn, beans, and dry milk, it reduced subsidies for corn and wheat millers and eliminated most retail food price controls by 1991.[23] The government also revised Mexican land-tenure laws to permit greater flexibility in owning, selling, and renting land.

The Mexican government continues, however, to support its domestic sugar industry. In recent years, Mexico's public development bank, Financiera Nacional Azucarera SA (FINASA), is estimated to have provided over $1.3 billion of loans on very easy terms to the Mexican sugar industry.[24]

In anticipation of joining NAFTA, Mexico established in 1993 its Program of Direct Support for the Countryside (Programa de Apoyos Directos para el Campo, or Procampo). Procampo provided income support to farmers, over a 15-year transitional period, through hectare-based direct payments to producers.[25] Partly due to budget austerity following the peso crisis, government expenditure on Procampo steadily declined from $1.4 billion in 1994 to just over $1 billion in 1998. The number of agricultural producers who benefited from Procampo also declined by 14 percent, from 3.29 million in 1994 to 2.95 million in 1998.[26] To complement Pro-

---

22. After eliminating import licenses in 1988, Mexico imposed tariffs on 67 agricultural products, including milk powder, sugar, beans, wheat, barley, corn, coffee, animal fats, meat, and edible offal. See WTO (1997, 2003).

23. Although Mexico's market price support for agricultural staples such as corn declined slightly, output payments as a share of total producer support increased from zero to 5 percent during 1985–2001. During 1998–99 alone, the market price support was equivalent to 18 percent of total production value of barley, corn, rice, sorghum, soybeans, and wheat. Prices Mexican farmers received were on average 17 percent higher than the world market, though well below the OECD average. See OECD's *Agricultural Policies in OECD Countries*, 1998–2002.

24. The government of Mexico maintains other programs, including a 1997 sugar policy that penalized producers who sold sugar in the domestic market, encouraging Mexican producers to export sugar abroad. See Haley and Suarez (1999).

25. To increase support for small farmers, the minimum Procampo rate was paid on one hectare for all farmers, including those who farm less than one hectare. In 2000, Procampo payments accounted for more than 75 percent of payments under publicly funded policies that are regarded as minimally trade-distorting. Procampo was a decoupled program that substituted for previous direct price supports for farmers growing barley, beans, corn, cotton, rice, sorghum, soy, sunflower, and wheat. In 2002, expenditure on Procampo accounted for only 1.2 percent of public spending. See OECD's *Agricultural Policies in OECD Countries*, 1998–2002.

26. If inflation is taken into account, Procampo government payments declined in real terms from about $100 per hectare to less than $62 per hectare. Some critics argue that 85 percent of Procampo funding benefits large-scale farmers in the north. See Taylor (2003). See also Hugh Dellios, "10 Years Later: NAFTA Harvests a Stunted Crop," *Chicago Tribune*, December 14, 2003, A1.

campo, Mexico created its Alliance for the Countryside program (Alianza para el Campo, or Alianza) in 1995 to improve agricultural productivity with modern equipment and technology. In 2002, Alianza provided $903 million to 4.3 million producers.[27] A third program, Produce Capitaliza, provides infrastructure and extension-type assistance and support to livestock producers for upgrading pastures. Counting all three subsidy programs, together with recent protective measures (discussed below), Mexico has significantly augmented its support programs since the late 1990s.[28] However, there remains a huge disparity in subsidy levels between the United States and Mexico. During 1998–2000, for example, average US subsidies given to each agricultural producer amounted to $20,803 per year; the comparable Mexican figure was an average $720 for each producer.[29] Of course the disparity reflects the fact that on average, US firms are large, run like modern business firms, whereas Mexican firms are small, operated as family enterprises. Relative to farm sales, the level of public subsidies is about the same in both countries. During 2001–03, annual average US farm support measured in producer support estimate terms reached $44.2 billion, about 20 percent of gross farm receipts; the comparable Mexican figure was $7.3 billion, or 21 percent of gross farm receipts (table 5.3).

Until 2002, agricultural trade disputes were addressed only under NAFTA Chapters 19 and 20. This changed when, in January 2002, US Corn Products International filed a Chapter 11 claim against the Mexican government's decision to impose a tax on high fructose corn syrup (HFCS). In addition to the HFCS case, another active agriculture case was initiated under Chapter 19, concerning the final antidumping (AD) duty determination by Mexico on US exports of bovine carcasses.[30] As of January 2004,

---

27. Alianza provides payments to first-hand buyers of wheat, corn, and sorghum in certain Mexican states. Other Alianza-based initiatives include liquid fertilization irrigation systems, quality seeds, livestock genetics and management practices, mechanization, and training programs. See USDA (2002a) and Larre, Guichard, and Vourc'h (2003).

28. Mexico's overall direct agricultural support, as measured by the OECD producer support estimate, increased from $4.5 billion in 1999 to $6 billion in 2000. Under pressure from the farm lobby and with the prospect of mid-term congressional elections in June 2003, the Mexican government provided an additional $1.3 billion in agricultural subsidies and protection. (This figure includes new import barriers on agricultural goods, especially US exports of apples and chicken parts.) See Larre, Guichard, and Vourc'h (2003) and OECD (2003). See also David Luhnow, "Of Corn, NAFTA, and Zapata," *Wall Street Journal*, March 5, 2003, A13.

29. See Sarmiento (2003) and "NAFTA Crisis Worsens," *Latin American Economic and Business Report*, February 11, 2003. See also David Luhnow, "Of Corn, NAFTA, and Zapata," *The Wall Street Journal*, March 5, 2003, A13.

30. While the US-Mexico HFCS dispute under Chapter 19 was settled in June 2002 (MEX-USA-98-1904-01), it was reopened under Chapter 11 by US Corn Products International. Parallel to the NAFTA dispute settlement process, the United States also brought the HFCS case against Mexico under the WTO in 1998. Other agricultural product disputes initiated under

most agricultural cases have been brought under Chapter 20. In fact, a total of 8 out of 10 cases proceeding in the framework of Chapter 20 are either directly or indirectly related to agriculture.[31] The two active agriculture cases under Chapter 20 panels concern US TRQs on tomato imports and sugar. A few agricultural disputes have been headed off through government or industry negotiations (Burfisher, Norman, and Schwartz 2002). Six key agricultural commodities in US-Mexico trade—sugar, meat (pork/beef/chicken), corn, beans, tomatoes, and avocadoes—that might eventually be addressed within the NAFTA dispute settlement mechanism are analyzed below.[32]

US-Canada Wheat Dispute

Types of Wheat Involved

Canadian wheat exports to the United States are small compared with total US wheat production. However, wheat exports to US and world markets are very important to Canada given its limited domestic market (table 5.4). Two types of wheat dominate the US wheat import menu: hard red spring wheat, which represents 73 percent of total US wheat imports, and durum wheat, which accounts for 23 percent (USITC 2001). A key difference between hard red spring and durum wheat products is their degree of substitutability for other wheat varieties. Durum wheat, used mainly for producing pasta, has few close substitutes. Hard red spring wheat, used to make breads and other baked goods, has important close substitutes, notably hard red winter wheat.[33]

Domestic US concerns are correlated with the growth of wheat imports from Canada. In 2003, Canada was the single largest supplier of hard red spring wheat, accounting for 93 percent of US imports of that type of wheat, and practically the only supplier of durum wheat to the United

---

Chapter 19 include apples (CDA-94-1904-01, CDA-95-1904-01), sows and boars (USA-94-1904-01), beer (CDA-95-1904-01), sugar (CDA-95-1904-04), prepared baby food products (CDA-USA-98-1904-01), cattle (USA-CDA-99-1904-06, USA-CDA-99-1904-07), bovine carcasses (MEX-USA-2000-1904-02, MEX-USA-2002-1904-01), and tomatoes (USA-CDA-2002-1904-04, USA-CDA-2002-1904-06). See appendix tables 4A.4 and 4A.5 in chapter 4 on NAFTA dispute settlement.

31. While only three Chapter 20 panels have been initiated, we assign several other disputes to the framework of Chapter 20, prior to the panel stage. See appendix 4A.3 in chapter 4 on NAFTA dispute settlement.

32. Trade disputes over avocadoes have partly been resolved through negotiated agreements. As a result, Mexican avocado exports have increased steadily under NAFTA. See "Free Trade on Trial," *The Economist*, December 30, 2003. We thank Tim Josling for this observation.

33. Hard red spring wheat is also comparatively higher in protein and gluten content than durum wheat.

Table 5.4 Volume of durum wheat exports by principal exporters, 1994–2003 (millions of tons, percent of world exports in parentheses)

Year	Canada	United States	European Union	Others	Total
1994–95	4.0 (58.7)	1.0 (14.5)	1.6 (23.0)	.3 (3.8)	6.9 (100)
1995–96	3.2 (62.0)	.8 (15.9)	.2 (4.5)	.9 (17.6)	5.2 (100)
1996–97	4.1 (65.4)	1.0 (16.7)	.4 (6.4)	.7 (11.4)	6.3 (100)
1997–98	4.2 (58.9)	1.2 (16.2)	.3 (4.0)	1.5 (20.9)	7.2 (100)
1998–99	3.9 (63.3)	1.0 (16.9)	.3 (4.7)	.9 (15.1)	6.1 (100)
1999–2000	3.6 (57.5)	.9 (14.9)	.3 (4.7)	1.4 (22.8)	6.2 (100)
2000–01	3.5 (52.2)	1.2 (17.6)	.7 (10.1)	1.3 (20.1)	6.7 (100)
2001–02	3.6 (49.7)	1.2 (16.8)	.6 (8.1)	1.9 (25.4)	7.3 (100)
2002–03[a]	3.0 (45.2)	1.0 (15.1)	1.3 (19.8)	1.3 (19.9)	6.6 (100)

a. Data for 2002–03 are preliminary.

Note: Data include semolina.

Sources: Statistics Canada, Agriculture Economics Statistics, 2004; USDA (2004b); and Canadian Wheat Board statistical tables 2003–04.

States, representing nearly 90 percent of total US wheat imports. During 1993–2003, US imports of Canadian hard red spring wheat increased steadily from over 1 million metric tons to nearly 2 million metric tons in 2001 but declined to 779,000 metric tons in 2003 on account of adverse weather.[34] Similarly, imports of Canadian durum wheat rose to 595,000 metric tons in 2002 but declined sharply to 40,000 metric tons in 2003 (tables 5.5 and 5.6).[35]

---

34. Widespread drought in western Canada in 2002–03 was the primary reason for declining production and exports of Canadian hard red spring wheat. In fact, drought and poor harvest weather in three of the world's largest wheat exporters (Australia, Canada, and the United States) created opportunities for nontraditional exporters, including Russia and Ukraine. See CWB (2003) and Vocke and Allen (2005).

35. North Dakota is the main US producing state, accounting for 47 percent of US hard red spring wheat production and 81 percent of US durum wheat production. Montana is the other key wheat producer, accounting for 22 percent of US hard red spring wheat production and 9 percent of US durum wheat production. See USDA (2002e).

Competition for Third-Country Markets

The United States remains the world's leading wheat exporter, with foreign sales averaging about $3.5 billion, representing about 24 percent of total world exports during 1998–2002.[36] Over the same period, Canada was also a major wheat exporter, with exports averaging $2.4 billion, accounting for about 16 percent of total world exports. Canada is a particularly keen competitor of the United States in wheat sales to developing countries. Anecdotes suggest the strength of Canadian competition. Between 1991 and 1996, for example, Moroccan imports of US wheat declined from over 60 percent of total Moroccan wheat imports to less than 20 percent; meanwhile, Moroccan imports of Canadian wheat increased from close to zero to about 20 percent of the market.[37] Faced with such episodes, the US wheat industry, led by the North Dakota Wheat Commission, has raised alarms over declining US wheat exports to eight key developing-country markets: Algeria, Brazil, Colombia, Guatemala, Peru, Philippines, South Africa, and Venezuela (table 5.7).

Wheat Industry Concerns about Pricing

The CWB handles about 18 percent of the world wheat and barley trade.[38] The United States claims that CWB export pricing practices lack transparency.[39] Of course the same can be said of the pricing practices of large private grain companies. Both private companies and state trading enterprises, like the CWB, deliberately keep their transaction prices a secret to facilitate price discrimination between customers. The key question is whether state trading enterprises should be held to a higher standard than large private grain traders. If the answer is "yes," then the United States has grounds to complain. If the answer is "no," then the complaint loses force. The main rationale for "yes" is that state trading enterprises implement public policy while also operating as commercial firms. The inherent dilemma is that the government policy component cannot be easily sepa-

---

36. These data are based on USDA Foreign Agricultural Service (FATUS) database, 2004; and UN Food and Agriculture Organization FAOSTAT database, 2004.

37. See "North Dakota Files Section 301 to Lure Canada to Negotiating Table," *Inside US Trade*, September 15, 2000.

38. Data are based on Statistics Canada database, www.statcan.ca (accessed in May 2004); conversation with Sergio Novelli, market analyst at Agriculture and Agri-Food Canada, April 2003; and Edward Alden and Ken Warn, "US Seeks to Dismantle Canada Wheat Sales," *Financial Times*, December 18, 2002.

39. The CWB "posted" wheat prices are based on export deals that have already been negotiated. The CWB uses the Minneapolis Grain Exchange for guidance to establish its own prices. See Gardner (2000). See also "Wheat Industry Letter," *Inside US Trade*, March 30, 2001.

Table 5.5 US hard red spring wheat trade with NAFTA partners, 1993–2003 (volume in thousands of metric tons and value in millions of dollars)

Country	1993 Volume	1993 Value	1994 Volume	1994 Value	1995 Volume	1995 Value	1996 Volume	1996 Value	1997 Volume	1997 Value
US exports to										
Canada	26	4	3	1	14	3	78	17	75	13
Mexico	952	132	623	91	753	139	1,513	319	1,031	171
NAFTA subtotal	978	136	626	92	767	142	1,591	336	1,106	185
Total world (including NAFTA)	34,516	4,490	29,329	3,820	31,303	5,230	30,105	6,084	24,425	3,911
US imports from										
Canada	1,289	142	2,110	226	1,188	170	1,061	191	1,783	272
Mexico	0	0	0	0	0	0	0	0	0	0
NAFTA subtotal	1,289	142	2,110	226	1,188	170	1,061	191	1,783	272
Total world (including NAFTA)	1,295	143	2,141	230	1,207	172	1,064	192	1,784	273

Note: Data are based on hard red spring wheat by HTS code 1001.90.

Source: USDA Foreign Agricultural Service (FATUS) database, 2004.

rated from the commercial component (Sumner 1999). A pragmatic solution is to adopt transparent pricing practices, which would enable competitors to make an informed guess about the public policy component.[40]

Nearly all Canadian farmers sell their wheat and barley for export through the CWB. Based on what little is known about CWB pricing practices, the CWB initially compensates farmers about 70 to 75 percent of the expected final return for grain. The balance is paid after sales are consummated. As a "single-desk seller," the CWB does not have to worry about competition from other Canadian grain trading firms.[41] The "sin-

40. The August 2004 WTO Council Declaration agreed to put the question of disciplines on export sales of state trading enterprises like the CWB on the agenda of the Doha Round. A recent WTO ruling, however, dismissed US claims against the CWB, weakening the case for including state trading enterprises under new export subsidy disciplines. In particular, the Appellate Body rejected US claims that the CWB violates GATT Article 17.1, which requires state trading enterprises to offer other WTO member companies the opportunity to compete for purchases and sales. The Appellate Body determined that under Article 17.1, the CWB can use its "special privileges" to export wheat as long it is done "solely in accordance with commercial considerations" and "in a manner consistent with the general principles of non-discriminatory treatment." The Appellate Body then upheld the panel ruling that Article 17 applies only to companies seeking to buy from or sell to a state trading enterprise and not to buy or sell in competition with such an enterprise, as the United States had claimed. See Pruzin, Yerkey, and Menyasz (2004); and WTO (2004b).

41. The CWB uses any surplus revenue to finance price reductions for selected customers (or markets). See Carter and Loyns (1996, 1998).

| 1998 | | 1999 | | 2000 | | 2001 | | 2002 | | 2003 | |
Volume	Value	Volume	Value	Volume	Value	Volume	Value	Volume	Value	Volume	Value
12	2	7	1	22	3	38	6	8	2	22	4
1,500	204	1,823	215	1,795	205	2,128	269	2,324	351	2,509	380
1,511	206	1,830	216	1,816	209	2,165	275	2,332	353	2,531	383
25,536	3,465	27,381	3,406	26,072	3,155	24,381	3,184	23,380	3,476	24,139	3,736
1,564	205	1,570	187	1,561	185	1,636	211	1,200	161	779	104
14	1	0	0	0	0	0	0	0	0	0	0
1,578	206	1,570	187	1,561	185	1,636	211	1,200	161	779	104
1,579	207	1,571	187	1,562	185	1,637	211	1,311	173	836	110

gle desk" feature may have other significant advantages, but these are debated.[42]

State Trading Enterprises and the CWB

The wheat dispute in NAFTA is unique because of the different marketing systems and political influence of key wheat producers in the United States and Canada. Private farmers are the base of wheat production in both countries, but marketing systems differ. In the United States, large private grain companies, such as Cargill and Bunge, buy most of the crop and sell wheat around the world.[43] In Canada, the CWB acquires virtually

---

42. The CWB's ability to extract a premium on wheat sales is the most debated issue. Some studies argue that since the CWB is most active in markets where price counts more than quality, Canadian grain has been priced competitively but not necessarily at a CWB price premium. See Kraft, Furtan, and Tyrchniewicz (1996) and Carter and Loyns (1998). See also GAO (1998).

43. According to a recent USITC report, Cargill and Continental each own a 29 percent share of US grain storage capacity; Archer Daniels Midland is the third largest company with a 28 percent share. Four large US firms account for 47 percent of US wheat exports. Private firms are gaining importance in the Canadian industry as well. Two US companies own 70 percent of Canadian milling capacity. Among Canadian pasta plants, for example, 90 percent are foreign-owned, of which 67 percent are owned by US investors. See USITC (2001) and Qualman and Wiebe (2002).

Table 5.6   US durum wheat trade with NAFTA partners, 1993–2003
(volume in thousands of metric tons and value in
millions of dollars)

	1993		1994		1995		1996		1997	
Country	Volume	Value	Volume	Value	Volume	Value	Volume	Value	Volume	Value
US exports to										
Canada	0	0	14	2	4	1	0	0	0	0
Mexico	23	4	3	1	58	9	47	7	36	4
NAFTA subtotal	23	4	17	3	62	10	47	8	36	4
Total world (including NAFTA)	1,232	189	1,209	235	1,143	234	995	212	1,454	285
US imports from										
Canada	513	70	376	55	313	66	250	56	433	86
Mexico	0	0	0	0	0	0	0	0	0	0
NAFTA subtotal	0	70	376	55	313	66	250	56	433	86
Total world (including NAFTA)	513	70	376	55	313	66	250	56	433	86

Note: Data are based on durum wheat by HTS code 1001.10.

Source: USDA Foreign Agricultural Service (FATUS) database, 2004.

all wheat and barley, and (like its private competitors) sells on a global basis.[44] As a crown corporation, the CWB enjoys special privileges:[45]

- Financing is guaranteed by the Canadian government, which compensates for any shortfalls in sales revenue from wheat or barley.

- The government of Canada also guarantees certain export credit sales of the CWB.[46]

- The CWB can borrow money at favorable interest rates.[47]

---

44. Three commissioners appointed by the Canadian government manage the CWB. The only province that does not operate through the CWB is Ontario, which established its own marketing board controlled independently by farmers. However, most of Ontario's exports are soft wheat and represent only 5 percent of total Canadian wheat exports. See Carter and Loyns (1998) and GAO (1998).

45. Crown corporations are companies designated by the government of Canada to administer and manage public services.

46. Government expenditure for wheat and barley operations decreased from $3.2 billion in 1990 to $922 million in 1996 but then increased to reach $1.2 billion in 2003. See GAO (1998) and Treasury Board of Canada Secretariat's Web site, www.tbs-sct.gc.ca/est-pre/p2_0304e. asp (accessed October 2004).

47. The CWB control over transportation and merchandising are additional factors in Canada's competitive trade policy. Under the Wheat Access Facilitation Program (1990), the CWB controls 1,100 primary elevators that handle US wheat exports to Canada.

1998		1999		2000		2001		2002		2003	
Volume	Value	Volume	Value	Volume	Value	Volume	Value	Volume	Value	Volume	Value
0	0	10	2	2	0	14	2	6	1	2	0
96	11	23	3	18	3	72	9	81	13	145	22
96	11	34	5	20	3	86	12	87	14	147	23
1,320	225	1,214	191	1,647	219	1,354	190	876	154	1,099	199
427	77	644	86	291	43	437	67	595	91	40	8
0	0	0	0	10	1	25	3	10	1	36	5
427	77	644	86	301	44	462	71	605	93	75	13
427	77	644	86	301	44	462	71	605	93	75	13

The CWB's influence on the Canadian wheat industry is evidenced by its control over the "middleman sector" between producers (farmers) and users (millers or foreign buyers). The US wheat industry's middleman sector comprises several producer cooperatives and small and large grain trading firms. By contrast, Canada's middleman sector is based on the CWB producer pool system, which amounts to a monopoly over the marketing of western Canadian wheat.[48] In turn, the CWB has created a network of accredited exporters, who act as marketing agents.[49] In 1998,

48. Under the producer pool system, the CWB has the flexibility to market over long periods. The US government argues that a pooling system makes it difficult for end users of wheat to manage their risk because they are prevented from selling surplus wheat stocks except to the CWB. The CWB sets initial prices for four marketing pools at the beginning of the crop year; the Canadian government guarantees the pools. The CWB-controlled pool system has proven costly. In January 2003, the Saskatchewan Wheat Pool nearly filed for bankruptcy with debt reaching $191 million. In June 2002, the Canadian House of Commons recommended that grain farmers be free from obligations to sell all of their wheat and barley crops to the CWB. See "Saskatchewan Wheat Pool in Financial Crisis," Canadian Broadcasting Corporation, January 31, 2003, www.cbc.ca (accessed in March 2003); and "Canadian Committee Recommends Change to Wheat Board Operation," Inside US Trade, June 21, 2002.

49. Accredited exporters are Canadian grain companies, Canadian subsidiaries of international grain companies, or other international grain companies. They are instrumental in allowing the CWB to sell into markets that previously depended on centralized buyers but now have many private companies sourcing grain. While they may sell grain to many customers, they have to buy Canadian grain solely from the CWB. Conversation with Brenda Brindle, general manager, Alberta Grain Commission, March 2003; and Martin, Mayer, and Bouma (2002).

Table 5.7 Comparison of US and Canadian wheat exports to third-country markets
(thousands of tons)

Country	1997–98	2002–03
US exports to		
Algeria	197	244
Brazil	—	570
China	323	202
Colombia	405	734
Japan	3,204	3,038
Morocco	488	153
Peru	208	566
Philippines	913	1,438
South Africa	133	181
Turkey	260	0
Venezuela	558	618
Canadian exports to		
Algeria	2,314	734
Brazil	621	170
China	1,331	177
Colombia	597	273
Japan	1,449	1,088
Morocco	368	311
Peru	636	148
Philippines	411	515
South Africa	257	n.a.
Turkey	216	118
Venezuela	600	228

— = less than 500 metric tons
n.a. = not available

Sources: USITC (2001); USDA (2004b); Canadian Grain Commission (2003); and UN Comtrade database, 2004.

the CWB estimated that accredited exporters made 30 percent of its sales.[50]

The primary means for US wheat producers to sell their wheat directly to the Canadian market is through the Canadian Wheat Access Facilitation Program. On paper, this program allows US wheat producers to negotiate sales contracts with prospective Canadian buyers on price, quantity, and delivery of wheat. Private companies participating in the program include Agricore, Pioneer, Cargill Limited, and Louis Dreyfus.[51] However, according to US wheat producers, the reality is that the pro-

---

50. While historical figures on exports of accredited exporters are not available, it is widely believed that values have grown significantly over the past 10 years. According to Bruce Gardner (2000), the CWB negotiates each export deal, and wheat transaction prices are closely held secrets.

51. See the Canadian Grain Commission's Web site at www.grainscanada.gc.ca (accessed in January 2003).

gram entails excessive regulation, making it costly for Canadian elevator operators to buy US grain through the program.[52]

Differences between Canada and the United States dominate NAFTA wheat disputes.[53] The crux of the current wheat dispute centers on different government policies and marketing strategies used by Canada and the United States. After the CUSFTA was implemented in 1989, all wheat trade barriers were eliminated, causing a surge in US imports of Canadian wheat. The US Congress then requested the US International Trade Commission (USITC) to investigate the "conditions of competition" between Canadian and US durum wheat. The USITC determined that the CWB had not sold durum wheat below its acquisition cost. In the terminology of trade remedy law, Canadian durum wheat sales were neither dumped nor subsidized.

Following this decision, the United States requested a binational panel under CUSFTA Chapter 18; the panel's final decision in 1993 concurred with the USITC determination.[54] The binational panel determined there was "no compelling evidence" of CWB dumping but suggested that a bilateral working group be established to audit the CWB. Audits of sales during 1989–92 revealed that only three durum wheat contracts out of 105 were sold below acquisition price, thereby violating the CUSFTA (GAO 1998).

In 1994, yet another USITC investigation in the wheat dispute led to a three-way split decision. The final negotiated settlement, also referenced

---

52. In a recent USITC survey, major US wheat exporters complained that exports to Canadian mill elevators are "difficult, burdensome, and infrequent." An example of successful bilateral efforts to facilitate wheat trade is the US-Canada in-transit program (1999), which uses Canadian railroads to ship US grains through Canada to final destinations in the United States. See Paddock, Destorel, and Short (2000).

53. Mexico is the third largest export destination for both Canadian and US wheat producers (Mexico imports about a third of its wheat needs). Recently, US wheat producers edged ahead of their Canadian competitors in Mexico's wheat market. In 2001, US wheat exports (3 million bushels) to Mexico were twice those of Canada. Under NAFTA, Canada has no restrictions on imports of Mexican wheat, but the United States imposes a declining schedule of tariff rates on durum wheat. Mexican nondurum wheat exports to the United States are tariff-free, but Mexican durum wheat exports face declining US tariffs starting at 0.77 cents per kilogram. Mexico phased out its wheat tariffs on US and Canadian wheat exports from 15 percent in 1994 to zero in 2004. See USDA *World Agricultural Supply and Demand Estimates Report on Grains* (March 2003) and Canadian Grain Commission (2003). See also NAFTA Provisions, Chapter 7a on Agriculture, available at www.sice.oas.org/summary/nafta/nafta7a. asp (accessed in May 2003).

54. The CUSFTA binational panel used the definition of "acquisition cost" provided by Ann Veneman, USDA deputy secretary, and Clayton Yeutter, US Trade Representative. Both officials defined "acquisition cost" as the CWB's initial payment. In 1988, when Veneman and Yeutter testified before the US House Subcommittee on Trade and the Senate Finance Committee, respectively, both officials confirmed that the CWB only made initial payments, and the measure of Canadian "acquisition cost" should not include final payments made after the crop is marketed. See Carter and Loyns (1998); see also the final report of the CUSFTA binational panel decision on "The Interpretation of and Canada's Compliance with Article 701.3 with Respect to Durum Wheat Sales," CDA-92-1807-01, February 8, 1993, available at www.nafta-sec-alena.org/app/DocRepository/1/Dispute/english/FTA_Chapter_18/Canada/cc92010e.pdf (accessed in September 2004).

as the US-Canada Memorandum of Understanding on Grains, joined a Canadian agreement to limit wheat exports with a US decision not to pursue the wheat dispute under GATT.[55] But the memorandum of understanding was short-lived: In September 1995, the agreement was dropped due to pressure from US wheat interests, which believed they could profit more from selling wheat at market prices.[56]

One Unsuccessful Answer: The Export Enhancement Program

Canadian wheat exports to the United States increased significantly after the Canadian government eliminated freight subsidies for overseas sales in 1995. Taking into account higher transpacific freight charges, the net returns from shipping to the US market exceeded the net returns from shipping to Asian or Latin American markets. Just as freight subsidies arguably subsidized Canadian wheat exports, the US EEP, established in 1983, arguably subsidized US wheat exports. Designed to counter unfair foreign trading practices in world agricultural markets, the EEP provided cash bonuses to US wheat exporters.[57] But the EEP boomeranged: It encouraged Canada to maintain its own agricultural export subsidies for wheat, further depressing world wheat prices and making the net returns from Canadian wheat exports to the US market still more attractive.[58]

The Current US-Canada Wheat Dispute

The US-Canada wheat dispute heated up in March 2003, when the United States filed formal charges against the CWB in the WTO.[59] The United

---

55. The memorandum of understanding was instrumental in creating a one-year TRQ that limited access to wheat imports at the lower NAFTA tariff levels. When this "peace clause" ended in September 1995, the US government announced it would closely monitor Canadian grain exports to the United States. See USDA (2000).

56. US wheat interests believed that market prices would exceed US-Canada memorandum of understanding prices. See Alston, Gray, and Sumner (2000).

57. Since mid-1995, rising world prices and the Uruguay Round Agreement on Agriculture have prevented the United States from using the EEP to support wheat exports. In any event, according to Gardner (2000), the EEP was never large enough to achieve significant gains in US wheat exports. See also Hanrahan (2004).

58. Consequently, in 1998, August Schumacher, former undersecretary of agriculture for farm and foreign agricultural services, stated that reviving the EEP for wheat exports would not raise farmgate prices. Instead, the EEP could lead to outcomes that are "only marginally helpful or even detrimental to American farmers." See "USDA Fends Off Pressure to Reactivate EEP Despite Falling Prices," *Inside US Trade*, July 10, 1998.

59. On March 7, 2003, the United States initiated a request to establish a WTO panel regarding Canadian wheat exports. Canada has so far not initiated a case against US wheat exports under either NAFTA or WTO dispute settlement mechanisms. See "US Request For Wheat Board Panel Blocked, US Faces Panel on Cotton," *Inside US Trade*, March 21, 2003.

States contended that as a consequence of the CWB's monopoly on certain grain sales, the CWB engages in unfair price discrimination, and that the CWB itself receives direct and indirect government subsidies. Specifically, the US government raised the following arguments:

- The CWB practices "discriminatory" trade policies that violate Canada's GATT obligations under Article 17.[60]

- US wheat exports into Canada receive less favorable treatment than like Canadian grain.[61]

- Canada's limits on the revenue that railroads can receive on the shipment of domestic grain constitute a violation of Canada's GATT Article 3 obligations.[62]

In August 2004, the WTO Appellate Body ruled against US claims that the Canadian government violated WTO rules by allowing the CWB to sell wheat on noncommercial terms.[63] While the Appellate Body's final report undermines US efforts to overhaul CWB operations, Canada still faces significant transition problems as ongoing WTO nego-

---

60. The US government alleges that the CWB is given exclusive rights that conflict with Canada's obligations under GATT Article 17. Article 17, paragraph 1(b) requires state trading enterprises to make sales "solely in accordance with commercial considerations" and to give other WTO members opportunities to compete for such sales. According to the United States, some privileges given by the Canadian government to the CWB include exclusive right to sell western Canadian wheat, government guarantees of the CWB's financial operations, and rights to purchase and export Canadian wheat at prices determined by both the Canadian government and the CWB. For complete details, see "Request for the Establishment of a Panel by the United States," www.wto.org/english/tratop_e/ dispu_e/dispu_e. htm (accessed in April 2003).

61. Under the Canada Grain Act (1970), imported grain must be segregated from domestic Canadian grain throughout the handling system. Even though Canadian elevators are mandated under the joint Wheat Access Facilitation Program (WAFP) to facilitate US wheat exports, US wheat cannot be stored in the same grain elevators. The United States argues that such handling restrictions act as a de facto ban on US wheat exports into Canada through Canadian grain elevators. In response, Canada argues that phytosanitary and varietal registration measures are designed to guarantee the purity of wheat varieties.

62. The United States assumes that removing existing caps on railway freight rates for transporting domestic grain would give US wheat producers better access to the Canadian market.

63. According to the US government, the CWB does not function as a commercial actor because it uses monopoly privileges to undercut prices and gain market share in wheat. While the WTO ruled against US claims that the CWB used "special privileges" to make sales on a noncommercial basis, the WTO did support some US claims. Specifically, the WTO determined that the Canadian grain distribution system and "rail revenue cap" were inconsistent with national treatment obligations. See WTO (2004b).

tiations focus on stronger discipline in the operations of state trading enterprises.[64]

In a separate case, the North Dakota Wheat Commission asked the US government to impose countervailing duties (CVDs) and AD duties up to $500 million on Canadian wheat imports.[65] While the commission could not provide evidence on actual CWB prices, it argued that Canadian exports of durum and hard red spring wheat are suppressing domestic US wheat prices.[66] Moreover, according to US wheat producers, the Canadian government and the CWB provide direct export subsidies on Canadian wheat ranging from 14.7 to 25.5 percent, plus indirect transportation and financial subsidies. Following the USITC's preliminary determination of material injury to domestic wheat farmers, the US Department of Commerce imposed preliminary CVD rates at around 4 percent on Cana-

---

64. Bob Friesen of the Canadian Farmers Association argues that the CWB is a necessary supply management mechanism that stabilizes rural infrastructure by directly subsidizing Canadian farmers to the extent of about $130 million per year. Bill Kerr of the University of Saskatchewan argues that if the CWB is eliminated, companies like Cargill, which can easily move grains from North Dakota to Canada, and vice versa, could dominate Canada's wheat market. Third parties to the WTO wheat dispute, including Australia, the European Union, and China, concur that the US proposal to limit state trading enterprises puts their countries at a competitive disadvantage compared with countries like the United States that historically have relied on private grain firms. Kerr points out that when the United States succeeded in eliminating Canadian government transportation subsidies, Canadian agricultural exports into the US market actually increased. In other words, revamping the CWB might lead to greater dominance by US marketing firms but more Canadian exports to the United States. Based on Kerr's presentation at the North American Committee Conference on Agriculture, Washington, March 21, 2003. See also Pruzin, Yerkey, and Menyasz (2004); "Appellate Body Rejects US Appeal of WTO Wheat Board Decision," *Inside US Trade*, September 3, 2004; and WTO (2004b).

65. For its part, the North Dakota Wheat Commission filed a Section 301 petition to pressure the USTR to investigate whether the CWB violated a trade agreement. In response to complaints from US wheat producers, the US Department of Commerce and US International Trade Commission launched investigations to determine whether Canadian wheat was dumped or subsidized in the US market. See Steven Chase and Barrie McKenna, "US Targets Wheat Board, Files Challenge at WTO over 'Monopoly,'" *Toronto Globe and Mail*, December 18, 2002; Peter Morton, Tony Seskus, and Ian Jack, "US Moves to Dismantle Wheat Board," *Financial Post*, December 18, 2002; "USA: US Commerce Department Delays Canada Wheat Duty Ruling," *Reuters*, January 31, 2003; Joel Baglole, "The Economy: US-Canada Trade Dispute Erupts over Sales of Wheat," *Wall Street Journal*, October 1, 2002; "North Dakota Files Section 301 to Lure Canada to Negotiating Table," *Inside US Trade*, September 15, 2000; and "Canada May Contest Final US Finding on Wheat in NAFTA Panel," *Inside US Trade*, May 9, 2003.

66. Pressured by North Dakota farmers led by the North Dakota Wheat Commission, the US government initiated a WTO dispute. A preliminary WTO ruling dismissed the US complaint against the CWB but allowed the United States to bring a second panel request if it provided more specific arguments. By August 2005, the US Department of Commerce issued a redetermination that imposed a combined AD and CVDs of 11.4 percent. See "Commerce Launches Cases on Canadian Durum, Hard Spring Wheat," *Inside US Trade*, October 25, 2002. See North Dakota Wheat Commission, "Commerce Department Reaffirms Canadian Subsidization of Wheat Sales to US Market," August 9, 2005.

dian exports of hard red spring and durum wheat products into the United States.[67] In May 2003, it imposed an additional AD duty of 8 percent on Canadian durum wheat and 6 percent on Canadian hard red spring wheat products.[68] Some studies estimate that total US subsidies per ton of wheat are three times higher than Canadian subsidies ($108 subsidies versus $31).[69] However, the fact that the United States subsidizes the same product is no legal defense against a CVD petition.

Wheat Recommendations

While multinational grain companies may resemble state trading enterprises, the Canadian government guarantees CWB loans and covers its losses. WTO negotiations are pointed toward the elimination of "trade-distorting practices with respect to exporting state trading enterprises," according to the August 2004 decision of the WTO General Council. Specifically, the decision targets the elimination of "export subsidies provided to or by them, government financing, and the underwriting of losses." In addition, the "future use of monopoly powers" in state trading enterprises will be the subject of further WTO negotiations.[70]

Given the draft WTO agriculture text, the Canadian government may need to substantially recast how the CWB does business. Our primary recommendation is for Canada to follow the example of the Australian Wheat Board and gradually privatize the CWB.[71] By deregulating the domestic wheat market over a period of up to 10 years, the CWB can move toward a producer-owned company. For example, the Canadian government might provide significant capital funds to set the CWB on the road to privatization.

If reforming the CWB is not feasible, our alternative recommendation is to negotiate a bilateral US-Canada memorandum of understanding that

---

67. In addition to CVD of 3.94 percent on Canadian durum and hard red spring wheat, the US Commerce Department imposed 8.15 percent AD duties on Canadian durum wheat and 6.12 percent on Canadian hard red spring wheat in May 2003. See BNA (2003d).

68. See "Canadian Wheat Hit with New US Tariffs," Canadian Broadcasting Corporation, May 2, 2003, www.cbc.ca/stories/2003/05/02/wheat_030502 (accessed in May 2003).

69. See Jeffrey Simpson, "The American Way of Trading," *Globe and Mail*, January 22, 2003; and "Commerce Launches Cases on Canadian Durum, Hard Spring Wheat," *Inside US Trade*, October 2002.

70. See the WTO General Council Decision, WT/L/579, Annex A, para. 18, August 2, 2004. www.wto.org/english/tratop_e/dda_e/draft_text_gc_dg_31july04_e.htm (accessed in June 2005).

71. In 1999, the Australian Wheat Board was privatized and is now known as the Australian Wheat Board Limited. The Australian government provided significant funding for the board to reform itself within 10 years and also gave special levies to fund capital assets such as grain storage and handling facilities.

establishes a TRQ for Canadian wheat exports. This memorandum of understanding could resemble the 1994 one. For example, the within-quota limit for Canadian total wheat exports to the United States might be 1.5 million metric tons or a percentage of the US market, whichever is higher, with a sublimit on durum wheat exports. Canadian wheat exports above the limit would be subject to a tariff, say 10 percent. While the memorandum of understanding is in effect, Canadian wheat would not be subject to AD or CVD penalties.

In order for the WTO Doha Round to succeed, the United States, Canada, and the European Union must curtail their amber and blue box supports for agriculture, including wheat. Farm subsidies in the amber box (trade-distorting, such as price supports) and blue box (trade-distorting but with production limits) will need to be sharply reduced, but to some extent the funds may be redirected to the green box (decoupled, nondistorting subsidies, such as income supports). Whatever formula is finally agreed on, it is virtually certain that the Doha Round will *not* altogether eliminate amber and blue box farm subsidies.[72]

Therefore, after the WTO package is concluded, the United States, Canada, and Mexico should take an additional bold step: a NAFTA agreement that after the Doha agreement has been fully implemented, remaining amber and blue box subsidies for wheat will be phased out altogether over an additional 10 years. Each country could choose, if it wished, to cushion the impact on farm values by redirecting the funds to green box supports. Green box supports could, for example, take the form of a contractual acreage payment that declines year to year, scaled to the historic wheat acreage in each farm, whether or not the acreage is planted to wheat in future years. This NAFTA agreement would serve as a valuable example not only for other subsidized crops in North America but also for support programs in Europe and elsewhere. More immediately, it would pave the way for completely free wheat trade within North America.

The Sugar Saga

The United States and Mexico share a long tradition of maintaining artificially high internal sugar prices.[73] Moreover, since 1998, as world sugar prices have declined, government assistance to sugar has increased.

---

72. For more detailed analysis of the Doha Round negotiations on agriculture, see Josling and Hathaway (2004).

73. Sugar has been a highly protected product for centuries—literally since the regime of Emperor Napoleon Bonaparte. In the interest of space, we pass over the rich history of policy intervention and start our NAFTA account in the 1990s. However, it is worth noting that while the United States and Mexico generously protect their domestic sugar producers, Canada does not.

Among OECD countries, US policies ensure the third highest domestic sugar prices, after the European Union and Japan.[74] But the industrial countries are not alone: Colombia, Mexico, South Africa, and Turkey all maintain domestic sugar prices higher than the United States.[75] Major sugar exporters include Australia, Brazil, China, Colombia, Cuba, the European Union, Guatemala, India, Japan, Mexico, South Africa, Thailand, and Turkey. The fact that several major exporters maintain exceptionally high domestic price levels testifies to the mammoth distortion in sugar production and trade.

While liberalization in sugar trade would be highly desirable, there are good reasons for maintaining high sugar prices as a means of discouraging sugar consumption. Sugar-related illnesses are estimated to kill 300,000 adults annually in the United States. A recent World Health Organization (WHO) and Food and Agriculture Organization (FAO) joint report on diet and nutrition confirmed links between sugar and obesity, diabetes, heart, and dental diseases.[76] Daily consumption of nondiet soda, a popular drink throughout North America and heavy in sugar or HFCS, is closely linked to weight gain and type 2 diabetes.[77] In turn, excessive weight and obesity

---

74. Average agricultural protection pales in comparison with government support for sugar. During 2001–03, total support to US producers, measured by the producer support estimate, was about 20 percent and remained below the OECD average; support for US sugar producers averaged above 55 percent during the same period. In the European Union, total support for producers in 2001–03 was about 35 percent, higher than the OECD average of 31 percent; support for EU sugar producers was about 55 percent. In Japan, total support was 58 percent, nearly twice the OECD average; support for Japanese sugar producers was 40 percent. See OECD's *OECD Agricultural Policies 2004: At a Glance* and Center for International Economics (2002).

75. According to the USDA, the domestic wholesale price for raw sugar in the United States was 18 cents per pound in 2000, and American businesses that need sugar to make their products pay close to 21 cents per pound. By comparison, the following countries support even higher domestic sugar prices, measured in cents per pound and ranked from highest to lowest: Japan (65.4), European Union (30.4), Turkey (27.9), Mexico (25.6), Colombia (21.1), and South Africa (20.9). The world sugar price is about 7 cents a pound. See LMC International (2003); Haley and Suarez (2000); and the editorial in the *New York Times*, November 29, 2003.

76. According to a 2004 study cosponsored by the US Centers for Disease Control and Prevention (CDC), the United States spends about $75 billion annually on obesity-related illnesses. A recent US CDC study confirmed that obesity-related deaths reached almost 200,000 in 2000. The WHO recommends sugar be restricted to 10 percent of calories consumed. The sugar industry, by contrast, insists a 25 percent sugar intake is safe. See WHO (2003). See also Edward Alden and Neil Buckley, "'Big Sugar' Fights to Maintain the Status Quo," *Financial Times*, February 26, 2004; Fiona Symon, "Cost of Obesity in the US," *Financial Times*, January 22, 2004; and Betsy McKay, "New Doubt Cast on Death Toll from Obesity," *Wall Street Journal*, December 3, 2004, A15.

77. See Rob Stein, "A Regular Soda a Day Boosts Weight Gain," *Washington Post*, August 25, 2004, A1. The longitudinal study on nondiet soda, involving 50,000 US nurses, was conducted with the assistance of the Harvard School of Public Health.

increase a person's risk of cancer.[78] After the WHO published a critical report in 2003, the global sugar and food industries rallied to dilute WHO efforts to combat obesity.[79]

In the short run, sugar demand is highly inelastic, but consumers are probably more responsive to sugar price increases in the long run.[80] Even though there are persuasive health reasons for keeping sugar prices high—and even raising them as a means of discouraging consumption—that does *not* mean that high prices should confer a windfall on sugar producers, the world norm today. It makes no more sense to enrich "Big Sugar" than it would to foster a Tobacco Monopoly or Whisky Trust. Instead, high sugar taxes, used to augment public revenues, should be preferred. That said, we turn to the actual practice of sugar policy under NAFTA.

NAFTA and Sugar

Within NAFTA (as in the world at large) the basic fight is over who gets rich from the high sugar prices that result from multiple means of protection. Since the government does not receive revenues, the contest is between competing producer interests.

North America contains two major sugar producers, the United States and Mexico.[81] The United States is the world's fourth largest sugar producer; Mexico is the seventh largest producer. Both countries extensively protect and support domestic sugar production. The key difference is that for most of the past decade Mexico has been a net sugar exporter, while the United States is a net importer (table 5.8). Over the past five years, US net sugar imports from the world averaged 1.3 million metric tons per

---

78. See Philip Abelson and Donald Kennedy, "The Obesity Epidemic," *Science*, June 4, 2004.

79. The US sugar lobby is the largest agricultural industry donor to political campaigns, giving more than $20 million to federal politicians since 1990. For details about the political economy of the US sugar industry, see Elliott (2005). In response to the 2003 WHO report, the US Sugar Association claimed the WHO used faulty science and threatened to ask congressional appropriators to challenge future US contributions to the WHO (running at some $400 million annually). See Edward Alden, Neil Buckley, and John Mason, "Sweet Deals: 'Big Sugar' Fights Threats from Free Trade," *Financial Times*, February 27, 2004. We thank Tim Josling for comments on an earlier draft.

80. Tobacco taxes illustrate the potential for limiting sugar consumption through vigorous application of the price mechanism. During 1990–93, when the Canadian government used taxes to double the real price of cigarettes, annual cigarette consumption per capita declined from about 81 packs to 52. Through high sugar prices, a similar decrease in sugar consumption might be achieved. See World Bank (1999).

81. Canada is a minor producer; imports cover almost all of the domestic consumption (see table 5.8).

Table 5.8 World production, supply, and distribution of centrifugal sugar (thousands of metric tons, raw value)

Country/year	Production	Imports	Exports	Domestic consumption[a]
United States[b]				
1992–93	7,111	1,827	389	8,343
1993–94	6,945	1,604	415	8,334
1994–95	7,191	1,664	472	8,470
1995–96	6,686	2,536	327	8,667
1996–97	6,536	2,517	191	8,868
1997–98	7,276	1,962	162	8,903
1998–99	7,597	1,655	209	9,079
1999–2000	8,203	1,484	112	9,318
2000–01	7,956	1,443	128	9,306
2001–02	7,174	1,393	124	8,978
2002–03	7,600	1,554	129	8,864
2003–04	8,070	1,437	145	8,573
Canada				
1992–93	123	1,110	42	1,200
1993–94	123	1,155	43	1,321
1994–95	182	1,090	50	1,158
1995–96	164	1,156	34	1,220
1996–97	157	1,062	19	1,190
1997–98	105	1,056	21	1,235
1998–99	95	1,129	13	1,240
1999–2000	73	1,207	13	1,265
2000–01	121	1,211	13	1,242
2001–02	88	1,239	14	1,254
2002–03	54	1,190	18	1,315
2003–04	98	1,350	157	1,275
Mexico				
1992–93	4,330	78	7	4,217
1993–94	3,823	94	0	4,393
1994–95	4,556	49	235	4,344
1995–96	4,642	234	646	4,343
1996–97	4,818	191	966	4,301
1997–98	5,486	31	1,076	4,391
1998–99	4,982	41	524	4,422
1999–2000	4,979	37	318	4,445
2000–01	5,220	43	155	4,481
2001–02	5,169	52	413	5,004
2002–03	5,229	65	46	5,092
2003–04	5,464	103	66	5,195
North America total				
1992–93	11,564	3,015	438	13,760
1993–94	10,891	2,853	458	14,048
1994–95	11,929	2,803	757	13,972
1995–96	11,492	3,926	1,007	14,230
1996–97	11,511	3,770	1,176	14,359
1997–98	12,867	3,049	1,259	14,529
1998–99	12,674	2,825	746	14,741
1999–2000	13,255	2,728	443	15,028
2000–01	13,297	2,697	296	15,029

(table continues next page)

Table 5.8 World production, supply, and distribution of centrifugal sugar (thousands of metric tons, raw value) *(continued)*

Country/year	Production	Imports	Exports	Domestic consumption[a]
2001–02	12,431	2,684	551	15,236
2002–03	12,883	2,809	193	15,271
2003–04	13,632	2,890	368	15,043
World total[c]				
1992–93	113,237	28,566	28,782	86,101
1993–94	111,015	30,538	29,734	85,849
1994–95	117,517	32,313	30,618	100,762
1995–96	122,568	33,228	34,920	103,073
1996–97	123,108	33,915	37,153	106,918
1997–98	125,265	33,494	37,208	109,265
1998–99	131,112	36,299	37,346	113,576
1999–2000	136,532	36,208	41,448	115,920
2000–01	130,495	38,786	37,686	117,531
2001–02	134,888	37,835	41,228	121,489
2002–03	147,336	39,309	45,724	123,521
2003–04	144,635	37,237	45,107	125,119

a. Domestic consumption reflects changes (not shown) in sugar stocks.
b. The US production, supply, and distribution estimates conform to those released in the World Agricultural Supply and Demand Estimates (WASDE), with the WASDE "miscellaneous" category allocated to domestic consumption. All data are presented on a fiscal year (October-September) basis. The US data include Puerto Rico.
c. Total distribution includes unrecorded imports.

Source: USDA Production, Supply, and Distribution database, 2002–04.

year;[82] Mexico's net exports to the world averaged a little less than 0.2 million tons.

Mexico has high tariffs of 18.33 percent on sugar imports from Canada and 17.31 percent on sugar imports from the United States. The United States has a minimal tariff rate of 0.85 percent on Canadian sugar exports and 1.02 percent on Mexican sugar exports. However, severe quantitative limits buttress US tariffs. By contrast, Canada is a net sugar importer and does not have TRQs or special export programs for sugar products. Canada imports between 85 and 90 percent of its sugar needs at the world market price, and domestic sugar prices move closely in parallel with world prices. Since 2001, Canada has eliminated its import tariffs on sugar imports from Mexico and the United States. As a result, low market prices of Canadian sugar attract US food processing companies, which are starting to relocate and take advantage of Canada's free-market sugar policy.[83] Practically the

---

82. To put the import figures in perspective, in 2001, US sugar production was 7.2 million metric tons raw value, and the United States imported 1.4 million metric tons. Domestic sugar consumption, taking into account stock drawdowns, reached 9.3 million metric tons. See USDA (2002b), Haley and Suarez (2002), and LMC International (2003).

83. For example, in 2003, Kraft Foods planned to close its Michigan-based Life Savers manufacturing plant and shift production to Montreal. Relocating to Canada is expected to save Kraft about $10 million per year. See "Sweet Subsidy," *Time,* February 25, 2002.

only Canadian concern is the absence of parity with Mexican access to the US refined sugar market, which is a consequence of the absence of US-Canadian agricultural liberalization.[84]

Since NAFTA, Mexico has successfully adapted technology and incentives to boost sugarcane recovery rates. Mexican sugar exports to the United States increased in raw value from an average of 2,000 metric tons per year during 1990–93 to 32,000 metric tons in 1994–2000.[85] Nevertheless, Mexican exports have been held back by the long-standing dispute over the NAFTA side letter agreement on sugar and the sugar-sweetener dispute. Mexican sugar producers want to gain completely free access to the US sugar market, and the US sugar producers want to prevent the projected flood of Mexican sugar into the United States.[86]

Similarly, US sweetener exporters want to gain free access to Mexico's market for soft drink sweeteners (table 5.9). Sweeteners, mainly HFCS, are a sugar substitute.[87] HFCS becomes progressively more popular as domestic policies push up the price of cane and beet sugar. Before January 2002, when the Mexican government imposed an HFCS tax, US sweetener producers successfully exported a small amount of HFCS to Mexico.[88] Since then, US exports of HFCS have dwindled. These sugar and sweetener disputes under NAFTA are direct offshoots of domestic sugar policies.

Domestic Sugar Policies

United States

US sugar policy is based on three mechanisms: loans that support domestic sugar production; TRQs, which restrict foreign sugar imports; and

---

84. In 1997, Canada's refined sugar exports to the United States were capped at 10,300 tons compared with Mexico's allocation of 27,954 tons. See Canadian Sugar Institute (2003). Both quotas gradually increase over time.

85. Based on US cane and beet sugar imports from Mexico. According to Haley and Suarez (1999) at the USDA, new technologies have led sugarcane recovery rates to rise from 9.08 percent in 1992 to 10.77 percent in 1997. See also Zahniser (2002).

86. Total Mexican sugar exports to the world declined from 1.1 million metric tons raw value in 1998 to 66,000 metric tons in 2004, mainly because of rising Mexican consumption. In the same period, total US sugar exports (which are historically small in absolute terms) declined from 162,000 to 124,000 metric tons. Canada is even less of a sugar exporter than the United States, and Canadian sugar exports declined from 21,000 to 14,000 metric tons in this period. Based on USDA Production, Supply, and Distribution database, November 2003. See Haley and Suarez (2002).

87. Other sugar substitutes include crystalline fructose, and high-intensity low-calorie sweeteners (aspartame).

88. From 1991 to 2001, the value of US exports to Mexico of HFCS and crystalline fructose increased from about $5.3 million (8,634 metric tons) in 1991 to $42 million in 2001 (117,124 metric tons). See Haley and Suarez (2002).

Table 5.9 US high-fructose corn syrup trade with NAFTA partners, 1993–2003 (volume in thousands of metric tons and value in millions of dollars)

Country	1993 Volume	1993 Value	1994 Volume	1994 Value	1995 Volume	1995 Value	1996 Volume	1996 Value	1997 Volume	1997 Value
US exports to										
Canada	50	15.9	17	9.0	25	7.2	23	6.7	66	16.2
Mexico	49	9.4	91	24.6	46	17.5	152	27.6	187	76.3
US imports from										
Canada	224	48.9	165	42.3	96	24.4	149	34.0	140	30.0
Mexico	0	0.1	0	0.0	0	0.0	0	0.0	3	0.9

Note: Data are based on HFCS-42 sweeteners and HFCS-55 syrups (HTS codes 1702.40.0000 and 1702.60.0050).

Source: USDA Foreign Agricultural Service (FATUS) database, 2004.

a reexport program to boost US sugar exports to world markets.[89] The economic cost for maintaining the sugar program is huge. According to the US General Accounting Office (GAO 2000), US sugar programs cost the economy about $900 million annually.[90] US sugar programs indirectly benefit sweetener producers, since artificially high sugar prices encourage the production of HFCS from corn.[91]

The 2002 Farm Act continued the price support loans provided under the 1996 Freedom to Farm Act, with one important difference: The 2002 Farm Act also requires the US Department of Agriculture (USDA) to operate the overall US sugar program at no budget cost to the government.[92] This trick is accomplished by giving the USDA authority to restrict sugar

---

89. The US government is slowly moving toward more direct income support programs. In August 2000, the USDA implemented the payment-in-kind program to reduce the US government's sugar inventory and lower the potential for loan forfeitures. Under the program, US sugar cane and beet producers can choose to divert acreage from sugar production in exchange for sugar held by the Commodity Credit Corporation. See USDA (2002b).

90. As of 1997, there were 973 farms in the entire United States growing sugarcane and 11,800 farms growing sugar beets. High yields in Florida and rising acreage and yields in Louisiana contribute to the growth of cane sugar production (see table 5.8). High domestic sugar prices in turn provide an incentive for US farmers to grow sugar beets instead of other crops, such as wheat. In 1998, the US General Accounting Office estimated that the sugar program cost domestic sweetener users about $1.9 billion per year (GAO 2000). See also Goombridge (2001).

91. Executives from the Corn Refiners Association, which represent HFCS manufacturers, argue that HFCS producers do not benefit from the sugar program because domestic HFCS prices are not directly linked to sugar prices. However, given the high rate of substitution between HFCS and sugar, the indirect benefit of high sugar prices is substantial. See GAO (2000); Gokcekus, Knowles, and Tower (2003); and David Orden's testimony (July 26, 2000).

92. Sugar loans (maximum term nine months) are nonrecourse, which means that when a loan matures, the USDA must accept sugar forfeited as collateral instead of cash repayment.

1998		1999		2000		2001		2002		2003	
Volume	Value	Volume	Value	Volume	Value	Volume	Value	Volume	Value	Volume	Value
166	47.4	101	30.3	92	25.7	79	25.4	90	29.1	92	30.5
186	53.1	165	54.9	132	40.7	111	34.9	5	1.6	2	1.0
53	30.7	147	31.8	147	28.9	182	36.9	167	33.1	151	34.5
1	1.2	2	1.9	2	2.5	1	1.3	0	0.2	26	6.2

imports and manage domestic marketing allotments and sugar payment-in-kind programs so that domestic sugar prices do not fall below effective price support levels, thereby removing the incentive for producers to forfeit their collateral.[93]

US import restrictions take the form of a TRQ. Under the TRQ, a low in-quota tariff of 1.66 cents per pound is levied on imports within the quota volume. A higher overquota tariff of 7.56 cents per pound (in 2003) was levied on Mexican imports that exceed the quota volume.[94] Under the 2002 Farm Act, the United States can restrict imports that exceed the minimum import quota of 1.2 million tons bound in the WTO. The US government assigns the raw cane sugar TRQs among 40 nations, based on sugar trade during 1975–81. In addition, the United States has a separate (albeit disputed) agreement under NAFTA that creates a separate TRQ for Mexican raw cane sugar. There are also TRQs on refined sugar, with separate allocations given to Canada and Mexico.[95]

By forfeiting sugar, the processor withdraws sugar from the market, thereby supporting higher US domestic sugar prices. By contrast, recourse loans would not allow sugar processors to simply forfeit sugar; instead, processors would have to repay the loan, plus interest, or declare bankruptcy. See Haley and Suarez (2002).

93. The current forfeiture price or loan rate is 18 cents per pound for cane sugar and 22.9 cents per pound for beet sugar. Unlike most commodity programs, sugar loans are made to processors rather than to producers, because sugarcane and sugar beets are perishable. See Haley and Suarez (2002). For a detailed analysis of the new sugar program provisions under the 2002 Farm Act, see Jurenas (2003).

94. The US above-quota, or second-tier, tariff on Mexican sugar declined from 15.2 cents per pound of raw cane sugar in 1995 to 7.56 cents in 2003 under NAFTA schedules. In contrast, the US above-quota tariff on sugar imported from the rest of the world declined from 17.62 cents in 1995 to 15.36 cents in 2002 pursuant to WTO commitments. See Roney (2003).

95. All other countries claim refined sugar TRQs on a first-come, first-served basis.

US sugar reexport programs, established in 1984, are another policy for bolstering the sugar market. There are two reexport programs—one is the Refined Sugar Re-Export Program for licensed raw sugarcane refiners; the other is the Sugar Containing Product Re-Export Program, which benefits food processors.[96] Both reexport programs are controversial because raw cane sugar imports under these programs are not subject to TRQs.[97] However, these reexport programs allow the US processors to remain competitive in world markets. Of the two programs, the US Sugar-Containing Product Re-Export Program is more contentious for Canada because benefits extend to a broader range of industrial sugar users and affect a greater volume of sugar exports.[98] In 1996, Canada initiated a NAFTA Chapter 20 consultation with the United States over the reexport programs. In 1997, Canada dropped the NAFTA consultations in exchange for a mutual understanding that preserved a fixed share of existing quotas. The bilateral agreement did not, however, address Canadian market access concerns. As of 2001, Canada's access to the US refined sugar market was significantly lower than Mexico's—10,300 tons compared with Mexico's 140,742 tons.

Mexico

The Mexican government subsidizes sugar through a combination of high import tariffs, domestic sugar production quotas, debt restructuring initiatives, and tax breaks. As a result, Mexico increased sugar production from 3.8 million metric tons in 1994 to 5.3 million metric tons in 2003. As of 2003, Mexico was exporting about 0.4 million metric tons of sugar per year.[99]

---

96. The Refined Sugar Re-Export Program allows licensed firms to import sugar at world prices (i.e., below US sugar prices) for refining and export, or for sale to licensed manufacturers of sugar-containing products that will be sold on world markets. While there are no limits on the quantity of sugar imports, the program had only eight licensed raw sugarcane refiners. Under the US Sugar-Containing Products Re-Export Program, US firms can buy sugar from any licensed refiner (refiners that will use world-priced sugar) for use in products that will be reexported onto the world market. According to the USDA's Foreign Agricultural Service, about 325 food-processing firms are licensed to participate in this program. See Haley and Suarez (2002) and USDA FAS (2002).

97. Imports and exports under the two programs averaged between 300,000 and 400,000 short tons raw value between fiscal years 1995 and 1999.

98. Eligible participants under the Sugar-Containing Products Re-Export Program include major industrial sugar users, small firms, and agricultural cooperatives. The total number of food processing firms benefiting from this program increased from 150 during the 1980s to 325 in 2002. During the same period, the volume of quota-exempt sugar exports jumped by about 160 percent from 50,000 tons to 130,000 tons. See also USDA FAS (2002).

99. Based on average Mexican sugar exports since 1998. See David Orden's testimony (July 26, 2000). See also LMC International (2003).

Import tariffs and other government controls serve to maintain high domestic sugar prices.[100] For example, Mexico's applied tariffs on sugar imports from the United States were around 17 percent in 2001 and about 18 percent on imports from Canada.[101]

While Mexico finished privatizing its sugar mills and partially deregulating its sugar industry in 1992, it increased protection for sugar by raising tariffs on raw sugar from 65 to 136 percent and from 73 to 127 percent on refined sugar (Mitchell 2004). As a result, domestic sugar prices increased by 60 percent and sugar production increased by 50 percent from 1990 to 2002. To manage the oversupply of sugar, the Mexican government has since 1997 acquired predetermined amounts of sugar for sale in export markets.[102] Nevertheless, in 2001, Mexican sugar production was so great that domestic sugar prices dropped by 40 percent, driving several Mexican sugar mills into bankruptcy.[103] To alleviate the resulting financial distress, the Mexican government created a $270 million last minute line of credit to pay farmers.

A government-controlled development bank also offers loans on easy terms to help the sugar industry pay its debt. Since 1998, FINASA has granted *quitas* or borrowing concessions to cane millers. As of 1999, FINASA held over $1.3 billion of concessional Mexican sugar industry debt.[104]

As Mexican government programs kept domestic sugar prices high in the late 1990s, one result was to attract imports of HFCS for use as a sweetener, especially in the soft drinks industry.[105] A combination of Mex-

---

100. Mexico's domestic wholesale price for refined sugar was 25.6 cents per pound in 2002, even higher than the US price of 21.5 cents per pound in 2003, which makes Mexico the fifth highest country in terms of price support for domestic sugar producers. US wholesale refined sugar price estimates are based on futures contract prices for number 14 raw cane sugar on the New York Coffee, Sugar, and Cocoa Exchange. For sugar price market information, see www.csce.com (accessed in November 2004). See also LMC International, Inc. (2003) and GAO (2000).

101. Applied tariffs do not include Mexico's AD duties of 20 percent on HFCS imports from the United States. Based on the World Bank's World Integrated Trade Solution (WITS) database, April 2003. See Mitchell (2004).

102. Domestic sugar production over the government-allocated sugar quota is either held in stocks, sold for nonfood uses, or exported. The Mexican government helps keep at least 600,000 metric tons raw value sugar from the domestic market. See Haley and Suarez (1999).

103. Among 60 Mexican sugar mills, some 30 are under receivership with a debt totaling $2 billion with the Mexican government alone. See Andrea Mandel-Campbell, "Commodities and Agriculture: Debt Mountain Threatens Mexican Sugar," *Financial Times*, June 28, 2001.

104. All outstanding sugar industry debt was supposed to be transferred from FINASA to another agency, FIDELIQ. But in 2003, FINASA was still offering concessions at 21.8 percent of any outstanding principal repaid by borrowers.

ico's large HFCS market and excess supply of HFCS among US sweetener producers makes Mexico a natural market for US exports.[106] To curb the use of HFCS, the Mexican government imposed AD duties in 1998 on US imports of sweetener products. After these measures were successfully contested and removed, Mexico then imposed in January 2002 a 20 percent tax on HFCS used in soft drinks.[107] As a result, US HFCS producers have struggled to enter the Mexican HFCS market. From 1998 to 2003, US HFCS exports to Mexico declined from 186,000 metric tons ($53.1 million) to 2,000 metric tons ($1 million) (table 5.9).

Sugar Side Letter Controversy

Under the original NAFTA sugar provisions, Mexico's maximum duty-free access to the US sugar market was supposed to increase from 25,000 metric tons raw value to at least 150,000 metric tons beginning in 2000.[108] After that, the Mexican quota would increase by 10 percent per year. Quantitative restrictions on US imports of Mexican sugar could end by 2009. However, if Mexico became a "net surplus producer" for two consecutive years, it would gain quota-free access to the US market starting in 2001. These terms provoked a squall in Congress at the time of NAFTA ratification and led former USTR Mickey Kantor to negotiate a NAFTA side letter agreement on sugar.

The controversial NAFTA sugar side letter changed key provisions for Mexican sugar exports to the US market. Unlike the original provision, which did not impose caps on Mexican sugar exports to the United States, the revised side letter curtailed Mexico's duty-free access to the US market to a maximum of 250,000 metric tons annually. More important, the side letter changed the formula for calculating surplus production, making it harder for Mexico to qualify as a net surplus producer. The original NAFTA provisions calculate Mexico's status as a net surplus sugar pro-

---

105. Before the Mexican government imposed taxes on HFCS exports from the United States, Mexican soft drink producers were using corn syrup as a close substitute for sugar. HFCS is also a leading competitor for the US sweetener market and, even as HFCS prices declined, domestic production expanded from 6.8 million tons in 1992 to 9.5 million tons in 1999. See GAO (2000) and Bolling (2002).

106. Mexico is the world's second largest market for soft drinks.

107. Most corn syrup used in Mexico is imported from the United States or made in Mexico by two subsidiaries of US companies. Since 1994, Arancia has been associated with the US firm Corn Products International. The other Mexican company, Almidones Mexicanos, is affiliated with Archer Daniels Midland Co. See "Mexico's New Soft Drink Tax Raises Stakes in Sweetener Fight with US," *Inside US Trade*, January 11, 2002.

108. In addition, under the original NAFTA agreement, Mexican sugar exports were also limited to no more than Mexico's net surplus production of sugar, defined as domestic sugar production less domestic sugar consumption. See Haley and Suarez (2002).

ducer based on its domestic sugar production minus domestic sugar consumption. The two countries disagree, however, on whether the side letter indicates that Mexico's sugar production needs to exceed its domestic consumption of both sugar and HFCS.[109]

Even more confusing, there are two versions of the side letter. The US version of the side letter is dated November 3, 1993, and was sent to Congress as part of its NAFTA legislative package. Unlike the US version of the side letter, Mexico's amended side letter, dated November 4, 1993, does not include revised calculations for Mexico to reach net sugar producer status. In essence, the dispute revolves around two issues: the amount of Mexican sugar access to the US market beginning in fiscal 2001 and the mechanism through which Mexican sugar would have unlimited access to the US market (see table 5.10 for a comparison between sugar provisions under the original NAFTA and revised side letters).[110]

Mexico and the United States have never been able to agree on key details of the side letter and whether it limits Mexican sugar imports to 250,000 tons annually. Moreover, Mexico claims it never signed the November 3 side letter that helped ratify NAFTA (table 5.10).[111] Instead, the Mexican government argues that its November 4 side letter does not include HFCS consumption in the formula used to define net producer status. The Mexican version allows Mexico to export its total net surplus production of sugar duty-free to the United States beginning in October 2000. US sugar and sweetener producers are fighting this interpretation: If the US version of the sugar side letter is abandoned, the NAFTA tier-two tariff would allow Mexican sugar exports to enter the United States outside current quota restraints and at a progressively lower tariff.[112]

---

109. Under the original NAFTA sugar side letter, Mexico would gain unlimited access to the US sugar market in 2001 instead of being permitted to ship 250,000 tons annually until gaining unlimited market access by 2009. In response, the US sugar industry, led by eight sugar associations, voiced concerns to US congressional members about the potential for Mexican sugar to replace HFCS in the US market. As a result, US negotiators reneged on the original draft NAFTA sugar agreement and submitted to Congress a controversial second side letter that Mexico claims it never signed. We thank Tim Josling and Kim Elliott for this observation and for providing written comments to an earlier draft. See "Sugar Lobby Eschews Legislative Fix, Keeps Up Push for Side Letter," *Inside US Trade*, October 22, 1993; and "US-Mexico Talks Fail to Resolve Conflicting Views on Sugar Access," *Inside US Trade*, April 24, 1998.

110. See "US, Mexican NAFTA Sugar Side Letters Reveal Two Key Differences," *Inside US Trade*, March 20, 1998; Pav Jordan, "Mexico Senator Says NAFTA Sugar Side Letter Invalid," *Reuters*, October 11, 2000; and "Text: US-Mexico Draft Side Letter on NAFTA Sugar," *Inside US Trade*, November 5, 1993.

111. For details about the two versions of the side letter, see "US, Mexican NAFTA Sugar Side Letters Reveal Two Key Differences," *Inside US Trade*, March 20, 1998. See also "US Abandons Side Letter as It Forges Ahead with Sugar Talks," *Inside US Trade*, August 16, 2002.

112. As of April 2003, the tier-two tariff for sugar is 7.5 cents per pound and will be reduced by 1.5 cents a pound per year until the sugar tariff is eliminated in 2008. See "Zoellick To Raise Mexico Sugar in Hopes of Resolution This Year," *Inside US Trade*, February 28, 2003.

Table 5.10 Comparison of sugar side letter provisions

Original side letter	Revised side letter	November 3, 1993 US version	November 4, 1993 Mexican version
Fiscal 1994–2008 (first 15 years):		**Fiscal 2000–08:**	Unlimited Mexican access to the US sugar market (i.e., no stipulation to exclude paragraph 16)
■ Maximum Mexican sugar exports limited to no more than net surplus production of sugar, equivalent to the difference between domestic sugar production and consumption	■ Changed definition of surplus production of sugar that would limit Mexico's ability to export sugar to the United States	■ If Mexico reaches net surplus producer status, the United States would allow maximum Mexican sugar exports of 250,000 tons	
■ Minimum Mexican sugar export of 7,258 metric tons raw cane sugar duty-free into United States	■ Revised surplus production status defined by whether Mexican sugar production was greater than Mexican consumption of both sugar and high-fructose corn syrup (HFCS)	■ Beginning fiscal 2001 marketing year (year 7), Mexico can export up to 150,000 tons	
		■ From fiscal 2002 to fiscal 2008 (years 8 to 14), Mexico can ship 110 percent of previous marketing year's ceiling according to original NAFTA terms	
Fiscal 1994–2000 (first six years):	**Fiscal 1994–2000** (first six years):		
■ Maximum duty-free access for Mexican sugar exports at no more than 25,000 metric tons raw value (mtrv)	■ Maximum duty-free access for Mexican sugar exports equal to the projected net surplus production up to 25,000 metric tons	■ Denies Mexico unlimited access to the US sugar market by stipulating that paragraph 16 of Section A of NAFTA Annex 703.2 (waiver for quantitative limits) would "not apply"	

By fiscal 2001
(year 7):

- Maximum duty-free access for Mexican sugar exports raised to 150,000 metric tons
- Maximum duty-free access for Mexican sugar exports will increase by 10 percent every year

Condition for unlimited Mexican sugar exports into the United States:

- Mexico must achieve net surplus producer status for two consecutive marketing years

---

- If Mexico does not qualify as a net surplus sugar producer, it can still export maximum 7,258 metric tons duty-free (as bound in US WTO schedule).
- No conditions provided for unlimited Mexican sugar exports into the United States.
- 2001–07: Maximum duty-free access for Mexican sugar exports to the United States is measured by its surplus of up to 250,000 metric tons.

Vague definition for calculating Mexican net surplus producer status:

- Only indicates that calculation should include "consumption" of HFCS

Vague definition for calculating Mexico net surplus producer status:

- Only indicates that calculation should include HFCS
- Mexican officials claim surplus producer status suggests both HFCS production and consumption are used to determine net producer status (i.e., making it easier to achieve net sugar surplus producer status)

Note: The side letters use the term "marketing year," which closely coincides with fiscal year.

Sources: USDA (2002c); "US-Mexico Draft Side Letter on NAFTA Sugar," Inside US Trade, November 5, 1993.

US-Canada Agreement on Sugar

NAFTA allows Mexico and Canada to maintain their tariffs on sugar. However, before NAFTA, the United States and Canada had negotiated their own bilateral agreement on sugar. The CUSFTA barred the United States from imposing trade restrictions on Canadian food exports containing 10 percent or less sugar.[113] This changed when the United States created a quota for refined sugar imports under the WTO, which significantly reduced Canada's access to the US sugar market.[114] In 1997, a bilateral understanding was reached. The United States would allow Canada an extra quota for refined sugar access on the condition that Canada would not challenge US reexport programs under the NAFTA dispute settlement mechanisms.[115]

Sugar Disputes under NAFTA

After Mexico imposed AD duties on HFCS imports in 1998, US firms initiated two claims against Mexico, invoking NAFTA dispute settlement Chapters 11 and 19.[116] The United States initiated its first sugar dispute against Mexico under NAFTA Chapter 19 in 1998.[117] According to the US

---

113. According to CUSFTA Article 707, the United States "shall not introduce or maintain any quantitative import restriction or import fee on any good originating in Canada containing 10 percent or less sugar by dry weight for purposes of restricting the sugar content of such good."

114. In 1994, the United States imposed a global TRQ of 22,000 tons of refined sugar under the WTO.

115. The 1997 bilateral understanding allowed Canada to export up to 10,300 tons of refined sugar and a maximum of 59,250 tons of sugar-containing products. Canada could also compete for the unallocated portion of the global sugar TRQ of about 7,500 tons of refined sugar. See AAFC (2001).

116. Partly in response to US tariffs on Mexican broom corn brooms, Mexico increased HFCS import duties in December 1996. After the United States complied with the NAFTA Chapter 20 determination on the *Broom Corn Brooms* case, Mexico reduced the 12.5 percent ad valorem rate on US HFCS imports to the NAFTA-specified rate of 6 percent in 1998. However, the US-Mexico HFCS dispute did not come to an end. Soon afterward, in May 1998, the United States initiated a Chapter 19 HFCS dispute against Mexico, which was settled in June 2002, and brought two separate cases under the WTO. In October 2001, the WTO Appellate Body upheld the panel determination that Mexico had not complied with requirements of the WTO Antidumping Agreement to justify imposing AD duties on HFCS. In 2000, Mexico initiated bilateral discussions with the United States over US sugar TRQs. The United States also initiated cases under NAFTA Chapter 11—one filed by US Corn Products International in January 2002 and another by Archer Daniels Midland Co. and A. E. Staley Manufacturing Co. in October 2003. See WTO (2001).

117. Mexico's administrative agency, SECOFI, imposed different AD duties on exports of HFCS grades 42 and 55. Specifically, SECOFI applied temporary AD duties on specific US HFCS exporters, ranging from $63.75 to $175.50 per metric ton. US exporters directly tar-

Corn Refiners' Association, the Mexican government encouraged domestic sugar and soft drink bottling industries to limit HFCS imports in exchange for a 20 percent price discount on sugar for soft drinks.[118] In August 2001, the NAFTA Chapter 19 panel decided Mexico should remove its tariffs against US HFCS exports and refund collected AD duties to the United States. Mexico complied with the NAFTA panel ruling but also limited the quantity of US HFCS exports.[119]

The dispute did not end there. In January 2002, the Mexican Congress passed legislation that imposed a 20 percent tax on soft drinks made with HFCS, and the US-based Corn Products International, Inc. initiated a second sugar-related dispute under NAFTA Chapter 11. The consequences of the newly imposed HFCS tax were immediate. As of early 2002, US HFCS exports plummeted by 69 percent from 117,000 metric tons in fiscal 2001 to about 36,000 metric tons in 2002.[120]

Arancia CPC, a subsidiary of Corn Products International, claims the HFCS tax costs the company between $35 million and $40 million in annual operating income and forced it to shut down its HFCS plant in Mexico.[121] Arancia CPC claims the HFCS tax led soft drink bottlers to cancel

---

gctcd by SECOFI include A. E. Staley Manufacturing, Cargill, Inc., Archer Daniels Midland Co., and CPC International, Inc. In January 1998, SECOFI imposed permanent import tariffs on HFCS products. US producers argue that both the AD tariffs and the permanent tariffs are inconsistent with NAFTA. See Haley and Suarez (1999). See also "US Mulls WTO Case In Response to Mexican AD Decision on HFCS," *Inside US Trade*, January 30, 1998.

118. A restraint agreement between Mexican sugar producers and soft drink bottlers was intended to limit the usage of HFCS to 350,000 tons per year. See Haley and Suarez (1999). See also "NAFTA Panel Finds Against Mexican Duties on US Corn Sweetener," *Inside US Trade*, August 10, 2001.

119. Mexico allows US HFCS exports up to 148,000 metric tons at a low tariff rate of 1.5 percent. Any US HFCS exports above that amount will face an AD duty of 210 percent. This would adversely affect US HFCS producers as the United States historically exports more than 148,000 metric tons of HFCS per year into Mexico. See "Mexico Ends Antidumping Duties on Corn Syrup," *Kiplinger Agriculture Letter* 73 no. 9, May 3, 2002. See also final NAFTA Chapter 19 panel decision, available at www.nafta-sec-alena.org/images/pdf/ma98010e. pdf (accessed in April 2003).

120. Even with duties applied between 1998 and 2001, US producers still exported about 120,000 tons of HFCS into Mexico per year. Mexico's new HFCS tax does not apply to soft drinks made with cane sugar, which Mexico produces in excess. Under pressure from the USTR and US agricultural groups, President Fox temporarily suspended the tax until Mexico's Supreme Court overturned his decision in July 2002. See "Mexico Reinstates HFCS Tax," *Food & Drink Weekly* 8, no. 28, July 22, 2002. See Haley and Suarez (2003).

121. According to the US National Corn Growers Association and the Corn Refiners Association, US corn producers have lost market opportunities for more than 20 million bushels of corn. Jaime Gallo of Arancia CPC claims that the HFCS tax potentially jeopardizes 18,000 direct and indirect jobs. See Josefina Real, "New Tax Forces Shutdown of Mexico Fructose Plant," *Reuters*, January 10, 2002; BNA (2003b, 2003c).

sweetener orders and estimated the tax cost $220 million in losses for the domestic Mexican fructose industry in 2002.

Recent US-Mexican sweetener negotiations suggest a possible breakthrough. The January 2004 US draft proposal suggests that Mexico forgo its right under NAFTA to unlimited access to the US sugar market after 2008. In return, Mexican overquota sugar exports would face either the high MFN tariff or lower tier-two NAFTA agreed tariff rate.[122] The fact that a proposed deal has been floated suggests that Mexico is willing to agree to reduced access to the US sugar market, though the market access numbers are far from agreed.[123]

Sugar Recommendations

The sprawling web of sugar claims and litigation reflects the difficulty of liberalizing trade in an agricultural commodity that has been protected and subsidized for decades. The fundamental problem is that neither the United States nor Mexico subscribes to free-market principles when it comes to sugar. Both countries seek to maintain sugar prices well above world levels—not to discourage consumption but rather to augment the revenues of cane, beet, and HFCS producers.

Given this objective, sugar side letters, tariffs, taxes, penalty duties, and litigation all essentially revolve around the division of economic rent created by the overarching regime of protection and subsidies. The original NAFTA text seemed to promise that Mexican and US sugar producers could eventually compete—free of border barriers—under a common umbrella of protection against the world sugar market. After the deal was sealed, both countries had second thoughts, centered on the intrusion of HFCS into the domain of cane and beet sugar. These doubts were compounded by ingenious and differentiated means of subsidization by the

---

122. The US sugar industry wants to prevent Mexican sugar exports from exceeding the 268,000-ton level. Higher Mexican shipments could push total US imports above the 1.523 million ton threshold and jeopardize the operation of the current US sugar program. The concern is that if US sugar imports exceed 1.523 million short tons, the US secretary of agriculture must lift marketing allotments that limit the quantity that domestic producers can sell in the United States. One potential result is that the high price of US sugar would sharply decline, which is something that US sugar producers want to avoid. See "US, Mexico Sweetener Talks Advance on Most Critical Hurdle," *Inside US Trade*, February 6, 2003. Under the draft US-Mexico sweetener agreement, Mexico sugar exports could reach 114,000 tons in 2004 and increase to 268,000 tons in the next two years. See "US, Mexico Sweetener Talks Advance on Most Critical Hurdle," *Inside US Trade*, February 2004.

123. Mexico and the United States also disagree on how to change reexport programs to prevent the circumvention of trade limits through sugar-containing products. See "US, Mexican Sweetener Industries Set for Fresh HFCS Talks Next Week," *Inside US Trade*, May 21, 2004.

Mexican and US governments. The result is a tangled web of claims and litigation with no resolution in sight. Indeed, Mexico cites the failure to resolve the sugar question as an argument to scale back its NAFTA commitments in other key commodities.[124]

Our recommendation differs sharply from the prevailing direction of NAFTA policy, which is focused, as we have said, on dividing the pie of protection and subsidy benefits between producer groups. In view of the significant adverse health effects of excessive sugar consumption, we urge NAFTA members to appoint a commission to recommend an appropriate excise tax on sugar and HFCS designed—like cigarette taxes—to both curtail consumption and raise revenue to offset the healthcare burden. Once the excise tax is imposed, free trade should be allowed in sugar and HFCS, but a portion of the excise tax revenue should be devoted to helping farmers and processors adjust, over a period of about 10 years. The excise tax should also provide significant funding for environmental purposes, including a reduction of sugar acreage in the ecologically sensitive Florida Everglades. Excise tax funds could be used to purchase sugar acreage and return the land to its natural condition. The funds could also be used to compensate sugar plantations that do not use environmentally harmful phosphorous fertilizers.[125]

To manage the transition toward free trade in HFCS and sugar, the United States and Mexico should also establish a comprehensive interim agreement. As an example, the United States could agree to a higher quota for Mexican sugar exports of 268,000 metric tons (compared with the existing 250,000 metric tons), starting in 2006, with an equivalent amount of US HFCS exports to Mexico. To mollify US sugar industry concerns, Mexican sugar shipments could be split 60 percent raw and 40 percent refined. Similarly, US HFCS exports could be split as 60 percent soft drink industry and 40 percent bakery industry.[126]

---

124. As of January 2003, all tariffs on pork, poultry, and rice were eliminated under NAFTA. However, Mexico recently hinted that without a sweetener deal allowing Mexican sugar exports duty-free into the United States by 2008, Mexico might impose trade barriers on pork and poultry. See "Mexico Weighs Request for Roll-Back of NAFTA Farm Tariff Cuts," *Inside US Trade*, January 3, 2003.

125. For a detailed analysis of the environmental harm caused by sugar cultivation, see Humphreys, van Bueren, and Stoeckel (2003).

126. So far, transition proposals have been stalemated by US efforts to protect cane refiners and Mexican attempts to limit the presence of US HFCS in Mexico's soft drinks industry. The United States, for example, prefers that Mexican sugar exports to the United States be split 80 percent raw and 20 percent refined; Mexico proposes that US HFCS exports follow a 50/50 split between soft drinks and bakery industries. See Jurenas (2003).

The Corn Saga

Newspaper stories frequently blame NAFTA for the plight of Mexican farmers, especially poor corn farmers.[127] The implication is that NAFTA can be held responsible for destroying the rural way of life in Mexico and driving illegal migrants to US cities. Even the Carnegie Endowment for International Peace cites the liberalization of corn trade as a great NAFTA failure (Audley et al. 2003). But multiple adversities are behind the plight of rural Mexican corn farmers. In this section, we try to distinguish fact from fantasy in the Mexican corn saga.

The place to start is with the facts on corn production, acreage, and trade. Basically, there are two types of corn: yellow and white. Yellow corn—the kind that the United States produces in abundance—is predominantly used as livestock feed. White corn—the kind that Mexico mainly produces—is largely used for human consumption (though white corn is sometimes used as livestock feed in Mexico as well). Under NAFTA, yellow and white corn are treated as the same commodity, even though Mexican farmers cultivate primarily white corn and US producers have the strongest advantage in yellow corn.

Mexican tariffs on corn under NAFTA are supposed to be eliminated by January 1, 2008.[128] Starting from the implementation of NAFTA in January 1994, liberalization was to be achieved by gradually expanding the TRQ. The initial TRQ on corn in 1994 was set at 2.5 million tons per year. This figure was set to expand by 3 percent per year, reaching 3.8 million tons by 2008 (table 5.11).

The overquota tariff rate for US and Canadian corn exports to Mexico was set at 215 percent in 1994 ($206 per metric ton). This overquota tariff will gradually decline to zero by January 1, 2008 (box 5.3). But while Mexico's corn import quotas under NAFTA reached only 3.1 million tons in 2001, Mexican corn imports actually surpassed 5 million tons annually from 1998 to 2003. In fact, the Mexican government allowed tariff-free corn imports to exceed NAFTA-mandated TRQs almost every year since 1994 (table 5.11), partly to satisfy the demands of the Mexican livestock and starch industries.[129] The Mexican government waived at least $2 bil-

---

127. For example, one journalist recounted the trials of Domingo Tena, a corn farmer from Michoacan state, now working in Chicago. Hugh Dellios, "10 Years Later, NAFTA Harvests a Stunted Crop," *Chicago Tribune*, December 14, 2003, A1.

128. According to Tim Josling, the Mexican government invoked the spirit of NAFTA both to phase out quantitative restrictions on corn more quickly than the letter requires and to push for agricultural reforms generally.

129. Under NAFTA, the Mexican government allocates TRQs directly to privileged users, often on a first-come, first-served basis. At one time, Conasupo indirectly allocated corn quotas to tortilla producers. See Yunez-Naude (2003) and Seidband (2004).

Table 5.11 US overquota corn exports to Mexico, 1994–2008

Year	Tariff rate quota level set by NAFTA (millions of metric tons)	Actual US corn exports Volume (millions of metric tons)	Actual US corn exports Value (millions of dollars)
1994	2.5	3.1	340
1995	2.6	2.9	359
1996	2.7	6.3	1,003
1997	2.7	2.6	317
1998	2.8	5.2	590
1999	2.9	5.1	527
2000	3.0	5.2	511
2001	3.1	5.7	626
2002	3.2	5.4	639
2003	3.3	5.7	688
2004	3.4	n.a.	n.a.
2005	3.5	n.a.	n.a.
2006	3.6	n.a.	n.a.
2007	3.7	n.a.	n.a.
2008	3.8	n.a.	n.a.

n.a. = not applicable

Source: USDA (2002a); USDA Foreign Agricultural Service (FAIUS) database, 2004.

lion in tariff revenues, at least two-thirds on yellow corn imports, using the argument that cheaper corn imports were necessary to meet growing domestic livestock demand and control inflation. In fact, domestic demand for yellow feed corn increased more than fourfold, from 1.7 million metric tons in 1990 to 9.5 million metric tons in 2002 (table 5.12).[130] Mexican per capita consumption of beef rose from 12.3 to 16.4 kilograms in the same period. By contrast, US per capita consumption of beef remained about 29 kilograms during this period (table 5.13).[131]

---

130. According to Lloyd Day, USDA spokesperson, roughly 80 percent of US corn exports to Mexico is yellow corn used primarily to feed growing demand for Mexican livestock. See Olga R. Rodriguez, "Oxfam Reports on US Subsidies in Mexico," Associated Press, August 28, 2003.

131. Data are based on USDA Economic Research Service Food Consumption Per Capita Data System, 2003.

Box 5.3   Timeline of NAFTA corn tariff phaseouts

Canadian tariffs

On US corn:

- were completely eliminated on January 1, 1998, after a nine-year phaseout period

On Mexican corn:

- will be completely eliminated on January 1, 2008

Mexican tariffs

On US corn:

- immediate elimination of import licensing requirement on January 1, 1994

- immediate establishment of duty-free tariff rate quotas (TRQs)

- in-quota tariffs set at 2.5 million metric tons on January 1, 1994: In-quota tariffs will gradually increase by 3 percent per year during a 14-year transition period, until TRQ is completely eliminated by January 1, 2008; TRQ in 2001: 3.1 million metric tons

- overquota tariffs based on gradual transition period: Overquota tariff equaled $206 per metric ton but not less than 215 percent, of which 24 percent was gradually eliminated in 2000; remaining overquota tariff will phase out by 2008; 1994: overquota tariff equaled greater of 206.4 percent ad valorem or 19.7 cents per kilogram; 2001: overquota tariff equaled greater of 127.1 percent ad valorem or 12.1 cents per kilogram; 2001 scheduled overquota tariffs replaced with minor overquota tariffs of 1 percent on yellow corn and 3 percent on white corn until end of 2001

On Canadian corn:

- immediate elimination of import licensing requirement on January 1, 1994

- immediate establishment of duty-free TRQs

- in-quota tariffs set at 1,000 metric tons on January 1, 1994

- in-quota tariffs will gradually increase by 3 percent per year during a 14-year transition period, until TRQ is completely eliminated by January 1, 2008

- TRQ in 2001: 1,230 metric tons

- no overquota tariffs

US tariffs

On Canadian corn:

- were completely eliminated on January 1, 1998, after a nine-year phaseout period

On Mexican corn:

- were eliminated on January 1, 1994

Source: Zahniser and Link (2002).

Table 5.12 Corn feed used for domestic consumption in NAFTA countries
(millions of metric tons)

Year	Canada	Mexico	United States
1990	5.8	1.7	117.1
1991	5.4	2.6	121.9
1992	4.8	3.6	133.4
1993	6.0	5.5	118.9
1994	6.3	5.4	138.7
1995	5.9	8.1	119.2
1996	6.3	7.1	134.0
1997	6.8	7.2	139.2
1998	7.1	7.5	138.9
1999	7.0	8.3	143.9
2000	7.9	8.8	148.4
2001	9.7	8.4	148.9
2002	10.3	9.5	141.3
2003	9.0	11.0	147.3

Source: USDA Production, Supply, and Distribution database, 2004.

Corn Production

US corn production is concentrated in midwestern states with regular rainfall patterns and relies on heavy machinery, chemicals, and high-yielding varieties. Mexican corn production, by contrast, is carried out mostly by small-scale, labor-intensive farmers, who cultivate multiple varieties.[132] Between 70 and 80 percent of total Mexican corn production is on rain-fed farms. About 30 percent of these rain-fed farms are *ejidos*, collective communities that are usually poor (Rosson and Adock 2003). As a consequence, average Mexican corn production yields in 2003 were a fraction (2.8 tons per hectare) of average US corn production yields (9.8 tons per hectare; see table 5.14).[133] Nevertheless, Mexican corn production in-

---

132. Before NAFTA, about 60 percent of cultivated agricultural land was used for corn, and that land yielded about 60 percent of total agricultural output (measured by sales value). After NAFTA, some 67 percent of cultivated land was used for corn, but the monetary yield fell to about 36 percent of the value of agricultural output. See Nadal (2000).

133. A comparison with Argentina, a major corn producer and among the top three world corn exporters, reveals the low productivity of Mexican corn farmers. In 1960, average corn production yields in Argentina and Mexico were about 2 and 1 tons per hectare, respectively. By 2001, average corn production in Argentina reached about 6 tons per hectare while Mexican corn farmers yielded about 2.8 tons per hectare. Based on UN Food and Agriculture Organization FAOSTAT database, 2003.

Table 5.13   Per capita beef consumption (kilograms)

Country	1990	2002	Percent change 1990–2002
Canada	34.0	30.0	−12
Mexico	12.3	16.4	33
United States	29.0	28.7	−1

Source: USDA Production, Supply, and Distribution database, 2004.

creased by 44 percent from 14.6 million metric tons to 21 million metric tons between 1990 and 2003. US corn production rose just 27 percent, from 201.5 million metric tons to 257 million metric tons, while Canadian corn production increased 35 percent, from 7.1 million metric tons to 9.6 million metric tons (see table 5.14).

Corn Prices

The Mexican government embarked on its program of unilateral liberalization of corn and Mexican domestic corn prices fell in dollar terms from $4.69 per bushel in 1995 to $3.65 per bushel in 1997 (and have since remained at about that level; see table 5.15). Even though corn prices have fallen by about 20 percent since 1995, Mexican corn production remained high.[134] Since 1994, the area under corn has remained fairly constant at 7 million to 8 million hectares (see table 5.16). In other words, lower corn prices did not prompt Mexican farmers to permanently reallocate land to other crops or to leave farm life altogether.

Corn Trade

The United States is the largest corn exporter in the world. US global corn exports increased by 17 percent from 40.7 million metric tons (worth $4.5 billion) in 1993 to 47.6 million metric tons in 2002 ($5.1 billion).[135] US corn exports to NAFTA partners, expressed as a share of total corn exports, steadily increased from 3 percent in 1993 ($0.2 billion) to 21 percent in 2002 ($1.1 billion; see tables 5.17 and 5.18).[136] US corn exports comprise

---

134. Although Oxfam argues that real corn prices declined by more than 70 percent between 1994 and 2001, a careful analysis suggests Mexican corn prices declined by about 10 percent in dollar terms over this period (see table 5.15). See Oxfam (2003) and Nadal (2000).

135. US global corn exports declined slightly in 2003 to 43.2 million metric tons ($4.9 billion).

136. In 1993, the United States imported just $61 million worth of corn from the world, mostly from NAFTA countries (about 67 percent). By 2002, the total value of US corn imports reached $137 million, of which $34 million was from NAFTA partners. US corn exports to

Table 5.14 Corn yield and production in NAFTA countries

Country	1960	1970	1980	1990	2003
Yield (tons per hectare)					
Canada	5.1	5.8	6.2	7.6	8.6
Mexico	1.1	1.3	2.0	2.2	2.8
United States	4.3	5.0	6.3	8.2	9.8
Production (millions of metric tons)					
Canada	.7	2.6	5.7	7.1	9.6
Mexico	6.2	8.9	12.4	14.6	21.0
United States	91.4	105.5	168.6	201.5	257.0

Source: UN FAOSTAT database, 2004; USDA (2004b).

about 40 percent of total US grain exports to Mexico (USDA 2003a). Although there is some concern in Canada that rising US corn exports could injure Canadian corn producers, Canada plays a relatively minor role in corn disputes under NAFTA (table 5.19).[137] The corn saga is essentially a US-Mexico drama.

Mexico consistently ranks as the second or third largest market for US corn, buying virtually 100 percent of its imports from the United States (Seidband 2004). During 1993–2003, the value of US corn exports to Mexico increased from $75 million (0.3 million metric tons) to $688 million (5.7 million metric tons). Most of the increase was in yellow corn, and the value of US yellow corn exports to Mexico as a proportion of total corn exports increased from about 39 to 73 percent (tables 5.17 and 5.18).[138]

Background of US-Mexico Corn Dispute

Corn is a staple in the Mexican diet (notably tortillas) and currently represents around 36 percent of the value of agricultural output in Mexico (Nadal 2000). About 68 percent of the Mexican agricultural workforce,

Canada meet feed grain demand and ethanol and sweetener production; these exports reached 4 million metric tons valued at $395 million in 2002, more than five times their value in 1994. US corn imports from Canada were 0.2 million metric tons in 2002. Based on Statistics Canada (2003) and USDA Foreign Agricultural Service (FATUS) database. See also Myles and Cahoon (2004).

137. Canada does not trade much corn with Mexico. During 1993–2002, Canada exported on average about 74 percent of its corn to the United States and about 99 percent of its corn imports were from the United States.

138. Almost all US corn imports from Mexico during 1993–2003 were white corn for human consumption. The total value of US corn imports from Mexico increased from $0.5 million (about 1,000 metric tons) in 1993 to nearly $3 million (about 6,000 metric tons) in 2003 (see table 5.18). See USDA Foreign Agricultural Service (FATUS) database, 2003.

Table 5.15　NAFTA prices for corn
(US dollars per bushel)

Year	Canada	Mexico[a]	United States[b]
1991	2.22	4.39	2.37
1992	2.26	4.57	2.07
1993	2.52	4.84	2.50
1994	2.23	4.11	2.26
1995	3.81	4.69	3.24
1996	2.71	3.96	2.71
1997	2.53	3.65	2.43
1998	1.86	3.65	1.94
1999	1.81	3.54	1.82
2000	2.02	3.78	1.85
2001	2.15	3.72	1.91
2002	2.32	3.69	2.32
2003	2.15	3.75	2.20

a. White corn prices are calculated as weighted average of Conasupo buying prices for maize producers.
b. Data are average price.

Sources: Mexico: 1991–94 estimates are based on Nadal (2000); 1995–2000 data are minimum prices for corn producers based on OECD, *Agricultural Policies in OECD Countries, 1998–2002;* and 2001–03 data are based on SECOFI, Mexico's Ministry of Economy, 2003–04, Sistema de Información Empresarial Mexicano, www.secofi-siem.gob.mx/portalsiem (accessed in June 2003). United States: 1991–2001 data are based on CRB (2003); and 2002–03 data are based on *Grain Price Outlook,* University of Purdue and University of Illinois at Urbana-Champaign (2000). Canada: Data are based on AAFC (2003a).

and about the same percentage of cultivated land in Mexico, is engaged in growing corn (Nadal 2000; Veeman, Veeman, and Hoskins 2001). At the turn of the 20th century, some 2,000 families owned 87 percent of the rural land in Mexico. The Mexican revolution, in 1910, distributed much of this land to ejidos. Today about 3.5 million farmers hold over 103 million hectares, and the individual *ejidatorios* on average cultivate small plots of about 5 hectares or less.[139] Ejidos are responsible for about 62 percent of total domestic corn production, about 70 percent on rain-fed land. Most ejido holdings are too fragmented to enable economies of scale and use

---

139. About 50 percent of Mexico's farmers till plots of 5 hectares or less (1 hectare = 2.741 acres). These farmers cultivate about 15 percent of total ejido land, and they earn less than a third of their income from agriculture. See Williams (2004). More than 20 percent of ejidatorios have farms split among three or more plots. See Giugale, Lafourcade, and Nguyen (2001).

Table 5.16   Area under corn in NAFTA countries, 1960–2003 (millions of hectares)

Year	Canada	Mexico	United States
1960	0.2	5.4	28.9
1965	0.3	7.5	22.4
1970	0.5	8.0	23.2
1975	0.6	7.9	27.4
1980	1.0	8.1	29.5
1985	1.1	6.2	30.4
1990	1.1	6.6	27.1
1995	1.0	7.8	26.4
2000	1.1	7.1	29.3
2001	1.3	7.8	27.8
2002	1.3	7.1	28.1
2003	1.2	7.7	28.8

Source: USDA Production, Supply, and Distribution database, 2004.

modern farming techniques. As a consequence, the Mexican agricultural sector provides temporary and part-time employment but does not provide a decent standard of living.

In recent years, Mexican government policy has favored the larger, and more successful, industrialized farmers concentrated in northern Mexico rather than the small, impoverished ejido farmers in southern and central Mexico.[140] Larger, more successful export-oriented farmers represent only 3 percent of private farmers but own almost 30 percent of total private land (Soloaga 2003, World Bank 2001). By contrast, in the poor ejidos, subsistence farming is the rule, and about half of the agricultural production is destined for household consumption.[141] To the extent that poor Mexi-

---

140. About 42 of every 100 Mexicans live in poverty in rural areas, and the majority of the poorest people are concentrated in southern states. Nevertheless, Mexican Agricultural Minister Javier Usabiaga is pursuing a strategy of support for successful Mexican farmers, mostly in northern states, who are expected to give temporary seasonal work to poorer farmers. See "NAFTA Crisis Worsens," *Latin American Economic and Business Report*, February 11, 2003. See also Lustig (2001) and Wiggins et al. (2002). Similarly, the top 10 percent of US farmers receive 65 percent of all agricultural subsidy payments in the United States. See the editorial in the *New York Times*, November 10, 2003.

141. Some studies estimate as much as 55 percent of agricultural production under 5 hectares of land is used for household consumption. See Taylor (2003) and Yunez-Naude (2003).

Table 5.17 US yellow corn trade with NAFTA partners, 1993–2003
(volume in thousands of metric tons and value
in millions of dollars)

	1993		1994		1995		1996		1997	
Country	Volume	Value	Volume	Value	Volume	Value	Volume	Value	Volume	Value
US exports to										
Canada	785	77	695	69	1,001	109	847	135	1,027	117
Mexico	241	29	2,310	247	2,411	301	5,401	881	2,311	282
NAFTA subtotal	1,026	106	3,005	316	3,412	410	6,248	1,015	3,338	399
Total world (including NAFTA)	39,432	4,145	34,581	3,800	58,921	7,161	50,968	8,239	41,123	5,103
US imports from										
Canada	323	30	356	39	258	29	332	51	200	24
Mexico	0	0	0	0	0	0	0	0	0	0
NAFTA subtotal	323	30	356	39	258	29	332	51	200	24
Total world (including NAFTA)	323	30	356	39.0	258	29	332	51	234	27

Note: Besides yellow, most other corn products are white.

Source: USDA Foreign Agricultural Service (FATUS) database, 2004.

can farm households eat what they produce, they are isolated from the price effects of NAFTA and trade with the United States.

In addition to small and inefficient land holdings, there are multiple reasons for low agricultural productivity in the central and southern states. Poor transportation and irrigation networks are part of the problem. It is three times more costly to deliver corn by rail from Sinaloa to Mexico City than by shipping from New Orleans via Veracruz.[142] Access to credit is notoriously difficult. Credit provided to the agricultural sector was 21 percent larger in 1983–90 than in 1996–2000.[143] Rural financial markets are "personalized" operations with little or no collateral required but at very high costs (Giugale, Lafourcade, and Nguyen 2001; Oxfam 2003). Without government guarantees, Mexican commercial banks hesitate to provide loans because of the historically high default rate on agricultural loans and the record of large-scale debt forgiveness. As a partial answer, the Mexican government created Financiera Rural in 2002, which aims to provide access to microcredits for farmers to buy machinery, equipment, and technology.

---

142. See "Floundering In a Tariff-Free Landscape," *The Economist*, November 28, 2002.

143. Moreover, most credit on easy terms goes to large farmers. Procede, established in 1993, provided property titles for rural households that could be used as collateral for loans. However, even though Procede issued more than 3 million property rights certificates, households did not get much credit in return. See Davis et al. (2000) and Larre, Guichard, and Vourc'h (2003).

1998		1999		2000		2001		2002		2003	
Volume	Value	Volume	Value	Volume	Value	Volume	Value	Volume	Value	Volume	Value
1,123	115	938	82	1,446	128	2,940	256	3,980	377	3,453	372
4,298	474	3,790	382	3,829	370	4,650	492	4,012	452	4,348	506
5,421	588	4,729	464	5,274	498	7,590	748	7,992	828	7,801	878
39,958	4,243	50,278	4,802	46,152	4,395	46,474	4,468	45,096	4,714	41,397	4,644
210	21	324	29	177	17	121	12	189	19	235	34
0	0	0	0	1	0	0	0	0	0	0	0
210	21	324	30	177	17	121	12	189	19	235	34
223	43	343	56	194	49	133	37	210	44	257	74

Domestic Corn Policies

Mexico

Throughout the 1980s, the state-owned enterprise known as the National Company of Popular Subsistence (La Compañía Nacional de Subsistencias Populares, or Conasupo) controlled Mexican corn trade and determined the level of imports. Conasupo's first concern was to guarantee high prices for domestic corn producers. At the same time, Conasupo subsidized millers to produce cheap tortillas for domestic consumption. Broad agricultural reforms were introduced in 1990, but direct price supports for corn were maintained.[144] After the 1995 peso crisis, Conasupo replaced these direct price supports with a policy of "last resort buyer."[145] As a "last resort buyer," Conasupo bought corn at average international prices based on the Chicago Commodity Exchange (with some regional variation). It bought white corn for human consumption and sold it to *nixtamaleros* (makers of corn dough used to produce tortillas) and corn

---

144. However, in the 1990 reforms, import controls and basic price supports were removed for copra, cottonseed, grain barley, rice, soy, sorghum, sunflower, and wheat.

145. As a result of the "last resort buyer" program, Conasupo purchases of corn declined from 45 percent of domestic production of grain in 1994 to 12 percent in 1998. See Yunez-Naude (2002a).

Table 5.18 US white corn trade with NAFTA partners, 1993–2003
(volume in thousands of metric tons and value
in millions of dollars)

Country	1993 Volume	1993 Value	1994 Volume	1994 Value	1995 Volume	1995 Value	1996 Volume	1996 Value	1997 Volume	1997 Value
US exports to										
Canada	55	21	54	24	54	26	38	26	37	33
Mexico	76	46	777	126	476	82	947	142	284	61
NAFTA subtotal	131	67	831	150	530	109	986	168	321	95
Total world (including NAFTA)	1,232	359	1,405	397	1,191	360	1,420	386	736	323
US imports from										
Canada	8	11	15	16	13	12	16	16	20	14
Mexico	1	0	2	1	3	1	3	1	5	2
NAFTA subtotal	9	11	16	17	15	13	19	17	25	16
Total world (including NAFTA)	30	31	41	45.6	37	37	55	65	67	76

Note: Besides yellow, most other corn products are white.

Source: USDA Foreign Agriculture Service (FATUS) database, 2004.

millers at a somewhat lower price (table 5.20).[146] Conasupo was dismantled in December 1998, but government market price supports to Mexican corn producers were increased.[147]

Mexican price support programs were maintained through various channels, including Conasupo, the Agricultural Marketing Board (ASERCA), and Alianza. From 1997 to 2000, ASERCA complemented Conasupo for corn-market interventions.[148] In 2003, the Mexican government emphasized ASERCA's target income program for a broader range of crops, aimed at compensating producers for the gap between target and market prices (Larre, Guichard, and Vourc'h 2003). Alianza also subsidized farmers' input use (Yunez-Naude 2003). Established in 1996, Alianza provides matching grants, with the aim of boosting agricultural productivity.

---

146. Mexican corn millers received an in-cash subsidy, administered by ASERCA, for corn bought from the domestic market.

147. According to the OECD, market price supports badly distort production and trade and are not efficient at transferring income to producers. Mexican market price support programs accounted for 62 percent of producer support in 2001.

148. Established in 1991, ASERCA largely replaced Conasupo for direct interventions in sorghum and wheat. However, cotton, rice, and soy producers in selected regions have also been included in ASERCA programs. See Lederman, Maloney, and Serven (2003).

1998		1999		2000		2001		2002		2003	
Volume	Value	Volume	Value	Volume	Value	Volume	Value	Volume	Value	Volume	Value
78	40	57	35	80	41	136	54.9	166	54	64	16
979	137	1,306	170	1,350	162	1,005	134	1,372	187	1,309	182
1,057	176	1,363	205	1.431	202	1,140	189	1,538	242	1,372	198
1,360	375	1,753	324	1,820	300	1,503	286	2,481	394	1,765	290
18	13	46	8	43	12	24	10	46	13	31	5
8	3	11	5	8	3	11	4	5	2	6	3
26	16	56	13	50	15	35	14	52	15	37	8
78	99	116	100	99	111	77	97	90	93	80	77

United States

On a crop-by-crop basis, corn is the largest recipient of US government subsidies, averaging $3.7 billion annually during 1994–2003.[149] This should not be surprising, since corn is also the leading US crop in terms of area cultivated (about 76 million acres in 2001) and value of production ($21 billion in 2002).[150] Indirectly, large agribusinesses, such as Cargill and Archer Daniels Midland (which market about 70 percent of US corn exports), benefit from corn subsidies because they can sell a larger crop at lower prices.[151]

---

149. US corn subsidies, which rise when the price falls, were very high in 2000, totaling $10.1 billion. They dropped to $1.7 billion in 2003. The Commodity Credit Corporation figures include direct government payments, countercyclical payments, and market loan payments. Based on USDA Table 35, CCC Net Outlays by Commodity and Function, www.fsa.usda. gov/dam/bud/bud1.htm (accessed in July 2005).

150. See Foreman (2001) and USDA's National Agricultural Statistics Service (NASS) statistical database, January 2004.

151. The Mexican government indirectly subsidizes both companies. Cargill, for example, receives support from the Mexican government for the sale and transport of grain. Cargill and Archer Daniels Midland, Co. also hold stakes in the largest Mexican tortilla and flour processing firms (Maesca and Minsa), which historically have benefited from public subsidies.

Table 5.19 Canadian corn trade with NAFTA partners, 1993–2003
(volume in thousands of tons and value in
millions of US dollars)

Country	1993 Volume	1993 Value	1994 Volume	1994 Value	1995 Volume	1995 Value	1996 Volume	1996 Value	1997 Volume	1997 Value
Canadian exports to										
Mexico	0	0	0	0	0	0	0	0	0	0
United States	517	44	234	58	392	43	303	70	151	40
NAFTA subtotal	517	44	234	58	392	43	303	70	151	40
Total world (including NAFTA)	522	49	350	63	622	65	364	102	163	50
Canadian imports from										
Mexico	0	0	0	0	0	0	0	0	0	0
United States	580	92	1,112	89	840	129	817	153	1,469	146
NAFTA subtotal	580	92	1,112	89	840	129	817	153	1,469	147
Total world (including NAFTA)	580	93	1,113	90	841	130	821	154	1,495	148

Sources: Statistics Canada, Strategic Policy Branch; AAFC (2003a); and UN Comtrade database, 2004.

US corn producers receive payments from three key programs: direct payments, marketing loan programs, and countercyclical payments.[152] US export credit guarantee programs, such as the Supplier Credit Guarantee Program, also underwrite credits that pay for US food and agricultural products sold to foreign buyers. The dollar volume of agricultural export credit programs (for all crops) totals about $3.4 billion per year. In 2002, exports to Mexico received about one-fifth of total US export credits, close to $680 million.[153]

Potential Disputes

So far corn disputes have not erupted between the United States and Mexico.[154] However, agrarian unrest within Mexico and calls to renegotiate

---

152. Direct payments are based both on land area cultivated and past (rather than current) output. For example, a US corn producer can receive direct payments without necessarily producing corn that year. The marketing loan program is designed to promote agricultural exports. Finally, when the effective corn price is below the target price, US corn producers are entitled to countercyclical payments irrespective of their production level. See USDA (2003b).

153. Based on total US export credits under the Facility Guarantee Program, which reached $3.4 billion in fiscal 2002. See the program's details at www.fas.usda.gov/excredits/facility.html (accessed in May 2004). See also Oxfam (2003).

154. However, two cases related to HFCS are pending under NAFTA Chapter 11 (investment disputes).

1998		1999		2000		2001		2002		2003	
Volume	Value	Volume	Value	Volume	Value	Volume	Value	Volume	Value	Volume	Value
0	0	0	0	0	0	0	0	0	0	0	0
418	36	320	41	132	30	233	23	358	36	267	43
418	36	320	41	132	30	233	23	358	36	267	43
861	43	481	96	144	38	241	25	377	41	268	44
0	3	0	14	0	108	0	73	0	141	0	32
937	150	1,080	113	2.920	165	3,907	303	3,978	419	3,458	373
937	153	1,080	127	2,921	274	3,907	377	3,978	559	3,458	406
941	157	1,084	118	2,936	170	3,917	319	3,978	429	3,461	383

NAFTA's corn and bean provisions suggest that US-Mexico corn disputes are waiting in the wings. In April 2003, Mexican farmers pressured President Vicente Fox to create a $270 million emergency fund and sign a national agriculture agreement that pledged to limit Mexican white corn imports.[155] Recently, when the Mexican Senate voted to extend the HFCS tax on soft drinks, it also agreed to a prospective overquota tariff of 72.6 percent on imports of US white corn.[156]

Canada is also concerned about US corn exports. In 2000, Canada almost levied AD duties on US corn.[157] In 2002, the Canadian Grain Commission banned US corn exports that contain traces of Starlink corn, a

---

155. In April 2003, agriculture protesters numbering 60,000 demonstrated against the prospect, at the end of 2008, of tariff-free NAFTA agricultural trade in corn, beans, powdered milk, and sugar. The National Agriculture Agreement also seeks to study the effects of NAFTA and the US Farm Act of 2002. See Pav Jordan, "Mexico to Seek Some NAFTA Changes," *Reuters News*, April 28, 2003.

156. Reports suggest US yellow corn exports to Mexico might also be subject to higher overquota tariffs depending on the domestic supply and demand situation determined by the Mexican Commerce and Agriculture Ministries. See "Mexico Extends HFCS Tax," *Inside US Trade*, January 2, 2004.

157. The Manitoba Crown Growers filed an AD and CVD action against the United States in August 2000. The Canadian government did not levy duties on US corn imports, partly because most US corn exports are used to feed the expanding Canadian livestock industry.

Table 5.20 State-owned Conasupo corn prices and subsidies in Mexico (US dollars per ton)

Category	1996	1997	1998	1999	2000
Average Conasupo purchasing prices for					
White corn	180	166	143	—	—
Yellow corn	95	108	126	—	—
Average Conasupo selling prices to Tortilla factories					
Mexico City	53	59	116	—	—
Other	60	59	116	—	—
Flour companies[a]	60	59	116	—	—
DICONSA shops[b]					
White corn	155	157	119	—	—
Yellow corn	147	129	116	—	—
Feed sector [c]	111	105	91	—	—
Retail corn price ceilings for					
Tortilla[d]	n.a.	227	194	397	438
Flour[e]	n.a.	152	466	497	540

— = not applicable because Conasupo was dismantled in December 1998.

n.a. = not available

Conasupo = La Compañía Nacional de Subsistencias Populares (Mexico's National Company of Popular Subsistence)

a. Since 1985, flour companies have purchased most of their corn grains directly from producers and received payments from Conasupo to lower selling prices to tortilla factories.
b. DICONSA shops are government retail shops that distribute corn and other staple products to rural consumers at low prices.
c. Since 1996, corn grain sales from Conasupo to the feed sector have declined significantly.
d. Retail prices of tortilla and flour were different in Mexico City from the rest of the country up to 1996.
e. Excludes flour sold in bulk, defined as 1 kg or more, for which retail prices were liberalized in 1995.

Source: OECD, Agricultural Policies in OECD Countries, 1998–2002.

biotech variety that, according to the commission, has not been proven safe for animal or human consumption.[158]

According to the Canadian International Trade Tribunal (CITT) 2001 annual report, US dumping and subsidization significantly reduced domestic Canadian corn prices. On the other hand, CITT found that corn used to feed livestock benefited farmers through lower costs of production. Nev-

---

158. The challenge is how to separate genetically modified corn used for feed grain from that approved for human consumption. As an example, while Starlink corn was never allowed for human consumption because of fears that it might trigger allergic attacks in humans, the Starlink gene inadvertently contaminated grain elevators and food processing plants. By 2000, traces of Starlink were found in taco shells and corn products across the United States, prompting prices for US corn to drop in export markets. We thank Tim Josling for this observation and for providing written comments to an earlier draft. See Erin Galbally, "Second Round of Concern Over Starlink Corn," Minnesota Public Radio, April 25, 2001.

ertheless, subsidized US corn gives US livestock producers a significant feed cost advantage over Canadian livestock producers (Loyns 2002).

Corn Recommendations

To evaluate the liberalization of corn under NAFTA, three issues are central: the NAFTA agreement itself, agricultural subsidies, and corn prices in Mexico. Under NAFTA terms, Mexican barriers to corn imports were to be liberalized over a 15-year transition period, which gradually phased out the TRQs. There is no evidence of US government pressure to liberalize the Mexican corn sector faster than the NAFTA timetable. On its own initiative, Mexico eliminated price supports for corn during the mid- to late 1990s, and corn prices (expressed in US dollars) fell by 22 percent between 1995 and 1998. Lacking alternatives, poor Mexican farmers continued producing corn despite the falling prices; in fact, they increased both the acreage and labor devoted to corn cultivation.

US agricultural subsidies are enormous, second only to the European Union's, and US corn producers benefit from this largesse.[159] While the United States should be held accountable for the fact that agricultural subsidies help drive down the price of corn in Mexico (as well as other commodities in other markets), subsidies are not responsible for the relatively low productivity of Mexico's corn sector. In general, the growth of Mexican agricultural production is lower than its population growth rate. However, the Mexican agricultural sector has historically served as the repository for excess labor, and Mexico has been relatively slow to adopt agricultural technology that would both boost productivity per hectare and reduce demand for farm labor (de Janvry and Sadoulet 2001).

In the long run, international competitive pressure and improved domestic farm technology, throughout Mexican agriculture, will induce rural emigration—sending people both to urban Mexico and the United States. Rural-urban migration is an important transmission mechanism for reducing poverty, and within Mexico, this process still has a long way to go.[160] International comparisons suggest that the Mexican agricultural labor force as a proportion of total labor remains very high. In 2000, the share of workers in Mexican agriculture was about 21 percent, compared with 17 percent in Brazil, 10 percent in Korea, and 2 percent in the United States and Canada.[161] One study estimates that radical free trade in agriculture—the elimination of all tariffs, all Mexican agricultural support pro-

---

159. Some experts estimate US subsidies for corn are as high as 30 cents a bushel. See Steven Chase, "Corn Farmers Flock to Cancun," *Globe and Mail*, September 10, 2003.

160. Recent studies suggest that rural emigration contributed to a very substantial decline in the number of Mexican rural poor. See de Janvry and Sadoulet (2001).

161. Data are based on UN Food and Agriculture Organization FAOSTAT database, 2004.

grams, and all US export subsidy programs—would lead to a decline in Mexican corn production by 19 percent and reduce total farm employment by an estimated 800,000 rural workers. These workers would in turn emigrate to urban Mexico and the United States.[162] If the estimate is accurate, free trade would reduce the share of Mexican workers engaged in agriculture from 21 to 19 percent.

We recommend that the Mexican government set its sights on free trade in corn over a period of six years, between 2008 and 2014. The liberalization period should be stretched out from the original NAFTA timetable through negotiation. During this period, as a consequence of WTO negotiations in the Doha Round, the United States will very likely cut its corn (and other agricultural) subsidies, perhaps by a large dollar amount and percentage. Export subsidies on agricultural products are likely to be eliminated altogether. If the United States continues to subsidize corn, either through distorting amber or blue box supports,[163] Mexico should be permitted to impose safeguard measures, with a lower injury threshold (e.g., "market disruption") than customary for safeguard actions.

Conclusions and Recommendations

Agriculture remains the make-or-break issue for multilateral and regional trade agreements. This is equally true for bilateral FTAs. To resolve the agricultural hurdle, the US-Chile FTA has long phaseout periods for sensitive agricultural products (notably dairy, sugar, avocadoes, and orange juice). In the US-Australia FTA and the Central American Free Trade Agreement (CAFTA), sugar is either excluded altogether or liberalized very little, and barriers on other sensitive products (dairy, beef, rice, and poultry) are phased out over long periods. Compared with other free trade pacts, the US-Mexico component of NAFTA ranks among the better agreements so far as farm products are concerned. By adhering to built-in timetables and by launching new negotiations on residual barriers (especially between the United States and Canada), NAFTA can achieve nearly free agricultural trade—what may be called "approximate free trade"—within a decade.

As a prelude to our recommendations, we note that NAFTA is far from an integrated economic area. Much remains to be done. According to one estimate, in 2000, the intensity of within-country trade was still 12 times greater than the intensity of between-country trade among the NAFTA

---

162. Under this scenario, Mexican horticultural exports would increase and partly compensate for the decline in corn and basic crop production. See Yunez-Naude (2002b).

163. Amber box subsidies either support prices or increase production quantities, or both. Blue box measures are government payments (such as deficiency payments) linked to production restraint programs. See WTO (2004c).

partners (Vollrath 2004). Since agricultural markets are subject to some of the highest barriers, the trade intensity difference is probably greater for farm products.

While much remains to be done, it makes little sense to alter the scheduled profile of farm barriers within NAFTA while Doha and FTAA talks are still under way—probably until 2007. However, NAFTA partners should use this window to chart a course toward "approximate free trade" over the decade 2007–17.

The starting point is to recognize that domestic agricultural subsidies will not be negotiated down across the board within NAFTA, because the United States and Canada will agree to "disarm" only with the assurance of comparable commitments from the European Union and other major agricultural producers. At most, trial programs, such as we have advocated for amber and blue box wheat supports, might be negotiated within NAFTA. Moreover, because agricultural subsidies have been capitalized into hundreds of billions of dollars of farmland values,[164] they can be reduced only slowly, even in the context of WTO negotiations. A likely outcome of the Doha Round will be a partial transformation of amber and blue box subsidies (those that support agricultural prices and production) into green box subsidies (decoupled from price levels and production decisions).

With this context in mind, NAFTA partners should seek to phase out existing border barriers and eliminate them totally by 2017. However, to deal with the subsidy problem, NAFTA partners should negotiate their own "WTO-plus" commitments to eliminate or substantially reduce amber and blue box subsidies on a product-by-product basis beyond the reforms undertaken in the Doha Round. In addition, on a purely national basis, each partner should retain its privilege to invoke special agricultural safeguards, triggered by a market disruption test that could be applied for one year. (The market disruption test could have a lower threshold, and the safeguards period could be longer, if amber and blue box subsidies were a factor.) "Snapback" tariffs should be the preferred means to revert to the previous level of protection, if an import surge caused a severe drop in domestic market prices.

As a second goal, by 2017, NAFTA members should adopt a common external tariff (CET) on agricultural products. In the final chapter, we recommend that a CET on nonagricultural products be accomplished on a much faster timeline. The slower phase-in of an agricultural CET reflects the high sensitivity of this sector.[165] By harmonizing their national tariff rates toward a negotiated CET, NAFTA countries will eliminate differences in the most-

---

164. Over 1994–2003, US agricultural subsidies and market access barriers have averaged $40.3 billion annually on a producer support estimate basis. Even if these supports are discounted at the high rate of 15 percent, taking into account market and political uncertainties, they could have created some $270 billion of higher US farmland values.

165. To be saleable, the CET would need to be phased in very slowly for key agricultural imports (such as sugar). See Hufbauer and Schott (2004).

favored nation (MFN) tariffs applied on imports from third countries.[166] The CET goal should be reached by a NAFTA accord that all countries would implement—over the course of 10 years—the lowest rate applied by a NAFTA member for each tariff line and eliminate quota barriers.[167]

A third area that needs to be addressed is the application of SPS restrictions that hamper trade in farm products across NAFTA borders. SPS regulations can act as a de facto nontariff barrier, especially on horticultural and meat products. We recommend, on a product-by-product basis, that the NAFTA partners create common SPS standards (or mutual recognition) and a common inspection service. Both the common standards and common inspection service could start on a bilateral basis and eventually reach a trilateral basis.[168] To illustrate, while cross-border US-Canada markets for live cattle are well integrated, the partners still do not have common beef grading standards nor do they recognize the equivalency of their individual beef grades. The beef story was a key driving force for a common US-Canada SPS regime, which ultimately led to the NAFTA Security and Prosperity Partnership pledge signed in March 2005.[169] The broader goal, over a 10-year period, should be the establishment of common NAFTA standards and joint inspection services, beginning with low-controversy products (such as onions or mangoes) and ultimately reaching high-controversy products (such as genetically modified varieties and meats).

References

AAFC (Agriculture and Agri-Food Canada). 2001. The Canadian Cane and Beet Sugar Industry Profile (May). www.agr.gc.ca/index_e.phtml (accessed in April 2003).

---

166. The CET in agriculture and other sectors will eliminate a major rationale for protective rules of origin. Rules of origin are justified as a means of preventing "trade deflection," namely the practice of routing imports through the lowest-tariff country in an FTA. Unstated is the intentional protective effect of rules of origin. Despite this intent, it is our hope that once the CET is established, rules of origin would be waived for tariff-free trade within NAFTA.

167. In 2001, the simple average MFN tariff rate for agricultural products was 4.7 percent in the United States, 3 percent in Canada, and 23.4 percent in Mexico. See WTO *World Trade Report*, 2003. These figures suggest that Mexico would have to cut its MFN tariffs much further than Canada or the United States in order to achieve a common external tariff by harmonizing down.

168. As an example, the United States and Mexico recently resolved outstanding SPS issues in poultry, allowing most Mexican states to export poultry products into the US market. See "NAFTA: The Future of Poultry," *NAFTA Works* 9, no. 2, February 2004.

169. In March 2005, US President Bush, Mexican President Fox, and Canadian Prime Minister Martin announced the establishment of a "Security and Prosperity Partnership of North America," which includes promoting a "safer and more reliable food supply while facilitating agricultural trade." Specifically, the NAFTA trilateral agreement addressed the need to "pursue common approaches to enhanced food safety and . . . recovery from foodborne and animal and plant disease hazards." See White House press release, "Security and Prosperity Partnership of North America Prosperity Agenda," March 23, 2005; and John D. McKinnon, "Canada, Mexico, US Reach Deal to Bolster Trade," *Wall Street Journal*, March 24, 2005, A4.

AAFC (Agriculture and Agri-Food Canada). 2002a. *Agriculture, Food and Beverages: Canada's International Business Strategy, 2001–2002*. Ottawa.

AAFC (Agriculture and Agri-Food Canada). 2002b. *Mexico: Agri-Food Country Profile*. Ottawa (May).

AAFC (Agriculture and Agri-Food Canada). 2003a. *Market Analysis Division Online*. Ottawa (November). www.agr.gc.ca/mad-dam/e/index2e.htm.

AAFC (Agriculture and Agri-Food Canada). 2003b. Crop Insurance. www.agr.gc.ca (accessed in January 2003).

Alston, Julian M., Richard Gray, and Daniel A. Sumner. 2000. Wheat Disputes Under NAFTA. In *Trade Liberalization Under NAFTA: Report Card on Agriculture*, ed., R.M.A. Loyns, Karl Meilke, Ron D. Knutson, and Antonio Yunez-Naude. October. Winnipeg, Manitoba: Friesen Printers.

Anson, Jose, Olivier Cadot, Jaime deMelo, Antoni Estevadeordal, Akiko Suwa Eisenmann, and Bolorma Tumurchudur. 2003. Rules of Origin in North-South Preferential Trading Arrangements With An Application to NAFTA. Centre for Economic Policy Research Discussion Paper 4166 (December). London: Centre for Economic Policy Research.

Antle, J. M., and V. H. Smith. 2000. *The Economics of World Wheat Markets*. New York: Oxford University Press.

Audley, John, Sandra Polaski, Demetrios G. Papademetriou, and Scott Vaughan. 2003. NAFTA's Promise And Reality: Lessons from Mexico for the Hemisphere. Washington: Carnegie Endowment for International Peace (November).

BNA (Bureau of National Affairs). 2003a. Canadian Government Doubles Funds For Promotion of Agricultural Exports. *BNA International Trade Reporter* (March 13).

BNA (Bureau of National Affairs). 2003b. House Lawmakers Urge Mexican Envoy To Help Resolve Trade in Sweeteners. *BNA International Trade Reporter* 20, no. 12 (March 20).

BNA (Bureau of National Affairs). 2003c. US Executive Urges Sweetener Accord With Mexico. *BNA International Trade Reporter* 20, no. 9 (February 27).

BNA (Bureau of National Affairs). 2003d. US Obtains WTO Dispute Panel to Rule on Canadian Wheat Board. *BNA International Trade Reporter* 20, no. 14 (April 3).

Bolling, Chris. 2002. Globalization of the Soft Drink Industry. *Agricultural Outlook*. Washington: US Department of Agriculture Economic Research Service (December).

Bradford, Scott C., Paul L. E. Grieco, and Gary Clyde Hufbauer. 2005. The Payoff to America from Global Integration. In *The United States and the World Economy: Foreign Economic Policy for the Next Decade*, C. Fred Bergsten and the Institute for International Economics. Washington: Institute for International Economics.

Burfisher, Mary, Terry Norman, and Renee Schwartz. 2002. *NAFTA Trade Dispute Resolution: What Are the Mechanisms?* Washington: US Department of Agriculture, Economic Research Service.

Burfisher, Mary E., Sherman Robinson, and Karen Thierfelder. 1998. *Farm Policy Reforms and Harmonization in the NAFTA*. Washington: US Department of Agriculture, Economic Research Service.

Canada House of Commons. 2002. Partners in North America: Advancing Canada's Relations with the United States and Mexico. Report of the Standing Committee on Foreign Affairs and International Trade. Ottawa, Ontario.

Canadian Grain Commission. 2003. *Canadian Grain Exports, Crop Year 2001–02*. Winnipeg, Manitoba.

Canadian Sugar Institute. 2003. *International Trade Challenge*. www.sugar.ca (accessed in April 2003). Toronto, Ontario.

Carter, Colin A., and R. M. A. Loyns. 1996. The Economics of Single-Desk Selling of Western Canadian Grain. Alberta: Agriculture, Food, and Rural Development (March).

Carter, Colin A., and R. M. A. Loyns. 1998. The Canadian Wheat Board: Its Role in North American State Trading. Presentation at the Institute of International Studies, Stanford University (October). Photocopy.

Center for International Economics. 2002. *Targets for OECD Sugar Market Liberalization*. October. Canberra, Australia. www.thecie.com.au/publications/CIE-OECD_sugar_market_liberalisation.pdf (accessed in June 2003).

Cline, William. 2004. *Trade Policy and Global Poverty*. Washington: Institute for International Economics.

Coalition for Sugar Reform. 2003. The Federal Government's Sugar Program. www.sugar-reform.org (accessed in April 2003). Washington.

CRB (Commodity Research Bureau). 2003. *Commodity Yearbook*. New York: John Wiley and Sons, Inc.

CWB (Canadian Wheat Board). 2003. *Grain Marketing Report* (March-April). www.cwb.ca/en/publications/farmers/mar-apr-2003/03-04-03-06.jsp (accessed on May 10, 2005). Winnipeg, Manitoba.

Davis, Benjamin, Alain de Janvry, Elisabeth Sadoulet, and Todd Diehl. 2000. Policy Reforms and Poverty in the Mexican Ejido Sector. In *Policy Harmonization and Adjustment in the North American Agricultural and Food Industry*, ed. R. M. A. Lyons et al. Texas A&M University, University of Guelph, and El Colegio de Mexico.

DeFerranti, David, Guillermo Perry, Francisco H. G. Ferreira, and Michael Walton. 2003. *Inequality in Latin America and the Caribbean: Breaking with History?* World and Latin American and Caribbean Studies. Washington: World Bank.

de Janvry, Alain, and Elisabeth Sadoulet. 2001. Priorities and Strategies in Rural Poverty Reduction: Experiences from Latin America and Asia. The Japan Program/INDES Conference. Washington: Inter-American Development Bank.

de Janvry, Alain, Gregory Graff, Elisabeth Sadoulet, and David Zilberman. 2001. Technological Change in Agriculture and Poverty Reduction. *World Development Report on Poverty and Development*. Washington: World Bank.

Dohlman, Erik, and Linwood Hoffman. 2000. *The New Agricultural Trade Negotiations: Background and Issues for the US Wheat Sector*. Washington: US Department of Agriculture, Economic Research Service (March).

Dyer, George A., and Dwight D. Dyer. 2003. Policy, Politics, and Projections in Mexican Agriculture. Ninth Annual NAFTA Agricultural and Food Policy Information Workshop, Montreal, April.

Elliott, Kimberly A. 2005. *Big Sugar and the Political Economy of US Agricultural Policy*. Center for Global Development Brief. Washington: Center for Global Development.

Foreman, Linda F. 2001. *Characteristics and Production Costs of US Corn Farms*. USDA Statistical Bulletin 974 (August). Washington: US Department of Agriculture.

Frazao, Elizabeth, ed. 1999. *America's Eating Habits*. Agricultural Information Bulletin 750 (May). Washington: US Department of Agriculture Economic Research Service.

GAO (US General Accounting Office). 1998. *US Agriculture Trade: Canadian Wheat Issues*. Washington.

GAO (US General Accounting Office). 2000. *Sugar Program: Supporting Sugar Prices Has Increased Users' Costs While Benefiting Producers*. Washington.

Gardner, Bruce L. 2000. *The Effectiveness of Policy in Achieving a Single North American Market for Agricultural Products*. University of Maryland, Center for Agricultural and Natural Resource Policy (November).

Giugale, Marcelo M., Olivier Lafourcade, and Vinh H. Nguyen, eds. 2001. *Mexico: A Comprehensive Development Agenda for the New Era*. Washington: World Bank.

Gokcekus, Omer, Justin Knowles, and Edward Tower. 2003. *Sweetening the Pot: How American Sugar Buys Protection*. Duke University Economics Working Paper 3-08 (May). Durham, NC: Duke University.

Goombridge, Mark A. 2001. *America's Bittersweet Sugar Policy*. Trade Briefing Paper No. 13. Washington: Cato Center for Trade Policy Studies.

Haley, Stephen, and Nydia Suarez. 1999. US-Mexico Sweetener Trade Mired in Dispute. *Agricultural Outlook*. Washington: US Department of Agriculture.

Haley, Stephen, and Nydia Suarez. 2000. Weak Prices Test US Sugar Policy. *Agricultural Outlook*. Washington: US Department of Agriculture.

Haley, Stephen, and Nydia Suarez. 2002. *Sugar and Sweetener Situation and Outlook Yearbook*. Washington: US Department of Agriculture Economic Research Service.

Haley, Stephen, and Nydia Suarez. 2003. *Sugar and Sweetener Outlook Yearbook*. Washington: US Department of Agriculture, Economic Research Service.

Hanrahan, Charles E. 2004. *Agricultural Export and Food Aid Programs*. Washington: Congressional Research Service.

Hathaway, Dale. 2003. *The Impacts of US Agricultural and Trade Policy on Trade Liberalization and Integration*. National Center for Food and Agricultural Policy. Washington: Inter-American Development Bank.

Hufbauer, Gary C., and Jeffrey J. Schott. 2004. The Prospects for Deeper North American Economic Integration: A US Perspective. *C. D. Howe Commentary* 195. Ontario: C. D. Howe Institute.

Humphreys, John, Martin van Bueren, and Andrew Stoeckel. 2003. *Greening Farm Subsidies: The Next Step in Removing Perverse Farm Subsidies*. Canberra, Australia: Centre for International Economics.

Josling, Tim, and Dale Hathaway. 2004. *This Far and No Further? Nudging Agricultural Reform Forward*. Institute for International Economics Policy Brief PB04-1 (March). Washington: Institute for International Economics.

Jurenas, Remy. 2003. *Sugar Policy Issues*. Issue Brief for Congress (July 14). Washington: Congressional Research Service.

Kraft, D. F., W. H. Furtan, and E. W. Tyrchniewicz. 1996. *Performance Evaluation of the Canadian Wheat Board*. Winnipeg: Canadian Wheat Board (January).

Knutson, Ronald D., and Rene Ochoa. 2004. Achieving Market Integration. *AgExporter* XVI, no.1 (January).

Larre, Benedicte, Stephanie Guichard, and Ann Vourc'h. 2003. *OECD Economic Surveys: Mexico*. Paris: Organization for Economic Cooperation and Development (November).

Lederman, Daniel, William F. Maloney, and Luis Serven. 2003. *Lessons from NAFTA for Latin American and Caribbean (LAC) Countries*. Washington: World Bank (December).

LMC International, Ltd. 2003. Review of Sugar Policies in Major Sugar Industries: Transparent and Non-Transparent or Indirect Policies. Prepared for the American Sugar Alliance (January). New York.

Loyns, R. M. A. 2002. Manitoba Corn Growers Association Inc. vs. US Corn Exports. Presentation at the Eighth Workshop of Policy Disputes, March 8.

Lustig, Nora. 2001. Life Is Not Easy: Mexico's Quest for Stability and Growth. *Journal of Economic Perspectives* 15, no. 1 (Winter): 85–106.

Martin, Larry, Holly Mayer, and Jerry Bouma. 2002. *Benefits and Costs of a Voluntary Wheat Board for the Province of Alberta*. Calgary, Alberta: George Morris Centre.

Mitchell, Donald. 2004. *Sugar Policies: Opportunity for Change*. World Bank Policy Research Working Paper 3222. Washington: World Bank.

Morrison, Rosanna Mentzer, ed. 2001. Global Food Trade. *USDA Food Review* 24, no. 3. Washington: US Department of Agriculture.

Myles, George C., and Matthew Cahoon. 2004. Canada and NAFTA: A 10-Year Measure of Success in Canadian-US Agricultural Trade. *AgExporter* XVI, no.1 (January).

Nadal, Alejandro. 2000. *The Environmental and Social Impacts of Economic Liberalization on Corn Production in Mexico*. World Wildlife Fund and Oxfam.

North American Commission for Environmental Cooperation. 2002. *Free Trade and the Environment: The Picture Becomes Clearer*. Montreal.

Orden, David. 1994. *Agricultural Interest Groups and the North American Free Trade Agreement*. NBER Working Paper No. 4790. Cambridge, MA: National Bureau of Economic Research.

Orden, David. 2003. *US Agricultural Policy: The 2002 Farm Bill and the WTO Doha Round Proposal*. Washington: International Food Policy Research Institute.

OECD (Organization for Economic Cooperation and Development). 2000. *Market Access, Domestic Support, and Export Subsidy Aspects of the Uruguay Round Agreement on Agriculture: Implementation in OECD Countries*. Joint Working Party of the Committee for Agriculture and the Trade Committee. Paris.

OECD (Organization for Economic Cooperation and Development). 2003. *Evolution of Agricultural Support in Real Terms in OECD Countries from 1986 to 2002*. Working Party on Agricultural Policies and Markets. Paris (May 28).

Oxfam. 2003. *Dumping Without Borders: How US Agricultural Policies Are Destroying the Livelihoods of Mexican Corn Farmers*. Oxfam Briefing Paper 50. Boston: Oxfam America.

Paddock, Brian, Julien Destorel, and Cameron Short. 2000. *Potential for Further Integration of Agri-Food Markets in Canada and the United States*. Ottawa: Agriculture and Agri-Food Canada.

Polopolus, Leo, Jose Alvarez, and William Messina, Jr. 2002. *Sugar and the North American Free Trade Agreement*. Gainesville, FL: University of Florida.

Pruzin, Daniel, Gary Yerkey, and Peter Menyasz. 2004. US Loses Appeal Against WTO Ruling on Canada Wheat Board, Eyes WTO Talks. *BNA International Trade Reporter* 21, no. 36.

Qualman, Darrin, and Nettie Wiebe. 2002. *The Structural Adjustment of Canadian Agriculture*. Ottawa: Canadian Centre for Policy Alternatives National Office.

Roney, Jack. 2003. Implementation of US Sugar Policy: Views of the US Sugar Producing Industry. American Sugar Alliance, presentation at the US Department of Agriculture (March). Washington: US Department of Agriculture.

Rosson, Parr, and Flyn Adock. 2003. *The North American Free Trade Agreement: Deepening Economic Integration and Responses to Competition*. Texas A&M University, Department of Agricultural Economics.

Sarmiento, Sergio. 2003. NAFTA and Mexico's Agriculture. *CSIS Hemisphere Focus* XI, no. 8 (March 4).

Seidband, Debbie. 2004. US Wheat and Corn Exports to Mexico Thrive Under NAFTA. *AgExporter* XVI, no. 1 (January).

Soloaga, Isidro. 2003. Mexico Policy. Paper presented at the Roles of Agriculture International Conference. UN Food and Agriculture Organization, Rome, October.

Sumner, Daniel. 1999. Chapter 6 Growing Opportunities: US Interests in Agricultural Trade Agreement. In *2000 WTO Negotiations: Issues for Agriculture in the Northern Plains and Rockies*, ed., Linda M. Young, J. Johnson, and V. Smith. Bozeman: Trade Research Center, Montana State University.

Taylor, J. Edward. 2003. The Microeconomics of Globalization: Evidence from China and Mexico. In *Agricultural Trade and Poverty*. Paris: Organization for Economic Cooperation and Development.

USDA (US Department of Agriculture). 2000. *NAFTA Commodity Supplement*. Washington: US Department of Agriculture Economic Research Service.

USDA (US Department of Agriculture). 2002a. Effects of NAFTA on Agriculture and Rural Economy. *Outlook Report* (July). Washington: US Department of Agriculture Economic Research Service.

USDA (US Department of Agriculture). 2002b. *Economic Research Service Briefing Room: Sugar and Sweetener Trade* (April 24). Washington.

USDA (US Department of Agriculture). 2002c. *Economic Research Service Briefing Room: Sugar and Sweetener Policy* (June 12). Washington.

USDA (US Department of Agriculture). 2002d. Export Assistance, Food Aid and Market Development Programs: Agricultural Export Assistance Update. Washington.

USDA (US Department of Agriculture). 2002e. World Wheat Situation and Outlook. Washington. www.fas.usda.gov/grain/ (accessed in June 2003).

USDA (US Department of Agriculture). 2003a. *Feed Grain Exports by Selected Destinations*. Washington: US Department of Agriculture Economic Research Service.

USDA (US Department of Agriculture). 2003b. *Economic Research Service Briefing Room: Corn Policy*. Washington.

USDA (US Department of Agriculture). 2004a. Farm Income and Costs. Washington: US Department of Agriculture Economic Research Service.www.ers.usda.gov/briefing/farmincome/ (accessed in September 2004).

USDA (US Department of Agriculture). 2004b. US Export Data. Grain and Feed Division. Washington. www.fas.usda.gov/grain/default.htm (November 2004).

USDA (US Department of Agriculture). 2004c. *Economic Research Service Briefing Room: Mexico: Trade*. Washington (accessed in September 2004).

USDA FAS (US Department of Agriculture Foreign Agricultural Service). 2002. *Import Requirements for Sugar and Sugar Containing Articles*. Washington.

USITC (US International Trade Commission). 2001. *Wheat Trading Practices: Competitive Conditions Between US and Canadian Wheat.* Washington (December 18).

Veeman, Michele, Teerence Veeman, and Ryan Hoskins. 2001. NAFTA in the Next Ten Years. Paper presented at a NAFTA conference, University of Alberta, May.

Vocke, Gary. 2001. *Wheat: Background and Issues for Farm Legislation.* Washington: US Department of Agriculture Economic Research Service.

Vocke, Gary, and Edward Allen. 2005. *Wheat Situation and Outlook Yearbook.* Market and Trade Economics Division. Washington: US Department of Agriculture Economic Research Service (March). www.ers.usda.gov/publications/so/view.asp?f=field/whs-bby/ (accessed on May 10, 2005).

Vollrath, Thomas. 2004. Gauging NAFTA's Success and Confronting Future Challenges. *AgExporter* XVI, no. 1 (January).

Wiggins, Steve, Nicola Keilbach, Kerry Preibisch, Sharon Proctor, Gladys Rivera Herrejón, and Gregoria Rodríguez Muñoz. 2002. Agricultural Policy Reform and Rural Livelihoods in Central Mexico. *Journal of Development Studies* 38, no. 4 (April).

Williams, David. 2004. Mexico's NAFTA Experience. *AgExporter* XVI, no. 1.

World Bank. 1999. *Curbing the Epidemic: Governments and the Economics of Tobacco Control.* Washington.

World Bank. 2001. *Mexico Land Policy: A Decade After the Ejido Reform.* Report No. 22187-ME. Washington.

WHO (World Health Organization). 2003. *Diet, Nutrition and the Prevention of Chronic Diseases.* Joint WHO/FAO Expert Consultation Report. WHO Technical Report Series Number 916. Geneva.

WTO (World Trade Organization). 1997. *Trade Policy Review: Mexico.* Geneva.

WTO (World Trade Organization). 2001. Mexico: Antidumping Investigation of HFCS from the United States. Appellate Body Report—WT/DS132/RW, October 22. Geneva. www.worldtradelaw.net (accessed in April 2003).

WTO (World Trade Organization). 2003. Notification of Mexico Tariff Quotas. Geneva: Committee on Agriculture.

WTO (World Trade Organization). 2004a. *United States Subsidies on Upland Cotton.* Report of the WTO Panel (September 8). Geneva. www.wto.org/english/tratop_e/dispu_e/267r_a_e.pdf (accessed in April 2005).

WTO (World Trade Organization). 2004b. *Canada Measures Relating to Exports of Wheat and Treatment of Imported Grain.* WTO Appellate Body Report. Geneva.

WTO (World Trade Organization). 2004c. *Domestic Support in Agriculture.* Background Fact Sheet. Geneva. www.wto.org/english/tratop_e/agric_e/agboxes_e.htm (accessed in September 2004).

Yunez-Naude, Antonio. 2002a. *Lessons from NAFTA: The Case of Mexico's Agricultural Sector.* Washington: World Bank.

Yunez-Naude, Antonio. 2002b. Mexico's Basic-Crops Subsector: Structure and Competition Under Free Trade. In *Structural Change as a Source of Trade Disputes Under NAFTA*, eds., R. M. A. Loyns, Karl Meilke, Ronald D. Knutson, and Antonio Yunez-Naude. Winnipeg, Canada: Friesen Printers.

Yunez-Naude, Antonio. 2003. The Dismantling of CONASUPO: A Mexican State Trader in Agriculture. *World Economy* 26: 97–122. Oxford: Blackwell Publishing.

Zahniser, Steven, and John Link, eds. 2002. *The Effects of NAFTA on Agriculture and the Rural Economy.* Agriculture and Trade Report WRS0201. Washington: US Department of Agriculture Economic Research Service.

Zahniser, Steven. 2002. NAFTA's Impact on US Agriculture: Trade and Beyond. *Agricultural Outlook* (October). Washington: US Department of Agriculture Economic Research Service.

Zahniser, Steven, ed. 2005. NAFTA at 11: The Growing Integration of North American Agriculture. *Agricultural Outlook* (February). Washington: US Department of Agriculture Economic Research Service.

Appendix 5A

Table 5A.1 US tariffs on dutiable agricultural imports from Canada and Mexico, 2003ᵃ (percent)

HTS code	Description	Canada	Mexico
Dairy			
040130	Milk and cream, not concentrated, not sweetened, fat content 0 to 6 percent but not 0 to 45 percent, not subject to general note 15 or additional note 5 to Chapter 4	44	0
040130	Milk and cream, not concentrated, not sweetened, fat content 0 to 45 percent, not subject to general note 15 or additional note 6 to Chapter 4	20	0
040210	Milk and cream in powder/granules/other solid forms, fat content by weight not exceeding 1.5 percent whether/not sweetened, nesoi	49	0
040221	Milk and cream, concentrated, not sweetened, in powder, granules, or other solid forms, with fat content 0 to 1.5 percent but not 0 to 3 percent, not subject to general note 15/Chapter 4 US note 7	51	0
040221	Milk and cream, concentrated, not sweetened, in powder/granules/other solid forms, fat content 0 to 3 percent but not 0 to 35 percent, not subject to general note 15 or Chapter 4 US note 7	43	0
040221	Milk and cream, concentrated, not sweetened, in powder, granules, or other solid forms, with fat content 0 to 35 percent, not subject to general note 15 or Chapter 4 US note 9	47	0
040229	Milk and cream, concentrated, sweetened, in powder, granules, or other solid forms, with fat content 0 to 1.5 percent, not subject to general note 15 or Chapter 4 US note 10	50	0
040291	Milk and cream, concentrated, in nonsolid forms, not sweetened, in airtight containers, not subject to general note 15 or additional US note 11 to Chapter 4	41	0
040291	Milk and cream, concentrated, in other than powder, granules, or other solid forms, unsweetened, other than in airtight containers	45	0
040299	Condensed milk, sweetened, in airtight containers, not subject to general note 15 or additional US note 11 to Chapter 4	43	0
040299	Condensed milk, sweetened, not in airtight containers, not subject to general note 15 or additional US note 11 to Chapter 4	44	0
040299	Milk and cream (except condensed milk), concentrated in nonsolid forms, sweetened, not described in general note 15 or additional US note 10 to Chapter 4	58	0
040310	Yogurt, in dry form, whether or not flavored or containing additional fruit or cocoa, not subject to general note 15 or additional US note 10 to Chapter 4	46	0

HTS	Description		
040390	Sour cream, fluid, not over 45 percent by weight butterfat, not subject to general note 15 or additional US note 5 to Chapter 4	42	0
040390	Sour cream, dried, not over 6 percent by weight butterfat, not subject to general note 15 or additional US note 12 to Chapter 4	68	0
040390	Sour cream, dried, 0 to 6 percent but not over 35 percent by weight butterfat, not subject to general note 15 or additional US note 8 to Chapter 4	54	0
040390	Sour cream, dried, 0 to 35 percent but not over 45 percent by weight butterfat, not subject to general note 15 or additional US note 9 to Chapter 4	77	0
040390	Sour cream, 0 to 45 percent by weight butterfat, not subject to general note 15 or additional US note 6 to Chapter 4	27	0
040390	Curdled milk/cream/kephir and other fermented or acidified milk/cream subject to general note 15 or Chapter 4 US note 10	17	0
040410	Modified whey (except protein concentrated), whether/not concentrated or sweetened, not subject to general note 15	53	0
040410	Whey (except modified whey), dried, whether or not concentrated or sweetened, not subject to general note 15 or additional US note 12 to Chapter 4	41	0
040490	Dairy products of natural milk constituents (except protein concentrated), described in additional US note 1 to Chapter 4 and not subject to general note 15 or Chapter 4 US note 10	59	0
040510	Butter not subject to general note 15 and in excess of quota in Chapter 4 additional US note 6	102	0
040520	Butter substitute dairy spreads, over 45 percent butterfat weight, not subject to general note 15 and in excess of quota in Chapter 4 additional US note 14	82	0
040520	Other dairy spreads of a type provided in chapter 4 additional US note 1, not subject to general note 15 and in excess of quota in Chapter 4 additional US note 10	54	0
040590	Fats and oils derived from milk, other than butter or dairy spreads, not subject to general note 15 and in excess of quota in Chapter 4 additional US note 14	119	0
040610	Chongos, unripened or uncured cheese, including whey cheese and curd, not subject to general note 15 or additional US note 16 to Chapter 4	57	0
040610	Fresh (unripened/uncured) blue-mold cheese, cheese/substitutes for cheese concentrated or processed from blue-mold cheese, not subject to Chapter 4 US note 17 or to general note 15	14	0
040610	Fresh (unripened/uncured) cheddar cheese, cheese/substitutes for cheese concentrated or processed from cheddar cheese, not subject to Chapter 4 US note 18 or general note 15	35	0
040610	Fresh (unripened/uncured) American-type cheese, cheese concentrated or processed from American-type, not subject to additional US note 19 to Chapter 4 or general note 15	61	0

(table continues next page)

Table 5A.1 US tariffs on dutiable agricultural imports from Canada and Mexico, 2003ᵃ (percent) *(continued)*

HTS code	Description	Canada	Mexico
040610	Fresh (unripened/uncured) edam and gouda cheeses, cheese/substitutes for cheese concentrated or processed therefrom, not subject to Chapter 4 US note 20 or to general note 15	60	0
040610	Fresh (unripened/uncured) Italian-type cheeses from cow's milk, cheese/substitutes concentrated or processed therefrom, not subject to Chapter 4 US note 21 or to general note 15	29	0
040610	Fresh (unripened/uncured) Swiss/emmenthaler cheeses excluding eye formation, gruyere-process cheese, and cheese concentrated or processed from such	39	0
040610	Fresh cheese, and substitutes for cheese, nesoi, with 0.5 percent or less by weight of butterfat, not described in additional US note 23 to Chapter 4 or general note 15	30	0
040610	Fresh cheese, and substitutes for cheese, concentrated cow's milk, nesoi, 0 to 0.5 percent by weight of butterfat, not described in additional US note 16 to Chapter 4 or general note 15	25	0
040620	Blue-veined cheese (except Roquefort or Stilton), grated or powdered, not subject to general note 15 or additional US note 17 to Chapter 4	38	0
040620	Cheddar cheese, grated or powdered, not subject to general note 15 or additional US note 18 to Chapter 4	19	0
040620	Colby cheese, grated or powdered, not described in general note 15 or additional US note 19 to Chapter 4	49	0
040620	Edam and gouda cheese, grated or powdered, not subject to general note 15 or additional US note 20 to Chapter 4	35	0
040620	Romano, reggiano, provolone, provoletti, sbrinz, and goya, made from cow's milk, grated or powdered, not subject to Chapter 4 US note 21 or to general note 15	24	0
040620	Cheese containing or processed from blue-veined cheese (except Roquefort), grated/powdered, not subject to additional US note 17 to Chapter 4	68	0
040620	Cheese containing or processed from cheddar cheese, grated or powdered, subject to additional US note 18 to Chapter 4	0	0
040620	Cheese containing or processed from cheddar cheese, grated or powdered, not subject to additional US note 18 to Chapter 4	19	0
040620	Cheese containing or processed from American-type cheese (except cheddar), grated or powdered, subject to additional US note 19 to Chapter 4	0	0
040620	Cheese containing or processed from American-type cheese (except cheddar), grated or powdered, not subject to additional US note 19 to Chapter 4	56	0

040620	Cheese containing or processed from edam or gouda cheeses, grated or powdered, subject to additional US note 20 to Chapter 4	0	0
040620	Cheese containing or processed from edam or gouda cheeses, grated or powdered, not subject to additional US note 20 to Chapter 4	12	0
040620	Cheese containing or processed from Italian-type cheeses made from cow's milk, grated or powdered, not subject to additional US note 21 to Chapter 4	60	0
040620	Cheese containing or processed from Swiss, emmenthaler or gruyere-process cheeses, grated or powdered, not subject to additional US note 22 to Chapter 4	55	0
040620	Cheese (including mixtures), nesoi, not over 0.5 percent by weight of butterfat, grated or powdered, not subject to additional US note 23 to Chapter 4	34	0
040620	Cheese (including mixtures), nesoi, 0 to 0.5 percent by weight of butterfat, w/cow's milk, grated or powdered, not subject to additional US note 16 to Chapter 4	21	0
040620	Blue-veined cheese (except Roquefort), processed, not grated or powdered, not subject to general note 15 or additional US note 17 to Chapter 4	37	0
040630	Cheddar cheese, processed, not grated or powdered, not subject to general note 15 or in additional US note 18 to Chapter 4	14	0
040630	Colby cheese, processed, not grated or powdered, not subject to general note 15 or additional US note 19 to Chapter 4	83	0
040630	Edam and gouda cheese, processed, not grated or powdered, not subject to general note 15 or additional US note 20 to Chapter 4	61	0
040630	Gruyere-process cheese, processed, not grated or powdered, not subject to general note 15 or additional US note 22 to Chapter 4	18	0
040630	Processed cheese concentrated/processed from blue-veined cheese (except Roquefort), not grated/powdered, not subject to additional US note 17 to Chapter 4, not to general note 15	48	0
040630	Processed cheese concentrated/processed from cheddar cheese, not grated/powdered, not subject to additional US note 18 or general note 15	40	0
040630	Processed cheese concentrated/processed from American-type cheese (except cheddar), not grated/powdered, subject to additional US note 19 to Chapter 4 or general note 15	0	0

(table continues next page)

Table 5A.1 US tariffs on dutiable agricultural imports from Canada and Mexico, 2003[a] (percent) *(continued)*

HTS code	Description	Canada	Mexico
040630	Processed cheese concentrated/processed from American-type cheese (except cheddar), not grated/powdered, not subject to additional US note 19 to Chapter 4 or general note 15	56	0
040630	Processed cheese concentrated/processed from edam or gouda, not grated/powdered, not subject to additional US note 20 to Chapter 4 or general note 15	0	0
040630	Processed cheese concentrated/processed from edam or gouda, not grated/powdered, not subject to additional US note 20 to Chapter 4 or general note 15	84	0
040630	Processed cheese concentrated/processed from Italian-type cheese, not grated/powdered, not subject to additional US note 21 to Chapter 4 or general note 15	33	0
040630	Processed cheese concentrated/processed from Swiss/emmenthaler/gruyere-process, not grated/powdered, not subject to additional US note 22 to Chapter 4 or general note 15	39	0
040630	Processed cheese (including mixtures), nesoi, not over 0.5 percent by weight butterfat, not grated or powdered, not subject to Chapter 4 US note 23 or general note 15	27	0
040630	Processed cheese (including mixtures), nesoi, with cow's milk, not grated or powdered, not subject to additional US note 16 to Chapter 4 or general note 15	49	0
040640	Blue-veined cheese, nesoi, not subject to general note 15 of the HTS or to additional US note 17 to Chapter 4	43	0
040690	Cheddar cheese, nesoi, not subject to general note 15 of the HTS or to additional US note 18 to Chapter 4	26	0
040690	Edam and gouda cheese, nesoi, not subject to general note 15 of the HTS or to additional US note 20 to Chapter 4	46	0
040690	Goya cheese from cow's milk, not in original loaves, nesoi, not subject to general note 15 or to additional US note 21 to Chapter 4	45	0
040690	Sbrinz cheese from cow's milk, nesoi, not subject to general note 15 or to additional US note 21 to Chapter 4	95	0
040690	Romano, reggiano, parmesan, provolone, and provoletti cheese, nesoi, from cow's milk, not subject to general note 15 or Chapter 4 US note 21	28	0
040690	Swiss or emmenthaler cheese with eye formation, nesoi, not subject to general note 15 or to additional US note 25 to Chapter 4	40	0
040690	Colby cheese, nesoi, not subject to general note 15 or to additional US note 19 to Chapter 4	34	0
040690	Cheeses and substitutes for cheese (including mixture), nesoi, with romano/reggiano/parmesan/provolone/etc., from cow's milk, not subject to Chapter 4 US note 21 or general note 15	71	0

HTS	Description		
040690	Cheeses and substitutes for cheese (including mixture), nesoi, with or from blue-veined cheese, not subject to additional US note 17 to Chapter 4 or general note 15	36	0
040690	Cheeses and substitutes for cheese (including mixture), nesoi, with or from cheddar cheese, not subject to additional US note 18 to Chapter 4 or general note 15	16	0
040690	Cheeses and substitutes for cheese (including mixture), nesoi, with or from American cheese except cheddar, not subject to additional US note 19 to Chapter 4 or general note 15	44	0
040690	Cheeses and substitutes for cheese (including mixture), nesoi, with or from edam or gouda cheese, not subject to additional US note 20 to Chapter 4 or general note 5	48	0
040690	Cheeses and substitutes for cheese (including mixture), nesoi, with or from Swiss, emmenthaler, or gruyere, not subject to Chapter 4 US note 22 or general note 15	69	0
040690	Cheeses and substitutes for cheese (including mixture), nesoi, with butterfat not over 0.5 percent by weight, not subject to additional US note 23 to Chapter 4 or general note 15	18	0
040690	Cheeses and substitutes for cheese (including mixture), nesoi, with cow's milk, with butterfat 0 to 0.5 percent by weight, not subject to Chapter 4 US note 16 or general note 15	26	0
Sugar			
170111	Cane sugar, raw solid form, without flavoring or coloring, nesoi, not subject to general note 15 or additional US note 5 to Chapter 17	89	27
170112	Beet sugar, raw, in solid form, without added flavoring or coloring, nesoi, not subject to general note 15 or additional US note 5 to Chapter 17	44	13
170191	Cane/beet sugar and pure sucrose, refined, solid, w/added coloring but not flavor, not subject to general note 15 or additional US note 5 to Chapter 17	38	11
170191	Cane/beet sugar and pure sucrose, refined, solid, w/added flavoring, 0 to 65 percent by weight sugar, described in Chapter 17 US note 2, subject to Chapter 17 US note 7	6	6
170191	Cane/beet sugar and pure sucrose, refined, solid, w/added flavoring, 0 to 65 percent by weight sugar, described in Chapter 17 US note 2, not subject to general note 15/Chapter 17 US note 7	83	0
170191	Cane/beet sugar and pure sucrose, refined, solid, w/added flavoring, 0 to 10 percent by weight sugar, described in Chapter 17 US note 3, not subject to general note 15/Chapter 17 US note 8	61	0

(table continues next page)

Table 5A.1 US tariffs on dutiable agricultural imports from Canada and Mexico, 2003[a] (percent) *(continued)*

HTS code	Description	Canada	Mexico
170199	Cane/beet sugar and pure sucrose, refined, solid, w/o added coloring or flavoring, not subject to general note 15 or additional US note 5 to Chapter 17	0	16
170230	Glucose and glucose syrup not containing or containing in dry state less than 20 percent fructose; blended, see additional US note 9 (Chapter 17)	6	6
170230	Glucose and glucose syrup not containing or containing in dry state less than 20 percent fructose; blended syrups (Chapter 17 note 4), nesoi	28	0
170240	Blended syrup described in additional US note 4 (Chapter 17), containing in dry state 20 to 50 percent by weight of fructose, see additional US note 9 (Chapter 17)	6	6
170240	Blended syrup described in additional US note 4 (Chapter 17), containing in dry state 20 to 50 percent by weight of fructose, nesoi	20	0
170260	Other fructose and fructose syrup containing in dry state >50 percent by weight of fructose, blended syrup (see additional US note 4 to Chapter 17) and see additional US note 9	6	6
170260	Other fructose and fructose syrup containing in dry state >50 percent by weight of fructose, blended syrup (see additional US note 4 to Chapter 17), nesoi	159	0
170290	Cane/beet sugars and syrups (including invert sugar); nesoi; w/soluble nonsugar solids, 6 percent or less soluble solids, not subject to general note 15 or Chapter 17 US note 5	0	15
170290	Blended syrups described in additional US note 4 to Chapter 17, nesoi, subject to additional US note 9 to Chapter 17	6	6
170290	Blended syrups described in additional US note 4 to Chapter 17, nesoi, not subject to additional US note 9 to Chapter 17	93	0
170290	Sugars nesoi w/o 65 percent by dry weight sugar, described in additional US note 2 to Chapter 17 and subject to additional US note 7 to Chapter 17	6	6
170290	Sugars nesoi w/o 65 percent by dry weight sugar, described in additional US note 2 to Chapter 17 and not subject to additional US note 7 to Chapter 17	17	0

Peanuts

120210	Peanuts (groundnuts), not roasted or cooked, in shell, subject to general note 15 of the HTS	164	164
120210	Peanuts (groundnuts), not roasted or cooked, in shell, subject to additional US note 2 to Chapter 12	164	164
120210	Peanuts (groundnuts), not roasted or cooked, in shell, subject to additional US note 2 to Chapter 12	164	164
120210	Peanuts (groundnuts), not roasted or cooked, in shell, not subject to general note 15 or additional US note 2 to Chapter 12	164	164
120220	Peanuts (groundnuts), not roasted or cooked, shelled, subject to general note 15 of the HTS	132	132
120220	Peanuts (groundnuts), not roasted or cooked, shelled, subject to additional US note 2 to Chapter 12	132	132
120220	Peanuts (groundnuts), not roasted or cooked, shelled, subject to additional US note 2 to Chapter 12	132	132
120220	Peanuts (groundnuts), not roasted or cooked, shelled, not subject to general note 15 or additional US note 2 to Chapter 12	132	132

nesoi = not elsewhere specified or included.

a. In the case of US imports from Canada, the figures show out-of-quota tariffs, which are not scheduled for reduction. Major exceptions to agricultural trade liberalization include US imports of Canadian dairy products, peanuts, peanut butter, cotton, sugar, and sugar-containing products, and Canadian imports of US dairy products, poultry, eggs, and margarine. In the case of US imports from Mexico, the figures show out-of-quota tariffs, which again are not scheduled for reduction. Agricultural commodities not subject to tariff and quota elimination until 2008 include Mexican exports of frozen concentrated orange juice, sugar, and peanuts, and US exports to Mexico of corn, dried beans, and nonfat dry milk. However, in-quota imports are subject to lower (often zero) tariffs, and the quotas are gradually expanded. All other agricultural products that are duty-free from both Canada and Mexico are not listed in this table.

Sources: USDA Economic Research Service (correspondence with John Wainio, 2003); and Zahniser (2005).

Table 5A.2 US agricultural trade with NAFTA partners, 1992–2003 (millions of dollars)

Commodity	1992	1993	1994	1995	1996	1997	1998	1999	2000	2001	2002	2003
NAFTA												
US exports[a]												
Agriculture, total	8,742	8,926	10,136	9,316	11,563	11,957	13,144	12,682	14,050	15,525	15,905	17,193
Animals and animal products	2,150	2,114	2,383	1,847	2,145	2,702	2,864	2,813	3,212	3,545	3,422	3,569
Grains and feeds	1,877	1,772	2,186	2,093	3,196	2,374	2,909	2,831	3,048	3,634	3,811	4,048
Fruits and preparations	788	837	871	795	810	881	880	937	1,041	1,071	1,140	1,223
Fruit juices	166	170	184	210	227	230	256	267	277	266	272	298
Nuts and preparations	170	171	169	179	198	203	206	223	247	228	246	270
Vegetables and preparations	1,230	1,321	1,516	1,373	1,487	1,701	1,917	1,872	2,036	2,186	2,362	2,504
Oilseeds and products	1,007	1,028	1,184	1,193	1,562	1,827	1,630	1,559	1,594	1,781	2,045	2,360
Cattle, live, including calves	173	110	172	67	91	169	148	166	261	259	125	48
Tomatoes	139	121	119	100	95	122	111	109	143	135	123	135
Sugar and related products	215	231	254	230	266	294	331	304	326	326	304	343
Cut flowers	129	127	135	132	134	149	155	156	161	163	158	193
Beverages, excluding fruit juices	163	165	226	166	173	200	211	226	234	255	239	260
Nonagricultural, total	114,706	123,789	143,272	149,371	163,102	192,167	201,155	215,013	242,795	220,702	213,546	215,633
Agriculture as percent of total exports	7	7	7	6	7	6	6	6	5	7	7	7
US imports[b]												
Agriculture, total	6,520	7,376	8,191	9,464	10,553	11,555	12,473	12,871	13,738	15,128	15,866	16,587
Animals and animal products	2,226	2,464	2,323	2,737	2,797	3,048	3,124	3,286	3,780	4,413	4,338	3,722
Grains and feeds	828	1,008	1,372	1,403	1,669	1,862	1,707	1,815	1,875	2,063	2,271	2,324
Fruits and preparations	391	380	438	570	616	639	808	993	852	934	967	1,126
Fruit juices	37	42	66	94	88	90	107	96	89	76	91	85
Nuts and preparations	77	72	79	87	70	75	113	101	112	76	98	126
Vegetables and preparations	1,072	1,379	1,491	1,746	2,066	2,201	2,727	2,715	2,979	3,389	3,524	4,102
Oilseeds and products	361	439	662	639	810	794	865	697	630	610	620	775
Cattle, live, including calves	1,245	1,341	1,151	1,409	1,121	1,119	1,144	1,000	1,152	1,461	1,447	867
Tomatoes	139	310	326	423	618	576	668	609	573	652	725	992
Sugar and related products	244	250	310	304	354	389	451	494	483	620	762	859

Cut flowers											
16	18	21	31	30	39	41	43	47	47	45	366
Beverages, excluding fruit juices											
373	387	460	494	607	715	865	1,019	1,199	1,390	1,523	1,623
Nonagricultural, total											
124,105	140,237	167,516	165,419	218,278	239,417	253,140	291,831	347,107	329,369	325,826	341,496
Agriculture as percent of total imports											
5	5	5	5	5	5	5	4	4	4	5	5
US agricultural exports to world											
43,237	42,965	46,164	56,192	60,408	57,134	51,801	48,378	51,246	53,658	53,005	59,561
US nonagricultural exports to world											
386,636	400,581	440,821	495,745	523,389	593,770	589,674	597,676	666,043	618,888	582,238	598,477
Agriculture as percent of total exports											
10	10	9	10	10	9	8	7	7	8	8	9
US agricultural imports from world											
24,796	25,117	27,024	30,255	33,511	36,148	36,894	37,673	38,974	39,366	41,935	47,376
US nonagricultural imports from world											
496,385	545,738	625,317	704,360	752,505	820,334	863,635	971,052	1,156,376	1,083,150	1,102,205	1,192,123
Agriculture as percent of total imports											
5	4	4	4	4	4	4	4	3	4	4	4

Mexico

US exports[a]

Agriculture, total											
3,799	3,618	4,587	3,521	5,441	5,177	6,151	5,624	6,410	7,404	7,252	7,879
Animals and animal products											
1,254	1,173	1,357	818	1,083	1,529	1,662	1,569	1,802	2,097	2,021	2,157
Grains and feeds											
1,064	888	1,234	1,060	2,069	1,165	1,639	1,578	1,686	2,061	2,048	2,208
Fruits and preparations											
77	110	185	85	95	117	128	190	246	259	242	234
Fruit juices											
7	8	12	6	7	8	15	16	29	24	27	22
Nuts and preparations											
37	37	44	33	45	44	46	60	78	71	73	81
Vegetables and preparations											
158	172	250	141	250	281	432	376	457	559	565	633
Oilseeds and products											
717	656	852	833	1,100	1,247	1,161	1,046	1,027	1,097	1,304	1,471
Cattle, live, including calves											
149	63	99	14	56	132	85	58	81	103	75	21
Tomatoes											
10	10	14	1	2	13	4	4	22	20	12	8
Sugar and related products											
66	59	81	59	108	101	99	97	105	78	50	66
Fresh cut flowers											
0	0	0	0	0	0	0	0	0	0	0	0
Beverages, excluding fruit juices											
52	71	103	43	43	42	36	41	54	78	68	77

(table continues next page)

Table 5A.2 US agricultural trade with NAFTA partners, 1992–2003 (millions of dollars) *(continued)*

Commodity	1992	1993	1994	1995	1996	1997	1998	1999	2000	2001	2002	2003
Nonagricultural, total	36,272	37,095	45,038	41,798	49,902	63,927	70,189	76,377	94,805	84,146	79,496	76,017
Agriculture as percent of total exports	9	9	9	8	10	7	8	7	6	8	8	9
US imports[b]												
Agriculture, total	2,378	2,718	2,894	3,835	3,764	4,109	4,686	4,881	5,077	5,265	5,518	6,301
Animals and animal products	374	459	386	601	174	230	271	362	477	485	378	579
Grains and feeds	53	60	85	105	128	158	156	161	168	197	215	258
Fruits and preparations	321	314	358	475	508	530	676	854	701	763	784	900
Fruit juices	26	31	58	80	74	65	91	71	67	51	62	43
Nuts and preparations	63	51	55	66	45	48	86	72	83	43	67	99
Vegetables and preparations	809	1,058	1,125	1,306	1,499	1,484	1,791	1,679	1,779	2,020	2,047	2,405
Oilseeds and products	42	29	27	32	37	32	50	43	39	44	37	39
Cattle, live, including calves	341	430	352	546	122	177	206	293	406	408	301	471
Tomatoes	133	304	315	406	580	517	567	490	412	485	552	761
Sugar and related products	31	38	69	91	121	129	158	176	175	215	296	267
Fresh cut flowers	10	12	13	19	15	16	18	18	22	21	21	15
Beverages, excluding fruit juices	169	186	219	275	360	484	631	759	884	1,030	1,178	1,271
Nonagricultural, total	31,213	35,556	45,249	57,315	69,859	80,260	87,691	103,436	128,720	124,394	127,785	130,023
Agriculture as percent of total imports	7	7	6	6	5	5	5	5	4	4	4	5
Canada												
US exports[a]												
Agriculture, total	4,943	5,308	5,550	5,794	6,122	6,780	6,993	7,058	7,640	8,121	8,654	9,314
Animals and animal products	897	941	1,025	1,029	1,062	1,173	1,202	1,244	1,410	1,448	1,376	1,412
Grains and feeds	814	884	952	1,032	1,127	1,209	1,270	1,253	1,363	1,573	1,761	1,840
Fruits and preparations	711	727	686	709	715	764	752	746	794	812	898	989
Fruit juices	159	162	171	204	220	222	241	251	248	242	245	276
Nuts and preparations	133	134	126	145	154	159	160	163	169	157	173	189
Vegetables and preparations	1,072	1,149	1,266	1,232	1,237	1,421	1,485	1,497	1,579	1,626	1,798	1,871
Oilseeds and products	290	372	332	360	463	580	469	512	566	684	749	889

Cattle, live, including calves	24	48	73	53	35	37	63	109	180	156	50	27
Tomatoes	129	111	105	98	94	109	107	104	121	115	112	126
Sugar and related products	149	172	173	172	158	193	232	207	221	248	254	278
Fresh cut flowers	16	17	17	15	15	20	22	24	25	27	27	29
Beverages, excluding fruit juices	110	94	123	126	130	158	175	185	180	177	171	183
Nonagricultural, total	78,435	86,693	98,234	107,573	113,200	128,240	130,966	138,636	147,990	136,556	134,050	139,616
Agriculture as percent of total exports	6	6	5	5	5	5	5	5	5	6	6	6
US imports[b]												
Agriculture, total	4,143	4,658	5,298	5,629	6,789	7,446	7,787	7,990	8,661	9,863	10,348	10,286
Animals and animal products	1,852	2,005	1,937	2,136	2,623	2,818	2,853	2,924	3,303	3,928	3,960	3,144
Grains and feeds	775	948	1,287	1,298	1,541	1,704	1,551	1,654	1,706	1,866	2,056	2,065
Fruits and preparations	70	66	80	95	108	109	132	139	150	171	183	226
Fruit juices	11	11	9	14	14	25	16	25	21	24	28	41
Nuts and preparations	13	21	24	22	26	27	26	29	28	34	32	27
Vegetables and preparations	263	321	366	439	568	716	936	1,037	1,200	1,369	1,476	1,696
Oilseeds and products	319	410	635	607	773	762	816	654	591	566	583	736
Cattle, live, including calves	903	911	799	863	999	943	938	708	746	1,052	1,146	396
Tomatoes	6	6	10	17	37	59	101	120	161	167	173	231
Sugar and related products	213	212	241	213	234	260	293	317	308	405	466	593
Fresh cut flowers	4	4	5	7	10	14	15	15	17	18	17	20
Beverages, excluding fruit juices	204	201	241	219	247	231	235	260	315	360	345	352
Nonagricultural, total	92,892	104,681	122,267	135,104	148,419	159,157	165,449	188,396	218,387	204,974	198,041	211,473
Agriculture as percent of total imports	4	4	4	4	4	4	4	4	4	5	5	5

a. US domestic exports.
b. US imports for consumption.

Sources: USDA Foreign Agriculture Service (FATUS) database, 2004; and USITC Interactive Tariff and Trade Dataweb, 2004; and US Department of Commerce, International Trade Administration, 2004.

6

The Automotive Sector

Disputes in the automotive sector led to the first postwar trade agreement between the United States and Canada—the 1965 Canada–United States Automotive Agreement (commonly known as the 1965 Auto Pact). Clearing up residual automotive trade and investment frictions was central to the 1989 Canada-US Free Trade Agreement (CUSFTA). Likewise, no industrial sector was more critical to the success of NAFTA than the automotive sector.

By far, motor vehicles and parts account for a larger share of intraregional trade in North America than any product sector. Three-way auto trade in 2003 was $125 billion, representing 20 percent of total trade among NAFTA partners. Between 1993 and 2003, the value of NAFTA auto trade almost doubled, accounting for 18 percent of the total growth in NAFTA trade over this period (calculated using data in appendix table 6A.1). Trade in vehicles and parts with non-NAFTA countries also increased sharply; North American auto-sector imports grew almost twice as fast as auto exports to the rest of the world. Together, the auto sector in 2003 accounted for 12 percent of merchandise trade between non-NAFTA and NAFTA countries.

To a considerable extent, NAFTA, like its predecessors, deepened integration of the North American automotive market. The same "Big Three" automotive producers (General Motors, Ford, and Chrysler) operated in all three NAFTA countries well before negotiations commenced for the 1965 Auto Pact, the 1989 CUSFTA, and the 1994 NAFTA. When the NAFTA negotiations began, all three trade ministers understood (with relief) that the elimination of trade barriers and investment incentives would not prompt huge segments of the automotive industry to shut down in one North American location and move to another. Instead, they expected that plants would continue to accelerate the ongoing process of specialization and that intraindustry trade would flourish—exactly as happened in the wake of the 1965 Auto Pact. Our analysis shows that these expectations have been borne out.

Besides being an important sector in its own right, the auto industry provides a substantial market for other industries, particularly those processing raw materials (such as textiles, rubber, steel, and aluminum). Accordingly, the performance of the auto industry has a direct and substantial impact on the entire economy—and on trade policy.

Policy in the Auto Sector

Policy integration of the North American auto industry followed the production and distribution initiatives of the Big Three. The policy process began with the 1965 Auto Pact, expanded through the Mexican Automotive Decree of 1977,[1] and culminated in the extension of the North American auto regime to Mexico in 1994, when NAFTA entered into force. Big Three investment in the Mexican automotive sector long preceded NAFTA negotiations, and a de facto hexagonal trade regime in vehicles and auto parts already existed between Mexico, the United States, and Canada. NAFTA institutionalized the existing degree of integration and created a more stable and competitive environment for auto production and trade. The more integrated North American market also attracted new investment from European and Japanese automakers. Today, Volkswagen produces the new Beetle in Mexico for the world market and is investing $100 million to begin producing the Golf there in 2005; Nissan produces the Sentra in Mexico to supply the Western Hemisphere. Toyota invested $140 million to open its first Mexican assembly plant in Tijuana in 2004. The plant, located near its pickup bed factory, will produce the Tacoma pickup truck.[2]

---

1. The 1977 Automotive Decree made participation by foreign firms in the domestic Mexican market contingent upon exports. Contrary to economic doctrine, the decree's trade-balancing requirements and ownership limitations accelerated Mexican auto industry rationalization. See Moran (1998) and Samuels (1990).

2. Rather than representing a zero-sum game, integration of the auto sector under NAFTA could spawn more investment in US auto plants. As an example, when its Tijuana plant expanded, Toyota overhauled its Long Beach plant by investing several hundred million dollars. This represented the first vehicle production investment in southern California since 1992. By 2003, Toyota added about 12,000 workers to its US employment base. Based on extensive written comments provided by Theodore Moran, February 2005. See also "Toyota Plans to Move Production of Parts of Pickup to Mexico," *Wall Street Journal*, January 4, 2002, A8; and John O'Dell, "Toyota to Add Assembly Site in Southland," *Los Angeles Times*, June 7, 2002.

The 1965 Auto Pact

The 1965 agreement linked the auto industries of Canada and the United States by ending Canadian policies aimed at self-sufficiency in automobiles and major components.[3] The higher level of integration and better access to the world's largest auto market allowed Canada to develop an internationally competitive auto industry. The Auto Pact created a tariff-free region for automotive trade; at the same time, it provided a degree of "safe-harbor" protection to ensure that the major firms continued their investment and production in Canada. The Auto Pact allowed the Big Three to rationalize production between Canada and the United States and form a single integrated production and marketing system. The ensuing rationalization enabled some parts and assembly firms to choose a unique production location to supply the regional market. As a consequence, each country specialized to a greater degree in particular automotive lines (e.g., trucks or large cars) and components (e.g., engines or transmissions).

In the margins of the Auto Pact, Canada imposed safeguards to ensure that Canadian production corresponded to a high percentage of Canadian consumption of vehicles and parts.[4] Under the Auto Pact, Canadian vehicles and parts entered the United States duty-free, based both on the place of origin (Canada) and the extent of regional content (at least 50 percent North American, meaning Canadian or US components). However, US and other vehicles and parts entered Canada duty-free from any country, based on the fulfillment by the importing manufacturer of the Auto Pact performance criteria (volume of Canadian production and Canadian value added requirement), not on the place of origin.

The Canada-US Free Trade Agreement

As a result of the Auto Pact, the US and Canadian automotive sectors were already largely integrated by the 1980s. The primary changes in CUSFTA for the automotive sector pertained to imports from outside North America. Under the Auto Pact, Canadian firms could import automobiles or parts from Europe or Japan and then sell them in the US market without

---

3. According to Paul Wonnacott (1965), the Canadian government ran a narrowly focused trade-balancing policy in parts under the pre-1965 auto regime. The idea was to encourage the manufacture of engines and transmissions in Canada, but allow the importation of other parts. We thank Paul Wonnacott and others for providing written comments to an earlier draft of this chapter.

4. The US government acquiesced to Canadian value added requirements because they were viewed as transitional arrangements. As a continuing source of bilateral trade friction, Canadian value added requirements almost led to the repudiation of the Auto Pact in August 1971.

paying duties at any step along the way, provided that the European and Japanese exporters maintained a certain production-to-sales ratio and a value added threshold through their Canadian manufacturing subsidiaries. Japanese auto firms, apart from Honda, never chose to meet these requirements, but Volvo and European subsidiaries of the Big Three did.

CUSFTA terminated duty-free entry based on a production-to-sales ratio test but "grandfathered" firms that already enjoyed duty-free preferences in the auto sector (allowing them to continue doing so). Also, before CUSFTA, Canada offered foreign firms reduced tariffs if they met certain value added thresholds for production in Canada. The United States regarded these tariff waivers as a disguised subsidy, and CUSFTA phased them out.[5] Finally, CUSFTA set a stronger origin threshold for "North American" production: Fifty percent of the cost of manufacturing must occur in Canada or the United States in order for the final product to qualify for duty-free treatment. CUSFTA effectively set the standard for future FTA content requirements, unlike the Canadian value added tests under the post-1965 agreement.[6]

Mexico

The Big Three started investing in mexico in the 1930s. In the 1960s, Nissan and Volkswagen joined them as mexican producers. During the 1960s and 1970s (the era of import substitution), mexico decided that its domestic motor industry should supply essentially the entire domestic market. In 1962 the Mexican government prohibited imports of finished ve?hicles and imposed high local-content requirements on the foreign companies producing cars in Mexico (Ford, GM, Chrysler, Nissan, and Volkswagen). The Mexican Automotive Decree of 1977 made continued participation by foreign firms contingent on exports—essentially a trade-balancing requirement. By 1980, the Mexican policy package had created a 500,000-unit motor vehicle industry producing vehicles with 50 percent local content, plus substantial exports of parts and components (to meet

---

5. Japanese and European automobile producers ultimately won a WTO case, claiming that the Canadian practice of giving US auto firms duty-free entry if they meet the Canadian production and value added tests, while phasing out the tariff waivers for third-country producers, was discriminatory (Canada—Certain Measures Affecting the Automotive Industry, WT/DS139 [brought by Japan], and WT/DS142 [brought by the European Commission]). In response, Canada abandoned the production and value added tests, effectively "ending" the Auto Pact for good. Canada now imposes a 6.1 percent tariff on all non-NAFTA automobile imports. However, imports from Mexico and the United States, which constituted 82 percent of Canadian automotive imports in 2002, enter duty-free under NAFTA.

6. We thank Paul Wonnacott for emphasizing this point to us.

the trade-balancing requirements). But the industry as a whole was uncompetitive when benchmarked against international standards.[7]

When Mexico joined the General Agreement on Tariffs and Trade (GATT) in 1986, its schedule of tariff liberalization conspicuously excluded autos. However, the Mexican government soon recognized that its protective auto regime, while eminently successful in jump-starting domestic production, had fostered a high-cost and uncompetitive industry. The Mexican Automotive Decree of 1989 substantially liberalized Mexican rules on the auto industry, even though the national value added requirement and native ownership requirement remained huge impediments to industry rationalization.[8]

NAFTA

NAFTA had only an indirect impact on Canada-US automotive-sector integration, because each country already enjoyed relatively unfettered access to the other's market.[9] The difficult negotiating issues for the automotive sector all pertained to Mexico.

First, the rule-of-origin threshold was raised in two phases to 56 percent in 1998 and ultimately to 62.5 percent in 2002 for most automotive products, a substantial increase from the 50 percent threshold in CUSFTA. The threshold was raised to prevent foreign automotive producers (especially Japanese producers) from using Mexico as an export platform to sell into the United States. Canada resisted pushing the rule of origin threshold too high because it did not want to disrupt existing production chains, which rely to some extent on non–North American components.

The second order of business for the five established auto firms was to gain better access to the Mexican market. Although Mexico had taken steps to liberalize its automotive sector since joining GATT in 1986, full liberalization of the Mexican auto industry culminated with NAFTA. The agreement ultimately dismantled the protectionist auto regime but al-

---

7. See Womack, Jones, and Roos (1991, 264). Even in this period, some Mexican plants (e.g., Ford in Hermosillo) manufactured good-quality autos at competitive costs for export to the US market.

8. Moran (1998) contends that unlike the ownership and value added requirements in the Mexican policy package, the trade-balancing requirements fostered rationalization and lower costs. Requirements under the Mexican Automotive Decree of 1989, however, remained onerous enough that very few vehicles were imported into Mexico. We thank G. Mustafa Mohatarem for extensive written comments on the Mexican auto regime and other issues.

9. Under the surface, however, US-Canadian tensions were mounting over secret deals between Canada and Big Three firms involving production incentives. These issues were quietly resolved in the context of NAFTA talks.

lowed a long phaseout period. National-content requirements were transformed into regional-content requirements, and a ten-year phaseout period (starting in 1995) was scheduled for the Mexican Automotive Decree of 1989. These measures gave the Mexican auto industry breathing room to meet import competition; meanwhile NAFTA ensured immediate and unfettered access of Mexican automotive products to the US and Canadian markets.

Mexican tariffs on cars and light trucks imported from the United States and Canada were lowered from 20 to 10 percent in 1994. Duties were phased out for light trucks in 1998 and for cars in 2003. Duties on parts were fully phased out in 2003 (75 percent of US parts exports have entered the Mexican market duty-free since 1998). However, Mexico maintained its most favored nation (MFN) tariffs on autos and parts imported from non-NAFTA sources. As Mexico has extended its network of bilateral trade agreements, however, these tariffs have been reduced or eliminated.[10]

NAFTA also required the gradual phaseout of nontariff auto trade barriers. In 1994, Mexico lowered the trade-balancing requirement from $1.75 of exports for every dollar of imports to $0.80 of exports per dollar imported. The requirement was phased down to $0.55 in 2003 and then eliminated in 2004. The national value added requirement dropped from 36 percent in 1994 to 29 percent in 2003 and was eliminated at the start of 2004. The national-content requirement was lowered from 30 to 20 percent both for the auto parts industry and "national suppliers" (maquiladoras qualify as national suppliers if they are not owned by the assembler they supply). Finally, import quotas were eliminated for heavy trucks and buses in 1998, and the surviving import ban on used cars will be eliminated by 2009.

Before the 1990s, the Mexican auto parts industry was relatively modest and highly protected from international competition.[11] Mexican firms feared NAFTA would mean the end of the domestic parts industry, and in fact many small companies did suffer from intense competition.

Despite these pressures, however, Mexico's auto parts industry as a whole is in good health and competitive internationally. NAFTA allowed

---

10. For example, the EU-Mexico trade pact contains special provisions for the automotive sector. Mexico agreed to eliminate its Automotive Decree by 2004, and improve access for EU vehicles. Mexican tariffs on vehicles were reduced from 20 to 3.3 percent when the pact entered into force in July 2001 and eliminated in 2003. Favorable access is also accorded to European car parts and components. A transitional relaxation of EU rules of origin will allow Mexican industry to comply with European content standards. See the "Communication from the Commission to the Council and the European Parliament, accompanying the final text of the draft decisions by the EC-Mexico Joint Council," http://europa.eu.int/comm/external_relations/news/2000/01_00/doc_00_2.htm (accessed on April 29, 2005).

11. According to Nunez (1990), by 1984, the Mexican automotive parts industry included 310 firms, 40 with sales over $10 million and 50,500 employees.

a long and generous transition period for Mexican parts suppliers—permitting Mexican firms to retain some protection from imports, both by phasing out the national-content requirement over 10 years and by maintaining the 49 percent maximum foreign investment share in national-supplier firms for five years (until 1999).

In fact, the Mexican parts industry adapted faster to competition than negotiators expected. Mexican producers established strategic alliances with foreign companies. Instead of replacing local suppliers, foreign suppliers teamed with Mexican auto parts manufacturers; the former provide the technical and design know-how, and the latter provide the plant and workforce. Links with foreign companies have given Mexican producers the technology to sell competitively in North America and have made Mexico a more attractive location for assembly plant investment from Europe and Japan.

Mexican trade diplomats are trying to enlarge the scope of automotive export destinations to take advantage of markets outside North America (in 2003, 93 percent of Mexican auto exports were destined for the United States and Canada; calculated using data in appendix table 6A.1). The slew of trade agreements that Mexico has negotiated with other partners has become a central feature of the nation's trade strategy.

In fact, Mexico has constructed a large network of FTAs with countries in Europe, East Asia, and Latin America as part of an aggressive strategy to become a global trade and investment hub. As of May 2005, Mexico has entered into FTAs with the European Union, Israel, Japan, Chile, Costa Rica, Colombia, Venezuela, Bolivia, Uruguay, Nicaragua, Guatemala, Honduras, El Salvador, and the European Free Trade Association (EFTA) countries, in addition to NAFTA. FTA talks are ongoing with the four South American nations of the Southern Cone Common Market (Mercosur). On the regional level, Mexico is one of the 34 countries negotiating the Free Trade Area of the Americas (FTAA). These trade agreements encourage new investment in Mexico, in the auto industry and elsewhere, to serve the North American market and to open opportunities in the Western Hemisphere, Europe, and Asia.

As a precursor to free trade with Mercosur, Mexico and Brazil signed a bilateral auto pact in July 2002 to export 140,000 automobiles to each other's markets at a duty of 1.1 percent. Before the agreement, Brazil and Mexico could trade only 50,000 units annually at a duty of 8 percent, while additional exports faced a 35 percent tariff in Brazil and a 23 percent tariff in Mexico.[12] The tariffs and the quota of 140,000 autos will be progressively liberalized and eliminated in 2005.

---

12. Nevertheless, in 2003, over 95 percent of Mexican auto and parts exports were still destined for the United States and Canada.

North American Auto Trends

What has happened to the auto industry since NAFTA went into effect, and what, if anything, has NAFTA done to change the North American auto industry? In this section, we look at data on production, sales, employment, wages, investment, and trade to discover the answers. Overall, the effect of NAFTA appears to be very positive, particularly for the Big Three and for Mexico.

Production and Sales

Table 6.1 shows production and sales figures for the auto industry in Canada, Mexico, and the United States between 1993 and 2003. Auto production in the United States has remained rather flat since NAFTA went into effect, averaging 12.1 million units per year over this period, with a peak level of 13.1 million units in 1999. Canada's auto production also peaked in 1999 at 3.1 million units, which was 35 percent above the 1993 level. While auto production in the United States and Canada trailed off during the recession of 2001, Mexico's auto production was slower to decline but had fallen to 1.6 million units in 2003. Within Mexico, roughly 60 percent of the units were produced by the Big Three in 2003; Nissan and Volkswagen accounted for about 15 percent each (Ward's Communications 2004).[13]

Although the United States exports automobiles to most parts of the world, the US appetite for imported cars is particularly strong, and automobile sales in the United States run well ahead of production (table 6.1). In 2003, the number of automobile units sold in the United States was 17 million, down from the 2000 peak of 17.8 million but well above the 1993 figure of 14.2 million. Domestic auto sales exceeded US production by 45 percent. By contrast, domestic production exceeded sales by 1 million units in Canada and 600,000 units in Mexico. Nonetheless, domestic purchases of autos have grown sharply in all three countries under NAFTA. Sales in Mexico plummeted during the peso crisis but reached 1 million units in 2002 and 2003 (some 5 percent of NAFTA sales compared with 3.8 percent in 1995).

---

13. Two new foreign-owned assembly plants are scheduled to open in Mexico in 2005 (Toyota and Volkswagen), compared with only one new assembly plant built in Canada since 1990. As a result of weak demand, operations like Ford's Oakville assembly plant sharply reduced the number of shifts. See "Ford to Build a New Plant in Oakville," CBC News, October 29, 2004; and Steve Arnold, "Weak Sales Are Idling Auto Plants," *The Hamilton Spectator*, November 16, 2004. In an effort to maintain its footing in the auto industry, in March 2005, the Canadian government provided $435 million to attract a $2.5 billion GM upgrade in Ontario. See "GM to Boost Production Plant in Canada," *Wall Street Journal*, March 3, 2005.

Table 6.1   Auto production and sales in North America, 1993–2003

Year	United States Millions of units	United States Percent of NAFTA	Canada Millions of units	Canada Percent of NAFTA	Mexico Millions of units	Mexico Percent of NAFTA	NAFTA Millions of units
Production							
1993	10.9	76.5	2.3	15.9	1.1	7.6	14.2
1994	12.3	78.1	2.3	14.8	1.1	7.2	15.7
1995	12.0	78.2	2.4	15.7	0.9	6.1	15.4
1996	11.9	76.6	2.4	15.5	1.2	7.9	15.5
1997	12.2	75.6	2.6	16.0	1.4	8.4	16.1
1998	12.0	74.9	2.6	16.0	1.5	9.1	16.1
1999	13.1	74.0	3.1	17.3	1.5	8.7	17.6
2000	12.8	72.4	3.0	16.7	1.9	10.9	17.7
2001	11.5	72.3	2.5	16.0	1.9	11.7	15.8
2002	12.3	73.5	2.6	15.7	1.8	10.8	16.7
2003	12.1	74.6	2.6	15.7	1.6	9.7	16.2
Sales							
1993	14.2	88.8	1.2	7.5	0.6	3.8	16.0
1994	15.4	89.1	1.3	7.3	0.6	3.6	17.3
1995	15.1	91.8	1.2	7.1	0.2	1.1	16.5
1996	15.5	90.9	1.2	7.1	0.3	2.0	17.0
1997	15.5	88.9	1.4	8.2	0.5	2.9	17.4
1998	16.0	88.4	1.4	7.9	0.7	3.7	18.1
1999	17.4	88.6	1.5	7.8	0.7	3.6	19.7
2000	17.8	87.7	1.6	7.8	0.9	4.5	20.3
2001	17.4	87.3	1.6	8.0	0.9	4.7	20.0
2002	17.1	86.2	1.7	8.7	1.0	5.1	19.9
2003	17.0	86.6	1.6	8.3	1.0	5.1	19.6

Source: Ward's Communications (2004).

Viewed from the US perspective, mercantilist thinkers would be alarmed. But since NAFTA entered into force, we have not heard the same hue and cry from the Big Three or the United Auto Workers (UAW) about imports that was common in the 1980s and early 1990s—a time when automobile imports from Japan were characterized as a scourge.[14] The Big

14. There is concern, however, that NAFTA facilitated increasing production by foreign-owned companies (transplants) in the United States. (Nissan, Volkswagen, and other foreign companies are major investors in Mexico and the southern United States.) While Big Three production declined significantly under NAFTA, total US production, including transplants, experienced a much smaller overall decline. Transplants, rather than imports, now account for a larger portion of market share lost by the Big Three. Based on extensive written comments provided by G. Mustafa Mohatarem in March 2005. A more likely cause for the rise in transplants (a trend that began in the 1980s) is voluntary export restraints imposed by Japan to calm trade frictions with the United States, which inter alia encouraged Japanese firms to produce in the United States (Cooney and Yacobucci 2005, 56). Nonetheless job loss

Table 6.2 Self-sufficiency index, North America, 1997–2003
(billions of dollars)

Year	Domestic shipments Autos	All manu-facturing	Imports Autos	All manu-facturing	Exports Autos	All manu-facturing	Self-sufficiency index (percent) Autos	All manu-facturing
1997	504.3	4,269.3	159.6	975.6	121.1	798.2	92.9	96.0
1998	525.1	4,328.4	169.4	1,055.2	122.5	818.1	91.8	94.8
1999	601.1	4,505.2	201.0	1,175.0	137.9	868.6	90.5	93.6
2000	581.8	4,734.7	224.4	1,362.9	145.9	983.9	88.1	92.6
2001	527.0	4,464.9	215.7	1,281.5	137.3	917.5	87.1	92.5
2002	682.1	4,396.9	231.6	1,288.9	142.3	883.6	88.4	91.6
2003			237.7	1,356.7	144.9	907.7		

Notes: Imports and exports include intra-NAFTA trade, which is cancelled out in the self-sufficiency index calculation. Auto trade is defined as SITC 78 (road vehicles). Manufacturing trade is defined as SITC 5-8. Shipments data are an aggregation of national statistics. Auto shipments data are defined as NAICS 3361, 3362, and 3363 for Canada and the United States and as Mexican Class 3841 for Mexico. NAICS data for the United States are available starting in 1997.

Sources: UN Comtrade Database, 2004; US Census Bureau (2003, 2005); INEGI (2005); and Statistics Canada (2005).

Three have substantial production capacity in Canada and Mexico. Consequently, Canadian and Mexican "export platforms" for sales to the US market do not harm the Big Three; indeed, they actually improve operating margins by reducing production costs. That of course does not put an end to labor concerns, but it is a side benefit of NAFTA.[15]

To examine the extent to which the North American region supplies its own market, we constructed a NAFTA self-sufficiency index (table 6.2). This index is the ratio of North American production to consumption, where consumption is calculated as the total value produced within NAFTA plus imports from third countries and minus exports to third countries. In 1997, the self-sufficiency index in the auto industry was 93 percent (meaning that the North American auto industry supplied 93 percent of North American auto consumption).[16] By 2002 the index had fallen to 88 percent. Throughout this period, North America has been less self-sufficient in autos than in manufacturing as a whole. Depending on one's

concerns persist. Representative Marcy Kaptur's (D-OH) claims that the Big Three auto-producing states (Ohio, Michigan, and Indiana) lost over 115,621 jobs under NAFTA. See "An Open Letter to President George W. Bush and Mexican President Vicente Fox," September 6, 2001, www.uaw.org/atissue/01/090601kaptur.html (accessed March 2005).

15. As an example, in 2002, Canadian Auto Workers (CAW) plant workers won pay increases of 9 percent over three years and an average hourly wage of C$22.40. But there is growing concern that big companies are unable to meet pension obligations for assembly workers. See Greg Keenan, "CAW Renews Drive to Unionize Toyota," Globe and Mail, July 13, 2004.

16. The detailed NAICS data, which underlie this index, go back only to 1997.

point of view, the trend indicates that North America's ability to meet its own automotive needs is regrettably decreasing or that its level of integration with the rest of the world is happily increasing.

Employment and Wages

Although Big Three managers may not be concerned when production shifts from the United States to Mexico, autoworkers in the United States are far from indifferent. Contrary to the contemporary fear when NAFTA was ratified, however, NAFTA has not harmed US autoworkers to the extent imagined. Their fortunes are primarily tied to the business cycle and to a lesser extent to the dollar exchange rate versus the yen and the euro. Meanwhile, working conditions have improved for autoworkers in Canada since the 1965 Auto Pact and for their counterparts in Mexico since NAFTA went into effect in 1994.

Table 6.3 shows total employment in the auto assembly and auto parts sectors, as well as manufacturing as a whole, between 1994 and 2004 for Canada, Mexico, and the United States. Not surprisingly, fluctuations in employment correspond to changes in production. In all three countries, total auto employment trends followed the business cycle, rising through the 1990s, and receding in the economic slowdown of 2001–02. In the auto industry, as well as the entire manufacturing sector, employment in the United States and Mexico is substantially below levels in the late 1990s. Canada experienced a decline in autoworkers as well, although less severe. In fact, Canada is the only NAFTA country where auto and manufacturing employment are greater today than when NAFTA entered into effect.

Since table 6.3 does not reveal a pronounced migration of US auto jobs to Mexico, we investigate the question further. Using quarterly data from the first quarter of 1994 to the third quarter of 2003, we estimated a regression model to explain the level of US auto employment. The three independent variables are US real GDP (to capture the business cycle and real income growth), time (as a proxy for productivity gains), and Mexican auto employment. We expect US auto employment to be positively correlated with real GDP and negatively correlated with time. To the extent that Mexican auto production substitutes for US production, we also expect US auto employment to be negatively correlated with Mexican auto employment.

The model gives a reasonably good fit, with an R-squared coefficient of 0.56.[17] The model coefficients, taken together, predict a loss of 74,000 US auto jobs between 1994 and 2003, while the actual loss was 43,000. However, the model is most interesting when we consider each independent

17. The R-squared statistic, which ranges from 0 to 1, indicates the regression model's goodness of fit.

Table 6.3 Employment in the auto sector and manufacturing industry, 1994–2004

Year	Assembly[a]	Bodies[b]	Parts[c]	Total auto	Manufacturing
Canada					
1994	56,200	—	72,542	128,742	1,716,245
1995	56,050	—	77,130	133,180	1,748,443
1996	57,508	—	80,210	137,718	1,788,952
1997	54,524	—	81,127	135,651	1,855,391
1998	57,687	—	87,281	144,968	1,916,170
1999	56,913	—	93,175	150,088	1,955,914
2000	55,712	—	98,154	153,866	2,253,900
2001	51,435	—	95,060	146,495	2,229,500
2002	50,985	—	98,114	149,099	2,291,000
2003	48,735	—	103,413	152,148	2,283,400
2004	47,897	—	101,254	149,151	2,297,000
Mexico					
1994	46,838	—	75,225	122,063	1,409,238
1995	38,926	—	64,616	103,542	1,298,665
1996	40,777	—	69,782	110,559	1,332,931
1997	43,987	—	79,752	123,739	1,409,849
1998	49,047	—	89,664	138,711	1,459,307
1999	52,168	—	90,008	142,176	1,475,223
2000	53,950	—	94,539	148,489	1,495,822
2001	51,628	—	86,285	137,913	1,432,840
2002[d]	47,262	—	80,497	127,759	1,360,866
2003[d]	41,101	—	74,345	115,446	1,290,526
2004[d]	38,569	—	74,316	112,885	1,260,103
United States					
1994	281,500	151,400	735,600	1,168,500	17,021,000
1995	294,700	159,900	786,900	1,241,500	17,241,000
1996	285,300	155,100	799,900	1,240,300	17,237,000
1997	286,800	158,200	808,900	1,253,900	17,419,000
1998	283,600	169,700	818,200	1,271,500	17,560,000
1999	291,300	184,200	837,100	1,312,600	17,322,000
2000	291,400	182,700	839,500	1,313,600	17,263,000
2001	278,700	159,400	774,700	1,212,800	16,441,000
2002	265,400	152,200	733,600	1,151,200	15,259,000
2003	264,600	153,000	707,800	1,125,400	14,510,000
2004	256,100	164,500	688,500	1,109,100	14,329,000

a. For United States and Canada: NAICS 3361. For Mexico: 205 Clases de Actividad Económica 384110.
b. For United States: NAICS 3363. Canada and Mexico do not provide separate employment statistics for bodies; instead, employment in auto bodies is included in other automotive categories.
c. For United States and Canada: NAICS 3362. For Mexico: 205 Clases de Actividad Económica 384121, 384122, 384123, 384124, 384125, and 384126.
d. Preliminary estimates.

Sources: Statistics Canada, 2005, www.statcan.ca; INEGI (2005); BLS (2005).

Table 6.4 Compensation cost per hour for autoworkers, 1993–2002 (US dollars per hour)

Year	United States	Canada[a]	Mexico
1993	25.52	20.83	3.98
1994	26.64	20.65	4.09
1995	26.55	20.81	2.56
1996	27.23	21.02	2.51
1997	28.00	20.86	2.93
1998	26.44	20.50	3.02
1999	26.73	19.97	3.45
2000	27.99	21.14	4.18
2001	29.84	20.83	5.04
2002[b]	31.67	21.12	5.12

a. Canadian data for 2000–02 are estimated using the Canadian compensation cost for all manufacturers.
b. Revised BLS methodology contributed to the increase in US compensation rate in 2002.

Note: Industry defined as SIC 371 in all three countries.

Source: BLS (2004).

variable separately. While the coefficients for GDP and time are highly significant and show the expected signs, the coefficient for Mexican employment is not significant, though it does show the expected sign. The magnitudes of the two significant coefficients (GDP and time) are surprisingly large. The time coefficient suggests that technology is removing jobs from the US auto industry at a rate of 117,000 per year. Taking this coefficient by itself (and with a tablespoon of salt), the process of innovation appears to have removed 1.1 million jobs from the industry between 1994 and 2003! Fortunately demand has grown, and the model calculates that 371 auto jobs are created for every billion dollars of additional real GDP (measured in 2000 US dollars). With GDP growth of $2.8 trillion over the period, the coefficient suggests that demand growth created more than 1 million jobs.

The estimated effect of Mexican employment, which is not statistically significant, is to remove 896 auto jobs from the United States for every 1,000 Mexican auto jobs created. Since Mexican auto employment fell by 9,600 jobs over the period, the supposed impact was to *create* about 8,600 US auto jobs. This effect is negligible. The much larger technology and demand effects easily overwhelm any influence of Mexican employment, positive or negative. This analysis suggests that so far as auto jobs are concerned, the fear of southward migration is vastly overstated in popular discussion.

Hourly compensation figures (inclusive of fringe benefits) in table 6.4 tell a less cheerful story from the standpoint of US autoworkers. The earnings figures are expressed in current US dollars and are compiled by the Bureau of Labor Statistics for the purpose of comparison across national boundaries. Although autoworkers in the United States took home more dollars in 2002 (the latest year available) than in 1993, the earnings gain of

24 percent only matched cumulative inflation of 24 percent over the same period. In other words, the real purchasing power of auto wages remained the same. For most US workers, by contrast, the 1990s was a decade when real wages increased. Autoworkers did not do as well, but the auto premium is still large: In 2002 the average autoworker's hourly compensation was $10.34 per hour above the average blue-collar manufacturing worker.

In nominal dollar terms, wages in the Mexican auto industry regained their 1993 level only in 2000, after falling precipitously in 1995. A hasty interpretation would say that nothing improved in the first years of NAFTA. But wages throughout Mexico were unsustainably high in 1993 given the overvalued peso and perilous condition of the Mexican financial system just before the financial crisis of 1994–95. Between January 1990 and January 1994, the peso increased in real value by 35 percent (taking into account both inflation and exchange rates), causing Mexican workers to be paid that much more in dollar terms. The fundamentals of the Mexican economy simply did not support this real appreciation of the peso. The postcrisis path of earnings in the Mexican auto industry is consistent with the general increase in earnings in the Mexican manufacturing sector as a whole. Once the peso crisis settled down, real wages in the automotive sector and the manufacturing sector as a whole managed to increase (see chapter 2).

Mexicans who work in auto assembly earned roughly 30 percent more than the average manufacturing worker in 2002.[18] This differential was the same in 1994 when NAFTA went into effect. The earnings premium in Mexico reflects the fact that auto firms need to attract workers with higher-than-average skills and good work habits. The union influence is decidedly less in Mexico, compared with the United States or Canada.

It is clear from table 6.4 that Mexican autoworkers earn only a fraction of US pay levels. After the peso crisis, the compensation cost for a Mexican autoworker was less than 10 percent that of a US autoworker. Since then, Mexican compensation has steadily risen, to 16 percent of US compensation in 2002.

Although US union leaders argue that Mexico is putting downward pressure on the earnings of US autoworkers (and this may be partly true), another explanation is that the wage premium paid to unionized autoworkers—the amount they earn in excess of the average for manufacturing workers—was compressed in the early 1990s largely as a result of US nonunion auto plants.[19]

---

18. This percentage is calculated using total remuneration and employment data from INEGI (2005).

19. In recent years, the number of auto plants has significantly grown in southern US states, an area traditionally less receptive to unions than the industrial midwest. The UAW has struggled to organize these plants, without significant success ("Rural Alabama auto plant turns UAW battleground," *Detroit News*, October 27, 2003).

To test the hypothesis that international trade with low-wage countries puts downward pressure on US wage premiums, we attempted to find a correlation between the changes in trade balance for an industry and the changes in compensation premiums between 1992 and 2001. If the hypothesis is correct, compensation premiums in an industry should rise (fall) relative to other industries when the industry trade balance improves (worsens).

To start, we examine trends in the trade balance and compensation premiums in the manufacturing sector. First, we consider US industry-level trade balances with Mexico and with all low-wage countries.[20] Industry trade balances are expressed as a percentage of total domestic shipments (the value is negative in the case of a trade deficit). To control for year-on-year variation, we use three-year averages to gauge the shift in trade balances from 1992–94 to 1999–2001. A positive change represents a shift toward exports, while a negative change shows a shift toward imports.[21] Table 6.5a presents trade balance data for ten industries at the SITC two-digit level. Scaled by industry size, the auto industry is a heavy importer, both from Mexico and from all low-wage countries (the majority of the industry's trade deficit with low-wage countries is attributable to Mexico). Over the past ten years, the US auto industry has turned from a net exporter to a net importer with respect to low-wage countries.

Turning to compensation, we calculate the compensation premium of an industry in two ways: (1) as the dollar difference between the hourly compensation of an industry's production workers and the hourly compensation of all civilian employees and (2) relative to all blue-collar workers in manufacturing industries. (If the average industry worker is compensated below the reference rate, then the compensation premium is negative.) Table 6.5b presents data on compensation premiums for ten representative industries and compares the three-year average for 1992–94 with the three-year average for 1999–2001. A quick glance shows a wide variation in compensation premiums. Autoworkers do well, with a premium second only to iron- and steelworkers, another industry with a strong union structure. When examining the trend in premiums, however, things are less bright for the auto industry. Among the ten selected industries, autoworkers experienced the largest fall in premiums compared with all civilian employees.[22] Among the ten industries, autoworkers also had the smallest gain relative to all blue-collar manufacturing workers.

---

20. "Low-wage countries" are defined as those nations not in the Organization for Economic Cooperation and Development (OECD) before 1992. Six countries—the Czech Republic, Hungary, South Korea, Mexico, Poland, and Slovakia—have acceded to the OECD since 1992 but are still commonly considered low-wage countries.

21. Wage data are from BLS (2004), trade data from USITC's Interactive Tariff and Trade Dataweb 2004, and US shipments data from BEA (2002).

22. When weighted by the number of employees, the pay premiums of all industries (our representative ten industries plus all others) should sum to zero.

Table 6.5a   United States trade balances with Mexico and all low-wage countries

SITC code/industry	2001 trade balance (millions of dollars)		Domestic shipments, 2001 (millions of dollars)	Trade balance as percent of domestic shipments, 2001		Change in trade balance as percent of domestic shipments, 1992–94 to 1999–2001	
	Mexico	Low-wage countries		Mexico	Low-wage countries	Mexico	Low-wage countries
57 Plastics in primary forms	2,039	5,957	127,823	1.60	4.66	0.83	0.87
63 Cork and wood manufactures	10	–2,046	85,083	0.01	–2.40	–0.14	–0.86
64 Paper and paper products	1,629	2,668	219,016	0.74	1.22	0.18	–0.17
65 Textiles	1,819	–2,886	152,704	1.19	–1.89	0.90	–0.54
67 Iron and steel	380	–3,600	83,842	0.45	–4.29	–0.34	–3.54
74 Industrial machinery and equipment	550	3,839	348,502	0.16	1.10	–0.18	–1.11
77 Electrical machinery and equipment	–10,874	6,075	489,361	–2.22	1.24	–1.77	1.88
78 Road vehicles	–15,258	–21,251	495,591	–3.08	–4.29	–2.28	–4.65
82 Furniture	–2,244	–10,047	169,187	–1.33	–5.94	–1.06	–3.34
84 Clothing	–6,079	–52,466	173,544	–3.50	–30.23	–2.97	–8.34

Sources: USITC Interactive Tariff and Trade Dataweb 2005; BEA (2002).

Table 6.5b   Compensation premiums, United States (dollars per hour)

SITC code/SIC code/industry	Compensation cost per hour, 2001	Compensation premium, 2001		Change in premium, 1992–94 to 1999–2001	
		Relative to all civilians	Relative to blue-collar manufacturing	Relative to all civilians	Relative to blue-collar manufacturing
57/28 Plastics in primary forms	26.69	4.54	6.46	1.15	2.40
63/24 Cork and wood manufactures	16.13	–6.02	–4.10	–0.58	0.67
64/26 Paper and paper products	24.38	2.23	4.15	0.68	1.93
65/22 Textiles	15.20	–6.95	–5.03	–0.28	0.96
67/331-2 Iron and steel	31.13	8.98	10.90	0.46	1.70
74/35 Industrial machinery and equipment	22.13	–0.02	1.90	0.36	1.60
77/36 Electrical machinery and equipment	20.36	–1.79	0.13	0.15	1.39
78/371 Road vehicles	29.84	7.69	9.61	–0.82	0.43
82/25 Furniture	16.50	–5.65	–3.73	–0.11	1.13
84/23 Clothing	12.39	–9.76	–7.84	–0.66	0.58

Note: Compensation data compiled by SIC code were linked to SITC categories for comparison with trade data. A majority of domestic shipments for any given SITC industry are within the associated SIC category.

Table 6.5c Regression models linking compensation premiums to trade balances, 1993–2001[a]

	I	II	III	IV	V	VI
Low-wage balance	0.148*		0.132			
	(0.069)		(0.070)			
Low-wage balance, 1-year lag		−0.097	−0.078			
		(0.075)	(0.074)			
Mexico balance				−0.206		−0.214
				(0.205)		(0.200)
Mexico balance, 1-year lag					−0.444*	−0.447*
					(0.195)	(0.195)
SITC 57/SIC 28 Plastics in primary forms	0.094	0.416	0.210	0.382	0.496*	0.595*
	(0.219)	(0.226)	(0.245)	(0.224)	(0.219)	(0.237)
63/24 Cork and wood manufactures	−0.130	0.135	−0.030	0.092	0.178	0.250
	(0.212)	(0.220)	(0.232)	(0.215)	(0.210)	(0.220)
64/26 Paper and paper products	0.104	0.397	0.214	0.352	0.451*	0.533*
	(0.215)	(0.224)	(0.238)	(0.218)	(0.213)	(0.226)
65/22 Textiles	−0.121	0.158	−0.019	0.137	0.264	0.362
	(0.214)	(0.221)	(0.235)	(0.224)	(0.221)	(0.239)
67/331-2 Iron and steel	0.305	0.469*	0.355	0.477*	0.537*	0.602*
	(0.206)	(0.207)	(0.211)	(0.212)	(0.206)	(0.214)
74/35 Industrial machinery and equipment	0.020	0.288	0.121	0.242	0.326	0.396
	(0.212)	(0.220)	(0.233)	(0.214)	(0.209)	(0.219)
77/36 Electrical machinery and equipment	−0.033	0.313	0.096	0.191	0.242	0.267
	(0.220)	(0.231)	(0.252)	(0.205)	(0.201)	(0.202)
78/371 Road vehicles	0.124	0.279	0.193	0.207	0.259	0.267
	(0.202)	(0.212)	(0.213)	(0.204)	(0.200)	(0.200)
82/25 Furniture	0.060	0.193	0.078	0.156	0.217	0.263
	(0.205)	(0.212)	(0.217)	(0.209)	(0.204)	(0.208)
84/23 Clothing (reference case)						
Constant	0.003	−0.292	−0.106	−0.242	−0.330*	−0.405*
	(0.163)	(0.172)	(0.193)	(0.161)	(0.157)	(0.172)
R-squared	0.136	0.105	0.148	0.098	0.142	0.154

* = significant at 5 percent level

a. The dependent variable is the change from previous year of the industry premium (in dollars) over mean hourly compensation for all civilian employees. The independent variables are the change from the previous year of the industry trade balance normalized by domestic shipments, and industry-specific dummies.

Note: Standard errors are in parentheses.

Source: Authors' calculations using data from BEA (2002), BLS (2004, 2005), and USITC Interactive Tariff and Trade Dataweb 2005.

With that overview in mind, we used a simple fixed-effects regression model to detect whether a positive correlation exists between a larger trade deficit (or larger trade surplus) and a falling (or rising) compensation premium for our ten representative industries.[23] The analysis was performed using two measures of the compensation premium (civilian employees and blue-collar workers) and with and without lags in the trade balance. Data for this exercise, drawn from the experience of the ten SITC two-digit manufacturing industries mentioned above, consisted of 90 observations of year-on-year changes in compensation premiums and year-on-year changes in the US industry's trade balance, with both Mexico and all low-wage countries. In only one trial did we find a regression parameter that confirms the hypothesis of a positive link between trade balances and compensation premiums.[24] In table 6.5c, we present the results of the "successful" trial in the first column, along with several unsuccessful trials.[25]

The results from the one "successful" trial suggest that a 1 percent shift toward imports supplied by low-wage countries (normalized by the value of domestic shipments) results in a 14.8-cent decline in the industry's hourly compensation premium. Between 1992 and 2001, the auto industry experienced a 5.98 percent shift toward imports. Hence the 14.8-cent parameter suggests that auto trade with low-wage countries might explain an 89-cent decline in the hourly compensation premium for autoworkers. (The actual change in premium was an increase of 26 cents.) However, the R-squared statistic for this trial is very low, only 0.14. Roughly speaking, this indicates that the model accounts for only 14 percent of the variance in the data. Even in the "successful" trial, other influences on compensation premiums appear to swamp the effect of trade balances with low-wage countries as a group. Moreover, we were unable to detect support for the hypothesis when the independent variable was confined to the US trade balance with Mexico alone.

Foreign Direct Investment

Since the NAFTA ratification debate, no one has heard a "giant sucking sound"—in the form of capital (and associated jobs) moving from the United States to Mexico. Nevertheless, both Mexico and Canada have attracted substantial amounts of US foreign direct investment (FDI) in the

23. In a fixed-effects model, a distinct dummy variable for each industry is intended to capture all the forces that affect the compensation premium in that industry, except the impact of separately identified independent variables—here a changing trade balance.

24. In order to confirm the hypothesis, the coefficient on the trade balance should be positive and statistically significant.

25. Other unsuccessful trials, measuring the industry compensation premium relative to total blue-collar manufacturing employees, are not reported.

Table 6.6   US transportation FDI outflows versus domestic plant and equipment expenditures in the motor vehicles industry, 1994–2003 (billions of dollars)

Year	World	Canada	Mexico	NAFTA total	Rest of the world	Domestic plant and equipment
1994	5.2	2.1	1.0	3.1	2.1	18.0
1995	5.9	2.6	0.7	3.3	2.6	16.0
1996	0.7	−0.6	−0.2	−0.8	1.5	17.9
1997	4.7	2.0	0.1	2.2	2.5	18.3
1998	−1.4	−2.2	1.3	−0.9	−0.5	27.5
1999	4.5	0.2	1.4	1.6	2.9	24.9
2000	7.8	4.5	1.1	5.5	2.3	29.8
2001	1.9	2.1	−1.0	1.1	0.7	24.2
2002	2.5	2.1	0.6	2.7	−0.3	23.6
2003	1.5	0.6	—	0.6	0.9	24.2[a]
Total	33.3	13.4	5.0	18.4	14.9	224.4

— = Information suppressed to avoid disclosure of data of individual companies.
FDI = foreign direct investment

a. Estimated from total nonresidential domestic investment.

Note: FDI data are for all manufactured transportation equipment. Domestic data are total capital expenditure on structures and equipment for motor vehicles industry, defined as SIC 371 from 1994 to 1998 and NAICS 3361, 3362, 3363 from 1999 to 2001.

Sources: BEA (2005a), US Census Bureau (2004).

road vehicle sector. Since the 2001–02 economic downturn, however, FDI outflows have remained cool.

For a poor country like Mexico, whose principal development constraint was lack of capital, foreign firms may add to Mexican capital stock, contribute to "capital deepening," and thus raise the level of output. This conceptual approach, dating from the 1960s, views foreign firms primarily as providers of capital. More recent research, starting in the 1980s, considers the provider-of-capital model an overly narrow interpretation of the contribution of FDI to host-country development. In addition, FDI plays an important role in opening the host economy to global opportunities for best practice, production processes, quality control procedures, research and development, advanced marketing techniques, and improved access to international markets.[26]

Table 6.6 presents data on US domestic capital expenditure and FDI from 1994 to 2003. After NAFTA entered into force, US FDI flows to both the

---

26. This conception of FDI arises within the concept of newer growth models, associated with endogenous growth theory and dynamic comparative advantage. See Grossman and Helpman (1991) and Aghion and Howitt (1998). We thank Theodore Moran for extensive written comments on FDI and other issues, in the context of an earlier draft.

Table 6.7 Inward FDI in the automotive sector, 1999–2003 (billions of dollars)

Country/region	Mexico	United States[a]
From:		
United States	3.69	—
Canada	0.79	0.66
European Union	1.24	14.10
Japan	1.66	12.16
All others	−0.01	−0.34
Total	7.37	26.59

a. US inward FDI flows for all transportation equipment.

Sources: BEA (2005b), Secretaría de Economía (2005).

Canadian and the Mexican transportation industries accelerated rapidly, if erratically. In the wake of NAFTA, more than half of all US foreign investment in the transportation sector has been directed to NAFTA partners. In 2003, the stock of US FDI in the Canadian transportation industry, measured on a historical cost basis, reached $17.9 billion. The stock of US FDI in the Mexican transportation industry reached $4 billion in 2002.[27]

While FDI is significant, the scale of US auto investment in Canada and Mexico pales in comparison with domestic spending. Between 1994 and 2003, the US transportation industry invested $224 billion domestically, compared with $18 billion in other NAFTA countries. In 2003, domestic fixed assets in the motor vehicles, bodies, trailers, and parts manufacturing industry on a historical-cost basis were estimated at $88 billion. This is almost twice the $45 billion stock of *all* US transport-sector FDI in the rest of the world (including NAFTA) in the same year.[28] Moreover, domestic assets are roughly four times the US transport manufacturing sector FDI stock in Mexico and Canada combined (around $22 billion in 2002–03).

Table 6.7 presents recent FDI inflows to the United States and Mexico disaggregated by source country. The European Union and Japan contribute almost all inward FDI in the United States. Recent flows make up a significant portion of the total inward FDI position of $64 billion on a historical-cost basis. While Mexico does not report the inward stock of FDI in its auto sector, the United States does report the historical cost of its outward transport manufacturing FDI stock in Mexico as $4 billion (in 2002). In Mexico, over half of the incoming auto FDI comes from NAFTA sources. Not surprisingly, the bulk of non-NAFTA FDI flows come from the European Union and Japan. FDI flows from these sources are likely to

---

27. Data are from BEA (2005a). The Mexican position at year-end 2003 was suppressed to avoid disclosures of individual companies.

28. Figures are from BEA (2005c, Table 3.3ES) and BEA (2005a). Note that the FDI figure includes transport-sector manufacturing beyond motor vehicles.

increase, as Toyota and Volkswagen are planning to open new assembly lines in Mexico by the end of 2005. Currently, assembly plants account for 36 percent of Mexico's inward FDI in the automobile industry.

Trade

Trade is the most common indicator of economic integration. Among North American countries, trade has increased substantially since NAFTA, both for the motor vehicles and parts industry and for merchandise as a whole. But aggregate trade figures can obscure more complex trade relationships. In this section, we look at both the overall value of auto trade and intraindustry auto trade.

Overall Value

Appendix table 6A.1 summarizes the value of trade in the vehicles and parts industry and merchandise as a whole in 1993 and 2002 for Canada, Mexico, and the United States. In 1993, vehicles and parts made up 22 percent of Canadian total merchandise trade. In 2002, when the figure was 20 percent of total trade and the value had reached nearly $100 billion, Canada's trade surplus in the auto sector was $12 billion. Canadian auto trade is heavily concentrated in North America (91 percent of the sector total), almost all of which is with the United States. Between 1993 and 2002, Canadian vehicles and parts trade with NAFTA countries increased 60 percent, with slightly faster growth for imports (64 percent) than exports (58 percent).

The pattern of US auto trade was similar in the post-NAFTA period. Half of US auto trade was with Canada and Mexico in 1993, when auto trade with NAFTA partners totaled $65 billion. The United States then had a $14 billion auto trade deficit with its NAFTA partners. By 2002, all of these numbers had expanded: Auto trade with NAFTA partners nearly doubled to $123 billion, while the US trade deficit in vehicles and parts with NAFTA partners more than doubled to $34 billion. Mexico accounted for the fastest growth (total auto trade with Mexico grew 243 percent), but US auto trade with Canada also increased sharply, up 58 percent. By 2002, Canada accounted for $86 billion of two-way US auto trade, while Mexico accounted for $37 billion. The US trade deficit in the auto sector reflects not only the comparative advantage of other producers but also the strong US dollar that prevailed through 2002. Only since February 2002 has the dollar declined against other "major currencies" on a trade-weighted basis; as of March 2005, it was 28 percent below its peak (Federal Reserve Bank of St. Louis 2005).

The United States accounts for 80 percent of Mexico's total trade in automobiles. Between 1993 and 2003, Mexican auto trade with the United States increased fivefold (from a low base). The auto sector now accounts for 13 percent of Mexico's total trade and 16 percent of its exports. Still, Mexican automotive exports to the United States are only half as large as shipments from Canada. Mexico's two-way trade with NAFTA partners in the vehicles and parts sector is only 40 percent that of Canadian trade.

At the same time, the US auto trade deficit also expanded; the deficit with NAFTA countries grew 135 percent (in nominal dollar terms) between 1993 and 2003, while the US deficit with the world as a whole grew 155 percent. Although much of the deficit increase is due to the higher volume of trade, the balance of US auto and parts trade has also shifted toward imports. In 1993, the value of US exports in autos and parts to the world was equivalent to 48 percent of its world auto and parts imports. By 2003, the ratio had declined to 36 percent. The gap with NAFTA countries is narrower, and its growth has been less steep. NAFTA auto export value amounted to 65 percent of auto import value in 1993, declining to 58 percent in 2003.

Intraindustry Trade

Is the auto industry atypical in the sense that there is far more two-way trade within the auto sector compared with other industries? To determine the answer to this question, we calculated a familiar intraindustry trade index (ITI), defined as follows:

$$ITI_{ij} = 1 - \left[\frac{|X_{ij} - M_{ij}|}{X_{ij} + M_{ij}} \right]$$

In this formula, X and M stand for exports and imports, respectively, the subscript i indexes the country or region with which the United States is trading, and the subscript j indexes the product that is being traded. If the United States were to export $3 billion of product j to country i and not import any product j from country i—a situation that illustrates extreme specialization—then the index would equal zero. The same would be true if the United States only imported product j from country i and did not export any of product j to country i. By contrast, when US trade in a product with a country is balanced—i.e., if exports equal imports—then the ITI would equal 1.

Table 6.8 shows ITIs for road vehicles trade between the United States and several partners: Brazil, Germany, Japan, the United Kingdom, Canada, and Mexico. Between 1992 and 2004, the ITI declined for all countries except Canada. Canada's ITI remains over .75, showing that trade is largely two-way. Mexico's ITI has declined sharply from .87 to .58 but remains higher than all other partners besides Brazil, whose total trade volume is extremely small.

How does NAFTA intraindustry trade in autos compare with other broad industries? Table 6.9 presents the ITIs for the same ten manufactur-

Table 6.8   US intraindustry trade index in
            SITC 78 (road vehicles), selected
            countries

Country	1992	2004
Brazil	0.84	0.66
Germany	0.49	0.34
Japan	0.10	0.07
United Kingdom	0.77	0.42
Canada	0.78	0.79
Mexico	0.87	0.58

Source: Authors' calculations using data from USITC Interactive Tariff and Trade Dataweb 2005.

ing sectors used in our comparison of wage premiums. US-Canada ITIs have increased or remained steady in most sectors (including autos) since 1992, with three notable exceptions: furniture, clothing, and wood manufactures. By contrast, the sharp decline in auto ITI between the United States and Mexico placed it in the minority, along with furniture and textiles, while other categories remained steady or saw significant increases.[29]

Table 6.10 presents a finer set of ITIs, in order to examine subsectors of the auto industry in North America between 1997 and 2004. Over the past decade, the auto parts ITI with Canada rose substantially, signaling an expansion of NAFTA supply lines for auto manufacturers. The overall auto ITI for Canada is larger than any of the three categories individually; this is because the United States has a trade surplus in the parts category that offsets a trade deficit in assembly.[30] Intraindustry activity with Mexico is primarily focused in bodies and parts, not finished vehicles. However, while the ITIs of bodies and parts have been falling since 1997, the ITI of finished vehicles has been rising. Decrease in overall auto ITI reflects both internal trends in the three subsectors and the growth of the share of US-Mexican trade in finished vehicles versus bodies and parts.[31]

To summarize: First, US intraindustry auto trade is greater with Canada than with Mexico; second, auto trade is more two-way with NAFTA part-

---

29. One reason for declining auto ITI between the United States and Mexico is that while non-NAFTA imports supply the Mexican domestic auto market, Mexican auto plants produce vehicles for the US market. Based on extensive written comments provided by G. Mustafa Mohatarem, March 2005.

30. The United States also maintains a surplus in the bodies category, but trade in this category is small relative to the other two.

31. In 1997, 43 percent of US-Mexico auto trade was classified in NAICS 3361 (assembly); in 2004, the share was 47 percent.

Table 6.9 US intraindustry trade index with NAFTA partners, selected industries, 1992 and 2004

SITC industry	1992	2004
Canada		
57 Plastics in primary forms	0.69	0.97
63 Cork and wood manufactures	0.52	0.22
64 Paper and paper products	0.43	0.59
65 Textiles	0.57	0.88
67 Iron and steel	0.83	0.92
74 Industrial machinery	0.56	0.75
77 Electrical machinery	0.60	0.62
78 Road vehicles	**0.78**	**0.79**
82 Furniture	0.95	0.69
84 Clothing	0.87	0.67
Mexico		
57 Plastics in primary forms	0.19	0.31
63 Cork and wood manufactures	0.67	0.98
64 Paper and paper products	0.24	0.49
65 Textiles	0.66	0.64
67 Iron and steel	0.44	0.76
74 Industrial machinery	0.67	0.94
77 Electrical machinery	0.99	0.95
78 Road vehicles	**0.87**	**0.58**
82 Furniture	0.89	0.31
84 Clothing	0.77	0.32

Source: Authors' calculations using data from USITC Interactive Tariff and Trade Dataweb 2005.

ners than with other major trading partners; and third, intraindustry trade in NAFTA is focused on bodies and parts, not finished vehicles.

Conclusion

Owing to the 1965 Auto Pact, US-Canada integration in the auto industry received a head start over other sectors. Although a latecomer to the process, Mexico started to dismantle its protectionist auto programs in the late 1980s and had begun the process of integration before NAFTA came into force. Thus, the North American auto industry has reached a more mature state of development than many of its peers. Auto trade accounts for a fifth of trade among NAFTA partners. Supply lines routinely cross national boundaries, as individual firms in the three countries pursue specializations and sell into the North American market based on their comparative advantage.[32] While the Big Three were the first to benefit from

---

32. Trefler (2004) uses plant-level manufacturing data to show that productivity enhancements in Canada have occurred both at the industry and the plant levels. He notes that "popular press reports that US-owned multinationals have been reorganizing their Canadian plants in order to produce fewer product lines, each with a global mandate." This is

Table 6.10 US intraindustry trade index in autos by NAICS subsector, NAFTA partners

Subsector	Partner	1997	2004
3361-Assembly	Canada	0.57	0.56
	Mexico	0.28	0.36
3362-Bodies	Canada	0.71	0.73
	Mexico	0.53	0.49
3363-Parts	Canada	0.70	0.81
	Mexico	0.88	0.64
All auto[a]	Canada	0.86	0.82
	Mexico	0.62	0.51

a. Defined as the sum of NAICS 3361, 3362, and 3363.

Source: Authors' calculations using data from USITC Interactive Tariff and Trade Dataweb 2005.

NAFTA and its precursors, foreign auto producers are now investing in all three countries.

We have argued that NAFTA codified the reality of integration within the North American auto industry. The US auto companies limited the loss of market share to Japanese and European imports in the 1980s and 1990s, in part on the basis of cost and quality advantages that came from offshore sourcing of parts and components (Womack, Jones, and Roos 1991). Despite the outcry of "runaway plants" and a "giant sucking sound," the data show that outsourcing strategies of the parent firms *support* the jobs of unionized workers in the United States.

The relevant comparison is not whether aggregate employment in the US auto industry has expanded or shrunk in the last three decades, nor whether a given plant in Mexico or Canada has taken over functions formerly carried out in Michigan, but what would have happened to the parent firms, workers, and communities if the Big Three had not invested outside the United States.[33] In 2004, Ford launched a new version of its best-selling F150 truck. Ford's Essex Engine Plant in Windsor, Canada is the exclusive source of the Triton V-8 engines for the F150. Ford's partner IMMSA of Monterrey, Mexico is the maker of the M450 chassis for the F150. Ford's fortune in the global market (against challenges from Toyota, Nissan, and DaimlerChrysler) depends on the intimate relationship be-

---

consistent with Baldwin, Beckstead, and Caves (2002), who find that for foreign-owned plants operating in Canada, increases in exports are associated with reductions in the number of commodities produced. Thus plant rationalization may have contributed to rising productivity. Although Trefler's study focuses exclusively on Canada, there is reason to believe that rationalization, or specialization, is also occurring in Mexico.

33. We thank Theodore Moran for providing the example in this paragraph, which draws heavily on written comments he provided to an earlier draft.

tween the Ford assembly workers in Michigan, IMMSA in Mexico, and Ford's Essex plant in Canada. Despite the UAW's opposition to NAFTA, the fate of Ford workers depends on trade-and-investment relationships that are enhanced by the agreement.

Ten years after NAFTA, the development that attracts most attention is security. The growth of cross-border supply lines in the industry has promoted efficiency; however, new security concerns have put these lines at risk. The costs of the "security tax" cannot be measured simply by border delays and increased paperwork. They also include the risk of a prolonged shutdown of border trade in the aftermath of an actual terrorist attack or a highly specific threat. This risk, if perceived to be high, will certainly chill investment in Mexico and Canada. Thus far, increased border security has not adversely affected the auto industry. The industry has a strong interest in the implementation of border security measures that are predictable, efficient, and most important, effective. Moreover, big firms are able to build security into their operations. But who can accurately foretell the public reaction to a terror event within the United States whose perpetrators were found to use the Canadian or Mexican border as a point of entry? Assuming the NAFTA partners can keep themselves free of terrorism, the auto industry provides a look ahead for other North American industries. Dire forecasts as to the consequences of free trade for US workers have not been borne out in the auto industry. In terms both of compensation and overall employment, the Mexican bogeyman appears more phantasm than reality. Worker fortunes are tied more strongly to productivity developments and growth in North American demand than to the pace of industrial integration. "Capital flight" within the auto industry has scarcely slowed domestic investment within the United States. Instead, trade has allowed firms in each country to specialize in the areas of the auto industry where they are most efficient—to the benefit of all three countries. While North America is somewhat less self sufficient in the auto sector today than a decade ago, it seems likely that in the absence of NAFTA far more auto jobs would have been lost to Asian and European competitors.

References

Aghion, Philippe, and Peter Howitt. 1998. *Endogenous Growth Theory*. Cambridge, MA: MIT Press.

Baldwin, John R., Desmond Beckstead, and Richard Caves. 2002. *Changes in the Diversification of Canadian Manufacturing Firms (1973-1997): A Move to Specialization*. Statistics Canada Analytical Studies Branch Research Paper Series 179 (February). Ottawa: Statistics Canada.

BEA (Bureau of Economic Analysis). 2002. Shipments of Manufacturing Industries, 1977–2001. Washington: US Department of Commerce. www.bea.gov/bea/dn2/gpo.htm (accessed on January 27, 2004).

BEA (Bureau of Economic Analysis). 2005a. U.S. Direct Investment Abroad: Balance of Payments and Direct Investment Position Data. Washington: US Department of Commerce. www.bea.gov/bea/di/di1usdbal.htm (accessed on April 29, 2005).

BEA (Bureau of Economic Analysis). 2005b. Foreign Direct Investment in the United States: Balance of Payments and Direct Investment Position Data. Washington: US Department of Commerce. www.bea.gov/bea/di/di1fdibal.htm (accessed on May 2, 2005).

BEA (Bureau of Economic Analysis). 2005c. Fixed Asset Tables. Washington: US Department of Commerce. www.bea.gov/bea/dn/FA2004/SelectTable.asp (accessed on April 29, 2005).

BLS (Bureau of Labor Statistics). 2004. Hourly Compensation Costs for Production Workers in Manufacturing, 30 Countries or Areas, 40 Manufacturing Industries, Selected Years 1975–2002. Washington: US Department of Labor. www.bls.gov/fls/flshcind.htm (accessed on March 15, 2005).

BLS (Bureau of Labor Statistics). 2005. Current Employment Survey. Washington: US Department of Labor. www.bls.gov/ces/home.htm (accessed on March 15, 2005).

Cooney, Stephen, and Brent D. Yacobucci. 2005. US Automotive Industry: Policy Overview and Recent History. Washington: Congressional Research Service (April 25).

Federal Reserve Bank of St. Louis. 2005. FRED II—Trade Weighted Exchange Index: Major Currencies. St. Louis, MO. http://research.stlouisfed.org/fred2/series/twexmmth/13 (accessed on January 15, 2004).

Grossman, Gene M., and Elhanan Helpman. 1991. Innovation and Growth in the Global Economy. Cambridge, MA: MIT Press.

INEGI (Instituto Nacional de Estadística Geografía e Informática). 2005. Banco de Información Económica. http://dgcnesyp.inegi.gob.mx/bdine/bancos.htm (accessed on March 23, 2005).

Moran, Theodore H. 1998. Foreign Direct Investment and Development: The New Policy Agenda for Developing Countries and Economies in Transition. Washington: Institute for International Economics (November).

Nunez, Perez. 1990. The Automotive Industry. In Foreign Direct Investment and Industrial Development in Mexico. Paris: Organization for Economic Cooperation and Development.

Samuels, Barbara. 1990. Managing Risk in Developing Countries. Princeton, NJ: Princeton University Press.

Secretaría de Economía. 2005. Comportamiento de la Inversión Extranjera Directa en Mexico. www.economia.gob.mx/?P=1164 (accessed on March 23, 2005).

Trefler, Daniel. 2004. The Long and Short of the Canada-US Free Trade Agreement. American Economic Review 94, no. 4 (September): 870–95.

US Census Bureau. 2003. Statistics for Industry Groups and Industries. 2001 Annual Survey of Manufacturers. Washington. www.census.gov/prod/2003pubs/m01as-1.pdf (accessed on January 27, 2004).

US Census Bureau. 2004. Annual Capital Expenditure Surveys. Washington. www.census.gov/csd/ace/ace-pdf.html (accessed on January 30, 2004).

US Census Bureau. 2005. 2002 Economic Census. Washington. www.census.gov/econ/census02/data/us/US000.HTM (accessed on April 29, 2005).

Ward's Communications. 2004. Ward's Motor Vehicle Data 2004. Southfield, MI: Ward's Communications.

Womack, James P., Daniel T. Jones, and Daniel Roos. 1991. The Machine That Changed the World: The Story of Lean Production. New York: HarperPerennial.

Wonnacott, Paul. 1965. Canadian Automotive Protection: Content Provisions, the Bladen Plan, and Recent Tariff Changes. The Canadian Journal of Economics and Political Science 31, no. 1 (February): 98–116.

Appendix 6A

Table 6A.1 Trade in road vehicles and parts, 1993 and 2003 (billions of dollars)

Partner/sector	Imports			Exports			Total trade			Trade balance	
	1993	2003	Percent growth	1993	2003	Percent growth	1993	2003	Percent growth	1993	2003
Canada											
With world											
All merchandise	131	240	83	145	272	88	276	512	85	13	32
Vehicles and parts	25	45	80	35	55	56	60	100	66	10	9
Auto share (percent)	19	19		24	20		22	19			
With Mexico											
All merchandise	3	9	213	1	2	150	3	10	201	−2	−7
Vehicles and parts	1	2	110	0	0	135	1	3	112	−1	−2
Auto share (percent)	41	28		15	14		36	26			
With United States											
All merchandise	88	145	65	117	233	100	205	379	85	29	88
Vehicles and parts	20	34	71	34	53	57	54	87	63	14	18
Auto share (percent)	23	24		29	23		26	23			
With NAFTA											
All merchandise	91	154	70	117	235	100	208	389	87	27	81
Vehicles and parts	21	37	74	34	53	57	55	90	64	12	16
Auto share (percent)	23	24		29	23		26	23			
With non-NAFTA											
All merchandise	41	86	111	27	37	36	68	123	81	−13	−49
Vehicles and parts	4	8	114	1	1	24	5	10	93	−3	−7
Auto share (percent)	9	10		4	4		7	8			
NAFTA's share of total trade (percent)	69	64		81	86		75	76			
NAFTA's share of auto trade (percent)	85	82		97	97		92	90			
Mexico											
With world											
All merchandise	65	171	162	52	165	219	117	337	187	−13	−6
Vehicles and parts	2	17	816	7	27	285	9	44	396	5	10
Auto share (percent)	3	10		14	16		8	13			
With United States											
All merchandise	48	106	120	43	147	242	91	253	177	−5	41
Vehicles and parts	1	10	665	6	25	330	7	35	393	4	15
Auto share (percent)	3	10		13	17		8	14			
With Canada											
All merchandise	1	4	317	2	3	81	3	7	173	1	−1
Vehicles and parts	0	1	8,850	1	1	57	1	2	182	1	0
Auto share (percent)	1	26		53	46		33	34			
With NAFTA											
All merchandise	49	110	123	44	150	237	94	260	177	−5	40
Vehicles and parts	1	11	738	7	26	296	8	37	371	5	15
Auto share (percent)	3	10		15	17		8	14			
With non-NAFTA											
All merchandise	16	61	283	7	16	110	23	77	228	−9	−46
Vehicles and parts	1	6	1,015	0	1	138	1	7	597	0	−5
Auto share (percent)	3	10		7	7		4	9			
NAFTA's share of total trade (percent)	76	64		86	91		80	77			
NAFTA's share of auto trade (percent)	72	66		93	96		89	84			

(table continues next page)

artner/sector	Imports 1993	2003	Percent growth	Exports 1993	2003	Percent growth	Total trade 1993	2003	Percent growth	Trade balance 1993	2003
nited States											
ith world											
All merchandise	603	1,305	116	465	724	56	1,068	2,029	90	−138	−581
Vehicles and parts	85	175	106	41	63	53	127	239	89	−44	−112
Auto share (percent)	14	13		9	9		12	12			
ith Canada											
All merchandise	114	228	100	100	169	69	214	397	86	−13	−58
Vehicles and parts	33	53	57	21	35	71	54	88	62	−13	−17
Auto share (percent)	29	23		21	21		25	22			
ith Mexico											
All merchandise	41	140	243	42	97	134	82	237	188	1	−42
Vehicles and parts	6	26	310	5	10	108	11	35	224	−2	−16
Auto share (percent)	15	18		11	10		13	15			
ith NAFTA											
All merchandise	154	367	138	142	267	88	296	634	114	−13	−100
Vehicles and parts	40	78	97	25	45	77	65	123	89	−14	−33
Auto share (percent)	26	21		18	17		22	19			
ith non-NAFTA											
All merchandise	449	938	109	323	457	41	772	1,394	81	−126	−481
Vehicles and parts	46	97	113	16	18	15	61	115	88	−30	−79
Auto share (percent)	10	10		5	4		8	8			
AFTA's share of total trade (percent)	26	28		31	37		28	31			
AFTA's share of auto trade (percent)	47	45		62	71		51	52			
orth America											
ith world											
All merchandise	800	1,716	115	661	1,161	76	1,461	2,877	97	−138	−555
Vehicles and parts	112	238	112	83	145	74	195	383	96	−29	−93
Auto share (percent)	14	14		13	12		13	13			
ith NAFTA											
All merchandise	147	316	115	152	326	115	299	642	115		
Vehicles and parts	31	63	103	33	62	89	64	125	96		
Auto share (percent)	21	20		22	19		21	20			
ith non-NAFTA											
All merchandise	653	1,400	115	509	835	64	1,162	2,235	92	−143	−565
Vehicles and parts	81	174	115	50	83	65	131	257	96	−31	−92
Auto share (percent)	12	12		10	10		11	12			
AFTA's share of total trade (percent)	18	18		23	28		20	22			
AFTA's share of auto trade (percent)	28	27		40	43		33	33			

tes: Trade in SITC 78 (Road Vehicles) includes vehicles and parts. For world and intra-NAFTA trade, a good traded tween NAFTA countries is counted twice, once as an import and once as an export. Sums may not add up due to unding.

urce: Compiled by authors from country data from UN Comtrade database, 2005, http://unstats.un.org/unsd/comtrade ccessed on May 2, 2005).

7

Energy

Energy trade is an important component of the North American economy. Each NAFTA country relies importantly on its neighbors to buy or sell energy resources to fuel regional economic growth. Though each of them produces substantial amounts of oil and gas, the region as a whole is a small net energy importer—primarily due to large-scale US oil imports. Canada and Mexico together supply about one-third of total US oil imports. Canada also accounts for the bulk of US imports of natural gas and electricity.

Yet, despite this natural interdependence, bilateral energy relations have had a stormy past, and NAFTA disciplines left substantial aspects of the energy economy untouched. Why?

Historically, political considerations strongly color energy policies in North America—reflecting both economic and sovereignty concerns:

- In the 1980s, Canada experimented with energy independence in its National Energy Program (NEP). Even after that initiative fell flat, Canadian opponents of North American integration frequently cited sovereign control over energy resources as a reason to oppose the Canada-US Free Trade Agreement (CUSFTA). While muted today, such sentiments make some Canadian politicians reluctant to embrace the concept of a "continental energy policy," a term President George W. Bush introduced in his 2000 election campaign that has drawn more attention in Canada than the United States.

- In Mexico, sovereignty concerns are even more extreme. The Mexican Constitution reserves to the state the exclusive right to exploit subsoil resources, creating barriers to both energy integration and market-oriented reforms. Equally troubling, Mexican policymakers have abetted the Organization of Petroleum Exporting Countries (OPEC) cartel on numerous occasions over the past decade to restrict exports and manipulate world oil prices—actions that are antithetical to North American economic integration.

- In the United States, which accounts for a quarter of world energy consumption, politicians call for the end of US dependence on foreign energy sources whenever there is an energy price spike. Such demands have intensified since the terrorist attacks of September 2001, prompting new subsidy-laden energy legislation that Congress finally passed in July 2005. At the same time, US politicians give short shrift to conservation policies—including energy taxes—that could constrain the vast appetite of US consumers for their gas-guzzling sport utility vehicles (SUVs).[1]

Political sensitivities notwithstanding, economic forces are driving the energy sector toward integration. Since the 1980s, deregulation of the energy sector in the United States and Canada has fostered strong growth in energy trade. The CUSFTA and NAFTA have facilitated bilateral trade but have been less influential in harmonizing energy policies and prices, which are still set within national and subnational borders.

Can the North American energy sector become as integrated as the auto sector, which is widely considered the most integrated industry in North America? Integration in the auto sector accelerated in the 1960s after the negotiation of the bilateral Canada–United States Automotive Agreement (commonly known as the 1965 Auto Pact). In contrast, economic integration of the energy sector is fairly recent. Efforts to advance the concept of a North American energy market will clearly take time, especially considering the political dimension. This chapter examines the energy policy framework in North America, and what can be done to promote investment, production, and trade in the region.

Energy Policies in North America

Energy policies in North America are made at both the national and subnational levels in each country. The CUSFTA and NAFTA have facilitated integration of the US and Canadian energy markets, though differences in regulatory policies significantly hinder market integration in the electricity sector. Despite these differences, policy coordination is advancing inter

---

1. While driving habits are conventionally viewed as inelastic to price signals, automakers are concerned that the recent decline in SUV sales is an indicator of the high long-term elasticity of vehicle choice to gas prices ("Rising Gasoline Prices Threaten Viability of Biggest SUVs," *Wall Street Journal*, March 22, 2005, B1).

alia through the work of the North American Electric Reliability Council (NERC), which is charged with developing, promoting, and enforcing standards for competition in the electricity sector and ensuring that differences in transmission systems and regulation do not impede the flow of electricity. NERC is primarily an exercise between the United States and Canada; broad based, Mexico's constitutional ban constrains cooperation on energy policy with its neighbors. Nonetheless, the experience of NERC illustrates that energy policy can converge in North America, although the convergence will probably be slow and incomplete. This section summarizes how energy policy has evolved in each of the three countries over the past few decades.

Canada

Between 1950 and 1973, Canada's energy sector was loosely regulated and largely geared toward producer interests. During the 1970s and early 1980s, the Canadian government turned interventionist in response to higher energy prices. In 1975, the Canadian government established Petro-Canada as a public energy company; it received federal subsidies and enjoyed special exploration rights. The government also instituted a "made in Canada" price for oil, which was substantially below prevailing world prices. Canadian oil exports were taxed to absorb the difference between the "made in Canada" price and the world price.

In 1980, Prime Minister Pierre Trudeau initiated the National Energy Program, which had three objectives: energy independence, a strong Canadian petroleum industry, and energy price fairness throughout Canada.[2] To achieve these goals, the Canadian federal government blocked or delayed foreign purchases of Canadian companies through investment restrictions enforced by the Foreign Investment Review Agency and pressured US firms to sell their Canadian assets to Canadian firms.[3] The NEP also put price ceilings on oil and natural gas and subsidized oil exploration based on how much of the operation was owned by Canadians. The government also taxed oil and gas exports. These policies evoked strong US opposition, especially regarding the forced divestment of Canadian holdings.

The NEP was controversial and failed to achieve its objectives.[4] Starting in 1984 with the election of a new Progressive Conservative government

---

2. This section draws on Watkins (1991).

3. In a much-heralded case, Conoco was pressured to sell its stake in Hudson Bay Oil and Gas to Dome Petroleum (Verleger 1988).

4. The National Energy Program prompted strong opposition from Alberta (and other provinces), which challenged the constitutionality of the export tax. The Canadian Supreme Court ruled in Alberta's favor, spurring important changes in the NEP. We are grateful to Helmut Mach of the government of Alberta for this point and other comments on an earlier draft of this chapter.

in Ottawa, privatization and deregulation became the themes of Canadian energy policy. In 1985, the Canadian government signed the Agreement on Natural Gas Prices and Markets with British Columbia, Alberta, and Saskatchewan, which allowed for competitive pricing (OECD 2000). This agreement was the first of a series of federal-provincial agreements that removed price controls and export restrictions on oil and natural gas. Real gas prices in the industrial sector in Canada fell by more than a third and remained constant for the household sector between 1985 and 1997. In 1991, the government began divesting its stake in shares of Petro-Canada; over the years, sales continued, and the government sold its final 19 percent stake in the company in 2004. Today, Canada's federal government advocates a "market-based" energy policy and tries to minimize government intervention.

The provinces have jurisdiction over resource management (except in frontier and offshore areas), intraprovincial commerce, and environmental issues; they also own all subsoil resources. The federal government has jurisdiction over nuclear power, interprovincial commerce, and international trade. The federal government attempts to direct research on energy-related issues. Provincial power over energy resources poses an additional hurdle to integration of the North American energy market, because different provinces have somewhat different energy strategies. By comparison, while individual states within the United States have some say over electric power management, their influence is much less than that of the Canadian provinces.

One example of divergent provincial practices is deregulation. Across Canada, oil, coal, and upstream natural gas markets are market-oriented. The downstream gas market has been completely deregulated in Ontario but is only slowly being deregulated in other provinces. The same is true with electricity generation: Some provinces are deregulating faster than others. Despite the slow pace of deregulation in some sectors and provinces, Canada's overall energy policy is market-oriented. Natural Resources Canada runs federal policy with a mandate to build on market-oriented policy in support of sustainable energy development and to strengthen and expand Canada's commitment to energy efficiency.

United States

US energy policy over the past few decades has featured bouts of government intervention with subsequent deregulation.[5] President Richard Nixon introduced price controls on crude oil in 1971; following the oil shock of 1973–74, the administration announced the improbable goal of achieving energy independence by 1980. President Gerald Ford's ill-starred Whip Inflation Now program continued price controls on oil. These

---

5. This section draws on Joskow (2001).

failed, but Ford successfully pushed new fuel efficiency standards for automobiles and created the Strategic Petroleum Reserve. President Jimmy Carter then created the US Department of Energy (DOE) to coordinate the various elements of US energy policy. During his tenure, the government implemented both price controls and quantitative limits on using natural gas and oil to generate electricity, which boosted reliance on coal for US electricity generation. Carter also signed the Natural Gas Policy Act in 1978, which deregulated natural gas prices for new supplies.[6] In 1979, following the fall of the Shah of Iran, the Carter administration replaced price controls with a tax on windfall profits generated from prices above those that earlier controls mandated. Although the tax ceased to collect revenue after the fall in oil prices in the early 1980s, it remained on the books until 1988. In addition to selective price controls and energy taxes, Carter announced proposals to reduce energy consumption, promote energy efficiency, and expand domestic production.

Under the promarket philosophy of the Reagan administration, the federal government took a hands-off attitude toward energy policy, and the states were allowed more room to determine their own energy initiatives. Several states gave large subsidies for "clean" energy production (e.g., solar, wind, and hydropower) to promote environmental objectives. In the early 1990s, President George H. W. Bush pursued further deregulation to combat the high prices charged by vertically integrated electricity monopolies. The goal was to separate generation from distribution. To that end, Bush signed the Energy Policy Act of 1992, which created standards for renewable energy, promoted energy efficiency, and encouraged energy development.

The reforms produced mixed results. States still control the electric transmission lines; local politics often impedes the efficient distribution of power within and between states. The business of generating electricity has become more competitive with deregulation, but retail distribution and sale are still subject to patchwork state regulation and local monopolies. More recently, fraud—and the widespread perception of fraud—by Enron and other companies has created a public backlash against deregulation.[7]

The United States has made halting attempts at reforming its much-criticized electricity transmission system. In December 1999, the Federal Energy Regulatory Commission (FERC) proposed that transmission providers should be organized into regional transmission organizations (RTOs). These groups (FERC initially envisioned 4 or 5) would combine a region's providers into a single operating entity.[8] In addition to managing

---

6. In the 1980s, prices were deregulated for natural gas supplies that the Natural Gas Policy Act had grandfathered.

7. See "US Energy Policy Back in the Spotlight," *Financial Times*, March 8, 2002.

8. When the RTO system was proposed, roughly 130 operators controlled sections of the US electricity transmission system.

transmission within the region, each RTO would be responsible for negotiating interregional exchanges with other RTOs. Although not subject to FERC orders, Canadian operators can join RTOs and thereby receive equal access to US transmission systems.[9]

Participation in an RTO was initially voluntary, but only two had been created (in the midwest and northeast) by June 2002. In 2003, FERC attempted to make RTO participation mandatory, but southern and northwestern utilities and their state regulators opposed the proposal. They feared that increased integration would result in higher prices in these traditionally energy-rich regions and that a surrender of the local utility monopoly on transmission lines would make it impossible to profit from past and future infrastructure investment.[10] The coalition has significant clout in Washington and managed to include a provision in the Energy Policy Act of 2005 that legislates a delay in mandatory RTO participation until 2007.[11] White House support for the "voluntary approach" to grid reform has effectively stalled the FERC initiative to make RTOs mandatory. As of 2005, six RTOs—including independent system operators (ISOs), which are very similar—were operating. However several of these operate over significantly smaller geographic areas than FERC initially envisioned. Three RTOs are confined to operations within a single state (California, New York, and Texas).[12]

In contrast to his father's Energy Policy Act, President Bush's 2001 National Energy Policy has been criticized for emphasizing energy development much more than conservation. The stated purpose of the National Energy Policy is to "help the private sector, and, as necessary and appropriate, State and local governments, promote dependable, affordable, and environmentally sound production and distribution of energy for the future" (NEPD 2001, xviii). This mission statement recognizes the leading role of the private sector in energy development and the roles of state and local governments in energy regulation. In this sense, the US and Canadian approaches to energy policy are similar. There are, however, two major differences. First, Canadian provinces own subsoil resources, while

---

9. For example, B. C. Hydro has been actively involved in the creation of RTO-West.

10. The southeast and northwest enjoy surplus energy as a result of depression-era development projects (the most famous being the Tennessee Valley Authority) and low production costs relative to other regions.

11. For example, Southern Co., a major power utility, has given $481,500 in campaign contributions to members of the House Energy and Commerce Committee, and $105,000 to Senator Richard C. Shelby (R-AL) since 1989. Senator Shelby was instrumental in the delay of FERC's plan to make RTO participation mandatory ("Short-Circuited: How Unlikely Coalition Scuttled Plan to Remake Electrical Grid," *Wall Street Journal*, November 4, 2003, A1).

12. For RTO boundaries and regulations, see www.ferc.gov/industries/electric/indus-act/rto.asp (accessed on May 25, 2005).

most subsoil resources in the United States are privately owned. Second, US federal agencies that oversee interstate gas and electricity markets have more clout than Canadian federal agencies. But "states' rights" concerns still constrain the ambition of federal regulators.

While much of the administration's National Energy Policy can be implemented without congressional input, there has been a five-year battle over legislation relating to the plan. Box 7.1 presents highlights of the Energy Policy Act of 2005 (HR 6), which passed Congress in late July 2005. The bill promotes US energy production but does not significantly reduce imports or shift US energy purchases toward Canada and Mexico. Similar legislation was introduced in the previous session of Congress but was successfully filibustered in the Senate in November 2003 (receiving only 57 of the required 60 votes for cloture).[13]

In essence, the 2003 US energy bill failed under the weight of excessive public subsidies to energy producers, lack of concrete incentives for energy conservation, and the strong opposition of Democratic members to the provision on MTBE liability protection.[14] MTBE protection was dropped from the 2005 bill in order to secure passage. Both bills focused on subsidies for expanding US production of traditional energy sources—oil, coal, and natural gas.[15] The bill also included subsidies for nontraditional sources—ethanol, biodiesel, hybrid cars and hydrogen fuel cells—in hopes that they would become commercially viable in the future. It is worth noting that ethanol production has been subsidized as an "infant industry" since 1978. Only domestically produced ethanol (mostly from corn) is eligible for the tax credit; in contrast, foreign ethanol is subject to a tariff of over 50 cents a gallon.[16]

The energy bill sought to ensure that America had secure sources of energy to meet growing demand. Provisions that would limit consumption, such as a more efficient corporate average fuel economy (CAFE) standard,

---

13. The *Wall Street Journal* called that bill "a 1,700-page monstrosity" that "may not have all that much to do with energy any more" ("The Grassley Rainforest Act," November 18, 2003, A20). The editorial criticized the pork barrel legislative process and the "GOP leadership [that] greased more wheels than a Nascar pit crew."

14. MTBE, a gasoline additive and suspected carcinogen, was banned in California in 1999, sparking the famed Methanex dispute under NAFTA Chapter 11 (see chapter 4 on dispute settlement). Several other states have followed California's lead, and the MTBE provisions in the energy bill were motivated by fears of defective product lawsuits against MTBE producers.

15. The nonpartisan Congressional Budget Office (CBO) projected that the tax incentives in the Energy Policy Act of 2005 conference report would reduce revenue by $12.5 billion, while the legislation would increase outlays by $1.6 billion (CBO 2005). The Bush administration had requested that the tax incentives be confined to $8 billion.

16. This tariff is intended to protect the US industry from Brazil, the world's leading ethanol producer. As NAFTA members, Canada and Mexico are exempted.

were viewed with suspicion.[17] Provisions that might raise the price of energy (in economic terms the surest way to promote conservation) were rejected outright. Conservation was an afterthought in the bill, though it does contain boutique programs, notably the $1.7 billion program to help automakers develop—within 20 years—a "freedom car" that runs on hydrogen fuel cells.

---

17. The CAFE standard regulates fuel economy in automobiles sold in the United States by setting a corporate sales-weighted standard for two categories. To avoid fines, the average fuel economy of a firm's passenger cars must be at least 27.5 miles per gallon (mpg), and light trucks—including pickups, minivans, and SUVs—must be at least 20.7 mpg.

Box 7.1 *(continued)*

Nuclear loan guarantees	For the construction of 8,400 megawatts of new nuclear plants, subject to approval by the secretary of energy.
Clean coal	$2 billion incentive program for deployment of "clean coal" technology; labeled the "highest and largest" tax incentives in the bill by Senate Energy and Natural Resources Committee Chairman Pete Domenici.
Strategic Petroleum Reserve	To be permanently authorized and increased in size to 1 billion barrels from 700 million barrels.
Renewable energy	Increase in tax credits for wind, solar, geothermal, biomass, and other renewable energy sources.
Hydrogen fuel cells	Authorizes $1.7 billion for research and development of fuel cell technology.
Combined heat and power programs	To receive a 10 percent investment tax credit and accelerated depreciation rates.
MTBE phase out	Phases out the use of MTBE, a gasoline additive that had been found to contaminate groundwater. Liability protection to MTBE producers (included in the 2003 bill) was dropped from the 2005 act to secure the support of Senate Democrats.
Liquefied natural gas (LNG) terminals	Gives FERC the final authority to approve sites of onshore LNG terminals, eliminating the ability of states and localities to veto proposed onshore LNG sites.
North American Energy Freedom	Embraces the goal of energy self sufficiency for the North American continent by 2025 and establishes the United States Commission on North American Energy Freedom to give recommendations to Congress and the President on creating a coordinated and comprehensive energy policy for the continent.

Source: Thomas Legislative Database, Library of Congress, thomas.loc.gov (accessed on August 2, 2005).

The US energy bill would only slightly affect NAFTA partners. Improvements in the natural gas infrastructure within the United States will provide incentives for both Mexico and Canada to expand exports to supply what promises to be a growing demand for clean energy. Canada will be disappointed about the lack of a mandate for the RTO system. However, Canadian firms are allowed to join RTOs as equal partners, and several, including B. C. Hydro, have already joined or are involved in talks. The specter of large energy subsidies has not upset NAFTA members as much as one might think. Canadian firms stand to profit from subsidies for hydrogen fuel cell research, alternative energy sources, and hydroelectric power.[18] While Canada generally opposes farm subsidies, the Canadian corn lobby sees ethanol support as something to imitate rather than complain about.

Mexico

Articles 27 and 28 of the 1917 Mexican Constitution declared subsoil minerals the property of the people and prohibited foreign activity in strategic energy sectors. These provisions of the Mexican Constitution were given teeth in 1938 when President Lázaro Cárdenas nationalized the oil industry and expropriated all foreign oil assets—an extremely popular action in Mexico. In 1958, Mexico passed a law giving the national oil company, Petróleos Mexicanos (Pemex), control over downstream oil operations such as transportation and marketing (Hufbauer and Schott 1992).

Mexico benefited in the 1970s as high oil prices coincided with the discovery of offshore oil reserves, enabling the country to dramatically increase its oil production and exports. Mexico sought to leverage its newfound oil wealth to develop an integrated oil industry. Extensive debt-financed investments were approved for exploration and development of crude oil and products, natural gas, and petrochemicals. Pemex employment grew rapidly. Mexico's luck ran out in the early 1980s when oil prices fell in response to global recession, making it impossible to service the country's burgeoning debt.

During the late 1980s and 1990s, the Mexican energy policy refocused on the exploitation of crude oil and gas. In 1995, the natural gas sector was opened to foreign investment in downstream operations such as transportation and storage. However, drilling for natural gas is still reserved for nationals. There has been much less reform in the oil sector. Foreign interests can contract their services to Pemex for exploration and extraction of oil reserves but cannot own any of the oil produced. This constraint all but eliminates the potential for substantial foreign participation in the oil sector.[19]

Today, Pemex remains a powerful force in Mexico as a symbol of national sovereignty, the cash cow of public finance, and an employer of about 140,000 people. Pemex seeks to maintain its oversized workforce and minimize domestic oil prices—goals that make Pemex economically inefficient and difficult to reform.[20] About 60 percent of Pemex's revenues

---

18. See "Canada Plugs into US Energy Bill," *Gas & Oil Connections* 8, no. 18, September 19, 2003.

19. The energy sector accounts for 57 percent of Mexican public-sector investment. Most of the public energy investment is in oil.

20. Whereas Pemex employs almost 140,000 people, by contrast the Venezuelan state oil company (PDVSA)—not a bastion of efficiency—has about 40,000 employees (EIA 2003b).

are diverted to the Mexican treasury, contributing about one-third of federal revenues but draining the company of needed investment funds. Indeed, in 2000 the money diverted to the federal budget was more than five times the amount spent on investment (WTO 2002). The 2002 budget tried to correct this imbalance by providing almost $15 billion for new energy investment. Most of this money has gone into existing fields, rather than new exploration.[21]

Mexico's Constitution mandates state control of electricity generation, transmission, and distribution. The state monopoly, Comisión Federal de Electricidad (CFE), maintains a legal monopoly on the sale of electricity to Mexican consumers.[22] This system is to blame for severe inefficiencies and underinvestment, which threatens the Mexican economy with high-energy costs today and chronic blackouts in the medium term.

To be sure, the Mexican Constitution has been reinterpreted several times in recent years to permit private activity in some aspects of the energy sector. In response to escalating costs, the Salinas administration reinterpreted the Constitution in 1991 to allow private companies to produce power for their own use, for sale to CFE, or for export. These companies subsequently have grown to account for a significant share of Mexican generation capacity. In an attempt to increase private-sector activity in the electricity sector, President Vicente Fox decreed in 2001 that CFE and Luz y Fuerza del Centro could buy increased amounts of electricity from "self-supplying" private firms that generated their own electricity and had been able to sell no more than 20 megawatts of excess to the Mexican government at marginal cost. However, the Mexican Supreme Court ruled in April 2002 that the Fox decree was unconstitutional.[23] In response, the Fox administration presented new energy reform proposals to the Mexican Congress in August 2002 that would amend Articles 27 and 28 of the Mexican Constitution to allow private electricity generators to sell directly to other large industrial consumers of the CFE. In an attempt to avoid the red-hot sovereignty issue, these proposals did not call for the privatization of existing CFE assets but instead fostered reforms that would encourage new investment because the firms could serve a larger and more competitive market. The case for reform was persuasive: Mexico already suffers frequent power outages; it will need much more en-

---

21. Between 2000 and 2004, Pemex invested a total of $40 billion. Less than $5 billion was spent on exploration ("Mexican Oil Chief Seeks Expansion," *New York Times*, March 3, 2005, 8).

22. There is one exception: Luz y Fuerza del Centro, a separate wholly owned government monopoly, has the exclusive rights to sell electricity to consumers in and around Mexico City. However, CFE and Luz y Fuerza are not allowed to compete, and Luz y Fuerza purchases much of its power from CFE.

23. In its deliberations, the Supreme Court questioned whether private generation was legal at all, but it was not asked to decide this question. See "Meeting Mexico's Electricity Needs," *North American Free Trade and Investment Report* 14, no. 2, January 31, 2004.

ergy investment to keep pace with the expected growth in energy demand over the next decade (EIA 2005b). Nonetheless, the energy reforms have been blocked in the Mexican Congress.[24]

While reforms are urgently needed, they would provide only a small portion of the resources that Mexico needs to upgrade its energy sector. Between 1994 and 2002, $5.3 billion of foreign direct investment had gone into the Mexican energy sector. Some $1.5 billion of this total had been directed toward small-scale electricity generation and international trade infrastructure, with about 60 percent of the investment coming from the United States and slightly less than 40 percent from France. The remaining $3.8 billion had gone to build-lease-transfer power-generating projects, with Europe providing 60 percent, the United States 20 percent, Japan 13 percent, and Canada 7 percent of the funding (Barnés de Castro 2002). Even taking these new investments into account, as of 2003, private entities own only around 30 percent of generating capacity.[25]

In 1999, the Mexican government estimated that $59 billion of investment in electricity generation and infrastructure improvements, through 2009, would be required to keep pace with demand. By this metric, the government is well behind.[26] Due to political and constitutional constraints, liberalization or privatization of the electricity industry is unlikely. The Partido Revolucionario Institucional (PRI), with the strong support of labor unions, has vowed to use its control of the Mexican Congress to block any attempt to increase foreign participation in the industry. Instead, these allies propose to force Pemex to invest in the creation of 4,000 MW of generating capacity over the next eight years.[27]

---

24. Some Congressional leaders would like to eliminate private generation entirely. In 2003, a group of PRI Congressmen asked the Auditoría Superior de la Federacíon (ASF), the auditing entity of the Mexican Congress, to review the procedures that allow private parties to sell electricity under its authority to review the government's use of the federal budget. The ASF determined that all generation permits granted between 1996 and 2002 were in violation of the Constitution. The Energy Ministry challenged the ASF finding in the Mexican Supreme Court. In April 2005, the Court ruled in a 6-5 decision that ASF had exceeded its authority by reviewing legal matters outside its scope. A definitive ruling in favor of ASF and against the permits would have had an immediate effect on the electricity industry. "Mexico Court Decision Eases Restrictions on Private Power Generation," *North American Free Trade and Investment Report* 15, no. 9, May 15, 2005.

25. CFE reported a generating capacity of 40,354 MW in March 2003. The Comisión Reguladora de Energía (CRE), the regulatory agency for energy generators, listed 235 permits for private generation with a total capacity of 19,443 MW in October 2003. However, included in this total are 29 permits (totaling 1,091 MW) owned by Pemex, the state oil firm. See "Meeting Mexico's Electricity Needs," *North American Free Trade and Investment Report* 14, no. 2, January 31, 2004.

26. See "Mexico's Power Generation Sector: Constitutional Challenge Against Permits Granted to Private Parties," *North American Free Trade and Investment Report* 14, no. 13, July 15, 2004.

27. Ibid. and "Meeting Mexico's Electricity Needs," *North American Free Trade and Investment Report* 14, no. 2, January 31, 2004.

Overall, the Pemex and CFE monopolies impose significant constraints on the development of Mexican energy resources and on Mexican economic growth. Pemex's political status as a symbol of Mexican sovereignty makes reform extremely difficult, and Mexico's energy policies remain the least market-oriented in North America.

Medium-Term Energy Outlook

This section examines supply of and demand for energy in North America. It discusses how much energy North America will need and what energy sources will fill this need.

Energy Balances

Tables 7.1a and 7.1b show energy production, imports, exports, and consumption of various energy sources for the three countries in North America in 2002. The United States accounted for almost a quarter of the world's energy consumption, and the share for North America as a whole was 29 percent. The US and North American shares in world consumption are fairly constant across the different sources of energy. Canada and Mexico currently produce more energy than they consume, but the large energy deficit of the United States overwhelms their relatively small surpluses. Thus, North America as a whole consumes 18 percent more energy than it produces.

Turning to oil, the United States imports more than it produces domestically and claims 83 percent of North American oil consumption. In 2002, net imports accounted for 53 percent of US oil consumption. In contrast, Canada and Mexico are net exporters of oil. Mexico has large reserves but actually produces little more oil than Canada and much less than the United States, reflecting the underachievement of Mexico in exploiting its own oil resources.[28] Still, Mexico is a net exporter: In 2002, Mexico consumed 55 percent of its own oil, while net exports accounted for 45 percent of production.[29]

As in the oil market, the United States accounts for a very large share of total North American natural gas consumption and production. It accounts for 71 percent of total North American gas production, but 83 percent of North American consumption—leading to net imports of 3.5 billion cubic feet (Bcf) in 2002 (or 16 percent of consumption). Here again, Canada produces much more natural gas than it consumes and exports

---

28. Mexico's oil reserves are much smaller than Canada's. However, most of Canada's reserves are in the form of oilsands, which are only in the early stages of being exploited. In contrast, Mexico's reserves are mostly mature.

29. Stock changes in 2002 were approximately zero.

Table 7.1a Energy production and consumption, 2002 (in quadrillion BTUs)

Product	North America	United States	Canada	Mexico	World
Total energy					
Production	99	71	18	10	405
Consumption	117	98	13	7	405
Oil[a]					
Production	30	17	5	8	157
Consumption	45	38	4	4	159
Dry natural gas[b]					
Production	28	20	7	1	99
Consumption	28	23	3	2	93
Coal[c]					
Production	24	23	2	0	97
Consumption	24	22	2	0	98
Electricity[d]					
Production	16	12	4	0	57
Consumption	16	12	4	0	57

more than half of its production, primarily to the United States. Mexico produces very little natural gas, flares a relatively large portion of its associated gas, and is not active in natural gas trade, despite Mexico's acute need for natural gas to generate electricity.

Coal is the only fossil fuel where the United States is self-sufficient. Canada is very active in coal trade, although only little of this trade is with the United States. Mexico imports a significant share of its total coal consumption, much of it from the United States, to supplement its relatively meager domestic coal production.

Electricity can be generated from a number of sources, including oil, natural gas, and coal. About two-thirds of North American electricity comes from these fossil fuels. The remaining third comes from nuclear and renewable sources. In the United States, 17 percent of electricity comes from nuclear power, and 12 percent from other renewable sources. In Canada, over half of electricity production comes from hydroelectric power, while a full 70 percent comes from nonfossil fuels (nuclear is 13 percent of the total). Mexico is most reliant on fossil fuels for electricity, since only 20 percent of its electricity comes from other sources.

Only a small share of total production is traded. The United States makes up the largest share of North American electricity consumption; net imports, however, account for less than 1 percent of total US electricity consumption. Canada is a small net exporter of electricity to the United States but hopes to increase exports in the future. Mexico lacks

Table 7.1b Energy production, trade, and consumption, 2002

Product/country	Production	Imports	Exports	Consumption
Oil (thousand barrels per day)				
North America	15,542	12,956	5,024	23,835
United States	9,000	11,530	984	19,761
Canada	2,949	1,088	2,079	2,093
Mexico	3,593	338	1,961	1,981
World	76,858			78,206
Dry natural gas (billion cubic feet)				
North America	27,014	4,352	4,322	26,991
United States	19,047	4,008	516	22,534
Canada	6,633	131	3,804	2,959
Mexico	1,334	213	2	1,498
World	90,717			90,270
Coal (million short tons)				
North America	1,179	47	40	1,152
United States	1,094	17	40	1,066
Canada	73	29	0	72
Mexico	12	2	0	14
World	5,252			5,262
Electricity (billion kilowatt hours)[e]				
North America	4,592	49	49	5,014
United States	3,839	36	13	4,337
Canada	549	13	36	487
Mexico	204	0	0	190
World	15,290			14,284

BTUs = British thermal units

a. 1 quadrillion BTUs is equal to about 180 million barrels of oil or 500,000 barrels per day for one year.
b. 1 quadrillion BTUs is equal to about 1 trillion cubic feet of natural gas.
c. 1 quadrillion BTUs is equal to about 50 million short tons of coal.
d. To avoid double counting total energy production, this table includes electricity generated only from primary sources that are not counted elsewhere (nuclear, hydroelectric, geothermal, wind, etc.). 1 quadrillion BTUs is equal to about 100 billion kilowatt hours.
e. Total electricity generation includes secondary production from plants that consume fossil fuels (oil, natural gas, and coal) and primary production from nuclear and renewable sources.

Note: Sums may not add up due to rounding.

Source: EIA (2004b).

both the investment to generate electricity at home and the infrastructure necessary to import sufficient power from the United States.

Overall, the United States is driving North American energy consumption, but Mexico has the most acute energy needs relative to the size of its economy. While energy is traded within North America, in most sectors the scope of trade is well short of levels that would confer maximum mutual benefits on the NAFTA partners. We now turn to some of the projections for energy consumption and production over the next 25 years.

Demand

In 2002, North America consumed 117 quadrillion British thermal units (BTUs) of energy, with the United States accounting for 83.7 percent of this total, Canada 11.1 percent, and Mexico 5.9 percent (table 7.1). These shares of energy consumption are roughly in line with the respective shares of North American GDP. At market exchange rates, the United States made up 88.4 percent of North America's GDP in 2002, Canada accounted for 6.1 percent, and Mexico 5.5 percent.[30]

Based on projections for real GDP growth and a number of other factors, the DOE projects how much energy the countries of North America will need in the future. These projections are displayed along with recent consumption history in table 7.2. The demand for energy is projected to grow relatively slowly in the United States and Canada during the next 20 years—about half the rate of real GDP growth. Mexico's demand for energy, however, may grow only moderately less than the growth of real Mexican GDP and more than twice that in the United States. Overall, energy consumption in North America is projected to be almost 50 percent greater in 2025 than in 2000. As explained later, the principal difficulty will be meeting the Mexican demand for energy, which might double by 2025.

Although the total demand for energy in North America is projected to increase substantially, the share of each type of energy in total demand will likely remain about the same. According to DOE projections, renewable energy will likely experience the fastest growth rate (albeit from a low base), followed by oil and natural gas, which will remain the largest sources of North America's energy. Under current policies, reflected in DOE projections, the use of nuclear power is projected to grow slowly; if so, it will continue to lose market share through 2025. Renewable energy is projected to grow at an average of 1.8 percent through 2025, which is slightly higher than the growth rate for North American energy consumption as a whole—1.5 percent (table 7.2). Coal is projected to grow at 1.5 percent per year, in line with the overall growth rate. In making these projections, the Energy Information Administration (EIA) assumed that oil prices would decline through 2006 and then remain in the range of $27/bbl (the OPEC basket price, in 2002 dollars) through 2025. But prices have been rising rather than

---

30. GDP data are from the International Monetary Fund's *World Economic Outlook* database, April 2003. Energy intensity can be expressed as the ratio of a country's physical energy consumption to its GDP. On this measure, Canada is the highest of the three countries in North America, and the United States and Mexico are virtually tied.

Table 7.2 Demand for energy in North America, 1990–2025

	1990	2000	2005	2010	2015	2020	2025	Average annual change 2001–25 (percent)
Total energy consumption (quadrillion BTUs)								
North America	100.6	118.7	124.6	134.5	144.6	155.0	166.6	1.5
United States	84.6	99.3	103.2	111.8	119.7	127.9	136.5	1.4
Canada	11.0	13.2	14.2	15.4	16.5	17.5	18.4	1.6
Mexico	5.0	6.2	7.2	7.3	8.3	9.6	11.6	2.8
World	348.4	398.9	433.3	470.8	517.3	567.8	622.9	1.8
Energy consumption by source (quadrillion BTUs)								
Total (North America)	100.6	118.7	124.6	134.5	144.6	155.0	166.6	1.5
Oil	40.4	46.3	48.3	53.3	58.3	62.1	67.3	1.6
Natural gas	23.1	28.8	30.6	32.6	35.3	38.7	40.9	1.6
Coal	20.7	24.5	24.9	27.4	28.6	30.7	34.2	1.5
Nuclear	6.9	8.7	9.4	9.6	9.8	10.0	9.7	0.4
Renewable	9.5	10.6	11.3	11.6	12.7	13.5	14.4	1.8
Net electricity consumption (billion kilowatt hours)								
North America	3,369	4,297	4,422	4,839	5,306	5,792	6,314	1.9
United States	2,827	3,605	3,684	4,055	4,429	4,811	5,207	1.8
Canada	435	510	539	578	630	680	728	1.6
Mexico	107	182	198	206	247	301	379	3.9
World	10,546	13,629	14,960	16,358	18,453	20,688	23,072	2.3

Notes: Data for 1990 and 2000 are historical as reported in EIA (2004a). Data for 2005 and beyond are projected based on the EIA reference case for income and population growth. 2005 projections are from EIA (2003a); 2010–25 projections are from EIA (2004a). The reference case assumes income and population growth of 3.1 and 0.9 percent, respectively, for North America, 3 and 0.8 percent for the United States, 2.7 and 0.6 percent for Canada, 3.9 and 1.1 percent for Mexico, and 3 and 1 percent for the world.

Source: EIA (2003a, 2004a).

falling, and continued high oil prices could affect both the total energy consumption and the composition energy sources.[31]

Much of the growth in demand for natural gas will reflect the increased consumption of electricity. While the growth of electricity consumption is projected to be slightly higher than the growth in total energy consumption for the United States and Canada, Mexico's growth of electricity consumption will likely average 3.9 percent annually, which is about 1.1 percentage points greater than its projected growth in total energy consumption (table 7.2). Mexico will need additional electricity as it con-

---

31. On April 4, 2005, the OPEC basket price stood at $53/bbl. It has been above the announced OPEC target price band (a maximum price of $28/bbl) since December 2, 2003 (EIA 2005d).

nects rural areas to electricity grids and as current customers demand more electricity to fuel economic expansion.

Supply

Table 7.3 shows the annual growth rate of production and consumption of various energy sources in each of the three countries from 1990 to 2001, as well as the projected annual growth rate of consumption through 2025. These projections assume that renewable energy and nuclear power remain minimal sources of supply. They may or may not be compatible with radical new CO_2 capture and sequestration technologies that could reduce greenhouse emissions from oil, coal, and natural gas. In the DOE scenario of "steady as she goes," as the North American economy integrates and as the demand for energy increases in Mexico, trade will become an increasingly important aspect of energy supply.

Oil

The United States needs to import substantial amounts of oil in order to meet its energy needs. Crude oil production in the United States declined 2.2 percent annually from 1990 to 2001, while consumption increased 1.2 percent annually. If the growth of oil consumption remains at about the same rate (or increases) in the United States through 2025, and if production remains relatively static, the United States will need substantially greater oil imports.

Concerns about US dependence on foreign oil often overlook the fact that the United States gets 40 percent of its imported oil from Canada, Mexico, and Venezuela; in fact, the United States now imports more oil from Canada than from any other country. The growth in Canadian oil production was double the growth in its consumption during 1990–2001, and much of the excess went to the United States. Canada's consumption of oil is projected to increase at about the same rate through 2025. While Canada's production of oil from conventional sources is expected to remain constant and eventually decline, technological innovations will allow further development of the oilsands in northern Alberta, so Canada will continue to be an important exporter of oil.

At the beginning of 2005, the EIA recorded that Canada had 178 billion barrels of proven oil reserves—that is, economically viable for exploitation (EIA 2005a).[32] The United States stood at 21.5 billion barrels (EIA 2005c). Mexico has fewer *proven* oil reserves (18.9 billion barrels),

---

32. In 2003, the EIA decided to classify the nearly 180 billion barrels of oil reserves in the form of oilsands as "conventional" or commercially viable ("There's Oil in Them Thar Sands!" *The Economist*, June 28, 2003, 75).

Table 7.3 Average annual growth rates of energy production and consumption (percent)

Product/country	Production 1990–2001	Consumption 1990–2001	Consumption 2001–25
Oil			
North America	−0.4	1.2	1.6
United States	−2.2	1.2	1.5
Canada	2.4	1.0	1.6
Mexico	1.9	0.8	2.5
Dry natural gas			
North America	0.0	1.6	1.6
United States	0.7	1.5	1.4
Canada	4.9	1.8	2.2
Mexico	2.9	3.2	3.9
Coal			
North America	0.4	1.6	1.6
United States	0.4	2.0	1.0
Canada	0.8	2.1	0.8
Mexico	2.5	3.7	2.4
Nuclear			
North America	2.3	2.3	0.4
United States	2.5	2.5	0.3
Canada	0.3	0.3	1.2
Mexico	9.7	9.7	1.1
Renewable			
North America	−0.2	−0.2	1.8
United States	−1.7	−1.6	2.1
Canada	1.1	1.1	1.3
Mexico	1.7	1.6	1.7

Sources: For 1990–2001 production and consumption: EIA (2003b); for 2001–25 consumption: EIA (2004a).

although it is thought to have substantially more reserves (some 54 billion barrels) that are not considered as there is no plan to explore them in the short term (EIA 2005b).[33] At current rates of production (3.8 million barrels per day), Mexico's proven reserves will last roughly 13 years. However, Mexico's annual demand for oil in physical terms is projected to grow about three times faster from 2001 to 2025 than from 1990 to 2001. This means that Mexico will need to substantially increase both its proven reserves and its production just to meet its own demand, much less continue to supply the United States with 1.4 million barrels per day of profitable oil exports.

Based on these projections for oil demand and supply, trade will become an even more important vehicle for meeting energy needs. One op-

---

33. Most of these are deep-water reserves in the Gulf of Mexico.

tion for reducing US dependence on Middle Eastern and West African oil is to increase energy imports from NAFTA members. However, in 2001, North America as a whole imported 13 million barrels of petroleum per day. By 2025, the EIA predicts that North America will import 21.4 million barrels per day—about 65 percent higher than the 2001 figure (EIA 2004a, 40).[34] Unless North America sharply increases its rate of oil production, the United States will increasingly depend on oil from regions marked by either political fragility or outright instability: the Middle East, Russia, and West Africa. Hence, the United States will likely become even more dependent on foreign oil; the question is whether it draws substantially more of this oil from Canada and Mexico—and, to a lesser extent, from regional suppliers such as Venezuela and Colombia.

Natural Gas

The natural gas market in North America is similar to the market for oil in many respects. In the United States, consumption of natural gas increased between 1990 and 2001 at double the rate of production, necessitating substantial imports.

Canada increased its production of natural gas by almost 5 percent annually between 1990 and 2001, while consumption increased 1.8 percent annually. Canada's excess production makes it the primary supplier of natural gas to the United States. While Canada is expected to continue to be a major natural gas exporter, level production and rising domestic consumption will keep exports from growing significantly over the next decade. Indeed, the DOE projects that US imports by ship of liquefied natural gas (LNG) will exceed imports from Canada by 2015 (EIA 2004a).

Mexico experienced the highest rates of growth in consumption of natural gas in 1990–2001, primarily due to electricity generation. Mexican natural gas consumption is projected to double by 2025. However, Mexico's proven natural gas reserves are relatively small (15 trillion cubic feet, or Tcf) compared with the United States (187 Tcf) and Canada (56 Tcf) and need to be substantially augmented as demand increases over the next decade (EIA 2005a, 2005b, 2005c). Mexico's existing proven reserves will be exhausted by 2025.

One way of supplementing output is to reduce flaring. Mexico flares 11.7 percent of its gross production of natural gas (Rosellón and Halpern 2001). If Mexico's flaring rate were reduced to that of the United States (0.5 percent), Mexico would have 146 Bcf more gas annually. Another possibility for Mexico is to increase net natural gas imports from southwest United States. Doing so will require major investments in pipeline infra-

---

34. As mentioned above, the EIA projects oil prices in the range of $27/bbl in 2025 (in 2002 dollars). If oil prices are substantially higher, as seems likely, imports will possibly be less, depending on production within North America.

structure. By 2025, the United States is projected to supply about 40 percent of Mexico's natural gas needs, compared with 7 percent in 2001 and around 15 percent in 2003 (EIA 2004a).

Several projects have been proposed to supply California and northern Mexico with natural gas imported from Asia, Australia, and even New Zealand. These projects contemplate the importation of LNG to regasification terminals in Mexico and then piping the gas to western United States. Locating the terminals in Mexico avoids certification and public relations problems that would arise in California. One such project, backed by ChevronTexaco, plans to begin operation in 2007, eventually processing 1.4 Bcf of natural gas a day.[35] In Canada, one LNG terminal is scheduled to begin operation in Nova Scotia in 2007, with two others proposed; there is also interest in building Pacific terminals in British Columbia ("Canada Offers Fertile Ground for LNG Terminal Developers," *Natural Gas Week*, January 3, 2005). A large portion of the LNG received at Canadian terminals would be gasified and exported to the United States via pipelines. However, concerns about the vulnerability of regasification terminals and LNG tankers to accidents and terrorist attacks have provoked strong community resistance to such projects, both in Mexico and Canada, as well as in the United States.[36]

Coal

Coal is another fuel that North America may be required to import in the future. Between 1990 and 2001, consumption of coal in all three countries grew faster than production, although both Canada and the United States were small net coal exporters in 2001. While coal resources are abundant, coal mining takes a heavy toll on the environment. Environmental restrictions, not reserves, will limit the expansion of production. However, the Bush administration has proposed the "Clear Skies" legislation, which would ease some of the current coal regulations, and recent legislative proposals would subsidize "clean coal" technology. Both programs have drawn the ire of environmental groups—indeed, "Clear Skies" was not

35. See "Baja Natural Gas Plant Proposed, ChevronTexaco Hoping to Pipe Fuel from Australia," *San Francisco Chronicle*, October 31, 2003, B3.

36. Plans for LNG terminals have been abandoned in Eureka, California, and were voted down by city councils in Fall River, Massachusetts, and Harpswell, Maine, due to terror concerns. FERC has the final decision on locating terminals in the United States, but local council decisions carry significant weight. In Mexico, a project in Baja California proposed by Marathon Oil has been abandoned, although other terminals are still planned. While government and industry officials assert that the risks of LNG are small, it is currently imported to only four locations in the United States, including Boston Harbor. James A. Fey of MIT has posited that an LNG spill and explosion could incinerate a 5 square mile area surrounding the point of ignition ("Fears of Terrorism Crush Plans for Liquefied-Gas Terminals," *Wall Street Journal*, May 14, 2004, A1).

included in the 2003 Energy Act for fear the provision would sink the entire bill.

In Canada, the government of Ontario has announced the goal of shutting down all coal-fired generators, which currently supply one quarter of Ontario's electricity, by 2007. However, the plan has been criticized as too costly and scientifically unjustified (McKitrick, Green, and Schwartz 2005). Others have suggested the regulation may run afoul of World Trade Organization (WTO) and NAFTA trade obligations, since much of Ontario's coal supply is imported from the United States (John Spears, "Electricity Laws May Break Trade Rules, Lawyer Says," *Toronto Star*, February 15, 2005, D6).

Mexico has a century of coal reserves at current production levels but remains a net importer of coal for two reasons. First, coal mining in Mexico is relatively costly, and second, Mexico's coal is of low quality, meaning it must be mixed with higher-quality coal from the United States and other countries before it can be utilized for energy production.

Nuclear and Renewable Energy

Public opinion in North America vehemently opposes nuclear energy. This could change but probably only in the wake of severe oil shortages or the stark impact of global warming. Although production and consumption of nuclear energy in Mexico grew substantially (from small bases) between 1990 and 2001, the DOE projects future growth through 2025 to do no more than maintain the current proportion of nuclear power in the total energy picture, as in the United States and Canada. Highly emotional political opposition—centered on meltdown and terrorist scenarios—diminishes the prospects for building nuclear power plants for cross-border electricity transmission in North America. This is a political fact, notwithstanding the emphasis on nuclear power expressed in the Report of the National Energy Policy Development Group (NEPD 2001) and despite the highly adverse climatic consequences of carbon dioxide emissions.

In the United States, consumption of renewable energy declined from 1990 to 2001 but is projected to turn around through 2025. Canada and Mexico are projected to increase their consumption of renewable energy through 2025 at the same annual rates as in 1990–2001. Although the volume of renewable energy usage is currently small, the prospects for the United States importing renewable energy from Canada could be improved if state regulations regarding renewable energy portfolios could be clarified and harmonized. We return to this topic in our recommendations.

Greenhouse Emissions

Despite the increased use of natural gas, carbon dioxide emissions will increase in step with total energy consumption, because (under DOE pro-

Table 7.4 Carbon dioxide emissions (billion metric tons)

Region/country	1990	2000	2010	2015	2020	2025	Average annual change 2001–25 (percent)
North America	5.8	6.7	7.7	8.3	8.9	9.7	1.6
United States	5.0	5.8	6.6	7.0	7.5	8.1	1.5
Canada	.5	.6	.7	.7	.8	.8	1.6
Mexico	.3	.4	.4	.5	.6	.7	2.8
World	21.6	23.5	27.7	30.4	33.5	37.1	1.9

Notes: Data for 1990 and 2000 are historical. 2010–25 projections are from EIA (2004a). The reference case assumes, for income and population growth respectively, 3.1 and 0.9 percent for North America, 3 and 0.8 percent for the United States, 2.7 and 0.6 percent for Canada, 3.9 and 1.1 percent for Mexico, and 3 and 1 percent for the world.

Source: EIA (2004a).

jections) North America will continue to rely primarily on oil to meet its energy needs (table 7.4). Only in Canada is the ratio of carbon dioxide emissions to energy consumption likely to decline.[37] It remains to be seen how Canada will live up to its Kyoto Protocol obligations, and what effect this will have on the North American energy market. In order for the greenhouse pollution outlook to change, natural gas, renewable energy, and nuclear power would have to be substituted for oil and coal on a much faster trajectory than is currently predicted by the DOE. Alternatively, radical new technologies will need to be developed that cheaply capture carbon dioxide (CO_2) from the exhaust of oil and coal combustion and pump the greenhouse substance deep into the earth. In addition, it may become economically feasible to capture and sequester the CO_2 byproduct from the generation of hydrogen (H_2) from natural gas (CH_4). Clean-burning hydrogen might then be used to fuel hydrogen fuel cells in automobiles. This new source of energy—which emits only water as a byproduct—would eliminate automotive greenhouse emissions.

NAFTA and Energy Trade

The NAFTA Text

Chapter 6 of NAFTA, which addresses "energy and basic petrochemicals," for the most part extended to Mexico the energy trade provisions that were established by the United States and Canada in their 1988 free

---

37. However, some analysts argue that even Canada's greenhouse gas emissions will get worse for three reasons: greater reliance on higher-polluting oil production from the oilsands, more coal-fired electric power plants to replace nuclear facilities, and higher Canadian demand for SUVs. See Rubin and Buchanan (2002).

trade agreement. The accord, however, does not create an integrated energy market in North America.

NAFTA liberalized energy trade much more than energy investment. NAFTA eliminates tariffs and quantitative restrictions on trade in energy products, although Mexico was allowed to keep its licensing system, which reserves petroleum trade to Pemex and electricity trade to the CFE. To maintain Pemex's monopoly on oil and gas exploration and development, as well as distribution of electricity and petroleum products, Mexico insisted on an exemption from most of the investment provisions and various other portions of the energy chapter.[38] However, Mexico did agree to gradually open purchase contracts issued by Pemex and CFE to US and Canadian bidders and to allow performance contracts for oilfield service firms (Hufbauer and Schott 1992). Also, Mexico agreed to liberalize foreign investment in coal and some basic and secondary petrochemicals.

Importantly, NAFTA Article 609 clarified that federal and subfederal energy regulations affecting "the transportation, transmission or distribution, purchase or sale of an energy or basic petrochemical is explicitly covered by NAFTA's national treatment obligations." Each NAFTA country is allowed to restrict energy exports for reasons of conservation, supply shortages, price volatility, and national security. However, these criteria are narrowly defined, and the "emergency clause" has not yet been invoked. NAFTA also prohibits minimum and maximum import and export prices, although it does not prohibit Mexico's public energy monopolies from setting the prices charged to business firms and individual households. These small inroads into Mexico's public energy monopoly provide a foundation for future reforms.

Energy Trade

Energy trade is an important element of North American commerce. Based on US imports from NAFTA countries in 2002, disaggregated by two-digit SITC categories, the top six traded sectors were road vehicles, petroleum, electrical machinery, telecommunications/sound recording, miscellaneous products under special tariff headings, and gas. When coal and electricity are thrown in the mix, energy accounts for 12 percent of total US imports from NAFTA countries.

Tables 7.5 and 7.6 show US energy trade (both volume and value) with Mexico and Canada between 1989 and 2004. Since energy trade between Canada and Mexico is very small, as is Mexican and Canadian energy trade with the rest of the world, we focus on their trade with the United States. Since energy prices are volatile, it is useful to focus on the volume

---

38. Petrochemicals are listed in NAFTA Chapter 6 (the exemption chapter) at the insistence of Mexico, which wanted the broadest definition of energy-related products so that certain petrochemicals would be exempt from NAFTA obligations.

of energy trade in North America rather than the value to get a handle on underlying trends (although fluctuations in energy prices obviously affect the volume to some extent). The volume of US energy imports from Canada has doubled for many products since 1989, although the two trade agreements are not responsible for most of this increase. US energy imports from Mexico have increased in some sectors but not in others. Natural gas is the only sector where US exports to both Canada and Mexico have grown substantially.

Coal

Coal is not an actively traded commodity in North America because each country has large domestic supplies. However, it is the one energy commodity where the United States enjoyed an overall trade surplus of some $285 million in 2004. Trade in coal between the United States and Mexico has generally been 2 million metric tons or less annually in each direction. Canada usually exports 2 million to 3 million metric tons to the United States but imports close to 20 million metric tons from the United States. US exports of coal to Canada have remained fairly constant in the past few years while total US coal exports have declined substantially.

Crude Oil, Refined Oil, and Liquefied Propane and Butane

The United States exports very little crude oil, and most US exports of crude go to Canada. In contrast, US imports of crude are substantial. Canada has usually sold a slightly greater volume of crude to the United States than Mexico has, but together Canada and Mexico averaged a little less than a third of total US imports of crude between 1989 and 2004.

The United States supplements its oil supply with imports of refined as well as crude oil, although US imports of refined oil are much lower than that of crude. Canada provides a substantial amount of refined oil to the United States (although the Canadian share is only about 10 percent of total US refined oil imports). Mexico has inadequate refining capacity so it is not surprising that the United States buys very little refined oil from Mexico. Indeed, due to the difficulty of obtaining sufficient funding for building refineries in Mexico, Pemex looked to the United States for some of its refined products. For example, Pemex and Shell each own 50 percent of the refinery in Deer Park, Texas, which is the sixth largest refinery in the United States. About 70 percent of the crude oil refined at Deer Park is imported from Mexico, and the refinery exports a significant amount back to Mexico.[39] As the demand for oil in Mexico will likely grow at a faster rate than Mexican refining capacity (currently estimated at 1.7 million barrels

---

39. Deer Park is one of the few refineries in the world that can convert very heavy crude into light products, such as gasoline. Mexican refineries are not capable of processing some of the heavy crudes pumped from Mexican oilfields. See Shell Deer Park (2003).

Table 7.5a US energy import values, 1989–2004 (in millions of dollars)

Product/country	1989	1990	1991	1992	1993	1994	1995	1996	1997	1998	1999	2000	2001	2002	2003	2004
Coal (SITC 32X)																
Canada	112	131	128	154	166	184	187	193	195	204	203	253	281	252	263	342
Mexico	2	1	0	0	0	0	0	0	0	0	2	0	0	1	0	0
Non-NAFTA	301	156	181	265	346	462	515	413	459	522	461	551	740	739	915	2,076
Total	415	288	309	419	513	646	703	606	654	726	665	805	1,023	993	1,178	2,418
Crude oil (SITC 333)																
Canada	3,133	4,414	4,643	4,814	4,999	4,917	6,139	7,367	7,424	5,560	6,552	12,654	10,048	11,077	13,964	18,702
Mexico	3,999	4,821	4,341	4,272	4,185	4,594	5,682	7,033	6,565	3,819	5,265	9,838	7,953	10,464	13,614	17,172
Non-NAFTA	27,909	34,598	28,390	29,018	29,063	29,019	30,256	30,449	24,405	16,088	19,825	34,054	31,376	32,543	45,188	63,069
Total	35,041	43,833	37,374	38,104	38,247	38,530	42,077	44,849	38,394	25,467	31,642	56,546	49,378	54,084	72,766	98,943
Refined oil (SITC 334)																
Canada	1,555	1,990	1,858	1,599	1,661	1,571	1,676	2,478	2,383	1,725	2,141	3,628	4,109	4,075	5,255	6,499
Mexico	121	205	164	222	478	267	216	368	430	439	375	660	587	571	978	1,591
Non-NAFTA	11,115	13,562	10,169	9,077	8,424	8,109	7,059	13,317	14,707	12,078	15,558	28,359	24,655	21,140	25,320	36,281
Total	12,792	15,757	12,191	10,898	10,563	9,948	8,951	16,163	17,520	14,243	18,074	32,647	29,351	25,786	31,353	44,371
Propane and butane (SITC 342)																
Canada	336	479	583	528	631	533	605	817	812	555	629	1,132	1,263	992	1,505	1,619
Mexico	45	121	93	37	45	47	39	124	105	82	74	93	70	73	22	17
Non-NAFTA	102	207	187	141	275	293	292	932	1,181	1,067	1,115	1,885	1,800	1,607	2,515	3,403
Total	483	807	863	706	952	873	936	1,872	2,098	1,705	1,818	3,110	3,134	2,672	4,042	5,039
Natural gas (SITC 343)																
Canada	1,695	2,012	2,334	2,729	3,245	3,903	3,246	3,915	5,069	5,184	6,070	10,361	15,355	11,428	18,249	19,481
Mexico	0	0	0	0	0	15	1	5	3	7	31	45	16	27	1	1
Non-NAFTA	66	137	93	79	146	97	27	84	154	154	304	611	954	900	2,510	3,881
Total	1,761	2,149	2,427	2,808	3,391	4,014	3,275	4,004	5,226	5,345	6,404	11,017	16,325	12,355	20,760	23,363
Electricity (SITC 351)																
Canada	558	463	487	590	662	960	856	902	978	1,039	1,334	2,711	2,681	1,160	1,382	1,261
Mexico	0	0	0	0	0	0	0	0	0	0	0	0	0	0	0	0
Non-NAFTA	0	0	0	0	0	0	0	0	0	0	0	0	0	0	0	0
Total	558	463	487	590	662	960	856	902	978	1,039	1,334	2,711	2,681	1,160	1,382	1,261
Total																
Canada	7,388	9,488	10,034	10,414	11,365	12,068	12,709	15,671	16,861	14,268	16,928	30,738	33,737	28,985	40,618	47,904
Mexico	4,167	5,148	4,597	4,531	4,708	4,923	5,938	7,529	7,103	4,347	5,747	10,637	8,627	11,136	14,615	18,781
Non-NAFTA	39,493	48,661	39,019	38,580	38,255	37,980	38,149	45,195	40,906	29,909	37,263	65,460	59,525	56,929	76,748	108,710
Total	51,049	63,298	53,650	53,525	54,329	54,971	56,797	68,396	64,871	48,525	59,938	106,835	101,891	97,050	131,981	175,395

Table 7.5b   US energy import volume, 1989–2004

Product/country	1989	1990	1991	1992	1993	1994	1995	1996	1997	1998	1999	2000	2001	2002	2003	2004
Coal (million metric tons)																
Canada	2	2	1	2	2	2	2	2	2	2	2	3	3	3	3	3
Mexico	0	0	0	0	0	0	0	0	0	0	0	0	0	0	0	0
Non-NAFTA	4	2	3	4	8	9	9	7	9	10	10	13	18	16	24	29
Total	5	4	5	6	9	11	11	10	11	12	12	16	21	19	27	32
Crude oil (million barrels)																
Canada	196	217	267	291	328	348	379	396	424	459	422	499	484	515	543	575
Mexico	255	254	275	281	301	339	367	386	392	364	364	396	424	491	535	545
Non-NAFTA	1,678	1,751	1,588	1,694	1,897	2,021	1,914	1,605	1,363	1,378	1,291	1,286	1,394	1,412	1,628	1,764
Total	2,128	2,222	2,130	2,266	2,527	2,708	2,660	2,387	2,179	2,202	2,078	2,181	2,302	2,418	2,706	2,884
Refined oil (million barrels)[a]																
Canada	75	76	77	70	77	78	77	96	96	93	98	103	132	133	140	138
Mexico	8	9	9	13	34	20	14	17	22	31	24	23	21	25	34	42
Non-NAFTA	614	614	547	495	519	523	411	637	726	858	896	944	947	823	817	924
Total	697	698	633	578	629	621	501	750	844	982	1,017	1,069	1,100	981	991	1,104
Propane and butane (million barrels)																
Canada	32	33	41	42	48	49	57	52	48	57	53	58	57	71	67	58
Mexico	5	9	7	3	4	4	3	10	9	12	9	6	6	6	1	0
Non-NAFTA	12	17	14	11	24	26	24	67	96	120	111	115	112	114	137	158
Total	48	58	62	55	76	78	84	129	153	188	172	179	175	191	205	216
Natural gas (billion cubic meters)																
Canada	31	36	45	57	64	72	81	82	84	88	94	97	109	110	108	108
Mexico	0	0	0	0	0	0	0	0	0	0	0	0	0	0	0	0
Non-NAFTA	2	3	2	2	4	0	1	2	3	3	6	11	12	13	27	38
Total	33	39	47	58	67	75	81	84	87	90	101	109	121	123	135	146
Electricity (thousand megawatt hours)																
Canada	18	16	20	26	29	44	40	42	43	39	45	47	38	38	31	27
Mexico	0	0	0	0	0	0	0	0	0	0	0	0	0	0	0	0
Non-NAFTA	0	0	0	0	0	0	0	0	0	0	0	0	0	0	0	0
Total	18	16	20	26	29	44	40	42	43	39	45	47	38	38	31	27

a. Refined oil (SITC 334) excludes some quantity where the quantity was measured in kilograms rather than in barrels.

Note: US imports for consumption, does not include trans-shipments.

Source: USITC Interactive Tariff and Trade Dataweb (2005).

Table 7.6a US energy export values, 1989–2004 (in millions of dollars)

Product/country	1989	1990	1991	1992	1993	1994	1995	1996	1997	1998	1999	2000	2001	2002	2003	2004
Coal (SITC 32X)																
Canada	763	592	432	560	376	386	457	514	564	688	665	657	648	651	627	708
Mexico	24	25	22	20	29	28	50	88	123	106	92	62	53	50	55	85
Non-NAFTA	3,600	3,991	4,266	3,745	2,793	2,548	3,205	3,248	2,878	2,397	1,503	1,454	1,211	966	929	1,910
Total	4,387	4,608	4,720	4,325	3,198	2,962	3,713	3,849	3,565	3,191	2,259	2,174	1,912	1,670	1,621	2,703
Crude oil (SITC 333)																
Canada	49	171	34	22	15	43	1	166	303	417	271	154	176	87	124	218
Mexico	0	0	0	1	0	0	0	4	0	0	0	1	0	1	0	0
Non-NAFTA	13	12	2	3	5	2	0	290	477	253	501	289	1	0	0	28
Total	62	183	35	27	20	44	1	460	780	670	772	444	177	88	124	246
Refined oil (SITC 334)																
Canada	434	594	446	395	422	429	492	560	651	561	626	886	905	797	986	1,255
Mexico	431	529	612	791	670	672	739	952	1,365	1,304	1,729	3,183	2,400	2,190	2,149	2,606
Non-NAFTA	2,308	3,546	3,927	3,349	3,405	2,685	2,733	3,251	2,719	1,723	2,114	2,881	2,910	3,027	3,943	5,864
Total	3,173	4,669	4,984	4,535	4,497	3,785	3,964	4,763	4,736	3,588	4,469	6,950	6,215	6,014	7,078	9,725
Propane and butane (SITC 342)																
Canada	14	27	31	22	32	27	55	51	41	39	48	97	57	45	72	102
Mexico	84	101	77	114	114	114	139	146	180	125	164	444	214	259	230	208
Non-NAFTA	14	32	148	121	82	54	122	105	76	40	87	122	67	166	169	114
Total	112	160	256	258	229	195	316	302	297	204	299	663	338	470	471	424
Natural gas (SITC 343)																
Canada	11	0	10	40	37	62	33	80	143	71	58	153	189	382	1,078	1,933
Mexico	56	41	41	191	80	44	87	33	35	30	18	111	201	471	73	13
Non-NAFTA	160	158	242	121	127	147	146	148	142	142	142	148	146	141	149	140
Total	227	199	293	351	244	254	266	261	320	243	218	411	536	994	1,330	2,086
Electricity (SITC 351)																
Canada	180	491	54	64	61	30	47	69	124	185	206	398	1,258	304	716	829
Mexico	0	0	0	0	0	0	0	0	0	0	0	0	0	0	0	0
Non-NAFTA	0	0	0	0	0	0	0	0	0	0	0	0	0	0	0	0
Total	180	491	54	64	61	30	47	69	124	185	206	398	1,258	304	716	829
Total																
Canada	1,451	1,876	1,006	1,102	943	977	1,085	1,439	1,826	1,960	1,874	2,344	3,234	2,265	3,603	5,045
Mexico	595	695	752	1,118	893	859	1,016	1,223	1,704	1,566	2,003	3,800	2,869	2,972	2,517	2,912
Non-NAFTA	6,095	7,738	8,585	7,339	6,413	5,435	6,205	7,042	6,292	4,555	4,346	4,895	4,335	4,303	5,190	8,056
Total	8,141	10,309	10,343	9,559	8,249	7,271	8,307	9,704	9,822	8,080	8,223	11,039	10,437	9,540	11,310	16,013

Table 7.6b US energy export volume, 1989–2004

Product/country	1989	1990	1991	1992	1993	1994	1995	1996	1997	1998	1999	2000	2001	2002	2003	2004
Coal (million metric tons)																
Canada	16	15	11	14	9	9	10	12	15	20	19	18	17	16	19	17
Mexico	0	0	0	0	0	0	1	2	2	2	1	1	1	1	1	1
Non-NAFTA	77	82	89	80	60	56	71	70	61	51	34	35	28	20	20	26
Total	93	97	100	94	69	66	82	84	73	72	54	54	45	37	40	44
Crude oil (million barrels)																
Canada	3	6	1	1	1	2	0	6	10	21	15	6	5	3	5	7
Mexico	0	0	0	0	0	0	0	0	0	0	0	0	0	0	0	0
Non-NAFTA	1	1	0	0	0	0	0	13	24	19	28	11	0	0	0	1
Total	4	7	2	1	1	2	0	19	34	40	42	17	5	3	5	8
Refined oil (million barrels)																
Canada	21	19	15	14	16	15	15	16	20	19	150	19	19	24	30	31
Mexico	26	24	29	36	32	34	34	40	58	69	77	99	79	67	56	54
Non-NAFTA	116	137	175	166	168	140	131	129	110	86	88	85	107	112	118	151
Total	162	180	219	216	216	189	179	184	187	174	315	203	205	203	204	236
Propane and butane (million barrels)																
Canada	2	2	2	2	2	2	4	3	2	3	3	4	3	3	3	4
Mexico	5	5	4	8	6	7	9	8	11	8	9	17	9	12	9	8
Non-NAFTA	1	2	8	7	6	4	8	7	4	3	4	5	3	7	7	3
Total	8	9	14	17	14	14	20	18	17	15	17	26	15	22	19	15
Natural gas (billion cubic meters)																
Canada	0	0	0	1	1	1	1	1	1	1	1	1	2	4	6	11
Mexico	1	1	1	3	1	1	1	1	1	1	1	1	2	4	1	0
Non-NAFTA	3	2	2	2	2	2	2	2	3	2	2	2	3	2	2	3
Total	4	2	2	6	3	3	4	4	6	4	3	4	7	11	9	14
Electricity (thousand megawatt hours)																
Canada	9	16	2	2	3	1	2	2	5	9	11	12	19	12	22	22
Mexico	0	0	0	0	0	0	0	0	0	0	0	0	0	0	0	0
Non-NAFTA	0	0	0	0	0	0	0	0	0	0	0	0	0	0	0	0
Total	9	16	2	2	3	1	2	2	5	9	11	12	19	12	22	22

Note: Refined oil (SITC 334) excludes some quantity where the quantity was measured in kilograms rather than barrels.

Source: USITC Interative Tariff and Trade Dataweb (2005).

per day), Mexico will probably continue to be a net importer of refined oil from the United States (EIA 2005b).

North American trade in liquefied propane and butane is small. The United States exports a few million barrels annually to both Canada and Mexico and receives a few million barrels annually from Mexico. Canada accounts for the dominant portion of total US imports of liquefied propane and butane, but the total is not large.

Natural Gas

The growth in natural gas trade in North America is the fastest of any energy commodity. The United States is a net importer of natural gas but at times during the 1990s has provided a significant amount of natural gas to Mexico. Mexican consumption of natural gas is expected to increase steeply in the future, at an annual rate of 6.2 percent from 2001 to 2025. While some of this gas will have to come from overseas, if greater pipeline capacity existed along the US-Mexico border, the United States could expand exports of natural gas to Mexico.

US natural gas imports have grown more than tenfold in value terms (and almost fivefold in quantity terms) since 1989, and most of the new supply has come from Canada. Natural gas trade between the United States and Canada is two-way; however, a significant amount of US exports represents Canadian gas transported from west to east that crosses the US border as it flows from Canadian gas wells to Canadian customers. While deregulation has boosted natural gas trade, and while pipeline capacity has increased, more pipeline construction will be necessary to create an integrated natural gas market between the United States and Canada.[40] Eventually, reserves in Alaska's North Slope and Canada's Mackenzie Delta may be tapped to supply natural gas across the continent.

Electricity

Almost all US trade in electricity is with Canada, and the United States is a net importer. However, electricity trade is two-way, due to shifting seasonal demand (north to Canada in the winter, south to US cities in the summer). Canada has a comparative advantage in electricity generation due to its many fast-flowing rivers that provide hydroelectric power. Mexico, which is plagued by frequent power outages, does not currently have adequate transmission infrastructure to import heavily from the United States. Likewise, Mexico lacks the infrastructure to export a significant volume of electricity to the United States. However, some private

---

40. The challenge is not only cross-border but also between regions of each country. As evidence of market segmentation, Bradley and Watkins (2003) cite significant price differences between natural gas sold at high prices in the Pacific northwest (where prices were very high during the 2001 energy crisis) compared with the slack market in the US mountain states during the same period.

companies, such as California-based Sempra Energy, have started producing electricity in Mexico for the US market.[41] Better transmission infrastructure would promote electricity trade between the United States
and Mexico, but it is not clear that new transmission lines will be built
anytime soon.

North American Policy Cooperation: Recent Initiatives

The Energy Consultative Mechanism (ECM) between the United States
and Canada, which has been in existence since 1980, provides a formal
mechanism for the two countries to discuss developments in the energy
sector and to facilitate cooperation in research and development. The
group, which comprises senior staff of Natural Resources Canada, the
Canadian Department of Foreign Affairs, and the US Departments of Energy and State, meets once a year but publishes no proceedings or reports.

In April 2001, the three NAFTA countries created the North American
Energy Working Group (NAEWG) to collaborate on energy policy issues
and to enhance North American energy trade and interconnections consistent with sustainable development.[42] The high political profile soon
faded, however. The NAEWG's work has focused on sharing information
on technical standards and regulations rather than on big-picture infrastructure projects or energy security issues.

As of March 2005, the NAEWG had issued four major reports,[43] focusing on North America's energy supply, demand, infrastructure, electricity
regulation, and energy efficiency. The first report, "North America: The Energy Picture," provides basic statistics and discusses the legal and policy
regulatory frameworks in each of the three countries. The second, "North
America: Regulation of International Electricity Trade," expands on the
previous report's section on electricity regulation. The third report, "North
American Energy Efficiency Standards and Labeling," documents North
American attempts to harmonize efficiency standards by 2003. The most
recent report, "North American Natural Gas Vision," was released in January 2005.

While NAEWG's level of activity is an improvement over the ECM,
much more could be done. The flavor of this working group is that of a

---

41. The Termoeléctrica de Mexicali natural gas power plant in Baja California Norte has a
capacity of 600MW and can supply both Mexico and southern California. Environmental
groups have challenged the plant, along with similar projects, but it has been approved in
court and is currently operating ("Judge Lets Power Flow from Mexico," Los Angeles Times,
July 10, 2003, C2).

42. See NAEWG (2002a) for details.

43. In addition to these four, NAEWG released "Guide to Federal Regulation of Sales of Imported Electricity in Canada, Mexico, and the United States" in January 2005 as a follow-up
publication to its earlier work on electricity trade.

talkfest—long on discussion, short on recommendations. We suggest that the NAEWG be given a higher profile, hold public meetings, and issue clear recommendations, even if the parties agree only on narrow issues.

By necessity, cooperation has been strongest in the area of electricity regulation. NERC, founded in 1968, develops voluntary reliability standards, relying on peer pressure and mutual self-interest to see that its regulations are followed. NERC itself has taken the position that voluntary standards are no longer adequate and advocates legislative changes to create a mandatory set of electric reliability standards across North America.[44]

In response to the northeast blackout of August 14, 2003, Ottawa and Washington sprang into action, establishing the US-Canada Power System Outage Task Force. This group was charged with determining the root causes of the blackout and developing a plan to prevent any recurrence of regionwide power outages. Box 7.2 summarizes the final report from the task force, which addresses the causes of the northeast blackout. The emphasis on preventing mass outages is clearly appropriate. To this end, a bilateral electricity reliability organization (ERO) to develop and enforce mandatory electric reliability rules throughout the United States and Canada was first suggested in 1997 as a successor organization to NERC. The ERO would be an important step forward. This step would require that the US Congress grant FERC power to delegate some of its regulatory authority to an international body. The concept of an ERO has sufficient promise and salience that it should become the top item on the agenda of energy cooperation.

Recommendations

What the August 2003 blackout proved for electricity—that effective policy and regulation on one side of the border is a national security priority on both sides—is also true in the oil, natural gas, nuclear, and other energy sectors. However, while more integrated North American energy policies may be in the best interests of all involved, getting from here to there is no small task.

NAFTA solidified already extensive energy relationships between the United States and Canada, which operate through physical and regulatory interconnections. The agreement also made tentative steps toward bringing Mexico into the market for trade and procurement of energy-related goods. However, private investment in Mexican hydrocarbons or electricity remains largely off-limits. NAFTA did not create the uneven nature of

---

44. NERC operates primarily in the United States and Canada, although its members also include energy suppliers to a portion of Baja California Norte, Mexico. NERC's position with respect to mandatory reliability standards is explained on its Web site, www.nerc.com (accessed on March 1, 2005).

Box 7.2   Causes of the August 2003 blackout

In April 2004, the US-Canada Power System Outage Task Force released its final report on the causes of the August 14, 2003 blackout, which affected 50 million people in the northeastern United States and Ontario. The report found that the blackout originated in Ohio. Three high-voltage transmission lines owned and operated by FirstEnergy (FE), a local utility company, failed after making contact with trees that had encroached into line easements. Due to computer failure, the line failures did not raise alarms, and FE controllers remained unaware of the problem. Since FE did not take action to rebalance the load on its system, the failures caused power to surge and overload other transmission lines in FE's control area, which in turn caused a cascade of failures throughout the region. The report faulted FE for not maintaining its transmission lines and for operating the transmission system in an insecure manner and the Midwest Independent System Operator (MISO), FE's RTO, for failing to provide effective diagnostic support and communicate the problem to other regional reliability coordinators.

To prevent future blackouts, the task force issued 46 specific recommendations. The first was to "make reliability standards mandatory, with penalties for noncompliance" (US-Canada Power System Outage Task Force 2004, 140). Second was to develop a regulator-approved independent funding mechanism for the North American Electric Reliability Council (NERC) to ensure its independence, and third was to strengthen the institutional framework for reliability management in North America. Most recommendations were far more technical in nature. The task force noted that "the August 14 blackout shared a number of contributing factors with prior large-scale blackouts, confirming that the lessons and recommendations from early blackouts had not been adequately implemented" (Task Force 2004, 147). This comment suggests systemic problems that require policy reform.

Previous blackouts have been caused by

- inadequate vegetation management (tree trimming);
- failure to ensure operation within secure limits;
- failure to identify emergency conditions and communicate that status to neighboring systems;
- inadequate operator training; and
- inadequate regional-scale visibility over the power system.

The new causes in the August 14 blackout were

- inadequate interregional visibility over the power system;
- dysfunction of a control area's System Control and Data Acquisition (SCADA) system and Emergency Management System (EMS); and
- lack of adequate backup capability to these systems.

North American energy integration, but it does institutionalize differences between the more market-oriented policies of Canada and the United States on one side and the more statist policies of Mexico on the other.

In our opinion, this bifurcation was an appropriate recognition of reality. The minimal steps taken by Mexico under NAFTA provide some small precedent for liberalization, and the alternative—retarding integration between Canada and the United States in order to include Mexico—is undesirable. Today, tension remains between cohesion and progress in North American energy policy. Our view is that even though it is in the interest of all member countries to narrow the policy gap in the long term, future demands for energy are too pressing to hold US-Canada integration hostage to the Mexican political environment. Instead, we advocate continuing two-track integration and offer two sets of recommendations. The first concentrates on meeting the energy needs of Canada and the United States through enhanced cooperation. The second seeks politically viable ways that the three countries can help expand energy production in Mexico.

Furthering US-Canada Policy Cooperation

When the National Energy Policy Development Group, chaired by Vice President Dick Cheney, released its assessment of the US energy policy (NEPD 2001), its recommendation to create a "North American framework" provoked a great deal of discussion in Canada (although relatively little in the United States, where the hot issue of the report was the recommendation to allow oil drilling in the Arctic National Wildlife Refuge). Exactly what the framework would entail is ambiguous, and some Canadians are wary that a continental energy policy would undermine Canadian sovereignty. There is no reason for this to be the case. Canada's own energy policies, driven by the constitutional mandate that accords most direct responsibilities to the provinces, are an example of how to maintain local sway while ensuring interregional cooperation.

Enhanced cooperation can come from many sources, but we believe that an agreement has the best chance of being implemented if it comes from a bilateral cabinet-level initiative. The ECM—which involves the US Departments of State and Energy alongside Natural Resources Canada and the Canadian Department of Foreign Affairs—has up to this point distinguished itself primarily by its low profile; instead, ECM meetings should be used to provide public and political impetus to a series of initiatives to promote US-Canada energy linkages. Several items are ripe for cooperation, provided the two sides communicate with one another at a senior political level.

Joint Regulation of Electricity Reliability

The electricity grid connections between the United States and Canada are so tightly integrated that they constitute a single electricity infrastructure. In the post–September 11 environment, the United States has an obvious interest in ensuring the security of those portions of the grid in Canada. The August 2003 blackout showed Canadians by example that substandard operation of the grid in Ohio can turn the lights out in Ottawa and Toronto.[45] Given the importance of electricity in the daily lives of Canadians and Americans, it is remarkable that grid reliability is regulated with only a voluntary set of standards (many of which were not followed in August 2003). There is broad support for developing mandatory reliability standards. NERC and FERC both agree that the creation of a bilateral ERO, mandated to develop and enforce reliability standards, would be desirable. Legislation enabling FERC to participate in the creation of an ERO was passed in July 2005 in the Energy Policy Act of 2005, and President Bush signed the measure into law in August. So the time is now right for an international initiative to establish joint regulation of the electricity grid.

If some level of joint regulation is successful in the realm of electricity management, the system could be expanded to other parts of the energy infrastructure, such as natural gas pipelines.

Renewable Portfolio Standards

Many US states have renewable portfolio standards (RPS), which either require the use of renewable energy or give incentives to use renewable energy. However, different states use different definitions of renewable energy. Some of these state definitions exclude particular types of energy-generating processes conventionally considered "renewable," particularly hydroelectric power in general or hydroelectric power from dams above a certain capacity. Also, some states have potentially abusive licensing standards or require the renewable energy be generated in-state.[46]

Canada's abundance of hydroelectric-generating capacity means it has much to gain from these emerging policies, but their potential use as trade barriers is a cause for concern.[47] In the United States, the federal government has already expressed some interest in developing a federal stan-

---

45. To be fair, equipment malfunction in Ontario caused the 1965 blackout, which affected much of the US northeast, including New York City.

46. NAFTA reiterates GATT language that trade-restrictive measures that attempt to protect the environment can be justified in some circumstances, but they cannot be applied in an arbitrary manner or function as a disguised restriction on trade.

47. Such "in-state" requirements are obviously a disguised restriction on extra-state commerce and thus a restriction on international trade. Licensing standards do not obviously violate NAFTA, but they could be used to restrict trade if states treated applications from Canada or Mexico less favorably. The definition of renewable energy is a tougher case. For example, New Jersey considers hydroelectric power generated by facilities with less than 30 megawatts of capacity to be renewable, but 96 percent of Canadian hydroelectric power is produced by facilities with more than 30 megawatts of capacity. Although there have been no legal cases on electricity issues to date, the 30-megawatt requirement could be considered "arbitrary" or a disguised restriction on trade, especially if most of New Jersey's hydroelectric power generators have less than 30 megawatts of capacity. Although the capacity of the plant has little to do with whether the energy is in fact renewable, some environmentalists fear that large dams adversely affect plants, animals, and fish.

dard, although a provision creating a federal RPS was removed from the Energy Policy Act of 2005 due to Republican objections an RPS would increase electricity costs ("Provisions to Curb Oil Use Fall Out of Energy Bill, *New York Times,* July 26, 2005, 14). If Canadian provinces are willing to adhere to an RPS—and there is no reason to believe they would not—expanding this to a binational standard should be relatively straightforward and would ensure that Canadian renewable energy is credited under the RPS. For the United States, an environment-friendly agreement with Canada would demonstrate its environmental credentials despite the US decision not to participate in the Kyoto Protocol.

Key Energy Projects

Both the United States and Canada should be more forthcoming about consultations over major energy projects than their record in the fractious deliberations over the Alaskan North Slope and Canadian Mackenzie Delta pipeline projects (box 7.3). It now appears that two pipelines will be constructed to bring natural gas from northern reserves to southern markets. Alaskan gas will take the "southern route" while a separate pipeline will connect the Mackenzie Delta to the existing Alberta gas pipeline infrastructure. While the pipeline routing dispute has subsided, it generated bilateral friction that contributed to unnecessary delays in infrastructure investments and set back the larger vision of energy security in North America.[48] We believe Dobson (2002) is correct in saying that infrastructure planning could and should be done within the context of existing regional mechanisms. The two governments should let private investors pursue their international energy projects, consistent with environmental, public safety, and security concerns.

Like the pipeline debate, most large energy projects in North America will have an international dimension. The next large projects on the horizon are the construction of LNG terminals in NAFTA countries (both to supply the local market and to import and regasify LNG for export via pipeline) and the exploitation of the oilsands in Alberta. Beyond LNG and the oilsands are nuclear power plants. While nuclear power currently dwells in the dark regions of political and environmental incorrectness, it could fast become more acceptable if atmospheric CO_2 concentrations rise and global warming becomes a political as well as a scientific fact.[49]

---

48. For a summary of Canadian concerns, see Paul Kergin, "Trust the Market (and Canada)," *Wall Street Journal,* May 15, 2002, A18.

49. Almost a quarter century since the partial meltdown at Three Mile Island, the de facto US freeze on building nuclear power capacity may be starting to thaw. Three operators have applied to the Nuclear Regulatory Commission for site approval to build additional reactors at existing plants in North Anna, VA, Clinton, IL, and Port Gibson, MS ("Nuclear Power Hopes to Find a Welcome Mat Again," *New York Times,* January 27, 2005, 16).

Box 7.3   Northern natural gas pipelines

In the United States, legislation attached to the Military Construction Appropriation Act of 2004 (PL 108-324) provides loan guarantees of roughly $18 billion to build a gas pipeline from northern Alaska to Chicago via the "southern route," which would run south across Alaska and then cut east through British Columbia and Alberta on its way to the Chicago hub.[1] An alternate "northern route" would have run southeast underwater into the northwestern territories and then through Alberta on its way to Chicago. The northern route is somewhat more direct and would cost $2 billion less to build than the southern route (Welch 2002).

The US Congress preferred the "southern route" both because it was thought to be more environment-friendly—much of this route parallels the Trans-Alaska oil pipeline or the Alaska-Canada Highway, so the construction infrastructure is already in place—and because a greater percentage of the line would go through the United States, thus creating more jobs for US union workers.

In addition to carrying gas from Alaska's North Slope, the "northern route" could have also been used to transport natural gas from Canada's Mackenzie Delta. Canadians initially feared that a standalone Mackenzie Delta pipeline might not be economically viable and that subsidies from the US government (at one point a guaranteed price floor for gas delivered via the North Slope pipeline was being considered) would price a private Canadian pipeline out of the market.[2] However, a private consortium has emerged to connect the Mackenzie Delta to Alberta's existing pipeline system. Notably, the Mackenzie pipeline consortium includes some Canadian aboriginal groups, who have joined with energy companies in support of a pipeline because they believe they have the political clout necessary to benefit from the extraction and transportation of natural resources on their lands.

---

1. This legislation, which also includes $400 million worth of tax breaks in the form of accelerated depreciation schedules and credits, was initially part of the Energy Policy Act of 2003 (HR 6) but was moved separately when the larger bill became bogged down in the Senate.

2. Jack Mintz of the C. D. Howe Institute pointed out that it was not just the potential for US subsidies but a more favorable tax system that advantaged US pipelines over Canadian ones. Canadian pipelines are depreciated for tax purposes at a rate of 4 percent per year using a declining balance method, resulting in a 50-year depreciation schedule, much longer than historical pipeline replacement life, even though the reserves in the Mackenzie Delta are expected to last only for 20 years. By contrast, the US tax depreciation schedule for pipelines is 15 years, and the Alaska pipeline will be allowed a special seven-year schedule (*National Post*, February 3, 2005).

Obviously, the home country will take the lead in developing LNG or nuclear projects on its territory or approving permits for infrastructure construction on its soil. The United States and Canada have differing philosophies regarding the level of government support for infrastructure projects and differing attitudes toward nuclear power. However, informal consultations can avoid misunderstandings on projects with cross-border dimensions and avoid duplication of efforts.

Currently, almost all of Canada's oil exports are destined for the United States and arrive through pipelines. Exploitation of the oilsands, now technologically and commercially viable (with oil at $50/bbl), should significantly expand Canadian production and exports. Currently, Alberta oilsands yield more than 1 million barrels per day (bpd), and production is projected to double by 2010 (Alberta Department of Energy 2005). However, not all of the increased production may supply North American markets. In April 2005, the state-owned China National Offshore Oil Company (CNOOC) bought a 16.7 percent share in MEG Energy Corporation, a Calgary firm exploiting a 2-billion-barrel oilsands lease near Christina Lake, which hopes to produce 25,000 bpd by 2008. In addition, Canadian pipeline firm Enbridge and PetroChina, a division of China National Petroleum Company, agreed to cooperate on the construction of a 720-mile pipeline from the Alberta oilsands to the coast of British Columbia. This pipeline would cost $2 billion and have a planned capacity of 400,000 bpd or 20 percent of projected oilsands output by 2010. The deal depends importantly on agreement on long-term supply contracts with Chinese and other customers.[50]

Chinese investment plans in Canadian oil are only in an embryonic state, but because the Chinese companies are state-owned, commentators have already stirred concerns about Chinese government ownership of Canadian natural resources.[51] Speaking in Beijing, Canadian Prime Minister Paul Martin said he "shares those concerns" and that "the decision will be based on its benefits to Canada and the protections for Canada, and the nature of the owner and what the owner has to bring" ("Martin Echoes Takeover Concerns," *Toronto Star*, January 22, 2005, D1). The scene is thus set for a new bout of federal/provincial friction on energy policy if larger Chinese investments—with the approval of Alberta and British Columbia—provoke policy action from the federal government in Ottawa.

Finally, US-Canada cooperation could advance exploitation of another promising energy source: coalbed methane (CBM) gas. CBM is gas that eons ago was trapped during the conversion of plant material into coal. The presence of CBM gas has long been known (it is the primary cause of coal mine explosions), but commercial production has become feasible only in the past few decades. Unfortunately, CBM extraction also produces large amounts of water, often with a high saline content. Disposal of this water poses an environmental challenge.[52] In 2002, CBM production in the United States was 4.7 Bcf per day; it is projected to rise to 5.6 Bcf in 2025. Over the same period, Canadian production is expected to rise from 0.5

---

50. See "China Buys into Oilsands," *Edmonton Journal*, April 13, 2005, H1; "Enbridge, PetroChina Sign Oilsands Pipeline Deal," *Reuters*, April 14, 2005; and "China is Emerging as a Rival to US for Oil in Canada," *New York Times*, December 23, 2004, 1.

51. Similar concerns surfaced in the United States in mid-2005 when CNOOC sought to buy Unocal.

52. The leading technique is to inject the water back into the coalbed, which significantly raises production costs.

Bcf per day to 2.2 Bcf per day (NAEWG 2005a, 14). CBM and other "unconventional sources" will remain minor contributors to total production of natural gas. As a benchmark, in 2003, North America produced roughly 75 Bcf of natural gas per day. However, in a maturing industry, CBM gas could partially compensate for depleting oil and gas reserves. Both the United States and Canada should fund additional research on the recovery and development of CBM deposits.

Expanding Mexican Production and US-Mexico Energy Trade

The basic problem in Mexico is that the country will need much more energy in the near future but is unlikely to meet growing demand because of inadequate investment in oil and gas fields and electricity generation and distribution. The current tax system and constitutional constraints on energy-related private activity effectively deny the needed financial resources for energy investment in Mexico. Frequent electricity "brownouts," which disrupt industrial production throughout the country, underscore both the need for tax and energy reforms in Mexico and the cost of the long-standing political impasse over policy reforms in the Mexican Congress.[53] Supply shortfalls threaten to dampen economic growth, further limiting revenue available for new energy investment.

According to Luis Ramírez Corzo, the director general of Pemex, present levels of investment (about $10 billion a year) will allow the company only to maintain production levels and continue to export. Raising investment to $20 billion could boost exports in both oil and natural gas.[54] To do so, however, Pemex needs advanced oilfield technologies to exploit deepwater reserves in the Gulf of Mexico, which are not on offer from private companies under the limited fee-based service contracts permitted by Mexico's constitutional provisions. Avoiding the Constitution's "no-go" zone, Ramírez has set an ambitious agenda that includes rewriting the Pemex union contract, freeing Pemex finances from government management, creating an independent board of directors, creating "alliances" with foreign oil companies, and convincing the government to siphon less oil revenue to meet its fiscal targets.[55] The Pemex chief even suggested

---

53. One reason for the impasse is Pemex's status as a national symbol and cash cow of the Mexican treasury. Pemex made up 37 percent of federal budget revenues in 2000. If Pemex were privatized or partially privatized, alternative tax sources would be needed to compensate for the fiscal drain.

54. Much of the increase in investment would target 54 billion barrels of "possible" oil reserves in deepwater areas of the Gulf of Mexico. Mexico's proven reserves stand at 18.9 billion barrels in 2005, down from 28.4 billion barrels in 1999. See "Into Deep Water," *The Economist*, February 26, 2005, 36, and EIA (2005b).

55. See "Mexican Oil Chief Seeks Expansion," *New York Times*, March 3, 2005, 8.

that some natural gas resources should be open to exploitation by the private sector.[56]

Unfortunately, for a variety of political reasons, we do not believe that reforms to give private companies—Mexican or foreign—the requisite incentive to invest or operate in Mexico are likely in the near term.[57] There is an important qualification to this pessimistic prognosis: If world energy prices stay in the $40 to $60 per barrel range (presumably as a result of rapid demand growth in China and India and political tensions in the Middle East), and if energy demand greatly exceeds supply in Mexico, the Mexican people might become more willing to reconsider the utility of the energy provisions in their Constitution. In this case, Mexico may be able to implement a mix of job security arrangements (guaranteed employment of energy workers either with new foreign employers or in their current jobs) and wage insurance programs for displaced workers, which would make full-scale reform politically acceptable. The chances of this scenario seem small in the near future. But as time passes, and Mexico's energy problems and the associated drag on development become more severe, reforms will become unavoidable.

Meanwhile, the prognosis is slightly better for tax reform, which would allow Pemex to keep a larger share of its revenues. In 2003, the Chamber of Deputies passed a bill to reduce the government's take of Pemex revenues by as much as $2.5 billion in 2006; however, the legislation is stalled in the Mexican Senate.[58] In 2003, Pemex provided almost one-third of the Mexican government revenue (SHCP 2004, annex A), so any reduction in revenues from Pemex must be gradual and matched with painful increases in tax revenues from other sources.

In any case, the Mexican impasse is primarily an internal matter and is tightly interwoven with Mexican history and national identity. Any démarche from the United States as to Mexican subsoil resources is likely to be rebuffed as "neoimperialism."[59] North America, speaking through the NAEWG, will be better served by analyzing the international implications

---

56. Ramírez would allow mature natural gas fields that were unassociated with oil fields to be exploited by the private sector, so that Pemex could focus investment elsewhere. "Pemex Chief Calls for Opening Mexico's Energy Sector," *North American Free Trade and Investment Report* 15, no. 9, May 15, 2005.

57. Jorge Castaneda and Nathan Gardels have proposed a "North American Energy Security Fund" that would issue securities to finance oil exploration backed by future oil revenues rather than the oil itself ("How to Tap Mexico's Potential," *Financial Times*, March 8, 2005, 15). We doubt, however, that the potential return to investors would be sufficient to attract much private funding.

58. See "Mexican Oil Chief Seeks Expansion," *New York Times*, March 3, 2005, 8.

59. In May 2003, the US Congress passed a nonbinding resolution suggesting that any immigration agreement with Mexico be predicated on opening Pemex to US investment. While the resolution went virtually unnoticed in the United States, it caused outrage in Mexico. President Fox quickly responded that "Pemex forms not just a part of our economy but of

of substantial reform in the Mexican energy sector, and how best to manage a future energy crisis in Mexico, rather than trying to advocate Mexican policy adjustment from the perspective of Washington or Ottawa.

This is not to say that the United States and Canada should abandon Mexico to its present rigid energy policy. Through the NAEWG and other channels, the United States and Canada should make a concerted effort to build trust with Mexico on energy issues. Mexico should reciprocate by abandoning collusive dealings with OPEC.

LNG Terminals and Natural Gas Pipelines

As discussed earlier, several companies have expressed interest in locating LNG regasification terminals in Mexico. If built, the terminals would connect to pipelines to serve northern Mexico as well as to export to southwest United States. Unlike most portions of the energy sector, private investment in natural gas transportation was legalized in Mexico in 1995.[60] Since then, the number of interconnections between Mexico and the United States has increased from 7 to 15 (NAEWG 2005a, 67). Currently, Mexico is a net importer of natural gas from the United States, but the LNG terminals are expected to reduce Mexican imports from the United States after they open. (Mexico's first LNG terminal is expected to begin operation in 2007; others are in the planning stages.) The free flow of natural gas between the United States and Mexico is in the interest of both countries and requires cooperation on continuing to build interconnections and pipeline infrastructure. Private participation in LNG imports offers US companies an opportunity to gain a foothold in Mexico in an area where the government welcomes them. To the public at large, LNG can powerfully demonstrate the benefits of private investment in Mexico.

Streamlined Cross-Border Permits

Presidential permits—actually given by the DOE after receiving approvals from the State and Defense Departments—are required before a US firm can construct, connect, or operate an electricity transmission line across an international border. The Bush administration's National Energy Policy report (NEPD 2001), as well as a United States Energy Association report (USEA 2001), recommended that the US government accelerate the approval of presidential permits. Two executive orders have already attempted to implement this policy.[61] New permits should be particularly

our history. . . . It has not been nor will be for sale" ("US Congressional Committee Sparks Controversy with Proposal that Immigration Accord with Mexico be Tied to Pemex Opening," SourceMex, May 21, 2003).

60. At present, Pemex still owns 84 percent of the natural gas transmission infrastructure (NAEWG 2005a, 17).

61. See Executive Order 13212 of May 18, 2001, *Federal Register* 66, no. 99, May 22, 2001, 28357; and Executive Order 13337 of April 20, 2004, *Federal Register* 69, no. 87, May 5, 2004, 25299.

helpful for future development along the southern border, which would enable the United States to export electricity (and natural gas) to Mexico.

Clean Energy Technology Exports to Mexico

The USEA (2001) has recommended that the United States "develop with the Mexican Government a coordinated plan of actions to foster the rapid development and introduction of clean energy systems in Mexico." The recommendation has its pros and cons. Encouraging the use of environment-friendly energy is a noble goal, but Mexico is primarily concerned with obtaining enough energy to meet its growing needs. Ensuring that the energy generation meets US environmental standards is a secondary concern. An aggressive US attempt to promote clean energy trade might be perceived by Mexican nationalists as a covert attempt to undermine Pemex and CFE, while hypocritically relying on environmentally questionable energy at home. On the other hand, "clean energy" systems can also increase production. For example, better equipment will reduce flaring in Mexican gasfields and pipelines, and antifraud mechanisms will eliminate waste.

To avoid a nationalist backlash, the United States should not deny imports of Mexican electricity that are generated in accordance with US environmental standards (even if those standards are below "best practice" methods), nor should the United States insist that Mexico meet "state of the art" environmental standards beyond those already widely applied in the United States. Meanwhile the NAEWG should undertake a project to study the ways of advancing clean energy technology trade in North America. The voice of Canada, an international leader in environment-friendly energy, should be prominent. Addressing these issues in a trilateral forum would put the focus on the shared goal of environmental protection rather than the narrower goal of US export promotion.

Energy Cooperation: Final Thoughts

To date, NAFTA has not played much more than a token role in trade and investment decisions in the energy sectors of the three countries. Trade is extensive, with Canadian and Mexican resources feeding the energy-hungry appetite of US consumers. NAFTA's modest approach to regional energy cooperation has had its downside; in particular, the trade pact has not spurred the efficiency gains that mark regional ties in other sectors. Because NAFTA sidestepped sensitive investment issues, trade in energy products has remained distorted and suboptimal.

Going forward, the short-term problems in North America are energy shortages in Mexico and to a lesser extent, localized energy shortages in the United States (e.g., California in 2001). Unless energy production in North America sharply increases, the long-term problem is that North America will continue to be at risk of supply shortages originating in the Middle East, Russia, and West Africa—the three large oil- and gas-exporting regions. So long as the North American energy market remains integrated with the world energy market, world price volatility will inevitably spill over into North American price volatility.[62] However, increased North American production can reduce the region's vulnerability to external supply shocks.

Although the United States and Canada have largely integrated their energy markets, the ultimate goal of a unified North American energy market is still a long way off. The United States and Canada should continue to deepen cooperation in the areas of infrastructure planning and regulation. They should encourage Mexico to pursue tax and energy policies that will generate domestic revenues that can fund expansion of oil and gas production and electricity generation. Such reforms are needed first and foremost to provide a strong foundation for Mexican economic growth. In so doing, Mexico would also contribute to North American energy security and thus to the long-term health of the North American economy—on which Mexico is so dependent.

Exploiting the Canadian oilsands and expanding production of US and Mexican oil and gas should be cornerstones of a new and concerted North American energy security policy. We return to this crucial issue in our concluding chapter.

References

Alberta Department of Energy. 2005. Submission to the US Senate Committee on Energy and Natural Resources. Hearing on Oil Shale and Oil Sands Resources. Edmonton, Alberta. (April 12).
Barnés de Castro, Francisco. 2002. Outlook and Opportunities in Mexico's Energy Sector. Mexico City: El Colegio de Mexico, Conference on NAFTA, February 11.
Bradley, Paul G., and G. Campbell Watkins. 2003. Canada and the U.S.: A Seamless Energy Border? C. D. Howe Institute Commentary 178. *The Border Papers*. Toronto: C.D. Howe Institute (April). www.cdhowe.org/pdf/commentary_178.pdf (accessed on November 26, 2002).
CBO (Congressional Budget Office). 2005. Cost Estimate for HR 6, Energy Policy Act of 2005, July 27. www.cbo.gov/ftpdocs/65xx/doc6581/hr6prelim.pdf (accessed on August 2, 2005).
Dobson, Wendy. 2002. Shaping the Future of the North American Economic Space: A Framework for Action. C. D. Howe Institute Commentary 162. *The Border Papers*. Toronto: C. D. Howe Institute (April).
EIA (Energy Information Administration). 2003a. *International Energy Outlook 2003*. Washington: EIA.
EIA (Energy Information Administration). 2003b. *International Energy Annual 2001*. Washington: EIA.

---

62. The final chapter of this book addresses US-Canadian cooperation in the management of strategic petroleum reserves, which may serve as a partial buffer against external supply shocks.

EIA (Energy Information Administration). 2004a. *International Energy Outlook 2004*. Washington: EIA.

EIA (Energy Information Administration). 2004b. *International Energy Annual 2002*. Washington: EIA.

EIA (Energy Information Administration). 2005a. Country Analysis Briefs: Canada. www.eia.doe.gov/emeu/cabs/canada.html (accessed on March 14, 2005).

EIA (Energy Information Administration). 2005b. Country Analysis Briefs: Mexico. www.eia.doe.gov/emeu/cabs/mexico.html (accessed on March 14, 2005).

EIA (Energy Information Administration). 2005c. Country Analysis Briefs: United States. www.eia.doe.gov/emeu/cabs/usa.html (accessed on March 14, 2005).

EIA (Energy Information Administration). 2005d. OPEC Brief. www.eia.doe.gov/emeu/cabs/opec.html (accessed May 2, 2005).

Hufbauer, Gary Clyde, and Jeffrey J. Schott. 1992. *North American Free Trade: Issues and Recommendations*. Washington: Institute for International Economics.

Joskow, Paul L. 2001. *US Energy Policy During the 1990s*. NBER Working Paper 8454. Cambridge, MA: National Bureau of Economic Research.

McKitrick, Ross, Kenneth Green, and Joel Schwartz. 2005. Pain Without Gain: Shutting Down Coal-Fired Plants Would Hurt Ontario. The Fraser Institute (January). www.fraserinstitute.ca/admin/books/files/PainWithoutGain.pdf (accessed on February 16, 2005).

NEPD (National Energy Policy Development Group). 2001. *Reliable, Affordable, and Environmentally Sound Energy for America's Future*. Report of the National Energy Policy Development Group. Washington: Department of Energy. www.energy.gov/engine/doe/files/dynamic/1952003121758_national_energy_policy.pdf (accessed on March 2, 2005).

NAEWG (North American Energy Working Group). 2002a. North America: The Energy Picture (June). www.eia.doe.gov/emeu/northamerica/engindex.htm (accessed on May 12, 2003).

NAEWG (North American Energy Working Group). 2002b. North America: Regulation of International Electricity Trade (December). www.fossil.energy.gov/coal_power/elec_reg/pdf/electricitytraderegulation.pdf (accessed on May 12, 2003).

NAEWG (North American Energy Working Group). 2002c. North American Energy Efficiency Standards and Labeling (December). www.eere.energy.gov/buildings/appliance_standards/pdfs/naewg_report.pdf (accessed on May 12, 2003).

NAEWG (North American Energy Working Group). 2005a. North American Natural Gas Vision (January). www2.nrcan.gc.ca/es/es/naewg/pdf/NAEWG%20Gas%20Vision%202005.pdf (accessed on March 1, 2005).

NAEWG (North American Energy Working Group). 2005b. Guide to Federal Regulation of Sales of Imported Electricity in Canada, Mexico, and the United States (January). www.neb-one.gc.ca/energy/EnergyReports/GuideFedRegSalesElec_CanadaMexicoUS_e.pdf (accessed on March 1, 2005).

OECD (Organization for Economic Cooperation and Development). 2000. *Energy Policy of IEA Countries: Canada 2000 Review*. Paris.

Pastor, Robert A. 2001. *Toward a North American Community: Lessons from the Old World for the New*. Washington: Institute for International Economics.

Rosellón, Juan, and Jonathon Halpern. 2001. *Regulatory Reform in Mexico's Natural Gas Industry: Liberalization in the context of a dominant upstream incumbent*. World Bank Working Paper 2537. Washington (January). http://econ.worldbank.org/files/1427_wps2537.pdf (accessed on April 20, 2005).

Rubin, Jeff, and Peter Buchanan. 2002. *Kyoto Discord: Who Bears the Cost?* CIBC World Markets, Occasional Report #36 (November 20).

SHCP (Secretaría de Hacienda y Crédito Público). 2004. Quarterly Report on Public Finances and Public Debt: Fourth Quarter of 2003 (February 4).

Shell Deer Park. 2003. Deer Park Refining L.P. www.shelldeerpark.com/refinery.htm (accessed on March 16, 2005).

US-Canada Power System Outage Task Force. 2004. *Final Report on the August 14 Blackout in the United States and Canada: Causes and Recommendations.* http://reports.energy.gov/BlackoutFinal-Web.pdf (accessed on March 16, 2005).

USEA (United States Energy Association). 2001. *Toward an International Energy Trade and Development Strategy.* www.usea.org/finaltdreport.htm (accessed on March 16, 2005).

Verleger, Philip K. 1988. Implications of the Energy Provisions. In *The Canada–United States Free Trade Agreement: The Global Impact,* ed. Jeffrey J. Schott and Murray G. Smith. Washington: Institute for International Economics.

Watkins, G.C. 1991. Deregulation and the Canadian Petroleum Industry: Adolescence or Maturity? In *Breaking the Shackles: Deregulating Canadian Industry,* eds., Walter Block and George Lermer. Vancouver: The Fraser Institute. http://collection.nlc-bnc.ca/100/200/300/fraser/deregulating/ (accessed on June 22, 2002).

Welch, David H. 2002. *Alaska Gas Pipeline Project.* www.csis.org/americas/canada/021501 welchPPT/index_files/frame.htm (accessed on March 16, 2005).

WTO (World Trade Organization). 2002. *Trade Policy Review—Mexico.* Report by the Secretariat. Geneva.

8

Mexico-US Migration

PHILIP MARTIN

Migration was a defining feature of the Mexico-US relationship for most of the 20th century, but legal immigration remained low until the 1990s. About 37 percent of all Mexican immigrants to the United States in the 20th century arrived in the United States in the 1990s (table 8.1). Over the past century, most Mexican migrants were negatively selected: They were usually from rural areas, where levels of education were lower than average; most had their first US jobs in seasonal agriculture (Martin 1993). US policy supported the recruitment of rural Mexicans under bilateral agreements in force between 1917–21 and 1942–64, but most 20th century Mexican migrants arrived and were employed outside these guestworker programs.

US government-sanctioned recruitment of Mexican workers for US jobs, followed by toleration of unauthorized migration, has a long history. The US government approved the recruitment of Mexican *bracero* workers during World Wars I and II to obtain additional farm and railroad workers by making "exceptions" to immigration rules that otherwise would have blocked their entry. The United States unilaterally ended both wartime bracero programs, in part because US labor and civil rights groups argued that the presence of Mexican migrants depressed wages and increased unemployment for similar US workers.

Both bracero programs were followed, with a lag, by rising illegal immigration from Mexico. At first it was very easy to cross the border: The

Philip Martin is a professor at the University of California, Davis, and chair of the university's Comparative Immigration and Integration Program.

Table 8.1   Mexican immigration and apprehensions, 1890–2003

Decade	Number of immigrants Annual average	Number of immigrants Decade total	Decade as percent of 1890–2000 total	Deportable aliens decade total
1890–1900	97	971	0	n.a.
1901–10	4,964	49,642	1	n.a.
1911–20	219,000	219,004	4	n.a.
1921–30	45,929	459,287	8	128,484
1931–40	2,232	22,319	0	147,457
1941–50	6,059	60,589	1	1,377,210
1951–60	22,981	229,811	4	3,598,949
1961–70	45,394	453,937	8	1,608,356
1971–80	64,029	640,294	11	8,321,498
1981–90	165,584	1,655,843	27	11,883,328
1991–2000	224,942	2,249,421	37	14,667,599
2002	219,380	n.a.	n.a.	n.a.
2003	115,864	n.a.	n.a.	n.a.
Total	n.a.	6,041,118	100	41,732,881

n.a. = not applicable

Note: Deportable aliens are measured by apprehensions, which in turn record events, so one person caught three times is three apprehensions; 95 to 98 percent of those apprehended are Mexicans.

Source: US Department of Homeland Security, *Yearbook of Immigration Statistics* (2003).

US Border Patrol was not established until 1924, so Mexican workers with US experience had little difficulty entering the United States and returning to the farms on which they had worked as braceros. By 1930, Mexicans were estimated to be 70 to 80 percent of the 72,000-strong seasonal workforce in California (Fuller 1940, 19871).[1] However, the Great Depression led to "repatriations" of Mexicans to free up jobs for Americans and practically stopped Mexican immigration, so that there were fewer Mexican-born US residents in 1940 (378,000) than there had been in 1930 (641,000), according to the US Census.

Since 1990, the share of Mexican immigrants in the civilian labor force has increased, but most Mexican-born workers in the United States are

---

1. During the 1920s, California farmers argued they needed continued access to Mexican farmworkers. The Farm Bureau asserted that "California's specialized agriculture [requires] a kind of labor able to meet the requirements of hard, stoop, hand labor, and to work under the sometimes less advantageous conditions of heat, sun, dust, winds, and isolation" (quoted in Fuller 1940, 19840). A Chamber of Commerce spokesperson testified to Congress in 1926: "We have gone east, west, north, and south and [the Mexican] is the only manpower available to us" (quoted in Fuller 1940, 19859).

now employed outside of agriculture.[2] In 2000, about 6.3 percent of male and 5 percent of female Mexican immigrants worked as farm laborers (Borjas and Katz 2005). Among the roughly 8 million Mexican-born US workers, two-thirds are unauthorized, and only an eighth are employed in US agriculture.[3] However, agriculture remains a major port of entry for the "new-new" unauthorized Mexicans from southern Mexican states such as Oaxaca and Chiapas, who often find their first US jobs in the fields, as more experienced Mexican workers move on to construction, manufacturing, and service jobs. As Mexico-US migration networks continue to mature, more Mexicans are moving directly from Mexican to US urban areas, bypassing the traditional agriculture port of entry.

While the number of legal Mexican immigrants increased from 2.2 million in the 1990s to nearly 9.2 million in 2000, fewer Mexican immigrants now work in the US agricultural sector and more work in the construction and retail sectors.[4] During 1990–2000, the shares of male and female Mexican immigrants working in the agricultural sector declined from about 21 to 16 percent and from 10 to 8 percent, respectively. The share of male Mexican immigrants employed in construction, however, increased from about 15 percent in 1990 to 26 percent in 2000. Similarly, the share of female Mexican immigrants employed in retail jumped from about 13 percent in 1990 to 20 percent in 2000.[5]

Postwar Migration Policy

John Steinbeck's 1940 novel *The Grapes of Wrath* gave an emotional impetus to the prescription for farm labor reform widely prevailing in the late 1930s—namely, to restructure southwestern agriculture in a manner that reduced its dependence on migrant and seasonal workers. Alternatively, if factories in the fields were to continue as a way of doing business,

2. In 1990, Mexican immigrants represented about 2 percent of the US labor force (2.6 million). By 2000, the share had doubled to about 4 percent (4.9 million). These data are based on US Census Bureau (2000). As another example, the share of Mexican immigrants in the Californian workforce jumped from just 2.4 percent in 1970 to 14.8 percent in 2000. See also Grieco and Ray (2004) and Borjas and Katz (2005).

3. The estimated number of unauthorized foreigners in the United States was 10.3 million as of March 2004, of which 57 percent, some 6 million, were Mexicans. See Passel (2005).

4. The share of legal Mexican immigrants in the total US immigrant population has increased since the 1950s: It rose from 12 percent in the 1950s (about 300,000 legal Mexican immigrants) to 25 percent (2.2 million) in the 1990s to about 30 percent by 2000 (9.2 million). The ratio of Mexican immigrants to the Mexican labor force has also increased: In 1970, Mexican immigrants represented about 3 percent of the Mexican labor force; by 2000, they represented about 16 percent. See Borjas and Katz (2005) and Mishra (2003).

5. See Card and Lewis (2005) and Borjas and Katz (2005). We thank Gordon Hanson and Luis Rubio for these observations and written comments to an earlier draft.

reformers wanted the workers to be treated as factory workers and covered under nonfarm labor laws.

In 1940, a congressional subcommittee chaired by Senator Robert LaFollette Jr. (Progressive-WI) recommended the second option, treating large farms as factories and covering their workers under federal labor laws, an approach that was expected to raise farm wages and encourage mechanization.[6] However, decades of low farm wages had been capitalized into higher land prices, and landowners were unwilling to see land prices fall as a consequence of higher wages. They used the outbreak of World War II to win a new bracero program (Craig 1971; Martin 1996, chapter 2). During the war, braceros, prisoners of war, interned Japanese, and state and local prisoners all supplemented the farm workforce, and their presence in the fields sent an unmistakable signal to US farmworkers that getting ahead in the US labor market meant getting out of farm work.

The bracero program expanded in the 1950s, when irrigation opened new land for farming in the southwest, the cost of shipping produce by truck from west to east fell with the interstate highway system, and the baby boom increased the demand for labor-intensive fruits and vegetables.[7] Western farmers assumed that Mexican or other foreign workers would continue to be available at US minimum wages and invested accordingly. However, the United States unilaterally ended the bracero program in 1964 amid predictions that labor-intensive agriculture would have to shrink for lack of seasonal workers and that the commodities most dependent on bracero workers would have to follow them to Mexico.[8]

The commodity in the spotlight in the early 1960s was the processing tomato used to make catsup. In 1960, about 80 percent of the 45,000 peak-harvest workers employed to pick the 2.2 million–ton processing-tomato crop in California were braceros. Growers testified that "the use of braceros is absolutely essential to the survival of the tomato industry." They were wrong. Today, 5,000 workers use machines to sort 12 million tons of tomatoes. The higher wages that followed the end of the bracero program spurred labor-saving mechanization. The state government facilitated mechanization, encouraging the University of California to develop a mechanical system for harvesting tomatoes.[9]

---

6. See "Violations of Free Speech and the Rights of Labor," hearings before a Subcommittee of the US Senate Committee on Education and Labor (The LaFollette Committee), 1940–41.

7. California has been the number one farm state since 1950 and has displaced New Jersey as the garden state, supplying fruits and vegetables to eastern US centers.

8. Based on the number of US-Mexico border patrol apprehensions, the number of illegal Mexican aliens increased after the bracero program ended. Apprehensions increased from 41,600 in 1964 to 348,200 in 1970 and about 1.7 million in 1986. See Borjas and Katz (2005).

9. California also established random sampling stations to test machine-harvested tomatoes and determine the price paid to the grower. Processing tomatoes today are worth about 2.5 cents a pound. When tomatoes were picked in 50-pound lugs by braceros, and each lug was

Figure 8.1 Ratio of US farm to manufacturing worker hourly earnings, 1965–2001

percent

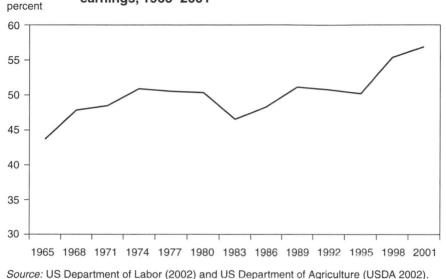

Source: US Department of Labor (2002) and US Department of Agriculture (USDA 2002).

Labor displacement and the reduction in the number and size of farms growing tomatoes led to a cutback in mechanization research. The number of workers hired for the harvest fell by 90 percent, and the number of farms growing tomatoes dropped 70 percent. Tomato-harvesting machines were costly, and only farmers with large acreages could justify purchasing them. Suits were brought against the University of California, alleging that taxpayer monies were spent on mechanization that displaced farmworkers and small farmers (Martin and Olmstead 1985). Agricultural researchers turned their attention elsewhere, and tomato mechanization proved to be the exception rather than the vanguard of a labor-saving trend, as had been expected in the 1970s.

Mexico-US migration was low during the late 1960s and early 1970s—the "golden age" for US farmworkers. Farm wages rose sharply without braceros. Cesar Chavez and the United Farm Workers (UFW) won a 40 percent wage increase for grape pickers in 1966, increasing entry-level wages from $1.25 to $1.75 an hour in the UFW's first contract (figure 8.1). However, some of the ex-braceros had become US immigrants during the 1960s, when a US employer could issue a letter asserting that a foreigner

worth $1.25, the loss was relatively minor if a lug was rejected for having too many green tomatoes or too much dirt. But with machine-picked tomatoes arriving in 25-ton truckloads, a load is worth $1,250, and random-sampling stations were crucial to overcome the perennial struggle between growers and packers over deductions for poor quality.

was "essential" to fill even a seasonal farm job, and a foreigner could use this offer of employment to become an immigrant. Ex-braceros who became immigrants in this manner received visas printed on green cards and were known as green-card commuters: Mexicans who lived in Mexico and worked seasonally in the United States.

As green-card commuters aged out of seasonal harvest work in the late 1970s, many sent their sons north, using false or altered green cards, or simply entered the United States illegally. A smuggling infrastructure soon evolved to provide information and move rural Mexicans to rural America and was strengthened in the early 1980s by events in the United States and Mexico. In the United States, the UFW sought another 40 percent wage increase in 1979, when federal wage-price guidelines called for maximum 7 percent wage increases. With no workers available from UFW hiring halls, growers turned to labor contractors, many of whom were green-card commuters, and they returned to their villages to recruit workers and bring them to the United States. The contractors stayed in business after the strikes were settled, and competition between union hiring halls and labor contractors to supply seasonal workers decidedly favored the contractors. The number of workers under UFW contracts dropped from 60,000–70,000 in the early 1970s to 6,000–7,000 a decade later (Mines and Martin 1984).

The Immigration Reform and Control Act of 1986

In Mexico, the peso devaluation in 1982–83 made work in the United States even more attractive. Apprehensions of Mexicans just inside the Mexico-US border reached their all-time peak of 1.7 million in 1986, meaning that the US Border Patrol was apprehending on average three Mexicans a minute, 24 hours a day, seven days a week.

In 1986, the United States also enacted the Immigration Reform and Control Act (IRCA, also known as the Simpson-Mazzoli Act). The purpose of IRCA was to reduce illegal immigration, both by imposing sanctions on US employers who knowingly hired unauthorized foreigners and by legalizing some unauthorized foreigners in the United States. Contrary to expectations, the IRCA actually increased Mexico-US migration.

The IRCA included two legalization or amnesty programs. One of these—a legalization program for unauthorized farmworkers called the Special Agricultural Worker (SAW) program—was rife with fraud. Over 1 million Mexican men became US immigrants under the SAW program by presenting letters from employers saying they had worked 90 days or more in 1985–86 on US farms as unauthorized workers (Martin 1994). Since about 6 million adult men lived in rural Mexico in the mid-1980s, it appears that the SAW program gave about one-sixth of them immigrant

Figure 8.2 Legalized and unauthorized US farmworkers, 1989–2000

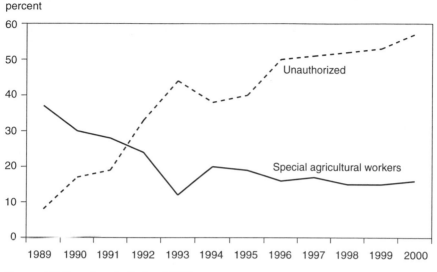

percent

Source: US Department of Labor (2002).

visas. Their families were deliberately excluded from legalization, under the theory that Mexican men wanted to commute to seasonal farm jobs and keep their families in Mexico, as earlier green-card commuters had done (Martin 1994).

The SAW participants did not behave as expected. Many switched to nonfarm US jobs and settled in US cities with their families; many others had never been farmworkers. State and local government outlays for education, health, and other public services to newly legalized immigrants and their often unauthorized families rose during the early 1990s (a period of recession). Unsuccessful suits were then brought against the federal government seeking reimbursement for the costs of providing services to these newcomers, and the perception that immigrants did not pay their way culminated in California's Proposition 187 in 1994 and later federal welfare reforms in 1996. Meanwhile, SAW participants moved on to nonfarm jobs and were replaced in the fields by newly arrived unauthorized workers (figure 8.2), so that between 1995 and 2000, almost 90 percent of the Mexicans who arrived were unauthorized (table 8.2).

Mexican Immigrants and Current Trends

In previous decades, about 80 percent of Mexicans settled in California and Texas, but beginning in the 1990s, fewer than half the Mexican immigrants

Table 8.2 Mexican-born US residents by period of entry and authorization (millions)

Period of entry	Total	Authorized	Unauthorized	Percent unauthorized
Pre-1980	2.2	2.2	n.a.	n.a.
1980–84	1.0	0.9	0.1	10
1985–89	1.7	1.0	0.7	41
1990–94	1.9	0.4	1.5	79
1995–2000	3.0	0.4	2.6	87

n.a. = not applicable

Note: There is no reliable estimate of the number of unauthorized Mexican-born US residents before 1980.

Source: Jeff Passel, Urban Institute (based on 2000 US Census).

settled there.[10] Instead, more Mexican immigrants settle in far-flung US cities, away from the Mexican border. During 1990–2000, the increase in Mexican immigration was concentrated in ten major US cities: Atlanta, Charlotte, Denver, Greensboro, New York, Portland, Raleigh-Durham, Salt Lake City, Seattle, and Washington, DC (Card and Lewis 2005).[11]

Another changing pattern is that Mexican immigrants to the United States are now more educated on average than nonmigrants remaining in Mexico (even after adjusting for illegal immigration).[12] Contrary to the "negative selection" hypothesis that less skilled workers are more likely to migrate to rich countries, recent economic studies suggest a greater proportion of Mexican immigrants are either high school graduates or have some college education. While Mexican immigrants are generally less educated than native US workers, Mexican immigrants with 12 to 15 years of schooling represent a significant share of Mexican immigrants living in the United States (Chiquiar and Hanson 2005).[13]

---

10. The share of Mexican immigrants settling in California or Texas declined from about 75 percent in 1970 to 65 percent in 1990 and less than 50 percent in 2000. For example, the share of Mexican immigrants living in Los Angeles fell from 31.7 percent in 1980 to 17.4 percent in 2000. See Card and Lewis (2005).

11. The share of Mexican immigrants in the Colorado workforce increased from 1 percent in 1980 to nearly 5 percent in 2000. See Borjas and Katz (2005).

12. We thank Gordon Hanson for this observation.

13. In 2000, Mexican immigrants with high school education represented 31 percent of the Mexican labor force in the United States, and those with some college education represented about 33 percent. However, the share of male Mexican immigrants who are college graduates increased only slightly from 1.4 percent in 1940 to just 3.4 percent in 2000. See Mishra (2003) and Borjas and Katz (2005).

Mexican immigration has a positive impact on wage levels in Mexico.[14] Economic studies suggest that during 1970–2000, Mexican immigration to the United States helped raise average Mexican wages by about 8 percent. Upward pressure on Mexican wage levels especially benefited Mexican workers with higher education levels.[15] Moreover, Mexican immigration plays a pivotal role in raising the level of remittances, which in turn help encourage Mexican capital accumulation, small business investment, and educational attainment. In 2003, Mexican immigrant remittances reached nearly $13 billion, equivalent to about 2 percent of Mexican GDP (Hanson 2005).

NAFTA and the Migration Hump

NAFTA went into effect on January 1, 1994, locking in place policies that lowered barriers to trade and investment between Canada, Mexico, and the United States. Studies on NAFTA's prospective impact agreed that the bulk of the additional jobs due to NAFTA would be created in Mexico. One hoped-for side effect of NAFTA was a reduction in unauthorized migration. This did not happen. Instead, the number of unauthorized Mexicans living in the United States rose from an estimated 2.5 million in 1995 to 4.5 million in 2000, representing an annual increase of 400,000 a year.[16] Moreover, between 1991 and 2000, some 2.2 million Mexicans were admitted as legal immigrants, over 200,000 a year. Why was NAFTA accompanied by an increase rather than a decrease in immigration?

Greater Mexican emigration was partly a consequence of the 1995 peso crisis and efforts to reform the Mexican rural *ejido* land tenure system. In particular, the peso crisis appeared to adversely affect Mexican states with a high propensity to emigrate (central and western Mexico) more than

14. According to Daniel Chiquiar and Gordon Hanson, male Mexican immigrants belong disproportionately to the middle and upper tiers of the Mexican wage distribution profile. In particular, they are concentrated in the third and fourth highest wage quintiles, while female Mexican immigrants are concentrated in the two lower-wage quintiles. See Chiquiar and Hanson (2005).

15. Mishra (2003) estimated that Mexican immigration to the United States accounted for about 37 percent of the increase in relative wages of high school graduates and about 14 percent of the increase in relative wages of college graduates in Mexico during 1990–2000. While Mexican real wages on average declined during 1970–2000, there was a big difference in the extent of decline between the upper and lower quintiles.

16. In the 1990s, some 15 million foreigners, 95 percent of them Mexicans, were apprehended just inside the US border. Individuals are often caught several times. The US Border Patrol reported 1.2 million apprehensions in fiscal 2004. Each person apprehended is fingerprinted. About 741,115 individuals were apprehended, including 36 percent who were apprehended at least twice.

states with a low propensity. Ejido reforms, by consolidating land hold-ings, tended to raise household incomes in southern Mexican states that specialize in agriculture, while prompting some rural workers to migrate north.[17] However, in addition to these events, which corresponded with NAFTA but were not caused by NAFTA, other and more fundamental forces were at work.

Pre-NAFTA Studies

Contrary to official rhetoric, some pre-NAFTA studies actually anticipated simultaneous job creation and displacement in Mexico. Scholars predicted that the displacement of workers from previously protected Mexican sectors such as agriculture might lead to additional Mexico-US migration. Hinojosa-Ojeda and Robinson (1991), for example, estimated that NAFTA would displace about 1.4 million rural Mexicans, largely because NAFTA-related changes in Mexican farm policies and freer trade in agricultural products would lead some farmers to quit farming. The authors projected that 800,000 displaced farmers would stay in Mexico, while 600,000 would migrate (illegally) to the United States over five to six years.

Hinojosa-Ojeda and McCleery (1992) developed a computable general equilibrium (CGE) model to project adjustments in the Mexican economy after NAFTA. They estimated that as of 1982, there were 2.5 million unauthorized Mexicans in the United States, that the cost of migrating illegally from Mexico to the United States was $1,200 (in the form of smuggling costs and lost earnings), and that the US earnings premium was $3,000 a year (unauthorized Mexicans then earned $4,000 a year in the United States versus $1,000 a year in Mexico). Hinojosa-Ojeda and McCleery sketched three migration scenarios—no more unauthorized Mexico-US migration, 4 million Mexican illegals, and 5 million Mexican illegals—and argued that the middle scenario could be achieved with NAFTA and a new guestworker program (what they called managed interdependence).

In an earlier report (Martin 1993), I examined NAFTA's likely impacts on Mexican and US agriculture. Most Mexican-born US residents are from rural areas in Mexico, and most find their first US jobs on farms. After examining how demand-pull factors in the United States and supply-push factors in Mexico would likely evolve after NAFTA, I concluded that the flow of Mexicans to the United States, running at 200,000 settlers and 1 million to 2 million sojourners a year in the early 1990s, would increase by 10 to 30 percent for 5 to 15 years, producing a hump when Mexico-US migration is viewed over time. The upward slope of the hump in the 1990s was due primarily to previous demographic growth in Mexico, in-

---

17. We thank Gordon Hanson and Luis Rubio for these comments. See also Hanson (2005), Schmidt and Gruben (1992), Robinson, Burfisher, and Thierfelder (1995), and World Bank (2001).

Figure 8.3 The migration hump

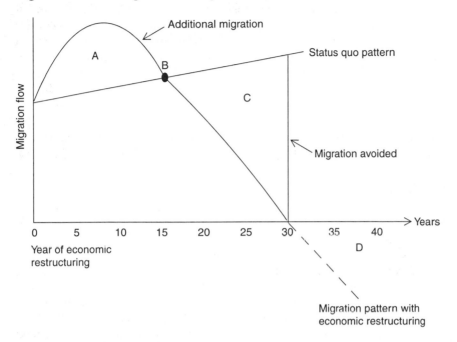

sufficient jobs in Mexico, and strong US demand for Mexican workers. The downward slope of the hump was projected to occur when the number of new entrants to the Mexican labor market fell and economic growth created more and better-paid jobs in Mexico.

Picturing the Hump

The migration hump is pictured in figure 8.3, where the volume of migration is measured on the Y-axis and time on the X-axis. The solid line through B represents the status quo migration flow (without NAFTA and other changes), and the arced line above A depicts the migration hump. Economic integration leads to an increase in migration over the status quo trajectory. Economic integration also speeds up job growth in Mexico so that migration falls and the volume of migration returns to the status quo level at B, in this case after 15 years. As growth continues, migration continues to fall, and area C represents the migration avoided by economic integration. Eventually, some migrants may return from the United States, shown by the area represented by D. This has occurred in previous emigration countries, including Ireland, Italy, Spain, and South Korea.

The critical policy parameters in a migration hump are A, B, and C: How much additional migration results from economic integration (A)? How soon does migration return to the status quo level (B)? And how much migration is avoided by economic integration and other changes (C)? Generally, a preexisting migration relationship and three additional factors must be present for economic integration to lead to a migration hump: a continued demand-pull for migrants in the destination country, an increased supply-push in the country of origin, and migration networks that can move workers across borders. Comparative static analysis—that is, comparison before and after the equilibrium points—usually ignores the adjustments that occur during economic integration, implicitly assuming that international trade will substitute for migration both in the short and the long terms. The migration hump, by contrast, illustrates the short-run dynamic relationship between economic integration and migration.

Contrast with Trade Theory

In standard Heckscher-Ohlin trade theory, capital-rich country N will import labor-intensive goods from labor-rich country S. Trade liberalization shifts additional production of labor-intensive goods to country S and capital-intensive goods to country N. These production shifts in turn put upward pressure on country S wages, discouraging emigration.

By contrast with the standard trade story, when technology differs between countries, trade and migration can be complements, not substitutes. Historically, corn in Mexico was highly protected; a guaranteed price of corn twice the world price served as the social safety net in rural areas. Mexico had about 3 million corn farmers in the mid-1990s, but the 75,000 corn farmers in Iowa produced twice as much corn as Mexico at half the price. In this example, more US exports of corn will stimulate more Mexican exports of labor.

The productivity story can be taken further. Suppose Mexican workers are more productive in the United States than they are in Mexico because of better public and private infrastructure. Migration can then complement trade. This occurred when much of the Mexican shoe industry shifted from León, Mexico, to Los Angeles, California, in the 1980s. The somewhat surprising result was that shoes produced with Mexican workers in Los Angeles were exported to Mexico in larger volumes when NAFTA lowered barriers to trade. By converting less productive Mexican workers into more productive US workers, NAFTA discouraged the production of a labor-intensive good in Mexico and encouraged migration to the United States.

Formal-Sector Jobs and Migration

Mexico needs formal-sector job creation to reduce emigration. As Mexico's population almost doubled between 1970 and 2000, from 53 million

Table 8.3   Mexico and United States: Population and labor force, 1970–2050 (millions)

	Mexico	United States
Population in 1970	53	203
Labor force in 1970	15	83
Percent of population	28	41
Population in 2000	100	281
Labor force in 2000	40	141
Percent of population	40	50
Labor force increase, 1970 to 2000 (percent)	167	70
Population in 2050	151	414
Labor force in 2050	70	207
Percent of population	46	50
Labor force increase, 2000 to 2050 (percent)	75	47
Employment in 2000		
Formal-sector jobs	15	125
Filled by Mexicans	15	6
Agriculture jobs	6	3
Filled by Mexicans	6	2

Sources: US Census Bureau (2000); Mexico's Consejo Nacional de Población (Conapo); 2050 projections from PRB (2004); IMSS (2000).

to 100 million, the number of Mexican-born US residents increased more than tenfold, from 0.8 million to about 9 million. In other words, about 9 percent of Mexicans live in the United States, and half the Mexican-born US residents are unauthorized. More important, 30 percent of Mexicans with formal-sector jobs work in the United States.[18] Thus, in 2000, about 20 million of the 40 million–strong Mexican labor force had formal-sector jobs—counting the 5.5 million Mexican-born workers in the United States (table 8.3).

Job Growth

Much of the recent formal-sector job growth in Mexico took place in *maquiladoras*, foreign-owned plants (largely in border areas) that import components duty-free, assemble them into goods, and then export the goods. Value added (mainly wages) by maquiladoras in Mexico typically

18. The usual indicator of formal-sector employment in Mexico is based on enrollment in the pension system (IMSS). About 13 million Mexican workers are forecast to be enrolled in the IMSS in 2005. Many Mexican workers are self-employed farmers, unpaid family workers, or subsist in the informal sector. If 5.5 million Mexicans are employed in the United States, and about 13 million are enrolled in the IMSS in Mexico, then 30 percent of Mexicans with formal-sector jobs are in the United States. For details, see Banamex at www.banamex.com/esp/pdf_bin/esem/pronos_130105i.pdf (accessed in April 2003).

amounts to 10 to 20 percent of the total value of the finished good.[19] The number of maquiladoras and their employment increased sharply after several peso devaluations and reached a peak of 1.3 million in 2000 before contracting sharply during the economic downturn in 2001–03 (see table 1.10 in chapter 1).

Maquiladoras never fulfilled their original goal of creating jobs for ex-braceros. The braceros were young men, while most maquiladora workers are young women (over 60 percent in 2000). Maquiladoras prefer hiring young women from the interior, many in their first jobs, believing that young women are more likely to be satisfied with assembly-line work. Nonetheless, maquiladoras have very high worker turnover. In many maquiladoras, two workers must be hired during the year to keep one job slot filled, an annual turnover rate of 100 percent.[20]

During the late 1990s, many Mexicans migrated northward with maquiladora expansion, but there is little smoking-gun evidence of "stepping-stone migration," as would occur if internal migrants to border areas became US migrants. The clearest evidence of such migration involves indigenous Mexicans, Mixtecs, and Oaxacans from southern Mexico who were recruited to work in Mexico's export-oriented vegetable industry in Sinaloa and Baja California in the 1980s and 1990s. Their seasonal jobs end in the spring, just as the demand for farmworkers in the United States rises, and some were recruited and later continued on their own to work in US agriculture. One survey of Mixtec workers in the United States in the late 1980s found that two-thirds had worked in northern Mexico's export-oriented agriculture before arriving in the United States (Zabin et al. 1993).

Demography

Mexican population growth peaked at 3.3 percent a year in 1970. In 1974, the Mexican government launched a family planning program, which greatly decreased fertility—from an average 7 children per woman in 1965 to 2.5 children in 2000. As a result, Mexico's population is now growing by less than 2 percent a year. Declining population growth reduces migration both directly and indirectly because households with fewer children tend to keep them in school longer, reducing the need for jobs.

---

19. The maquiladora or Border Industrialization Program was launched in 1965 to provide jobs to ex-braceros and their families who had moved to the border to be closer to US farm jobs. They had no source of income with the end of the bracero program. Many braceros had originally moved to the border area to increase their chances of being selected. The US employers had to pay for transportation from the workers' place of recruitment to the US job, so they preferred border-area workers.

20. Job turnover has remained high, even in the 2001–02 downturn, partly because the managers get together and pay the same wages, and workers shift jobs frequently because there is little penalty for doing so.

While past population growth presents Mexico with a major job creation challenge, the number of Mexicans turning 15 (the age of labor force entry in Mexico) should drop 50 percent between 1996 and 2010, from 1 million to 500,000 a year. Meanwhile, if Mexican economic reforms continue, sustained growth can create jobs for new labor force entrants so that fewer Mexicans will feel compelled to emigrate. Mexico averaged 2.7 percent GDP growth since 1992, but formal-sector employment averaged 3 percent, which should persuade more Mexicans (particularly young workers) to stay in Mexico (see table 8.4). The key to keeping youth home is continuous economic and job growth, which creates optimism for economic betterment without migration. If the US Border Patrol buildup is completed by 2010, just as emigration pressures fall, one must be careful to credit the real reasons for the drop in immigration: demography and jobs.

Managing Mexico-US Migration

The migration hump has both an upside and a downside. Looking at the upside of migration in the 1990s, some observers saw ever-rising levels of Mexico-US migration. But Mexico-US migration may fall for demographic and economic reasons, and the policy question is how to manage Mexico-US migration until emigration pressures subside.

President Fox's Initiative

How should Mexico-US migration be managed until the X is crossed and emigration begins to fall? (see figure 8.3) Mexican President Vicente Fox, elected in July 2000, made a migration agreement one of his government's top priorities. In February 2001, Presidents Fox and Bush established a high-level working group to create "an orderly framework for migration that ensures humane treatment [and] legal security, and dignifies labor conditions."[21] President Fox subsequently proposed a four-point migration plan, which included legalization for unauthorized Mexicans in the United States, a new guestworker program, cooperative measures to end border violence, and changes in US law that would exempt Mexicans from US immigrant visa ceilings.[22]

---

21. "Mexico: Bush, Fox Meet," *Migration News* 8, no. 3 (March 1, 2001), http://migration.ucdavis.edu/mn/more.php?id=2318_0_2_0 (accessed in July 2005).

22. In presenting Mexico's proposal, Foreign Minister Jorge Castaneda in June 2001 said, "It's the whole enchilada or nothing." While the US government seemed willing to embrace historic changes in Mexico-US migration management, it was not prepared to serve the "whole enchilada." US Secretary of State Colin L. Powell in September 2001 reported, "We've made a great deal of progress with respect to principles. We are now getting ready to move from principles into specifics and programs and how would one design such programs." See "Fox

Table 8.4 Mexican GDP and employment growth, 1992–2004

Year	GDP growth (percent)	Labor force (millions)	Labor force growth (percent)	Employment (millions)	Employment growth (percent)	Formal-sector employment (millions)
1992	3.6	31.2	3.6	30.3	3.5	11.3
1993	2.0	32.4	3.7	31.3	3.6	11.3
1994	4.4	33.2	2.7	31.8	1.6	11.4
1995	−6.2	35.0	5.2	33.0	3.5	11.0
1996	5.1	35.7	2.1	34.1	3.6	11.4
1997	6.8	37.5	5.1	36.2	6.1	12.3
1998	4.9	38.3	2.2	37.2	2.7	13.3
1999	3.7	38.4	0.2	37.6	1.1	14.2
2000	6.6	39.1	1.9	38.3	1.8	15.0
2001	−0.1	39.2	0.1	38.3	0.1	15.2
2002	0.7	40.2	2.7	39.3	2.5	15.3
2003	1.3	40.7	1.3	39.7	1.1	15.6
2004[a]	n.a.	n.a.	n.a.	n.a.	n.a.	16.1
Average	2.7	36.2	2.6	35.1	2.6	13.2

n.a. = not available

a. Data for the total population in 15–24 age group are from two sources: For 1992–2003, data are based on OECD (2005); 2004 data are based on the Mexican Ministry of Labor (Secretaría del Trabajo y Previsión Social [STPS]).

In addition to sponsoring a new public policy framework, Mexico has pioneered in recognizing the contributions that its citizens living in the United States can make to foster economic development in Mexico. President Fox has called migrants in the United States heroes for their remittances of over $1 billion a month to Mexico and has said that migrants are indispensable to creating a modern and prosperous Mexico. Backing up such claims, the Mexican government began issuing matricula consular documents to Mexicans in the United States so that they have government-issued ID cards to open bank accounts, rent apartments, and function in a security-conscious United States.[23] Mexican federal, state, and local governments have created programs to match remittance savings that are in-

Visits Bush," *Migration News* 8, no. 10 (October 1, 2001), migration.ucdavis.edu/mn/more.php?id=2463_0_2 (accessed in July 2005). By promising a far-reaching agreement on migration, the Fox administration may have made a political blunder that made more modest migration reforms nonnegotiable. We thank Luis Rubio for this observation on an earlier draft.

23. Mexico's 47 US consulates issue matricula consular cards to Mexicans in the United States for $29. Over 600,000 were issued in 2001 and 1 million in 2002. Consular officials also educate Mexicans on low-cost options for remitting funds. Cited in "Mexico: Ag, Remittances, Social Security," *Migration News* 10, no. 1 (January 2003), migration.ucdavis.edu/mn/more.php?id=23_0_2_0 (accessed in July 2005).

Formal-sector employment growth (percent)	Labor force (excluding formal sector) (millions)	Labor force growth (excluding formal sector) (percent)	Total population, 15–24 age group (millions)	Total population growth, 15–24 age group (percent)
2.5	20.0	4.2	17.8	0.9
0.2	21.1	5.7	18.0	0.9
1.1	21.8	3.5	18.2	1.3
−4.2	24.0	10.1	18.8	3.5
3.7	24.3	1.4	18.9	0.5
8.0	25.2	3.8	19.0	0.4
8.0	25.1	−0.7	19.1	1.0
6.8	24.2	−3.3	18.9	−1.7
5.8	24.1	−0.4	19.3	2.4
1.1	24.0	−0.5	19.0	−1.8
1.2	24.9	3.7	19.1	0.9
1.7	25.2	1.0	19.3	0.8
2.9	n.a.	n.a.	19.7	1.9
3.0	23.3	2.4	18.8	0.8

Sources: World Bank *World Development Indicators* 2005; OECD (2005); IMSS (2005); and STPS (2005).

vested to spur economic development. In 2004, these programs provided $60 million to match $20 million in remittances donated by Mexicans abroad to build or improve streets and water systems.[24]

However, the September 11, 2001 terrorist attacks froze Mexico-US migration discussions, as the American public refocused on border security. A new emphasis on ensuring that foreign terrorists do not arrive legally or illegally, the movement of the Immigration and Naturalization Service (INS) into the new Department of Homeland Security, and a recession in both Mexico and the United States combined to reduce the impetus for a new Mexico-US migration agreement. Nonetheless, Mexico-US migration continues at historically high levels despite stepped-up border controls.

Congressional Initiatives

Within the United States, three major US migration policy options have been debated: guestworkers, earned legalization, and legalization. In January 2004, President Bush unveiled a Fair and Secure Immigration Reform (FSIR) proposal, which would permit the 6 million to 8 million unautho-

24. Agustin Escobar, personal correspondence, January 2005. See also IMF *World Economic Outlook* (2005).

rized foreigners in the United States with jobs—perhaps two-thirds of the total of unauthorized foreigners—to become legal guestworkers if their US employers certified their employment and if the foreigner paid a registration fee of $1,000 to $2,000. As temporary workers with renewable three-year work permits, they would be free to travel in and out of the United States, get Social Security numbers and driver's licenses, and apply for immigrant visas. However, at the end of six years, these guestworkers would have to return to their countries of origin, albeit with a new incentive: credit in their home country's social security system for the legal work they did in the United States.[25] As under current law, US employers would be able to request immigrant visas for guestworkers or unauthorized workers who fill jobs for which US workers cannot be found, and President Bush promised to urge Congress to raise the total number of employment immigrant visas available (both skilled and unskilled workers), currently 140,000 a year.[26]

If the currently unauthorized workers who came forward were not sufficient to fill vacant jobs, the Bush proposal would allow US employers to recruit additional foreign workers. After advertising jobs on a new Internet labor exchange and justifying a refusal to hire any US workers who respond, the employer could go abroad and recruit guestworkers, who would receive three-year renewable visas like those issued to unauthorized workers in the United States. Guestworkers from outside the United States, however, would not have to pay the registration fee charged to unauthorized workers in the United States. After his reelection in November 2004, President Bush pledged to work for congressional approval of legislation "to make sure that where there's a willing worker and a willing employer, that job ought to be filled legally in cases where Americans will not fill that job."[27]

---

25. The Bush plan has not been transformed into legislation. It could, however, work as follows: First, an employer acknowledges in a letter or affidavit the unauthorized worker's employment history. After paying a fee and undergoing a security check, the unauthorized worker then uses the employer's letter or affidavit to become a registered guestworker for three years.

26. Bush promised to propose an increase in the number of green cards or immigrant visas available for foreigners in cases where US employers cannot find US workers. There still could be, however, long waits for employers seeking immigrant visas for needed foreign workers. The current limit is 10,000 immigrant visas a year for unskilled workers. If the number of such visas were raised to 100,000 a year, and 5 million unauthorized workers sought to become guestworkers with immigrant visas, it would take 50 years to convert all of them to immigrants. "Bush: Legalization, AgJOBS," *Migration News* 11, no. 1 (January 4, 2004), http://migration.ucdavis.edu/mn/more.php?id=2967_0_2_0 (accessed in July 2005).

27. According to Sidney Weintraub, the illegal Mexican immigration debate is essentially about wage subsidies for employers, at the expense of low-skilled US nationals, and price subsidies for the general public, in the form of cheap goods and services made by foreign workers. Weintraub offers an alternative to Bush's guestworker program: substantial US de-

The Bush plan would turn unauthorized workers into guestworkers. Conversely, many Democrats, the AFL-CIO,[28] and groups such as La Raza want legalization for unauthorized foreigners in the United States, which gives them immigrant visas—as the IRCA legalization of 1987–88 did. The most recent Democratic proposal is the Safe, Orderly, Legal Visas and Enforcement Act (SOLVE), introduced in May 2004. SOLVE would legalize unauthorized workers who have been in the United States at least five years and with at least two years' employment, if they can pass English, background, and medical exams. Those in the United States less than five years could apply for "transitional status" valid for up to five years and then apply for "earned immigrant status" after they satisfy residence, employment, and other criteria. Under SOLVE, the number of low-skilled guestworkers would be capped at 350,000 a year. Before they could be admitted, the US Department of Labor would have to check that employers paid prevailing wages and that the presence of guestworkers did not adversely affect similar US workers. Guestworkers could apply for immigrant visas after two years.

The third option is earned legalization. Senators Edward Kennedy (D-MA) and Larry Craig (R-ID) introduced the Agricultural Job Opportunity, Benefits, and Security Act (AgJOBS) in September 2003, a proposal endorsed by a majority of senators to test an earned legalization program for farmworkers. Under AgJOBS, unauthorized foreigners could become legal residents and workers if they did at least 100 days of farmwork in a 12-month period. Then, after satisfying a three-part farmwork test that includes at least 360 days of farmwork over six years (including 240 days in the first three years), AgJOBS workers and their families could become immigrants through a process that could take five years. AgJOBS would also make it easier for farm employers to recruit additional guestworkers by revising the H-2A program to eliminate the requirement that farmers provide free housing to out-of-area workers[29] and by freezing the adverse-effect wage rate that farmers must pay to avoid depressing wages for US workers.[30]

---

velopment aid on the condition that Mexico increase its own tax collections for development purposes. As Weintraub notes, Mexican federal tax revenues are less than 12 percent of GDP, one of the lowest ratios in Latin America. See Sidney Weintraub, "Development Aid Can Ease Illegal Immigration," *Financial Times*, April 18, 2005.

28. The AFL-CIO has also called for an end to enforcement of employer sanction laws and stepped up enforcement of labor laws, but no new guestworker program.

29. AgJOBS would allow employers to provide workers with "a monetary housing allowance" if the state's governor certifies that "sufficient housing" exists; the allowance would be $150 to $250 per month in California.

30. Farmers currently, and under AgJOBS, would have to pay foreign H-2A workers the higher of the federal or state minimum wage, the prevailing wage in the occupation and area of intended employment, or the adverse-effect wage rate.

Pilot Guestworker Programs

Major legislation will be controversial and take time to enact. Meanwhile, pilot guestworker programs could play an important role in managing Mexico-US migration until the downward side of the migration hump appears. They could be used to test concepts such as the inducement to return to Mexico, included in the Bush proposal, or tracking guestworkers and their employment, as the Bush plan and AgJOBS would require.[31]

The United States has about 20 nonimmigrant programs that allow the admission of foreigners to work for temporary periods, issuing visas that range from A for ambassadors to TN for NAFTA professionals with a bachelor's degree or more. Most Mexicans entering the United States legally as guestworkers arrive with H-2A and H-2B visas—farmworkers and unskilled nonfarmworkers, respectively—to work temporarily in seasonal or temporary US jobs (the "double-temporary" criteria).

The H-2A and H-2B programs are certification programs, meaning that a US employer must convince the US Department of Labor on a job-by-job basis that US workers are not available. In other words, each job vacancy to be filled by a foreign worker with an H-2A or H-2B visa needs a DOL certification that US workers are not available to fill the job, and the border gate to foreign workers stays closed until the government certifies that US workers are unavailable. The alternative process, used in the H-1B program to admit foreigners with a bachelor's degree or higher to fill US jobs (for up to six years), allows a US employer to open the border gate by attesting that foreign workers are needed to fill vacant jobs. Under the H-1B program, there is generally no enforcement of employer attestation unless DOL receives complaints.

The purpose of nonimmigrant or guestworker programs is to add workers temporarily to the labor force but not to add settled residents to the population. The "guest" adjective implies that the foreigner is expected to leave the country when his job ends. Under H-1B, H-2A, and H-2B programs, foreign workers are tied to a single US employer by contracts—the employer's job offer becomes the contract—and workers must generally leave the United States if they are discharged. In most cases, guestworkers are envisioned as a transitional presence in an industry or occupation, employed until jobs are mechanized or otherwise eliminated by trade or restructuring.

The United States and Mexico could usefully experiment with new guestworker pilot programs to determine whether alternatives to the current H-2A and H-2B programs are viable and whether Mexico-US coop-

---

31. Hufbauer and Vega-Cánovas (2003) called for a general guestworker program that would issue up to 300,000 visas a year to Mexicans after they underwent a background check, require them to have at least eight months of employment in the United States, and allow them to naturalize after five years (the normal period legal immigrants must live in the United States to naturalize).

eration can reduce unauthorized migration so that workers and employers are legal rather than illegal.

US industries that currently hire large numbers of unauthorized Mexican workers might be candidates for new-style guestworker programs that modify the H-2A and H-2B programs. One example is meatpacking. In 2002, the US meat- and poultry-processing industries employed an average 520,000 workers to "disassemble" cattle, hogs, and poultry. There is very high worker turnover, with some plants hiring two workers a year to keep one job slot filled. Most meatpacking firms are enrolled in the voluntary Basic Pilot employee verification program, under which employers submit the government-issued A-numbers of newly hired non-US citizen workers for verification of their right to work in the United States. Many meatpackers, including Tyson Foods, also employ workers supplied by temp agencies, and data for these workers are not necessarily submitted to Basic Pilot.[32]

A pilot guestworker program could relax the requirements of the H-2B program that the US job be temporary in exchange for a requirement that meatpacking firms hire all workers directly and screen them for legal status under Basic Pilot. A pilot program, labeled H-2BB, could isolate the Social Security and unemployment insurance taxes paid by US employers and guestworkers and (1) use the employer's contributions to enforce program rules, subsidize mechanization research, and train US workers; and (2) return the worker's Social Security contributions when he surrenders his work permit in Mexico. Both efforts could be supplemented with other steps to ensure compliance and achieve longer-term goals. For example, Mexico could select guestworkers from among those participating in Oportunidades, a program that gives poor Mexicans cash payments. Payments or required health checkup dates could be adjusted to ensure compliance with guestworker rules.

An L-1 Visa Option

The US L-1 visa is available to "key employees"—executives, managers, and workers with "specialized knowledge"—to allow them to move from a job in a multinational corporation abroad to a job in an affiliated US firm. On a pilot basis, multinational firms with operations in both Mexico and the United States could be permitted to use L-1X visas to bring unskilled Mexican workers to the United States for employment and training in the

---

32. In 2001, the US federal government charged Tyson Foods (with 120,000 employees, the largest US meatpacker) with conspiracy to smuggle unauthorized workers into the United States after plant managers made arrangements with INS undercover agents to pay $200 for each worker who went to work in Tyson plants as employees of temp firms. The federal government sought $100 million in fines and changes in Tyson's hiring methods. Tyson maintained that a few rogue managers were responsible for working with undercover federal agents acting as smugglers and was acquitted of the charges in March 2003.

expectation that the Mexican worker would return to Mexico and be employed in the firm's Mexican operation after one to three years. Such a program involving hotels, medical care providers, and other services would provide continuity in employee seniority within a single firm and make the multinational firm a partner in ensuring that program rules are followed. By opening legal channels for Mexican workers who have contacts with US employers in Mexico, unauthorized migration might be discouraged.

Migrant Workers in Agriculture

A third pilot guestworker program could involve agriculture. Seasonal employment on US crop farms has served as the port of entry for many Mexican-born US residents, and 85 percent of the almost 2 million hired seasonal employees on US crop farms were born in Mexico. An agricultural pilot program could test methods of using payroll taxes collected from participating guestworkers and their US employers to encourage worker returns as well as promote mechanization.

For example, 95 percent of US raisins are grown around Fresno, California, by about 3,500 farmers, many of whom have relatively small plots that average 40 acres. Workers receive about $0.01 a pound for cutting and laying 25 pounds of green grapes on paper trays to dry in the sun. There is a "labor shortage" every year because in order to raise the sugar content of their grapes, farmers wait as long as possible to begin harvesting, yet they know that the longer they wait to begin harvesting, the more likely rain will diminish the value of the drying grapes. When the sugar content is high enough, farmers want 50,000 workers during the four- to six-week harvest.

The alternative is dried-on-the-vine (DOV) systems, which allow mechanical harvesting of raisin grapes. DOV systems increase the hours of labor needed for pruning in the winter months, when unemployment is high, and reduce the need for harvest workers. However, the upfront cost of retrofitting vineyards for mechanical DOV harvesting is about $1,500 per acre, or a total of $225 million for the 150,000 acres of raisin grapes. If the DOV system were adopted, peak September employment in the raisin industry would fall from 50,000 to 10,000, and a magnet for unauthorized Mexican workers would disappear.

Social Security and UI Funds

A pilot guestworker program in which employer contributions for Social Security and unemployment insurance (UI) were set aside could generate significant funds to transform the industry, provide transitional jobs for Mexican migrants, and spur development in the migrants' areas of origin. The 20 percent of wages paid by employers and workers for Social Security (15 percent of gross wages) and UI (5 percent) could generate significant funds to achieve these goals. For example, if raisin harvesters average $5,000 each, 20 percent payroll taxes are $1,000 per worker per season. Hence the employment of 50,000 guestworkers could generate a total of $50 million to subsidize mechanization and encourage returns.

More broadly, if there are 6 million unauthorized Mexican workers and they were converted to guestworkers earning an average of $15,000 a year, the 20 percent payroll taxes accounted for by Social Security and UI would generate $3,000 a year per worker, or a total of $18 billion a year from gross earnings of $90 billion. This significant sum could be used to promote labor-saving mechanization and worker training in the United States, as well as encourage returns and foster economic development in Mexico.

Don't Forget Enforcement

None of these pilot programs can achieve their goals unless illegal migration is reduced. During the 1990s, the United States stepped up border control efforts and relaxed the enforcement of laws aimed at having US employers hire only legal workers. Since the September 11 terrorist attacks, immigration authorities have stepped up workplace enforcement in selected sectors, including airports, nuclear reactors, and other sensitive industries, but not at US workplaces. The Mexican and US governments have announced new cooperative agreements to patrol the border to prevent terrorists from slipping into the United States and prevent deaths of migrants attempting entry through the deserts.

Cooperative border control efforts and workplace enforcement that reduce illegal immigration and employment are indispensable keys to testing the effectiveness of pilot guestworker programs. As long as Mexicans can enter the United States illegally and find jobs, there will be little incentive for Mexican workers or US employers to participate in pilot guestworker programs, even if they promise return bonuses for workers and other assistance for employers. Reducing illegal migration and employment is a prerequisite for any new guestworker or migration arrangement.[33]

The pilot guestworker programs could be open to foreigners outside the United States as well as authorized foreigners already in the United States. However, they would not encompass most of the 10 million unauthorized foreigners in the United States, including 6 million to 7 million workers.

---

33. In addition, steps should be taken to expedite legitimate traffic across the border. This goal can be achieved with prescreening and trusted traveler and transporter programs that allow expedited entries. Both countries can benefit by expanding the number of people and firms in such trust-expedite programs so that limited enforcement resources can be targeted on others who may pose a danger. As Hufbauer and Vega-Cánovas (2003) suggest, inspecting trusted travelers before they arrive at the border and inspecting goods away from the border facilitate the movement of trusted travelers and goods. Hufbauer and Vega-Cánovas include in their trusted traveler proposal an immigration component, calling for the creation of a NAFTA retirement visa that would allow retirement in any of the three NAFTA countries.

Instead of starting with them, the pilot program and enforcement approach should allow tests of new concepts to keep guestworkers guests and to prevent unauthorized migration for employment. This approach could help to prevent another immigration surprise: Experience shows that for most major immigration reforms, the unanticipated consequences are more important and long lasting than the anticipated consequences.

Conclusions and Recommendations

The number of international migrants is relatively small. In a world of 6 billion, the United Nations estimated the number of international migrants—that is, persons living outside their country of birth or citizenship—at 175 million in 2000, or 3 percent of global residents. Mexico-US migration is larger, with about 9 percent of Mexican-born persons living in the United States.

The economic integration symbolized by NAFTA should eventually reduce economically motivated Mexico-US migration. NAFTA went into effect in January 1994, in part to enable Mexico to export, in the words of former President Carlos Salinas, tomatoes rather than tomato pickers. However, during the 1990s, Mexico-US trade and migration increased together, producing a migration hump, because of large numbers of new labor force entrants, very uneven economic and job growth in Mexico, and an economic boom in the United States.

High levels of Mexico-US migration over the past decade should not obscure the fact that Mexico-US migration may soon diminish for demographic and economic reasons. A combination of the sharp drop in Mexican fertility in the 1980s and 1990s, the potential for sustained economic and job growth in Mexico, and the winding down of the large-scale exodus from Mexican agriculture should reduce Mexico-US migration after 2010.

While demographic and economic forces are taking hold, policy initiatives should seek to reduce the frictions inherent in US-Mexico migration. The options most often mentioned—large-scale guestworker programs at one extreme and legalization at the other—may simply add to illegal immigration, as has occurred in the past. Instead, pilot guestworker programs that make incremental changes to existing foreign worker programs—by adding economic mechanisms to encourage employers to mechanize and guestworkers to return—would allow the United States and Mexico to test new methods of managing declining migration pressures.

References

Borjas, George J., and Lawrence F. Katz. 2005. The Evolution of the Mexico-Born Workforce in the United States. In *Mexican Immigration*, ed. George Borjas. Chicago, IL: University of Chicago Press (forthcoming).

Card, David, and Ethan G. Lewis. 2005. The Diffusion of Mexican Immigrants During the 1990s: Explanations and Impacts. In *Mexican Immigration*, ed. George Borjas. Chicago, IL: University of Chicago Press (forthcoming).

Chiquiar, Daniel, and Gordon H. Hanson. 2005. International Migration, Self-Selection, and the Distribution of Wages: Evidence from Mexico and the United States. *Journal of Political Economy* 113 (April): 239–81.

Craig, Richard B. 1971. *The Bracero Program: Interest Groups and Foreign Policy*. Austin, TX: University of Texas Press.

Fuller, Varden. 1940. The Supply of Agricultural Labor as a Factor in the Evolution of Farm Organization in California. Unpublished Ph.D. dissertation, University of California, Berkeley, 1939. Reprinted in *Violations of Free Speech and the Rights of Labor*, hearings before a Subcommittee of the US Senate Committee on Education and Labor (The LaFollette Committee). Washington: US Senate: 19778–894.

Grieco, Elizabeth, and Brian Ray. 2004. *Mexican Immigrants in the US Labor Force*. Washington: Migration Policy Institute (March).

Hanson, Gordon H. 2005. *Emigration, Labor Supply and Earnings in Mexico*. Working Paper. San Diego, CA: University of California San Diego (January).

Hinojosa-Ojeda, Raúl, and Sherman Robinson. 1991. *Alternative Scenarios of U.S.-Mexican Integration: A Computable General Equilibrium Approach*. Working Paper 609 (April). University of California, Berkeley, Department of Agricultural and Resource Economics.

Hinojosa-Ojeda, Raúl, and Robert McCleery. 1992. U.S.-Mexico Interdependence, Social Pacts and Policy Perspectives: A Computable General Equilibrium Approach. In *U.S.-Mexican Relations: Labor Market Interdependence*, eds. Jorge Bustamante, Clark Reynolds, and Raúl Hinojosa-Ojeda. Stanford, CA: Stanford University Press.

Hufbauer, Gary Clyde, and Gustavo Vega-Cánovas. 2003. Whither NAFTA: A Common Frontier? In *The Rebordering of North America*, eds. Peter Andreas and Thomas J. Biersteker. New York: Routledge Press.

IMSS (Instituto Mexicano del Seguro Social). 2000. Subdirección General de Finanzas. www.imss.gob.mx/imss (accessed May 2005).

IMSS (Instituto Mexicano del Seguro Social). 2005. Asegurados en el IMSS por Sector de Actividad Económica, Anual 1983–2004. Centro de Estudios de las Finanzas Públicas. www.cefp.org.mx/intr/e-stadisticas/copianewe_stadisticas.html (accessed in May 2005).

Martin, Philip L. 1993. *Trade and Migration: NAFTA and Agriculture*. Washington: Institute for International Economics.

Martin, Philip L. 1994. Good Intentions Gone Awry: IRCA and U.S. Agriculture. *The Annals of the Academy of Political and Social Science* 534 (July): 44–57.

Martin, Philip L. 1996. *Promises to Keep: Collective Bargaining in California Agriculture*. Ames, IA: Iowa State University Press.

Martin, Philip L., and Alan L. Olmstead. 1985. The Agricultural Mechanization Controversy. *Science* 227, no. 4687 (February): 601–6.

Mines, Richard, and Philip L. Martin. 1984. Immigrant Workers and the California Citrus Industry. *Industrial Relations* 23, no. 1 (January): 139–49.

Mishra, Prachi. 2003. Emigration and Wages in Source Countries: Evidence from Mexico. Columbia University, New York. Photocopy (August).

OECD (Organization for Economic Cooperation and Development). 2005. Labor Force Statistics Database. Paris. www.oecd.org/topicstatsportal/0,2647,en_2825_495670_1_1_1_1_1,00.html (accessed in April 2005).

Passel, Jeffrey S. 2005. *Estimates of the Size and Characteristics of the Undocumented Population*. Washington: Pew Hispanic Center. www.pewhispanic.org/reports/report.php?ReportID=44 (accessed on March 21, 2005).

PRB (Population Reference Bureau). 2004. *United Nations World Population Prospects: 1950–2050*. Washington. www.prb.org/datafind/datafinder5.htm (accessed in May 2005).

Robinson, Sherman, Mary Burfisher, and Karen Thierfelder. 1995. *The Impact of the Mexican Crisis on Trade, Agriculture, and Migration.* International Food Policy Research Institute Discussion Paper 8 (September). Washington: IFPRI.

Schmidt, Ronald H., and William C. Gruben. 1992. *Ejido Reform and the NAFTA.* Federal Reserve Bank San Francisco Weekly Letter 92-34 (October 2). San Francisco. Federal Reserve Bank of San Francisco.

STPS (Mexico Secretaría del Trabajo y Previsión Social). 2005. *Encuesta Nacional de Empleo, 1998–2004.* www.stps.gob.mx/01_oficina/05_cgpeet/302_0074.htm (accessed in May 2005).

US Census Bureau. 2000. 2000 Census. Washington. www.census.gov/main/www/cen 2000.html (accessed on April 18, 2005).

USDA (US Department of Agriculture). 2002. Farm Labor Data Sources. Washington. www. ers.usda.gov/Briefing/FarmLabor/farmlabor (accessed in November 2002).

US Department of Labor. 2002. The National Agricultural Workers Survey (NAWS). Washington. www.dol.gov/asp/programs/agworker/naws.htm (accessed in November 2002).

World Bank. 2001. *Mexico Land Policy: A Decade after the Ejido Reform.* World Bank Report No. 22187-ME (June 15). Washington.

Zabin, Carol, Michael Kearney, David Runsten, and Ana Garcia. 1993. *Mixtec Migrants in California Agriculture: A New Cycle of Rural Poverty.* Davis, CA: California Institute for Rural Studies.

9

Recommendations for North American Economic Integration

NAFTA is unique among US free trade agreements. It involves two of America's largest trading partners—countries that share long land borders with the United States. Geography gives NAFTA enormous regional coherence, while presenting the opportunity and challenge of closer ties that are advantageous to all three parties.

As this volume has documented, NAFTA has succeeded in advancing economic integration in North America. In some dimensions, it has surpassed expectations. North American trade has increased much more rapidly than forecast by most economic models. Liberalization in the auto sector has sparked a movement toward specialization, with productivity improving in all three countries. Direct investment in Mexico has been robust. Trade disputes have been well managed, albeit with a few notable exceptions.

In other areas, however, NAFTA's footprint has been small. Attempts to draft common NAFTA rules on subsidies and antidumping (AD) and countervailing duties (CVDs) were abandoned. Side agreements on labor and the environment saved NAFTA from congressional defeat but were not backed by meaningful financial resources or authoritative judicial mechanisms. Energy policy was included in the pact, but Mexico was exempted from the most important provisions regarding investment. By opting out of these energy obligations, Mexico missed an opportunity to attract much-needed investment and technology for expanding its energy production. Mexican energy policy is causing the country two self-inflicted wounds, as it deals with energy shortages at home while forgoing additional revenue from oil and gas exports to the United States and other countries.

While NAFTA encouraged structural reform of the three economies, it left the task of managing the adjustment process to each government. National adjustment programs have been generally limited and underfunded. In the United States, inadequate adjustment policies continue to feed worker discontent about globalization in general and US trade policies in particular. In Mexico, the adjustment burden was far greater and the resource constraints severe. Mexico compounded these problems by failing to use the opportunities NAFTA opened to build new infrastructure and create adequate alternative employment for the agricultural workforce. The Mexican political system has been unable to produce tax and energy reforms, which would generate new resources to fund investments in physical infrastructure and social services, especially education. As a result, Mexico continues to suffer from a high "TECC" problem: high transport, energy, and capital costs. These factors have limited Mexico's ability to take full advantage of NAFTA and have put Mexican industries at a competitive disadvantage against foreign competitors, particularly China.

For some observers, our nuanced assessment of NAFTA's benefits and shortcomings, set forth in previous chapters, will prove too complicated to digest. Many of them may continue to rely on the US media's aggressive but simplistic sound bites that denigrate NAFTA for the "broken promises" of its political creators. Others may discount the aggregate gains because of continuing concerns about high levels of illegal immigration, slow progress on environmental problems, weak enforcement of labor standards, declining real wages in Mexico, and increased transshipments of illegal drugs. Accounts of these injustices are customarily, if loosely, associated with NAFTA and globalization.

Anti-NAFTA reverberations still echo in the US political arena. The "No More NAFTAs" rallying cry has been revived most recently in the contentious congressional debate over ratification of the Central American Free Trade Agreement (CAFTA). For better or worse, part of the NAFTA legacy is more bitter and divisive trade politics in the United States (Destler 2005). However, NAFTA also has focused attention on US trade relations with Latin America and the Caribbean, engaging the interests of a growing segment of the American electorate of Hispanic heritage. Given the sharp divisions in Congress on trade, Hispanic electoral considerations now are given greater weight. Republicans and Democrats alike energetically court the Hispanic vote in presidential, congressional, and statehouse races. NAFTA politics thus remain complex and contentious.

This chapter presents our assessment of the potential for closer ties in North America, building on the strong base of North American trade and investment, which we analyzed in the previous chapters. We neither propose nor foresee the deep integration being pursued in Europe (which is driven by the ultimate goal, among European elites, of political union) as the model for North America.[1] Given sovereignty concerns and large disparities in size and wealth among the three countries, plus new security imperatives, we do not expect or seek extensive legal harmonization or anything approaching free migration. Rather, we take a more pragmatic approach and target the reduction or elimination of *specific* barriers to the movement of goods, services, capital, and people where the economic benefits to the NAFTA partners are almost certainly large.[2]

Weighing the achievements and shortcomings, we have given NAFTA a positive, but not uncritical, assessment. In economic terms, NAFTA has more than delivered what it promised, and most of our criticisms seek to strengthen and deepen the accord, not cut back on commitments. Unlike some critics who would like to reopen—and thus effectively unravel—the NAFTA compact, we look for areas where NAFTA can be expanded to address unfinished business and new challenges that arose after September 11, 2001.

Post–September 11 Challenges

Since September 11, the NAFTA partners have had to face a new and overriding challenge: addressing the added security measures to deal with potential terrorist threats. In response, the United States has erected new speed bumps on NAFTA's superhighways and around its ports. Heightened security measures impose two burdens on NAFTA trade: They make it more costly and cumbersome to move goods and people across borders and create a zone of uncertainty around investment in Canada and Mexico. Many producers, recognizing their strongest interests are in the large US market, may tilt investment away from Canada and Mexico.

Security considerations pose a particular challenge to businesses that have integrated their operations on a regional basis—one of the great virtues of the trade association. Many manufacturers, particularly in the auto industry, closely link their production facilities in the United States, Canada, and Mexico and suffer when even temporary border delays block shipments between nearby plants. Since NAFTA, much of the increase in US-Mexico trade has been spurred by US companies that established manufacturing plants in Mexico, seeking lower labor costs for slices of the value added chain. Maquiladora exports in 2003 (about $78 billion) represented about half of total Mexican exports of manufactured

---

1. The setback to European political union, delivered in May and June 2005 by "no" votes in France and the Netherlands on the constitutional treaty, hints at the much stronger opposition that even a slight move toward political union would face in North America.

2. Our recommendations in this chapter revise and extend the analysis put forward in Hufbauer and Schott (2004). See also Goldfarb (2003b), who summarizes a number of ideas other commentators propose for deeper integration.

goods ($141 billion) (Banamex 2004). Maquiladora exports, as well as enormous quantities of merchandise arriving daily from Canada, are all vulnerable to security delays.

Moreover, in the United States, the issues of closer economic relations have been subordinated, at least temporarily, to the immediate demands of national security. Four years later, the aftershocks of attacks in New York and Washington still reverberate through public discourse. Security considerations color all aspects of regional and international relations. US-Canada cooperation has deepened as the two countries implement their Smart Border initiative (with some 35 working agendas). Similar measures have been put in place on the Mexican border.

This new reality poses additional challenges and opportunities for North America. NAFTA provides a solid foundation for new North American initiatives. The political imperative to work together has never been greater. But melding the security and economic objectives of the three countries is now more complex.

To deal effectively with security issues noted above, the NAFTA countries must reassess their go-slow approach to closer economic relations. The North American agenda is rich with proposals to support and smooth the integration of the three economies. At present, some 30-odd regional committees and working groups address NAFTA initiatives in an ad hoc manner. The new "Security and Prosperity Partnership of North America," announced by Presidents George W. Bush and Vicente Fox and Prime Minister Paul Martin at the Crawford Summit on March 23, 2005, reorganizes these specific efforts under several broad themes but treads lightly on more comprehensive and longer-run initiatives to deepen economic integration.[3]

What forces will catalyze political leaders to move the North American project forward? In the early 1960s, the political impetus for governmental action came from US and Canadian automakers. In the 1980s, Canadian business leaders promoted the Canada-US Free Trade Agreement (CUSFTA). In 1990, Mexican President Carlos Salinas dared the United States to accept Mexico as an FTA partner and convinced Canada to join the ensuing trade negotiations. The impetus in 2005 comes from the push for border security.[4] The NAFTA partners must work more closely together now for two reasons: first, to prevent terror attacks, and second, in case of additional terrorist attacks down the road, to be less disposed to

---

3. Documents pertaining to the Security and Prosperity Partnership are available on its Web site, www.spp.gov (accessed on June 30, 2005).

4. Despite high oil prices, concerns about energy security have not yet prompted new collaborative energy projects. However, all three countries pledged at the Crawford Summit to pursue national initiatives "to increase reliable energy supplies for the region's needs and development." See Prosperity Agenda, White House Press Office, March 23, 2005, www.spp. gov/spp/prosperity_agenda/index.asp?dName=prosperity_agenda (accessed on June 30, 2005).

respond with knee-jerk actions that disrupt goods and people moving across borders and thereby spawn enduring political acrimony. But preemptive preparations need economic fuel as well. The key is to find the right combination of economic and security initiatives that will spur political leaders of all three countries into action.

Hufbauer and Vega-Cánovas (2003) argue that we need a common vision on NAFTA—one that builds on past successes and that posits a new agenda for a Common Frontier (also labeled a Security Perimeter) involving policy convergence in areas such as customs and energy regulation, migration, and even monetary cooperation. These issues have long percolated in the substratum of trilateral relations but have been deferred due to heavy resistance by powerful political constituencies in each country.

Wendy Dobson (2002) puts forward similar themes from a Canadian perspective. She argues that Canada and the United States should pursue a "strategic bargain" that would involve deepening the existing NAFTA relationship, "without full-scale harmonization" of policies of the kind that emerge from traditional customs union and common-market negotiations, which dilute the political independence of member countries.

According to Dobson (2002, 30), "only a Big Idea is likely to attract US attention." In the context of trade politics, Dobson's view draws from the experience of past GATT rounds (progressively bigger events), as well as the history of the CUSFTA and NAFTA. Where small proposals foundered, large bargains eventually succeeded—not because they were easy to negotiate but because they enlisted the attention of US presidents and enabled cross-sector agreements that balanced competing political interests and mobilized enough US business interest to spur congressional support. While small bargains in the form of bilateral FTAs have flourished in recent years, in most cases these accords are seen as way-stations to bigger deals like the Free Trade Area of the Americas (FTAA) or the long-run pursuit of a Middle East FTA. The balance of postwar trade history still leans heavily toward Dobson's thesis of a Big Idea as the way to get noticed and supported in Washington.

Fitting the bill, border security has certainly attracted the attention of official Washington. However, border security alone does not give Canada or Mexico added leverage to negotiate reforms in US policies long resistant to change. Cooperation on security benefits all three countries, and the costly alternative to cooperating with the United States on security matters—for both Canada and Mexico—is less efficient and more intrusive border restrictions by the United States.

Still, the border security issue establishes a higher priority for new negotiations on an agenda of complementary economic and security concerns. In this regard, Dobson's idea of a "strategic bargain" makes sense, especially since the two countries already have extensive economic integration in autos, steel, and energy infrastructure. To date, however, the Bush administration has given scant attention to proposals to deepen economic integration in North America—with the notable exception of border security pacts. Big ideas have simply not resonated among Washington officials riveted on Afghanistan, Iraq, the broader Middle East, and the war on terror.

Upgrading NAFTA

After a decade of progress, the three NAFTA partners still have important unfinished business. Economic growth in Mexico has lagged well behind its potential even while the United States enjoys a cyclical recovery; the region remains vulnerable to volatile energy prices and supply shortfalls; illegal immigration still confronts political leaders on both sides of the Rio Grande; and civil society continues to demand that governments redress labor and environmental abuses, particularly along the US-Mexico border.

For better or worse, many of these issues are linked politically. For the United States, faster economic growth in Mexico is critical to strengthening security on its southern border, while deeper cooperation with Canada on border security initiatives is essential to ensure the efficient flow of goods and people across the long northern border. Mexico's economic prospects depend on reforms of Mexican tax and energy policies and extensive new investment in a sector that has been closed to foreign participation for seven decades.

Energy should be a standalone priority for Mexico, though political realities may require attention to the plight of Mexican migrants to the United States—both those settled for a long time and the annual flow of new immigrants—as an unstated quid pro quo. Moreover, plans for needed energy infrastructure investments will have to balance economic payoffs, sovereignty concerns, and environmental impacts.

Indeed, if Mexico is to take full advantage of NAFTA's opportunities, it will need to invest heavily in several key areas to not only redress energy shortfalls but also upgrade transport and telecommunications networks and public services like water and sewage treatment. Doing so would create better opportunities for economic development in the poorer regions of southern Mexico and would reduce the "Mexico cost" that weighs heavily on the international competitiveness of Mexican industry.

To generate the significant sums required for such investments, Mexico will need to attract both domestic and foreign funds. First, however, the Mexican government must pursue domestic economic reforms that generate substantial new revenues for the Mexican Treasury and create a more conducive policy environment for new investment. Only then should consideration be given to regional initiatives that pool contributions from the United States and Canada for Mexican infrastructure projects. Without prior domestic reforms, proposals to leverage foreign assistance to Mexico—including a North American Investment Fund—would likely be rejected out of hand.[5] Indeed, it would be counterproductive to ask Washington and Ottawa to subsidize Mexican infrastructure investment unless the Mexican government is first willing to tap its own resources.

New initiatives in the areas of trade, energy, migration, and finance could help deal with pressing problems in each country, while promoting closer security ties to better handle the aftershocks of future terrorist attacks. At the same time, more could be done to strengthen NAFTA's environmental and labor provisions, and its institutional foundations, building on the experience of recent trade pacts. We examine in brief what might be achieved on each topic.

Deepening the Trade Bargain

We have devoted an entire chapter to each of the three largest markets for North American trade: agriculture (chapter 5), autos (chapter 6), and energy (chapter 7). These chapters provide a detailed picture of the past, present, and future of the industry in North America with our sector-specific recommendations. In this concluding chapter, we go further and suggest several broad initiatives that would deepen trade in all economic areas by progressing toward a common external tariff (CET) and streamlining NAFTA rules of origin.

The CUSFTA, followed by NAFTA, went a long way toward removing border barriers to merchandise trade between the three countries. However, key problems have proven immune to negotiated fixes, most notably issues surrounding softwood lumber, wheat, and sugar, as well as the broader questions raised by agricultural subsidies and contingent protection. Negotiators may want to tilt against these windmills again,[6] but we believe a more fruitful strategy would address a less contentious source of distortion in North American trade and investment—differences in the most-favored nation (MFN) tariffs applied against imports from third countries. Indeed, it is plausible to foresee acceptance of a CET in the NAFTA region for a wide range of merchandise by the end of this decade.[7]

---

5. We strongly doubt members of the US Congress would agree to finance Mexican projects, particularly given the constraints that the large US budget deficit imposes on projects in their own districts. Instead, we favor a large increase and restructuring of the North American Development Bank (NADBank) project finance, which supports new investment in both countries (see chapter 3 and below).

6. In our view, the disputes just mentioned, together with trucking, fisheries, avocadoes, and several others, are best addressed through mid-level dispute resolution procedures, with only occasional intervention from top political leaders.

7. For a discussion of a CET between Canada and the United States, see Goldfarb (2003a). She believes the CET would work to the economic advantage of both countries, though it faces a number of obstacles.

As a technical matter, the NAFTA partners could move toward a CET if the two members with higher MFN tariffs would lower their rates toward the level of the member with the lowest MFN rate, thereby gradually harmonizing their MFN tariffs on industrial goods. This approach has two advantages: It promotes new trade liberalization and provides the most direct way to reduce trade distortions generated by NAFTA rules of origin.

Trade Liberalization. There is already a high degree of convergence between US and Canadian MFN tariffs. Mexican levies are generally much higher, though they are applied to only a small share of Mexican imports due to Mexico's extensive network of FTAs. The notable exceptions from Mexico's FTA network are countries in East Asia, although Mexico and Japan recently concluded an FTA, which entered into force in April 2005. Mexican officials have been reluctant to discuss harmonization of MFN tariffs in the NAFTA region because of their higher-bound rates; they would therefore have to change tariff schedules more than the United States and Canada to implement a CET. In addition, Mexicans fear increased competition from China if they lower their MFN tariff shield.

Neither concern should deflect progress toward a NAFTA CET, for two reasons. First, a CET probably would be implemented incrementally over a fixed period. Initial steps could comprise World Trade Organization (WTO) commitments undertaken in the context of the current Doha Round negotiations in the WTO, which may include tariff elimination for specific sectors under "zero-for-zero" pacts. Second, Mexico has and already uses other trade policy tools besides MFN tariffs to protect domestic firms against aggressive Chinese competition. Safeguard measures and AD actions already are an integral part of Mexico's policy toolkit; in addition, like the United States, Mexico could invoke—at least through 2013—special safeguard provisions, accepted by China in its protocol of accession to the WTO, to limit import surges.[8]

We do not envisage that a CET would limit any NAFTA member from concluding additional bilateral or regional FTAs with other countries, nor would it alter the terms of existing FTAs. Thus, for example, the United States would be free to negotiate an FTA with Switzerland, Korea, or the entire Middle Eastern region. However, an FTA between one NAFTA member and a third country could raise legitimate "rule of origin" issues—namely a concern that the third country could transship goods to the other two NAFTA members by taking advantage of its FTA privileges. We address this concern in the next section.

Rules of Origin. The record-keeping and transactions costs of meeting rules-of-origin requirements are substantial. Rules of origin are included

---

8. The special safeguards applicable to imports from China are described in Hufbauer and Wong (2004). Paragraphs 238 and 241 of China's Protocol of Accession to the WTO authorizes these safeguards.

in trade pacts for two basic reasons. The more principled argument is that rules of origin are necessary to prevent the low-tariff NAFTA member from importing goods from third countries and then reexporting them—as is or as components of larger assemblies—to the high-tariff members (trade deflection). The political, and protectionist, rationale for rules of origin is far more crass: to throw up a nontariff barrier against imports from countries outside the trade arrangement.

A common MFN tariff at least does away with the principled trade deflection rationale, giving liberal-minded trade ministers a better chance of overriding the protectionist support for rules of origin. Technically this could be done by a NAFTA provision that says that rules of origin no longer apply after all three NAFTA members get to a stage where 90 percent of their MFN eight-digit Harmonized Tariff System (HTS) rates in any two-digit HTS group fall within plus or minus one percentage point of the average for the three countries.[9]

Moreover, to deal with the possibility of trade deflection by way of shipments from an FTA partner to a NAFTA member, we suggest the following rule. If any NAFTA member suspects that trade deflection is occurring on a substantial scale in a two-digit product group, it could invoke the old rules of origin (a "snap-back" provision). However, the snap-back would be subject to review under the provisions of Chapter 20.

Even with the FTA snap-back, to be saleable in the United States, the CET would need to exclude key agricultural imports, and it might require long phase-in periods for highly sensitive industrial products.[10] Otherwise, the protected farmers and companies would overwhelm the tax-cut argument with cries of "giveaways to Brazil and the European Union" (agriculture) and "giveaways to China" (textiles and clothing). However desirable, we don't see talks dealing with all agricultural tariffs—much less farm quotas and subsidies—even though the three countries will need to accept some liberalization of farm trade barriers in the context of WTO and FTAA negotiations. The political problems that kept these barriers intact in the CUSFTA and NAFTA are still alive. A CET may be possible for

---

9. Within the two-digit HTS group 87, labeled "Vehicles, other than railway or tramway rolling stock, and parts and accessories thereof," there are 68 HTS tariff lines with eight-digit identities—such items as 8701.10.00, "Pedestrian controlled tractors," and 8708.94.50, "Steering wheels for other vehicles." Under our proposal, if 90 percent of these eight-digit lines (namely 61 lines) have MFN tariff rates by the three NAFTA countries that are within one percentage point of the average for the line, then there would be no rule of origin on any item within the two-digit HTS group. Shipments of any included item from one NAFTA member to another would clear customs with no inquiry as to where the item was originally made.

10. In chapter 5 on agriculture, we lay out a path that would lead to the eventual adoption of an agricultural CET. NAFTA should be able to achieve a CET in other products (primarily manufactures) well before the ground is suitably prepared for common tariffs on agricultural products.

selected farm products like Brussels sprouts, apples, and flaxseed. But to list the eligible products is to reveal the limitations. The dairy complex, field crops, cattle, and pork are all beyond the scope of a CET in this decade.

Similarly, it will be difficult to extend a CET to highly protected industrial sectors like textiles and clothing. It is a hard political fact that the US textile and clothing industries are gearing up for the fight of their lives with the removal of Multi-Fiber Arrangement (MFA) quotas. The industries are mounting at least two counterattacks. They are already confronting China with multiple safeguard suits. India and other big suppliers may soon be targets as well, not only for safeguard suits but also for AD actions. Meanwhile, the industries will insist that any reduction or elimination of tariff barriers be concentrated in FTAs and unilateral measures like the Caribbean Basin Initiative (CBI) and the African Growth and Opportunity Act (AGOA)[11]—not the WTO—and that tariff reductions be accompanied by tight rules of origin. The two industries will do their best to ensure that only fiber, yarn, and cloth made within the preference zone (which excludes China, India, and other major suppliers) is eligible for reduced or zero tariffs. In light of these strategies, the US textile and clothing industries will resist any reduction of US MFN tariffs in a CET framework, and they will adamantly oppose the elimination of rules of origin. Similarly, Mexico is applying its own draconian safeguards against Chinese apparel imports. Mexico, like the United States, will be loath to reduce its high MFN rate structure, since it serves as the first line of defense against Asian clothing exporters. Because of the political muscle at work, a CET proposal would likely have to defer downward harmonization of textile and clothing tariffs for a long transition period.

Trade Remedies. In any event, movement toward a CET would not address Canadian and Mexican concerns about AD and CVD actions. In light of statements by members of Congress regarding the sanctity of existing US unfair trade laws, we would bluntly say that one can almost forget about AD/CVD reform in new NAFTA talks.[12] In our view, the best course is to pursue integration policies that reduce demand for AD/CVD actions rather than attempt to constrain the supply head-on.

Still, apart from the softwood lumber case—which involves a substantial amount of trade and eventually will be negotiated as a standalone set-

---

11. The CBI is a one-way preference arrangement for the Caribbean islands and Central America. AGOA provides similar one-way trade preferences. Tight rules of origin on textiles and clothing are integral to both agreements.

12. Recall that in May 2001, almost two-thirds of the Senate urged President Bush not to put US AD laws on the table in new WTO talks. Nonetheless, US officials agreed to include AD on the negotiating agenda to promote "greater transparency, certainty, and predictability in the ways in which the rules are administered." See Deputy USTR Peter F. Allgeier's testimony before the Subcommittee on Trade of the House Committee on Ways and Means, May 17, 2005.

tlement—how important is the contingent protection to NAFTA countries? As of October 1, 2004, the United States had 351 AD and CVD orders in place. Of these, only 15 are against Canada and 11 against Mexico. AD/CVD orders against NAFTA countries make up only 7 percent of all orders, despite the fact that these countries account for roughly one-third of all US trade.[13]

Granted, the potential use of AD/CVD actions may deter Canadian or Mexican firms from competing aggressively in the US market. Moreover, any firm considering a major new investment may be influenced, at the margin, to locate in the United States. Nevertheless, we are not convinced that doing something to limit the continuing troublesome impact of the AD and CVD regimes is worth the negotiating cost and effort to Canada and Mexico.[14] Instead, a better strategy would rely on the calibrated use of WTO and NAFTA dispute settlement provisions to keep US AD/CVD measures in line with WTO and NAFTA obligations. In recent years, WTO panels have ruled against the United States in a number of cases (involving steel, lumber, and other products) where the US Commerce Department or US International Trade Commission contravened WTO rules by using inappropriate methodologies to determine dumping or injury. Negotiations under way in the Doha Round of WTO talks could further clarify the procedures for conducting investigations. Meanwhile, in appropriate cases, Canada and Mexico can continue to call on NAFTA Chapter 19 procedures to review final AD/CVD determinations.

If Canada and Mexico were determined to face down the United States over AD/CVDs, a plausible approach would be to negotiate time-limited (say renewable every five years) sector holidays from AD duties. The holidays would be negotiated in consultation with affected industries and would probably cover only areas that had not recently experienced a flurry of AD cases. In a sense, this proposal would codify the market demand for AD actions. However, sector holidays would provide a modest degree of assurance for new investment and plant expansion aimed at the regional market within NAFTA.

A task force report issued by the Council on Foreign Relations (2005) recommends that the NAFTA partners ensure future free trade in natural resource products (such as lumber) by concluding a new agreement.[15] The new agreement would ensure security of market access and security of supply, and include rules on resource pricing that address, for example, longstanding US concerns about Canada's timber management practices.

---

13. By contrast, Chinese exporters were subject to 57 AD/CVD orders, accounting for 16 percent of the US total, compared with China's 9 percent share of total US merchandise trade.

14. For further analysis of AD/CVD disputes, see Macrory (2002) and chapter 4 on dispute settlement.

15. Michael Hart, a member of the task force, principally inspired this recommendation.

Since very little progress has been made on US-Canada lumber disputes, despite a quarter century of litigation, a new approach seems well worth trying.

Looking a decade ahead, it seems likely that tariff and trade remedy issues will occupy less space on the North American trade agenda, while domestic regulatory measures—with intended or unintended trade consequences—will become more important. Pharmaceutical trade between the United States and Canada is already an explosive issue in the US Congress and state legislatures; food safety and environmental standards are a perennial question; geographic indications and other labeling issues are on the horizon.

As a modest step toward mutual recognition and convergence, we suggest that leading regulatory agencies in the member countries invite senior representatives from their NAFTA counterparts to participate when they deliberate on new regulations that could affect NAFTA commerce. The farm sector is an ideal candidate for increased regulatory cooperation (Josling, Roberts, and Orden 2004). Cooperation on common standards of food health and safety (sanitary and phytosanitary measures) would spread best practices across North America, as well as reduce unnecessary barriers to trade. Joint inspection regimes would further boost confidence in the regional food supply. As a start, the three countries could establish a "crisis center" for immediate consultation on BSE ("mad cow") and other high-profile food safety concerns.

Going with the Energy Flow

Since September 11, and especially since the Iraq war began and crude oil prices soared, US policymakers have rediscovered their latent concerns over the adequacy of regional energy supplies. Development of oil and gas fields, as well as construction of new energy distribution channels, is a high priority—though for somewhat different reasons—in both Canada and Mexico as well. Yet energy security initiatives, including expansion of North American production of oil and gas, have failed in Congress due to parochial demands of politicians. As a result, three important problems continue to fester.

First, the region is not producing enough oil and gas given its vast reserves. Coupled with a sharp decline in spare production capacity worldwide, North America is now more vulnerable to volatile energy price swings. New production in North America could help reduce the high security premium now embedded in crude oil contracts.

Second, differing product standards and inadequate investment in new refineries have led to supply bottlenecks for petroleum products, most notably gasoline. Here again, new NAFTA projects could boost local supplies and help protect against supply disruptions elsewhere.

Third, the blackout that deprived 50 million Americans and Canadians of electricity in August 2003 underscored the problems of aging electrical transmission systems. The regulatory reforms needed to spur new infrastructure investment have long been debated, but efforts to implement reforms usually run afoul of some federal or state/provincial rules. Hopefully, the electric shock of the northeast blackout in August 2003 will energize the reform process. The US-Canada Power System Outage Task Force, created after the August 2003 blackout, reported that system failure was preventable and would have been prevented if grid operators had followed voluntary reliability standards. Noting that many of the causes of the 2003 blackout had been exposed through investigations of prior blackouts but remained unaddressed, the task force laid out 46 specific recommendations for the United States and Canada.[16] First among these was to make reliability standards mandatory with penalties for noncompliance.

What more could be done? Dobson (2002) proposes a constructive starting point: use the existing bilateral and trilateral mechanisms to coordinate efforts at regulatory reforms that would encourage production and distribution of natural gas.[17] Working together in this area seems like a no-brainer. However, the proposed projects are big and expensive, and politicians invariably compete for the spoils. Witness the wrangling over recent energy bills in the US Congress and the US subsidies enacted to influence the route of a natural gas pipeline from Alaska's North Slope to Chicago so as to maximize US jobs (at the expense of Canadian jobs).[18] Canadians initially worried that the legislated route, which bypasses the Mackenzie Delta gas reserves, would leave Canadian reserves untapped. These concerns have abated since a privately funded consortium proposed a second pipeline to connect the Mackenzie Delta reserves to the existing Alberta pipeline infrastructure.[19] In contrast to US willingness to intervene and support infrastructure projects, Canadian officials argue that the market should guide planning of pipeline routes and other infrastructure "megaprojects." However, pure market forces, without the breath of government intervention, are seldom allowed unfettered play when it comes to major energy projects—in the United States, Canada, or else-

---

16. The full report is available at https://reports.energy.gov/BlackoutFinal-Web.pdf (accessed on November 1, 2004).

17. This recommendation was put forward by President Bush's task force on energy policy and got renewed attention after the Enron crisis broke. See the comprehensive analysis by Bradley and Watkins (2003). For the purpose of advancing natural gas production and distribution, the groups created in the wake of the power outage could be consolidated into the North American Energy Group, established by the NAFTA members in 2001.

18. Members of Congress also argued that their preferred route would minimize environmental damage since the pipeline would not go underwater, and large portions would parallel the Alaskan Oil Pipeline and the Trans-Alaska Highway.

19. See box 7.3 in chapter 7 for a discussion of the pipeline controversy.

where. Environmental, employment, indigenous population, and security concerns are all given voice through public officials.

The pipeline saga illustrates the current limits of US-Canada cooperation on infrastructure. While the US-Canada energy infrastructure is already fairly well integrated, distribution of energy faces numerous obstacles both within and between countries, and new interconnections are frequently contentious. Better cooperation will require more formal contacts at the regulatory level, with the clear support of both governments.

The United States will not achieve energy independence (given existing sources and reserves of energy), but it can strengthen energy security by working cooperatively with its immediate neighbors. For example, it should be possible for the United States to include Canada in its future storage plans for strategic reserves of oil and gas. Abandoned potash mines located in Saskatchewan, and similar sites, could be used for northern reserves. When public attitudes become more receptive to nuclear power (largely as a consequence of global warming), Canada and the United States might well find common interests in locating new generation facilities and disposing of spent radioactive fuel.

Progress with Mexico on the energy front will be more difficult. Fundamentally, there are two obstacles. The first of these is popular Mexican resistance to amend the constitutional prohibition against foreign participation. Unfortunately, the Mexican Congress seems reluctant to proceed on even modest reforms, even though they could boost investment in electricity-generating plants. It is even less willing to welcome foreign energy companies in developing deep Mexican oil reserves (in the Gulf of Mexico) or gas reserves (in the northern states). The second is the political clout of Petróleos Mexicanos (Pemex) and the Comisión Federal de Electricidad (CFE) workers worried about losing their jobs. Even if the petroleum sector booms, it won't relieve the featherbedding that accounts for huge excess employment and drives up costs. We think that Mexico could design transitional arrangements to guarantee the job security of many current energy-sector workers, either in their present place of employment or in new foreign ventures, then buy out others through wage insurance programs (funded by oil industry contributions), similar to those recently incorporated in the US Trade Act of 2002.

Even accompanied by labor provisions, it will be a huge political hurdle to amend the Mexican Constitution to enable limited foreign participation. Indeed, we don't believe that incremental energy reforms are saleable unless linked to other important political issues, such as migration. Despite the multiple political roadblocks, we believe that Mexico will soon have little choice but to reform its archaic energy laws, if its development strategies are to succeed and Mexican growth is to reach a consistent annual rate of 5 percent or higher. Necessity may prove to be the mother of reform.

In sum, North America has a large and growing demand for energy as it simultaneously faces stagnant or decreasing production in most of the continent. While energy imports are destined to rise, increased investment in oil and gas field development—combined with enhanced cooperation between the NAFTA countries on energy distribution and regulation—could alleviate potential shortages and help dampen oil price pressures. The creation of a high-profile energy panel to discuss regulation, trade, and infrastructure projects would be a welcome start. Where possible, Canada and the United States should go forward in harmonizing regulatory standards and streamlining permit processes for cross-border infrastructure projects. In addition, Mexico should act in its own best interest and adjust its policies to promote greater development of its energy resources and increased investment in pipelines and power plants. Toward that end, Canada and the United States should be ready to help Mexico increase its energy production through technical assistance and the provision of advanced oilfield technologies for developing deepwater reserves.

Controls on Coming and Going

Mexico is keenly interested in the treatment accorded to migrant workers, both those already resident in the United States and those who seek entry, legally or otherwise. According to Philip Martin, in chapter 8 of this volume, the number of Mexican workers employed in the United States is about 5.5 million. Annually in the late 1990s, approximately 150,000 Mexicans entered the United States legally, mainly under family reunification visas, and 400,000 entered illegally, most in search of work.

As a cooperative prologue to the thorny problem of migrant workers, we believe that Ottawa, Washington, and Mexico City can forge common visa standards for most non-NAFTA visitors and immigrants. This goal is highly significant from a security standpoint. For people arriving from outside the NAFTA region, the North American countries need a shared system for excluding non-NAFTA nationals who pose a security threat.[20] Legal immigrants are already thoroughly scrutinized before they enter; the real problem is visitors. Annually, Canada admits about 4.4 million non-US visitors, Mexico admits about 3.3 million, and the United States admits about 29 million non-NAFTA visitors (Rekai 2002). These numbers are up to 30 times larger than the annual intake of legal immigrants.

---

20. As Rekai (2002) points out, Canada and the United States have very different systems for admitting immigrants as permanent residents. About two-thirds of Canadian immigrants are admitted on employment criteria and one-third on family reunification grounds. The proportions for the United States are reversed. In addition, Canada has a more lenient attitude toward refugees than the United States. Canada does not keep good track of refugees after they are granted asylum, prompting US concerns that some may be involved in terrorist sleeper cells.

Non-NAFTA visitors who threaten security can be better excluded if a few core measures are adopted. The NAFTA partners should agree on documentation requirements, length-of-stay requirements, visa waiver country lists, and watch lists for potentially troublesome visitors.[21] Officials in each country should have electronic access to the immigration records of its partners. These suggestions seem obvious. However, US security agencies, such as the FBI, CIA, ATF, and Customs, have yet to agree on a common watch list for potentially troublesome visitors to the United States, so it will take political energy to forge a common North American approach.

As well, NAFTA partners should create a special force to handle all third-country immigration controls at the individual's first port of entry into NAFTA space. Common document and biometric identification standards should be applied.

Likewise, the partners should create a more efficient system for handling legitimate travelers among the three NAFTA countries. The Smart Border accord negotiated between Canada and the United States contains useful elements: high-tech identity cards for permanent residents, using biometric identifiers, and preclearance programs for frequent travelers, known as INSPASS at airports and CANPASS at land borders and bridges (dedicated commuter lanes). The same system should be extended to cover visitors arriving from Mexico.

The most difficult problem between Mexico and the United States—but one with the highest political, security, and economic payoff if satisfactorily resolved—is the issue of unauthorized Mexican workers. Within this category are two groups: those who already reside in the United States, numbering as many as 4.5 million in 2000,[22] and those who will come to the United States to work. What kind of assurances could an immigration agreement provide? The place to start is with the sustained flow of migrant workers arriving in the United States. The United States should take up President Vicente Fox's challenge to substantially enlarge the annual quota of Mexicans legally authorized to enter the United States on temporary, renewable work permits. In recent years, legal immigration from Mexico to the United States has numbered about 130,000 to 170,000 people annually (US Department of Justice 2002). Illegal immigration figures are speculative, but in chapter 8 of this volume, Philip Martin places the annual number at around 400,000 in the late 1990s.

One way to tackle the flow problem is to start with an expanded number of legal visas. Martin recommends a guest worker visa that could be initiated by a US employer. Mexicans admitted under these visas would be

---

21. As part of the Smart Border accord, Canada and the United States have already agreed to harmonize their visa waiver lists.

22. See Pastor (2001) and chapter 8 on migration by Philip Martin. We cite Martin's figures, which are somewhat higher than Pastor's.

refunded part of their Social Security and unemployment insurance payments when they returned to Mexico and surrendered the visa. Perhaps 150,000 people, including unskilled workers, could be admitted from Mexico annually on a work-skill basis. These workers could be issued a high-tech identity card, including biometric data. However—and this is where security gets underlined—to obtain a guest worker visa, the Mexican applicant would have to undergo a background check. The overall guest worker program should be renewable, say every two years, based on progress in reducing illegal crossings, drawing on an approach sketched in the next paragraph.

Coupled with the substantial, but closely regulated, increase in temporary work permits, the United States and Mexico should embark on a joint border patrol program to reduce the flow of illegal crossings. Of great concern to the United States is not only the migration of Mexican workers illegally but also the lack of security on Mexico's southern border with Guatemala and Belize, a passage for illegal workers traversing from Central America. No border patrol program will eliminate illegal crossings, but a joint program could reduce the flow. Biennial renewal of the guest worker visa program should be conditioned, in our view, on progress in reducing the illegal flow.[23]

Meanwhile, employer sanctions should extend beyond a meaningless paper chase. Inspection by the employer of a high-tech identity card would suffice to meet the firm's obligations. However, if an employer hires a worker (after a defined cutoff date) on the basis of other documentation, the firm would be at risk for substantial penalties if it were found to have accepted counterfeits that a reasonable employer would suspect to be fraudulent.

That raises the situation of perhaps 4.5 million unauthorized Mexicans who live and work in the United States. We do not have a magic solution. The foundation for our tentative suggestions is the proposition that these people have made permanent homes in the United States and are not going to pack up their lives and return to Mexico. Under a set of appropriate circumstances, therefore, they should be granted residence permits with eligibility for citizenship. The appropriate circumstances we envisage have two components—a threshold relating to the total number of illegal crossings and standards for individual applicants.

First, the resident permit program would be launched when the presidents of the United States and Mexico jointly certify every two years that the annual rate of illegal crossings—measured by border apprehensions—had not exceeded, say, 50,000 persons. In recent years, the number of

---

23. As part of a detailed plan for dealing with immigration to the United States from Latin America, Hanson (2005) also suggests temporary worker permits. However, he would offer permanent residence, and eventual citizenship, to all workers who enter under the plan and comply with the terms of their visas (primarily by staying employed).

apprehensions has exceeded 100,000 annually, so this would entail a dramatic reduction in illegal crossings. The resident permit program would be suspended for new applicants in years when the presidents could not make this certification. The same trigger should, in our view, apply to continuation of the guest worker visa program.

Individual eligibility for the residence permit would require evidence that the person resided in the United States before the *announcement* of the program. Applicants for a residence permit who could provide satisfactory evidence of residence in the United States before the announcement of the program would not be subject to deportation, whether or not they met other eligibility requirements, so long as they periodically reported a place of residence to the Department of Homeland Security and committed no felony after the issuance of the residence permit. These persons would be issued high-tech residence permits meeting the documentation requirements for employment. Holders of residence permits would also be immediately eligible for public Social Security and Medicare benefits, as well as private health and pension benefits, based on their contributions. They could apply for citizenship after five years.

To be sure, these proposals leave many questions unanswered.[24] Issuing residence permits to Mexicans covertly living and working in the United States can be said to reward illegal behavior. Not issuing residence permits to Central Americans and others living and working illegally can be said to discriminate. A guest worker program that does not offer US citizenship can be criticized for dangling forbidden fruit. A call for Mexican cooperation on border control raises Mexican constitutional issues.[25] After listing these and other difficulties, it is tempting to abandon proposals for migration reform and claim, with Dr. Pangloss, that we already live in the best of all possible worlds. "Don't ask, don't tell," it might be said, is the only answer to the conundrum of illegal immigration. But we hold the view that piecemeal and imperfect reforms are better than letting the US-Mexico migration issues fester.

Where the Buck Stops

There is scope for deeper financial cooperation within NAFTA, but little prospect for a common currency. This conclusion stems from the predominance of the US economy in the region—accounting for almost 90 percent of North American GDP—and the reluctance of US policymakers to share control over monetary policy with their North American neigh-

---

24. We are grateful to Sidney Weintraub for raising these points in comments on an earlier draft of this chapter.

25. In the past, Mexico's constitutional freedom of movement within the country has been interpreted to prohibit Mexican authorities from interfering with illegal border crossings.

bors. Simply put, the United States would insist on calling the shots on monetary policy if the three countries got together on a common North American currency.

Owing to the relative size of the three economies, currency integration would have little economic effect on the United States (Truman 2003). While the favorable effects are far larger for Canada and Mexico, they would have to cede significant monetary control to the United States in any formal monetary union. If Canada or Mexico wants to have a common currency, nothing stands in either country's way of unilaterally adopting the US dollar. But doing so would not give Canada and Mexico a say in US monetary policy. As a result, dollarization—or a new North American currency—is far from imminent.[26]

Nonetheless, closer cooperation on monetary policy among the three NAFTA countries would be desirable. To that end, we recommend that the Federal Reserve Board of Governors invite representatives of the Banco de Mexico and the Bank of Canada to participate in its key meetings—those where interest rate decisions are made—on a nonvoting basis. Reciprocal invitations should be forthcoming from the Banco de Mexico and the Bank of Canada.

At the same time, the NAFTA partners could usefully coordinate their approaches to the regulation of financial services. Mexico has experienced a series of bank failures, while the collapse of Enron, Arthur Andersen, Global Crossing, and WorldCom, followed by a string of Wall Street and CEO scandals, starkly revealed the seamy underside of US finance. Canada has a cumbersome capital-market regulatory regime, which is run by the provinces.[27] Mexico and the United States are both well along on their own cleanup acts, but more could be done in a North American context. In Canada, the trend toward harmonized securities regulation among the provinces is long overdue. A single national system would help even more.[28]

North American regulatory task forces should exchange views on the reform of accounting standards and corporate governance. They could provide a voice for convergent regulation of banks, insurance companies, securities firms, pension funds, mutual funds, and other asset management

---

26. For an extensive analysis of these issues, see Robson and Laidler (2002) and Truman (2003).

27. In the United States, the states have a regulatory role as well, but for securities, the Securities and Exchange Commission (SEC) is clearly the dominant voice (as the confrontation between the SEC and New York Attorney General Eliot Spitzer showed). The state regulatory voice is strongest for insurance, an anachronism that dates to the 1930s.

28. Canada's 13 provincial securities regulators have created uniform legislation and a mutual recognition ("passport") system so that securities registered in one province can be issued and traded in the other provinces. A joint body of Canadian securities administrators provides oversight. The federal finance minister has established a Wise Persons' Committee to study whether a single regulator or a perfected passport system should be the next step.

companies throughout North America. Mutual recognition of standards for issuing securities should command greater support, particularly in the Securities and Exchange Commission.[29] If the NAFTA members agreed in principle to mutual recognition of *federal* standards, but not state or provincial standards, it would give a useful push to rationalization of the Canadian system.[30]

Updating Environment and Labor Provisions

The NAFTA labor and environmental side agreements were never designed to make substantial progress in addressing labor and environmental problems.[31] Negotiated primarily to provide political cover for Democratic members of the US Congress to support NAFTA, the side agreements were far from ambitious and were never funded at the level necessary to effectively deal with labor and environmental problems. The labor side agreement is largely hortatory. The environmental side agreement is somewhat stronger, but no NAFTA country, least of all the United States, wants intrusive surveillance of its domestic environmental policies. Instead, the side agreements have managed to spotlight selective labor and environmental abuses. Labor unions and some nongovernmental organizations have seized on these shortcomings as a broad rallying cry against "NAFTA failures."

Against this background it will be difficult to assemble a political consensus within the United States for deeper integration within NAFTA unless new measures are taken to address labor and environmental issues. We think constructive steps are possible as part of a larger bargain.

First, US and Mexican environmental groups are rightly distressed that so little has been achieved in improving the day-to-day environment in the border zone and many cities in the interior of Mexico. Fears expressed by NAFTA critics in 1993 that the pact would spur the downward harmonization of environmental and health standards, and create pollution havens in Mexico, were imaginary bogeymen. But environmental problems have been decades in the making. The missing ingredient is money: The North American Development Bank (NADBank) is woefully under-

---

29. Since 1991, the Canadian provinces and the SEC have had a system for mutual recognition of prospectuses and other disclosure materials, known as the Multi-Jurisdictional Disclosure System (MJDS). In the wake of the Enron debacle and other Wall Street scandals, however, the SEC has not devoted bureaucratic resources to updating the MJDS and coordinating the evolution of financial standards.

30. If NAFTA talks got under way on these matters, it would make great sense for the United States to engage the European Union on the same issues. Conceivably a transatlantic accord could result, to the benefit of North America as well as Europe.

31. For a more comprehensive treatment of the two side agreements, see chapters 2 and 3.

funded, and Mexican municipalities are starved of revenues. We think a revamped matching program is the answer. The NADBank's capital base should be increased incrementally from $4.5 billion to $10 billion. Instead of a 50-50 split between the United States and Mexico, the funding should be 75-25. For its part, the Mexican federal government should assist municipalities to levy and collect property taxes and dedicate the revenues to environmentally sound infrastructure improvement—basic needs like water, sanitation, and paved roads.[32] NADBank loans for municipal environmental projects should be conditioned on meaningful local tax efforts. As US contributions to NADBank would increase by more than $5 billion under our proposal, with substantial new placements directed to Mexican communities, Mexico could reciprocate by adopting tax reforms and infrastructure investments that improve regional transport networks and enhance border security.

Second, it galls Mexico that trade sanctions are held out as a remedy for persistent Mexican violations of NAFTA environmental or labor obligations. To be sure, NAFTA panels have never gotten close to recommending trade sanctions, but the theoretical remedy is written in the side agreements. This amounts to discriminatory deterrence. The United States agreed on monetary fines as the remedy for Canadian violations, and it also agreed on monetary fines as the remedy of first recourse in the US-Chile and US-Singapore FTAs.[33] As part of the new package, the United States should align NAFTA procedures with those in its new FTAs and agree to monetary fines as either the ultimate or penultimate remedy for Mexican violations.[34]

Third, US labor advocates object that Mexico does not effectively enforce core labor standards. The US definition of core standards differs somewhat from the International Labor Organization (ILO) definition, though they have elements in common: prohibitions on discrimination based on gender, ethnicity, race, or religion; freedom from coerced labor; and prohibitions against the worst forms of child labor.[35] We think Mexico, as well as Canada and the United States, could agree to establish NAFTA oversight of core labor standards (appropriately defined) by an independent, trilateral monitoring board that regularly reported to the

---

32. In 2000, Mexican property taxes were just 0.3 percent of GDP, compared with 3 percent in the United States and 3.5 percent in Canada (OECD 2002, table 22).

33. Trade sanctions are an ultimate, and highly theoretic, backup remedy in the US-Chile and US-Singapore FTAs.

34. See Elliott (2001) for a complete discussion on using fines rather than trade sanctions in the context of labor standards disputes.

35. Some labor leaders would argue that US "right-to-work" laws do not conform to the ILO's interpretation of freedom of association. In our opinion, robust NAFTA enforcement of labor standards would need to be accompanied by explicit recognition that right-to-work laws do not contravene freedom of association.

Commission for Labor Cooperation (CLC) on an expeditious and nonpolitical basis. From the standpoint of trade politics, this reform should be highly valued by US labor unions and should more than compensate for the loss of trade sanctions.

Finally, the three countries should renegotiate the language of NAFTA Chapter 11. As we have explained in chapter 4 on dispute settlement, NAFTA Chapter 11 arbitrations in investor-state disputes have not resulted in the rollback of state and provincial environmental standards. However, sentiment is widespread in the environmental community that past and future arbitration awards will have just this result. The remedy, we think, is to update the NAFTA text to reflect the interpretive notes issued by the NAFTA Free Trade Commission as well as definitional changes developed in recent FTA negotiations (see chapter 4).[36]

Strengthening NAFTA's Institutions

By design, most of NAFTA's institutions were constructed in a way that guarantees the primacy of national sovereignty. There is still no appetite for supranationalism in North America. We do not recommend new North American institutions to administer and implement the regional compact. However, we do counsel specific reforms of existing NAFTA institutional arrangements.[37] The benefit of 10 years' experience leads us to believe that bolstering NAFTA's institutions will make them more effective and pose no threat to national sovereignty. In addition, we believe revisions to dispute settlement procedures and to the labor and environment side accords merit priority attention.

First, we would consolidate the three national NAFTA sections into a single staff, which should be jointly funded. The current system of national staffs has resulted in funding disparity, with the US section chronically underfunded. The joint funding model should also be used to pay for panelists and other expenses relating to the operation of dispute settlement mechanisms. To raise the profile of NAFTA institutions, the unified staff should be housed in a single NAFTA headquarters building, where NAFTA disputes could be heard. Second, in chapter 4, we recommend that the dispute settlement provisions of NAFTA be both strengthened and simplified. Currently, NAFTA disputes are addressed in a de-

---

36. For example, in the CAFTA, the "measures tantamount to expropriation" test is revised, the arbitration procedures are more transparent, and a new appellate mechanism is adopted.

37. By contrast, Pastor (2001) argues for more comprehensive institutional reforms including integration of the North American transportation infrastructure, creating a development fund to address regional income disparities, a permanent North American court on trade and investment, a North American passport with a larger temporary worker program, and the eventual adoption of a common currency.

centralized system governed by four chapters (in addition to the two side agreements on labor and environment). Decentralization has caused some controversy over which chapter should be applied to a given dispute. To avoid this, we suggest consolidation of the processes. Rather than four separate methods for selecting panelists, a single roster should be selected for six-year terms. Panelists should have a broad background in international economic law and be capable of hearing cases under any chapter. In addition to panel consolidation, the hearing processes and evidentiary standards should be fine-tuned.

Second, the NAFTA partners need to reexamine both the dispute settlement provisions and how they are used. Chapter 11—on investor-state disputes—has attracted the most criticism. We note above how it should be clarified and updated. Chapters 19 and 20 also merit attention.

Chapter 19—on AD and CVD—was established before the WTO Dispute Settlement Understanding of the Uruguay Round. We believe the WTO process has helped dissuade AD/CVD initiations. In any event, Chapter 19 is handicapped by lengthy panel proceedings (often a result of deliberate inaction on the part of national governments) and the absence of a common NAFTA standard on AD/CVD reviews. Rather than addressing these concerns within NAFTA, we encourage countries to turn to the WTO dispute settlement process, which has been operating reasonably well for the past decade. While not without its own difficulties, including extensive delays in some high-profile cases, the WTO process is a better mechanism for addressing AD and CVD disputes, since it operates against a common standard that applies to all three countries (and all other WTO members as well). The most serious problem with the WTO system for reviewing AD and CVD disputes is that, unlike NAFTA, it does not lead to the refund of duties that were wrongfully assessed. However, this defect could be corrected by a NAFTA agreement that stipulates refunds in appropriate WTO cases between the NAFTA parties.

Chapter 20 is the broadest of the dispute settlement provisions; it governs the implementation of NAFTA. The focus of Chapter 20 has been on consultation rather than arbitration. While in theory a Chapter 20 award can result in withdrawal of equivalent NAFTA benefits, this has never occurred, and there is no mechanism to determine "equivalent benefits." We suggest raising the profile of Chapter 20 "reports" to "decisions" and inserting language to indicate that Chapter 20 decisions "shall be binding." Rather than determining "equivalent benefits," we ask arbitration panels to impose monetary fines—which are less destructive than trade sanctions—as the preferred penalty to ensure compliance.

Finally, with regard to the side agreements on labor and the environment, we also see an opportunity for improving the institutions that make the agreement work. The side agreements were an afterthought to the NAFTA negotiations, and, as noted above, the institutions created by these agreements suffer from funding shortfalls. Many of these institutions have been charged with being all things to all people. We prefer that they concentrate on doing a few things well:

- As noted above, NADBank and the Border Environment Cooperation Commission (BECC) simply do not have the funding required to do the job of environmental cleanup and sustainable development in the border region. This funding must be increased, and the United States will have to shoulder more of the burden. NADBank and the BECC should target upgrading border infrastructure to the standards of non-border communities in the United States and Mexico and streamline project finance procedures so that local communities can utilize NAD-Bank funds more effectively.

- The CLC also requires more funding. Again, we suggest scaling funding commitments so that the United States increases its contribution. We recommend that the labor review process be revamped into a monitoring system based on agreed labor standards in four areas: discrimination, child labor, coerced labor, and workplace health and safety. The monitoring should be carried out by an independent board that both reports to the CLC and publishes its findings. Published reports will put a useful spotlight on glaring deficiencies. Moreover, by focusing on the foremost tier of North American Agreement on Labor Cooperation (NAALC) standards, the CLC will have a better chance of being heard.

- The Commission for Environmental Cooperation (CEC) should concentrate on becoming a resource for North American environmental statistics, which can be used to assess environmental trends in Canada, Mexico, and the United States. In addition, concise reports and an annual "environmental report card" should replace the current longer reports, which the broader NAFTA community rarely reads. Those reports should concentrate on "naming and shaming" the worst environmental problems. The CEC should continue to run the citizen submission process under Article 14. However, the process should be streamlined and strengthened so that the "factual records" identify noncompliance and provide corrective recommendations within a reasonable period.

Conclusion

What does this all add up to? Over the near term, the agenda for North American integration is likely to be more limited than the ambitious vision of Dobson's "strategic bargain." In terms of trade initiatives, through 2007, the three countries probably will pay more attention to the broad-based initiatives in the WTO Doha Development Agenda and the FTAA.

After 2007, if the WTO and the FTAA achieve only modest reforms, the United States might well expand its already extensive network of bilateral FTAs. Mexico and Canada could do the same. Nevertheless, because of critical border and energy security imperatives, all three countries will need to encourage engagement on the broad North American trade and economic agenda.

As was the case with the CUSFTA and NAFTA, Canada and Mexico will need to supply the initiative. While Canadians might argue that many economic issues warrant a bilateral approach limited to Canada and the United States, domestic US politics make Mexican participation imperative. It makes sense, therefore, for the prime minister of Canada and the president of Mexico to try to reach agreement on their own major agenda items and then make a joint démarche to Washington. It is entirely possible that President Bush would welcome a friendly North American initiative, especially if the WTO and the FTAA are bogged down and a Middle East FTA looks like a long and difficult slog.

In large measure, our North American agenda is about enlightened self-interest. An international agreement can provide the political impetus to craft successful policies. When the United States moves to rationalize its own immigration law, it will be the primary beneficiary of a more secure border and a more accountable workforce. In Canada, improved border security measures will protect against disruptions in US-Canada trade— a matter of growing concern for firms already producing in Canada, as well as those considering additional investments. Mexican energy reforms will boost industrial production by stimulating new investment in oil and gas field development, power generation, and transmission, which in turn will provide Mexican homes and industries with more reliable sources of energy. Allaying energy shortages will spur investment in the manufacturing and technology sectors, which are critical to Mexico's development strategy. In other words, it would make economic sense for many of our proposals to be implemented on a unilateral basis. But in the real world of give-and-take politics, these reforms may be possible only in the context of a fresh round of NAFTA negotiations.

References

Banamex. 2004. Productive Sector Finances. www.banamex.com/eng/finanzas/sec_prod/sector_productivo.html (accessed on November 18, 2004).

Bradley, Paul G., and G. Campbell Watkins. 2003. Canada and the US: A Seamless Energy Border? Commentary 178. *The Border Papers*. Toronto: C. D. Howe Institute (April).

Council on Foreign Relations. 2005. *Building a North American Community: Report of the Independent Task Force on the Future of North America*. New York: Council on Foreign Relations.

Destler, I. M. 2005. *American Trade Politics*, 4th ed. Washington: Institute for International Economics.

Dobson, Wendy. 2002. Shaping the Future of the North American Economic Space: A Framework for Action. Commentary 162. *The Border Papers*. Toronto: C. D. Howe Institute (April).

Elliott, Kimberly Ann. 2001. *Fin(d)ing Our Way on Trade and Labor Standards?* International Economics Policy Brief PB 01-5. Washington: Institute for International Economics.

Goldfarb, Danielle. 2003a. The Road to a Canada-US Customs Union: Step-by-Step or in a Single Bound? Commentary 184. *The Border Papers*. Toronto: C. D. Howe Institute (June).

Goldfarb, Danielle. 2003b. Beyond Labels: Comparing Proposals for Closer Canada-US Economic Relations. Backgrounder 76. *The Border Papers*. Toronto: C. D. Howe Institute. (October).

Hanson, Gordon H. 2005. Challenges for US Immigration Policy. In *The United States and the World Economy*, ed. C. Fred Bergsten. Washington: Institute for International Economics.

Hufbauer, Gary Clyde, and Gustavo Vega-Cánovas. 2003. Whither NAFTA: A Common Frontier? In *The Rebordering of North America: Integration and Exclusion in a New Security Context*, eds. Peter Andreas and Thomas J. Biersteker. New York and London: Routledge.

Hufbauer, Gary Clyde, and Jeffrey J. Schott. 2004. The Prospects for Deeper North American Integration: The US Perspective. Commentary 195. *The Border Papers*. Toronto: C. D. Howe Institute (January).

Hufbauer, Gary Clyde, and Yee Wong. 2004. *China Bashing 2004*. International Economics Policy Brief PB04-5 (September). Washington: Institute for International Economics.

Josling, Tim, Donna Roberts, and David Orden. 2004. *Food Regulation and Trade: Toward a Safe and Open Global System*. Washington: Institute for International Economics.

Macrory, Patrick. 2002. NAFTA Chapter 19: A Successful Experiment in International Dispute Resolution. Commentary 168. *The Border Papers*. Toronto: C. D. Howe Institute (September).

OECD (Organization for Economic Cooperation and Development). 2002. *Revenue Statistics 1965–2001*. Paris.

Pastor, Robert. 2001. *Toward a North American Community*. Washington: Institute for International Economics.

Rekai, Peter. 2002. US and Canadian Immigration Policies: Marching Together to Different Tunes. Commentary 171. *The Border Papers*. Toronto: C. D. Howe Institute (November).

Robson, William B. P., and David Laidler. 2002. No Small Change: The Awkward Economics and Politics of North American Monetary Integration. Commentary 167. *The Border Papers*. Toronto: C. D. Howe Institute (July).

Truman, Edward M. 2003. North American Monetary and Financial Integration: Notes on the US Perspective. *International Management* 8, no. 1 (Fall): 75–79.

US Department of Justice, Statistics Division. 2002. *Legal Immigration, Fiscal Year 2000*. Annual Report 6. Washington: Office of Policy and Planning (January).

Acronyms

AD	antidumping
AFL-CIO	American Federation of Labor and Congress of Industrial Organizations
AgJOBS	Agricultural Job Opportunity, Benefits, and Security Act
AGOA	African Growth and Opportunity Act
Alianza	Alianza para el Campo
AMS	aggregate measurement of support
ASERCA	Apoyos y Servicios a la Comercialización Agropecuaria
ASF	Auditoría Superior de la Federacíon
Banamex	Banco Nacional de Mexico
bcf	billion cubic feet
BECA	Border Environmental Cooperation Agreement
BECC	Border Environment Cooperation Commission
BEIF	Border Environment Infrastructure Fund
BIE	Banco de Información Económica database (INEGI)
BLS	Bureau of Labor Statistics
BRRA	Bus Regulatory Reform Act
BTU	British thermal unit
CAFE	corporate average fuel economy
CAFTA	Central American Free Trade Agreement
CAW	Canadian Auto Workers
CBI	Caribbean Basin Initiative
CBM	coalbed methane
CDC	US Centers for Disease Control
CEC	North American Commission for Environmental Cooperation

CET	common external tariff
CFE	Comisión Federal de Electricidad
CIC	Citizenship and Immigration Canada
CIMARIs	Integrated Centers for Handling, Recycling, and Disposal of Hazardous Waste
CITT	Canadian International Trade Tribunal
CLC	Commission on Labor Cooperation
CNOOC	China National Offshore Oil Company
COFIDAN	Corporación Financiera de América del Norte
Conasupo	La Compañía Nacional de Subsistencias Populares
CPS	Current Population Survey
CRE	Comisión Reguladora de Energia
CT	Congreso del Trabajo
CTM	Confederación de Trabajadores Mexicanos
CUSFTA	Canada-US Free Trade Agreement
CWB	Canadian Wheat Board
CVD	countervailing duty
DOC	US Department of Commerce
DOE	US Department of Energy
DOL	US Department of Labor
DOT	US Department of Transportation
DOV	dried on vine
DSB	WTO Dispute Settlement Body
DSU	WTO Dispute Settlement Understanding
ECC	Extraordinary Challenge Committee
ECE	Evaluation Committee of Experts
ECM	Energy Consultative Mechanism
EEP	Export Enhancement Program
EIA	Encuesta Industrial Anual
EIM	Encuesta Industrial Mensual
EIS	environmental impact statement
EKS	environmental Kuznets curve
EPA	US Environmental Protection Agency
ERO	electricity reliability organization
ESI	Environmental Sustainability Index
FAO	Food and Agriculture Organization
FDI	foreign direct investment
FERC	Federal Energy Regulatory Commission
FINASA	Financiera Nacional Azucarera SA
FSIR	Fair and Secure Immigration Reform
FSLMRA	Federal Service Labor-Management Relations Act
FTA	free trade agreement
FTAA	Free Trade Area of the Americas
FTC	Free Trade Commission (NAFTA)
GATT	General Agreement on Tariffs and Trade

HFCS	high-fructose corn syrup
HS	Harmonized System
HTS	Harmonized Tariff System
ICSID	International Center for Settlement of Investment Disputes
IDP	NADBank Institutional Development Cooperation Program
ILO	International Labor Organization
IMSS	Instituto Mexicano del Seguro Social
INE	Instituto Nacional de Ecologia
INEGI	Instituto Nacional de Estadistica, Geografia, e Informatica
INET	Indigenous Network of Economies and Trade
INS	Immigration and Naturalization Service
IRCA	Immigration Reform and Control Act
IT	information technology
ITA	US International Trade Administration
ITI	intraindustry trade index
JPAC	Joint Public Advisory Committee
LCE	Ley de Comercio Exterior
LGEEPA	Ley General del Equilibrium Ecológico y la Protección al Ambiente
LIRLF	Low Interest Rate Lending Facility
LNG	liquefied natural gas
MAI	Multilateral Agreement on Investment
MEA	Multilateral Environmental Agreement
Mercosur	Mercado Común del Sur
MFA	Multi-Fiber Arrangement
MFN	most-favored nation
MJDS	Multi-Jurisdictional Disclosure System
MOU	memorandum of understanding
mtrv	metric tons raw value
NAAEC	North American Agreement on Environmental Cooperation
NAALC	North American Agreement on Labor Cooperation
NADBank	North American Development Bank
NAEWG	North American Energy Working Group
NAFTA	North American Free Trade Agreement
NAFTA-TAA	NAFTA Transitional Adjustment Assistance
NAICS	North American Industry Classification System
NAO	national administrative offices
NEP	National Energy Program
NERC	North American Electric Reliability Council
NGO	nongovernmental organization
NLRA	National Labor Relations Act

NLRB	National Labor Relations Board
OECD	Organization for Economic Cooperation and Development
OPEC	Organization of Petroleum Exporting Countries
OSHA	Occupational Safety and Health Administration
PAFN	Programa Ambiental de la Frontera Norte de Mexico
PAN	Partido Acción Nacional
PCB	polychlorinated biphenyls
Pemex	Petróleos Mexicanos
PITEX	Programa de Importación Temporal para Producir Artículos de Exportación
PRB	Population Reference Bureau
PRD	Partido de la Revolución Democrática
PRI	Partido Revolucionario Institucional
Procampo	Programa de Apoyos Directos para el Campo
Profepa	Procuraduría Federal de Protección al Ambiente
RPS	renewable portfolio standard
RTO	regional transmission organization
SAW	special agricultural worker
SCM	WTO Agreement on Subsidies and Countervailing Measures
SEC	Securities and Exchange Commission
Secofi	Secretaria de Comercio y Fomento Industrial
Sedesol	Direcion de Residuos Solidos Municipales
Semarnat	Secretaría de Medio Ambiente y Recursos Naturales
SIC	Standard Industrial Classification
SIMBAD	Sistema Municipal de Bases de Datos database (INEGI)
SITC	Standard International Trade Classification
SLA	US-Canada Agreement on Trade in Softwood Lumber
SMD	standard market design
SOLVE	Safe, Orderly, Legal Visas and Enforcement Act
SPS	sanitary and phytosanitary
STPS	Secretaria del Trabajo y Prevision Social
SUV	sport utility vehicle
SWEP	Solid Waste Environmental Program
SWL	softwood lumber
TAA	Trade Adjustment Assistance
tcf	trillion cubic feet
Telmex	Telefonos de Mexico
TFP	total factor productivity
TN	temporary visa (NAFTA)
TRIMs	WTO Agreement on Trade-Related Investment Measures
TRQs	tariff rate quotas
UAW	United Auto Workers
UFW	United Farm Workers

UI	unemployment insurance
UNCITRAL	United Nations Commission on International Trade Law
UNICEF	United Nations Children's Fund
UNT	Unión Nacional Trabajadores
USCIS	US Citizenship and Immigration Services
USITC	US International Trade Commission
USTR	United States Trade Representative
WAFP	Wheat Access Facilitation Program
WHO	World Health Organization
WTO	World Trade Organization

Additional Readings

Labor

Bergsten, C. Fred. 2002. Renaissance for United States Trade Policy? *Foreign Affairs* (November).

Globerman, Steven. 2000. Trade Liberalization and the Migration of Skilled Professionals and Managers: The North American Experience. *World Economy* 23, no 7 (July).

Hanson, Gordon H. 2005. *Globalization, Labor Income, and Poverty in Mexico.* NBER Working Paper 11027 (January). Cambridge, MA: National Bureau of Economic Research.

Martin, Gary. 2000. Employment and Unemployment in Mexico in the 1990s. *Monthly Labor Review.* November. www.bls.gov/opub/mlr/2000/11/art1full.pdf (accessed on September 3, 2002).

Nissen, Bruce. 2002. Alliances Across the Border: The US Labor Movement in the Era of Globalization. www.labournet.org/discuss/global/nissen.html (accessed on June 24, 2002).

Statistics Canada. 2000a. Brain Drain and Brain Gain: The Migration of Knowledge Workers Into and Out of Canada (May 24). www.statcan.ca/Daily/English/000524/d000524a.htm (accessed on June 24, 2002).

Environment

Charnovitz, Steve. 1993. NAFTA: An Analysis of its Environmental Provisions. *Environmental Law Reporter* 23 (February): 10067–73.

CEC (Commission for Environmental Cooperation). 2002. The Environmental Effects of Free Trade: North American Symposium on Assessing the Linkages between Trade and Environment. Montreal. www.cec.org (accessed on September 25, 2002).

EPA (US Environmental Protection Agency). 1998. US-Mexico Border Environmental Program Appendix 1: A Brief Description of US-Mexico Border Environmental Agreements and International Institutions. Washington. yosemite1.epa.gov/oia/MexUSA.nsf/0/fc9b8cbfd7cd8cb4882563dc0003520e?OpenDocument (accessed on May 2, 2005).

EPA (US Environmental Protection Agency). 2000. US-Mexico Border XXI Program. Progress Report 1996–2000. Washington.

Esty, D. 2001. Bridging the Trade-Environment Divide. *Journal of Economic Perspectives* 15, no. 3. Nashville, TN: American Economic Association.

GAO (US General Accounting Office). 1999. US-Mexico Border: Issues and Challenges Confronting the United States and Mexico. Washington.

Grossman, Gene M., and Alan B. Krueger. 1995. Economic Growth and the Environment. *The Quarterly Journal of Economics* 110, no. 2 (May).

Hogenboom, Barbara. 1998. *Mexico and the NAFTA Environment Debate: The Transnational Politics of Economic Integration.* Utrecht, Netherlands: International Books.

Johnson, Pierre Marc, and Andre Beaulieu. 1996. *The Environment and NAFTA: Understanding and Implementing the New Continental Law.* Peterborough, Ontario: Island Press.

Kirton, John. 1997. The Commission for Environmental Cooperation and Canada-US Environmental Governance in the NAFTA Era. *American Review of Canadian Studies* 27, no. 3 (Autumn): 459–86.

Markell, David L. 2000. The Commission for Environmental Cooperation's Citizen Submission Process. *Georgetown International Law Review* 12 (Spring).

OECD (Organization for Economic Cooperation and Development). 2000. Assessing the Environmental Effects of Trade Liberalization Agreements. Paris.

Segger, Marie-Claire Cordonnier, Mindahi Bastida Muños, Mónica Araya, Anna Karina Gonzales, Nicolas Lucas, and Jorje Zalles. 2002. *Ecological Rules and Sustainability in the Americas.* Winnipeg: International Institute for Sustainable Development.

Dispute Settlement

Appleton, Barry. 2000. NAFTA Ruling Will Force Governments to Disclose. *The Lawyers Weekly* (September).

Bhala, Raj. 2001. The Power of the Past: Towards *de jure stare decisis* in WTO Adjudication (Part Three of a Trilogy). *The George Washington International Law Review* 33, nos. 3 and 4.

Caron, David C., ed. 2004. International Decisions. *American Journal of International Law* 98, no.1 (January).

Ikenson, Daniel. 2004. Zeroing In: Antidumping's Flawed Methodology Under Fire. *CATO Free Trade Policy Bulletin*, no. 11 (April 27).

Vega-Cánovas, Gustavo, Alejandro Posadas, Gilbert R. Winham, and Frederick W. Mayer. 2005. México, Estados Unidos y Canadá: Resolución de Controversias En La Era Post Tratado de Libre Comercio de América del Norte. Mexico: Universidad Nacional Autónoma de México.

Weiler, Todd, ed. 2004. *NAFTA Investment Law and Arbitration: Past Issues, Current Practice, Future Prospects.* Ardsley, NY: Transnational Publisher, Inc.

Migration

Feliciano, Zadia. 2001. The Skill and Economic Performance of Mexican Immigrants from 1910 to 1990. *Explorations in Economic History* 38 (July).

Heckscher, Eli. 1949. The Effects of Foreign Trade on the Distribution of Income. In *Readings in the Theory of International Trade*, ed. H. S. Ellis and L. A. Metzler. Philadelphia, PA: Blakiston.

Hamilton, B., and J. Whaley. 1984. Efficiency and Distributional Implications of Global Restrictions on Labor Mobility. *Journal of Development Economics* 14: 61–75.

Hinojosa-Ojeda, Raúl, and Sherman Robinson. 1992. Labor Issues in a North American Free Trade Area. In *North American Free Trade: Assessing the Impact*, ed. Nora Lustig, Barry P. Bosworth, and Robert Z. Lawrence. Washington: Brookings Institution.

Hufbauer, Gary Clyde, and Jeffrey J. Schott. 1992. *North American Free Trade: Issues and Recommendations*. Washington: Institute for International Economics.

IMF (International Monetary Fund). 2005. Chapter 2: Two Current Issues Facing Developing Countries. *IMF World Economic Outlook*. Washington (April).

Krauss, M. B. 1976. The Economics of the "Guest Worker" Problem: A Neo-Heckscher-Ohlin Approach. *Scandinavian Journal of Economics* 78: 470–76.

Martin, Philip L. 1983. Labor-intensive agriculture. Scientific American 249 (4 October): 54–59. Reprinted in *Immigration Law*, ed. Alexander Aleinikoff and David A. Martin. St. Paul, MN: West Publishing, 1985.

Massey, D. S., R. Alarcon, J. Durand, and H. Gonzalez. 1987. *Return to Aztlan: The Social Process of International Migration from Western Mexico*. Berkeley and Los Angeles: University of California Press.

Mundell, R. A. 1957. International Trade and Factor Mobility. *American Economic Review* 47: 32135.

Ohlin, Bertril. 1933. *Interregional and International Trade*. Cambridge, MA: Harvard University Press.

Riding, Alan. 1985. *Distant Neighbors: A Portrait of the Mexicans*. New York: Alfred A. Knopf.

Stolper, Wolfgang F., and Paul A. Samuelson. 1941. Protection and Real Wages. *Review of Economic Studies* 9 (November): 5873.

Taylor, J. Edward, and Philip L. Martin. 2001. Human Capital: Migration and Rural Population Change. In *Handbook of Agricultural Economics I*, ed., Bruce Gardener and Gordon Rausser. Amsterdam: Elsevier Science.

US Commission for the Study of International Migration and Cooperative Economic Development. 1990. *Unauthorized Migration: An Economic Development Response*. Washington.

Index

environmental data, 180
Environmental Health Coalition
  enforcement claim against Mexico, 191t
environmental Kuznets curve (EKC), 167–68
environmental policy
  hazardous waste disposal in Mexico, 172n
  Mexico's regulations, enforcement efforts,
    166–67
  in United States, 163–64
environmental side agreement. See North
    American Agreement on Environmental
    Cooperation
Environmental Sustainability Index (ESI), 180n
EPA. See United States, Environmental Protection
    Agency
ERO. See electricity reliability organization
ESI. See Environmental Sustainability Index
ethanol, 230n, 401
Ethyl Corporation
  Chapter 11 dispute against Canada, 260t
European Union
  agricultural support, 294t
  compared to NAFTA organization, 1n
  exports to Mexico, 74t
  FDI to Mexico, 31t–32t
  wheat exports, volume of, 298t
exchange rates
  peso, renminbi versus dollar, 75f
Executive Air Transport, Inc.
  labor claim against, 151t
Exon-Florio legislation, 203
expropriation
  of foreign investments, 206–207
  interpretation, scope of, 207n, 250, 250n

Fair and Secure Immigration Reform (FSIR)
    proposal, 457–59, 458n
Fair Labor Standards Act, 92
Fast and Secure Trade Program, 17
FDI. See foreign direct investment
Federal Service Labor Management Relations Act
    (FSLMRA), 118n
Feldman, Elliot J., 217, 217n, 219
Feldman, Marvin
  Chapter 11 dispute against Mexico, 260t
FERC. See United States, Federal Energy
    Regulatory Commission
financial services regulation, 485–86, 486n
Finland, 77t
Fireman's Fund Insurance Company
  Chapter 11 dispute against Mexico, 263t
FISI. See Canada, Farm Income Stabilization
    Insurance program
Ford Motor Company, 389
foreign direct investment (FDI)
  among NAFTA partners, 2, 30, 31t–32t, 91, 383t
    in auto sector, 382–85, 383t, 384t
  from EU, Japan, to NAFTA countries, 384,
    384t
  in US, 9091, 91n

foreign investors, investments
  and expropriation, 206–207
  treatment of, 203–207
Fox, Vicente, 14–15, 57, 59, 107, 470
  energy reform, 405
  migration initiative, 455–56, 456n
  on NADBank, 177
  and suspension of HFCS tax, 244, 244n, 325n
Frank, Robert J.
  Chapter 11 dispute against Mexico, 264t
Free Trade Area of the Americas (FTAA), 56
Free Trade Commission (FTC), 158
"freedom car," 402
Friends of the Earth
  enforcement claims against Canada, US, 193t,
    197t
Friends of the Old Man River, The
  enforcement claim against Canada, 188t, 197t
Friesen, Bill, 308n
FSIR. See Fair and Secure Immigration Reform
FSLMRA. See Federal Service Labor Management
    Relations Act
FTAA. See Free Trade Area of the Americas
FTC. See Free Trade Commission

GAMI Investments
  Chapter 11 dispute against Mexico, 265t
General Electric Corporation
  labor claim against, 146t, 147t
General Law of Ecological Equilibrium and
    Protection of the Environment (LGEEPA),
    166
Germany
  auto trade with US, 387t
  exports to Mexico, 74t, 75, 76t, 77t, 78, 78t
Gini coefficients, 52t, 51b
Gini index, 101, 101n
Glamis Gold Ltd.
  Chapter 11 dispute against US, 266t
Global Trade Analysis Project (GTAP) models,
    72
Gonzalez, Charlie, 177
Graham, Lindsey, 217
Grand River Enterprises
  Chapter 11 dispute against US, 267t
grapes, raisins, harvesting of, 462
gravity models, to evaluate impact of NAFTA, 70,
    71–72
Grupo Financiero Banamex, 203
GTAP. See Global Trade Analysis Project
Guatemala, 58t

Haas, Francis K.
  Chapter 11 dispute against Mexico, 263t
Han Young factory
  labor claim against, 149t
Harmonized Tariff System (HTS)
  and rules of origin, 475, 475n
hazardous waste, 165, 171, 172n
HAZTRAKS, 171

Other Publications from the Institute for International Economics

POLICY BRIEFS

65 The Benefits of Price Convergence:
Speculative Calculations
Gary Clyde Hufbauer, Erika Wada,
and Tony Warren
December 2001 ISBN 0-88132-333-0

66 Managed Floating Plus
Morris Goldstein
March 2002 ISBN 0-88132-336-5

67 Argentina and the Fund: From Triumph
to Tragedy Michael Mussa
July 2002 ISBN 0-88132-339-X

68 East Asian Financial Cooperation
C. Randall Henning
September 2002 ISBN 0-88132-338-1

69 Reforming OPIC for the 21st Century
Theodore H. Moran
May 2003 ISBN 0-88132-342-X

70 Awakening Monster: The Alien Tort
Statute of 1789
Gary C. Hufbauer and Nicholas Mitrokostas
July 2003 ISBN 0-88132-366-7

71 Korea after Kim Jong-il
Marcus Noland
January 2004 ISBN 0-88132-373-X

72 Roots of Competitiveness: China's Evolving
Agriculture Interests Daniel H. Rosen,
Scott Rozelle, and Jikun Huang
July 2004 ISBN 0-88132-376-4

73 Prospects for a US-Taiwan FTA
Nicholas R. Lardy and Daniel H. Rosen
December 2004 ISBN 0-88132-367-5

74 Anchoring Reform with a US-Egypt
Free Trade Agreement
Ahmed Galal and Robert Z. Lawrence
April 2005 ISBN 0-88132-368-3

75 Curbing the Boom-Bust Cycle: Stabilizing
Capital Flows to Emerging Markets
John Williamson
July 2005 ISBN 08813-330-6

BOOKS

IMF Conditionality* John Williamson, editor
1983 ISBN 0-88132-006-4
Trade Policy in the 1980s* William R. Cline, ed.
1983 ISBN 0-88132-031-5
Subsidies in International Trade*
Gary Clyde Hufbauer and Joanna Shelton Erb
1984 ISBN 0-88132-004-8
International Debt: Systemic Risk and Policy
Response* William R. Cline
1984 ISBN 0-88132-015-3
Trade Protection in the United States: 31 Case
Studies* Gary Clyde Hufbauer, Diane E. Berliner,
and Kimberly Ann Elliott
1986 ISBN 0-88132-040-4

Toward Renewed Economic Growth in Latin
America* Bela Balassa, Gerardo M. Bueno, Pedro-
Pablo Kuczynski, and Mario Henrique Simonsen
1986 ISBN 0-88132-045-5
Capital Flight and Third World Debt*
Donald R. Lessard and John Williamson, editors
1987 ISBN 0-88132-053-6
The Canada-United States Free Trade Agreement:
The Global Impact*
Jeffrey J. Schott and Murray G. Smith, editors
1988 ISBN 0-88132-073-0
World Agricultural Trade: Building a Consensus*
William M. Miner and Dale E. Hathaway, editors
1988 ISBN 0-88132-071-3
Japan in the World Economy*
Bela Balassa and Marcus Noland
1988 ISBN 0-88132-041-2
America in the World Economy: A Strategy for
the 1990s* C. Fred Bergsten
1988 ISBN 0-88132-089-7
Managing the Dollar: From the Plaza to the
Louvre* Yoichi Funabashi
1988, 2d. ed. 1989 ISBN 0-88132-097-8
United States External Adjustment and the World
Economy* William R. Cline
May 1989 ISBN 0-88132-048-X
Free Trade Areas and U.S. Trade Policy*
Jeffrey J. Schott, editor
May 1989 ISBN 0-88132-094-3
Dollar Politics: Exchange Rate Policymaking in
the United States*
I. M. Destler and C. Randall Henning
September 1989 ISBN 0-88132-079-X
Latin American Adjustment: How Much Has
Happened?* John Williamson, editor
April 1990 ISBN 0-88132-125-7
The Future of World Trade in Textiles and
Apparel* William R. Cline
1987, 2d ed. June 1999 ISBN 0-88132-110-9
Completing the Uruguay Round: A Results-
Oriented Approach to the GATT Trade
Negotiations* Jeffrey J. Schott, editor
September 1990 ISBN 0-88132-130-3
Economic Sanctions Reconsidered (2 volumes)
Economic Sanctions Reconsidered:
Supplemental Case Histories
Gary Clyde Hufbauer, Jeffrey J. Schott, and
Kimberly Ann Elliott
1985, 2d ed. Dec. 1990 ISBN cloth 0-88132-115-X
ISBN paper 0-88132-105-2
Economic Sanctions Reconsidered: History and
Current Policy Gary Clyde Hufbauer,
Jeffrey J. Schott, and Kimberly Ann Elliott
December 1990 ISBN cloth 0-88132-140-0
ISBN paper 0-88132-136-2
Pacific Basin Developing Countries: Prospects for
the Future* Marcus Noland
January 1991 ISBN cloth 0-88132-141-9
ISBN paper 0-88132-081-1

Currency Convertibility in Eastern Europe*
John Williamson, editor
October 1991 ISBN 0-88132-128-1

International Adjustment and Financing: The Lessons of 1985-1991* C. Fred Bergsten, editor
January 1992 ISBN 0-88132-112-5

North American Free Trade: Issues and Recommendations*
Gary Clyde Hufbauer and Jeffrey J. Schott
April 1992 ISBN 0-88132-120-6

Narrowing the U.S. Current Account Deficit*
Alan J. Lenz/*June 1992* ISBN 0-88132-103-6

The Economics of Global Warming
William R. Cline/*June 1992* ISBN 0-88132-132-X

US Taxation of International Income: Blueprint for Reform* Gary Clyde Hufbauer, assisted by Joanna M. van Rooij
October 1992 ISBN 0-88132-134-6

Who's Bashing Whom? Trade Conflict in High-Technology Industries Laura D'Andrea Tyson
November 1992 ISBN 0-88132-106-0

Korea in the World Economy* Il SaKong
January 1993 ISBN 0-88132-183-4

Pacific Dynamism and the International Economic System*
C. Fred Bergsten and Marcus Noland, editors
May 1993 ISBN 0-88132-196-6

Economic Consequences of Soviet Disintegration*
John Williamson, editor
May 1993 ISBN 0-88132-190-7

Reconcilable Differences? United States-Japan Economic Conflict*
C. Fred Bergsten and Marcus Noland
June 1993 ISBN 0-88132-129-X

Does Foreign Exchange Intervention Work?
Kathryn M. Dominguez and Jeffrey A. Frankel
September 1993 ISBN 0-88132-104-4

Sizing Up U.S. Export Disincentives*
J. David Richardson
September 1993 ISBN 0-88132-107-9

NAFTA: An Assessment
Gary Clyde Hufbauer and Jeffrey J. Schott/*rev. ed.*
October 1993 ISBN 0-88132-199-0

Adjusting to Volatile Energy Prices
Philip K. Verleger, Jr.
November 1993 ISBN 0-88132-069-2

The Political Economy of Policy Reform
John Williamson, editor
January 1994 ISBN 0-88132-195-8

Measuring the Costs of Protection in the United States
Gary Clyde Hufbauer and Kimberly Ann Elliott
January 1994 ISBN 0-88132-108-7

The Dynamics of Korean Economic Development*
Cho Soon/*March 1994* ISBN 0-88132-162-1

Reviving the European Union*
C. Randall Henning, Eduard Hochreiter, and Gary Clyde Hufbauer, editors
April 1994 ISBN 0-88132-208-3

China in the World Economy Nicholas R. Lardy
April 1994 ISBN 0-88132-200-8

Greening the GATT: Trade, Environment, and the Future Daniel C. Esty
July 1994 ISBN 0-88132-205-9

Western Hemisphere Economic Integration*
Gary Clyde Hufbauer and Jeffrey J. Schott
July 1994 ISBN 0-88132-159-1

Currencies and Politics in the United States, Germany, and Japan C. Randall Henning
September 1994 ISBN 0-88132-127-3

Estimating Equilibrium Exchange Rates
John Williamson, editor
September 1994 ISBN 0-88132-076-5

Managing the World Economy: Fifty Years after Bretton Woods Peter B. Kenen, editor
September 1994 ISBN 0-88132-212-1

Reciprocity and Retaliation in U.S. Trade Policy
Thomas O. Bayard and Kimberly Ann Elliott
September 1994 ISBN 0-88132-084-6

The Uruguay Round: An Assessment*
Jeffrey J. Schott, assisted by Johanna W. Buurman
November 1994 ISBN 0-88132-206-7

Measuring the Costs of Protection in Japan*
Yoko Sazanami, Shujiro Urata, and Hiroki Kawai
January 1995 ISBN 0-88132-211-3

Foreign Direct Investment in the United States, 3d ed., Edward M. Graham and Paul R. Krugman
January 1995 ISBN 0-88132-204-0

The Political Economy of Korea-United States Cooperation*
C. Fred Bergsten and Il SaKong, editors
February 1995 ISBN 0-88132-213-X

International Debt Reexamined* William R. Cline
February 1995 ISBN 0-88132-083-8

American Trade Politics, 3d ed., I. M. Destler
April 1995 ISBN 0-88132-215-6

Managing Official Export Credits: The Quest for a Global Regime* John E. Ray
July 1995 ISBN 0-88132-207-5

Asia Pacific Fusion: Japan's Role in APEC*
Yoichi Funabashi
October 1995 ISBN 0-88132-224-5

Korea-United States Cooperation in the New World Order*
C. Fred Bergsten and Il SaKong, editors
February 1996 ISBN 0-88132-226-1

Why Exports Really Matter!* ISBN 0-88132-221-0
Why Exports Matter More!* ISBN 0-88132-229-6
J. David Richardson and Karin Rindal
July 1995; February 1996

Global Corporations and National Governments
Edward M. Graham
May 1996   ISBN 0-88132-111-7

Global Economic Leadership and the Group of Seven   C. Fred Bergsten and C. Randall Henning
May 1996   ISBN 0-88132-218-0

The Trading System after the Uruguay Round*
John Whalley and Colleen Hamilton
July 1996   ISBN 0-88132-131-1

Private Capital Flows to Emerging Markets after the Mexican Crisis*   Guillermo A. Calvo, Morris Goldstein, and Eduard Hochreiter
September 1996   ISBN 0-88132-232-6

The Crawling Band as an Exchange Rate Regime: Lessons from Chile, Colombia, and Israel
John Williamson
September 1996   ISBN 0-88132-231-8

Flying High: Liberalizing Civil Aviation in the Asia Pacific*
Gary Clyde Hufbauer and Christopher Findlay
November 1996   ISBN 0-88132-227-X

Measuring the Costs of Visible Protection in Korea*   Namdoo Kim
November 1996   ISBN 0-88132-236-9

The World Trading System: Challenges Ahead
Jeffrey J. Schott
December 1996   ISBN 0-88132-235-0

Has Globalization Gone Too Far?   Dani Rodrik
March 1997   ISBN cloth 0-88132-243-1

Korea-United States Economic Relationship*
C. Fred Bergsten and Il SaKong, editors
March 1997   ISBN 0-88132-240-7

Summitry in the Americas: A Progress Report
Richard E. Feinberg
April 1997   ISBN 0-88132-242-3

Corruption and the Global Economy
Kimberly Ann Elliott
June 1997   ISBN 0-88132-233-4

Regional Trading Blocs in the World Economic System   Jeffrey A. Frankel
October 1997   ISBN 0-88132-202-4

Sustaining the Asia Pacific Miracle: Environmental Protection and Economic Integration   Andre Dua and Daniel C. Esty
October 1997   ISBN 0-88132-250-4

Trade and Income Distribution   William R. Cline
November 1997   ISBN 0-88132-216-4

Global Competition Policy
Edward M. Graham and J. David Richardson
December 1997   ISBN 0-88132-166-4

Unfinished Business: Telecommunications after the Uruguay Round
Gary Clyde Hufbauer and Erika Wada
December 1997   ISBN 0-88132-257-1

Financial Services Liberalization in the WTO
Wendy Dobson and Pierre Jacquet
June 1998   ISBN 0-88132-254-7

Restoring Japan's Economic Growth
Adam S. Posen
September 1998   ISBN 0-88132-262-8

Measuring the Costs of Protection in China
Zhang Shuguang, Zhang Yansheng, and Wan Zhongxin
November 1998   ISBN 0-88132-247-4

Foreign Direct Investment and Development: The New Policy Agenda for Developing Countries and Economies in Transition
Theodore H. Moran
December 1998   ISBN 0-88132-258-X

Behind the Open Door: Foreign Enterprises in the Chinese Marketplace
Daniel H. Rosen
January 1999   ISBN 0-88132-263-6

Toward A New International Financial Architecture: A Practical Post-Asia Agenda
Barry Eichengreen
February 1999   ISBN 0-88132-270-9

Is the U.S. Trade Deficit Sustainable?
Catherine L. Mann
September 1999   ISBN 0-88132-265-2

Safeguarding Prosperity in a Global Financial System: The Future International Financial Architecture, Independent Task Force Report Sponsored by the Council on Foreign Relations
Morris Goldstein, Project Director
October 1999   ISBN 0-88132-287-3

Avoiding the Apocalypse: The Future of the Two Koreas   Marcus Noland
June 2000   ISBN 0-88132-278-4

Assessing Financial Vulnerability: An Early Warning System for Emerging Markets
Morris Goldstein, Graciela Kaminsky, and Carmen Reinhart
June 2000   ISBN 0-88132-237-7

Global Electronic Commerce: A Policy Primer
Catherine L. Mann, Sue E. Eckert, and Sarah Cleeland Knight
July 2000   ISBN 0-88132-274-1

The WTO after Seattle   Jeffrey J. Schott, editor
July 2000   ISBN 0-88132-290-3

Intellectual Property Rights in the Global Economy   Keith E. Maskus
August 2000   ISBN 0-88132-282-2

The Political Economy of the Asian Financial Crisis   Stephan Haggard
August 2000   ISBN 0-88132-283-0

Transforming Foreign Aid: United States Assistance in the 21st Century   Carol Lancaster
August 2000   ISBN 0-88132-291-1

Fighting the Wrong Enemy: Antiglobal Activists and Multinational Enterprises   Edward M.Graham
September 2000   ISBN 0-88132-272-5
Globalization and the Perceptions of American Workers
Kenneth F. Scheve and Matthew J. Slaughter
March 2001   ISBN 0-88132-295-4
World Capital Markets: Challenge to the G-10
Wendy Dobson and Gary Clyde Hufbauer, assisted by Hyun Koo Cho
May 2001   ISBN 0-88132-301-2
Prospects for Free Trade in the Americas
Jeffrey J. Schott/*August 2001*   ISBN 0-88132-275-X
Toward a North American Community: Lessons from the Old World for the New
Robert A. Pastor/*August 2001* ISBN 0-88132-328-4
Measuring the Costs of Protection in Europe: European Commercial Policy in the 2000s
Patrick A. Messerlin
September 2001   ISBN 0-88132-273-3
Job Loss from Imports: Measuring the Costs
Lori G. Kletzer
September 2001   ISBN 0-88132-296-2
No More Bashing: Building a New Japan–United States Economic Relationship   C. Fred Bergsten, Takatoshi Ito, and Marcus Noland
October 2001   ISBN 0-88132-286-5
Why Global Commitment Really Matters!
Howard Lewis III and J. David Richardson
October 2001   ISBN 0-88132-298-9
Leadership Selection in the Major Multilaterals
Miles Kahler
November 2001   ISBN 0-88132-335-7
The International Financial Architecture: What's New? What's Missing?   Peter Kenen
November 2001   ISBN 0-88132-297-0
Delivering on Debt Relief: From IMF Gold to a New Aid Architecture
John Williamson and Nancy Birdsall, with Brian Deese
April 2002   ISBN 0-88132-331-4
Imagine There's No Country: Poverty, Inequality, and Growth in the Era of Globalization
Surjit S. Bhalla
September 2002   ISBN 0-88132-348-9
Reforming Korea's Industrial Conglomerates
Edward M. Graham
January 2003   ISBN 0-88132-337-3
Industrial Policy in an Era of Globalization: Lessons from Asia
Marcus Noland and Howard Pack
March 2003   ISBN 0-88132-350-0
Reintegrating India with the World Economy
T. N. Srinivasan and Suresh D. Tendulkar
March 2003   ISBN 0-88132-280-6

After the Washington Consensus: Restarting Growth and Reform in Latin America   Pedro-Pablo Kuczynski and John Williamson, editors
March 2003   ISBN 0-88132-347-0
The Decline of US Labor Unions and the Role of Trade   Robert E. Baldwin
June 2003   ISBN 0-88132-341-1
Can Labor Standards Improve under Globalization?
Kimberly Ann Elliott and Richard B. Freeman
June 2003   ISBN 0-88132-332-2
Crimes and Punishments? Retaliation under the WTO   Robert Z. Lawrence
October 2003   ISBN 0-88132-359-4
Inflation Targeting in the World Economy
Edwin M. Truman
October 2003   ISBN 0-88132-345-4
Foreign Direct Investment and Tax Competition   John H. Mutti
November 2003   ISBN 0-88132-352-7
Has Globalization Gone Far Enough? The Costs of Fragmented Markets
Scott Bradford and Robert Z. Lawrence
February 2004   ISBN 0-88132-349-7
Food Regulation and Trade: Toward a Safe and Open Global System
Tim Josling, Donna Roberts, and David Orden
March 2004   ISBN 0-88132-346-2
Controlling Currency Mismatches in Emerging Markets
Morris Goldstein and Philip Turner
April 2004   ISBN 0-88132-360-8
Free Trade Agreements: US Strategies and Priorities   Jeffrey J. Schott, editor
April 2004   ISBN 0-88132-361-6
Trade Policy and Global Poverty
William R. Cline
June 2004   ISBN 0-88132-365-9
Bailouts or Bail-ins? Responding to Financial Crises in Emerging Economies
Nouriel Roubini and Brad Setser
August 2004   ISBN 0-88132-371-3
Transforming the European Economy
Martin Neil Baily and Jacob Kirkegaard
September 2004   ISBN 0-88132-343-8
Chasing Dirty Money: The Fight Against Money Laundering
Peter Reuter and Edwin M. Truman
November 2004   ISBN 0-88132-370-5
The United States and the World Economy: Foreign Economic Policy for the Next Decade
C. Fred Bergsten
January 2005   ISBN 0-88132-380-2

DISTRIBUTORS OUTSIDE THE UNITED STATES

**Australia, New Zealand,
and Papua New Guinea**
D.A. Information Services
648 Whitehorse Road
Mitcham, Victoria 3132, Australia
tel: 61-3-9210-7777
fax: 61-3-9210-7788
email: service@adadirect.com.au
www.dadirect.com.au

United Kingdom and Europe
(including Russia and Turkey)
The Eurospan Group
3 Henrietta Street, Covent Garden
London WC2E 8LU England
tel: 44-20-7240-0856
fax: 44-20-7379-0609
www.eurospan.co.uk

Japan and the Republic of Korea
United Publishers Services Ltd.
1-32-5, Higashi-shinagawa,
Shinagawa-ku, Tokyo 140-0002 JAPAN
tel: 81-3-5479-7251
fax: 81-3-5479-7307
info@ups.co.jp
**For trade accounts only.
Individuals will find IIE books in
leading Tokyo bookstores.**

Canada
Renouf Bookstore
5369 Canotek Road, Unit 1
Ottawa, Ontario KIJ 9J3, Canada
tel: 613-745-2665
fax: 613-745-7660
www.renoufbooks.com

India, Bangladesh, Nepal, and Sri Lanka
Viva Books Pvt.
Mr. Vinod Vasishtha
4325/3, Ansari Rd.
Daryaganj, New Delhi-110002
India
tel: 91-11-327-9280
fax: 91-11-326-7224
email: vinod.viva@gndel.globalnet. ems.vsnl.
net.in

Southeast Asia (Brunei, Burma, Cambodia,
Malaysia, Indonesia,
the Philippines, Singapore, Thailand
Taiwan, and Vietnam)
APAC Publishers Services
70 Bedemeer Road #05-03
Hiap Huat House
Singapore 339940
tel: 65-684-47333
fax: 65-674-78916

**Visit our Web site at:
www.iie.com
E-mail orders to:
orders@iie.com**